A Commentary on Plutarch's Pericles

A COMMENTARY ON

Plutarch's Pericles

Philip A. Stadter

The University of North Carolina Press
Chapel Hill and London

Both the initial research and the publication of this work were made possible
in part through a grant from the Division of Research Programs of the
National Endowment for the Humanities, an independent federal agency
whose mission is to award grants to support education, scholarship, media
programming, libraries, and museums, in order to bring the results of
cultural activities to a broad, general public.

Library of Congress Cataloging-in-Publication Data

Stadter, Philip A.
    A commentary on Plutarch's Pericles / by Philip A. Stadter.
      p. cm.
    Contains also the Greek text of the Pericles.
    Bibliography: p.
    Includes indexes.
    ISBN 0-8078-1861-5 (alk. paper)
    1. Plutarch. Pericles. 2. Pericles, 499–429 B.C. 3. Athens (Greece)—
Biography. 4. Orators—Greece—Athens—Biography. 5. Statesmen—
Greece—Athens—Biography. 6. Greece—History—Athenian supremacy,
479–431 B.C. I. Plutarch. Pericles. 1989. II. Title.
PA4369.P43S73 1989   88-27029
938′.04′0924—dc19   CIP
[B]

Printed in the United States of America

93 92 91 90 89   5 4 3 2 1

Herberto Bloch
magistro humanissimo

CONTENTS

CONTENTS

LIST OF ILLUSTRATIONS

PREFACE

No apology is needed for a new commentary on the *Pericles*, for
the last thorough commentary to the Greek text in English was by
Holden, in 1894.* Since that time archaeological excavations, the
unearthing of inscriptions, and scholarly endeavor have provided
a rich banquet of new sources and interpretations. Holden wrote
before the excavations of the Athenian Agora or the publication
of the *Athenian Tribute Lists*, before the commentaries of Gomme,
Dover, and Andrewes to Thucydides or of Rhodes to the Aristotelian *Constitution of Athens*. Moreover, since the mid-1960s there has
been a fresh and healthy reexamination of Plutarch as writer and
man of his time. A new study is clearly needed.

Rather I must regret that contrary to what Plutarch himself
would have wished, this book treats only one life of the *Pericles–
Fabius* pair. Such are the limitations of time and my competence.
My intention has been to write a general commentary, in particular not limiting myself to historical questions—for many years
the sole reason to read Plutarch—but looking also to language
and biographical technique. Similarly, I have tried to address several levels of reader, from student to scholar, explaining what I
thought needed to be known, or giving references for further
investigation. Plutarch's language is sometimes difficult for students or those more accustomed to classical Greek authors, and so
I have tried to explain constructions and usages more than I
would for another author. The Introduction explores a number of

---

*Now available again in a reprint by Bolchazy-Carducci Publishers, Chi-
cago, n.d. See also the translation, introduction, and notes by Bernadotte
Perrin (1910). A careful treatment of Plutarch's Greek and many historical
comments are found in the German commentary of Siefert and Blass (1909), a
revision of that of Sintenis (1856). A helpful commentary for the Greekless
reader, based on Scott-Kilvert's Penguin translation, has now been prepared
by A. J. Podlecki (1987). I am grateful to the author for allowing me to see a
draft of that commentary before publication.

topics fundamental to understanding this life, especially my conviction that the historical value of the life cannot be appreciated without a clear understanding of its literary and artistic aspects.

The study of sources, although fascinating and treated at length in the Introduction and the text, is in some ways a chimera, as it can never give us the certainty that we pretend from it. Very little careful historical narrative was written concerning the fifth century. Even Thucydides has many omissions, and his major narrative begins when Pericles had only a few more years to live. Indeed, it is an illusion to believe that we can write much that is certain about the mid-fifth century: the gaps are too enormous in proportion to our few solid facts. Plutarch had a vision, a very persuasive vision, of the accomplishments of Pericles. His view has been extremely influential in establishing our interpretation of those years, and even when skepticism has challenged his statements and questioned his sources, his presentation has still set many of the parameters of the discussion. I hope that a thorough treatment of this life will aid in the ongoing revision of our history of these years.

Plutarch's power, however, derives not from historical acuteness but from his understanding of human nature and ability to involve his reader in the moral struggles of his hero. He created his own distinctive style of biography, anecdotal, rich in historical incident, notable especially for the clear and sympathetic delineation of character. This commentary attempts to deal with the life as an extraordinary example of the biographer's art.

A particular feature of the commentary is that in treating the language of Plutarch I have been able to use the computerized texts of Plutarch and other Greek authors produced by the *Thesaurus Linguae Graecae* and made accessible on the Ibycus system through David Packard's LEX program. These tools have allowed me to observe Plutarch's usage very closely in the *Pericles* and in his other works and to compare it with that of other authors. In convenience of access and completeness they far surpass Wyttenbach's index. The text of K. Ziegler's edition of the *Pericles* is reproduced here with the generous permission of BSB B. G. Teubner Verlagsgesellschaft, Leipzig. Translations in this volume are my own unless otherwise identified.

Much of the work for this commentary was done while visiting at Oxford University on a grant from the American Council of Learned Societies, with generous support also from the University of North Carolina at Chapel Hill. I am grateful to the President and Fellows of St. John's College for their hospitality during my stay, and to the supportive staff of the Ashmolean Library. D. A. Russell kindly and perceptively read a draft of the text; the fruits of his reading are on every page, though I do not think he has been able to keep me from all the errors of ignorance and obstinacy. I am indebted to the late Harry Levy, who first encouraged me to undertake this work, to Kenneth Reckford and Frank Frost, who read drafts at various stages, to Jay Bolter, for helping me to tame the computers which sometimes threatened to overwhelm the whole project, and to a series of graduate assistants, Mary Pendergraft, Rebecca McComb, and William Seavey. Other scholars and friends who have helped with suggestions, encouragement, and patient listening include A. Andrewes, E. Badian, G. Bowersock, E. Bowie, W. R. Connor, C. Gill, H. R. Immerwahr, G. Kennedy, D. M. Lewis, J. Linderski, M. Manfredini, C. B. R. Pelling, A. Podlecki, B. Scardigli, G. E. M. de Ste. Croix, L. Stephens, and R. Wallace. I am grateful to The University of North Carolina Press for shepherding this book to publication, and especially to Laura Oaks, who as copy editor brought a semblance of order to the chaos of my manuscript. The dedication expresses the special debt I feel to the scholar who first introduced me to Plutarch.

ABBREVIATIONS

The following abbreviations of reference works and commentaries are used in the text. Journals are abbreviated as in *L'Année Philologique*; classical authors as in the *Oxford Classical Dictionary*, 2nd ed., and LSJ, except where the abbreviation has been expanded for clarity. The *Lives* of Plutarch are cited by chapter and section of the Teubner edition, although for convenience I have indicated the comparisons separately. Note that the Loeb edition differs slightly in section numbers. The *Moralia* are cited by Latin title and Stephanus page. Thus *Thes.* 2.1, *Comp. Thes.–Rom.* 2.2, *De glor. Ath.* 349D.

ATL	Meritt, B. D., H. T. Wade-Gery, and M. F. McGregor. 1939–53. *The Athenian Tribute Lists.* 4 vols. Cambridge, Mass. (vol. 1); Princeton (vols. 2–4).
Beloch, *Gr. Gesch.*	Beloch, K. J. 1912–27. *Griechische Geschichte*². 4 vols. in 8. Strassburg (vols. 1–2); Berlin and Leipzig (vols. 3–4).
Boersma, *Building Policy*	Boersma, J. S. 1970. *Athenian Building Policy from 561/0 to 405/4 B.C.* Groningen.
Busolt, *Gr. Gesch.*	Busolt, G. 1893–1904. *Griechische Geschichte bis zur Schlacht bei Chaeronea*². 3 vols. in 4. Gotha.
Busolt and Swoboda	Busolt, G., and H. Swoboda. 1920–26. *Griechische Staatskunde*³. 2 vols. Munich.
CAF	Kock, T. 1880–88. *Comicorum Atticorum Fragmenta.* 3 vols. Leipzig. Fragments cited from this collection are designated K.
CAH	*Cambridge Ancient History.* 1923–. Cambridge.
CGFP	Austin, C. 1973. *Comicorum Graecorum Fragmenta in Papyris Reperta.* Berlin and New York.

Davies, *APF*	Davies, J. K. 1971. *Athenian Propertied Families, 600–300 B.C.* Oxford.
de Ste. Croix, *OPW*	de Ste. Croix, G. E. M. 1972. *The Origins of the Peloponnesian War*. Ithaca, N.Y.
Denniston	Denniston, J. D. 1954. *The Greek Particles*[2]. Oxford.
Dinsmoor, *Architecture*	Dinsmoor, W. B. 1950. *The Architecture of Ancient Greece*[3]. London.
FAC	Edmonds, J. 1957–61. *Fragments of Attic Comedy*. 3 vols. Leiden.
FCG	Meineke, A. 1839–57. *Fragmenta Comicorum Graecorum*. 5 vols. Berlin. Reprinted 1970.
FGrHist	Jacoby, F. 1923–. *Die Fragmente der griechischen Historiker*. Berlin and Leiden. Fragments of authors from this collection are cited in the form, e.g., 115 F90.
FVS	Diels, H., and W. Kranz. 1951–52. *Die Fragmente der Vorsokratiker*[6]. Zurich and Berlin.
Flacelière	Flacelière, R., and E. Chambry. 1964. *Plutarque: Vies*. Vol. 3, *Périclès–Fabius Maximus, Alcibiade–Coriolan*. Paris. Reprinted 1969.
Gomme, *HCT*	Gomme, A. W. 1945–56. *A Historical Commentary to Thucydides*. 3 vols. (to 5.24). Vols. 4 and 5 completed by K. J. Dover and A. Andrewes. Oxford.
Guthrie, *HGP*	Guthrie, W. K. C. 1962–81. *A History of Greek Philosophy*. 6 vols. Cambridge.
Harrison, *Law*	Harrison, A. R. W. *Law of Athens*. Vol. 1, *The Family and Property*, 1968. Vol. 2, *Procedure*, 1971. Oxford.
Hignett, *HAC*	Hignett, C. 1951. *A History of the Athenian Constitution to the End of the Fifth Century*. Oxford.
Hill, *Sources*	Hill, G. F. 1951. *Sources for Greek History between the Persian and Peloponnesian Wars*. New ed. by R. Meiggs and A. Andrewes. Oxford.

Holden	Holden, H. A. 1894. *Plutarch's Life of Pericles*. London and New York. Reprinted Chicago, n.d.
IG	*Inscriptiones Graecae*. 1873–. Berlin.
IG I²	*Inscriptiones Graecae. Inscriptiones Atticae anno Euclidis vetustiores*. 1924. Ed. min. ed. F. Hiller von Gaertringen. Berlin.
IG I³	*Inscriptiones Graecae. Inscriptiones Atticae anno Euclidis vetustiores*. Ed. tert., fasc. 1., *Decreta et Tabulae Magistratuum*. 1981. Ed. D. Lewis. Berlin and New York.
IG IV, I²	*Inscriptiones Graecae. Inscriptiones Epidauri*. 1929. Ed. min. ed. F. Hiller von Gaertringen. Berlin.
Jones, *Plutarch*	Jones, C. P. 1971. *Plutarch and Rome*. Oxford.
Kagan, *AW*	Kagan, D. 1974. *The Archidamian War*. Ithaca, N.Y.
Kagan, *OPW*	Kagan, D. 1969. *The Outbreak of the Peloponnesian War*. Ithaca, N.Y.
LSJ	Liddell, H. G., R. Scott, and H. J. Jones. 1940. *A Greek-English Lexicon*. Oxford.
MacDowell, *Law*	MacDowell, D. M. 1978. *The Law in Classical Athens*. Ithaca, N.Y.
Meiggs, *AE*	Meiggs, R. 1972. *The Athenian Empire*. Oxford.
Meiggs, *Trees*	Meiggs, R. 1982. *Trees and Timber in the Ancient World*. Oxford.
Meinhardt	Meinhardt, E. 1957. *Perikles bei Plutarch*. Frankfurt.
ML	Meiggs, R., and D. Lewis. 1969. *A Selection of Greek Historical Inscriptions to the End of the Fifth Century B.C.* Oxford.
MT	Goodwin, W. W. 1889. *Syntax of the Moods and Tenses of the Greek Verb*. London and New York. Reprinted 1965.

OCD^2	*Oxford Classical Dictionary*. 2nd ed. Oxford.
Overbeck, *Schriftquellen*	Overbeck, J. 1868. *Die antike Schriftquellen zur Geschichte der bildenden Künste bei den Griechen.* Leipzig. Reprinted Hildesheim 1959.
PA	Kirchner, J. E. 1901–3. *Prosopographia Attica.* 2 vols. Reprinted Berlin 1966.
PCG	Kassel, R., and C. Austin. 1983–. *Poetae Comici Graeci.* Vol. 3.2, *Aristophanes*, 1984. Vol. 4, *Aristophon–Crobylus*, 1983. Vol. 5, *Damoxenus–Magnes*, 1986. Berlin and New York. Fragments cited from this collection are designated K.A.
Pollitt, *Sources*	Pollitt, J. J. 1965. *The Art of Greece 1400–31 B.C.: Sources and Documents.* Englewood Cliffs, NJ.
P. Stras.	Preisigke, F. 1912–20. *Griechische Papyrus der kaiserlichen Universitäts- und Landesbibliothek zu Strassburg.* Leipzig.
RE	Pauly, A., G. Wissowa, and W. Kroll. 1894–1978. *Realencyclopädie der classischen Altertumswissenschaft.* Stuttgart.
Rhodes, *CAAP*	Rhodes, P. J. 1981. *A Commentary on the Aristotelian Athenaion Politeia.* Oxford.
Russell, *Plutarch*	Russell, D. A. 1972. *Plutarch.* London and New York.
Schwarze, *Beurteilung*	Schwarze, J. 1971. *Die Beurteilung des Perikles durch die attische Komödie und ihre historische und historiographische Bedeutung.* Zetemata 51. Munich.
SEG	*Supplementum Epigraphicum Graecum.* 1923–. Leiden.
SIG^3	*Sylloge Inscriptionum Graecarum*[3]. 1915–24. Ed. W. Dittenberger. Leipzig.
Smyth	Smyth, H. W. 1956. *Greek Grammar.* Rev. by Gordon M. Messing. Cambridge, Mass.

Tod, *GHI*	Tod, Marcus N. 1948. *A Selection of Greek Historical Inscriptions.* Vol. 2, *From 403 to 323 B.C.* Oxford.
Travlos, *Pictorial Dictionary*	Travlos, J. 1971. *A Pictorial Dictionary of Ancient Athens.* London.
Ziegler	Lindskog, Cl., and K. Ziegler. 1964. *Plutarchi Vitae Parallelae.* Vol. 1.2. Tert. recensuit K. Ziegler. Leipzig.
Ziegler, *RE*	Ziegler, K. *RE* s.v. Plutarchos 2, XXI, 1 (1951) 636–962. Earlier printed as *Plutarchos von Chaironeia.* Stuttgart 1949. Reprinted 1964.

INTRODUCTION

1. Plutarch

1. Life

Plutarch could hardly be unaware of history, for his home was Chaeronea, the small town in Boeotia whose fertile plain was the field of battle for Philip's defeat of the Athenians and Thebans in 338, and Sulla's of Mithridates in 86. His family were wealthy landowners, of an old family, who could afford to send the young Plutarch to Athens to study philosophy with the influential Platonist Ammonius. Greece was prospering after a long period of decline, partially supported by the benefactions of the philhellene emperor Nero, who about this time made his highly publicized trip to Greece, to compete in the games and announce the freedom of Greece (A.D. 67–68). Plutarch would have been about twenty. His studies at Athens made him a convinced Platonist and introduced him to the pursuits of the gentleman scholar, which he was to continue throughout his long life. Although we possess some declamations that appear to be juvenile works, Plutarch never became a traveling philosopher and sophist in the manner of Dio Chrysostom, his contemporary. Rather we find him lecturing on philosophy at Rome, or leading what seems to have been a philosophical school at his home in Chaeronea.

In the Greece of Plutarch's day, Rome was the final arbiter: wealth and prestige, even continued existence, for an individual as for a city, depended upon a smooth relation with the ruling power. Like most leading Greeks, Plutarch held Roman citizenship, with the name of L. Mestrius Plutarchus, reflecting the patronage of a Roman friend, the consular L. Mestrius Florus, either for his father or himself. Early in life Plutarch had undertaken an embassy to the proconsul of the province of Achaea, and his trips to Italy apparently were also connected with public business. Unlike a later generation, he did not attempt to enter the Roman *cursus honorum* to become part of the imperial power structure. Instead, he warned his friends that their struggles for power in the cities were always subject to the proconsuls: better to make peace with your rival, before Rome did it for you. Nevertheless, his circle of friends included a number of prominent and powerful Romans. Plutarch traveled with Mestrius Florus to the battlefield of Bedriacum in the Po valley; he dedicated the treatise *On Brotherly Love* to T. Avidius Quietus and C. Avidius Nigrinus, two brothers who both were in turn governors of Achaea, and inscribed other works to less important figures. Most influential would have been Q. Sossius Senecio, twice consul under Trajan (in 99 and 107), to whom Plutarch dedicated the *Parallel Lives* and other works. The Romans respected his learning, dignity, and common sense: late in life, we are told, Plutarch received the honor of *ornamenta consularia* and appointment as imperial procurator in Achaea. It was a suitable honor for one whose major work, the *Parallel Lives*, set side by side Roman and Greek statesmen as examples of the qualities needed in political life.

Most of Plutarch's mature years seem to have been divided between Chaeronea and Delphi, with regular sojourns in Athens, where he had been given citizenship, to visit libraries and talk to friends. In Chaeronea life centered around a group of friends and young people that seems to have formed an informal school of philosophy and spent hours debating on set topics. Plutarch was also proud of his willingness to serve, as Epaminondas had, in various minor civic capacities. Much of his time would have been devoted to his writing, most of which belongs to the later years of his life, after the death of Domitian in A.D. 96.

The sheer volume of his writing is stupefying: the extant works, perhaps half the total, fill some twenty-seven volumes in the Loeb Library series.[1] At Delphi he was a priest and administrator for many years, at a time when the shrine was prospering under the patronage of the emperors, especially Domitian, who rebuilt the

---

1. This mass of writing and Plutarch's willingness to talk about himself permit us an unusually rich perception of his interests, thinking, and surroundings—a benefit denied us, for instance, by the more limited and cryptic works of Herodotus or Thucydides.

temple, and Hadrian. His familiarity and concern with the shrine are evident especially in his four "Pythian" works, *On the E at Delphi, On the Present Lack of Metrical Oracles, On the Decline of Oracles,* and *On God's Slowness to Punish,* but are seen also in the frequent references to Delphi and its monuments throughout his works. When he died in the reign of Hadrian, probably shortly before A.D. 125, he was honored with a bust and an inscription from both cities, Chaeronea and Delphi.[2]

2. The Essays

Although Plutarch's works are conventionally and conveniently divided between the seventy-odd essays of the *Moralia* and the fifty short biographies of the *Lives,* the same tone, interests, and purposes are apparent throughout his writing, nor can we isolate periods that were devoted more to one type than the other. Like all educated men of his age, Plutarch was trained in rhetoric, the techniques of effective presentation and persuasion, but he thought of himself—and was seen by others—as a philosopher in the Platonic tradition. He was willing to consider every sort of question, from the nature of the moon or the role of *daimones* in human affairs to the rationality of animals and the paradoxes of the Stoics. But his fundamental perspective is ethical, and the basis of his philosophy is the consideration of the proper behavior of human beings. Human nature is far from perfect, but self-discipline and philosophy permit growth in virtue.

Much of his writing explicitly or implicitly is aimed at helping his readers understand their moral situation and improve themselves. Our lifetime is a period given by god to strengthen the good tendencies of our natures and curb the bad, using education and our own rational efforts to develop habits of virtue and right attitudes.[3] From these principles were born general essays like *Progress in Virtue* or *On Moral Virtue,* as well as a host of short pieces on particular topics, such as *Controlling Anger, Quiet of Mind, Brotherly Love, Scrupulousness.* In these works is founded Plutarch's reputation as physician of souls, the humane, patient sage who is

2. On Plutarch's life see Jones, *Plutarch,* 1–64, Russell, *Plutarch,* 1–17. On Ammonius see Jones 1966a; on Senecio, Jones 1970.
3. See especially Ingenkamp 1971 on Plutarch's advice for moral health.

aware of man's weaknesses yet constantly urges the necessity of improvement and, with a wealth of examples from literature and history, indicates practical means to achieve it. But Plutarch's understanding and thoughtfulness are evident as well in works less precisely didactic, such as the defense of love and marriage in the *Dialogue on Love* or the touching words to his spouse on the death of their daughter in the *Consolation to His Wife*. They are also expressed in the political sphere in works like *Distinguishing Friends from Flatterers*, which warns the officeholder against the ingratiations of false friends, and *How to Profit from Your Enemies*, which takes the enmity of others as a given in public life and instructs the reader on how to make it a source of moral growth.

Even the work that treats most particularly of the political environment of the Roman provinces, the *Advice on Political Life*, written for a friend in Sardis who was beginning a political career, emphasizes the moral aspect of public administration. Exactly because local power is so limited by the brute force of the Roman rule, the politician's objective must be concord with other leading men and with the irrational populace. Political life also must be an arena for developing one's personal virtue while working for the common good. By being willing to yield in small things, one can prevail in that which is more important and more honorable. A necessary element in politics as in all social contacts is *philanthrōpia*, an attitude of benevolence toward others that Plutarch considered the basis of Greek moral education.[4]

3. The *Parallel Lives*

Plutarch wrote a small number of independent lives of people who interested him, of which only two survive, the *Aratus* and the *Artaxerxes*. He also wrote individual lives of the emperors, which also are lost except for the short accounts of *Galba* and *Otho*. But his major achievement was the collection of *Parallel Lives*, pairs of Greek and Roman statesmen set side by side, of which twenty-two

---

4. For a full list of the *Moralia* see Russell, *Plutarch*, 164–72. For a breakdown by subject see Ziegler, *RE* 636–37. On the *Moralia* in general see Russell, *Plutarch*, 42–99; Barrow 1967, 72–149. On the *Advice on Political Life* see Renoirte 1951; the edition and commentary of Valgiglio 1976; Jones, *Plutarch*, 110–21; Carrière 1977.

survive and only a few are lost.[5] The collection apparently grew gradually, and somewhat to its author's surprise, as the encouragement of his friends and his own satisfaction led him to add one pair to another. His audience was first of all his friends, educated Greeks and philhellene Romans, all belonging to the upper class, wealthy, and familiar with Greek philosophy and literature.[6] As with the essays, the ultimate purpose is not historical but moral:

> I began to write lives on account of others, but have remained and "loved the land" also for my own sake, trying in some way through the narrative, as in a mirror, to set myself in order and assimilate my life to the virtues of my subjects. For it is in fact a living together, a sharing of a way of life, whenever we consider "what sort of a man he was," and through the narrative welcome and accept in turn each one as a visitor from another country, taking from his deeds the most important and finest for our understanding.
>
> "Ah, what greater delight could you have than this?"
>
> And what more effective for correction of character? Democritus said that one must pray that we meet with fair images and that the harmonious and useful ones be borne to us from our surroundings rather than the ignoble and evil, foisting on philosophy an opinion that is both false and leads the inexperienced to superstition. But we exercise ourselves in the school of history and the familiarity of writing, welcoming and constantly receiving into our souls the memory of the best and most famous men. If the obligatory contacts with those around us put before us something vulgar or ignoble, we can reject it and push it away, turning a mild and gentle mind toward the finest of our models. (*Aem.* 1.1–5)

---

5. This number includes the double pair *Agis–Cleomenes* and *Tiberius–Gaius Gracchus*. For further discussion of the nature, purpose, sources, and style of the *Lives* see Barrow 1967, 51–65, 150–161; Gossage 1967; Russell, *Plutarch*, 100–142; Wardman 1974.

6. The frequent explanations of Roman terms and practices in the Roman lives indicate, however, that Plutarch anticipated that his audience would be chiefly Greek and relatively uninformed on such matters.

In biography Plutarch found a means to develop his own character and that of his friends by reviewing the great men of the past and considering their virtues. Far from wishing to examine the power of the statesman, the brilliance of his political insight, the effectiveness of his strategy, or the extent of his influence, he directs his attention to the inner character that the man reveals. Ambition, honesty, or generosity are his subjects, not battles or political triumphs. As he states in an often-quoted passage in the *Alexander,*

> Frequently a small action, a word, a joke, reveal more of character than battles with innumerable casualties or enormous opposing armies or sieges of cities (1.2).

Depending on his sources and his view of his subject's character, Plutarch combined military and political history and personal anecdote in various portions.[7] Although they employ the same materials as history, Plutarch's biographies have a different purpose. History, in the hands of Thucydides and Polybius and to a lesser extent other writers, was meant to educate by explaining the true course of events, especially the causes behind events and the inner motivations of leaders and of states. Plutarch's biographies till a narrower but fertile field: he trains us to observe the human character in all the diverse circumstances of human history and to draw from our observations "as in a mirror" that which will help us shape our own character to a more noble model. Even statesmen who have few qualities to imitate may be useful for moral education. As Plutarch writes in the *Demetrius,* "we shall be more eager observers and imitators of better lives if we are not completely uninformed on those which are ignoble and subject to criticism" (1.6).[8]

7. The *Pericles,* for example, although rich in anecdotes, has no chapters devoted entirely or primarily to anecdotes, as are found, e.g., in the *Themistocles, Alcibiades, Phocion* or *Alexander.*

8. On the moral purpose of the *Lives* and their relation to history, see especially Wardman 1974, 1–37. Wardman, however, tends to blur distinctions in stating that the *Lives* "are to be regarded as a form of historical writing" (p. 153). The styles of ancient biography and history are quite different, as Wallace-Hadrill has noted (1983, 8–22). In particular, one might notice in biography the frequent citation of sources, including verbatim documents, and the avoidance of speeches.

The moral purpose of the lives explains also the distinctive organization into pairs, for the juxtaposition of two similar characters, often with similar historical and personal circumstances, permits the reader to see how the virtues, neatly defined in the abstract, take on particular form in individuals.[9] The subjects of the pairs are chosen because their qualities are the same:

> The virtues, because of various constitutions of individuals, take on certain differences, peculiar colors as it were, and they assimilate themselves to the underlying habits, bodily temperaments, nourishment, and manner of life of the individual: Achilles was brave in one way, Ajax in another, and the intelligence of Odysseus was not like that of Nestor. (*Mul. virt.* 243C)

There are many reasons why Plutarch might have chosen to place a Roman beside a Greek in each pair: to encourage Greek understanding of the Roman past by comparing Roman statesmen with their own heroes, or to recall to the rulers of the world that subject Greece also had its heroes, or even to put down the Romans by comparing them unfavorably, as he often does, with their Greek counterparts. But certainly the most important to Plutarch would have been exactly this juxtaposition, in an extended series, of the virtues of the two nations, allowing us to see and appreciate the qualities of each and realize how, despite their different constitutions and temperaments, each had produced men of virtue, worthy of imitation.[10]

There is no external evidence on the chronology of composition of the lives. All seem to have been written after the death of Domitian in A.D. 96. Plutarch tells us that *Demosthenes* and *Cicero* formed Book 5, *Pericles* and *Fabius* Book 10, and *Dion* and *Brutus* Book 12. Cross references within the Lives allow us to gain a fairly

---

9. See Erbse 1956; Wardman 1974, 234–44; B. F. Harris 1970, 190–200; Pelling 1986b; Frazier 1987.

10. The choice of individual subjects for these biographies is similarly problematic, and clearly varied at different stages of writing. In the initial ten pairs, he seems to have thought first of Boeotians, then founders and outstanding leaders. Later he became interested in Roman statesmen of the late Republic, and attempted to find matches for them in Greece. For an overview of the topic see Geiger 1981 and Russell 1982.

secure notion of the first ten pairs, and to make some guesses about the latter groups.[11] The series began with Epaminondas of Thebes, a fellow Boeotian and Plutarch's favorite statesman, who was paired with a Scipio, probably Aemilianus.[12] Two other generals with Boeotian connections followed: Pelopidas, another Theban, and Lucullus, who had once saved Chaeronea from Roman retaliation, matched with Marcellus and Cimon. The fourth pair celebrated Philopoemen, "the last of the Greeks," and Flamininus, "the liberator of Greece." With the fifth book Plutarch attempted a standard theme: the two orators famous as fighters for freedom, Demosthenes and Cicero. His preface reveals his self-consciousness at moving to a broader stage, which demanded consultation of research materials not available at Chaeronea and could have required an appreciation of Latin style that he refused to claim (*Dem.* 2). With *Lycurgus–Numa* and *Theseus–Romulus* he headed in a different direction: back to the great lawgivers and founders. *Themistocles–Camillus* and *Lysander–Sulla* continue the series of great men, as the former were saviors of their cities and second founders, and both the latter besieged and captured Athens, and Sulla captured Rome. *Pericles–Fabius* rounds out this part of the *Parallel Lives*, holding up to imitation men who through virtue steered their cities through great difficulties. At the end of the *Fabius* (27.3) Plutarch makes a suggestive reference back to Epa-

11. See Stoltz 1929; Jones 1966b, esp. 66–68; van der Valk 1982; and Stadter 1983–84, 358–59. Van der Valk's argument for *Solon–Publicola* as the ninth pair misses the close connection between Themistocles and Camillus as saviors of Athens and Rome, and Lysander and Sulla as conquerors of the two cities.

12. The pair is listed in the so-called "Lamprias catalogue" of Plutarch's works, no. 7. At no. 28 is a separate Scipio Africanus. The argument for the elder Scipio would be that the victory over Carthage at Zama established Rome as a major power, as did the victory at Leuctra over Sparta for Thebes, and that both were persecuted by political trials (cf. *On Self-praise* 540D–541A). On the other hand, Scipio Aemilianus also defeated Carthage, and in addition shared the philosophical interests that Plutarch considered so important to Epaminondas (cf. *Pel.* 4.1 and *On Socrates' Sign*). The arguments pro and con are summarized by Peper 1912, 129–31, Ziegler, *RE* 895–96, and Sandbach 1969, 15:74–76 (who favor the elder Scipio). Herbert 1957, however, argues convincingly for Aemilianus, already supported by Wilamowitz 1967, 2:260. On the difficulty of recovering the contents of the *Epaminondas* see Tuplin 1984.

minondas, the first hero in the series. After this pair he strikes out in several directions, as with increased confidence he examines other types of virtue, and even, in *Coriolanus–Alcibiades* and *Demetrius–Antony*, its corruption into vice.

There are no specific indications of chronology, but it is reasonable to accept Jones's conclusion that all the first ten pairs were written in the period ca. A.D. 96–114. The parallel lives written prior to the *Pericles*, then, would be the following:

1. *Epaminondas–Scipio Aemilianus*
2. *Pelopidas–Marcellus*
3. *Cimon–Lucullus*
4. *Philopoemen–Flamininus*
5. *Demosthenes–Cicero*
6. *Lycurgus–Numa*
7. *Theseus–Romulus*
8. *Themistocles–Camillus*
9. *Lysander–Sulla*

If we consider the lives of fifth-century Athenian statesmen, then, the *Pericles* comes after the *Cimon* and the *Themistocles*, but earlier than *Aristides*, *Nicias*, and *Alcibiades*. The fifth-century lives do not seem to form a unit, or to be meant to reflect a common historical perspective.

2. The *Pericles*

1. The Purpose of the *Pericles*

The *Parallel Lives* were meant to educate, to improve the reader by allowing him to contemplate the good qualities of these famous statesmen. Of no pair is this more true than *Pericles–Fabius*. In the preface to that pair Plutarch reminds us that the mind is nourished by contemplation, and especially by contemplation of "deeds of virtue, which instill in the inquirer a certain eagerness and zeal for imitation." Studying the creations of Phidias or Polyclitus delights us, but does not encourage us to imitate their lives.

> Instead, virtue at once disposes us by its actions both to admire the acts and to emulate the agents. . . . For what is no-

ble (*to kalon*) spontaneously draws us actively to itself and instills in us an immediate urge to action, not merely building character in the observer through a representation but producing a moral choice by a reasoned account of the action. (*Per.* 2.3–4)

Pericles and Fabius are precisely the sort of people whose lives call us to make a moral choice when we consider their actions. Their particular qualities are summarized at the end of the preface: "self-restraint (πρᾳότης) and honesty (δικαιοσύνη), and the ability to endure the foolishness of the mass of citizens and of their colleagues in office" (*Per.* 2.5).

The goals of the *Pericles* are threefold: to demonstrate through a presentation of his actions that Pericles in fact possessed and exercised the virtues of *praotēs* and *dikaiosynē*, to refute those who hold the contrary opinion, and to lead the reader to make a decision to put these virtues into practice in his own life.

2. The *Pericles–Fabius* Pair

The parallel with *Fabius* is essential to the implementation of Plutarch's purposes, although usually neglected because of the difference between our objectives and his.[13] Despite the obvious differences in their situations—Pericles as leading statesman in a democracy when Athenian imperialism was at its height, Fabius as one member of a senatorial oligarchy during Rome's greatest crisis—Plutarch saw points of comparison that reveal his personal evaluation of the two men. Among other factors, both held monarchical power for a time and wielded it firmly enough that they were denounced as tyrants. Both were honest, lacking in superstition, and brave in facing deaths in their families. Both used oratory as a tool of persuasion (ὄργανον πειθοῦς, *Per.* 8.1–4, 15.2–3, *Fab.* 1.7–9), and both were cautious in war.

Their great similarity, however, that which subsumed all others, was their ability, as Plutarch states in his preface, to endure the stupidities of the mass of common citizens and of their own colleagues, that is, their *praotēs*. Aristotle (*Eth. Nic.* 4.5.1, 1125b26)

13. See Stadter 1975 for a detailed treatment of this topic.

defined this virtue as a mean with regard to feeling (ὀργή). The man who is *praos* controls his emotions, being neither without feeling nor carried away by feeling, but subjecting all to *logos*. For Plutarch as well, the term describes a self-restraint that avoids any kind of excess[14] and reveals itself especially when one is under the pressure of *orgē*, whether internal or external. Pericles and Fabius manifested this quality in their lives: it could be recognized in their walk, or in their caution in war, but especially in their ability to withstand political pressure.[15] The philosophical teaching of Anaxagoras, which permitted Pericles to bear patiently and even kindly with the pest who followed him home from the agora (5.2), gave him the strength to oppose the rashness of Tolmides (18.2–3), to restrain the demos when they dreamed of impossible conquests in Egypt, Sicily, Etruria, and Africa (20.3–4), and finally to hold them in check when they raged to drive the Spartan army from Attica (33). For Plutarch, this is the great moment of Pericles' life, and parallel to Fabius' firmness in controlling the Roman eagerness to battle Hannibal and, especially, the rashness and taunts of Minucius. The contest, as in Thucydides, pits Pericles' reason against Athenian emotion, *gnōmē* against *orgē*. Like the helmsman of a ship who resists the anguished cries of the frightened passengers, trusting in his skill, Pericles refused to call an assembly and exercised his own judgment (λογισμοῖς). Despite the attacks of friends, enemies, and comic poets, "Pericles was moved by nothing, but mildly (πράως) and in silence endured infamy and hostility, . . . holding the city under control" (34.1).

The comparison also permits us to recognize the special qualities of Pericles, such as his foresight in offering his lands to the city to forestall dangerous slander (33.3). Through the comparison of the two men, the *megalophrosynē* of Pericles emerges as a quality for which Fabius offers no parallel. It was this greatmindedness that permitted him to envision and carry through the building program that made Athens the jewel of Greece. This proud vision

14. See Martin 1960; de Romilly 1979, 275–307; Aalders 1982. On *praotēs* and *epieikeia* as political virtues, see L. Robert, *Hellenica* 13:223–24.

15. Their style of walking: *Per.* 5.1, πραότης πορείας, *Fab.* 17.7, πράῳ βαδίσματι. Caution: *Per.* 18.1, ἐν δὲ ταῖς στρατηγίαις εὐδοκίμει μάλιστα διὰ τὴν ἀσφάλειαν, cf. also 18.2–4, 19.3, 20.3–4, 21, and 38.4. Fabius' caution was proverbial, but note esp. *Fab.* 5.3, 5.4, 10.7, 19.3, 25.3, 26.3–4.

inspired the Congress Decree, which would unite all Greece in common action. Like his calmness, it was learned from Anaxagoras, another indication of the value for a statesman of a philosophical education.[16]

The final *synkrisis* of the two lives reviews in a rather pedestrian manner some of the differences between the two men. As often in these comparisons, Plutarch's muse seems to leave him here,[17] and we find only a bare listing of military (*Comp.* 1–2) and political (3) accomplishments. Yet some features do stand out that are important to Plutarch's overall interpretation. Pericles' advice on the conduct of the Peloponnesian War demonstrates that his foresight was superior to that of Fabius (2.3). More importantly, Pericles' politics of struggle against his oligarchic opponents, leading finally to their ostracism, was justified by the firm hold that he won over the city, a hold that permitted him to pursue his wise policies without the restraints and difficulties from which Fabius suffered (3.2–4). Finally, his building program far outshone anything that Fabius could have dreamed of (3.7).

3. Pericles and Plutarch's Contemporaries:
   The *Advice on Public Life*

Plutarch's analysis of Pericles' virtues also served to make the statesman a more inviting model for the biographer's contemporaries. Whether attempting to win influence in one of the Greek cities under Roman rule, or undertaking to serve in the imperial administration—in these years men from Greek cities were beginning to be admitted to equestrian or even senatorial careers—the second-century statesman would need his full share of "self-restraint and honesty and the ability to endure the foolishness of the mass of citizens and their colleagues in office." The *Parallel Lives* were composed at the same time that Epictetus was warning those who would listen of the pressures of the imperial administration, and how important it was to preserve a realistic sense of the limits

---

16. For Anaxagoras see 4.6, 5.1. *Phronēma* and its compounds appear frequently in the *Pericles*, cf. my note to 5.1. It appears four times in the *Fabius*, 3.7, 5.6, 18.4, and 27.1.

17. See Russell, *Plutarch*, 110–113, and the articles cited in note 9 above.

of one's power to control others and one's own destiny. Plutarch took a different tack, indicating the directions in which his reader could improve his character so as to resist and triumph over these pressures.

The treatise *Advice on Public Life*, written for Menemachus of Sardis, a young man of good birth aspiring to an active political life, seems to belong to the same period and similarly gives major emphasis to the character of the statesman.[18] There is the same view that the demos is an irrational element that must be managed, and that the politician will have to be persuasive and courageous in resisting pressure. Factional strife is a vice that should be avoided or resolved as quickly as possible.[19] The political virtues that he commends in the *Pericles* are those he recommends for the contemporary politician: *praotēs*, *semnotēs* (dignity), *kathariotēs* (freedom from scandal or graft).[20] Not surprisingly, Pericles is the statesman most frequently cited as a model of political behavior and leadership. The politician must learn to adjust his behavior to his responsibilities, like Pericles (800C). Oratorical effectiveness will allow him to succeed, as it did Pericles (802B–C). The best model of the true statesman's administration and delegation of authority is that of Pericles (811C, 812C–D). In a sort of paradox, Pericles' awareness that he ruled "free men, Greeks, Athenians" becomes a paradigm for the contemporary statesman, who should remember his own situation, that he "rules as a subject, he rules a city subject to proconsuls and imperial legates" (813D–E).[21]

Other qualities proper to the contemporary politician are notable in Pericles as well. For example, the politician should not enter his career with the expectation of growing rich (798E): Pericles

18. See Jones, *Plutarch*, 110–21; Wardman 1974, 100–104; Carrière 1977, 237–51. Carrière stresses the practical, even Machiavellian, aim of the treatise, in teaching how to acquire and retain power.

19. Jones, *Plutarch*, 112, 117. Note Plutarch's unfavorable comments on Pericles' rivalries, at 11.3 (βαθυτάτην τομὴν τεμοῦσα τῆς πόλεως) and at *Comp. Per.–Fab.*3.2.

20. See Jones, *Plutarch*, 114. The term *katharos*, missing from the *Pericles*, appears in the *Comparison*: (Pericles) ἀδωρότατον ἑαυτὸν καὶ καθαρώτατον ἐφύλαξεν (3.6).

21. For other references to Pericles see 803A, 803B, 803F, 805C, 808A, 810D, 811E, 812E, 818D. After Pericles, with some fourteen anecdotes, come Epaminondas with ten and Phocion with nine.

did not increase his father's estate by a drachma (15.3). Most indicative of Plutarch's attitude toward Pericles' career is his advice to Menemachus that a politician cannot expect to change and improve the populace at once, but should slowly build his influence. Major changes require time and authority, which is won only after one has a reputation and the trust of the people (799B–C).[22] On the other hand, for the politician to be able to accomplish his goals, he must have power in his hands (813C), although he need not always hold a magistracy. The need for gradually winning a reputation and the trust of the people recalls the period of Pericles' struggle with his rivals, before he could run the state on his own. The struggle was unfortunate, but the victory meant that Pericles, unlike Fabius, could wield power effectively (*Comp.* 3.4).[23]

Thus the *Pericles* is written not only to inform the reader but also, through the historical example of Pericles, to give the reader assistance in living the life of an active member of the political community. But as Plutarch was well aware, Pericles was "monarch" of an independent state, not a city under Roman rule. No local statesman, or even proconsul, could aspire to the kind of Olympian role ascribed to Pericles in the final chapter of the life. There we must recognize Pericles' divine calmness and the monarchical power—σωτήριον ἔρυμα τῆς πολιτείας—as an inspiration for all, but a model especially for the Roman emperor.

4. The Structure of the *Pericles*

The structure of the *Pericles* reveals a redesign of the standard biographical form to reinforce the particular goals and challenges of the life. In a seminal study of the form of ancient biography, Friedrich Leo noted the presence in most of Plutarch's biographies of standard elements: family, birth, appearance, general statement of character, education, political activity, and death.[24] In the *Pericles*, the order of the introductory material is family

---

22. Note that Pericles achieves the δόξα καὶ πίστις recommended at 799C by refusal to profit from his power in the city (*Per.* 15.3).

23. Note the complaint against the error of Theseus and Romulus in changing the kingship: "The ruler must first of all preserve his own position (*archē*)" (*Comp. Thes.–Rom.* 2.2).

24. Leo 1901, 145–92.

(3.1–2), birth (3.3), appearance (3.3–7), and education (4–6). But the analysis of the rest of the life has given more difficulty to scholars. It does not fall neatly into the "chronological" and "eidological" segments outlined by Weizsäcker (respectively 9–14, 19–20, 22–38 and 15–18, 21), nor into the dichotomy between Pericles the demagogue (9–14) and Pericles the aristocratic leader (15–end) championed by Gomme.[25] Steidle has demonstrated that elements depicting and interpreting character occur throughout the narrative and that in fact strict chronological sequence is relatively insignificant in the *Pericles* and many other lives.[26] Major themes are found even in the earliest sections of the life: thus the sections on origin (3) and teachers (4–6) already treat character and politics; the new beginning at chapter 7 does not start a chronological sequence but a discussion of life-style; and so on. Steidle postulates a general division by topic: 7–16 on political and 18–37 on military leadership. The chronological sequence would begin at chapter 22.[27] This analysis, though superior to previous attempts, nevertheless is not completely satisfactory. The contrast between political and military leadership certainly was in Plutarch's mind, as it features in the *Comparison*. But military and foreign policy already appear in the first half of the life as examples of political leadership: cf. the battle of Tanagra (10.1–2) and the fleet exercises (11.4). On the other hand political actions figure heavily in the account of the Peloponnesian War, especially the indictments of chapters 31–32, and Pericles' wartime leadership was clearly more political than military.

The complexity of the *Pericles* results from Plutarch's integration of three different organizational principles, chronological,

25. Weizsäcker 1931 argued that the "chronological" sections of the *Lives* presented straightforward consecutive narrative, whereas the "eidological" gave anecdotal overviews of character, drawing material freely from different periods without regard to temporal sequence. Nesselhauf 1933, 123–25, slightly revised Weizsäcker's schema for the *Pericles*, noting that 19–20 were also achronological. For Gomme's analysis, which rightly noted the importance of Pericles' *metabolē*, see *HCT* 1:65–67.

26. Steidle 1951, 151–66, noted, e.g., the traits of character depicted in the Cimonian section, 9–10, including the defense against the slander of Idomeneus.

27. This structure is basically accepted by Meinhardt (who however begins the chronological sequence with the Sacred War, 21.2) and by Flacelière.

topical, and rhetorical. In addition, the smoothness of his transitions often renders analysis difficult. The chronological scheme gives a rough sequence: birth (3.3), entry into political life (7.1), rivalry with Cimon (9–10), rivalry with Thucydides son of Melesias (11–14), Sacred War (21), crisis of 446 (22–23), Samian War (25–28), Peloponnesian War (29–35), recall (37), and death (38). In this sequence chapters 11–14 overlap with 21–23. But many incidents are discussed out of chronological order: Pericles' contacts with Anaxagoras, the building program, the campaigns of chapters 18–20, and the citizenship law, to name a few.[28] The scheme according to topics gives a different arrangement: introductory material, including family, birth, appearance, formative influences, and character (3–6); background to his political career (7–8); the struggle for power in the city (9–14); qualities as a ruler, including control of demos, honesty, and greatmindedness (15–17); qualities as a general, including caution, foresight, and success (18–23); the Samian War (25–28); the Peloponnesian War (29–35); family life (36); recall and death (37–38). Many other topics of interest, such as the building program and Pericles' relation to Aspasia, are subordinated to these. Finally, an effective rhetorical presentation required another type of arrangement, which would give proper emphasis to the elements essential to Plutarch's understanding of his hero's character. These would include the philosophical underpinnings to Pericles' oratory (8.1–3), his readiness to resolve the dispute with Cimon (10.4–8), the grandeur of the building program (12–13), and his aristocratic policies and oratory (15.1–2). Due care also had to be taken to defuse the objections of the anti-Periclean tradition, for example on the causes of the war. In addition, the whole was united by a number of major themes woven in and out of the fabric of the life.

With these points in mind we can formulate a sample outline, recognizing that no single schema will set out all the elements of organization.

1. Pericles' formation (3–6):
   3.1–3, family and birth
   3.4–7, appearance

28. See the discussion of historical method, below.

This structure arises not from the aims of historical narrative (although Thucydides' narrative provides the major organizing element of section 6), but from the moral and rhetorical purposes already described.

5. Rhetorical Method

Persuasion is an essential element of the life. Plutarch wished to present Pericles as an object of imitation, but there was a significant strand of the ancient tradition that was hostile to Pericles. Its criticisms were threefold: (1) he was a demagogue who had ruined the Athenian people by catering to their desires without thinking of their true welfare, (2) he had dominated the city like a tyrant, in the tradition of Pisistratus, and (3) he had started the Peloponnesian War for base political motives, to escape from political attacks on his friends and himself. The first charge was the most disturbing to Plutarch because it had been eloquently stated by his beloved Plato. The second was contemporary, found in the mockery of the comic poets of the Periclean era, but later became a standard topic of school declamations. The third also could be found in the comedians, and was later incorporated into popular historical accounts.

This hostile perspective presented Plutarch with a challenge more proper to the world of epideictic rhetoric than to historical narrative.[29] How in the face of these charges was he to excite admiration and emulation for his subject? Plutarch chose to hinge his argument on a single question: how did Pericles use political power? The difficulty is phrased explicitly at 9.1:

> Thucydides (2.65) ascribes to Pericles a certain aristocratic
> method of governing, "in theory democracy, but in practice
> rule of the first man," but many others say that it was he who
> first seduced the people through cleruchies, theoric funds,
> and distributions of payments, by his policies giving them
> bad habits and making them wastrels instead of self-disci-
> plined and self-supporting. . . .

The question at stake here is not whether Pericles had power, but how he used it. Did he act aristocratically, that is, with the best end in view, or as a demagogue?

Although the question is posed explicitly only well into the life, it is of cardinal importance, for it represents Plutarch's fundamen-

---

29. For a fuller discussion of the influence of rhetorical theory in the composition of this life see Stadter 1987.

tal decision how to approach the rhetorical problem of the *Pericles*. Gomme mistakenly thought that Plutarch did not have the means to resolve the conflict between favorable and hostile views, between Thucydides and Plato.[30] In fact the biographer had already made his decision in favor of Thucydides, as is apparent from the introduction to the pair of lives. Rather he focuses on the question precisely as a rhetorical technique—to defuse a view opposite to his own. The structural elements of the life are arranged and composed to aid in this process of persuasion. The initial section on family, appearance, and educational influences (chapters 3–6) is standard to the genre, but Plutarch uses it to shape our attitude toward his hero. Pericles is the son of Xanthippus, the victor at Mycale, and the great-nephew of Clisthenes, the lawgiver, who expelled the tyrants. His life is shaped by philosophers, especially by Anaxagoras, who formed his character to highmindedness, sobriety, and self-control. There is, of course, a contrasting strain: the mockery of his physical appearance and his tyranny, the attacks of the boor and of Ion. The basic question already underlies the narrative, but the striking presentation of the effect of Anaxagoras' philosophy precludes our seeing in Pericles a simple demagogue. In the second section (chapters 7–8) we are reminded that Pericles was not *demotikos* by nature but found that an alliance with the demos was the only means to security and power. Moreover, his conduct as a politician is always serious and responsible, and his oratorical skill is used for the benefit of the polis: each time he ascends the speaker's platform, he prays that his words may fit the present need (8.6).

Like a master orator, therefore, Plutarch has rhetorically prepared his reader for the explicit statement of the main question at the beginning of chapter 9. Everything said so far has implied a positive response to that question, and indicated that Pericles is an admirable statesman. Now Plutarch is ready to turn to "the facts themselves" to see the reasons for Pericles' shift from one kind of policy to another (chapters 9–14). In so doing he concedes that Pericles did support the initiatives for which he was criticized, "cleruchies and theoric funds and pay distributions," but undertakes to give a special rationale for them. In fact he looks at only a

30. Gomme, *HCT* 1:56.

few carefully selected events in describing the rivalry with Cimon and with Thucydides son of Melesias. In both cases Pericles does not begin the combat, but reacts to the initiatives of his opponents; in both he is fighting for his right to lead. The various distributions to the citizens counter Cimon's demagoguery; the cleruchies respond to Thucydides' threat. More importantly, however, Pericles' means to gain power are justified both by their own value and the way he exercised the power that he acquired. Pericles' reasonableness permits him to recall Cimon after Tanagra, and the measures undertaken to defeat Thucydides—festivals, cleruchies, and especially the building program—were valuable and brought honor to the city. The account of Pericles' rivalry with his two opponents, far from being a disinterested examination of events, is an artfully presented argument for the statesmanship he demonstrated even while struggling to gain and hold power in the city.[31]

The middle sections (chapters 15–23), which present a synoptic view of Pericles as ruler of the city, do not restrict themselves to the period after Thucydides' ostracism but range freely back to earlier periods, as far as the battle of Coronea and the Corinthian Gulf expedition of the 450s. They are essentially a review of how Pericles used power, and so are a strongly positive answer to the question posed at 9.1. Pericles employed oratory to cure the city's ills, as a doctor would his drugs; he demonstrated integrity in handling money, ambition for the city (*megalophrosynē*, esp. at chapter 17), and a wise caution as general, leading to successes in numerous campaigns. These lead to an intermediary peak, the war against Samos (chapters 24–28), parallel to Fabius' secondary acme at the siege of Taranto, although placed before rather than after the hero's greatest moment. Whatever demagoguery might have been used in the struggle with his rivals, Pericles is shown by his responsible use of power to be eminently worthy of imitation.

The high point of Pericles' career is his conduct during the Peloponnesian War (chapters 29–35). Plutarch does not admire Pericles' conduct in refusing to repeal the Megarian decree, since from his distant perspective it was always a mistake for Greeks to

31. Breebaart 1971, 260–72, offers an important corrective to Gomme's explanation of 9.1.

fight against Greeks. He is not really satisfied with any of the reasons given for Pericles' intransigeance. But once the war begins, he presents Pericles' actions as wholly admirable. Pericles resisted the irrational eagerness of the mob, the urgings of his friends, and the insults of his enemies. By refusing to fight the Peloponnesian invaders as they ravaged Attica, he saved the city. Here Pericles acts according to Plutarch's highest ideals of statesmanship, putting philosophic calm and the good of the state above short-term goals and personal rewards. Here especially he displays the *praotēs*, "the ability to endure the foolishness of populace and colleagues, and thus greatly benefit his country" (cf. 2.5), that Plutarch considered his chief virtue.

Rhetorical needs are also reflected in the techniques used by Plutarch in the *Pericles*: selection, amplification, and evocation of ethos and pathos. Aristotle had recommended a selective narrative for epideictic oratory: there is no need to tell all, especially if it is well known (*Rhet.* 3.16.1–2, 1416b16–26). Plutarch's narrative was necessarily incomplete, because of the paucity of sources, but it is made more so by the rigor of his criteria for reporting. Not only is most of the historical context excluded (see below), but also valuable information on Pericles' family (e.g., the reputation of his sons as lazy spendthrifts, his guardianship of Alcibiades).[32] Amplification (*auxēsis*, the enlargement of a topic)[33] appears frequently in the *Pericles*: in the account of Anaxagoras' thought and its effect on Pericles (4.5–5.1); the assessment of Pericles' oratory (8.1–4); the exaltation of his aristocratic rule (15.1–3); and the admiration of his steadfastness against the mob (33.4–8). The major passage, however, is the section on the building program (12–13), which begins with what might have been a minor item, similar to the list of cleruchies, but takes on a life of its own. Here amplification functions as proof: what began as an item in a list of demagogic measures becomes a testimony to Pericles' vision and aristocratic concern for the city.

The *Pericles* portrays the *ēthos*, or character, of its subject, but

32. For the reputation of Pericles' sons, see my note to 36.2; for Alcibiades the note to 37.1 and *Alc.* 1.2, 3.1–2.

33. Cf. Aristotle's recommendation of its use in epideictic oratory, *Rhet.* 3.17.3, 1417b31–34 and 3.19.1, 1419b10–19.

also employs ethos as a means of persuasion. First of all Plutarch reveals his own character, establishing himself as humane, understanding, good. This ethos is most obvious in the introduction (1–2), but is felt throughout. Often he asks us to share his values, as when he cites Zeno on appearing virtuous (5.3), talks of omens from the gods (6.4–5), or notes that true virtue is revealed in daily life (7.6). Elsewhere he wants us to share his indignation at Idomeneus, the comic poets, or Stesimbrotus (10.7, 13.16). The familiarity thus established with his readers certainly is one of the sources of his success as biographer.

With a kind of rhetorical feedback, the very ethos that Plutarch ascribes to Pericles serves to convince us of the truth of the portrait. For Plutarch first allows us to form an idea of Pericles' character, especially in the early chapters, then uses this preliminary notion to explain to us his other actions. So we accept that despite seeking popular support, Pericles was not democratic by nature (7.4), and that he could not have killed Ephialtes, because he had nothing brutal about him (10.7). The image of self-restraint that is built up during the life becomes the proof of Plutarch's explanation of his refusal to fight the Peloponnesians invading Attica (33).

The more explicit appeal to the emotions recommended by rhetorical theorists, *pathos*, may be found in its proper place in the epilogue, in the expression of wonder and admiration of Pericles' Olympian calm.[34]

For this life, given the strength and authority of the anti-Periclean tradition, special rhetorical treatment of hostile stories and judgments was needed. No one had more authority for Plutarch than Plato, yet he had harshly criticized Pericles for corrupting the Athenians with jury pay (*Gorgias* 515E; cf. 9.1). Despite those clear words, Plutarch artfully makes Plato a supporter of Pericles. Plutarch begins from the brief and ironic passage in the *Phaedrus* on Anaxagoras' influence on Pericles, and credits to that influence the austere nobility he sees in Pericles (5.1; cf. *Phaedrus* 270A). Later he returns to Plato's statement on the exalted oratory of

---

34. Cf. Quintilian 6.2.20 and the comments of Kennedy 1963, 93–94. There is also a strong element of pathos in the narrative of the death of Pericles' children and his appeal for citizenship for his bastard son (36.7–9, 37.5).

Pericles, citing him for the philosophical element in Pericles' oratory (8.1, 15.2), so that it emerges as true *psychagōgia*, based on intimate knowledge of the human soul. In addition, the use of Platonic images of the statesman as doctor and helmsman implicitly assimilates Pericles to the Platonic ideal. Plato's hostile judgment is refuted by using Plato himself to testify on Pericles' behalf.

Despite his very positive assessment of Pericles, Plutarch records more hostile and disparaging statements about him than any other author. The accounts of the constant carping of his critics, and of the pressures to which he was subjected, fit the characterization of Pericles as even-tempered in difficult circumstances, as we have seen. Other unfavorable anecdotes do not usually reflect Plutarch's inability to chose between sources, but a combination of rhetorical and historical goals. Plutarch did not disdain facts, and he was willing to admit that Pericles could have faults (10.7). Moreover, he liked to report contemporary testimony, even if he doubted it. But he was also confident that he could disarm or refute criticism. Sometimes he would simply put a favorable interpretation on an unfavorable story, such as Pericles' boast that his victory over Samos was superior to Agamemnon's (28.7–8). His treatment of Pericles' relationship with Aspasia exemplifies another technique, misdirection and false dichotomy. The accusation that she had caused Pericles to start the Samian War is rephrased and generalized (24.2): why did Aspasia have so much influence on the leading men and philosophers of the day (24.2)? Soon Pericles' own relationship is narrowed to two choices: was he consulting her for her political wisdom, or was he truly in love? In either case, a potentially scandalous relationship has been drawn back within acceptable limits of behavior.

On other occasions Plutarch argues from necessity or probability—either that Pericles was forced to an action (e.g., to seek the support of the demos at the beginning of his career) or that an anecdote is improbable given Pericles' actions.[35] But Plutarch is

---

35. The argument from probability is used in the form of an enthymeme against Idomeneus: Idomeneus accused Pericles of murdering Ephialtes, who was his friend and co-worker; but Pericles spared even his rival Cimon; therefore it is impossible that he killed a friend. The reasoning is then confirmed by a reference to Aristotle (10.7–8).

most effective at attacking a statement by attacking its author. Ion of Chios said that Pericles was presumptuous and arrogant: but Ion "always expected virtue, like a complete tragic performance, to have a part for satyrs as well" (5.3). The comedians gossiped of his affairs with married women: "but who can wonder that men given to debauchery would offer their slanders against their betters in sacrifice to the envy of the crowd, as if to an evil spirit, when even Stesimbrotus of Thasos dared to report against Pericles an extreme and disgusting wrong toward his daughter-in-law?" (13.16). The rhetorical question here shows high indignation, as earlier in his response to Idomeneus. Duris' account of the brutal punishment meted out to the Samian trierarchs (28.2–3) is doubly refuted: Plutarch first appeals to other authorities—Thucydides, Aristotle, and Ephorus—but then attacks Duris, who "never is able to keep his narrative truthful, even when no personal feeling is involved, and here seems to have magnified his country's sufferings to slander the Athenians."

As these last examples indicate, the rhetorical techniques employed by Plutarch often influence his historical methods, which we must now examine.

6. Historical Method

A narrative of events long past requires not only sources of information but a process of assembling, recalling, evaluating, interpreting, selecting, and organizing this information for the particular purpose of the narrative. How did Plutarch go about this process?

Plutarch's youthful education would have introduced him to the classics of Greek literature, including the major historians and orators. His reading over the succeeding decades had gone far beyond the major authors, absorbing omnivorously works in all areas of ancient learning, including local histories of individual cities, antiquarian studies, and memoirs.[36] Yet the technical apparatus to manage this reading was relatively simple.

---

36. Plutarch's delight in the history of the past is evident throughout his works, but note, e.g., *Non posse* 1092E–F, "History (αἱ ἱστορίαι) also has many delightful diversions, and leaves desire always unsatiated with truth and un-

The papyrus book roll, copied individually on demand, was the fundamental unit, although in Plutarch's day the codex, with its rapid access to individual pages of text, was beginning to come into use.[37] Plutarch undoubtedly owned many rolls, but he lamented that many of the texts he desired were not available at Chaeronea and longed for the libraries of major centers like Athens, which held "an abundance of every sort of book" (*Dem.* 2.1). Nevertheless, we must remember that it would have been normal to acquire a book for one's personal use simply by having it copied from a text in the possession of a friend or library, and we can suppose that Plutarch and his friends had slaves trained for the purpose. A similar procedure would be to copy from a favored work selected passages, either short or quite extensive.[38] Thus while access to texts would have been a problem, it was not an insuperable one.

We know that Plutarch also kept notes from his reading.[39] Short-term notes might have been made on wax tablets or other temporary materials, but most notes would have been collected in a continuous sequence on papyrus rolls, arranged according to topics as in a commonplace book. Plutarch had nothing like the modern scholar's note cards (much less computer data bases), which permit easy rearrangement of material. Most notes would have been arranged in the order in which they were taken, al-

---

filled with pleasure," and the expansion of this idea in the following paragraphs.

37. Note, for example, that the Berlin papyrus of the Aristotelian *Constitution of Athens*, probably written in the second century A.D., was a codex with wide margins for scholia (see Chambers 1967). See in general Roberts and Skeat 1983; Turner 1968, 7–8, 10–16, 112–26.

38. Cf. the request of Cicero's son Marcus for a Greek secretary to help him in preparing notes: "I beg you to send me a copyist as quickly as possible, especially a Greek, for that will save me much trouble in writing out notes" (*Ad fam.* 16.21.8).

39. For notebooks on ethical topics, see *De tran. anim.* 464F; cf. 457D. The collections of *Sayings of Kings and Commanders* and *Sayings of Spartans* (*Mor.* 172A–242D) seem to derive from Plutarch's notebooks, although the introduction to the former is spurious. Many of the anecdotes recorded here are also found in the *Lives*; four sayings of Pericles are found at 186C–D, of which two are found in the *Pericles*. Concerning sayings of Pericles, see note to 8.7. Cf. also H. Martin 1969.

though for particular purposes notes might have been taken on small pieces of papyrus, organized, and then glued into a roll, or a piece with a note inserted into a roll at the proper place. More simple was to add a note in the margin of a text, or to give a cross reference to another roll where additional notes on the same subject were gathered.

Notes permitted the accumulation of many anecdotes or illustrative passages on the same topic, but memory was the dominant method of retaining information for both short and long term.[40] Memory training formed a major part of ancient rhetorical education, and it is obvious from Plutarch's works, especially his easy and elegant use of literary and philosophical quotations, that his memory was exceptionally capacious and well exercised. We can suppose that even if he had made notes on a topic, he often did not consult them—a troublesome and time-consuming task with a papyrus roll—but relied on his memory of his reading. Such long-term memory of readings over a period of decades should be distinguished from short-term memory of reading for a particular essay, which is more properly an element of composition.

Although the ancient world did not possess the invaluable indexes and reference works assembled by classical scholars in the last two centuries, Plutarch nevertheless had access to scholarly aids prepared by generations of librarians, grammarians, and antiquaries. He refers to chronological canons and lists of magistrates and victors at the games. We also know of reference works on the people who were named in Old Comedy, and commentaries to classical authors, including the orators, that explained references to people and practices. And of course, there were earlier collections of opinions of the philosophers, sayings of famous men, and literary texts and anecdotes on selected subjects.

Finally, Plutarch undoubtedly had personal assistance from slaves and friends. Trained slaves could be used as copyists, as already mentioned, or as scribes to take dictation, either of notes

40. See Zimmermann 1930; Gomme, *HCT* 1:78–81; Stadter 1965, 138; Hamilton 1969, xliv. Note Plutarch's comment after his reference to Cyrus' favorite courtesan, Aspasia: "These thoughts came to mind while I was writing, and it seemed unnatural to reject them and pass them by" (*Per.* 24.12). Book 2 of the *Symposiaca*, Plutarch tells us, was composed "as memory dictated" (629D).

or finished works.[41] Freedmen or slaves could be valuable personal secretaries or reference librarians.[42] Most important were Plutarch's friends and fellow literati, whose own memories and libraries would have been open to Plutarch's questions.[43] Nor should we forget the group of young people around Plutarch in Chaeronea, who would have been willing helpers in searching out a quotation or sharing anecdotes from their reading.

What practices can we detect in Plutarch's *Lives* that reveal how Plutarch presented his material once collected? Pelling has demonstrated that in one group of six Roman lives dealing with the period of the Civil War, Plutarch, like Livy and other ancient writers, first did all the reading that might seem necessary, then composed each life, using a single source for the basic articulation of the narrative.[44] This method probably lies behind the *Pericles* as well, with certain special features. First, Plutarch was immensely more familiar with fifth-century history than Roman republican history, so that the same kind of preliminary reading would not have been necessary: this had been done over the course of many decades. Nevertheless, we may imagine a rereading of the relevant sections of Thucydides, Stesimbrotus, Aristotle, Ephorus, and perhaps Theopompus and Idomeneus. Secondly, because there was no authoritative narrative source for much of Pericles' life, Plutarch seems not to have used an underlying history for the

41. Pliny the Elder had slaves read to him while he made notes and extracts (Pliny *Ep.* 3.5.10–17). Slaves could also have functioned as translators (Jones, *Plutarch*, 86) although I believe Plutarch's knowledge of Latin was sufficient to obviate the need for them in most circumstances.

42. Thus we find Cicero writing to his freedman Tiro, who had questioned the accuracy of a statement, that he had asked his slave, Dionysius, for advice concerning the facts, which he (Cicero) had taken from a book of Dicaearchus (*Ad Att.* 6.2.3).

43. Cf. *Dem.* 2.1: a large city not only contained books, but preserved the memory of much that had escaped writers. See also Theander 1950–51, 2–32, and 1959, 99–131. For a valuable characterization of scholars and scholarship in the second century A.D., and of their influence in upper-class society see Wallace-Hadrill's study of Suetonius (1983), 26–29.

44. Two studies by Pelling on the Roman lives of the period of the Civil War are especially valuable on this subject: "Plutarch's Method of Work in the Roman *Lives*" (1979), and "Plutarch's Adaptation of His Source Material" (1980), esp. 91–92 (on composition). See also Russell 1963 and Pelling 1985.

articulation of chapters 3–21. From the point where Thucydides' narrative became usable, with the crisis of 446 (*Per.* 22), his account provided the narrative framework, to which stories from other sources were attached.

Various errors suggest that here, as in the Roman lives, Plutarch would rely during composition on his short-term memory of what he had just read or reread rather than attempt to keep several papyrus rolls open at once or make use of extensive notes. Two such errors occur together at 35.2 and 35.3: he first placed the anecdote of the eclipse one year late, associating it with the expedition of 430 rather than 431, then he merged the expeditions to Epidaurus and Potidaea into one item (see my notes ad loc.). The two errors may be related. Plutarch did not mention the eclipse in the context in which Thucydides had put it (i.e., at 34.1) because he was concentrating on the measures that Pericles took in the first year of the war. He was then distracted by the elaborate paragraph on the plague, in which he tried to capture some of Thucydides' drama while summarizing the plague's effect. When he resumed with the next year in Thucydides, and the expedition against Epidaurus, he recalled the anecdote of Pericles and the eclipse and included that. But the distraction may have been enough to cause him, when he continued his narrative, to confuse the account of the two expeditions and blend them into one single event.

A gifted narrator, Plutarch also had the ability to flesh out the meager indications of his sources with realistic detail.[45] In focusing upon the life and character of one individual, he permitted himself certain narrative licenses, especially those that allowed a simplification of the historical narrative.[46] We have just mentioned an instance of conflation; compression of time is also found frequently—for instance, in the leap of six years between the end of chapter 23 and the beginning of 24. In the discussion of structure above, we noted his use of topical rather than chronological arrangement, as with the building program or the campaigns recounted in 19–20. Chronology was not his only, or even his most

45. Cf. Carney 1960, 27–31; Stadter 1965, 138–40; Pelling 1980, 129.
46. See Pelling 1980, 127–31, and the studies of Buckler (1978) and de Wet (1981). Note the contrast between 28.1 and Thuc. 1.117.3.

important, organizational principle.[47] Focus on the individual subject also meant that Plutarch often ascribed to Pericles actions that his sources attributed to the Athenians generally, as with the ships sent to Corcyra (29.1).[48] Many important events that could not be associated directly with the hero were passed over or narrated schematically—such as the Egyptian campaigns of the 450s, or the incidents of Corcyra and Potidaea. Plutarch's presentation of events reflects his aims in the life at hand and often is at odds with interpretations suggested in other lives.

In this context a comparison with the *Cimon*, which had been composed earlier but treats part of the same period, is illuminating. *Pericles* 9–10 treats the rivalry with Cimon, but it is obvious that there Cimon is presented only as a foil for Pericles, not with any effort to reveal his motivation or policy.[49] It is natural, for example, that Cimon's extraordinarily successful expeditions be given only the barest mention, although they fill long chapters of the *Cimon*[50] and Cimon's victory at the Eurymedon had permitted Pericles to lead an expedition beyond the Chelidonian islands into Persian waters (*Cim.* 13.4). But the nature and effects of Cimon's distributions to the needy in the city were certainly important for the development of Pericles' political program. The full catalogue of these distributions in the *Cimon* (10.1–8) is supplemented and ornamented by a citation of Aristotle for a variant version and quotations from Cratinus, Gorgias, and Critias, concluding with comparisons with the exemplary Spartan Lichas and the legendary mission of Triptolemus to share the discovery of grain with the

47. This can often be observed in the *Lives*: e.g., in the account of the battle of Plataea in *Aristides*, where Plutarch is following Herodotus quite closely, but chooses to reverse for better narrative effect in his own context Herodotus' order for the quarrel between the Tegeans and Athenians for the position on the left wing (Hdt. 9.26–28.1; *Arist.* 12) and the cavalry attack of Masistius (Hdt. 9.20–24; *Arist.* 14).

48. Cf. also 21.2 (Delphi), 25.2, 25.5 (Pericles is not mentioned by Thucydides, although he is by Diodorus). In the same way, the reply to the Tegeans at Plataea is ascribed to Aristides, not to the Athenians (*Arist.* 12; cf. Hdt. 9.27.1, 28.1).

49. The same, in reverse, is true of the *Cimon*, in which Pericles is mentioned only five times (13.4, 14.5, 15.2, 16.1, 17.8).

50. *Cim.* 7–8, 11–14.2. There are brief allusions at *Per.* 7.3, 9.5, 10.5, and 10.8.

cities of Greece. In the *Pericles*, these are reduced to two bare items: unfenced fields and dinners for needy citizens.[51] Most importantly, the two accounts give opposing interpretations to Cimon's behavior. The *Pericles* is brief but clear: Pericles has been defeated by demagoguery (*καταδημαγωγούμενος*, 9.2). But in the *Cimon*, "those who charged that these acts were flattery of the mob and demagoguery" are refuted firmly by appeal to Cimon's aristocratic policy, Laconian tendencies, and honesty (10.8). In the account of the Areopagus reforms, Ephialtes leads the attack in the *Cimon* (15.2), but Pericles himself does so in the *Pericles* (9.4–5), though Ephialtes is his agent. In *Cim.* 15.4 it is said that the charges which would lead to Cimon's ostracism were his relationship with Elpinice and his philo-Laconism; in *Per.* 9.5 they are reported as ill will toward the demos and philo-Laconism. But the *Pericles* omits the evidence for his pro-Spartan stance, and especially the missions to Ithome, given at length in *Cimon* (16.1–17.3). In treating the battle of Tanagra and Cimon's subsequent recall, Plutarch adjusts his account in the *Pericles* to make Pericles' role more explicit. Those who oppose Cimon are not enemies within the Council, as at *Cim.* 17.5, but "friends of Pericles," who reject him not as a potential traitor but simply as an exile (10.1). Pericles, we learn, fought especially well that day and was the most prominent of the army. Finally, only in the *Pericles* do we hear the story, somewhat demeaning to Cimon though not to Pericles, that Elpinice had arranged a pact with Pericles, with Cimon promising to go on campaign outside the city if he were recalled (10.5). Thus Plutarch in the *Pericles* not only gives more attention to his hero, referring to Cimon's actions only when they are necessary to understand those of Pericles, but he selectively records and interprets in such a way as to strengthen his own conception of his subject.[52] Although fully aware of other issues and events that had

51. Note that the variant of Aristotle is not cited here, but another passage from *Ath. pol.* will be cited later in the sentence. In each case the citation is meant to ornament the major story.

52. Note also the treatment of Cimon's trial after the siege of Thasos (*Cim.* 14.3–5, *Per.* 10.6): in the *Pericles* Pericles' part is softened, so that he is only "one of the accusers proposed by the demos," whereas in the *Cimon* he is "the most vehement of the accusers."

major effects on Athenian politics in these years, such as the earthquake at Sparta and the Messenian revolt, the expansion of Attic land power in the 450s, and the campaigns in Egypt and Cyprus, Plutarch narrows his account in the *Pericles* to the initiative by which Pericles succeeded in ostracizing Cimon, and then, when popular feeling demanded his recall, in getting him out of Athens.

Finally, Plutarch does not attempt to relate Pericles to the literary figures of his time, as is done so often in modern scholarship.[53] He does not suggest any tie between Pericles and Sophocles, Euripides, Herodotus, or Thucydides, and even in referring to Pericles' contact with philosophers and sophists, he implies that the influence was in one direction only. Pericles is not presented as an intellectual, but as a wise ruler.

7. Some General Principles for Reading Plutarch

The preceding observations suggest the following general principles for reading the *Pericles*, and the *Parallel Lives* in general:[54]

1. Plutarch's purposes, for the *Lives* in general, and for any particular life, strongly affect both narrative and interpretation. The major goal is usually moral rather than simply informational, but minor goals include information, delight, philosophical speculation, rhetorical persuasion.[55]

2. The *Parallel Lives* were composed in pairs, and the reasons behind the choice are important considerations in the interpretation of a life.

3. Plutarch's good nature tends to set his hero in the best light possible, or to accept the most noble explanation for an action, insofar as it accords with his own interpretation of the hero's character. Note especially his rules for fair-minded narrative in *De Herodoti Malignitate* (855B–856D) and his comparison with portrait painters in the introduction to the *Cimon* (2.3–4): "if there is

---

53. The attempt is made by most modern authors who present a general picture of the fifth century, but cf. especially Ehrenberg's *Sophocles and Pericles* (1954).

54. This list is heavily indebted to that given in Frost 1980, 55–59.

55. Cf., e.g., the study of B. F. Harris on autocratic power in Plutarch's *Lives* (1970).

some small feature that is unpleasant, [we prefer that they] not omit it completely, nor draw it too precisely. The former would destroy the resemblance, the latter would make it ugly."

4. Each life is shaped by the experiences and character of its hero, so that the structure and tone of one life differ markedly from another.

5. Considerations of chronology are secondary to those of character and subject.

6. All passages must be read in the context in which Plutarch reports them. This includes the dramatic and rhetorical structure of the life, and its relation to the life with which it is paired.

7. The nature of the narrative is dependent upon the genre, variety, and detail of the sources.

8. Plutarch's reading was extensive, and we normally can assume that he has read the authors that he cites. The mistakes that he makes are more likely to be his own than those of an anonymous intermediate source.

9. Plutarch considers it desirable to cite contemporary sources, even when he distrusts them.

10. Plutarch does not respect all sources equally. His opinion of a source should be considered in evaluating both the truth of an item and its role in the life.

11. Plutarch uses the information supplied by his source to make his own point, which is not necessarily that of his source.[56]

12. It is wise to resist the temptation to name lost writers as Plutarch's sources for specific passages, and especially to interpret Plutarch on the basis of their supposed bias or reliability. This is a game with few rewards and many pitfalls.

8. The Value of the *Pericles*

We must distinguish two criteria for evaluating Plutarch's contribution in this life, one historical, the other interpretative. Despite the rhetorical and methodological practices, mentioned above, that prohibit us from considering Plutarch as an absolutely reliable transmitter and evaluator of historical information con-

---

56. See especially his reinterpretation of Dionysius of Halicarnassus on the character of Coriolanus, as brought out by Russell 1963.

cerning Pericles and his contemporaries, our fund of knowledge of this period would be immensely impoverished if the *Pericles* had not been preserved. This life allows us to flesh out the bare bones of the Thucydidean analysis with detail that brings alive the political tensions and the personalities of the mid-fifth century. Without it, most of the anecdotes of Ion and Stesimbrotus and of the attacks of the comic poets would be lost. Thucydides son of Melesias would be only a name, the expeditions to the Chersonese and to Sinope would be forgotten, and the Congress Decree, like those of Charinus, Glaucon, and Dracontides, would vanish without a trace. With them would go lesser items that help us interpret major events: the details of the architectural history of the Eleusinian telesterion, of Pericles' administration of his family estates, or his quarrels with his children. We would know neither that Pericles had been elected general fifteen times consecutively, nor that in this period he was the object of constant political attacks. These notices derive in large part from contemporary sources, indicating the political climate in which Pericles wielded power, even when their biases render their presentation of facts unreliable. The Pericles of Plutarch, for all his heroic dimensions, is a more real person as politician and political leader than the cool and logical thinker portrayed by Thucydides.

Precisely because it makes use of information and anecdotes set aside by Thucydides, Plutarch's interpretation of Pericles has proved valuable and often convincing through the centuries. His conception of a politician who had to deal with the real world, who fought to assume and hold political power, and who was ridiculed and driven from power when his policy was most wise, still strikes a responsive chord in readers today. This is in many ways a very human leader, an orator of extraordinary power, who yet was called "squillhead" and dismissed as a self-important boor. Thucydides' analysis is truer and deeper, but Plutarch allows us to consider the man behind the strategy.

9. Style

Although Plutarch did not accept the pedantic Atticism that dictated the vocabulary and style of many of his contemporaries, he was a conscious stylist who shaped his language with care and subtlety.[57] Deeply committed to the great literature of the classical period yet open to stylistic and lexical development in the literary language, he created a personal and flexible means of expression, a middle ground between an artificial revival of ancient usage and those writers who surrendered more to the educated language of the Hellenistic and imperial period.[58]

Two features manifestly indicate his concern with style: his avoidance of hiatus, and use of prose rhythms. Isocrates had established the principle that hiatus—a sequence in which a word ending in a vowel is followed by one beginning with a vowel— should be shunned, and was followed by many literary authors. Plutarch is rather careful in this regard.[59] In the *Pericles* hiatus appears after καί (64 times), the article (65), δι' (16), περί (6), ἤ(3), ὧ (1), τί (2), numbers (3), full stops (3), and commas (2)—all common exceptions to the rule of avoidance. That is, except with καί and the article instances of hiatus are rare. Naturally, Plutarch does not alter quotations. Only two examples are found that do not fit the cases listed: ἐπεὶ αὐτήν (*Comp.* 2.1) and μέγα ἔργον (*Per.* 21.1). These have parallels in other works.[60]

In addition, Plutarch shows a marked preference for certain types of rhythmic patterns or clausulae at the end of sentences, another mark of literary sophistication. He favors especially - - - x with its by-form - - - - x, and - - - - - x (cf. for example, 1.2 τῷ θεωρεῖν, 1.4 καὶ βαναύσους, 2.5 ἐκ τῶν γραφομένων, and 1.2 ὠφε-

---

57. See in general Weissenberger 1895, 1–37; Ziegler, *RE* 931–38; Russell, *Plutarch*, 18–41; Carney 1960; Flacelière 1937, 27–36; Griffiths 1970, 10–16. On Atticism see Schmid's *Atticismus* (1887–97) and Lasserre 1979.

58. His use of the optative mood is typical: although it had almost disappeared from the *koinē*, Plutarch uses it regularly, but far less frequently than Plato. See Hein 1914. He differs from classical practice in the use of negatives, often employing μή and its compounds where οὐ would have been required. See my note to 6.2, and Stegmann 1882.

59. See Benseler 1841, 314–548; Schellens 1864; Flacelière 1969, 498–99.

60. The phrase μέγα ἔργον is found also at *Luc.* 16.2 and *Ages.* 18.4; μέγα occurs in hiatus six other times in Plutarch. Ἐπεί occurs in hiatus about seven times. Plutarch does not in the *Pericles* allow hiatus after ἔτι, μή, ἄχρι, μέχρι, or προ, as sometimes in other works. There are examples of hiatus before names, a common exception, but they are covered within the other cases (note however, νὴ Δί' Εὐβοίᾳ in *Comp.* 2.1.)

λίμων παραμελοῦντας), while avoiding other patterns, such as - - - x or - ᵛ - ᵛ x.⁶¹

Contrary to the practice of the strictest Atticists, Plutarch readily expands his vocabulary beyond the limits of classical Attic, creating new words, appropriating Hellenistic coinages, and importing words from the poetic and dialect vocabularies. Verbs with two adverbial prefixes are common, as regularly in later Greek: some twenty are found in the *Pericles*, half of which have the first element συν-. Among poetic words, note 6.1 θάμβος, 7.7 κόρος, 9.5 λάφυρα, 12.6 κομιστήρ. Dialect words include 36.9 κλαυθμός and 38.1 βληχρός. Plutarch enjoyed the effect of redoubling synonyms, as well as the *variatio* that avoided using the same word twice in the same context (e.g., ἐγκολαψάντων . . . ἐνεχάραξεν at 21.3).⁶² Poetic words often occur as the second of such pairs (cf. τὸ συνεχὲς φεύγων καὶ τὸν κόρον at 7.7). As in other Hellenistic authors, abstract nouns are much more frequent than in classical prose. Note in 13.1–2, for example, καλλιτεχνία, τάχος, διαδοχή, ἡλικία, τέλος, ἀκμή, πολιτεία, συντέλεια. In addition he employs a large number of neuter substantives: cf. τὸ φιλητικὸν . . . καὶ φιλόστοργον (1.1), τὸ φαινόμενον, τὸ δοκοῦν, τὸ βέλτιστον (1.2), τὸ ἀνθηρὸν . . . καὶ τερπνὸν (1.3).

Plutarch shares the general decline in variety of connecting particles found in Hellenistic Greek.⁶³ Three particles, δέ, γάρ, and οὖν, account for more than 70 percent of initial sentence connectives in the *Pericles*, with δέ substantially ahead (47 percent against 12.7 percent and 13.4 percent respectively). Some ten other particles and combinations represent another 14 percent (καί, καὶ γάρ, καὶ μέντοι γε, ἀλλά, μέντοι, καίτοι, οὐ μήν, οὐ μήν ἀλλά, γοῦν, δ᾽οὖν). Demonstratives often (eleven times) appear without connective particles, relatives less so (four times).⁶⁴ Διό introduces sentences eight times, εἶτα and πλήν twice each.

61. See de Groot 1915 and 1918, 40–58, and Sandbach 1939. There is a useful summary of the subject in *OCD*² s.v. prose-rhythm.
62. The redoubling of synonyms is a Demosthenic trait: see Lasserre 1979, 140.
63. See Blomqvist 1969.
64. For the use of demonstratives as connectives in historical narrative see Denniston, 258.

Although he varies the form and length of his sentences continually, Plutarch delights in long, loosely constructed sentences, rich in participles. Their construction is usually additive rather than complex, but because participles used circumstantially, substantively, attributively, and as genitive absolutes are intermingled, it is necessary to read with some attention. The informality and length of many sentences—often ten lines or more of modern text—occasionally makes them hard to follow, although more commonly the clauses follow on one another quite naturally. The seventeen-line sentence at 12.1–2 of our text is an example. It contains some nine finite verbs, fifteen participles, and five infinitives but unfolds in a fairly predictable way: first there is a relative clause, next the main clause τοῦτο . . . ἐβάσκαινον . . . καὶ διέβαλλον ἐν ταῖς ἐκκλησίαις, and then the participle βοῶντες introducing the series of clauses expressing the complaints, connected by μέν, δέ, καί, each clause more complex than the preceding. The first is supplemented simply by a participial phrase, τὰ κοινὰ . . . μεταγαγών, the second is introduced by a relative clause, with an appositive accusative and infinitive, and the third is expanded by the participle ὁρῶσα and the indirect statement that follows.

The sentence is made fuller by the frequent doubling of verbs and objects, often with little effect on sense: ἡδονὴν . . . κόσμον, δύναμιν . . . ὄλβον, ἐβάσκαινον . . . διέβαλλον, ἀδοξεῖ . . . κακῶς ἀκούει, ὑβρίζεσθαι . . . τυραννεῖσθαι, καταχρυσοῦντας . . . καλλωπίζοντας. Unusual word order supplies ornament, such as the mild hyperbaton and ABAB order of μεγίστην δὲ τοῖς ἄλλοις ἔκπληξιν ἀνθρώποις, and the chiasm of δεινὴν ὕβριν...ὑβρίζεσθαι καὶ τυραννεῖσθαι περιφανῶς.[65] The simile comparing the Acropolis to a painted woman adds color and force to the concluding clause. The

65. This sort of hyperbaton, frequently used by classicizing writers, derives from Demosthenes: see Lasserre 1979, 155–56. Phrases arranged in ABA order are quite common in the *Pericles*, especially at the ends of cola. Thus we find subject-verb-subject (Καλλικράτης εἰργάζετο καὶ Ἰκτῖνος, 13.7), object-verb-object (φιλομαθές τι κέκτηται καὶ φιλοθέαμον, 1.2), genitive-noun-genitive (κυνῶν ἔκγονα καὶ πιθήκων, 1.1), adjective-dative-adjective (προμήκη δὲ τῇ κεφαλῇ καὶ ἀσύμμετρον, 3.3), adjective-noun-adjective (δεινὸν ἀσέβημα καὶ μυσῶδες, 13.16), etc. Chiasmus is not unusual, e.g., 1.4 ἐπὶ τῶν μύρων καὶ τῶν ἀλουργῶν . . . τοὺς δὲ βαφεῖς καὶ μυρεψούς, 13.5 ἀειθαλὲς πνεῦμα καὶ ψυχὴν ἀγήρω.

whole is rounded off by a triplet of nouns, λίθους . . . ἀγάλματα
. . . ναούς, ending with a six-syllable word, χιλιοταλάντους, and
one of his favorite clausulae, - ᴗ ᴗ - -. The effect is of accumulation rather than suspense, of piling on of riches of words and
ideas, rather than of a tightly ordered and controlled structure of
thought.

10. Text

The text used is a photographic reproduction of that of C.
Lindskog and K. Ziegler, revised by Ziegler, in the Teubner edition
of the *Lives*, vol. 1.2, 3rd ed. (Leipzig 1964). All the lemmata are
those of Ziegler's text, but in the commentary I suggest alternatives that diverge from Ziegler's text at a number of points. Most
often I follow the text of R. Flacelière in the Budé edition (*Vies*,
vol. 3, Paris 1964), which differs only slightly from Ziegler's, usually by retaining manuscript readings.[66] These differences are
listed in Appendix 1.

Both editions are based on four manuscripts divided into two
families, S and UMA, although each cites additional manuscripts
on occasion. The *Parallel Lives*, because of their bulk, were early
divided into volumes containing groups of lives. Our manuscripts
reflect two editions arranged in different orders, one of two volumes, arranged chronologically according to the Greek statesmen,
in which *Pericles–Fabius* was seventh, the other of three volumes,
arranged by the native cities of the Greeks (Athenian, various,
Spartan), in which the pair was sixth. S, Seitenstettensis 34, of the
second half of the tenth century, is the chief representative of the
bipartite family, which was already being used by the patriarch
Photius in the ninth century. UMA preserve the tripartite tradition. Of these U, Vaticanus graecus 138, of the first half of the
eleventh century, is the oldest, preserving the *recensio Constantina*,
an edition in thirty-two-line pages prepared for the emperor Con-
stantine Porphyrogennetos;[67] A, Parisinus graecus 1671, was copied for the Byzantine scholar Maximus Planudes in Constantino-

---

66. M. Manfredini has kindly shared with me his unpublished collation of
the manuscripts of the *Pericles*.
67. See Irigoin 1976.

ple in 1296. M, Marcianus 385, of the fifteenth century, combines both traditions, but follows the tripartite family for the *Pericles*.[68] Recent studies promise to clarify further the early history of the two recensions of the text and the interrelations between the later manuscripts.[69]

3. Sources for the *Pericles*

Herodotus was the historian of the Persian Wars, Thucydides of the Peloponnesian War. The period in between, which included most of the active period of Pericles' life, never found its historian, although Thucydides gave a brief sketch of the growth of Athenian power in this period in his *Pentecontaetea* (1.89–117). Thus later writers, including Plutarch, were forced to piece together traditions and random bits of information, without the clear sequence of events and artistic shaping of the account that a master narrator provides. Furthermore, as far as we know, no authoritative biography of Pericles was written in the Hellenistic or later periods.[70] Plutarch's knowledge of Pericles nevertheless would date back to his earliest education, through stories he had heard

68. See the prefaces to volumes 1.1 and 1.2 of the Teubner edition and 1 and 3 of the Budé edition, with the reviews of Erbse 1961 and Cadell 1965. The fundamental study of the tradition is Ziegler 1907. For a sketch of Plutarch's readers and influence through the ages, see Hirzel 1912; cf. also Ziegler, *RE* 947–62; Barrow 1967, 162–72; Russell, *Plutarch*, 143–58.

69. See Irigoin 1982–83; the summary but still rich essay of M. Manfredini, "La tradizione manoscritta delle *Vite*" (1987); and Manfredini's special studies of the tradition of *Solon* (1977), *Lycurgus and Numa* (1981), and *Theseus–Romulus* and *Themistocles–Camillus* (1983).

70. Although it once was widely accepted that Plutarch regularly relied on Hellenistic biographies or variorum histories that collected the traditions he reported, this view has been discredited by studies of individual lives and of Plutarch's method of work. For the former opinion see esp. E. Meyer on the *Cimon* (1899), and more recently Homeyer 1963. For the view presupposed here see Gomme, *HCT* 1:82; Stadter 1965; Hamilton 1969, xliii–lxii; Frost 1980, 40–59. On the nature of Hellenistic biography see Momigliano 1971. For arguments against any kind of true political bibliography in the Hellenistic period see Geiger's *Cornelius Nepos and Ancient Political Biography* (1985). It is noteworthy that Nepos himself did not write a biography of Pericles. A certain Sabinus is cited as author of a biography of Pericles by schol. Aristid. 3:500 Dindorf.

from his father or his tutors, and read in Thucydides or Plato.[71] As he matured and extended his reading, the sources of his conception of the man would fall into several broad classes: narrative historians; references in Old Comedy; commentators to the classical writers; fifth-century authors, such as Ion of Chios and Stesimbrotus; notices in philosophers and the tradition of the philosophical schools; antiquarians; and his own observation. Some of these he would have reviewed specifically for this life, others he would recall from memory or notes taken over the years.[72] Whenever he could in the *Lives*, Plutarch took advantage of contemporary sources: Solon's poems, the speeches of Demosthenes, the letters of Alexander.[73] The same is true of the *Pericles*. Although later writers were used as necessary, Plutarch made a special effort to profit from contemporary sources, which would have included not only Thucydides, but the mocking of Old Comedy, the anti-Periclean jibes of Ion and Stesimbrotus, and decrees moved in the assembly by Pericles, his enemies, or his friends. Although often disagreeing with their content or implications, he nevertheless recorded these disparate opinions, fully aware of the value of contemporary witnesses, even when hostile, for creating a living portrait.

Of his many sources, the most influential were Thucydides and Plato; the most useful in terms of portraying character were a collection of fifth-century decrees and the jokes of Old Comedy. Unfortunately most of the authors he cited have now been lost, and Plutarch certainly did not cite all that he used. The modern reader is forced to steer an uneasy and often dangerous path between the Scylla of speculative reconstruction and the Charybdis of skeptical agnosticism. A review of the different authors, extant and lost, and of the other possible sources, is essential for navigation. In analyzing and reconstructing sources, it is necessary

71. See Frost 1980, 47–49.

72. Note the group of anecdotes concerning Pericles assembled in the *Sayings of Kings and Commanders, Mor.* 186C–D.

73. The principle is important, even when the source itself is suspect, as in the case of the letters of Alexander. The same applies, though in a more limited way, for the Roman lives, where he cites the memoirs of Scipio Nasica for *Aemilius Paulus* and uses Dellius for *Antony*, and for the Civil War lives employs Asinius Pollio and various works of Cicero and Caesar.

to treat authors preserved only in citations from other authors with special care, keeping in mind both their own purposes in writing and the reasons for which Plutarch chose to quote a particular passage.[74] Granted Plutarch's interests, it is right to begin with fifth-century writers.[75]

1. Contemporary Sources

a. *Herodotus and Thucydides.* Although Herodotus was a contemporary of Pericles, and perhaps knew him in Athens, he refers infrequently to events after 479. He names Pericles only once, recounting the portent of the lion-dream as the last item in his account of the Alcmeonid family (6.131). This dream, ambiguous in its suggestions of power and violence, is recalled but not expressly cited at *Per.* 3.3. Thucydides, on the other hand, made Pericles a major figure in his narrative of the Peloponnesian War, in which Pericles' foresight and cool evaluation of the implications and consequences of war serve as a foil to the growing irrationality of the Athenian demos and its leaders as the war progressed. Nevertheless, despite its brilliance this portrait covers only the span of a year and a half, between Pericles' speech refusing to repeal the Megarian decree in 432 (Thuc. 1.139–44) and his last speech and deposition from office in 430 (2.60–65). This part of the narrative totals only about forty-five modern pages and includes large sections in which Pericles does not figure directly, such as the attack on Plataea and the description of the plague. Thucydides also gives scattered short notices to Pericles (1.111.2; 1.114.1, 3; 1.116–17; 127.1) that Plutarch gathers into his life. As raw material for a biography, it is extremely limited in scope and detail.

Plutarch knew Thucydides' history well, and no doubt was familiar with it long before he undertook to write the *Parallel Lives.* He cites specific passages of Thucydides twenty-three times in the

74. Cf., e.g., Ambaglio 1980.

75. The fundamental work on the sources of the *Pericles* is Meinhardt's *Perikles bei Plutarch* (1957), with a full bibliography of earlier studies. See also the excellent observations of Gomme, *HCT* 1:54–84 on the fifth-century lives. Scardigli 1979 provides a valuable survey of the Roman lives, with a thorough treatment of source discussions. For the breadth of Plutarch's reading, see Ziegler, *RE* 911–28; Theander 1950–51; and Stadter 1965, 125–40.

Lives and thirty times in the *Moralia*, not including general references. His admiration for his work is apparent in the *Nicias* (1.1), where he asks his readers not to compare his account with that of Thucydides, who "published an inimitable account, even more pathetic, lively, and various than he usually is." In the *Pericles* Thucydides furnishes the overall vision of the statesman as farsighted and strong-minded, ruling the state as a monarch even in a democracy (cf. 9.1). More specifically, his narrative is the foundation for chapters 22–23 (Megara and Euboea), 25–28 (the Samian War), and 29–35 (the Peloponnesian War), although Plutarch has added a great deal. It is this Thucydidean core that furnishes the chronological framework for the second half of the life. However, Thucydides was interested in power, not character, and clear understanding, not temperament, so that the tone of Plutarch's account often belies its Thucydidean origin.[76]

b. *Ion of Chios.* A completely different type of account was provided by Ion of Chios (*FGrHist* 392). Ion was best known in his own day as a poet who wrote in various popular genres, especially tragedy.[77] He was born ca. 490, presented his first tragedy at Athens ca. 451, and on one occasion won both the tragic and the dithyrambic contests at Athens. His prose works included a *Foundation of Chios* and the *Epidemiai* or *Visits*. The latter work gave personal sketches and scenes of Ion's visits abroad, and of visits of other distinguished persons to his home on Chios. His wealth and culture permitted him to entertain and be entertained by the elite of Athens, where he must have visited often. His report of a dinner party at Athens attended by Cimon, which took place when he was only a young man, furnishes an engaging sketch of that politician. Plutarch cites the book (though not by name) several times in the *Cimon* (5.3, 9.1, 16.10 = F12–14) and twice in the *Pericles* (5.3, 28.7 = F15–16), as well as four times in the *Moralia*. Plutarch found Ion useful for personal detail, especially for the after-dinner story told by Cimon in *Cim.* 9. In the *Pericles* he is

76. See the discussion of structure in section 2.4 above, and Stadter 1973b. On Plutarch's reinterpretation of Thucydides, see de Romilly 1988.

77. See von Blumenthal 1939; Jacoby 1947 and his commentary to *FGrHist* 392; Huxley 1965; and Wehrli 1973. Strasburger 1986 exaggerates the importance of Ion and Stesimbrotus in the *Pericles*.

cited for additional color on Pericles' austerity—Ion clearly preferred Cimon's aristocratic good humor to Pericles' severe inten-
sity—and for a sentiment from the Samian funeral oration. He
has also been suggested as the source for two anecdotes in chapter
8 (the conversation of Archidamus and Thucydides, and Pericles'
reproof of Sophocles) and for the story of Anaxagoras at 16.7–
9.[78]

c. *Stesimbrotus.* The book of Stesimbrotus of Thasos (*FGrHist* 107)
was consciously used by Plutarch as a contemporary account
(ἡλικιῶτις ἱστορία, *Per.* 13.16) in the lives of Themistocles, Cimon,
and Pericles, even though he often rejected what it contained. Stesimbrotus' work *On Themistocles, Thucydides, and Pericles* is known
only from the eleven references in Plutarch and one notice in
Athenaeus (F10A = 589D–E). Wilamowitz and Jacoby argued
that it was a political pamphlet, pouring out all the hatred of the
Athenian empire and its leaders that might be expected from a
citizen of Thasos, whose secession had been violently suppressed
by Athens. However, Schachermeyr has demonstrated that the
fragments give no sign of an attack on the empire, but rather
suggest a contemptuous review of the education and training of
Athenian leaders—exactly what one would expect from a sophist
known to have lectured and written on Homer and Homeric interpretation. The emphasis on education and character, with frequent anecdotes, fitted Plutarch's needs exactly: like Ion, Stesimbrotus could personalize the excessively political account of Thucydides. In the *Pericles* Plutarch cites him for a quotation from one
of Pericles' speeches (8.9) and for Pericles' relations with his son
Xanthippus (13.16, 36.6), as well as for a variant from Thucydides'
account of the siege of Samos (26.1). The stories at *Per.* 10.6 and
29.2 are attributed to Stesimbrotus at *Cim.* 14.5 and 16.1 and
clearly derive from him. Other anecdotes, especially the stories
concerning Elpinice and Xanthippus, may be drawn from him:
see my notes to 16.3, 28.6, and 36. At the same time, Plutarch was

78. The poet Sophocles was the subject of one of the best anecdotes of the
Epidemiai: see F6 = Athen. 13.603E–604D.

disgusted by his scandalmongering (13.16) and doubted his accuracy (13.16, 26.1; cf. *Them.* 2.5, 24.6–7).[79]

d. *Old Comedy.* The *Pericles* is remarkable for its frequent citations from the authors of Old Comedy, only one of whom, Aristophanes, still survives.[80] A distinguishing feature of Attic Old Comedy was its direct involvement in the life of the polis, especially in the form of comments and attacks on prominent political figures, such as Aristophanes' ridicule of the general Lamachus in the *Acharnians* and his denunciation of Cleon in the *Knights*. Although for a brief period (440/39–437/36) there was a law limiting this mockery, Pericles was a major target of the comic poets during his lifetime.[81] It is extremely difficult for the modern observer to reach an accurate assessment of the meaning of these attacks, whether they should be considered a reflection of a deep resentment against Pericles by the conservative party or by masses of the people, or only a peculiar expression of Attic wit, meant chiefly for laughter and with little political or historical significance. As far as we know, all politically prominent figures were ridiculed by

79. See Jacoby, commentary to *FGrHist* 107; Gomme, *HCT* 1:36–37; Schachermeyr 1965, 3–23; Strasburger 1986; Accame 1982. Meister 1978 notes that Schachermeyr is wrong to separate political and moral arguments so rigidly, and stresses rather Stesimbrotus' importance as the beginning of biography. We must be careful to remember, however, that we know Stesimbrotus only through Plutarch, who was excerpting items as a biographer. It is dangerous to see a Plutarchean biographer in Stesimbrotus. He may well have included material of a quite different sort: compare Plutarch's very selective use of Plato's *Phaedrus* in the *Pericles*. On Stesimbrotus as a Homeric critic see Richardson 1975, 71–74. For a possible new fragment of his work on the mysteries see Burkert 1986.

80. Old Comedy fragments are cited according to the edition of T. Kock, *Comicorum Atticorum Fragmenta* (*CAF*, K.) (1880–88) and the still incomplete edition of R. Kassel and C. Austin, *Poetae Comici Graeci* (*PCG*, K.A.), vol. 3.2, *Aristophanes* (1984); vol. 4, *Aristophon–Crobylus* (1983); vol. 5, *Damoxenus–Magnes* (1986). The edition of A. Meineke, *Fragmenta Comicorum Graecorum* (*FCG*) (1839–57), is still important. J. Edmonds, *Fragments of Attic Comedy* (*FAC*) (1957–61) is sometimes inaccurate but useful for its English translation. Cf. also C. Austin, *Comicorum Graecorum Fragmenta in Papyris Reperta* (*CGFP*) (1973).

81. See esp. Schwarze, *Beurteilung.*

the comedians,[82] and Pericles, being most prominent, was ridiculed most often. Because comedy also had a religious and civic function of debunking the great, its attacks need not have been a direct reflection of the political opposition of either author or audience.

Where did Plutarch find these references? Although like most postclassical Greeks Plutarch much preferred Menander and the New Comedy to Aristophanes and the Old, he quotes Aristophanes some thirty times (twenty-two from extant works) and often refers to other Old Comedy authors.[83] We know from the papyrus fragments that the Old Comedy was still read in the second century A.D.,[84] although it was necessary to use a commentary. The difficulty of reading Aristophanes by that time is mentioned by a friend of Plutarch's in an account of a party given by the biographer in Chaeronea. Considering what is proper for after-dinner entertainment, he recommends New Comedy but excludes the Old, because it is too intense, too indecent, and "every person would need a grammar-teacher beside him, to explain who Laispodias is in Eupolis, and Cinesias in Plato [the comic poet], Lampon in Cratinus, and each of the others made fun of in comedy (kōmōidoumenoi), so that our dinner party would become a grammar-school, or the jokes would mean less."[85] Although a boorish sophist immediately responds by reciting several passages from

---

82. Note the comments of Dover 1972, 34–35. That exuberant criticism was appreciated by the audience but not reflected in the policy of the assembly is apparent from the case of the *Knights*. This virulent attack on Cleon won first prize in 424, yet Cleon was elected one of the ten generals for 424/23. See Dover 1972, 95–100. See also Ameling 1981.

83. See his *Comparison of Aristophanes and Menander*, of which only a fragmentary epitome is preserved, *Mor.* 853A–854D. On his references to Old Comedy see Helmbold and O'Neil 1959. Plutarch recalls or cites verses from Aristophanes, Cratinus, Eupolis, Hermippus, Pherecrates, Phrynichus, Plato Comicus, and Teleclides, as well as the anonymous verses listed under "Comica adespota."

84. See Pack 1965 and the analysis by Willis, "A Census of the Literary Papyri from Egypt" (1968); and, on Cratinus, Luppe 1967.

85. *Symp.* 712A. The *grammatikos* was an expert on literary texts. His knowledge and social standing could range from that of a learned literary scholar to that of a secondary-school teacher, one of whose main functions was exegesis of classical texts: see Marrou 1964, 223–42. Interestingly enough, all the

Aristophanes (*Symp.* 712D), the party seems to agree with the speaker.

The story illustrates the peculiar status of Old Comedy in the second century: it was read in school, along with other classics, but its frequent topical allusions inhibited its easy use in conversation, or in Plutarch's essays.[86] Old Comedy had to be read with exegetical material, such as the books of *kōmōidoumenoi* mentioned by Athenaeus and others.[87] It is a mistake, however, to think that these books replaced the reading of the actual texts among the well-educated. Rather, they permitted Old Comedy to be read by those who were not grammarians. Naturally, however, the same explanations of a passage reappear in different citations, whether in a scholiast to Plato, in Athenaeus, in Pollux' *Onomasticon*, or in Plutarch.[88] Plutarch, then, when citing Old Comedy in the *Pericles*

---

persons mentioned in this passage as being mocked in comedy are known from other citations: Laispodias is named at schol. Ar. *Birds* 1569, quoting Eupolis F102 K., from the *Demes*; Cinesias is named by Galen from Plato Comicus F184 K.; and Lampon is mentioned by Hesychius and others, citing Cratinus F57–58 K. = F62 K.A., from the *Drapetides* (cf. also F117 K. = F125 K.A.).

86. One thinks of the difficulty of citing verses of Dante's *Inferno* in company.

87. Athenaeus 11.482C; 13.586A, 591C; cf. Steinhausen 1910. Note that Galen, a generation later than Plutarch, wrote some ten books on "ordinary" words in Aristophanes, Eupolis, and Cratinus, another on peculiar words, and finally one entitled *Whether Old Comedy Is Useful Reading for Those Being Educated.* See his *De libris propriis* 18 (19:48 Kuhn) and DeLacy 1966, 265. In a papyrus letter of the second century A.D., a man writes to someone in Alexandria, "Make and send me copies of Books 6 and 7 of Hypsicrates' *Komoidoumenoi*" (Turner 1968, 87). There were also works on the courtesans of Athens, from which Plutarch may have learned some anecdotes of Aspasia. In his commentary to *FGrHist*, 347–51, Jacoby suggests that these may have formed a special subset of *kōmōidoumenoi*. Papyri have revealed special collections, *gnomologia*, taken from comedy: see Kalbfleisch 1925 (on poverty); Livrea 1985 (on miserliness and greed); and Carrara 1987. For an account of the ancient commentators (scholiasts) to the comic poets see Henderson 1987, lvi–lxix.

88. Steinhausen 1910 does not appreciate the interrelation between these collections and the study of Old Comedy, especially Aristophanes. Naturally, readings in school or later might be from anthologies of selected passages as well as whole plays. See Barns 1950, 1951.

---

and other fifth-century lives, was drawing on his own reading, fortified by the antiquarian material available in the commentaries and the books of *kōmōidoumenoi*.[89] The actual quotations, on such items as head shape, buildings, political power, and the cause of the war, represent his own selection from the numerous references to Pericles in Old Comedy.[90] We have already noted Plutarch's preference for contemporary sources. In the Old Comedy poets he found valuable contemporary information, especially on the opposition to Pericles that formed one of the main facets of his portrait.[91]

e. *Cratinus*. Cratinus, an older contemporary of Aristophanes, writing chiefly from the 440s to the 420s, is the comic writer most frequently quoted in the *Pericles* (at 3.5, 13.8, 13.10, and 24.9).[92] His *Nemesis* (*Per.* 3.5) featured a mythological plot, based on the story that Zeus, in the form of a swan, made love to Nemesis (also

89. This conclusion contrasts with that of Schläpfer 1950, 57–60, who thinks that Plutarch read only Aristophanes, in particular the *Knights, Clouds,* and *Frogs*. Like Ziegler, *RE* 918–19, he is misled by the small number of citations from Old Comedy outside the fifth-century lives, which must be ascribed rather to the peculiar nature of Old Comedy. Cf. also the conclusions of DiGregorio (1979, 1980) concerning Plutarch's knowledge of tragedy. We can see traces of the learning of the commentaries used by Plutarch even where the comic poets are not directly cited: e.g., in the notice on the vowel quantity in Damon's name (4.1), on Aspasia (24), and on the engineer Artemon (27.4).

90. Plutarch omits some material on Pericles, e.g., the *Dionysalexandros* of Cratinus (*CGFP* F70; *PCG* 4:140–47), which satirized the outbreak of a war (either the Samian or the Peloponnesian War) through the story of Paris and Helen, with Dionysus playing Paris; the reference in Teleclides' *Hesiods* to Pericles' love for a certain Chrysilla of Corinth (F17 K.); and the lines from Aristophanes' *Peace*, 605–11, on the accusations against Phidias.

91. The gibes and anecdotes of the comic poets were often treated as historical fact, with little sense of the various purposes to which they might have been put in the plays. The habit already existed in the fifth century, as Socrates protests in Plato's *Apology*, trying to correct the false impression given of him in the *Clouds*. In the fourth century Ephorus also used Aristophanes and other comic writers in his account of the origin of the Peloponnesian War. Theopompus may have used them in his excursus on the demagogues (Connor 1968, 102–3). On the whole Plutarch seems more careful.

92. See Schwarze, *Beurteilung*, 5–90; A. Körte, *RE* s.v. Kratinos 3, XI, 2 (1922) 1647–54; Norwood 1932, 114–44; Mattingly 1977, 231–45; *CAF* 1:11–130; *CGFP* 34–50; *PCG* 4:112–337.

called Leda), who thereupon laid an egg from which was hatched Helen, the cause of the Trojan War. Zeus, Plutarch tells us, was a Pericles-figure; Nemesis may have been Aspasia, though this seems unlikely.[93] The *Chirons* (*Per.* 3.5, 24.9) also used a mythological plot, although the contents are not clear. Chiron was the teacher of Achilles and the other heroes; the play, with its chorus of centaur companions of Chiron, seems to recall the heroic days of old. Pericles appears as a tyrant Zeus, and Aspasia as Hera. The *Thracian Women* (*Per.* 3.4, 13.10) may be connected with the introduction of the Thracian goddess Bendis into Athens; again Pericles appears behind the figure of Zeus. The *Archilochoi*, cited at *Cim.* 10.4 (= F1 K., F1 K.A.), is not mentioned in the *Pericles*. Unknown plays of Cratinus are cited at *Per.* 13.8 (= *De glor. Ath.* 351A) and at *Sol.* 25.2 (= F274 K., F300 K.A.).

f. *Aristophanes*. Aristophanes is cited twice in this life, from the *Acharnians* (*Per.* 30.4) on the cause of the Peloponnesian War, and from the *Babylonians* (*Per.* 26.4).[94] Plutarch often referred to Aristophanes, especially for topical quotations: of the twenty-three quotations from his extant works, seven are from the *Knights*, none from the apolitical *Ecclesiazusae*. However, because the poet began writing only in 427, two years after Pericles' death, few citations were suitable for this life.

g. *Teleclides*. Teleclides won his first victory in the Dionysia ca. 445.[95] We know eight titles, but not the sources of Plutarch's quotations at *Per.* 3.6 and 16.2. Plutarch cites him again at *Nic.* 4.5 (F41 K.).

h. *Eupolis*. Eupolis, the third of the canonical triad of Old Comedy writers, with Aristophanes and Cratinus, produced his first play in

93. Cf. Godolphin 1931; Luppe 1974. Note that a new temple to Nemesis was dedicated at Rhamnus in northeast Attica in the 430s.

94. Two words referring to Pericles' oratory at 8.4 are also from the *Acharnians* (531); see my note ad loc. For Aristophanes and Pericles see Schwarze, *Beurteilung*, 135–59; for the fragments, *CAF* 1:392–600 and *PCG* 3:2. Plutarch does not cite *Peace* 605–11, preferring to use the evidence of Glaucon's decree instead. Cf. my note to 31.2.

95. On Teleclides see Schwarze, *Beurteilung*, 93–100; *CAF* 1:209–24.

429 and died before the end of the Peloponnesian War. In his *Demoi*,[96] probably produced in 412, four famous Athenian states-men—Miltiades, Aristides, Solon, and Pericles—were brought up from the Underworld to give advice to the state. The demes of Attica would have formed the chorus. Plutarch cites the *Demoi* in this life for the shape of Pericles' head (*Per.* 3.7) and for his bastard son (24.10), but omits (because too well known?) a famous passage on his eloquence (F94 K., Fl02 K.A.), which formed part of a standard tradition on the power of oratory.[97]

i. *Hermippus.* Hermippus and the comic poet Plato are cited once each in this life. Hermippus won a victory at the Dionysia in 435 and continued writing into the teens. We know ten titles and some one hundred fragments, cited by scholiasts, lexicographers, and Athenaeus. Plutarch cites him only in this life (*Per.* 33.8), but his interpretation is fairly detailed and seems to derive from knowl-edge beyond the passage itself. The fragment probably belongs to the *Moirai*, produced in 430 or 429. The absence of other citations suggests that Plutarch did not know Hermippus' comedies well and may never have read him. Plutarch also refers to Hermippus' prosecution of Aspasia at *Per.* 32.1; see my discussion there.[98]

j. *Plato.* Plato the comic writer was a contemporary of Aristoph-anes, writing roughly in the period 425–400. We have some thirty titles of plays and 260 fragments. Plutarch cites him at *Per.* 4.4 for his reference to Damon, and elsewhere on Themistocles' tomb,

---

96. On the *Demoi* see Plepelits 1970; Sartori 1975; Schwarze, *Beurteilung*, 125–35; *CAF* 1:279–93; *PCG* 5:342–76. For the substantial new fragments on papyrus see Plepelits 1970; Page 1950; *CGFP* F92–94; and *PCG* F99–101. The *Demoi* is also quoted at *Alc.* 13.2 (F95 K., F116 K.A.), and referred to at *Symp.* 712A (F102 K., F107 K.A., quoted above).

97. Cf. Connor 1962b. Plutarch cites other plays of Eupolis at *Nic.* 4.6 (F181 K., F193 K.A.), *Cim.* 15.4 (F208 K., F221 K.A.), *De adul. et amic.* 54B (F346 K., F374 K.A.), *Symp.* 699A (F147 K., F158 K.A.), and *Max. cum princ.* 778A and *De adul. et amic.* 50D (F162 K., F175 K.A.). Plutarch does not mention that Eupolis referred to Aspasia under the name Helen in the *Prospaltoi* (F249 K., F267 K.A.). On Eupolis see Schwarze, *Beurteilung*, 113–35; for the fragments, *CAF* 1:258–369, and *PCG* 5:294–539.

98. On Hermippus see Schwarze, *Beurteilung*, 100–113; *CAF* 1:224–53; *PCG* 5:561–604.

the ostracism of Hyperbolus, Timon of Athens, and other subjects. He never names the plays cited.[99]

k. *Unnamed comic poets.* A number of citations simply refer to the comic poets: 4.3, 7.8, 8.4, 13.15–16, 16.1, 24.9. Some of these we can identify, such as those from Aristophanes' *Acharnians* at 8.4; others elude us.[100]

l. *Decrees.* Plutarch is one of the few ancient authors to use the Athenian fifth-century decrees that had been preserved by antiquarian curiosity.[101] They were in fact invaluable contemporary sources, as modern historians have discovered in exploring the implications of epigraphical texts, which often preserve events and attitudes not suggested by the literary tradition. The most important decrees in the *Pericles* are the Congress Decree summarized in chapter 17, the "humane" decree and the Charinus decree, which explain Pericles' stubbornness toward the Spartans in chapter 30, and the several decrees relating to the attacks on Pericles and his friends in chapters 31–32. Not every reference to a decree or a decision of the assembly is based on the decree itself; narrative sources occasionally refer to them or quote a phrase. Yet most seem to derive, like those quoted occasionally in other fifth-century lives, from the *Collection of Decrees* of Craterus of Macedon (*FGrHist* 342). Plutarch's two references to Craterus indicate that he knew his work and its value. On one occasion he defends the Peace of Callias against the minimalist interpretation of the historian Callisthenes, writing that "in the decrees that Craterus collected a copy of the treaty is listed as existing" (*Cim.* 13.5 = F13). In the *Aristides*, on the other hand, after giving Craterus' version

---

99. Cf. Schwarze, *Beurteilung*, 160–64; *CAF* 1:601–667. Other citations: *Them.* 32.6 (F183 K., cited via Diodorus the Perigete), *Nic.* 11.6–7 (F187 K.), *Alc.* 13.9 (F187 K.), *Ant.* 70.1 (F218 K.), *Symp.* 712A (F184 K.), *Praec. ger. rep.* 801A–B (F185 K.), and [*Vitae dec. or.*] 833C (F103 K.).

100. See Schwarze, *Beurteilung*, 164–68. Other fragments of Old Comedy are quoted at *Arist.* 5.8 (*CAF* 3:adespota F68) and *De aud.* 27C (F8), *An seni* 789E (F56), *Praec. ger. rep.* 807A (F11), *Non posse* 1101F (F55; perhaps not comic, cf. adespota iambica F37 West), and [*De mus.*] 1142B (F65).

101. See 8.7 and my note ad loc. On Plutarch's preference of decrees to the speeches reported in Thucydides, which he did not consider authentic, see Stadter 1973b.

of the death of Aristides, he criticizes him for omitting evidence he normally includes: "but Craterus presents no written evidence for this story, neither an indictment nor a decree, although he usually quite reasonably records such evidence and notes those who report it" (*Arist.* 26.1–4 = F12). Plutarch never cites other authors who might have recorded decrees, such as Theophrastus or Demetrius of Phaleron, for this sort of information. Craterus was not widely cited: apart from Plutarch, he is referred to chiefly by Stephanus of Byzantium, Harpocration, and the scholiastic tradition. His work was apparently quite specialized, treating fifth-century Athenian documents, including indictments and tribute lists, in nine books. The arrangement was at least in part chronological, but Plutarch's reference to narrative apart from the documents themselves suggests that there may have been a topical arrangement as well. Jacoby connects the collection with similar studies from the early years of the Peripatetic school, such as Aristotle's *Constitutions* or Theophrastus' *Laws*. Craterus' source would have been the city archives, where decrees, indictments, and probably other records could be consulted, rather than inscribed stelai, which only preserved a small percentage of such documents. Plutarch's decision to use such a collection allowed him to enrich markedly our knowledge of Pericles and his policy.[102]

102. See in general F. Jacoby, *RE* s.v. Krateros 1, XI, 2 (1922), 1617–22 (reprinted in Jacoby 1956, 165–67) and his commentary to *FGrHist* 342 (1955), with the review of Chambers (1957). P. Krech, *De Crateri Psephismaton Synagoge* (1888) is still useful, although he exaggerates in considering all references to decrees in Plutarch's fifth-century lives to be fragments of Craterus. Jacoby in 1922 thought Plutarch used Craterus directly, but in his *Atthis* (1949, 209) and in *FGrHist* (n. 52) he considers the use of a Hellenistic intermediary more likely. But as Gomme noted (*HCT* 1:75n.2), the reference at *Arist.* 26.4 indicates some personal acquaintance. For Craterus in Plutarch see Ewbank 1982, 168–71; for the *Pericles* see also Meinhardt, *Perikles*, 9, 12, 20, and 70–74 (list of passages). Frost 1961 and Ewbank 1982, 162–67, review other possible sources for documentary material in Plutarch. Some antiquarian writers cited documents: note Melanthios' quotation of the decree against Diagoras of Melos in his *On the Mysteries at Eleusis* (*FGrHist* 326 F36) and Polemo's citation of inscriptions for linguistic usage (Athen. 6.234D–E). Plutarch usually avoids quoting documents in his *Lives*, preferring to summarize or paraphrase, but he cites verbatim phrases from the indictment of Alcibiades (*Alc.* 22.4) and the decree of Dromoclides (*Demetr.* 13.1–3: "I will subjoin the precise expression from the decree, which runs as follows . . ."). He por-

2. Later Historians and Antiquarians

a. *Ephorus*. Ephorus of Cyme on the coast of Asia Minor wrote the first universal history, covering the history of the world from the Trojan War to 341 B.C. in thirty books. He was frequently cited in later writers; Diodorus especially seems to have relied on him heavily for his account of the fifth century.[103] Plutarch was very familiar with him and cites him frequently, especially in the *Alcibiades*, *Lysander*, *Dion*, and *Pelopidas*. His easy acquaintance with this historian is indicated by an anecdote he relates of a garrulous acquaintance at Chaeronea (*De garr.* 514C = F213): "Since he had read by chance two or three books of Ephorus, he wore out everybody and made every dinner unbearable by holding forth continually on the battle of Leuctra and its aftermath, and so won the nickname, 'Epaminondas.'" Plutarch was tolerantly amused: he himself knew Ephorus well. This conclusion is confirmed by the passages where he states firmly that Ephorus did not report something found in Duris (*Per.* 28.2, *Alc.* 32.2).[104]

In the *Pericles* Plutarch employs Ephorus as a useful supplement to Thucydides' accounts of Pericles' repulse of the Spartans from Attica in 446 and of the Samian War (22–23.1, 25–28). The Ephoran narrative forms a major part of the "worst reason" for Pericles' refusal to repeal the Megarian decree (31–32). It may also

---

trays himself as introducing casually into an after-dinner conversation a reference to the decree authorizing the expedition of the Athenians to the battle of Plataea, with the special point that it was passed in the prytany of the Aiantis tribe (*Symp.* 628E). He therefore knew not only a summary, but even the heading of the decree. The evidence for the archive at Athens and its availability is discussed, with a review of earlier studies, by Boegehold 1972. Documents in archives must be distinguished from inscribed copies: cf. J. and L. Robert 1961, 140–41, and Sherwin-White 1985. Recent discoveries have given evidence of public archives preserved on papyrus in several cities, although only the seals are preserved: see Habicht 1985, 34, and for a similar earlier archive in Judah, Avigad 1986. The philosopher Epicurus even deposited his writings in the Athenian archives for safe-keeping: see Clay 1982.

103. See *FGrHist* 70 with commentary; E. Schwartz, *RE* s.v. Ephoros, VI, 1 (1907) 1–16 (= Schwartz 1959, 3–26); Barber 1935; Herbert 1954.

104. See Theander 1950–51, 62–63; von der Muehll 1954. Note also the direct citations in *Them.* 27.1 and *De malig. Her.* 869A and 855F (= F190, 187, 189).

lie behind other items, including the conflict of Pericles and Thucydides (cf. 11.1, 11.5, 18.2, 19.2, 20.3, 25.2, 33.4). Ephorus is
explicitly cited only at 27.3 and 28.2.

b. *Theopompus.* Theopompus of Chios wrote two major historical
works: a *Hellenica* in twelve books, continuing Thucydides down to
394 B.C., and a *Philippica* in no fewer than fifty-eight books, treating principally the years 360–336, but including long digressions
on matters only distantly related. One of these was a section,
found at the end of Book 10, given in antiquity the title "On the
Demagogues of Athens." Only some sixteen fragments can be
reasonably ascribed to this book, treating of Themistocles, Cimon,
Thucydides son of Melesias, Cleon, Hyperbolus, and the fourth-
century politicians Callistratus and Eubulus. These fragments,
and the title given them in antiquity, have encouraged the hypothesis that Theopompus might have been an important source
for fifth-century Athenian politics, but in fact our evidence is
extremely thin, so that the exact extent of his treatment of the
demagogues cannot be determined.[105] Even less clear is the influence that his account had on the *Pericles.* Theopompus was a well-
known writer, and Plutarch was undoubtedly familiar with his
work, which he cites some twenty times.[106] Nevertheless, the extent of his borrowings from Theopompus in the *Pericles* is often
exaggerated.

First, the limitations of our knowledge of his treatment of the
fifth-century politicians must be acknowledged. Theopompus is
never cited directly for Pericles, or for other major figures such as
Aristides, Ephialtes, or Nicias; the one reference to Thucydides
son of Melesias insists on an erroneous name for his father. Sec-

---

105. See especially Connor 1968 and Ferretto 1984, not seen by me. For the
fragments and a commentary see *FGrHist* 115. The excursus on the demagogues is F85–100. Theopompus has often been held a major source of the
first part of the *Pericles*; see, e.g., Busolt, *Gr. Gesch.* 3.1:237, 239. Wade-Gery
1938 argues specifically for Theopompus as the basis for chapters 9–10.
Connor 1968 accepts this conclusion, but notes (pp. 35–36, 116) that there is
no evidence that Plutarch followed Theopompus for long sections of his
biographies. For arguments against taking Theopompus as a major source for
the life see Meinhardt, 23n. 50. Connor provides a full bibliography.

106. These include three times each in the *Themistocles* and the *Agesilaus*,
twice in the *Lysander*, and six times in the *Demosthenes*. For Plutarch's direct use
of Theopompus see Theander 1950–51, 58.

ond, he is cited by Plutarch in connection with fifth-century politicans only for Themistocles (*Them.* 19.1, 25.3, 31.3 = F85–87). At 31.3 Plutarch flatly rejects Theopompus' version, at 19.1 he contrasts it with "the majority of writers," at 25.3 he presents it without comment. The first two manifestly contradict Thucydides' account. Plutarch generally is very suspicious of Theopompus, whom he considers a fault-finder who frequently goes counter to the common tradition (cf. his comments at *Ages.* 33.1 = F323, *Dem.* 13.1 = F326, and *Lys.* 30.2 = F333). He in fact often contradicts more reliable sources.[107]

We must hesitate, therefore, before too readily assigning a major influence to Theopompus in the *Pericles*. There is no reason to think that Theopompus gave special treatment to Pericles, or that, in the words of Wade-Gery, "Perikles must have been one of the main villains of the piece, and Kimon and Thucydides were there as foils."[108] Considering its possible value, the excursus on the demagogues was seldom used by ancient scholars: even the Aristophanic scholiasts used it not for basic information but for minor variants or for confirmation of material easily derived from the plays themselves. The original worth of this section on the demagogues for the fifth century may well have been slight. However, Plutarch does appear to have used Theopompus alongside Aristotle's *Constitution of the Athenians* for the lavish generosity of Cimon (9.2; cf. *Cim.* 10.1 and F89) and Cimon's early recall from ostracism (10.4; cf. *Cim.* 17.8 and F88), and perhaps for his sketch of Thucydides the son of Melesias (11.1) and an anecdote about him (8.5). An item concerning Delphi (21.2) may be taken from a digression on the Delphic oracle, and the widespread tradition on Pericles' oratorical ability (see 7.1, 8.1, 8.3, 16.3) may also ultimately derive from him.

Two philosophers, Aristotle and Theophrastus, may be included here, since the works used by Plutarch reflect Peripatetic historical interests.

c. *Aristotle.* The collection of *Constitutions* (*Politeiai*) attributed to Aristotle and surely written under his direction, if not directly by

107. See Connor 1968, 119–24, on some of Theopompus' weaknesses as a historian.
108. Wade-Gery 1938, 133 (= 1958, 236).

him, was descriptive rather than theoretical, and thus more historical than philosophical in nature. It formed both a research tool for the political theory found in the *Politics* and other writings of the Peripatetics, and a compendium meant to be enjoyed by the curious reader, as Plutarch clearly did (cf. *Non posse* 1093C, where he expresses the delight he finds in the *Politeiai*). Some 158 *Constitutions* were written, many no doubt by Aristotle's students. Like Aristotle's other exoteric works, which were written for the general public, the *Constitutions* were known to the modern world only in fragments until the discovery of the papyrus text of the *Constitution of the Athenians* at the end of the nineteenth century. Despite some infelicities and errors this work is remarkable for its compact and readable presentation of the development of the Athenian governmental system. It is divided into two parts, first a historical overview, then a description of the mechanism of government in the author's day.[109] Plutarch cites it only twice in the *Pericles* (9.3, 10.8), in connection with the reform of the Areopagus and the death of Ephialtes. But his numerous citations or paraphrases in other lives, especially in the *Solon*, indicate that he was very familiar with the work.[110] It was natural for him to look at other constitutions in the collection for specific information on cities, as he does frequently in the *Quaestiones graecae*.[111] In the *Pericles* the *Constitution of the Samians* furnished unusual details from the Samian War (26.3, 28.2). Like the *Athenian Constitution*, this no doubt noted especially the changes in government. The Samian War marked a time of major upheaval in Samian politics and so naturally was treated in some detail. We cannot identify the source of

109. The *Constitution of the Athenians* has recently been the subject of a comprehensive commentary by Rhodes (*CAAP*). On the question of this work he concludes, *CAAP*, 61–63, that it might have been written by Aristotle, but more likely by a student working under his direction. For Aristotle's historical researches see Rhodes, *CAAP* passim; Weil 1960; Huxley 1972.

110. Citations at *Thes.* 25.3, *Sol.* 25.1, *Them.* 10.6, *Cim.* 10.2, *Nic.* 2.1. For the *Lycurgus* Plutarch found the *Constitution of the Lacedaemonians* equally useful, as his six citations show (cf. *Lyc.* 1.2, 5.12, 6.4, 14.2, 28.2, 31.4). The fragments of the other *Constitutions* are assembled by V. Rose, *Aristotelis Qui Ferebantur Librorum Fragmenta* (1886), 303–67. Those of the *Samian Constitution* are F570–78, pp. 353–57, including three from Plutarch (576 = *Qu. Gr.* 295E–296B; 577–78 = *Per.* 26.3, 28.2).

111. See Stadter 1965, 131–32.

the citation from Aristotle at *Per.* 4.1, which may be from a lost work, or an error for a reference to Plato.

Plutarch shows the influence of Aristotelian political categories in the way that he speaks of the contrast between *dēmos* and *oligoi* (cf. my notes to 7.1 and 7.3) and in his references to kingly (*basilikē*) and aristocratic (*aristokratikē*) constitutions (cf. note to 15.1). We know these theories best from Aristotle's *Politics*, but Plutarch seems to have had little acquaintance with Aristotle's esoteric works, the lectures for his school that form most of what we know of his works.[112] But these ideas are also present in the *Constitution of the Athenians*[113] and undoubtedly were found in other exoteric works, now lost, such as the *Statesman* and *On Kingship*, as well as later political writers and theorists.

d. *Theophrastus.* Theophrastus of Eresos (ca. 370–285/83), Aristotle's successor as head of the Peripatetic school at Athens, wrote or supervised the production of an enormous number of works in the fields of ethics, zoology, botany, psychology, and politics, only a few of which have survived. Plutarch cites him over fifty times in the *Lives* and the *Moralia*, calling him "the most curious and inquisitive of the philosophers" (*Alc.* 10.4), but the exact extent of his reading in Theophrastus is uncertain. He only cites two works by name, *On Kingship* and *Phenomena*, but the citations cover the full range of topics treated by the philosopher. One of Plutarch's lost works was a treatment of Theophrastus' Πολιτικὰ πρὸς τοὺς καίρους (Lamprias catalogue 53), which gave examples of practical decision-making in various cities and may be the source for the notice on Pericles' bribery of the Spartans at *Per.* 23.2. The anecdote at 38.2 may come from one of the works on ethics or psychology.[114]

---

112. See Sandbach 1982. For a contrary view see Verbeke 1960; Aalders 1977 and 1982, 61–65.

113. Cf. Rhodes, *CAAP* 88–89, note to 2.1.

114. See O. Regenbogen, *RE* s.v. Theophrastos 3, suppl. VII (1940) 1354–1562; Podlecki 1985; and the fragments collected by Wimmer 1862 and Fortenbaugh 1984. For the *Laws* see the edition and commentary by Szegedy-Maszak (1981). Raubitschek 1958 argued that a treatise on ostracism contained in the *Laws* was a source for most of the ancient tradition on ostracism, including Plutarch.

e. *Duris*. Duris of Samos (*FGrHist* 76), a writer of broad interests, wrote on literature (Homer, tragedy), painting, and sculpture, on laws and games, and three historical works: the *Chronicles of Samos*, the *Histories* or *Makedonika* (from 370/69 to 281 B.C.), and a work on Agathocles of Sicily. He was of a wealthy and noble family, which had apparently joined other Samians in exile during the Athenian occupation of Samos. When the family returned after Alexander's death, first his father and then he were tyrants of Samos. He was much involved in the Samian poetic revival of his day and certainly considered his histories an improvement on standard works. Plutarch used his *Histories* for the *Demosthenes*, *Alexander*, *Phocion*, and *Eumenes* (F38–40, 46, 50–51, 53); the *Samian Chronicles* for the *Pericles* (28.2–3 = F67), *Agesilaus*, *Alcibiades*, and *Lysander* (F69–71). The *Samian Chronicles* covered at least from the seventh century to the end of the fifth in two or more books. The Samian War appears in three fragments, all of which have an echo in the *Pericles*: F65, Aspasia as the cause of two wars, the Samian and the Peloponnesian (cf. *Per.* 24.1, 25.1, and 30.4); F66, the tattooing of prisoners of the war by both sides (cf. *Per.* 26.4); and F67, the cruel execution of Samian prisoners (*Per.* 28.2–3). As the preface to his *Histories* suggests, he strove for drama and exciting detail in his narrative: a good example is the long excerpt from the *Samian Chronicles* describing how the Athenian women blinded with their brooches the lone Athenian survivor of a battle (F24). But it was often overdone, as when he even gave the name of the spearman who wounded Philip: Didymus comments, "Of course, Duris had to recount marvels here" (F36). Plutarch complains of his exaggeration and theatricality at *Per.* 28.2–3 (F67).[115] With Phylarchus he is a representative of the genre of tragic history very popular in antiquity. Its qualities are sketched by Polybius, who characterized Phylarchus as "eager to draw out pity in his readers and to make them feel what is said . . . always trying to set events before their eyes," composing like a tragic playwright (Polybius 2.56.7–16).

Plutarch's judgment on Duris' history is based on familiarity with his work, although he may not have reread it for the *Pericles*:

---

115. Cf. also his comments on Duris' version of Alcibiades' entry into Athens in 408, *Alc.* 32.3 = F70.

---

the three incidents he used from Duris (Aspasia's responsibility, the tattooing, and the executions) were all such as to be easily remembered or recorded in notes.[116]

f. *Megarian local historians.* The reference at 30.4 to Megarians may refer to Megarian local historians, who are cited individually or as a group by Plutarch in connection with Theseus, Lycurgus, and Solon.[117] However, it is possible that Plutarch is thinking of contemporary Megarian friends.

g. *Atthidographers.* It is worth noting that in the *Pericles* Plutarch does not cite either Hellanicus of Lesbos, who in the fifth century wrote a history of Athens, or the various Atthidographers—writers of annalistic Athenian history—active in the fourth and third centuries. The tradition culminated in the *Atthis* of Philochorus (*FGrHist* 328) in seventeen books, which we know to have mentioned the reforms of Ephialtes, Pericles' reduction of Euboea, the grain distribution of 446, the ostracism of Thucydides, the trial of Phidias, and the outbreak of the Peloponnesian War. Apparently Plutarch did not consider them suitable for citation in his *Life*, although he may have found some useful material there. He does cite several in a list of Athenian historians in *De glor. Ath.* 345D, but it is clear that he gives pride of place to Thucydides, cited also at 347A–B and 347D.[118]

---

116. See in general E. Schwartz, *RE* s.v. Duris 3, V (1905) 1853–56 (= Schwartz 1959, 27–31); Jacoby, commentary to *FGrHist* 76; Ferrero 1963; Kebric 1977; Mastrocinque 1979. On tragic history see Ullman 1942 and F. W. Walbank 1955.

117. Cf. the edition of L. Piccirilli (1975) and *FGrHist* 484–87. *Per.* 30.4 = 5 F23 P., *FGrHist* 487 F13. For other Megarian citations see *Thes.* 10.2 = 5 F6a P., 487 F1; *Thes.* 20.1–2, 32.6–7 = Hereas 3 F1, 2 P., 486 F1, 2; *Lyc.* 1.8 = Dieuchidas 1 F5 P., 485 F5; *Sol.* 10.5 = Hereas 3 F3 P. (cf. 6 F12b); 486 F4. In the *Moralia* note the reference concerning Ino, *Symp.* 675E = 5 F4b P.

118. Atthidographers are cited only seven times in the six fifth-century lives: Hellanicus (323a F24b) at *Alc.* 21.1; Clidemus (323 F21, 22) at *Them.* 10.6 and *Arist.* 19.6; Phanodemus (325 F22–24) at *Cim.* 12.6, 19.2 and *Them.* 13.1; and Philochorus (328 F135b) at *Nic.* 23.8. A review of Jacoby's collection, *FGrHist* 323a-34, shows that although they are cited frequently in the *Theseus* (Philochorus six times, Hellanicus five, Clidemus and Demon twice, Bion and Ister once each), they appear only rarely elsewhere: Hellanicus (323a F28) at *De malig. Her.* 869A; Philochorus (328 F222) at *An seni* 785B, Androtion (324

h. *Scholiasts*. Undoubtedly Plutarch frequently used exegetical material for texts from the time he began reading. Its importance for his knowledge of Old Comedy has already been discussed. Plutarch seems in general very familar with the sort of material cited by scholiasts and grammarians not only on comic poets, but on Homer, Hesiod, and Plato. It is frequently difficult for us to establish which information came to him directly, and which from a learned scholiast. Comments like those on the length of the vowel in Damon (*Per.* 4.1), on the Samian tattoo (26.4), and Artemon περιφώρητος (27.4) suggest acquaintance with this literature. In addition, certain of Plutarch's friends were especially knowledgeable in literature, such as the *grammatikoi* Marcus (*Symp.* 628B, 740E), Apollophanes (*Symp.* 684E), and Demetrius of Tarsus (*De def. or.* 410A and frequently). The precise nature of Plutarch's relation to this world of learning is still to be investigated.

3. Philosophers

a. *Plato*. Plato represented one of the most important sources for the *Pericles*, despite the relatively little factual material he records. As has been seen (section 2.5 above), Plato's denigration of Pericles as a statesman established one of the two poles of Plutarch's

---

F34) at *Sol.* 15.3, Ister (334 F26) at *Alex.* 46.1, and a reference to Attic writers at *Symp.* 724A. Cf. Frost 1984. F. Jacoby's *Atthis* (1949) provides an analysis of the form and content of the Atthidographers, as an introduction and supplement to his edition and exhaustive commentary to the fragments. Hellanicus might have been useful to Plutarch, but he wrote only two books, of which the second covered at least the sixth and fifth centuries, perhaps from Solon to the fall of Athens. This would be 190 years, or (figuring thirty modern pages for a book) 6.3 years per page. Jacoby preferred to think that the book began with the first archon in 683/82, therefore 278 years or 9.3 years per page. Hellanicus would hardly have been able to consider politics in much detail. As a comparison, consider that Thucydides 1.98–117, from Eion to the Samian War, covers 40 years in 12 pages, a rate of 3.3 per page (including two pages for the war itself). Philochorus, perhaps the greatest of the Atthidographers, also offered a succinct account: Jacoby (commentary to *FGrHist* 328, p. 252) calculates that he may have covered about 60 years in Book 4 (roughly 462/61–404/3), which would average out to about 2 years per page.

---

portrait. Plato was Plutarch's favorite author, whom he knew thoroughly and quoted frequently, even, as in the *Amatorius*, engaging in a running debate with him on major topics.[119] Plato is cited in the *Pericles* at 7.8, 8.2, 13.7, 15.2, and 24.7, and certainly or probably lies behind comments at 4.2, 4.5, 5.1, 9.1, 15.2, and 24.5. The most important passages are those in the *Phaedrus* where Plato describes the power of Pericles' rhetoric and the influence of Anaxagoras (270A–271C), the estimate of the statesman in the *Gorgias* (455E, 503C, 515C–516E), and the sketch of Aspasia in the *Menexenus* (235E).[120]

b. *Aeschines*. Aeschines was a student of Socrates, who like Plato, Xenophon, and others, wrote philosophical dialogues with Socrates as protagonist. We know of works entitled *Alcibiades, Axiochos, Callias, Miltiades, Rhinon, Telauges,* and *Aspasia*. Plutarch cites him at *Arist.* 25.4–9, and *De rect. aud.* 39B–C, and refers to his life and works at *De adul. et amic.* 67D–E, and *De coh. ira* 462D–E. In the *Pericles* he cites him for notices on Aspasia's friendship with Pericles (24.6) and Pericles' tears at her trial (32.5). Both passages, and probably other items on Aspasia in chapters 24 and 32, must be drawn from the *Aspasia*.[121] Aeschines seems to have introduced Aspasia as a woman of intelligence (cf. F9 K., where she is shown discussing a point with Xenophon and his wife), but in the tradition of the Milesian courtesan Thargelia (F10 K.; cf. *Per.* 24. 3–4). Ehlers suggests that Aeschines tried to demonstrate the role of *erōs* in the development of *aretē*, using Aspasia as the example of the teacher who uses *erōs* to lead men to political excellence. Pericles' defense of Aspasia at her trial would have been evidence of her effect on him and her importance to him as a teacher of political

119. See in general R. M. Jones 1916; Ziegler, *RE* 744–51; Helmbold and O'Neil 1959, 56–63. Despite his reverence for Plato, he is not afraid to disagree with him: for another case of difference of historical interpretation, cf. *Them.* 4.4: Plutarch insists that introducing the navy saved Greece, whereas Plato (cf. *Laws* 707B) had considered it an evil.

120. Plutarch did not doubt the authenticity of the *Menexenus*, which was questioned in the nineteenth century but is now generally accepted. For recent discussion of the dialogue see Guthrie, *HGP* 4:321–23.

121. The fragments of Aeschines have been collected by Krauss 1911 and by Dittmar 1912. On the *Aspasia* see esp. Ehlers 1966.

aretē.[122] Just as with Plato's *Menexenus*, Plutarch uses the dialogue for information about Aspasia without considering Aeschines' philosophical purpose.

c. *Antisthenes.* This philosopher (ca.445–ca.360) also was a follower of Socrates and wrote Socratic dialogues, including one entitled *Aspasia.* Although Diogenes Laertius (6.10–19) lists some seventy titles of Antisthenes, the extant fragments give only a hazy idea of his thought. Most pleasures, he felt, were treacherous, and the only real happiness came from virtue. Pericles perhaps was presented as yielding to pleasure, as represented by Aspasia.[123] Plutarch quotes him some eleven times, usually for some aphoristic comment or moral advice, as at *Per.* 1.5. One or two notices on Aspasia may derive from him (cf. my notes to 24.9, 32.1), and others have been suggested as well (e.g., at 10.5). But the only historical fact for which Plutarch explicitly cites Antisthenes is the name of Alcibiades' nurse (*Alc.* 1.3).

d. *Heraclides.* Heraclides of Pontus, who was at the Academy in the time of Plato and Speusippus, retired after the latter's death (339) to his native city of Heraclea on the Black Sea. He wrote a large number of works, chiefly dialogues of the type used by Aristotle and later Cicero. However, he wrote well and used imaginative settings, in which mythological or historical figures expounded on their experiences: one work treats Empedocles' last day and apotheosis; another the experiences of the shaman Abaris. Plutarch found the *Abaris* useful for introducing young pupils to discussions on the soul (*De aud.* 14E = F73) but was aware that Heraclides might embroider a true story, making it "fabulous and artificial" (*Cam.* 22.3 = F102). He was a popularizer and was read more for pleasure than serious philosophy, but Plutarch cites him occasionally for the odd detail: at *Per.* 27.4 (= F60) for a description of the soft-living Artemon; at 35.5 (= F47) for the accuser of Pericles. He is cited four times in the *Solon* (F146–49), and nine other times.[124]

122. Cf. Ehlers 1966, 66, 69–71.
123. The fragments are collected in Caizzi 1966 and Giannantoni 1983; for his thought cf. Guthrie, *HGP* 3:304–11, and Rankin 1986.
124. F20, 68, 72, 73, 102, 139, 140, 156, 168. Cf. also F100. The fragments are collected in Wehrli 1953. In general see Diog. Laert. 5.86–93; *RE* s.v.

e. *Idomeneus.* A statesman in Lampsacus and a friend of Epicurus, Idomeneus of Lampsacus (ca. 325–265) wrote a book on the Socratic philosophers and another on demagogues (*FGrHist* 338). The latter work was cited especially by Athenaeus (F3, 4, 12, 14) and by Plutarch (F5–7 in the *Aristides,* F8–9 at *Per.* 10.7 and 35.5, F10–11 in the *Demosthenes,* and F15 in the *Phocion*). He was something of a scandalmonger, whom Plutarch uses for variants that he will reject, as at *Per.* 10.7, *Arist.* 10.7–9, *Dem.* 15.5, 23.4, and *Phoc.* 4.2. There is no reason to think that his stories, which regularly contradict the standard tradition, preserved accurate information.[125]

4. Orators and Rhetoricians

a. *The Attic orators.* The Attic orators, who often recall moments of glory in the Athenian past, have relatively little to say about Pericles. Isocrates refers to him most frequently, reminding his readers that Pericles had been taught by Damon and Anaxagoras (15.235), that he was Alcibiades' guardian (16.28; a relationship not mentioned in the *Pericles,* but noted in the *Alcibiades,* 1.2), and that he was responsible for the construction of the expensive Acropolis temples (7.66, 15.234). He knew that he had led the Samian expedition (15.111) and considered him a good manager (8.126, 15.234). Some of Plutarch's conception of Pericles may have been influenced by Isocrates, but there is no evidence that he was a direct source for the life. The other orators tell us even less.

b. *Rhetoricians.* The teaching of rhetoric in the Roman imperial period depended upon imitation of classical models in declamations or disputations on set subjects. Historical examples were regularly used as ornament or to support the argument, and historical figures and incidents were regularly assigned as practice subjects for speakers. Pericles, as the leading figure of Athens' most glorious period, appears frequently in rhetorical writing, and we must assume that Plutarch's background knowledge of

---

Herakleides 45, VIII (1913) 472–484 (Däbritz) and suppl. XI (1968) 675–86 (Wehrli); and Gottschalk 1980.

125. See Jacoby, *RE* s.v. Idomeneus 5, IX (1916) 910 and his commentary to *FGrHist* 338.

Pericles and attitudes toward him were shaped at least to some extent by acquaintance with such rhetorical exercises as a student.

c. *Valerius Maximus*. This author, who wrote under Tiberius, provides our earliest extant collection of rhetorical exempla. His nine books of *Memorable Deeds and Sayings*, arranged by topic and divided between Romans and foreigners, were known to Plutarch and are cited in his *Lives*.[126] Six items concern Pericles, including several similar to those in Plutarch.[127] He seems not to be a source for the *Pericles* but, like other orators and rhetoricians writing later than Plutarch, serves to indicate the level of familiarity with Pericles' life in the educated classes of the Roman Empire.

d. *Aristides*. The best example of the rhetorical treatment of Pericles' life is found in Aelius Aristides' oration *On the Four*. Aristides, a distinguished rhetor of the second century A.D., composed ca. 161–65 a display speech defending the four great Athenians—Miltiades, Themistocles, Cimon, and Pericles—against the attack made on them by Plato in the *Gorgias*.[128] Although much more diffuse and taken up with his own eloquence than Plutarch, his defense of Pericles shares several topics with the biographer, by whom he seems to have been heavily influenced. After a general introduction that emphasizes Pericles' self-control and philosophical training by Anaxagoras, Aristides addresses individually and at great length Plato's charges that Pericles made the Athenians talkative, lazy, cowardly, and greedy (cf. *Per.* 9.1). Thucydides provides the main counter-arguments, not only the evaluation at 2.65, which is recalled several times, but the Samian War and the expeditions of 446 against Megara and Euboea, and against the Peloponnese. The comic poets are cited for Pericles' eloquence and his forcefulness as a leader. This section of the speech, more a panegyric than a defense, concludes as Plutarch does with the topos on the epithet "Olympian." Despite the oration's length, Aristides

126. See *Brut.* 53.5–6 = Val. Max. 4.6.5; *Marc.* 30.2–5 (not found in our text of Valerius).

127. Val. Max. 3.1.ext. 1; 4.3.ext. 2; 5.10.ext. 1; 7.2.ext. 7; 8.9.ext. 2; 8.11.ext. 1: cf. my notes to *Per.* 32.3, 8.8, 36.7–8 and 39.2, 8.2, and 34.2.

128. Oration 3 Lenz and Behr 1:2–3 (Leiden 1978), oration 46 Dindorf vol. 2 (Leipzig 1829; reprinted Hildesheim 1964). Cf. Boulanger 1923 and Behr 1968.

has nothing to add to Plutarch's account. On the contrary, the very restricted use of comic citations and the complete absence of the decrees and of the anecdotes of Stesimbrotus and Ion rob his narrative of the vitality and sense of personality so strongly felt in the *Pericles*. Following the rules of encomia, he avoids all negative traits or actions, and so is silent on Pericles' role in the outbreak of the Peloponnesian War and on his relationship with Aspasia. The speech is a concert piece, meant to display the orator's skill, not to penetrate a character.

e. *Later rhetoricians.* The works of later rhetoricians reveal a number of standard themes based loosely (sometimes very loosely) on historical tradition. Pericles often appears as a subject. For example, it was known that Archidamus when invading Attica did not ravage Pericles' land (cf. *Per.* 33.3): the speaker is asked to defend Archidamus when the Spartans accuse him of being bribed.[129] Alternatively, he can be asked to defend Pericles from the charge of treason on the same occasion.[130] Cases are also invented in which Pericles is accused of attempting tyranny (cf. *Per.* 16.3), or causing the war (cf. *Per.* 29. 8), or (when washed ashore in Megara) for moving the Megarian decree.[131] These topics show a minimum of interest in historical accuracy, desiring only to make the set problem interesting by using the names of well-known historical figures. They sometimes echo items from Plutarch's life.

5. Personal Observation (Autopsy) and Oral Tradition

Plutarch not infrequently supplemented his reading with his own experience and autopsy, although traces of this are rather rarer in the *Pericles* than in some lives. The buildings of the Acropolis obviously affected him profoundly and were an impor-

129. *Rhetores Graeci*, ed. Walz, 3:486, 5:53, 7:310; Hermogenes, ed. Rabe, *Stasis* 31.2, 55.7.

130. Hermogenes *Peri eureseos* 141.19–143.24, 146.2, 4; *Rhet. Gr.* 8:188–198 Walz. The charge is often connected with Pericles' famous response, "I spent the money for what was necessary" (cf. *Per.* 23.1). These and the following examples have been called to my attention by D. A. Russell.

131. *Rhet. Gr.* 7:263 Walz; cf. 3:487, 4:408 (a thousand sets of armor are found in his house), 4:318, 4:398 (he could say, after all, that he had passed it for the Megarians' own good!).

tant reason behind his admiration for Pericles (cf. 12.1, 13.1–5, *Comp.* 3.7.) He probably knew the wolf at Delphi from autopsy (21.2). He speaks with familiarity of the portrait statues of Pericles (3.4) and of the figures on the Parthenos shield (31.3–4). We must expect that his own observation during his stays in Athens was supplemented by the stories of friends and guides. The same would have been true for Eleusis, where Plutarch was an initiate, but the source of the detailed architectural history of the teles-terion at Eleusis (13.7) remains problematic. The deme names for the architects suggest an ultimate source in the decrees authoriz-ing construction, which may have been preserved in a written source, such as a traveler's guide or handbook to monuments; or perhaps they were known to a friend of Plutarch, as knowledge-able on Eleusinian antiquities as he himself was on those of Delphi. The building program under Hadrian, which reveals careful emulation of classical models, seems to imply some investigation by Plutarch's contemporaries of the site's architectural history.[132]

Oral tradition, gathered either from friends or in the schools of rhetoric or philosophy, was probably source for more than the one passage where Plutarch expressly acknowledges, "This story is told in the lectures of the philosophers" (35.2). We may think also of the anecdotes of Pericles' management of his estate and his relation to Anaxagoras (16.3–9), of his need to ask for a special dispensation from his own law in favor of his bastard son (37.2–5), or of the memorable phrases from his speeches recalled at 8.7 or 33.5. The Megarians cited at 30.4 may well be his own contempo-raries, defending their city in conversation, rather than writers of Megarian local history. Plutarch puts in the mouth of his in-law Craton a story about Pericles also found in his *Apophthegmata* and *Precepts on Government* (*Symp.* 620C–D, cf. 186C, 813D). Although the anecdote undoubtedly comes from a literary source, as do the

---

132. We do not know of special accounts of Eleusinian buildings, but several are cited concerning the Athenian acropolis. Polemon of Ilion (ca. 210–170 B.C.) wrote *On the Dedications on the Acropolis* in four books (see *RE* s.v. Polemon 9, XXI, 2 [1952] 1288–1320), and Heliodorus the Periegete (*FGrHist* 373, 2nd cent. B.C.?) wrote no fewer than fifteen books *On the Acropolis at Athens*. The book *On Monuments* of Diodorus the Periegete is cited three times by Plutarch (*FGrHist* 372 F35, 37, 38), but Jacoby rightly notes that this concerned only Athenian grave monuments (*FGrHist* 3B:commentary, pp. 141–42).

others cited by Craton (from Plato's *Republic* and Xenophon's *Anabasis*), this like other examples from the *Symposiaca* illustrates the atmosphere in which such oral exchanges could take place.[133]

Finally, in considering Plutarch's sources, we must recall that Plutarch's overriding goal was not to set out precisely the various debts he owed to earlier writers, but to share with us, to the best of his ability, his own learning and fascination with moral qualities as he saw them in the great statesmen of the past. Thanks to the dramatic skill of Thucydides and Plato, and the peculiar assortment of comic poets and memoirists, antiquarians and philosophers who lie behind the *Pericles*, it proves to be among the most rewarding of Plutarch's *Lives*.

133. On Plutarch's observation of monuments and inscriptions and citation of oral tradition see Theander 1950–51, 2–32.

PERICLES

CONSPECTVS SIGLORVM

N = cod. Matritensis saec. XIV
N¹ = scriptura manus primae cod. **N**
N² = scriptura manus secundae cod. **N**
Nᵐ = scriptura marginis cod. **N** (ubi nil aliud adnotatur, in ipso textu **N** idem legitur quod in meo textu)
Nᵗ = scriptura ipsius textus cod. **N** (ubi nil aliud adnotatur, in margine **N** idem legitur quod in meo textu). eadem ratione in scripturis ceterorum codicum usus sum
U = Vaticanus 138 veteris manus saec. X/XI
U = Vaticanus 138 recentioris manus (in Demosthene et Cicerone) saec. XIV
N = N*U* (in Demosthene et Cicerone)
S = Seitenstettensis saec. XI/XII
M = Marcianus 385 saec. XIV/XV
A = Parisinus 1671 a. 1296
B = Parisinus 1672 saec. XIV ineuntis
C = Parisinus 1673 saec. XIII
E = Parisinus 1675 saec. XIV
Υ = UMA (BCE)
O = Pseudo-Appianus
Oᵛ = Pseudo-Appiani cod. Vaticanus saec. XIV/XV
Oᵐ = Pseudo-Appiani cod. Marcianus a. 1441
Oˡ = Pseudo-Appiani classis deterior

NOTAE

Am.	= Amyot	Ri.	= Richards
Anon.	= Anonymus	Scal.	= Scaliger
Br.	= Bryan	Sch.	= Schaefer
Cast.	= Castiglioni	Sint.	= Sintenis
Cob.	= Cobet	Sol.	= Solanus
Cor.	= Coraes	Va.	= Valckenaer
Emp.	= Emperius	Vulc.	= Vulcobius
Ha.	= Hartman	We.	= Westermann
Herw.	= van Herwerden	Wil.	= v. Wilamowitz-Möllen-
Kron.	= Kronenberg		dorff
Leop.	= Leopold	Wytt.	= Wyttenbach
Li.	= Lindskog	Xy.	= Xylander
Mu.	= Muret	Zie.	= Ziegler
Rei.	= Reiske		

Margini exteriori adscripsi paginas editionis Francofurtanae (a. 1599 et 1620), interiori Sintenisianae minoris (a. 1852—55, postea saepius repetitae) et Lindskogianae (a. 1914).

PERICLES

ΠΕΡΙΚΛΗΣ ΚΑΙ ΦΑΒΙΟΣ ΜΑΞΙΜΟΣ

1 L **1.** Ξένους τινὰς ἐν Ῥώμῃ πλουσίους κυνῶν ἔκγονα καὶ c
πιθήκων ἐν τοῖς κόλποις περιφέροντας καὶ ἀγαπῶντας
ἰδὼν ὁ Καῖσαρ ὡς ἔοικεν ἠρώτησεν, εἰ παιδία παρ'
5 αὐτοῖς οὐ τίκτουσιν αἱ γυναῖκες, ἡγεμονικῶς σφόδρα
νουθετήσας τοὺς τὸ φύσει φιλητικὸν ἐν ἡμῖν καὶ φιλόστοργον εἰς θηρία καταναλίσκοντας, ἀνθρώποις ὀφειλό-
μενον. ἆρ' οὖν, ἐπεὶ [κυνῶν τε καὶ πιθήκων ἔκγονα] φιλο- 2
299 8 μαθές τι κέκτηται καὶ φιλοθέαμον ἡμῶν ἡ ψυχὴ φύσει, d
10 λόγον ἔχει ψέγειν τοὺς καταχρωμένους τούτῳ πρὸς τὰ μη-
δεμιᾶς ἄξια σπουδῆς ἀκούσματα καὶ θεάματα, τῶν δὲ καλῶν
καὶ ὠφελίμων παραμελοῦντας; τῇ μὲν γὰρ αἰσθήσει, κατὰ
πάθος τὴν πληγὴν ἀντιλαμβανομένῃ τῶν προστυγχανόν-
των, ἴσως ἀνάγκη πᾶν τὸ φαινόμενον, ἄν τε χρήσιμον ἄν
15 τ' ἄχρηστον ᾖ, θεωρεῖν, τῷ νῷ δ' ἕκαστος, εἰ βούλοιτο,
χρῆσθαι καὶ τρέπειν ἑαυτὸν ἀεὶ καὶ μεταβάλλειν ῥᾷστα
πρὸς τὸ δοκοῦν πέφυκεν, ὥστε χρὴ διώκειν τὸ βέλτιστον,
ἵνα μὴ θεωρῇ μόνον, ἀλλὰ καὶ τρέφηται τῷ θεωρεῖν. ὡς 3
γὰρ ὀφθαλμῷ χρόα πρόσφορος, ἧς τὸ ἀνθηρὸν ἅμα καὶ e
20 τερπνὸν ἀναζωπυρεῖ καὶ τρέφει τὴν ὄψιν, οὕτω τὴν διά-
2 L νοιαν ἐπάγειν δεῖ θεάμασιν ἃ τῷ χαίρειν πρὸς τὸ οἰκεῖον
αὐτὴν ἀγαθὸν ἐκκαλεῖ. ταῦτα δ' ἔστιν ἐν τοῖς ἀπ' ἀρετῆς 4
ἔργοις, ἃ καὶ ζῆλόν τινα καὶ προθυμίαν ἀγωγὸν εἰς μίμησιν ἐμποιεῖ τοῖς ἱστορήσασιν· ἐπεὶ τῶν γ' ἄλλων οὐκ

cf. Ekkehard Meinhardt, Perikles bei Plutarch, Diss. Frankfurt am Main 1957

[S (U M A ═) Υ] 2 ἔκγονα Zie. ex l. 9 : τέκνα ‖ 8 κυνῶν—ἔκγονα del.
Rei. (cf. l. 2) ‖ 13 πάθος del. Li. τὴν πληγὴν del. Cor. κατὰ πάθος
τῆς πληγῆς Rei.; intellige κατὰ πάθος scil. τὴν πλ. ‖ 15 ἕκαστον:
em. Steph. ‖ 16 καὶ del. Cor. male post χρῆσθαι distinctione posita ‖
21 τῷ S ante corr., U²M : τὸ S¹ e corr., U¹A ‖ 24 ἱστορήσασιν
post Am. Rei.: ἱστορήμασιν

1

εὐθὺς ἀκολουθεῖ τῷ θαυμάσαι τὸ πραχθὲν ὁρμὴ πρὸς τὸ
πρᾶξαι, πολλάκις δὲ καὶ τοὐναντίον χαίροντες τῷ ἔργῳ
τοῦ δημιουργοῦ καταφρονοῦμεν, ὡς ἐπὶ τῶν μύρων καὶ
τῶν ἁλουργῶν τούτοις μὲν ἡδόμεθα, τοὺς δὲ βαφεῖς καὶ
5 μυρεψοὺς ἀνελευθέρους ἡγούμεθα καὶ βαναύσους. διὸ 5
f καλῶς μὲν Ἀντισθένης ἀκούσας ὅτι σπουδαῖός ἐστιν αὐλη-
τὴς Ἰσμηνίας, „ἀλλ' ἄνθρωπος" ἔφη „μοχθηρός· οὐ γὰρ ἂν
6 οὕτω σπουδαῖος ἦν αὐλητής·" ὁ δὲ Φίλιππος πρὸς τὸν υἱὸν
ἐπιτερπῶς ἔν τινι πότῳ ψήλαντα καὶ τεχνικῶς εἶπεν· „οὐκ
αἰσχύνη καλῶς οὕτω ψάλλων;" ἀρκεῖ γάρ, ἂν βασιλεὺς ἀ- 10
κροᾶσθαι ψαλλόντων σχολάζῃ, καὶ πολὺ νέμει ταῖς Μούσαις
ἑτέρων ἀγωνιζομένων τὰ τοιαῦτα θεατὴς γιγνόμενος.

153 **2.** Ἡ δ' αὐτουργία τῶν ταπεινῶν τῆς εἰς τὰ καλὰ
ῥᾳθυμίας μάρτυρα τὸν ἐν τοῖς ἀχρήστοις πόνον παρέχεται
καθ' αὑτῆς, καὶ οὐδεὶς εὐφυὴς νέος ἢ τὸν ἐν Πίσῃ θεασά- 15
μενος Δία γενέσθαι Φειδίας ἐπεθύμησεν, ἢ τὴν Ἥραν 300 S
τὴν ἐν Ἄργει Πολύκλειτος, οὐδ' Ἀνακρέων ἢ Φιλήμων
ἢ Ἀρχίλοχος ἡσθεὶς αὐτῶν τοῖς ποιήμασιν. οὐ γὰρ ἀναγκαῖον, εἰ τέρπει τὸ ἔργον ὡς χαρίεν, ἄξιον σπουδῆς εἶναι
2 τὸν εἰργασμένον. ὅθεν οὐδ' ὠφελεῖ τὰ τοιαῦτα τοὺς θεωμέ- 20
νους, πρὸς ἃ μιμητικὸς οὐ γίνεται ζῆλος οὐδ' ἀνάδοσις 3 L
κινοῦσα προθυμίαν καὶ ὁρμὴν ἐπὶ τὴν ἐξομοίωσιν. ἀλλ'
b ἥ γ' ἀρετὴ ταῖς πράξεσιν εὐθὺς οὕτω διατίθησιν, ὥσθ'
ἅμα θαυμάζεσθαι τὰ ἔργα καὶ ζηλοῦσθαι τοὺς εἰργασ-
3 μένους. τῶν μὲν γὰρ ἐκ τύχης ἀγαθῶν τὰς κτήσεις καὶ 25
ἀπολαύσεις, τῶν δ' ἀπ' ἀρετῆς τὰς πράξεις ἀγαπῶμεν,
καὶ τὰ μὲν ἡμῖν παρ' ἑτέρων, τὰ δὲ μᾶλλον ἑτέροις παρ'
4 ἡμῶν ὑπάρχειν βουλόμεθα. τὸ γὰρ καλὸν ἐφ' αὑτὸ πρακτικῶς κινεῖ καὶ πρακτικὴν εὐθὺς ὁρμὴν ἐντίθησιν, ἠθοποιοῦν

[S(UMA =)Υ] 1 ὁρμῆι ante ras. S ‖ 4 καὶ om. S ‖ 8 οὕτω S:
τῶ Υ ‖ 9 πόπωι ante corr. S | ψάλαντα UAψάλλοντα M | τεχνικῶς S
et ras. U: κατατεχνικῶς Υ κατατέχνως Rei. ‖ 11 ψαλόντων Υ | νέμη Υ ‖
15 ἑαυτῆς U ‖ 17 Φιλήμων] Φιλητᾶς Br. Ἱππώναξ Cob. ‖ 20 τὸν
εἰργασμένον] S²U²M: τῶν εἰργασμένων S¹U¹ τῶν εἰργασμένων A ‖
22 ὁρμὴν Rei.: ἀφορμὴν ‖ 24 ἅμα ⟨τῷ⟩ vel θαυμάζεσθαί ⟨τε⟩ Zie. |
εἰργασμένους Iunt. Ald.: ἐργασαμένους ‖ 25 τύχης S: τῆς τύχης Υ

οὐ τῇ μιμήσει τὸν θεατήν, ἀλλὰ τῇ ἱστορίᾳ τοῦ ἔργου τὴν
προαίρεσιν παρεχόμενον.

Ἔδοξεν οὖν καὶ ἡμῖν ἐνδιατρῖψαι τῇ περὶ τοὺς βίους 5
ἀναγραφῇ, καὶ τοῦτο τὸ βιβλίον δέκατον συντετάχαμεν,
5 τὸν Περικλέους βίον καὶ τὸν Φαβίου Μαξίμου τοῦ δια- c
πολεμήσαντος πρὸς Ἀννίβαν περιέχον, ἀνδρῶν κατά τε
τὰς ἄλλας ἀρετὰς ὁμοίων, μάλιστα δὲ πρᾳότητα καὶ δι-
καιοσύνην, καὶ τῷ δύνασθαι φέρειν δήμων καὶ συναρχόντων ἀγνωμοσύνας ὠφελιμωτάτων ταῖς πατρίσι γενομέ-
10 νων. εἰ δ᾽ ὀρθῶς στοχαζόμεθα τοῦ δέοντος, ἔξεστι κρίνειν ἐκ τῶν γραφομένων.

3. Περικλῆς γὰρ ἦν τῶν μὲν φυλῶν Ἀκαμαντίδης, τῶν
δὲ δήμων Χολαργεύς, οἴκου δὲ καὶ γένους τοῦ πρώτου
κατ᾽ ἀμφοτέρους. Ξάνθιππος γὰρ ὁ νικήσας ἐν Μυκάλῃ 2
15 τοὺς βασιλέως στρατηγοὺς ἔγημεν Ἀγαρίστην Κλεισθέ-
νους ἔγγονον, ὃς ἐξήλασε Πεισιστρατίδας καὶ κατέλυσε d
τὴν τυραννίδα γενναίως καὶ νόμους ἔθετο καὶ πολιτείαν
4 L
301 S ἄριστα κεκραμένην πρὸς ὁμόνοιαν καὶ σωτηρίαν κατέστησεν. αὕτη κατὰ τοὺς ὕπνους·ἔδοξε τεκεῖν λέοντα, καὶ μεθ᾽ 3
20 ἡμέρας ὀλίγας ἔτεκε Περικλέα, τὰ μὲν ἄλλα τὴν ἰδέαν τοῦ
σώματος ἄμεμπτον, προμήκη δὲ τῇ κεφαλῇ καὶ ἀσύμμετρον. ὅθεν αἱ μὲν εἰκόνες αὐτοῦ σχεδὸν ἅπασαι κράνεσι 4
περιέχονται, μὴ βουλομένων ὡς ἔοικε τῶν τεχνιτῶν ἐξο-
νειδίζειν. οἱ δ᾽ Ἀττικοὶ ποιηταὶ σχινοκέφαλον αὐτὸν ἐκά-
25 λουν · τὴν γὰρ σκίλλαν ἔστιν ὅτε καὶ σχῖνον ὀνομάζουσι.
τῶν δὲ κωμικῶν ὁ μὲν Κρατῖνος ἐν Χείρωσι (fr. 240 5
CAF I 86) „Στάσις δὲ (φησί) καὶ πρεσβυγενὴς Κρόνος e
ἀλλήλοισι μιγέντε μέγιστον τίκτετον τύραννον, ὃν δὴ

19 Herod. 6, 131

[S(UMA =)Υ] **4** τὸ δέκατον τοῦτο συνέγραψα Sᵐ (m. 1) ‖
7 πρᾳότητι καὶ δικαιοσύνῃ e corr. man. rec. S ‖ **10.11** εἰ–γραφομένων om. Sᵗ, in mg. add. S m. rec. ‖ **10** δέοντος Υ: πρέποντος
S² ‖ ἐξέσται Ri. ‖ **15** βασιλέως UM: βασιλέων SA ‖ **16** τοὺς Πεισ.
Rei. ‖ **20** ἰδέαν MA: εἰδέαν SU ‖ **24.25** οἱ δ᾽ Ἀττικοὶ...ὀνομάζουσι
del. Kron. cl. c. 13, 10 ‖ **26** Χείρωσι Sch.: χείρωσι ‖ **27** Κρόνος
Anon.: χρόνος

3

Κεφαληγερέταν θεοὶ καλέουσι", καὶ πάλιν ἐν Νεμέσει
(fr. 111 CAF I 49) · „μόλ᾽ ὦ Ζεῦ ξένιε καὶ καραϊέ."
6 Τηλεκλείδης δὲ „ποτὲ μὲν" ὑπὸ τῶν πραγμάτων ἠπορη-
μένον καθῆσθαί φησιν (fr. 44 CAF I 220) αὐτὸν ἐν τῇ
πόλει „καρηβαροῦντα, ποτὲ δὲ μόνον ἐκ κεφαλῆς ἐνδεκα- 5
7 κλίνου θόρυβον πολὺν ἐξανατέλλειν", ὁ δ᾽ Εὔπολις ἐν τοῖς
Δήμοις (fr. 93 CAF I 280) πυνθανόμενος περὶ ἑκάστου
τῶν ἀναβεβηκότων ἐξ Ἅιδου δημαγωγῶν, ὡς ὁ Περικλῆς
ὠνομάσθη τελευταῖος ·

    ὃ τί περ κεφάλαιον τῶν κάτωθεν ἤγαγες.   10

4. Διδάσκαλον δ᾽ αὐτοῦ τῶν μουσικῶν οἱ πλεῖστοι
f Δάμωνα γενέσθαι λέγουσιν, οὗ φασι δεῖν τοὔνομα βραχύνοντας τὴν προτέραν συλλαβὴν ἐκφέρειν, Ἀριστοτέλης
(fr. 364) δὲ παρὰ Πυθοκλείδῃ μουσικὴν διαπονηθῆναι
2 τὸν ἄνδρα φησίν. ὁ δὲ Δάμων ἔοικεν ἄκρος ὢν σοφιστὴς 15
καταδύεσθαι μὲν εἰς τὸ τῆς μουσικῆς ὄνομα πρὸς τοὺς
154 πολλοὺς ἐπικρυπτόμενος τὴν δεινότητα, τῷ δὲ Περικλεῖ 5 L
συνῆν καθάπερ ἀθλητῇ τῶν πολιτικῶν ἀλείπτης καὶ διδά-
3 σκαλος. οὐ μὴν ἔλαθεν ὁ Δάμων τῇ λύρᾳ παρακαλύμματι
χρώμενος, ἀλλ᾽ ὡς μεγαλοπράγμων καὶ φιλοτύραννος 20
4 ἐξωστρακίσθη καὶ παρέσχε τοῖς κωμικοῖς διατριβήν. ὁ 302 S
γοῦν Πλάτων (fr. 191 CAF I 655) καὶ πυνθανόμενον αὐτοῦ
τινα πεποίηκεν οὕτω ·

    πρῶτον μὲν οὖν μοι λέξον, ἀντιβολῶ · σὺ γὰρ
    ὥς φασι [ὦ] Χείρων ἐξέθρεψας Περικλέα.   25

5 διήκουσε δὲ Περικλῆς καὶ Ζήνωνος τοῦ Ἐλεάτου πρα-
γματευομένου ⟨μὲν⟩ περὶ φύσιν ὡς Παρμενίδης, ἐλεγκτι-
b κήν δέ τινα καὶ δι᾽ ἀντιλογίας εἰς ἀπορίαν κατακλείουσαν

11 Plat. Alc. I 118c ‖ 19 v. Aristid. 1, 7 Nic. 6, 1 Aristot.
Ἀθπ. 27, 4

[S(UMA =)Υ] 2 καραϊέ Meineke: κάριε S μακάριε Υ καράνιε
Kock ‖ 3 ἠπορημένων ante corr. S ‖ 5 δὲ om. U s. s. A ‖ 12. 13 οὔ
φασι . . . ἐκφέρειν del. Ha. ‖ 14 μουσικὴν ἂν διαπ. Υ ‖ 18 συνεῖναι
Rei. ‖ 25 ὦ del. Cob. ‖ 26 ἐλαιάτου S ‖ 27 μὲν add. Rei. ‖ 28 ἀντι-
ολογίας Υ | κατακλείουσαν εἰς ἀπορίαν Υ

ἐξασκήσαντος ἕξιν, ὥς που καὶ Τίμων ὁ Φλειάσιος εἴρηκε
διὰ τούτων (fr. V W.)·

    ἀμφοτερογλώσσου τε μέγα σθένος οὐκ ἀλαπαδνὸν
    Ζήνωνος, πάντων ἐπιλήπτορος.

5 ὁ δὲ πλεῖστα Περικλεῖ συγγενόμενος καὶ μάλιστα περι- 6
θεὶς ὄγκον αὐτῷ καὶ φρόνημα δημαγωγίας ἐμβριθέστερον, ὅλως τε μετεωρίσας καὶ συνεξάρας τὸ ἀξίωμα τοῦ
ἤθους, Ἀναξαγόρας ἦν ὁ Κλαζομένιος, ὃν οἱ τότ' ἄνθρωποι Νοῦν προσηγόρευον, εἴτε τὴν σύνεσιν αὐτοῦ μεγά-
10 λην εἰς φυσιολογίαν καὶ περιττὴν διαφανεῖσαν θαυμάσαντες, εἴθ' ὅτι τοῖς ὅλοις πρῶτος οὐ τύχην οὐδ' ἀνάγκην
διακοσμήσεως ἀρχήν, ἀλλὰ νοῦν ἐπέστησε καθαρὸν καὶ c
L ἄκρατον, ἐν μεμειγμένοις πᾶσι τοῖς ἄλλοις ἀποκρίνοντα
τὰς ὁμοιομερείας.

15 **5.** Τοῦτον ὑπερφυῶς τὸν ἄνδρα θαυμάσας ὁ Περικλῆς
καὶ τῆς λεγομένης μετεωρολογίας καὶ μεταρσιολεσχίας
ὑποπιμπλάμενος, οὐ μόνον ὡς ἔοικε τὸ φρόνημα σοβα-
ρὸν καὶ τὸν λόγον ὑψηλὸν εἶχε καὶ καθαρὸν ὀχλικῆς καὶ
πανούργου βωμολοχίας, ἀλλὰ καὶ προσώπου σύστασις
20 ἄθρυπτος εἰς γέλωτα καὶ πρᾳότης πορείας καὶ καταστολὴ περιβολῆς πρὸς οὐδὲν ἐκταραττομένη πάθος ἐν τῷ
λέγειν καὶ πλάσμα φωνῆς ἀθόρυβον καὶ ὅσα τοιαῦτα
πάντας θαυμαστῶς ἐξέπληττε. λοιδορούμενος γοῦν ποτε 2 d
καὶ κακῶς ἀκούων ὑπό τινος τῶν βδελυρῶν καὶ ἀκολάστων
25 ὅλην ἡμέραν ὑπέμεινε σιωπῇ κατ' ἀγοράν, ἅμα τι τῶν
303 8 ἐπειγόντων καταπραττόμενος, ἑσπέρας δ' ἀπήει κοσμίως
οἴκαδε παρακολουθοῦντος τοῦ ἀνθρώπου καὶ πάσῃ χρω-

---

3 vide ap. Wachsmuth ‖ 15 Plat. Phaedr. 270a

[S(UMA =) Υ] 1 ὥς που S: ὥσπας U ὥσπερ MA (in A ερ
s. s. m. 2) | φλιάσιος libri ‖ 3 ἀλαπαδνὸν MA (sed in A tota vox
in ras.) Diog. L. 9, 5, 25: ἀπατηλὸν SU ‖ 7 συνεξάρας S ‖ 9 νοῦν
s. s. U² ‖ 13 ἐν μεμιγνένοις SM: ἐμμεμιγμένοις U ἐν ἐμμεμιγμέ-
νοις A | ἄλλοις, s. s. ὅλοις m. 1, S ‖ 19 σύστασις S²: συστά-
σει S¹Υ

5

μένου βλασφημίᾳ πρὸς αὐτόν. ὡς δ' ἔμελλεν εἰσιέναι
σκότους ὄντος ἤδη, προσέταξέ τινι τῶν οἰκετῶν φῶς
λαβόντι παραπέμψαι καὶ καταστῆσαι πρὸς τὴν οἰκίαν
3 τὸν ἄνθρωπον. ὁ δὲ ποιητὴς Ἴων (FGrH 392 F 15) μοθωνικήν φησι τὴν ὁμιλίαν καὶ ὑπότυφον εἶναι τοῦ Περικλέους, 5
καὶ ταῖς μεγαλαυχίαις αὐτοῦ πολλὴν ὑπεροψίαν ἀνα-
e μεμεῖχθαι καὶ περιφρόνησιν τῶν ἄλλων, ἐπαινεῖ δὲ τὸ
Κίμωνος ἐμμελὲς καὶ ὑγρὸν καὶ μεμουσωμένον ἐν ταῖς
⟨συμ⟩περιφοραῖς. ἀλλ' Ἴωνα μὲν ὥσπερ τραγικὴν διδα-
σκαλίαν ἀξιοῦντα τὴν ἀρετὴν ἔχειν τι πάντως καὶ σατυρι- 10
κὸν μέρος ἐῶμεν, τοὺς δὲ τοῦ Περικλέους τὴν σεμνότητα
δοξοκοπίαν τε καὶ τῦφον ἀποκαλοῦντας ὁ Ζήνων παρε- 7 L
κάλει καὶ αὐτούς τι τοιοῦτο δοξοκοπεῖν, ὡς τῆς προσποιήσεως αὐτῆς τῶν καλῶν ὑποποιούσης τινὰ λεληθότως
ζῆλον καὶ συνήθειαν. 15

6. Οὐ μόνον δὲ ταῦτα τῆς Ἀναξαγόρου συνουσίας ἀπέ-
λαυσε Περικλῆς, ἀλλὰ καὶ δεισιδαιμονίας δοκεῖ γενέ-
f σθαι καθυπέρτερος, ἢν τὸ πρὸς τὰ μετέωρα θάμβος ἐνεργάζεται τοῖς αὐτῶν τε τούτων τὰς αἰτίας ἀγνοοῦσι καὶ
περὶ τὰ θεῖα δαιμονῶσι καὶ ταραττομένοις δι' ἀπειρίαν 20
αὐτῶν, ἣν ὁ φυσικὸς λόγος ἀπαλλάττων ἀντὶ τῆς φοβερᾶς
καὶ φλεγμαινούσης δεισιδαιμονίας τὴν ἀσφαλῆ μετ' ἐλπί-
2 δων ἀγαθῶν εὐσέβειαν ἐνεργάζεται. λέγεται δέ ποτε
κριοῦ μονόκερω κεφαλὴν ἐξ ἀγροῦ τῷ Περικλεῖ κομισθῆ-
ναι, καὶ Λάμπωνα μὲν τὸν μάντιν, ὡς εἶδε τὸ κέρας ἰσχυ- 25
ρὸν καὶ στερεὸν ἐκ μέσου τοῦ μετώπου πεφυκός, εἰπεῖν
155 ὅτι δυεῖν οὐσῶν ἐν τῇ πόλει δυναστειῶν, τῆς Θουκυδίδου
καὶ Περικλέους, εἰς ἕνα περιστήσεται τὸ κράτος παρ' ᾧ
γένοιτο τὸ σημεῖον· τὸν δ' Ἀναξαγόραν τοῦ κρανίου διακοπέντος ἐπιδεῖξαι τὸν ἐγκέφαλον οὐ πεπληρωκότα τὴν 30

cap. 6 cf. mor. 435 f Coriol. 38 et ibi l. l.

[S(UMA =)Υ] 4 μοχθωνικὴν U² ‖ 9 περιφοραῖς: em. Madvig ‖ ἴωνα (a s. s. m. 2) U ‖ 12 δοξοκομπίαν Υ ‖ 13 δοξοκομ-
πεῖν Υ ‖ 14 ἐμποιούσης Cob. ὑπεμποιούσης Zie. ‖ 16 συνηθείας S ‖
18 ἣν τὸ Cob. Sauppe: ὅση libri ὅσην τὸ Anon. ‖ ἐργάζεται Υ ‖
29 διακοπέντος, κο s. s. m. 1, S

6

304 S βάσιν, ἀλλ᾽ ὀξὺν ὥσπερ ᾠὸν ἐκ τοῦ παντὸς ἀγγείου συνω-
λισθηκότα κατὰ τὸν τόπον ἐκεῖνον ὅθεν ἡ ῥίζα τοῦ κέρα-
τος εἶχε τὴν ἀρχήν. καὶ τότε μὲν θαυμασθῆναι τὸν Ἀνα- 3
ξαγόραν ὑπὸ τῶν παρόντων, ὀλίγῳ δ᾽ ὕστερον τὸν Λάμ-
5 πωνα, τοῦ μὲν Θουκυδίδου καταλυθέντος, τῶν δὲ τοῦ δήμου
πραγμάτων ὁμαλῶς ἁπάντων ὑπὸ τῷ Περικλεῖ γενομένων. ἐκώλυε δ᾽ οὐδέν, οἶμαι, καὶ τὸν φυσικὸν ἐπιτυγχά- 4
8 L νειν καὶ τὸν μάντιν, τοῦ μὲν τὴν αἰτίαν, τοῦ δὲ τὸ τέλος b
καλῶς ἐκλαμβάνοντος· ὑπέκειτο γὰρ τῷ μέν, ἐκ τίνων
10 γέγονε καὶ πῶς πέφυκε θεωρῆσαι, τῷ δέ, πρὸς τί γέγονε
καὶ τί σημαίνει προειπεῖν. οἱ δὲ τῆς αἰτίας τὴν εὕρεσιν 5
ἀναίρεσιν εἶναι τοῦ σημείου λέγοντες οὐκ ἐπινοοῦσιν ἅμα
τοῖς θείοις καὶ τὰ τεχνητὰ τῶν συμβόλων ἀθετοῦντες,
ψόφους τε δίσκων καὶ φῶτα πυρσῶν καὶ γνωμόνων ἀπο-
15 σκιασμούς· ὧν ἕκαστον αἰτίᾳ τινὶ καὶ κατασκευῇ σημεῖον
εἶναί τινος πεποίηται. ταῦτα μὲν οὖν ἴσως ἑτέρας ἐστὶ
πραγματείας.

7. Ὁ δὲ Περικλῆς νέος μὲν ὢν σφόδρα τὸν δῆμον εὐλαβεῖτο. καὶ γὰρ ἐδόκει Πεισιστράτῳ τῷ τυράννῳ τὸ εἶδος c
20 ἐμφερὴς εἶναι, τήν τε φωνὴν ἡδεῖαν οὖσαν αὐτοῦ καὶ τὴν
γλῶτταν εὔτροχον ἐν τῷ διαλέγεσθαι καὶ ταχεῖαν οἱ
σφόδρα γέροντες ἐξεπλήττοντο πρὸς τὴν ὁμοιότητα. πλού- 2
του δὲ καὶ γένους προσόντος αὐτῷ λαμπροῦ καὶ φίλων
οἳ πλεῖστον ἐδύναντο, φοβούμενος ἐξοστρακισθῆναι τῶν
25 μὲν πολιτικῶν οὐδὲν ἔπραττεν, ἐν δὲ ταῖς στρατείαις ἀνὴρ
ἀγαθὸς ἦν καὶ φιλοκίνδυνος. ἐπεὶ δ᾽ Ἀριστείδης μὲν ἀπο- 3
τεθνήκει καὶ Θεμιστοκλῆς ἐξεπεπτώκει, Κίμωνα δ᾽ αἱ
στρατεῖαι τὰ πολλὰ τῆς Ἑλλάδος ἔξω κατεῖχον, οὕτω δὴ
φέρων ὁ Περικλῆς τῷ δήμῳ προσένειμεν ἑαυτόν, ἀντὶ τῶν d
30 πλουσίων καὶ ὀλίγων τὰ τῶν πολλῶν καὶ πενήτων ἑλόμενος

13 Val. Max. 8, 9 ext. 2

[S(UMA =)Υ] 1 ὀξὺν ὥσπερ ᾠὸν suspecta censet Ha. ‖
10 γέγονε Rei.: γεγονέναι ‖ 12 λέγοντες τοῦ σημείου: trp. Sint. ‖
23 αὐτοῦ S ‖ 26 ἐτεθνήκει Cob.

2 BT Plut. vit. I 2 ed. Ziegler [1673]

4 παρὰ τὴν αὑτοῦ φύσιν ἥκιστα δημοτικὴν οὖσαν. ἀλλ' ὡς 305 S
ἔοικε δεδιὼς μὲν ὑποψίᾳ περιπεσεῖν τυραννίδος, ὁρῶν δ'
ἀριστοκρατικὸν τὸν Κίμωνα καὶ διαφερόντως ὑπὸ τῶν
καλῶν κἀγαθῶν ἀνδρῶν ἀγαπώμενον, ὑπῆλθε τοὺς πολ- 9 L
λούς, ἀσφάλειαν μὲν ἑαυτῷ, δύναμιν δὲ κατ' ἐκείνου παρα- 5
5 σκευαζόμενος. εὐθὺς δὲ καὶ τοῖς περὶ τὴν δίαιταν ἑτέραν
τάξιν ἐπέθηκεν. ὁδόν τε γὰρ ἐν ἄστει μίαν ἑωρᾶτο τὴν
ἐπ' ἀγορὰν καὶ τὸ βουλευτήριον πορευόμενος, κλήσεις τε
δείπνων καὶ τὴν τοιαύτην ἅπασαν φιλοφροσύνην καὶ συνή-
e θειαν ἐξέλιπεν, ὡς ἐν οἷς ἐπολιτεύσατο χρόνοις μακροῖς 10
γενομένοις πρὸς μηδένα τῶν φίλων ἐπὶ δεῖπνον ἐλθεῖν·
πλὴν Εὐρυπτολέμου τοῦ ἀνεψιοῦ γαμοῦντος ἄχρι τῶν
6 σπονδῶν παραγενόμενος εὐθὺς ἐξανέστη. δειναὶ γὰρ αἱ
φιλοφροσύναι παντὸς ὄγκου περιγενέσθαι, καὶ δυσφύλα-
κτον ἐν συνηθείᾳ τὸ πρὸς δόξαν σεμνόν ἐστι· τῆς ἀληθινῆς 15
δ' ἀρετῆς κάλλιστα φαίνεται τὰ μάλιστα φαινόμενα,
καὶ τῶν ἀγαθῶν ἀνδρῶν οὐδὲν οὕτω θαυμάσιον τοῖς
7 ἐκτὸς ὡς ὁ καθ' ἡμέραν βίος τοῖς συνοῦσιν. ὁ δὲ καὶ τῷ
δήμῳ, τὸ συνεχὲς φεύγων καὶ τὸν κόρον, οἷον ἐκ διαλειμμάτων ἐπλησίαζεν, οὐκ ἐπὶ παντὶ πράγματι λέγων οὐδ' 20
f ἀεὶ παριὼν εἰς τὸ πλῆθος, ἀλλ' ἑαυτὸν ὥσπερ τὴν Σαλαμινίαν τριήρη, φησὶ Κριτόλαος, πρὸς τὰς μεγάλας χρείας
ἐπιδιδούς, τἄλλα δὲ φίλους καὶ ῥήτορας ἑτέρους καθιεὶς
8 ἔπραττεν. ὧν ἕνα φασὶ γενέσθαι τὸν Ἐφιάλτην, ὃς κατέλυσε τὸ κράτος τῆς ἐξ Ἀρείου πάγου βουλῆς, πολλὴν κατὰ 25
τὸν Πλάτωνα (respubl. 562c) καὶ ἄκρατον τοῖς πολίταις
ἐλευθερίαν οἰνοχοῶν, ὑφ' ἧς ὥσπερ ἵππον ἐξυβρίσαντα
156 τὸν δῆμον οἱ κωμῳδοποιοὶ λέγουσι (adesp. 41 CAF III 406)
„πειθαρχεῖν οὐκέτι τολμᾶν, 10
ἀλλ' ⟨ἐν⟩δάκνειν τὴν Εὔβοιαν καὶ ταῖς νήσοις ἐπιπηδᾶν". 30

6 mor. 800c ‖ 18 sq. mor. 812 c, d

[S(UMA=)Υ) 12 πλὴν S: πρὶν Υ ‖ 15 ἐστι Br.: ἐπὶ ‖ 16 ⟨μὴ⟩
μάλιστα Cor. ἥκιστα Cob. ‖ 18.19 τῷ δήμῳ Sauppe: τοῦ δήμου ‖
19 οἷον del. Cob. ‖ 23 ἑτέρους Xy.: ἑταίρους libri (ἑταίρους ῥήτορας Holzapfel Li.) ‖ 24 ὧν] ὃν U ‖ 28 κωμωδοποιοὶ SM κωμω-
δι̕οποιοὶ U κωμῳδιοποιοὶ A ‖ 30 ἀλλὰ δάκνειν: em. Zie. (ἀναδ. Sch.)

8. Τῇ μέντοι περὶ τὸν βίον κατασκευῇ καὶ τῷ μεγέθει
306 S τοῦ φρονήματος ἁρμόζοντα λόγον ὥσπερ ὄργανον ἐξαρτυόμενος, παρενέτεινε πολλαχοῦ τὸν Ἀναξαγόραν, οἷον
βαφὴν τῇ ῥητορικῇ τὴν φυσιολογίαν ὑποχεόμενος. τὸ γὰρ 2
5 „ὑψηλόνουν τοῦτο καὶ πάντη τελεσιουργόν", ὡς ὁ θεῖος
Πλάτων (Phaedr. 270a) φησί, „πρὸς τῷ εὐφυὴς εἶναι
κτησάμενος" ἐκ φυσιολογίας, καὶ τὸ πρόσφορον ἑλκύσας
ἐπὶ τὴν τῶν λόγων τέχνην, πολὺ πάντων διήνεγκε. διὸ 3
καὶ τὴν ἐπίκλησιν αὐτῷ γενέσθαι λέγουσι· καίτοι τινὲς b
10 ἀπὸ τῶν ⟨ἀναθημάτων⟩ οἷς ἐκόσμησε τὴν πόλιν, οἱ δ'
ἀπὸ τῆς ἐν τῇ πολιτείᾳ καὶ ταῖς στρατηγίαις δυνάμεως
Ὀλύμπιον αὐτὸν οἴονται προσαγορευθῆναι· καὶ συνδραμεῖν οὐδὲν ἀπέοικεν ἀπὸ πολλῶν προσόντων τῷ ἀνδρὶ τὴν
δόξαν. αἱ μέντοι κωμῳδίαι τῶν τότε διδασκάλων, σπουδῇ 4
15 τε πολλὰς καὶ μετὰ γέλωτος ἀφεικότων φωνὰς εἰς αὐτόν,
ἐπὶ τῷ λόγῳ μάλιστα τὴν προσωνυμίαν γενέσθαι δηλοῦσι,
„βροντᾶν" μὲν αὐτὸν καὶ „ἀστράπτειν" ὅτε δημηγοροίη,
„δεινὸν δὲ κεραυνὸν ἐν γλώσσῃ φέρειν" λεγόντων ⟨Ari-
stoph. Ach. 531. adesp. 10 CAF III 4)
20   Διαμνημονεύεται δέ τις καὶ Θουκυδίδου τοῦ Μελησίου 5
λόγος εἰς τὴν δεινότητα τοῦ Περικλέους μετὰ ᾽παιδιᾶς
εἰρημένος. ἦν μὲν γὰρ ὁ Θουκυδίδης τῶν καλῶν καὶ ἀγα- c
θῶν ἀνδρῶν, καὶ πλεῖστον ἀντεπολιτεύσατο τῷ Περικλεῖ
χρόνον. Ἀρχιδάμου δὲ τοῦ Λακεδαιμονίων βασιλέως πυν-
25 θανομένου πότερον αὐτὸς ἢ Περικλῆς παλαίει βέλτιον,
11 L „ὅταν" εἶπεν „ἐγὼ καταβάλω παλαίων, ἐκεῖνος ἀντιλέγων
ὡς οὐ πέπτωκε, νικᾷ καὶ μεταπείθει τοὺς ὁρῶντας."
   Οὐ μὴν ἀλλὰ καὶ οὕτως ὁ Περικλῆς περὶ τὸν λόγον εὐλα- 6
βὴς ἦν, ὥστ᾽ ἀεὶ πρὸς τὸ βῆμα βαδίζων ηὔχετο τοῖς θεοῖς

4 Cic. orat. 15 || 14 Cic. orat. 29 || 23 mor. 802 c Aristoph. eq.
571 sq.

[S(UMA=)Υ] 3 παρενέτεινε SUM παρέτεινε, ρε in ras., A παρ-
ενεῖρε Cob. παρενέσπειρε cl. Dion. 11,1 Zie., sed Sol. 3,4 cft. Erb-
se Gnom. 33,41 || 4 βαφὴν Br.: βαφῆι S βαφῇ Υ | ὑπερχεόμενος
S ἐπιχεόμενος Cor. || 7 καὶ τὸ πρόσφορον ἐκ φυσιολ. Ha. || 10 ἀνα-
θημάτων add. Zie. || 13 τῷ ἀνδρὶ αὐτῷ τὴν Υ || 20 μιλησίου: em.
Sint. || 28 οὕτως Holzapfel: αὐτὸς

2*

PLUTARCH

[μηδὲ] ῥῆμα μηδὲν ἐκπεσεῖν ἄκοντος αὐτοῦ πρὸς τὴν προ-
7 κειμένην χρείαν ἀνάρμοστον. ἔγγραφον μὲν οὖν οὐδὲν
ἀπολέλοιπε πλὴν τῶν ψηφισμάτων, ἀπομνημονεύεται δ᾽
d ὀλίγα παντάπασιν, οἷον τὸ τὴν Αἴγιναν ὡς λήμην τοῦ Πει-
ραιῶς ἀφελεῖν κελεῦσαι, καὶ τὸ τὸν πόλεμον ἤδη φάναι 5
8 καθορᾶν ἀπὸ Πελοποννήσου προσφερόμενον· καί ποτε 307 S
τοῦ Σοφοκλέους, ὅτε συστρατηγῶν ἐξέπλευσε μετ᾽ αὐτοῦ,
παῖδα καλὸν ἐπαινέσαντος, „οὐ μόνον" ἔφη „τὰς χεῖρας ὦ
Σοφόκλεις δεῖ καθαρὰς ἔχειν τὸν στρατηγόν, ἀλλὰ καὶ
9 τὰς ὄψεις." ὁ δὲ Στησίμβροτός (FGrH 107 F 9) φησιν, ὅτι 10
τοὺς ἐν Σάμῳ τεθνηκότας ἐγκωμιάζων ἐπὶ τοῦ βήματος
ἀθανάτους ἔλεγε γεγονέναι καθάπερ τοὺς θεούς· οὐδὲ γὰρ
ἐκείνους αὐτοὺς ὁρῶμεν, ἀλλὰ ταῖς τιμαῖς ἃς ἔχουσι καὶ
τοῖς ἀγαθοῖς ἃ παρέχουσιν ἀθανάτους εἶναι τεκμαιρόμεθα·
e ταῦτ᾽ οὖν ὑπάρχειν καὶ τοῖς ὑπὲρ τῆς πατρίδος ἀποθανοῦ- 15
σιν.

9. Ἐπεὶ δὲ Θουκυδίδης (2, 65) μὲν ἀριστοκρατικήν τινα
τὴν τοῦ Περικλέους ὑπογράφει πολιτείαν, „λόγῳ μὲν
οὖσαν δημοκρατίαν, ἔργῳ δ᾽ ὑπὸ τοῦ πρώτου ἀνδρὸς
ἀρχήν", ἄλλοι δὲ πολλοὶ πρῶτον ὑπ᾽ ἐκείνου φασὶ τὸν 20
δῆμον ἐπὶ κληρουχίας καὶ θεωρικὰ καὶ μισθῶν διανομὰς
προαχθῆναι, κακῶς ἐθισθέντα καὶ γενόμενον πολυτελῆ
καὶ ἀκόλαστον ὑπὸ τῶν τότε πολιτευμάτων ἀντὶ σώφρονος 12 L
καὶ αὐτουργοῦ, θεωρείσθω διὰ τῶν πραγμάτων αὐτῶν ἡ 25
2 αἰτία τῆς μεταβολῆς. ἐν ἀρχῇ μὲν γὰρ ὥσπερ εἴρηται πρὸς
f τὴν Κίμωνος δόξαν ἀντιταττόμενος ὑπεποιεῖτο τὸν δῆμον,
ἐλαττούμενος δὲ πλούτῳ καὶ χρήμασιν, ἀφ᾽ ὧν ἐκεῖνος
ἀνελάμβανε τοὺς πένητας, δεῖπνόν τε καθ᾽ ἡμέραν τῷ δεο-

4 v. Demosth. 1, 2 mor. 186 c. 803 a Aristot. rhet. 1411 a 14.
Strab. 9, 395 Athen. 3, 99 d Arsen. 418 ‖ 6 Cic. off. 1, 144 Val.
Max. 4, 3 ext. 1 ‖ 17 mor. 802 c ‖ 25 Plut. Cim. 10, 1 Aristot.
Ἀθπ. 27, 3 sq. Athen. 12, 533 a (Theopomp. FGrH 115 F)

[S(UMA =)Υ] 1 μηδὲ del. Zie. ‖ 12 οὐδὲ S: οὐ Υ ‖ 14 ἃ
παρέχουσιν Br.: ἅπερ ἔχουσιν | ἀθανάτους del. Sauppe ‖ 15 ταῦτ᾽
Cor.: ταῦτ᾽ libri, quod tuetur Sch.

10

μένῳ παρέχων Ἀθηναίων καὶ τοὺς πρεσβυτέρους ἀμφιεννύων, τῶν τε χωρίων τοὺς φραγμοὺς ἀφαιρῶν ὅπως ὀπωρίζωσιν οἱ βουλόμενοι, τούτοις ὁ Περικλῆς καταδημαγω- 157
γούμενος τρέπεται πρὸς τὴν τῶν δημοσίων διανομήν,
5 συμβουλεύσαντος αὐτῷ ⟨Δάμωνος τοῦ⟩ Δαμωνίδου τοῦ
Οἴηθεν, ὡς Ἀριστοτέλης (fr. 365) ἱστόρηκε. καὶ ταχὺ 3
θεωρικοῖς καὶ δικαστικοῖς λήμμασιν ἄλλαις τε μισθοφοραῖς καὶ χορηγίαις συνδεκάσας τὸ πλῆθος, ἐχρῆτο κατὰ
τῆς ἐξ Ἀρείου πάγου βουλῆς, ἧς αὐτὸς οὐ μετεῖχε διὰ τὸ
10 μήτ᾽ ἄρχων μήτε θεσμοθέτης μήτε βασιλεὺς μήτε πο-
308 S λέμαρχος λαχεῖν. αὗται γὰρ αἱ ἀρχαὶ κληρωταί τ᾽ ἦσαν 4
ἐκ παλαιοῦ, καὶ δι᾽ αὐτῶν οἱ δοκιμασθέντες ἀνέβαινον
εἰς Ἄρειον πάγον. διὸ καὶ μᾶλλον ἰσχύσας ὁ Περικλῆς ἐν 5
τῷ δήμῳ κατεστασίασε τὴν βουλήν, ὥστε τὴν μὲν ἀφαι-
15 ρεθῆναι τὰς πλείστας κρίσεις δι᾽ Ἐφιάλτου, Κίμωνα δ᾽ ὡς b
φιλολάκωνα καὶ μισόδημον ἐξοστρακισθῆναι, πλούτῳ μὲν
καὶ γένει μηδενὸς ἀπολειπόμενον, νίκας δὲ καλλίστας
νενικηκότα τοὺς βαρβάρους καὶ χρημάτων πολλῶν καὶ
λαφύρων ἐμπεπληκότα τὴν πόλιν, ὡς ἐν τοῖς περὶ ἐκείνου
20 (10, 1) γέγραπται. τοσοῦτον ἦν τὸ κράτος ἐν τῷ δήμῳ τοῦ
Περικλέους.

3 L **10.** Ὁ μὲν οὖν ἐξοστρακισμὸς ὡρισμένην εἶχε νόμῳ
δεκαετίαν τοῖς φεύγουσιν· ἐν δὲ τῷ διὰ μέσου στρατῷ
μεγάλῳ Λακεδαιμονίων ἐμβαλόντων εἰς τὴν Ταναγρικὴν
25 καὶ τῶν Ἀθηναίων εὐθὺς ὁρμησάντων ἐπ᾽ αὐτούς, ὁ μὲν
Κίμων ἐλθὼν ἐκ τῆς φυγῆς ἔθετο μετὰ τῶν φυλετῶν εἰς c
λόχον τὰ ὅπλα, καὶ δι᾽ ἔργων ἀπολύεσθαι τὸν Λακωνισμὸν
ἐβούλετο συγκινδυνεύσας τοῖς πολίταις, οἱ δὲ φίλοι τοῦ
Περικλέους συστάντες ἀπήλασαν αὐτὸν ὡς φυγάδα. διὸ 2

22sq. Cim. 17, 4–7. 18

[S(UMA=)Υ] 5 Δάμωνος τοῦ add. Zie. (post ⟨Δάμωνος⟩
Cob.) | δημωνίδου libri || 6 Οἴηθεν] cf. Aristot. || 10 μήτε βασιλεὺς
μήτε πολέμ. μήτε θεσμ. Sauppe || 11 τ᾽ om. S || 12 δι᾽ αὐτῶοι-
ᵈᵒκιμασθέντες U || 23. 24 λακεδαιμονίων στρατῷ μεγάλῳ: trp.
Sint. || 24 ταναγραικὴν Υ

καὶ δοκεῖ Περικλῆς ἐρρωμενέστατα τὴν μάχην ἐκείνην ἀγωνίσασθαι καὶ γενέσθαι πάντων ἐπιφανέστατος, ἀφει-
3 δήσας τοῦ σώματος. ἔπεσον δὲ καὶ τοῦ Κίμωνος οἱ φίλοι πάντες ὁμαλῶς οὓς Περικλῆς συνεπῃτίατο τοῦ Λακω-
νισμοῦ, καὶ μετάνοια δεινὴ τοὺς Ἀθηναίους καὶ πόθος 5 ἔσχε τοῦ Κίμωνος, ἡττημένους μὲν ἐπὶ τῶν ὅρων τῆς Ἀττικῆς, προσδοκῶντας δὲ βαρὺν εἰς ἔτους ὥραν πόλεμον.
d 4 αἰσθόμενος οὖν ὁ Περικλῆς οὐκ ὤκνησε χαρίσασθαι τοῖς πολλοῖς, ἀλλὰ τὸ ψήφισμα γράψας αὐτὸς ἐκάλει τὸν ἄνδρα, κἀκεῖνος ἐπανελθὼν εἰρήνην ἐποίησε ταῖς πόλεσιν· οἰκείως 10 γὰρ εἶχον οἱ Λακεδαιμόνιοι πρὸς αὐτόν, ὥσπερ ἀπήχθοντο
5 τῷ Περικλεῖ καὶ τοῖς ἄλλοις δημαγωγοῖς. ἔνιοι δέ φασιν οὐ πρότερον γραφῆναι τῷ Κίμωνι τὴν κάθοδον ὑπὸ τοῦ 309 S Περικλέους, ἢ συνθήκας αὐτοῖς ἀπορρήτους γενέσθαι δι' Ἐλπινίκης, τῆς Κίμωνος ἀδελφῆς, ὥστε Κίμωνα μὲν ἐκ- 15 πλεῦσαι λαβόντα ναῦς διακοσίας καὶ τῶν ἔξω στρατηγεῖν καταστρεφόμενον τὴν βασιλέως χώραν, Περικλεῖ δὲ τὴν
e 6 ἐν ἄστει δύναμιν ὑπάρχειν. ἐδόκει δὲ καὶ πρότερον ἡ Ἐλπι- 14 L νίκη τῷ Κίμωνι τὸν Περικλέα πρᾳότερον παρασχεῖν, ὅτε. τὴν θανατικὴν δίκην ἔφευγεν. ἦν μὲν γὰρ εἷς τῶν κατηγό- 20 ρων ὁ Περικλῆς ὑπὸ τοῦ δήμου προβεβλημένος, ἐλθούσης δὲ πρὸς αὐτὸν τῆς Ἐλπινίκης καὶ δεομένης, μειδιάσας εἶπεν ,,ὦ Ἐλπινίκη, γραῦς εἶ, γραῦς εἶ, ὡς πράγματα τηλικαῦτα διαπράσσειν.'' οὐ μὴν ἀλλὰ καὶ πρὸς τὸν λόγον ἅπαξ ἀνέ-
στη τὴν προβολὴν ἀφοσιούμενος, καὶ τῶν κατηγόρων 25
7 ἐλάχιστα τὸν Κίμωνα λυπήσας ἀπεχώρησε. πῶς ἂν οὖν τις Ἰδομενεῖ (FGrH 338 F 8) πιστεύσειε κατηγοροῦντι τοῦ Περικλέους, ὡς τὸν δημαγωγὸν Ἐφιάλτην, φίλον γενόμενον
f καὶ κοινωνὸν ὄντα τῆς ἐν τῇ πολιτείᾳ προαιρέσεως, δολο-

12 mor. 812f ‖ 18 Plut. Cim. 14, 5

[S(UMA =)Υ] 1 ἐρρωμενέστατα τὴν Cob.: ἐρρωμενεστάτην ‖
9 κατεκάλει Ha. ‖ 10 ἐπανελθὼν Cor.: ἀπελθὼν libri ἀνελθὼν Br.
Sch. κατελθὼν Sint. ‖ 17 καταστρεφόμενον Naber ‖ 24 διαπράσσειν Zie.: δράσειν libri πράσσειν Vulc. διαπράσσεσθαι Cim. 14, 5 ‖
29 δολοφωνήσαντος ante ras. S

φονήσαντος διὰ ζηλοτυπίαν καὶ φθόνον τῆς δόξης· ταῦτα
γὰρ οὐκ οἶδ' ὅθεν συναγαγὼν ὥσπερ χολὴν τἀνδρὶ προσβέβληκε, πάντῃ μὲν ἴσως οὐκ ἀνεπιλήπτῳ, φρόνημα δ'
εὐγενὲς ἔχοντι καὶ ψυχὴν φιλότιμον, οἷς οὐδὲν ἐμφύεται
5 πάθος ὠμὸν οὕτω καὶ θηριῶδες. Ἐφιάλτην μὲν οὖν, φοβε- 8 158
ρὸν ὄντα τοῖς ὀλιγαρχικοῖς καὶ περὶ τὰς εὐθύνας καὶ διώξεις τῶν τὸν δῆμον ἀδικούντων ἀπαραίτητον, ἐπιβουλεύ-
σαντες οἱ ἐχθροὶ δι' Ἀριστοδίκου τοῦ Ταναγρικοῦ κρυφαίως
ἀνεῖλον, ὡς Ἀριστοτέλης (fr. 367) εἴρηκεν.

10   Ἐτελεύτησε δὲ Κίμων ἐν Κύπρῳ στρατηγῶν. **11.** Οἱ δ'
ἀριστοκρατικοί, μέγιστον μὲν ἤδη τὸν Περικλέα καὶ πρόσθεν ὁρῶντες γεγονότα τῶν πολιτῶν, βουλόμενοι δ' ὅμως
15 L εἶναί τινα τὸν πρὸς αὐτὸν ἀντιτασσόμενον ἐν τῇ πόλει καὶ
τὴν δύναμιν ἀμβλύνοντα, ὥστε μὴ κομιδῇ μοναρχίαν εἶναι,
310 S Θουκυδίδην τὸν Ἀλωπεκῆθεν, ἄνδρα σώφρονα καὶ κηδεστὴν
16 Κίμωνος, ἀντέστησαν ἐναντιωσόμενον, ὃς ἧττον μὲν ὢν
πολεμικὸς τοῦ Κίμωνος, ἀγοραῖος δὲ καὶ πολιτικὸς μᾶλ- b
λον, οἰκουρῶν ἐν ἄστει καὶ περὶ τὸ βῆμα τῷ Περικλεῖ
συμπλεκόμενος, ταχὺ τὴν πολιτείαν εἰς ἀντίπαλον κατέ-
20 στησεν. οὐ γὰρ εἴασε τοὺς καλοὺς καὶ ἀγαθοὺς καλουμέ- 2
νους ἄνδρας ἐνδιεσπάρθαι καὶ συμμεμεῖχθαι πρὸς τὸν
δῆμον ὡς πρότερον, ὑπὸ πλήθους ἠμαυρωμένους τὸ ἀξίωμα, χωρὶς δὲ διακρίνας καὶ συναγαγὼν εἰς ταὐτὸ τὴν
πάντων δύναμιν ἐμβριθῆ γενομένην, ὥσπερ ἐπὶ ζυγοῦ
25 ῥοπὴν ἐποίησεν. ἦν μὲν γὰρ ἐξ ἀρχῆς διπλόη τις ὕπουλος 3
ὥσπερ ἐν σιδήρῳ, διαφορὰν ὑποσημαίνουσα δημοτικῆς
καὶ ἀριστοκρατικῆς προαιρέσεως, ἡ δ' ἐκείνων ἅμιλλα
καὶ φιλοτιμία τῶν ἀνδρῶν βαθυτάτην τομὴν τεμοῦσα τῆς c
πόλεως, τὸ μὲν δῆμον, τὸ δ' ὀλίγους ἐποίησε καλεῖσθαι.

5 Aristot. Ἀθπ. 25, 4

[S(UMA =)Υ] 2 ὁπόθεν Blaß | προσβέβληκε Rei.: προβέβληκε
libri προσβέβλυκε Cor. ‖ 8 Ταναγραίου Aristot. ‖ 14 ἀμβλύνοντα,
τα add. mg. m. 2, U ‖ 16 ἀνέστησαν Madvig ‖ 19 εἰς τἀντίπαλον
Rei. ‖ 22 ⟨τοῦ⟩ πλήθους Rei. ‖ 25 ἦν Anon.: ἢ | διπλόη Ruhnken:
διαπλοκή

4 διὸ καὶ τότε μάλιστα τῷ δήμῳ τὰς ἡνίας ἀνεὶς ὁ Περικλῆς ἐπολιτεύετο πρὸς χάριν, ἀεὶ μέν τινα θέαν πανηγυ-
ρικὴν ἢ ἑστίασιν ἢ πομπὴν εἶναι μηχανώμενος ἐν ἄστει,
καὶ διαπαιδαγωγῶν οὐκ ἀμούσοις ἡδοναῖς τὴν πόλιν, ἐξή-
κοντα δὲ τριήρεις καθ᾽ ἕκαστον ἐνιαυτὸν ἐκπέμπων, ἐν 5
αἷς πολλοὶ τῶν πολιτῶν ἔπλεον ὀκτὼ μῆνας ἔμμισθοι,
μελετῶντες ἅμα καὶ μανθάνοντες τὴν ναυτικὴν ἐμπει-
5 ρίαν. πρὸς δὲ τούτοις χιλίους μὲν ἔστειλεν εἰς Χερρόνησον
a. 447 κληρούχους, εἰς δὲ Νάξον πεντακοσίους, εἰς δ᾽ Ἄνδρον
d ⟨τοὺς⟩ ἡμίσεις τούτων, εἰς δὲ Θρᾴκην χιλίους Βισάλταις 10
a. 444/3 συνοικήσοντας, ἄλλους δ᾽ εἰς Ἰταλίαν ⟨ἀν⟩οικιζομένης 16 L
6 Συβάρεως, ἣν Θουρίους προσηγόρευσαν. καὶ ταῦτ᾽ ἔπραττεν ἀποκουφίζων μὲν ἀργοῦ καὶ διὰ σχολὴν πολυπράγμονος
ὄχλου τὴν πόλιν, ἐπανορθούμενος δὲ τὰς ἀπορίας τοῦ
δήμου, φόβον δὲ καὶ φρουρὰν τοῦ μὴ νεωτερίζειν τι παρα- 15
κατοικίζων τοῖς συμμάχοις.

12. Ὁ δὲ πλείστην μὲν ἡδονὴν ταῖς Ἀθήναις καὶ κόσμον ἤνεγκε, μεγίστην δὲ τοῖς ἄλλοις ἔκπληξιν ἀνθρώποις, 311 S
μόνον δὲ τῇ Ἑλλάδι μαρτυρεῖ μὴ ψεύδεσθαι τὴν λεγομέ-
e νην δύναμιν αὐτῆς ἐκείνην καὶ τὸν παλαιὸν ὄλβον, ἡ τῶν 20
ἀναθημάτων κατασκευή, τοῦτο μάλιστα τῶν πολιτευμάτων τοῦ Περικλέους ἐβάσκαινον οἱ ἐχθροὶ καὶ διέβαλλον ἐν ταῖς ἐκκλησίαις, βοῶντες ὡς ὁ μὲν δῆμος ἀδοξεῖ
καὶ κακῶς ἀκούει, τὰ κοινὰ τῶν Ἑλλήνων χρήματα πρὸς
αὐτὸν ἐκ Δήλου μεταγαγών, ἡ δ᾽ ἔνεστιν αὐτῷ πρὸς τοὺς 25
ἐγκαλοῦντας εὐπρεπεστάτη τῶν προφάσεων, δείσαντα
τοὺς βαρβάρους ἐκεῖθεν ἀνελέσθαι καὶ φυλάττειν ἐν
2 ὀχυρῷ τὰ κοινά, ταύτην ἀνῄρηκε Περικλῆς, καὶ δοκεῖ
δεινὴν ὕβριν ἡ Ἑλλὰς ὑβρίζεσθαι καὶ τυραννεῖσθαι περι-

8 cf. c. 19, 1 Diod. 11, 88, 3 Paus. 1, 27, 5 Andoc. 3, 9 ‖ 11 cf.
Plut. Nic. 5, 3 Diod. 12, 10, 3 Strab. 6, 263 Dion. Hal. Lys. 1
Phot. lex. s. v. Θουριομάντεις

[S(UMA =)Υ] 9 ἀνδρῶν ante ras. S ‖ 10 τοὺς add. Cob. | Βι-
σάλταις Steph.: βησάλταις ‖ 11 οἰκιζομένης: suppl. Eberhard ‖
15 τι del. Cob. ‖ 20 ἐκείνην Br.: ἐκείνης ‖ 21 τοῦτο Anon.: τούτωι S
τούτω Υ ‖ 25 ἢ δ᾽ ἔστιν Cob.

φανῶς, ὁρῶσα τοῖς εἰσφερομένοις ὑπ᾽ αὐτῆς ἀναγκαίως
πρὸς τὸν πόλεμον ἡμᾶς εἴην πόλιν καταχρυσοῦντας καὶ
καλλωπίζοντας ὥσπερ ἀλαζόνα γυναῖκα, περιαπτομένην f
λίθους πολυτελεῖς καὶ ἀγάλματα καὶ ναοὺς χιλιοταλάν-
5 τους. ἐδίδασκεν οὖν ὁ Περικλῆς τὸν δῆμον, ὅτι χρημάτων 3
μὲν οὐκ ὀφείλουσι τοῖς συμμάχοις λόγον, προπολεμοῦντες
αὐτῶν καὶ τοὺς βαρβάρους ἀνείργοντες, οὐχ ἵππον, οὐ 159
ναῦν, οὐχ ὁπλίτην, ἀλλὰ χρήματα μόνον τελούντων, ἃ τῶν
17 L διδόντων οὐκ ἔστιν, ἀλλὰ τῶν λαμβανόντων, ἂν παρέχωσιν
10 ἀνθ᾽ οὗ λαμβάνουσι, δεῖ δὲ τῆς πόλεως κατεσκευασμένης 4
ἱκανῶς τοῖς ἀναγκαίοις πρὸς τὸν πόλεμον, εἰς ταῦτα τὴν
εὐπορίαν τρέπειν αὐτῆς, ἀφ᾽ ὧν δόξα μὲν γενομένων ἀίδιος,
εὐπορία δὲ γινομένων ἑτοίμη παρέσται, παντοδαπῆς ἐργασίας φανείσης καὶ ποικίλων χρειῶν, αἳ πᾶσαν μὲν τέχνην
15 ἐγείρουσαι, πᾶσαν δὲ χεῖρα κινοῦσαι, σχεδὸν ὅλην ποι-
οῦσιν ἔμμισθον τὴν πόλιν, ἐξ αὐτῆς ἅμα κοσμουμένην καὶ
τρεφομένην. τοῖς μὲν γὰρ ἡλικίαν ἔχουσι καὶ ῥώμην αἱ 5
στρατεῖαι τὰς ἀπὸ τῶν κοινῶν εὐπορίας παρεῖχον, τὸν δ᾽ b
312 8 ἀσύντακτον καὶ βάναυσον ὄχλον οὔτ᾽ ἄμοιρον εἶναι λημ-
20 μάτων βουλόμενος. οὔτε λαμβάνειν ἀργὸν καὶ σχολάζοντα,
μεγάλας κατασκευασμάτων ἐπιβολὰς καὶ πολυτέχνους ὑποθέσεις ἔργων διατριβὴν ἐχόντων ἐνέβαλε φέρων εἰς τὸν
δῆμον, ἵνα μηδὲν ἧττον τῶν πλεόντων καὶ φρουρούντων
καὶ στρατευομένων τὸ οἰκουροῦν ἔχῃ πρόφασιν ἀπὸ τῶν
25 δημοσίων ὠφελεῖσθαι καὶ μεταλαμβάνειν. ὅπου γὰρ ὕλη 6
μὲν ἦν λίθος, χαλκός, ἐλέφας, χρυσός, ἔβενος, κυπάρισσος,
αἱ δὲ ταύτην ἐκπονοῦσαι καὶ κατεργαζόμεναι τέχναι τέκτο- c
νες, πλάσται, χαλκοτύποι, λιθουργοί, βαφεῖς χρυσοῦ,
μαλακτῆρες ἐλέφαντος, ζωγράφοι, ποικιλταί, τορευταί,
30 πομποὶ δὲ τούτων καὶ κομιστῆρες ἔμποροι καὶ ναῦται καὶ
κυβερνῆται κατὰ θάλατταν, οἱ δὲ κατὰ γῆν ἁμαξοπηγοὶ
καὶ ζευγοτρόφοι καὶ ἡνίοχοι καὶ καλωστρόφοι καὶ λινουρ-

[S(UA =)Υ] 10 δεῖν Cob. ‖ 12—13 γενομένων—γινομένων
Anon.: γινομένων—γενομένων ‖ 15 κινοῦσα U ‖ 28. 29 βαφεῖς,
χρυσοῦ μαλακτῆρες ⟨καὶ⟩ ἐλέφαντος Rei. ‖ 29 πορευταί U ‖ 32 λιθουργοί: em. Xy.

γοὶ καὶ σκυτοτόμοι καὶ ὁδοποιοὶ καὶ μεταλλεῖς, ἑκάστη δὲ
τέχνη, καθάπερ στρατηγὸς ἴδιον στράτευμα, τὸν θητικὸν ὄχλον καὶ ἰδιώτην συντεταγμένον εἶχεν, ὄργανον καὶ 18 L
σῶμα τῆς ὑπηρεσίας γινόμενον, εἰς πᾶσαν ὡς ἔπος εἰπεῖν
ἡλικίαν καὶ φύσιν αἱ χρεῖαι διένεμον καὶ διέσπειρον τὴν 5
εὐπορίαν.

d **13.** Ἀναβαινόντων δὲ τῶν ἔργων ὑπερηφάνων μὲν μεγέθει, μορφῇ δ᾽ ἀμιμήτων καὶ χάριτι, τῶν δημιουργῶν ἁμιλ-
λωμένων ὑπερβάλλεσθαι τὴν δημιουργίαν τῇ καλλιτεχνίᾳ,
2 μάλιστα θαυμάσιον ἦν τὸ τάχος. ὧν γὰρ ἕκαστον ᾤοντο 10
πολλαῖς διαδοχαῖς καὶ ἡλικίαις μόλις ἐπὶ τέλος ἀφίξεσθαι,
ταῦτα πάντα μιᾶς ἀκμῇ πολιτείας ἐλάμβανε τὴν συντέ-
3 λειαν. καίτοι ποτέ φασιν Ἀγαθάρχου τοῦ ζωγράφου μέγα
φρονοῦντος ἐπὶ τῷ ταχὺ καὶ ῥᾳδίως τὰ ζῷα ποιεῖν ἀκού-
4 σαντα τὸν Ζεῦξιν εἰπεῖν· ,,ἐγὼ δ᾽ ἐν πολλῷ χρόνῳ.‘‘ ἡ 15
γὰρ ἐν τῷ ποιεῖν εὐχέρεια καὶ ταχύτης οὐκ ἐντίθησι βάρος
e ἔργῳ μόνιμον οὐδὲ κάλλους ἀκρίβειαν, ὁ δ᾽ εἰς τὴν γένεσιν τῷ πόνῳ προδανεισθεὶς χρόνος ἐν τῇ σωτηρίᾳ τοῦ 313 S
γενομένου τὴν ἰσχὺν ἀποδίδωσιν. ὅθεν καὶ μᾶλλον θαυμά-
ζεται τὰ Περικλέους ἔργα, πρὸς πολὺν χρόνον ἐν ὀλίγῳ 20
5 γενόμενα. κάλλει μὲν γὰρ ἕκαστον εὐθὺς ἦν τότ᾽ ἀρχαῖον,
ἀκμῇ δὲ μέχρι νῦν πρόσφατόν ἐστι καὶ νεουργόν· οὕτως
ἐπανθεῖ καινότης ἀεί τις, ἄθικτον ὑπὸ τοῦ χρόνου διατη-
ροῦσα τὴν ὄψιν, ὥσπερ ἀειθαλὲς πνεῦμα καὶ ψυχὴν ἀγήρω
καταμεμειγμένην τῶν ἔργων ἐχόντων.   25

6 Πάντα δὲ διεῖπε καὶ πάντων ἐπίσκοπος ἦν αὐτῷ Φειδίας, καίτοι μεγάλους ἀρχιτέκτονας ἐχόντων καὶ τεχνίτας

13 mor. 94 f

[S(UMA=)Υ] 9 ὑπερβαλέσθαι: em. Sch. | τῆς δημιουργίας
Blaß ‖ 10 ἕκαστον Υ et ante ras. S: ἕκαστος post ras. S ‖ 13 ποτέ
Xy.: τότε ‖ 15 post χρόνῳ add. καὶ γὰρ εἰς πολὺν χρόνον mor. ‖
18 προσδανεισθεὶς Madvig ‖ 19 τὴν ἰσχὺν] τὸν τόκον Cob. ‖
20 πρός] εἰς Cob. πρὸς πολὺν χρόνον ἐν ὀλίγωι γενόμενω Sᵐ ‖
23 καινότης ἀεί τις S: τις καινότης ἀεὶ M τις καινότης ἀεί τις UA,
sed in A τις² erasum ‖ 27 ἔχων Naber

19 L τῶν ἔργων. τὸν μὲν γὰρ ἑκατόμπεδον Παρθενῶνα Καλ- 7
λικράτης εἰργάζετο καὶ Ἰκτῖνος, τὸ δ᾽ ἐν Ἐλευσῖνι τελε- f
στήριον ἤρξατο μὲν Κόροιβος οἰκοδομεῖν, καὶ τοὺς ἐπ᾽
ἐδάφους κίονας ἔθηκεν οὗτος καὶ τοῖς ἐπιστυλίοις ἐπέ-
5 ζευξεν· ἀποθανόντος δὲ τούτου Μεταγένης ὁ Ξυπεταιὼν
τὸ διάζωσμα καὶ τοὺς ἄνω κίονας ἐπέστησε, τὸ δ᾽ ὀπαῖον
ἐπὶ τοῦ ἀνακτόρου Ξενοκλῆς ὁ Χολαργεὺς ἐκορύφωσε· 160
τὸ δὲ μακρὸν τεῖχος, περὶ οὗ Σωκράτης (Plat. Gorg. 455e)
ἀκοῦσαί φησιν αὐτὸς εἰσηγουμένου γνώμην Περικλέους,
10 ἠργολάβησε Καλλικράτης. κωμῳδεῖ δὲ τὸ ἔργον Κρατῖνος 8
(fr. 300 CAF I 100) ὡς βραδέως περαινόμενον·

> πάλαι γὰρ αὐτό (φησί)
> λόγοισι προάγει Περικλέης, ἔργοισι δ᾽ οὐδὲ κινεῖ.

τὸ δ᾽ Ὠιδεῖον, τῇ μὲν ἐντὸς διαθέσει πολύεδρον καὶ πολύ- 9
15 στυλον, τῇ δ᾽ ἐρέψει περικλινὲς καὶ κάταντες ἐκ μιᾶς κορυ-
φῆς πεποιημένον, εἰκόνα λέγουσι γενέσθαι καὶ μίμημα
τῆς βασιλέως σκηνῆς, ἐπιστατοῦντος καὶ τούτῳ Περικλέους. διὸ καὶ πάλιν Κρατῖνος ἐν Θρᾴτταις παίζει πρὸς 10
αὐτόν (fr. 71 CAF I 35)·

20   ὁ σχινοκέφαλος Ζεὺς ὅδε
προσέρχεται [Περικλέης] τῳδεῖον ἐπὶ τοῦ κρανίου b
ἔχων, ἐπειδὴ τοὔστρακον παροίχεται.

φιλοτιμούμενος δ᾽ ὁ Περικλῆς τότε πρῶτον ἐψηφίσατο 11
314 S μουσικῆς ἀγῶνα τοῖς Παναθηναίοις ἄγεσθαι, καὶ διέ-
25 ταξεν αὐτὸς ἀθλοθέτης αἱρεθείς, καθότι χρὴ τοὺς ἀγωνιζο-
μένους αὐλεῖν ἢ ᾄδειν ἢ κιθαρίζειν. ἐθεῶντο δὲ καὶ τότε
καὶ τὸν ἄλλον χρόνον ἐν Ὠιδείῳ τοὺς μουσικοὺς ἀγῶνας.

20 L Τὰ δὲ Προπύλαια τῆς ἀκροπόλεως ἐξειργάσθη μὲν ἐν 12
πενταετίᾳ Μνησικλέους ἀρχιτεκτονοῦντος, τύχη δὲ θαυ-

1 Philoch. FGrH 328 F 121 Strab. 9, 395 Paus. 8, 41, 9 ‖
28 Harpocr. s. v. προπύλαια (Philoch. FGrH 328 F 36)

[S(UMA=)Υ] 4 ὑπέζευξεν S συνέζευξεν Zie. ‖ 5 Ξυπεταιὼν
Cob.: ξυπέτιος ‖ 6 διάζωμα Υ ‖ 13 λόγοισι Steph.: λόγοις | προάγει
Rei.: προσάγει ‖ 20 ὅδε MA: ὧδε SU ὁδὶ Bekker ‖ 21 Περικλέης
del. Cob. ‖ 23 πρῶτον CE: πρῶτα SΥ

μαστὴ συμβᾶσα περὶ τὴν οἰκοδομίαν ἐμήνυσε τὴν θεὸν
οὐκ ἀποστατοῦσαν, ἀλλὰ συνεφαπτομένην τοῦ ἔργου καὶ
c 13 συνεπιτελοῦσαν. ὁ γὰρ ἐνεργότατος καὶ προθυμότατος
τῶν τεχνιτῶν ἀποσφαλεὶς ἐξ ὕψους ἔπεσε καὶ διέκειτο
μοχθηρῶς, ὑπὸ τῶν ἰατρῶν ἀπεγνωσμένος. ἀθυμοῦντος 5
δὲ τοῦ Περικλέους, ἡ θεὸς ὄναρ φανεῖσα συνέταξε θερα-
πείαν, ᾗ χρώμενος ὁ Περικλῆς ταχὺ καὶ ῥᾳδίως ἰάσατο τὸν
ἄνθρωπον. ἐπὶ τούτῳ δὲ καὶ τὸ χαλκοῦν ἄγαλμα τῆς
Ὑγιείας Ἀθηνᾶς ἀνέστησεν ἐν ἀκροπόλει παρὰ τὸν βωμόν,
ὃς καὶ πρότερον ἦν ὡς λέγουσιν.   10

14   Ὁ δὲ Φειδίας εἰργάζετο μὲν τῆς θεοῦ τὸ χρυσοῦν ἕδος,
καὶ τούτου δημιουργὸς ἐν τῇ στήλῃ [εἶναι] γέγραπται·
d πάντα δ᾽ ἦν σχεδὸν ἐπ᾽ αὐτῷ, καὶ πᾶσιν ὡς εἰρήκαμεν
15 ἐπεστάτει τοῖς τεχνίταις διὰ φιλίαν Περικλέους. καὶ τοῦτο
τῷ μὲν φθόνον, τῷ δὲ βλασφημίαν ἤνεγκεν, ὡς ἐλευθέρας 15
τῷ Περικλεῖ γυναῖκας εἰς ταὐτὸ φοιτώσας ὑποδεχομένου
τοῦ Φειδίου. δεξάμενοι δὲ τὸν λόγον οἱ κωμικοὶ (adesp. 59
CAF III 410) πολλὴν ἀσέλγειαν αὐτοῦ κατεσκέδασαν, εἴς τε
τὴν Μενίππου γυναῖκα διαβάλλοντες, ἀνδρὸς φίλου καὶ ὑπο-
στρατηγοῦντος, εἴς τε τὰς Πυριλάμπους ὀρνιθοτροφίας, 20
ὃς ἑταῖρος ὢν Περικλέους αἰτίαν εἶχε ταῶνας ὑφιέναι
16 ταῖς γυναιξὶν αἷς ὁ Περικλῆς ἐπλησίαζε. καὶ τί ἄν τις
ἀνθρώπους σατυρικοὺς τοῖς βίοις καὶ τὰς κατὰ τῶν κρειτ-
e τόνων βλασφημίας ὥσπερ δαίμονι κακῷ τῷ φθόνῳ τῶν
πολλῶν ἀποθύοντας ἑκάστοτε θαυμάσειεν, ὅπου καὶ Στη- 21 L
σίμβροτος ὁ Θάσιος (FGrH 107 F 10b) δεινὸν ἀσέβημα 26
καὶ μυσῶδες ἐξενεγκεῖν ἐτόλμησεν εἰς τὴν γυναῖκα τοῦ 315 S
υἱοῦ κατὰ τοῦ Περικλέους; οὕτως ἔοικε πάντῃ χαλεπὸν
εἶναι καὶ δυσθήρατον ἱστορίᾳ τἀληθές, ὅταν οἱ μὲν ὕστερον
γεγονότες τὸν χρόνον ἔχωσιν ἐπιπροσθοῦντα τῇ γνώσει 30

3 Plin. n. h. 22, 44 ‖ 28 cf. Thuc. 1, 22

[S (U M A =) Υ] 9 ὑγείας libri ‖ 11 τῆς τοῦ θεοῦ S ‖ 12 εἶναι
del. Sint. στήλῃ καταγέγραπται Fuhr συναναγέγραπται Wil. ‖
16 ταὐτὸ Zie. cl. c. 32,1: τὰ ἔργα ‖ 18 ἀσέλγεια U¹ ‖ 19 συστρατηγοῦντος Cob. ‖ 27 μυθῶδες: em. Cob. ‖ 30 ἐπιπροσθοῦντα S:
ἐπίπροσθεν ὄντα Υ

τῶν πραγμάτων, ἡ δὲ τῶν πράξεων καὶ τῶν βίων ἡλικιῶτις
ἱστορία τὰ μὲν φθόνοις καὶ δυσμενείαις, τὰ δὲ χαριζομένη
καὶ κολακεύουσα λυμαίνηται καὶ διαστρέφῃ τὴν ἀλήθειαν.

14. Τῶν δὲ περὶ τὸν Θουκυδίδην ῥητόρων καταβοών-
5 των τοῦ Περικλέους ὡς σπαθῶντος τὰ χρήματα καὶ τὰς f
προσόδους ἀπολλύντος, ἠρώτησεν ἐν ἐκκλησίᾳ τὸν δῆμον,
εἰ πολλὰ δοκεῖ δεδαπανῆσθαι· φησάντων δὲ πάμπολλα,
„μὴ τοίνυν" εἶπεν „ὑμῖν, ἀλλ' ἐμοὶ δεδαπανήσθω, καὶ τῶν
ἀναθημάτων ἰδίαν ἐμαυτοῦ ποιήσομαι τὴν ἐπιγραφήν."
10 εἰπόντος οὖν ταῦτα τοῦ Περικλέους, εἴτε τὴν μεγαλοφρο- 2
σύνην αὐτοῦ θαυμάσαντες, εἴτε πρὸς τὴν δόξαν ἀντιφιλοτι- 161
μούμενοι τῶν ἔργων, ἀνέκραγον κελεύοντες ἐκ τῶν δημοσίων ἀναλίσκειν καὶ χορηγεῖν μηδενὸς φειδόμενον. τέλος 3
δὲ πρὸς τὸν Θουκυδίδην εἰς ἀγῶνα περὶ τοῦ ὀστράκου a. 443
15 καταστὰς καὶ διακινδυνεύσας, ἐκεῖνον μὲν ἐξέβαλε, κατέλυσε δὲ τὴν ἀντιτεταγμένην ἑταιρείαν.

15. Ὡς οὖν παντάπασι λυθείσης τῆς διαφορᾶς, καὶ τῆς
πόλεως οἷον ὁμαλῆς καὶ μιᾶς γενομένης κομιδῇ, περιήνεγκεν εἰς ἑαυτὸν τὰς Ἀθήνας καὶ τὰ τῶν Ἀθηναίων ἐξηρ-
20 τημένα πράγματα, φόρους καὶ στρατεύματα καὶ τριήρεις
22 L καὶ νήσους καὶ θάλασσαν καὶ πολλὴν μὲν δι' Ἑλλήνων, b
πολλὴν δὲ καὶ διὰ βαρβάρων ἥκουσαν ἰσχὺν καὶ ἡγεμονίαν,
ὑπηκόοις ἔθνεσι καὶ φιλίαις βασιλέων καὶ συμμαχίαις
πεφραγμένην δυναστῶν, οὐκέθ' ὁ αὐτὸς ἦν οὐδ' ὁμοίως
25 χειροήθης τῷ δήμῳ καὶ ῥᾴδιος ὑπείκειν καὶ συνενδιδόναι
316 8 ταῖς ἐπιθυμίαις ὥσπερ πνοαῖς τῶν πολλῶν, ἀλλ' ἐκ τῆς
ἀνειμένης ἐκείνης καὶ ὑποθρυπτομένης ἔνια δημαγωγίας
ὥσπερ ἀνθηρᾶς καὶ μαλακῆς ἁρμονίας ἀριστοκρατικὴν
καὶ βασιλικὴν ἐντεινάμενος πολιτείαν, καὶ χρώμενος αὐτῇ
30 πρὸς τὸ βέλτιστον ὀρθῇ καὶ ἀνεγκλίτῳ, τὰ μὲν πολλὰ

cap. 15 cf. Thuc. 2, 65

[S(UMA=)Υ] 25 ῥαιδίως S ῥαδίως Υ: em. Anon. ‖ 27 ⟨εἰς⟩
vel ⟨πρὸς⟩ ἔνια Rei. ‖ 29. 30 αὐτῇ–ὀρθῇ C: αὐτῷ–ὀρθῷ cet. ‖
30 ἀνεγκλήτῳ Υ

c βουλόμενον ἦγε πείθων καὶ διδάσκων τὸν δῆμον, ἦν δ᾽
ὅτε καὶ μάλα δυσχεραίνοντα κατατείνων καὶ προσβιβάζων
ἐχειροῦτο τῷ συμφέροντι, μιμούμενος ἀτεχνῶς ἰατρὸν
ποικίλῳ νοσήματι καὶ μακρῷ κατὰ καιρὸν μὲν ἡδονὰς
ἀβλαβεῖς, κατὰ καιρὸν δὲ δηγμοὺς καὶ φάρμακα προσφέ- 5
2 ροντα σωτήρια. παντοδαπῶν γὰρ ὡς εἰκὸς παθῶν ἐν ὄχλῳ
τοσαύτην τὸ μέγεθος ἀρχὴν ἔχοντι φυομένων, μόνος ἐμμελῶς ἕκαστα διαχειρίσασθαι πεφυκώς, μάλιστα δ᾽ ἐλπίσι
καὶ φόβοις ὥσπερ οἴαξι συστέλλων τὸ θρασυνόμενον αὐτῶν
καὶ τὸ δύσθυμον ἀνιεὶς καὶ παραμυθούμενος, ἔδειξε τὴν 10
ῥητορικὴν κατὰ Πλάτωνα (Phaedr. 271 c) ψυχαγωγίαν οὗ-
d σαν καὶ μέγιστον ἔργον αὐτῆς τὴν περὶ τὰ ἤθη καὶ πάθη
μέθοδον, ὥσπερ τινὰς τόνους καὶ φθόγγους ψυχῆς μάλ᾽
3 ἐμμελοῦς ἁφῆς καὶ κρούσεως δεομένους. αἰτία δ᾽ οὐχ ἡ
τοῦ λόγου ψιλῶς δύναμις, ἀλλ᾽, ὡς Θουκυδίδης (2, 65) 23 L
φησίν, ἡ περὶ τὸν βίον δόξα καὶ πίστις τοῦ ἀνδρός, ἀδωρο- 16
τάτου περιφανῶς γενομένου καὶ χρημάτων κρείττονος
ὃς τὴν πόλιν ἐκ μεγάλης μεγίστην καὶ πλουσιωτάτην ποιήσας καὶ γενόμενος δυνάμει πολλῶν βασιλέων καὶ τυράν-
νων ὑπέρτερος, ὧν ἔνιοι καὶ ἐπὶ τοῖς υἱέσι διέθεντο ⟨τοῖς⟩ 20
ἐκείνου, μιᾷ δραχμῇ μείζονα τὴν οὐσίαν οὐκ ἐποίησεν ἧς
ὁ πατὴρ αὐτῷ κατέλιπε.

e **16.** Καίτοι τὴν δύναμιν αὐτοῦ σαφῶς μὲν ὁ Θουκυδίδης
διηγεῖται, κακοήθως δὲ παρεμφαίνουσιν οἱ κωμικοί (adesp.
60 CAF III 411), Πεισιστρατίδας μὲν νέους τοὺς περὶ αὐτὸν 25
ἑταίρους καλοῦντες, αὐτὸν δ᾽ ἀπομόσαι μὴ τυραννήσειν κελεύοντες, ὡς ἀσυμμέτρου πρὸς δημοκρατίαν καὶ βαρυτέρας 317 S
2 περὶ αὐτὸν οὔσης ὑπεροχῆς. ὁ δὲ Τηλεκλείδης (fr. 42
CAF I 220) παραδεδωκέναι φησὶν αὐτῷ τοὺς Ἀθηναίους

15 Isocr. 8, 126

[S(UMA =)Υ] 2 προσβιάζων: em. Sch. ‖ 5 εὐλαβεῖς: em.
Rei. | προσφέροντι Υ ‖ 9 συστέλλων Zie.: προσστέλλων SU
προὔστέλλων Α προσυστέλλων Μ προσαναστέλλων Madvig ‖ 18 ὃς
SU: ὃς καὶ ΜΑ ‖ 19 δυνάμει S: καὶ δυνάμει Υ ‖ 20. 21 ⟨τοῖς⟩
ἐκείνου Sauppe: ἐκεῖνος libri, quod del. Li. cruce ad ἐπὶ τοῖς
posita ἐπί⟨τροπον⟩ τ. υ. δ. ἐκεῖνον Madvig ‖ 26 ἀπομόσειν S

πόλεών τε φόρους αὐτάς τε πόλεις, τὰς μὲν δεῖν, τὰς
δ᾽ ἀναλύειν,
λάινα τείχη, τὰ μὲν οἰκοδομεῖν τὰ δὲ τἄμπαλιν αὖ καταβάλλειν,
5 σπονδάς, δύναμιν, κράτος, εἰρήνην, πλοῦτόν τ᾽ εὐδαι-
μονίαν τε.

καὶ ταῦτα καιρὸς οὐκ ἦν οὐδ᾽ ἀκμὴ καὶ χάρις ἀνθούσης 3 f
ἐφ᾽ ὥρᾳ πολιτείας, ἀλλὰ τεσσαράκοντα μὲν ἔτη πρωτευ-
όντων ἐν Ἐφιάλταις καὶ Λεωκράταις καὶ Μυρωνίδαις καὶ
10 Κίμωσι καὶ Τολμίδαις καὶ Θουκυδίδαις, μετὰ δὲ τὴν
Θουκυδίδου κατάλυσιν καὶ τὸν ὀστρακισμὸν οὐκ ἐλάττω
24 L τῶν πεντεκαίδεκα ἐτῶν διηνεκῆ καὶ μίαν οὖσαν ἐν ταῖς
ἐνιαυσίοις στρατηγίαις ἀρχὴν καὶ δυναστείαν κτησάμενος,
ἐφύλαξεν ἑαυτὸν ἀνάλωτον ὑπὸ χρημάτων, καίπερ οὐ 162
15 παντάπασιν ἀργῶς ἔχων πρὸς χρηματισμόν, ἀλλὰ τὸν
πατρῷον καὶ δίκαιον πλοῦτον, ὡς μήτ᾽ ἀμελούμενος ἐκφύγοι μήτε πολλὰ πράγματα καὶ διατριβὰς ἀσχολουμένῳ
παρέχοι, συνέταξεν εἰς οἰκονομίαν ἣν ᾤετο ῥᾴστην καὶ
ἀκριβεστάτην εἶναι. τοὺς γὰρ ἐπετείους καρποὺς ἅπαν- 4
20 τας ἀθρόους ἐπίπρασκεν, εἶτα τῶν ἀναγκαίων ἕκαστον
ἐξ ἀγορᾶς ὠνούμενος διῴκει τὸν βίον καὶ τὰ περὶ τὴν
δίαιταν. ὅθεν οὐχ ἡδὺς ἦν ἐνηλίκοις παισὶν οὐδὲ γυναιξὶ 5
δαψιλὴς χορηγός, ἀλλ᾽ ἐμέμφοντο τὴν ἐφήμερον ταύτην
καὶ συνηγμένην εἰς τὸ ἀκριβέστατον δαπάνην, οὐδενὸς
25 οἷον ἐν οἰκίᾳ μεγάλῃ καὶ πράγμασιν ἀφθόνοις περιρρέον- b
τος, ἀλλὰ παντὸς μὲν ἀναλώματος, παντὸς δὲ λήμματος
δι᾽ ἀριθμοῦ καὶ μέτρου βαδίζοντος. ὁ δὲ πᾶσαν αὐτοῦ τὴν 6
τοιαύτην συνέχων ἀκρίβειαν εἷς ἦν οἰκέτης Εὐάγγελος,
29 ὡς ἕτερος οὐδεὶς εὖ πεφυκὼς ἢ κατεσκευασμένος ὑπὸ τοῦ
318 s Περικλέους πρὸς οἰκονομίαν. ἀπᾴδοντα μὲν οὖν ταῦτα τῆς 7

30 mor. 831 f

[S(UMA =)Υ] 1 πόλεις ante corr. S ‖ 3 τὰ δὲ τἄμπαλιν αὖ
Kock: τὰ δὲ αὐτὰ πάλιν libri τὰ δ᾽ ἔπειτα πάλιν Fuhr ‖ 8 ἐφ᾽ ὥραν
Rei. | τεσσαράκοντα ne addubites, cf. Cic. de or. 3, 34, 138 ‖ 9 μυρω-
νίδης ante corr. S μυρωνίδες U ‖ 12 διήνεγκε: em. Pflugk ‖ 30 ἀπᾴδοντα Valckenaer: ἅπαντα libri ἀπάρτητα Rei. ἀπαρτᾷ Madvig

21

Ἀναξαγόρου σοφίας, εἴγε καὶ τὴν οἰκίαν ἐκεῖνος ἐξέλιπε
καὶ τὴν χώραν ἀνῆκεν ἀργὴν καὶ μηλόβοτον ὑπ᾽ ἐνθουσια-
σμοῦ καὶ μεγαλοφροσύνης· οὐ ταὐτὸν δ᾽ ἐστὶν οἶμαι θεωρη-
τικοῦ φιλοσόφου καὶ πολιτικοῦ βίος, ἀλλ᾽ ὁ μὲν ἀνόργανον
c καὶ ἀπροσδεῆ τῆς ἐκτὸς ὕλης ἐπὶ τοῖς καλοῖς κινεῖ τὴν 5
διάνοιαν, τῷ δ᾽ εἰς ἀνθρωπείας χρείας ἀναμειγνύντι τὴν
ἀρετὴν ἔστιν οὗ γένοιτ᾽ ἂν οὐ τῶν ἀναγκαίων μόνον, ἀλλὰ
καὶ τῶν καλῶν ὁ πλοῦτος, ὥσπερ ἦν καὶ Περικλεῖ, βοη- 25 L
8 θοῦντι πολλοῖς τῶν πενήτων. καὶ μέντοι γε τὸν Ἀναξαγόραν αὐτὸν λέγουσιν ἀσχολουμένου Περικλέους ἀμελού- 10
μενον κεῖσθαι συγκεκαλυμμένον ἤδη γηραιὸν ἀποκαρτεροῦντα, προσπεσόντος δὲ τῷ Περικλεῖ τοῦ πράγματος,
ἐκπλαγέντα θεῖν εὐθὺς ἐπὶ τὸν ἄνδρα καὶ δεῖσθαι πᾶσαν
δέησιν, ὀλοφυρόμενον οὐκ ἐκεῖνον, ἀλλ᾽ ἑαυτόν, εἰ τοιοῦ-
9 τον ἀπολεῖ τῆς πολιτείας σύμβουλον. ἐκκαλυψάμενον οὖν 15
d τὸν Ἀναξαγόραν εἰπεῖν πρὸς αὐτόν· ,,ὦ Περίκλεις, καὶ οἱ
τοῦ λύχνου χρείαν ἔχοντες ἔλαιον ἐπιχέουσιν."

17. Ἀρχομένων δὲ Λακεδαιμονίων ἄχθεσθαι τῇ αὐξήσει τῶν Ἀθηναίων, ἐπαίρων ὁ Περικλῆς τὸν δῆμον ἔτι
μᾶλλον μέγα φρονεῖν καὶ μεγάλων αὐτὸν ἀξιοῦν πραγμά- 20
των γράφει ψήφισμα, πάντας Ἕλληνας τοὺς ὁποίποτε κατ-
οικοῦντας Εὐρώπης ἢ [τῆς] Ἀσίας παρακαλεῖν, καὶ μικρὰν
πόλιν καὶ μεγάλην, εἰς σύλλογον πέμπειν Ἀθήναζε τοὺς
βουλευσομένους περὶ τῶν Ἑλληνικῶν ἱερῶν, ἃ κατέπρησαν οἱ βάρβαροι, καὶ τῶν θυσιῶν, ἃς ὀφείλουσιν ὑπὲρ τῆς 25
e Ἑλλάδος εὐξάμενοι τοῖς θεοῖς, ὅτε πρὸς τοὺς βαρβάρους
2 ἐμάχοντο, καὶ τῆς θαλάττης, ὅπως πλέωσι πάντες ἀδεῶς
καὶ τὴν εἰρήνην ἄγωσιν. ἐπὶ ταῦτα δ᾽ ἄνδρες εἴκοσι τῶν
ὑπὲρ πεντήκοντα ἔτη γεγονότων ἐπέμφθησαν, ὧν πέντε
μὲν Ἴωνας καὶ Δωριεῖς τοὺς ἐν Ἀσίᾳ καὶ νησιώτας ἄχρι 30
Λέσβου καὶ Ῥόδου παρεκάλουν, πέντε δὲ τοὺς ἐν Ἑλλησ- 319 S
πόντῳ καὶ Θρᾴκῃ μέχρι Βυζαντίου τόπους ἐπῄεσαν, καὶ

1 Plat. Hipp. I 283a Him. ecl. 3,18

[S(UM A =)Υ] 2 ἀνῆκεν Him. Br.: ἀφῆκεν ‖ 5 ἐπὶ τοῖς καλοῖς
suspecta censet Ha. ‖ 21 ὁποίποτε SΥ: ὁπήποτε vulg. ‖ 22 ⟨τῆς⟩
Εὐρώπης Cob. | del. Zie. | παρακαλῶν Naber ‖ 24 βουλευσομένους
M A: βουλευσαμένους S U ‖ 27 συμπλέωσι S

πέντε ἐπὶ τούτοις εἰς Βοιωτίαν καὶ Φωκίδα καὶ Πελοπόννησον, ἐκ δὲ ταύτης διὰ Λοκρῶν ἐπὶ τὴν πρόσοικον
26 L ἤπειρον ἕως Ἀκαρνανίας καὶ Ἀμβρακίας ἀπεστάλησαν·
οἱ δὲ λοιποὶ δι᾽ Εὐβοίας ἐπ᾽ Οἰταίους. καὶ τὸν Μαλιέα 3
5 κόλπον καὶ Φθιώτας [καὶ] Ἀχαιοὺς καὶ Θεσσαλοὺς ἐπο-
ρεύοντο, συμπείθοντες ἰέναι καὶ μετέχειν τῶν βουλευμά- f
των ἐπ᾽ εἰρήνῃ καὶ κοινοπραγίᾳ τῆς Ἑλλάδος. ἐπράχθη δ᾽ 4
οὐδὲν οὐδὲ συνῆλθον αἱ πόλεις, Λακεδαιμονίων ὑπεναντιω-
θέντων, ὡς λέγεται, καὶ τὸ πρῶτον ἐν Πελοποννήσῳ τῆς
10 πείρας ἐλεγχθείσης. τοῦτο μὲν οὖν παρεθέμην ἐνδεικνύ-
μενος αὐτοῦ τὸ φρόνημα καὶ τὴν μεγαλοφροσύνην.

18. Ἐν δὲ ταῖς στρατηγίαις εὐδοκίμει μάλιστα διὰ τὴν 163
ἀσφάλειαν, οὔτε μάχης ἐχούσης πολλὴν ἀδηλότητα καὶ
κίνδυνον ἑκουσίως ἁπτόμενος, οὔτε τοὺς ἐκ τοῦ παρα-
15 βαλέσθαι χρησαμένους τύχῃ λαμπρᾷ καὶ θαυμασθέντας
ὡς μεγάλους ζηλῶν καὶ μιμούμενος στρατηγούς, ἀεί τε
λέγων πρὸς τοὺς πολίτας, ὡς ὅσον ἐπ᾽ αὐτῷ μενοῦσιν
ἀθάνατοι πάντα τὸν χρόνον. ὁρῶν δὲ Τολμίδην τὸν Τολ- 2
μαίου διὰ τὰς πρότερον εὐτυχίας καὶ διὰ τὸ τιμᾶσθαι
20 διαφερόντως ἐκ τῶν πολεμικῶν σὺν οὐδενὶ καιρῷ παρα-
σκευαζόμενον εἰς Βοιωτίαν ἐμβαλεῖν, καὶ πεπεικότα τῶν
ἐν ἡλικίᾳ τοὺς ἀρίστους καὶ φιλοτιμοτάτους ἐθελοντὰς b
στρατεύεσθαι, χιλίους γενομένους ἄνευ τῆς ἄλλης δυνάμεως, κατέχειν ἐπειρᾶτο καὶ παρακαλεῖν ἐν τῷ δήμῳ, τὸ
25 μνημονευόμενον εἰπών, ὡς εἰ μὴ πείθοιτο Περικλεῖ, τόν
γε σοφώτατον οὐχ ἁμαρτήσεται σύμβουλον ἀναμείνας,
χρόνον. τότε μὲν οὖν μετρίως εὐδοκίμησε τοῦτ᾽ εἰπών· 3
ὀλίγαις δ᾽ ὕστερον ἡμέραις ὡς ἀνηγγέλθη τεθνεὼς μὲν
29 αὐτὸς Τολμίδης περὶ Κορώνειαν ἡττηθεὶς μάχῃ, τεθνεῶ- a. 447
320 S
27 L τες δὲ πολλοὶ κἀγαθοὶ τῶν πολιτῶν, μεγάλην τοῦτο τῷ

---

18 Thuc. 1, 113 Diod. 12, 6

[S̲(UMA=)Υ] 5 καὶ del. Baehr ‖ 6 ⟨συν⟩ιέναι Wil. ‖
7 καινοπραγία (οι s. s. m. 1) E: καινοπραγία cet. ‖ 14 παραβάλλε-
σθαι: em. Sint. ‖ 22 ἐθελοντί: em. Cob. ‖ 23 ⟨συ⟩στρατεύεσθαι
Cob. ‖ 24 παρακαλεῖν suspectum Ha. κατακηλεῖν Zie.

3 BT Plut. vit. I 2 ed. Ziegler [1673]

23

Περικλεῖ μετ᾽ εὐνοίας δόξαν ἤνεγκεν ὡς ἀνδρὶ φρονίμῳ
καὶ φιλοπολίτῃ.

a. 447 **19.** Τῶν δὲ στρατηγιῶν ἠγαπήθη μὲν ἡ περὶ Χερρό-
c νησον αὐτοῦ μάλιστα, σωτήριος γενομένη τοῖς αὐτόθι
κατοικοῦσι τῶν Ἑλλήνων· οὐ γὰρ μόνον ἐποίκους Ἀθη- 5
ναίων χιλίους κομίσας ἔρρωσεν εὐανδρίᾳ τὰς πόλεις, ἀλλὰ
καὶ τὸν αὐχένα διαζώσας ἐρύμασι καὶ προβλήμασιν ἐκ
θαλάττης εἰς θάλατταν, ἀπετείχισε τὰς καταδρομὰς τῶν
Θρᾳκῶν περικεχυμένων τῇ Χερρονήσῳ, καὶ πόλεμον ἐνδελεχῆ καὶ βαρὺν ἐξέκλεισεν, ᾧ συνείχετο πάντα τὸν χρόνον 10
ἡ χώρα, βαρβαρικαῖς ἀναμεμειγμένη γειτνιάσεσι καὶ γέ-
2 μουσα λῃστηρίων ὁμόρων καὶ συνοίκων. ἐθαυμάσθη δὲ
a. 453 καὶ διεβοήθη πρὸς τοὺς ἐκτὸς ἀνθρώπους περιπλεύσας
Πελοπόννησον, ἐκ Πηγῶν τῆς Μεγαρικῆς ἀναχθεὶς ἑκα-
d τὸν τριήρεσιν. οὐ γὰρ μόνον ἐπόρθησε τῆς παραλίας 15
πολλὴν ὡς Τολμίδης πρότερον, ἀλλὰ καὶ πόρρω θαλάττης
προελθὼν τοῖς ἀπὸ τῶν νεῶν ὁπλίταις, τοὺς μὲν ἄλλους᾽
εἰς τὰ τείχη συνέστειλε δείσαντας αὐτοῦ τὴν ἔφοδον, ἐν δὲ
Νεμέᾳ Σικυωνίους ὑποστάντας καὶ συνάψαντας μάχην
3 κατὰ κράτος τρεψάμενος, ἔστησε τρόπαιον. ἐκ δ᾽ Ἀχαΐας 20
φίλης οὔσης στρατιώτας ἀναλαβὼν εἰς τὰς τριήρεις, ἐπὶ
τὴν ἀντιπέρας ἤπειρον ἐκομίσθη τῷ στόλῳ, καὶ παραπλεύσας τὸν Ἀχελῷον Ἀκαρνανίαν κατέδραμε καὶ κατέκλεισεν
Οἰνιάδας εἰς τὸ τεῖχος, καὶ τεμὼν τὴν γῆν καὶ κακώσας,
e ἀπῆρεν ἐπ᾽ οἴκου, φοβερὸς μὲν φανεὶς τοῖς πολεμίοις, 25
ἀσφαλὴς δὲ καὶ δραστήριος τοῖς πολίταις. οὐδὲν γὰρ οὐδ᾽ 28 L
ἀπὸ τύχης πρόσκρουσμα συνέβη περὶ τοὺς στρατευομένους.

a. 435? **20.** Εἰς δὲ τὸν Πόντον εἰσπλεύσας στόλῳ μεγάλῳ καὶ
κεκοσμημένῳ λαμπρῶς, ταῖς μὲν Ἑλληνίσι πόλεσιν ὧν 30
ἐδέοντο διεπράξατο καὶ προσηνέχθη φιλανθρώπως, τοῖς

---

3 cf. ad p. 14, 8 ‖ 12sq. Thuc. 1, 111, 2—3 Diod. 11, 85. 88,
1—2 Paus. 1, 27, 5

[S(UMA =)Υ] 8 ἀπετείχισε del. Madvig ‖ 16 πολλὴν Emp.:
πόλιν ‖ 24 οἰνεάδας: em. Sint.

δὲ περιοικοῦσι βαρβάροις ἔϑνεσι καὶ βασιλεῦσιν αὐτῶν
321 8 καὶ δυνάσταις ἐπεδείξατο μὲν τῆς δυνάμεως τὸ μέγεϑος
καὶ τὴν ἄδειαν καὶ τὸ ϑάρσος, ᾗ βούλοιντο πλεόντων καὶ
πᾶσαν ὑφ᾽ αὑτοῖς πεποιημένων τὴν ϑάλασσαν, Σινωπεῦσι
5 δὲ τρισκαίδεκα ναῦς ἀπέλιπε μετὰ Λαμάχου καὶ στρατιώτας ἐπὶ Τιμησίλεων τύραννον. ἐκπεσόντος δὲ τούτου καὶ f 2
τῶν ἑταίρων, ἐψηφίσατο πλεῖν εἰς Σινώπην Ἀϑηναίων ἐϑε-
λοντὰς ἑξακοσίους καὶ συγκατοικεῖν Σινωπεῦσι, νειμαμένους οἰκίας καὶ χώραν ἣν πρότερον οἱ τύραννοι κατ-
10 εἶχον. τἆλλα δ᾽ οὐ συνεχώρει ταῖς ὁρμαῖς τῶν πολιτῶν 3
οὐδὲ συνεξέπιπτεν, ὑπὸ ῥώμης καὶ τύχης τοσαύτης ἐπαι- 164
ρομένων Αἰγύπτου τε πάλιν ἀντιλαμβάνεσϑαι καὶ κινεῖν
τῆς βασιλέως ἀρχῆς τὰ πρὸς ϑαλάσσῃ. πολλοὺς δὲ καὶ 4
Σικελίας ὁ δύσερως ἐκεῖνος ἤδη καὶ δύσποτμος ἔρως
15 εἶχεν, ὃν ὕστερον ἐξέκαυσαν οἱ περὶ τὸν Ἀλκιβιάδην ῥήτορες. ἦν δὲ καὶ Τυρρηνία καὶ Καρχηδὼν ἐνίοις ὄνειρος,
οὐκ ἀπ᾽ ἐλπίδος διὰ τὸ μέγεϑος τῆς ὑποκειμένης ἡγεμονίας καὶ τὴν εὔροιαν τῶν πραγμάτων.

21. Ἀλλ᾽ ὁ Περικλῆς κατεῖχε τὴν ἐκδρομὴν ταύτην καὶ
20 περιέκοπτε τὴν πολυπραγμοσύνην, καὶ τὰ πλεῖστα τῆς
δυνάμεως ἔτρεπεν εἰς φυλακὴν καὶ βεβαιότητα τῶν ὑπαρχόντων, μέγα ἔργον ἡγούμενος ἀνείργειν Λακεδαιμονίους b
καὶ ὅλως ὑπεναντιούμενος ἐκείνοις, ὡς ἄλλοις τε πολλοῖς
29 L ἔδειξε καὶ μάλιστα τοῖς περὶ τὸν ἱερὸν πραχϑεῖσι πόλεμον.
25 ἐπεὶ γὰρ οἱ Λακεδαιμόνιοι στρατεύσαντες εἰς Δελφοὺς 2
Φωκέων ἐχόντων τὸ ἱερὸν Δελφοῖς ἀπέδωκαν, εὐϑὺς ἐκεί- a. 448
νων ἀπαλλαγέντων ὁ Περικλῆς ἐπιστρατεύσας, πάλιν εἰσή-
γαγε τοὺς Φωκέας, καὶ τῶν Λακεδαιμονίων ἣν ἔδωκαν 3
αὐτοῖς Δελφοὶ προμαντείαν εἰς τὸ μέτωπον ἐγκολαψάντων
30 τοῦ χαλκοῦ λύκου, λαβὼν καὶ αὐτὸς προμαντείαν τοῖς
Ἀϑηναίοις εἰς τὸν αὐτὸν λύκον κατὰ τὴν δεξιὰν πλευρὰν
ἐνεχάραξεν.

25 Thuc. 1, 112, 5

[S(UMA =)Υ] 3 ᾗͅι S ‖ 9 οἰκίαι ante corr. S ‖ 22 μέγα del.
Ha. ‖ 24 ἔδοξε U ‖ 29 ἐκκολαψάντων SΥ: em. Iunt.

3*

c   **22.** Ὅτι δ' ὀρθῶς ἐν τῇ Ἑλλάδι τὴν δύναμιν τῶν Ἀθη-
a. 446 ναίων συνεῖχεν, ἐμαρτύρησεν αὐτῷ τὰ γενόμενα. πρῶτον 322 8
μὲν γὰρ Εὐβοεῖς ἀπέστησαν, ἐφ' οὓς διέβη μετὰ δυνάμεως.
εἶτ' εὐθὺς ἀπηγγέλλοντο Μεγαρεῖς ἐκπεπολεμωμένοι καὶ
στρατιὰ Πελοποννησίων ἐπὶ τοῖς ὅροις τῆς Ἀττικῆς οὖσα, 5
Πλειστώνακτος ἡγουμένου βασιλέως Λακεδαιμονίων.
2 πάλιν οὖν ὁ Περικλῆς κατὰ τάχος ἐκ τῆς Εὐβοίας ἀνεκομίζετο πρὸς τὸν ἐν τῇ Ἀττικῇ πόλεμον, καὶ συνάψαι μὲν
εἰς χεῖρας οὐκ ἐθάρσησε πολλοῖς καὶ ἀγαθοῖς ὁπλίταις
προκαλουμένοις, ὁρῶν δὲ τὸν Πλειστώνακτα νέον ὄντα 10
κομιδῇ, χρώμενον δὲ μάλιστα Κλεανδρίδῃ τῶν συμβούλων,
d ὃν οἱ ἔφοροι φύλακα καὶ πάρεδρον αὐτῷ διὰ τὴν ἡλικίαν
συνέπεμψαν, ἐπειρᾶτο τούτου κρύφα, καὶ ταχὺ διαφθείρας χρήμασιν αὐτὸν ἔπεισεν ἐκ τῆς Ἀττικῆς ἀπαγαγεῖν
3 τοὺς Πελοποννησίους. ὡς δ' ἀπεχώρησεν ἡ στρατιὰ καὶ 15
διελύθη κατὰ πόλεις, βαρέως φέροντες οἱ Λακεδαιμόνιοι
τὸν μὲν βασιλέα χρήμασιν ἐζημίωσαν, ὧν τὸ πλῆθος 30 L
οὐκ ἔχων ἐκτεῖσαι μετέστησεν ἑαυτὸν ἐκ Λακεδαί-
μονος, τοῦ δὲ Κλεανδρίδου φεύγοντος θάνατον κατέγνω-
4 σαν. οὗτος δ' ἦν πατὴρ Γυλίππου τοῦ περὶ Σικελίαν Ἀθη- 20
ναίους καταπολεμήσαντος. ἔοικε δ' ὥσπερ συγγενικὸν
αὐτῷ προστρίψασθαι νόσημα τὴν φιλαργυρίαν ἡ φύσις,
e ὑφ' ἧς καὶ αὐτὸς αἰσχρῶς ἐπὶ κακοῖς ἔργοις ἁλοὺς ἐξέπεσε
τῆς Σπάρτης. ταῦτα μὲν οὖν ἐν τοῖς περὶ Λυσάνδρου
(c. 16. 17) δεδηλώκαμεν.   25

23. Τοῦ δὲ Περικλέους ἐν τῷ τῆς στρατηγίας ἀπολογισμῷ δέκα ταλάντων ἀνάλωμα γράψαντος ἀνηλωμένων
εἰς τὸ δέον, ὁ δῆμος ἀπεδέξατο μὴ πολυπραγμονήσας μηδ'

---

1 Thuc. 1, 114 ‖ 11 Thuc. 2, 21, 1 Diod. 13, 106, 10 Ephor.
FGrH 70 F 193 ‖ 20 Plut. Nic. 28, 4 et ibi l. l. ‖ 26 schol.
Aristoph. nub. 857

[S(UMA =)Υ] 4 ἐκπεπολεμωμένοι E: ἐκπεπολεμημένοι S A²
ἐκπεπολημένοι U M A¹ ‖ 5 Πελοποννησίων Blaß: πολεμίων ‖ 11 Κλε-
ανδρίδῃ] Κλέαρχος Diod. ‖ 12 οἱ ex εἰ corr. S (m. 1) ‖ 17 τὸ μὲν
πλῆθος Υ ‖ 23 κακοῖς] καλοῖς Sint. Li.

ἐλέγξας τὸ ἀπόρρητον. ἔνιοι δ᾽ ἱστορήκασιν, ὧν ἐστι καὶ 2
Θεόφραστος ὁ φιλόσοφος, ὅτι καθ᾽ ἕκαστον ἐνιαυτὸν εἰς
τὴν Σπάρτην ἐφοίτα δέκα τάλαντα παρὰ τοῦ Περικλέους,
οἷς τοὺς ἐν τέλει πάντας θεραπεύων παρῃτεῖτο τὸν πόλεμον,
323 s οὐ τὴν εἰρήνην ὠνούμενος, ἀλλὰ τὸν χρόνον ἐν ᾧ παρα-
6 σκευασάμενος καθ᾽ ἡσυχίαν ἔμελλε πολεμήσειν βέλτιον.   f
Εὐθὺς οὖν ἐπὶ τοὺς ἀφεστῶτας τραπόμενος καὶ δια- 3
βὰς εἰς Εὔβοιαν πεντήκοντα ναυσὶ καὶ πεντακισχιλίοις
ὁπλίταις, κατεστρέψατο τὰς πόλεις, καὶ Χαλκιδέων μὲν 4
10 τοὺς ἱπποβότας λεγομένους πλούτῳ καὶ δόξῃ διαφέροντας
ἐξέβαλεν, Ἑστιεῖς δὲ πάντας ἀναστήσας ἐκ τῆς χώρας,
Ἀθηναίους κατῴκισε, μόνοις τούτοις ἀπαραιτήτως χρη-
31 L σάμενος, ὅτι ναῦν Ἀττικὴν αἰχμάλωτον λαβόντες ἀπέκτει- 165
ναν τοὺς ἄνδρας.
15   24. Ἐκ τούτου γενομένων σπονδῶν Ἀθηναίοις καὶ Λακεδαιμονίοις εἰς ἔτη τριάκοντα, ψηφίζεται τὸν εἰς Σάμον a. 441?
πλοῦν, αἰτίαν ποιησάμενος κατ᾽ αὐτῶν ὅτι τὸν πρὸς Μιλησίους κελευόμενοι διαλύσασθαι πόλεμον οὐχ ὑπήκουον.
ἐπεὶ δ᾽ Ἀσπασίᾳ χαριζόμενος δοκεῖ πρᾶξαι τὰ πρὸς Σαμί- 2
20 ους, ἐνταῦθ᾽ ἂν εἴη καιρὸς διαπορῆσαι μάλιστα περὶ τῆς
ἀνθρώπου, τίνα τέχνην ἢ δύναμιν τοσαύτην ἔχουσα, τῶν
τε πολιτικῶν τοὺς πρωτεύοντας ἐχειρώσατο, καὶ τοῖς
φιλοσόφοις οὐ φαῦλον οὐδ᾽ ὀλίγον ὑπὲρ αὑτῆς παρέσχε
λόγον. ὅτι μὲν γὰρ ἦν Μιλησία γένος, Ἀξιόχου θυγάτηρ,
25 ὁμολογεῖται· φασὶ δ᾽ αὐτὴν Θαργηλίαν τινὰ τῶν παλαιῶν 3 b
Ἰάδων ζηλώσασαν ἐπιθέσθαι τοῖς δυνατωτάτοις ἀνδράσι.

7 sq. Thuc. 1, 114, 3 Diod. 12, 7. 22 schol. Aristoph. nub.
213 IG I² 39 = Dittenberger Syll.³ 64 ‖ 16 Thuc. 1, 115, 2 sq.;
cf. ad c. 25

[S(UMA =)Υ] 7 εὐθύς: αὖθις Sauppe ‖ 9 post πόλεις καὶ
lac. stat. Fuhr, coll. Thuc. (καὶ τὴν μὲν ἄλλην ὁμολογίᾳ κατεστήσαντο); pro μὲν scribebat δὲ Br. ‖ 10 ἱπποβάτας S, cf. Herod.
5, 77, 2 ‖ 12 κατῴκισε, μόνοις Rei.: μόνους κατῴκισε codd. (ἐγκατ-
ῴκισε Herw.) ‖ 18 κελευόμενοι A ras.: κελευόμενον UM et ante
ras. A κελευόμεθα S | ὑπήκοον S¹ ‖ 21 τοσαύτην Υ Sᵐ (m. 1):
++++
αὐτὴ Sʳ

27

4 καὶ γὰρ ἡ Θαργηλία, τό τ᾽ εἶδος εὐπρεπὴς γενομένη καὶ
χάριν ἔχουσα μετὰ δεινότητος, πλείστοις μὲν Ἑλλήνων
συνῴκησεν ἀνδράσι, πάντας δὲ προσεποίησε βασιλεῖ τοὺς
πλησιάσαντας αὐτῇ, καὶ ταῖς πόλεσι μηδισμοῦ δι᾽ ἐκείνων ὑπέσπειρεν ἀρχάς, δυνατωτάτων ὄντων καὶ μεγίστων. 5
5 τὴν δ᾽ Ἀσπασίαν οἱ μὲν ὡς σοφήν τινα καὶ πολιτικὴν ὑπὸ
τοῦ Περικλέους σπουδασθῆναι λέγουσι· καὶ γὰρ Σωκρά-
c της ἔστιν ὅτε μετὰ τῶν γνωρίμων ἐφοίτα, καὶ τὰς γυναῖκας ἀκροασομένας οἱ συνήθεις ἦγον ὡς αὐτήν, καίπερ
οὐ κοσμίου προεστῶσαν ἐργασίας οὐδὲ σεμνῆς, ἀλλὰ παι- 10
6 δίσκας ἑταιρούσας τρέφουσαν. Αἰσχίνης (p. 45. 46 Kr.) 324 S
δέ φησι καὶ Λυσικλέα τὸν προβατοκάπηλον ἐξ ἀγεννοῦς 32 L
καὶ ταπεινοῦ τὴν φύσιν Ἀθηναίων γενέσθαι πρῶτον Ἀσπα-
7 σίᾳ συνόντα μετὰ τὴν Περικλέους τελευτήν. ἐν δὲ τῷ
Μενεξένῳ τῷ Πλάτωνος (235 e), εἰ καὶ μετὰ παιδιᾶς τὰ 15
πρῶτα γέγραπται, τοσοῦτόν γ᾽ ἱστορίας ἔνεστιν, ὅτι δόξαν
εἶχε τὸ γύναιον ἐπὶ ῥητορικῇ πολλοῖς Ἀθηναίων ὁμιλεῖν.
d φαίνεται μέντοι μᾶλλον ἐρωτική τις ἡ τοῦ Περικλέους
8 ἀγάπησις γενομένη πρὸς Ἀσπασίαν. ἦν μὲν γὰρ αὐτῷ
γυνὴ προσήκουσα μὲν κατὰ γένος, συνῳκηκυῖα δ᾽ Ἱππο- 20
νίκῳ πρότερον, ἐξ οὗ Καλλίαν ἔτεκε τὸν πλούσιον· ἔτεκε
δὲ καὶ παρὰ τῷ Περικλεῖ Ξάνθιππον καὶ Πάραλον. εἶτα
τῆς συμβιώσεως οὐκ οὔσης αὐτοῖς ἀρεστῆς, ἐκείνην μὲν
ἑτέρῳ βουλομένην συνεξέδωκεν, αὐτὸς δὲ τὴν Ἀσπασίαν
9 λαβὼν ἔστερξε διαφερόντως. καὶ γὰρ ἐξιὼν ὥς φασι καὶ 25
εἰσιὼν ἀπ᾽ ἀγορᾶς ἠσπάζετο καθ᾽ ἡμέραν αὐτὴν μετὰ
τοῦ καταφιλεῖν. ἐν δὲ ταῖς κωμῳδίαις (adesp. 63 CAF III 63)
Ὀμφάλη τε νέα καὶ Δηάνειρα καὶ πάλιν Ἥρα προσαγο-
e ρεύεται. Κρατῖνος δ᾽ ἄντικρυς παλλακὴν αὐτὴν εἴρηκεν ἐν
τούτοις (fr. 241 CAF I 86)· 30

1 Athen. 13, 608 f al. ‖ 11 Schol. Aristoph. eq. 132 Schol. Plat.
Menex. 235e Harpocr. s. Ἀσπασία ‖ 19 Plat. Prot. 314e Meno
94b Athen. 12, 533c ‖ 25 Athen. 13, 589e

[S(UMA =)Υ] 3 πάντα U ‖ 9 συνῆγον S ‖ 12 ἀγεννοῦς MA:
ἀγενοῦς SU ‖ 15 τῷ] τοῦ ante corr. S

"Ἥραν τέ οἱ Ἀσπασίαν τίκτει [καὶ] Καταπυγοσύνη
παλλακὴν κυνώπιδα.

δοκεῖ δὲ καὶ τὸν νόθον ἐκ ταύτης τεκνῶσαι, περὶ οὗ πεποί- 10
ηκεν Εὔπολις ἐν Δήμοις (fr. 98 CAF I 282) αὐτὸν μὲν οὗτως
5 ἐρωτῶντα ·

ὁ νόθος δέ μοι ζῇ;

τὸν δὲ Μυρωνίδην ἀποκρινόμενον ·

καὶ πάλαι γ᾽ ἂν ἦν ἀνήρ,
εἰ μὴ τὸ τῆς πόρνης ὑπωρρώδει κακόν.

33 L οὗτω δὲ τὴν Ἀσπασίαν ὀνομαστὴν καὶ κλεινὴν γενέσθαι 11
11 λέγουσιν, ὥστε καὶ Κῦρον τὸν πολεμήσαντα βασιλεῖ περὶ
τῆς τῶν Περσῶν ἡγεμονίας τὴν ἀγαπωμένην ὑπ᾽ αὐτοῦ
μάλιστα τῶν παλλακίδων Ἀσπασίαν ὀνομάσαι, καλουμέ-
325 S νην Μίλτω πρότερον. ἦν δὲ Φωκαῒς τὸ γένος, Ἑρμοτίμου 12 f
15 θυγάτηρ · ἐν δὲ τῇ μάχῃ Κύρου πεσόντος ἀπαχθεῖσα
πρὸς βασιλέα πλεῖστον ἴσχυσε. ταῦτα μὲν ἐπελθόντα τῇ
μνήμῃ κατὰ τὴν γραφὴν ἀπώσασθαι καὶ παρελθεῖν ἴσως
ἀπάνθρωπον ἦν.

25. Τὸν δὲ πρὸς Σαμίους πόλεμον αἰτιῶνται μάλιστα a. 441?
20 τὸν Περικλέα ψηφίσασθαι διὰ Μιλησίους Ἀσπασίας δεηθείσης. αἱ γὰρ πόλεις ἐπολέμουν τὸν περὶ Πριήνης πόλεμον,
καὶ κρατοῦντες οἱ Σάμιοι, παύσασθαι τῶν Ἀθηναίων κε- 166
λευόντων καὶ δίκας λαβεῖν καὶ δοῦναι παρ᾽ αὐτοῖς, οὐκ
ἐπείθοντο. πλεύσας οὖν ὁ Περικλῆς τὴν μὲν οὖσαν ὀλιγαρ- 2
25 χίαν ἐν Σάμῳ κατέλυσεν, τῶν δὲ πρώτων λαβὼν ὁμήρους

14 Plut. Artax. 26, 5 Xen. Anab. 1, 10, 2 Aelian. v. h. 12, 1
Athen. 13, 576d schol. Aristid. p. 468 D. ‖ Cap. 25–28 cf.
Thuc. 1, 115–117 Diod. 12, 27–28

[S(UMA ═)Υ] 1 τέ οἱ Wil.; ϑ᾽ οἱ | Ἀσπασίαν del. Cob. |
καὶ del. Emp. | καταπυγοσύνην: em. Emp. ‖ 4 δημοσίοις: em.
Xy. ‖ 7 μυρωνίδην C: πυρωνίδην cet. et sic etiam pap. Oxy. 1240,
cf. Wil. Herm. 54, 69 ‖ 16 μὲν ⟨οὖν⟩ Cor.

⟨ἄνδρας⟩ πεντήκοντα καὶ παῖδας ἴσους εἰς Λῆμνον ἀπέστειλε. καίτοι φασὶν ἕκαστον μὲν αὐτῷ τῶν ὁμήρων διδόναι τάλαντον ὑπὲρ ἑαυτοῦ, πολλὰ δ᾽ ἄλλα τοὺς μὴ θέλοντας
3 ἐν τῇ πόλει γενέσθαι δημοκρατίαν. ἔτι δὲ Πισσούθνης ὁ Πέρσης, ἔχων τινὰ πρὸς Σαμίους εὔνοιαν, ἀπέστειλεν 5 αὐτῷ μυρίους χρυσοῦς, παραιτούμενος τὴν πόλιν. οὐ μὴν ἔλαβε τούτων οὐδὲν ὁ Περικλῆς, ἀλλὰ χρησάμενος ὥσπερ
b ἐγνώκει τοῖς Σαμίοις καὶ καταστήσας δημοκρατίαν, ἀπέ-
4 πλευσεν εἰς τὰς Ἀθήνας. οἱ δ᾽ εὐθὺς ἀπέστησαν, ἐκκλέψαντος αὐτοῖς τοὺς ὁμήρους Πισσούθνου, καὶ τἆλλα παρεσκεύ- 10 ασαντο πρὸς τὸν πόλεμον. αὖθις οὖν ὁ Περικλῆς ἐξέπλευσεν 34 L ἐπ᾽ αὐτοὺς οὐχ ἡσυχάζοντας οὐδὲ κατεπτηχότας, ἀλλὰ καὶ πάνυ προθύμως ἐγνωκότας ἀντιλαμβάνεσθαι τῆς θα-
5 λάττης. γενομένης δὲ καρτερᾶς ναυμαχίας περὶ νῆσον ἣν Τραγίας καλοῦσι, λαμπρῶς ὁ Περικλῆς ἐνίκα, τέσσαρσι 15 καὶ τεσσαράκοντα ναυσὶν ἑβδομήκοντα καταναυμαχήσας, ὧν εἴκοσι στρατιώτιδες ἦσαν.

26. Ἅμα δὲ τῇ νίκῃ καὶ τῇ διώξει τοῦ λιμένος κρατή-
c σας, ἐπολιόρκει τοὺς Σαμίους, ἁμῶς γέ πως ἔτι τολμῶντας ἐπεξιέναι καὶ διαμάχεσθαι πρὸ τοῦ τείχους. ἐπεὶ δὲ 326 S μείζων ἕτερος στόλος ἦλθεν ἐκ τῶν Ἀθηνῶν καὶ παντε- 21 λῶς κατεκλείσθησαν οἱ Σάμιοι, λαβὼν ὁ Περικλῆς ἑξήκοντα τριήρεις ἔπλευσεν εἰς τὸν ἔξω πόντον, ὡς μὲν οἱ πλεῖστοι λέγουσι, Φοινισσῶν νεῶν ἐπικούρων τοῖς Σαμίοις προσφερομένων, ἀπαντῆσαι καὶ διαγωνίσασθαι πόρρω- 25 τάτω βουλόμενος, ὡς δὲ Στησίμβροτος (FGrH 107 F 8), ἐπὶ Κύπρον στελλόμενος· ὅπερ οὐ δοκεῖ πιθανὸν εἶναι.
2 ὁποτέρῳ δ᾽ οὖν ἐχρήσατο τῶν λογισμῶν, ἁμαρτεῖν ἔδοξε. πλεύσαντος γὰρ αὐτοῦ, Μέλισσος ὁ Ἰθαγένους, ἀνὴρ φιλόσοφος στρατηγῶν τότε τῆς Σάμου, καταφρονήσας τῆς 30
d ὀλιγότητος τῶν νεῶν καὶ τῆς ἀπειρίας τῶν στρατηγῶν,

[S(UMA=)Υ] 1 ἄνδρας add. Herw. cl. Thuc. ‖ 10 παρεσκευάσαντο S Υ: παρασκευάσαντος CE vulg. ‖ 12 κατεπεπηχότας U¹ ‖ 15 τέσσαρσι καὶ om. U ‖ 28 τὸν λογισμὸν U ‖ 29 ἀποπλεύσαντος Cob. ‖ 31 καὶ (Am.) Cor.: ἢ

ἔπεισε τοὺς πολίτας ἐπιθέσθαι τοῖς Ἀθηναίοις, καὶ γενο- 3
μένης μάχης νικήσαντες οἱ Σάμιοι καὶ πολλοὺς μὲν αὐτῶν
ἄνδρας ἑλόντες, πολλὰς δὲ ναῦς διαφθείραντες, ἐχρῶντο τῇ
θαλάσσῃ καὶ παρετίθεντο τῶν ἀναγκαίων πρὸς τὸν πόλεμον
5 ὅσα μὴ πρότερον εἶχον. ὑπὸ δὲ τοῦ Μελίσσου καὶ Περικλέα φησὶν αὐτὸν Ἀριστοτέλης (fr. 535) ἡττηθῆναι ναυ-
μαχοῦντα πρότερον. οἱ δὲ Σάμιοι τοὺς αἰχμαλώτους τῶν 4
Ἀθηναίων ἀνθυβρίζοντες ἔστιζον εἰς τὸ μέτωπον γλαῦκας·
35 L καὶ γὰρ ἐκείνους οἱ Ἀθηναῖοι σάμαιναν. ἡ δὲ σάμαινα ναῦς
10 ἐστιν ὕπoωρος μὲν τὸ σίμωμα, κοιλοτέρα δὲ καὶ γαστρο- e
ειδής, ὥστε καὶ φορτοφορεῖν καὶ ταχυναυτεῖν. οὕτω δ᾽
ὠνομάσθη διὰ τὸ πρῶτον ἐν Σάμῳ φανῆναι, Πολυκράτους
⟨τοῦ⟩ τυράννου κατασκευάσαντος. πρὸς ταῦτα τὰ στίγματα λέγουσι καὶ τὸ Ἀριστοφάνειον (fr. 64 CAF I 408)
15 ᾐνίχθαι·

Σαμίων ὁ δῆμός ἐστιν ὡς πολυγράμματος.

27. Πυθόμενος δ᾽ οὖν ὁ Περικλῆς τὴν ἐπὶ στρατοπέδου
συμφοράν, ἐβοήθει κατὰ τάχος, καὶ τοῦ Μελίσσου πρὸς
αὐτὸν ἀντιταξαμένου κρατήσας καὶ τρεψάμενος, τοὺς πο-
327 S λεμίους εὐθὺς περιετείχιζε, δαπάνῃ καὶ χρόνῳ μᾶλλον ἢ
21 τραύμασι καὶ κινδύνοις τῶν πολιτῶν περιγενέσθαι καὶ
συνελεῖν τὴν πόλιν βουλόμενος. ἐπεὶ δὲ δυσχεραίνοντας 2
τῇ τριβῇ τοὺς Ἀθηναίους καὶ μάχεσθαι προθυμουμένους f
ἔργον ἦν κατασχεῖν, ⟨εἰς⟩ ὀκτὼ μέρη διελὼν τὸ πᾶν πλῆ-
25 θος ἀπεκλήρου, καὶ τῷ λαχόντι τὸν λευκὸν κύαμον εὐωχεῖ-
σθαι καὶ σχολάζειν παρεῖχε τῶν ἄλλων τρυχομένων. διὸ 3
καί φασι τοὺς ἐν εὐπαθείαις τισὶ γενομένους λευκὴν ἡμέραν
ἐκείνην ἀπὸ τοῦ λευκοῦ κυάμου προσαγορεύειν. Ἔφορος 167

16 vide ap. Kock

[S(UMA =)Υ] 2 πολλὰς μὲν αὐτάνδρους ἑλόντες ναῦς, πολλὰς
δὲ διαφθ. Rei. ‖ 7 τῶν om. Υ ‖ 10 ὑπόπρωρος: em. Cor. ‖
κοιλοτέρα] κυκλοτερὴς Ha. ‖ 11 ποντοπορεῖν: em. Cor. ‖ 13 τοῦ
add. Sint. ‖ 20 περιετείχιζε (χι s. s. m. 1) S ‖ 24 εἰς add. Rei. ‖
25 λαχόντι Br.: λαβόντι ‖ 26 τρυχομένων Sauppe: μαχομένων

167 (FGrH 70 F 194) δὲ καὶ μηχαναῖς χρήσασθαι τὸν Περικλέα,
τὴν καινότητα θαυμασταῖς, Ἀρτέμωνος τοῦ μηχανικοῦ
παρ⟨ασχ⟩όντος, ὃν χωλὸν ὄντα καὶ φορείῳ πρὸς τὰ κατεπείγοντα τῶν ἔργων προσκομιζόμενον ὀνομασθῆναι Περι-
4 φόρητον. τοῦτο μὲν οὖν Ἡρακλείδης ὁ Ποντικὸς (fr. 60 5
Wehrli) ἐλέγχει τοῖς Ἀνακρέοντος ποιήμασιν (fr. 16 D.)
ἐν οἷς „ὁ περιφόρητος" Ἀρτέμων ὀνομάζεται πολλαῖς
ἔμπροσθεν ἡλικίαις τοῦ περὶ Σάμον πολέμου καὶ τῶν 36 L
πραγμάτων ἐκείνων· τὸν δ᾽ Ἀρτέμωνά φησι τρυφερόν τινα
τῷ βίῳ καὶ πρὸς τοὺς φόβους μαλακὸν ὄντα καὶ κατα- 10
b πλῆγα τὰ πολλὰ μὲν οἴκοι καθέζεσθαι, χαλκῆν ἀσπίδα
τῆς κεφαλῆς αὐτοῦ δυεῖν οἰκετῶν ὑπερεχόντων, ὥστε
μηδὲν ἐμπεσεῖν τῶν ἄνωθεν, εἰ δὲ βιασθείη προελθεῖν,
ἐν κλινιδίῳ κρεμαστῷ παρὰ τὴν γῆν αὐτὴν περιφερόμενον
κομίζεσθαι καὶ διὰ τοῦτο κληθῆναι περιφόρητον. 15

28. Ἐνάτῳ δὲ μηνὶ τῶν Σαμίων παραστάντων, ὁ Περικλῆς τὰ τείχη καθεῖλε καὶ τὰς ναῦς παρέλαβε καὶ χρήμασι
πολλοῖς ἐζημίωσεν, ὧν τὰ μὲν εὐθὺς εἰσήνεγκαν οἱ Σάμιοι,
τὰ δ᾽ ἐν χρόνῳ ῥητῷ ταξάμενοι κατοίσειν ὁμήρους ἔδω-
2 καν. Δοῦρις δ᾽ ὁ Σάμιος (FGrH 76 F 67) τούτοις ἐπιτραγῳ- 20
δεῖ, πολλὴν ὠμότητα τῶν Ἀθηναίων καὶ τοῦ Περικλέους
c κατηγορῶν, ἣν οὔτε Θουκυδίδης ἱστόρηκεν οὔτ᾽ Ἔφορος
οὔτ᾽ Ἀριστοτέλης (fr. 536)· ἀλλ᾽ οὐδ᾽ ἀληθεύειν ἔοικεν,
ὡς ἄρα τοὺς τριηράρχους καὶ τοὺς ἐπιβάτας τῶν Σαμίων
εἰς τὴν Μιλησίων ἀγορὰν καταγαγὼν καὶ σανίσι προσ- 328 S
δήσας ἐφ᾽ ἡμέρας δέκα κακῶς ἤδη διακειμένους προσέ- 26
ταξεν ἀνελεῖν, ξύλοις τὰς κεφαλὰς συγκόψαντας, εἶτα
3 προβαλεῖν ἀκήδευτα τὰ σώματα. Δοῦρις μὲν οὖν οὐδ᾽
ὅπου μηδὲν αὐτῷ πρόσεστιν ἴδιον πάθος εἰωθὼς κρατεῖν

6 Athen. 12, 533e

[S(UM A =)Υ] 1 μηχαναῖς ⟨φησι⟩ Zie. ‖ 2 θαυμασταῖς Madvig: θαυμάσαντα ‖ 3 παρασχόντος Zie.: παρόντος libri πορόντος
Rei. πορίζοντος Cor. ‖ 14 παραφερόμενον: em. Ald. Iunt. ‖ 18 εὐθὺς
++ S ‖ ἤνεγκαν Υ ‖ 19 δ᾽ ἐν Υ: δὲ S ‖ καταθήσειν Cob. ‖ 23 ἀλη-
θέσιν S ‖ 25 ἀγαγὼν Υ ‖ 26 ἡμέραις Υ

τὴν διήγησιν ἐπὶ τῆς ἀληθείας, μᾶλλον ἔοικεν ἐνταῦθα
δεινῶσαι τὰς τῆς πατρίδος συμφορὰς ἐπὶ διαβολῇ τῶν
Ἀθηναίων.

Ὁ δὲ Περικλῆς καταστρεψάμενος τὴν Σάμον ὡς ἐπανῆλ- 4
5 θεν εἰς τὰς Ἀθήνας, ταφάς τε τῶν ἀποθανόντων κατὰ τὸν d
πόλεμον ἐνδόξους ἐποίησε, καὶ τὸν λόγον εἰπών, ὥσπερ
37 L ἔθος ἐστίν, ἐπὶ τῶν σημάτων ἐθαυμάσθη. καταβαίνοντα 5
δ᾽ αὐτὸν ἀπὸ τοῦ βήματος αἱ μὲν ἄλλαι γυναῖκες ἐδεξι-
οῦντο καὶ στεφάνοις ἀνέδουν καὶ ταινίαις ὥσπερ ἀθλητὴν
10 νικηφόρον, ἡ δ᾽ Ἐλπινίκη προσελθοῦσα πλησίον, ,,ταῦτ᾽" 6
ἔφη ,,θαυμαστά ⟨σου⟩ Περίκλεις καὶ ἄξια στεφάνων,
ὃς ἡμῖν πολλοὺς καὶ ἀγαθοὺς ἀπώλεσας πολίτας, οὐ Φοί-
νιξι πολεμῶν οὐδὲ Μήδοις, ὥσπερ οὑμὸς ἀδελφὸς Κίμων,
ἀλλὰ σύμμαχον καὶ συγγενῆ πόλιν καταστρεφόμενος."
15 ταῦτα τῆς Ἐλπινίκης λεγούσης, ὁ Περικλῆς μειδιάσας 7 e
ἀτρέμα λέγεται τὸ τοῦ Ἀρχιλόχου (fr. 27 D.) πρὸς αὐτὴν
εἰπεῖν·

> οὐκ ἂν μύροισι γραῦς ἐοῦσ᾽ ἠλείφεο.

θαυμαστὸν δέ τι καὶ μέγα φρονῆσαι καταπολεμήσαντα
20 τοὺς Σαμίους φησὶν αὐτὸν ὁ Ἴων (FGrH 392 F 16), ὡς τοῦ
μὲν Ἀγαμέμνονος ἔτεσι δέκα βάρβαρον πόλιν, αὐτοῦ δὲ
μησὶν ἐννέα τοὺς πρώτους καὶ δυνατωτάτους Ἰώνων ἑλόντος. καὶ οὐκ ἦν ἄδικος ἡ ἀξίωσις, ἀλλ᾽ ὄντως πολλὴν 8
ἀδηλότητα καὶ μέγαν ἔσχε κίνδυνον ὁ πόλεμος, εἴπερ,
25 ὡς Θουκυδίδης φησί (8, 76, 4), παρ᾽ ἐλάχιστον ἦλθε Σαμίων ἡ πόλις ἀφελέσθαι τῆς θαλάττης τὸ κράτος Ἀθηναίους.

29. Μετὰ ταῦτα κυμαίνοντος ἤδη τοῦ Πελοποννησια- f
329 8 κοῦ πολέμου, Κερκυραίοις πολεμουμένοις ὑπὸ Κορινθίων
ἔπεισε τὸν δῆμον ἀποστεῖλαι βοήθειαν καὶ προσλαβεῖν a. 433

---

28 Thuc. 1, 44sq. Diod. 12, 33 IG I 179 = Syll.³ 72

[S(UMA =)Υ] 7 ἐθαυμαστώθη Υ ‖ 11 σου add. (Rei.) Zie. ‖
12 ὅς] ὅτι Rei. | ἀπολέσας S ‖ 14 καταστρεφόμενος; Ri.

ἐρρωμένην ναυτικῇ δυνάμει νῆσον, ὡς ὅσον οὐδέπω Πελο
ποννησίων ἐκπεπολεμωμένων πρὸς αὐτούς. ψηφισαμένου
δὲ τοῦ δήμου τὴν βοήθειαν, ἀπέστειλε δέκα ναῦς μόνας
ἔχοντα Λακεδαιμόνιον, τὸν Κίμωνος υἱόν, οἷον ἐφυβρίζων·
πολλὴ γὰρ ἦν εὔνοια καὶ φιλία τῷ Κίμωνος οἴκῳ πρὸς 5
168 2 Λακεδαιμονίους. ὡς ἂν οὖν, εἰ μηδὲν ἔργον μέγα μηδ᾽
ἐκπρεπὲς ἐν τῇ στρατηγίᾳ τοῦ Λακεδαιμονίου γένοιτο, 38
προσδιαβληθείη μᾶλλον εἰς τὸν λακωνισμόν, ὀλίγας αὐτῷ
ναῦς ἔδωκε καὶ μὴ βουλόμενον ἐξέπεμψε, καὶ ὅλως διετέ
λει κολούων, ὡς μηδὲ τοῖς ὀνόμασι γνησίους, ἀλλ᾽ ὀθνείους 10
καὶ ξένους, ὅτι τῶν Κίμωνος υἱῶν τῷ μὲν ἦν Λακεδαιμό
νιος ὄνομα, τῷ δὲ Θεσσαλός, τῷ δ᾽ Ἠλεῖος. ἐδόκουν δὲ
3 πάντες ἐκ γυναικὸς Ἀρκαδικῆς γεγονέναι. κακῶς οὖν ὁ
Περικλῆς ἀκούων διὰ τὰς δέκα ταύτας τριήρεις, ὡς μικρὰν
μὲν βοήθειαν τοῖς δεηθεῖσι, μεγάλην δὲ πρόφασιν τοῖς 15
b ἐγκαλοῦσι παρεσχηκώς, ἑτέρας αὖθις ἔστειλε πλείονας
4 εἰς τὴν Κέρκυραν, αἳ μετὰ τὴν μάχην ἀφίκοντο. χαλεπαί
νουσι δὲ τοῖς Κορινθίοις καὶ κατηγοροῦσι τῶν Ἀθηναίων
ἐν Λακεδαίμονι προσεγένοντο Μεγαρεῖς, αἰτιώμενοι πάσης
μὲν ἀγορᾶς, ἁπάντων δὲ λιμένων ὧν Ἀθηναῖοι κρατοῦσιν 20
εἴργεσθαι καὶ ἀπελαύνεσθαι παρὰ τὰ κοινὰ δίκαια καὶ
5 τοὺς γεγενημένους ὅρκους τοῖς Ἕλλησιν· Αἰγινῆται δὲ
κακοῦσθαι δοκοῦντες καὶ βίαια πάσχειν, ἐποτνιῶντο κρύφα
πρὸς τοὺς Λακεδαιμονίους, φανερῶς ἐγκαλεῖν τοῖς Ἀθη
6 ναίοις οὐ θαρροῦντες. ἐν δὲ τούτῳ καὶ Ποτείδαια, πόλις 25
ὑπήκοος Ἀθηναίων, ἄποικος δὲ Κορινθίων, ἀποστᾶσα
c 7 καὶ πολιορκουμένη μᾶλλον ἐπετάχυνε τὸν πόλεμον. οὐ
μὴν ἀλλὰ καὶ πρεσβειῶν πεμπομένων Ἀθήναζε, καὶ τοῦ

9 Plut. Cim. 16,1 ‖ 13 Thuc. 1, 50, 5 ‖ 17 Thuc. 1, 67, 4 (1,
139, 1) schol. Aristoph. Pax 608 Diod. 12, 39, 4 ‖ 22 Thuc. 1,
67, 2 ‖ 25 Thuc. 1, 56—65 ‖ 27 cf. Thuc. 1, 139. 140, 4 Diod.
12, 39, 4

[S(UMA =)Υ] 10 κωλύων Υ σκώπτων Naber; aliquid excidisse putat Ha. fort. iure ‖ 15 μὲν om. in fine pag. U ‖ 16 ἑτέ
ρως U ‖ ἔστειλε, λ in ras. m. rec., S ‖ 20 πάντων Υ ‖ 23 βίαν S ‖
25 ποτίδαια codd. ‖ 28 καὶ πρεσβειῶν S: πρεσβειῶν τε Υ

βασιλέως τῶν Λακεδαιμονίων Ἀρχιδάμου τὰ πολλὰ τῶν
ἐγκλημάτων εἰς διαλύσεις ἄγοντος καὶ τοὺς συμμάχους
39 L πραΰνοντος, οὐκ ἂν δοκεῖ συμπεσεῖν ὑπό γε τῶν ἄλλων
330 S αἰτιῶν ὁ πόλεμος τοῖς Ἀθηναίοις, εἰ τὸ ψήφισμα καθε-
5 λεῖν τὸ Μεγαρικὸν ἐπείσθησαν καὶ διαλλαγῆναι πρὸς αὐτούς. διὸ καὶ μάλιστα πρὸς τοῦτο Περικλῆς ἐναντιω- 8
θεὶς καὶ παροξύνας τὸν δῆμον ἐμμεῖναι τῇ πρὸς τοὺς Μεγαρεῖς φιλονικίᾳ, μόνος ἔσχε τοῦ πολέμου τὴν αἰτίαν.

30. Λέγουσι δὲ πρεσβείας Ἀθήναζε περὶ τούτων ἐκ Λα-
10 κεδαίμονος ἀφιγμένης, καὶ τοῦ Περικλέους νόμον τινὰ d
προβαλομένου κωλύοντα καθελεῖν τὸ πινάκιον ἐν ᾧ τὸ
ψήφισμα γεγραμμένον ἐτύγχανεν, εἰπεῖν Πολυάλκη τῶν
πρέσβεών τινα· ,,σὺ δὲ μὴ καθέλῃς, ἀλλὰ στρέψον εἴσω
τὸ πινάκιον· οὐ γὰρ ἔστι νόμος ὁ τοῦτο κωλύων.`` κομ-
15 ψοῦ δὲ τοῦ λόγου φανέντος, οὐδέν τι μᾶλλον ὁ Περικλῆς
ἐνέδωκεν. ὑπῆν μὲν οὖν τις ὡς ἔοικεν αὐτῷ καὶ ἰδία 2
πρὸς τοὺς Μεγαρεῖς ἀπέχθεια, κοινὴν δὲ καὶ φανερὰν
ποιησάμενος αἰτίαν κατ' αὐτῶν, ἀποτέμνεσθαι τὴν ἱερὰν
ὀργάδα, γράφει ψήφισμα κήρυκα πεμφθῆναι πρὸς αὐτοὺς
20 καὶ πρὸς Λακεδαιμονίους τὸν αὐτόν, κατηγοροῦντα τῶν
Μεγαρέων. τοῦτο μὲν οὖν τὸ ψήφισμα Περικλέους ἐστὶν 3 e
εὐγνώμονος καὶ φιλανθρώπου δικαιολογίας ἐχόμενον· ἐπεὶ
δ' ὁ πεμφθεὶς κῆρυξ Ἀνθεμόκριτος αἰτίᾳ τῶν Μεγαρέων
ἀποθανεῖν ἔδοξε, γράφει ψήφισμα κατ' αὐτῶν Χαρῖνος,
25 ἄσπονδον μὲν εἶναι καὶ ἀκήρυκτον ἔχθραν, ὃς δ' ἂν ἐπιβῇ
τῆς Ἀττικῆς Μεγαρέων, θανάτῳ ζημιοῦσθαι, τοὺς δὲ
στρατηγοὺς ὅταν ὀμνύωσι τὸν πάτριον ὅρκον ἐπομνύειν,
40 L ὅτι καὶ δὶς ἀνὰ πᾶν ἔτος εἰς τὴν Μεγαρικὴν εἰσβαλοῦσι·

17 cf. Thuc. 1, 139, 2 || 22 mor. 812d Demosth. or. 12, 4 Paus. 1,
36, 3 Harpocrat. et Suda s. v. Ἀνθεμόκριτος Bekker Anecd. 1,
403, 29

[S(UMA =)Υ] 3 δοκεῖ M: δοκῇ UA, sed η in ras. U ἐδόκει S |
γε Υ: τε S | 7 ἐμμεῖναι S: ἐμμείνας Υ || 9. 10 πρέσβεις—ἀφιγμένους:
em. Br. || 11 προβαλλομένου: em. Rei. || 12 πολυάλκην A ||
20 κατηγορήσοντα Cor. || 27 πατρικὸν Υ || 28 ἐμβαλοῦσιν Υ, cf.
Thuc. 4, 66, 1

ταφῆναι δ' Ἀνθεμόκριτον παρὰ τὰς Θριασίας πύλας, αἱ
4 νῦν Δίπυλον ὀνομάζονται. Μεγαρεῖς δὲ τὸν Ἀνθεμοκρίτου
f φόνον ἀπαρνούμενοι, τὰς αἰτίας εἰς Ἀσπασίαν καὶ Περικλέα τρέπουσι, χρώμενοι τοῖς περιβοήτοις καὶ δημώδεσι
τούτοις ἐκ τῶν Ἀχαρνέων στιχιδίοις (v. 524 sq.)·   5

> πόρνην δὲ Σιμαίθαν ἰόντες Μεγάραδε   331 S
> νεανίαι κλέπτουσι μεθυσοκότταβοι·
> κᾆθ' οἱ Μεγαρῆς ὀδύναις πεφυσιγγωμένοι
> ἀντεξέκλεψαν Ἀσπασίας πόρνας δύο.

169 31. Τὴν μὲν οὖν ἀρχὴν ὅπως ἔσχεν οὐ ῥᾴδιον γνῶναι, 10
τοῦ δὲ μὴ λυθῆναι τὸ ψήφισμα πάντες ὡσαύτως τὴν αἰτίαν
ἐπιφέρουσι τῷ Περικλεῖ. πλὴν οἱ μὲν ἐκ φρονήματος μεγά-
λου μετὰ γνώμης κατὰ τὸ βέλτιστον ἀπισχυρίσασθαί
φασιν αὐτόν, πεῖραν ἐνδόσεως τὸ πρόσταγμα καὶ τὴν συγ-
χώρησιν ἐξομολόγησιν ἀσθενείας ἡγούμενον, οἱ δὲ μᾶλλον 15
αὐθαδείᾳ τινὶ καὶ φιλονικίᾳ πρὸς ἔνδειξιν ἰσχύος περιφρονῆσαι Λακεδαιμονίων.

2 Ἡ δὲ χειρίστη μὲν αἰτία πασῶν, ἔχουσα δὲ πλείστους
μάρτυρας, οὕτω πως λέγεται. Φειδίας ὁ πλάστης ἐργολάβος μὲν ἦν τοῦ ἀγάλματος ὥσπερ εἴρηται, φίλος δὲ 20
b τῷ Περικλεῖ γενόμενος καὶ μέγιστον παρ' αὐτῷ δυνηθείς,
τοὺς μὲν δι' αὐτὸν ἔσχεν ἐχθροὺς φθονούμενος, οἱ δὲ τοῦ
δήμου ποιούμενοι πεῖραν ἐν ἐκείνῳ ποῖός τις ἔσοιτο τῷ Περικλεῖ κριτής, Μένωνά τινα τῶν Φειδίου συνεργῶν πείσαντες 41 L
ἱκέτην ἐν ἀγορᾷ καθίζουσιν, αἰτούμενον ἄδειαν ἐπὶ μηνύσει 25
3 καὶ κατηγορίᾳ τοῦ Φειδίου. προσδεξαμένου δὲ τοῦ δήμου

6sq. Athen. 13, 570a Suda s. v. πεφυσιγγωμένοι ‖ 12 Thuc. 1,
140, 5 ‖ 18 Diod. 12, 39, 1 Philoch. FGrH 328 F 121

[S(UMA =)Υ] 1 θριασίου S θριασίους Υ: em. Rei. ‖ 5 ἀχαρ-
νέως Υ ‖ 6 ἰδόντες S ‖ 8 μεγαρεῖς Υ Suda | ὀδύναισι S ‖ 9 ἀντέ-
κλεψαν S | πόρνας S, cod. Rav. Aristoph.: πόρνα Υ, cet.
codd. Aristoph., Suda ‖ 14 πρόσταγμα Υ: πρᾶγμα S ‖ 16 πρὸς
ἔνδοξον ἰσχὺν Υ ‖ 23 τις Υ: τε S | τῷ om. Υ ‖ 25.26 καθίζουσιν |
αἰτούμενοι ἄδειαν ἐπὶ μηνύσει καὶ κατηγορᾷ καθίζουσιν αι | αἰτού-
μενοι ἄδειαν ἐπὶ μηνύσει καὶ κατηγορία U, sed αἰτούμενοι¹—αι
exp. m. 1

τὸν ἄνθρωπον καὶ γενομέι ης ἐν ἐκκλησίᾳ διώξεως, κλοπαὶ
μὲν οὐκ ἠλέγχοντο· τὸ γὰρ χρυσίον οὕτως εὐθὺς ἐξ ἀρχῆς
τῷ ἀγάλματι προσειργάσατο καὶ περιέθηκεν ὁ Φειδίας
γνώμῃ τοῦ Περικλέους, ὥστε πᾶν δυνατὸν εἶναι περιελοῦ-
5 σιν ἀποδεῖξαι τὸν στι θμόν, ὃ καὶ τότε τοὺς κατηγόρους c
ἐκέλευσε ποιεῖν ὁ Περικλῆς· ἡ δὲ δόξα τῶν ἔργων ἐπίεζε
φθόνῳ τὸν Φειδίαν, καὶ μάλισθ᾽ ὅτι τὴν πρὸς Ἀμαζόνας
μάχην ἐν τῇ ἀσπίδι ποιῶν αὐτοῦ τινα μορφὴν ἐνετύπωσε,
πρεσβύτου φαλακροῦ πέτρον ἐπηρμένου δι᾽ ἀμφοτέρων
10 τῶν χειρῶν, καὶ τοῦ Περικλέους εἰκόνα παγκάλην ἐνέθηκε
332 S μαχομένου πρὸς Ἀμαζόνα. τὸ δὲ σχῆμα τῆς χειρός, ἀνα- 4
τεινούσης δόρυ πρὸ τῆς ὄψεως τοῦ Περικλέους, πεποιημένον εὐμηχάνως οἷον ἐπικρύπτειν βούλεται τὴν ὁμοιότητα, παραφαινομένην ἑκατέρωθεν. ὁ μὲν οὖν Φειδίας 5
15 εἰς τὸ δεσμωτήριον ἀπαχθεὶς ἐτελεύτησε νοσήσας, ὡς δέ
φασιν ἔνιοι φαρμάκοις, ἐπὶ διαβολῇ τοῦ Περικλέους τῶν d
ἐχθρῶν παρασκευασάντων. τῷ δὲ μηνυτῇ Μένωνι γράψαντος Γλαύκωνος ἀτέλειαν ὁ δῆμος ἔδωκε, καὶ προσ-
έταξε τοῖς στρατηγοῖς ἐπιμελεῖσθαι τῆς ἀσφαλείας τοῦ
20 ἀνθρώπου.

32. Περὶ δὲ τοῦτον τὸν χρόνον Ἀσπασία δίκην ἔφευγεν
ἀσεβείας, Ἑρμίππου τοῦ κωμῳδιοποιοῦ διώκοντος καὶ
42 L προσκατηγοροῦντος, ὡς Περικλεῖ γυναῖκας ἐλευθέρας
εἰς τὸ αὐτὸ φοιτώσας ὑποδέχοιτο, καὶ ψήφισμα Διοπείθης 2
25 ἔγραψεν εἰσαγγέλλεσθαι τοὺς τὰ θεῖα μὴ νομίζοντας ἢ
λόγους περὶ τῶν μεταρσίων διδάσκοντας, ἀπερειδόμενος
εἰς Περικλέα δι᾽ Ἀναξαγόρου τὴν ὑπόνοιαν. δεχομένου δὲ 3
τοῦ δήμου καὶ προσιεμένου τὰς διαβολάς, οὕτως ἤδη e
ψήφισμα κυροῦται Δρακοντίδου γράψαντος, ὅπως οἱ λόγοι

7 Cic. Tusc. 1, 34 ‖ 21 Athen. 13, 589 e Schol. Aristoph. eq.
969. Schol. Hermog. 7, 165 Walz ‖ 24 mor. 169 f. Diod. 12, 39, 3
Diog. Laert. 2, 12

[S(U M A =) Υ] 2 ἐλέγοντο: em. Orelli ‖ 3 τῷ om. Υ ‖ 4 πᾶν Υ:
πάνυ S ‖ 8 ἐν τῇ ἀσπίδι μάχην S ‖ 10 Περικλέους ⟨δ᾽⟩ Blass ‖
18 γλύκωνος: em. Pareti Röm. Mitt. 24, 274 ‖ 21 ⟨καὶ⟩ Ἀσπασία
Rei. ‖ 22 κωμῳδοποιοῦ Υ ‖ 24 διοπίθης S

τῶν χρημάτων ὑπὸ Περικλέους εἰς τοὺς πρυτάνεις ἀπο- 42 L
τεθεῖεν, οἱ δὲ δικασταὶ τὴν ψῆφον ἀπὸ τοῦ βωμοῦ φέρον-
4 τες ἐν τῇ πόλει κρίνοιεν. Ἄγνων δὲ τοῦτο μὲν ἀφεῖλε τοῦ
ψηφίσματος, κρίνεσθαι δὲ τὴν δίκην ἔγραψεν ἐν δικα-
σταῖς χιλίοις καὶ πεντακοσίοις, εἴτε κλοπῆς καὶ δώρων 5
5 εἴτ᾽ ἀδικίου βούλοιτό τις ὀνομάζειν τὴν δίωξιν. Ἀσπασίαν
μὲν οὖν ἐξῃτήσατο, πολλὰ πάνυ παρὰ τὴν δίκην, ὡς Αἰσχίνης
(p. 48 Kr.) φησίν, ἀφεὶς ὑπὲρ αὐτῆς δάκρυα καὶ δεηθεὶς
τῶν δικαστῶν, Ἀναξαγόραν δὲ φοβηθεὶς ⟨τὸ δικαστή-
f 6 ριον⟩ ἐξέκλεψε καὶ προύπεμψεν ἐκ τῆς πόλεως. ὡς δὲ διὰ 10
Φειδίου προσέπταισε τῷ δήμῳ, [φοβηθεὶς τὸ δικαστή-
ριον] μέλλοντα τὸν πόλεμον καὶ ὑποτυφόμενον ἐξέκαυσεν, ἐλπίζων διασκεδάσειν τὰ ἐγκλήματα καὶ ταπεινώσειν
τὸν φθόνον, ἐν πράγμασι μεγάλοις καὶ κινδύνοις τῆς 333 8
πόλεως ἐκείνῳ μόνῳ διὰ τὸ ἀξίωμα καὶ τὴν δύναμιν 15
170 ἀναθείσης ἑαυτήν. αἱ μὲν οὖν αἰτίαι, δι᾽ ἃς οὐκ εἴασεν
ἐνδοῦναι Λακεδαιμονίοις τὸν δῆμον, αὗται λέγονται· τὸ
δ᾽ ἀληθὲς ἄδηλον.

a. 431 **33.** Οἱ δὲ Λακεδαιμόνιοι γινώσκοντες ὡς ἐκείνου κατα- 43 L
λυθέντος εἰς πάντα μαλακωτέροις χρήσονται τοῖς Ἀθη- 20
ναίοις, ἐκέλευον αὐτοὺς τὸ ἄγος ἐλαύνειν τὸ Κυλώνειον,
ᾧ τὸ μητρόθεν γένος τοῦ Περικλέους ἔνοχον ἦν, ὡς Θου-
2 κυδίδης (1, 127) ἱστόρηκεν. ἡ δὲ πεῖρα περιέστη τοῖς
πέμψασιν εἰς τοὐναντίον· ἀντὶ γὰρ ὑποψίας καὶ διαβολῆς
ὁ Περικλῆς ἔτι μείζονα πίστιν ἔσχε καὶ τιμὴν παρὰ τοῖς 25
πολίταις, ὡς μάλιστα μισούντων καὶ φοβουμένων ἐκεῖνον
3 τῶν πολεμίων. διὸ καὶ πρὶν ἐμβαλεῖν εἰς τὴν Ἀττικὴν τὸν

10 Diod. 12, 39, 3 Aristoph. Pax 605sq. Aristodem. 16, 1 ‖
19 Thuc. 1, 126. 127 ‖ 27 Thuc. 2, 13, 1 Polyaen. 1, 36, 2
Iustin. 3, 7, 9

[S(UMA =)Υ] 1 τοὺς om. S ‖ 3 ⟨τοῦ⟩ ἐν τῇ πόλει Rei. ‖
6 ἀδικίας S ἀδίκου Υ: em. Rei. ‖ 9 τὸ δικ. add., deinde (11)
φοβ. τὸ δικ. del. Madvig ‖ 10 ἐξέκλεψε Emp.: ἐξέπεμψεν | καὶ πρού-
πεμψεν om. S ‖ 11 τὸ S: ὡς τὸ Υ ‖ 15 μόνῳ om. U ‖ 16 ἀνατιθείσης
Cor. ‖ 21 τὸ κυλώνειον om. Υ fort. recte ‖ 22 τὸ μηπρόσθεν U ‖
23 ἱστόρηκεν S: εἴρηκεν Υ

38

43 L Ἀρχίδαμον ἔχοντα τοὺς Πελοποννησίους προεῖπε τοῖς
Ἀθηναίοις, ἂν ἄρα τἆλλα δῃῶν ὁ Ἀρχίδαμος ἀπέχηται τῶν b
ἐκείνου διὰ τὴν ξενίαν τὴν οὖσαν αὐτοῖς ἢ διαβολῆς τοῖς
ἐχθροῖς ἐνδιδοὺς ἀφορμάς, ὅτι τῇ πόλει καὶ τὴν χώραν καὶ
5 τὰς ἐπαύλεις ἐπιδίδωσιν.

Ἐμβάλλουσιν οὖν εἰς τὴν Ἀττικὴν στρατῷ μεγάλῳ 4
Λακεδαιμόνιοι μετὰ τῶν συμμάχων, Ἀρχιδάμου τοῦ βασιλέως ἡγουμένου, καὶ δῃοῦντες τὴν χώραν προῆλθον εἰς
Ἀχαρνὰς καὶ κατεστρατοπέδευσαν, ὡς τῶν Ἀθηναίων οὐκ
10 ἀνεξομένων, ἀλλ᾽ ὑπ᾽ ὀργῆς καὶ φρονήματος διαμαχου-
μένων πρὸς αὐτούς. τῷ δὲ Περικλεῖ δεινὸν ἐφαίνετο πρὸς 5
τοὺς ἑξακισμυρίους Πελοποννησίων καὶ Βοιωτῶν ὁπλίτας c
– τοσοῦτοι γὰρ ἦσαν οἱ τὸ πρῶτον ἐμβαλόντες – ὑπὲρ
αὐτῆς τῆς πόλεως μάχην συνάψαι· τοὺς δὲ βουλομένους
44 L μάχεσθαι καὶ δυσπαθοῦντας πρὸς τὰ γιγνόμενα κατεπράυ-
16 νε, λέγων ὡς δένδρα μὲν τμηθέντα καὶ κοπέντα φύεται
ταχέως, ἀνδρῶν δὲ διαφθαρέντων αὖθις τυχεῖν οὐ ῥᾴδιόν
ἐστι. τὸν δὲ δῆμον εἰς ἐκκλησίαν οὐ συνῆγε, δεδιὼς βια- 6
σθῆναι παρὰ γνώμην, ἀλλ᾽ ὥσπερ νεὼς κυβερνήτης ἀνέ-
334 S μου κατιόντος ἐν πελάγει θέμενος εὖ πάντα καὶ κατα-
21 τείνας τὰ ὅπλα χρῆται τῇ τέχνῃ, δάκρυα καὶ δεήσεις ἐπιβατῶν ναυτιώντων καὶ φοβουμένων ἐάσας, οὕτως ἐκεῖνος
τό τ᾽ ἄστυ συγκλείσας καὶ καταλαβὼν πάντα φυλακαῖς d
πρὸς ἀσφάλειαν, ἐχρῆτο τοῖς αὑτοῦ λογισμοῖς, βραχέα
25 φροντίζων τῶν καταβοώντων καὶ δυσχεραινόντων. καίτοι 7
πολλοὶ μὲν αὐτῷ τῶν φίλων δεόμενοι προσέκειντο, πολλοὶ
δὲ τῶν ἐχθρῶν ἀπειλοῦντες καὶ κατηγοροῦντες, χοροὶ δ᾽
ᾖδον ᾄσματα καὶ σκώμματα πρὸς αἰσχύνην, ἐφυβρίζοντες
αὐτοῦ τὴν στρατηγίαν ὡς ἄνανδρον καὶ προϊεμένην τὰ

6 Thuc. 2, 19. 20 Diod. 12, 42 mor. 784e ‖ 18 Thuc. 2, 22
Diod. 12, 42, 6 ‖ 25 Thuc. 2, 21

[S(UMA =)Υ] 2 δῃῶν ὁ vel δῃῶν ὁ Υ: ἤδη ὣν S ‖ 3 τὴν¹
om. S ‖ τὴν² om. Υ ‖ ἢ om. S, cf. Thuc. ‖ 12 τοὺς om. U ‖ ἐξακι-
σχιλίους S, cf. mor. ‖ 15 δυσπλοοῦντας S ‖ γινόμενα Υ ‖ 19 νέος U ‖
21 καὶ Υ: τε καὶ S ‖ 26 αὑτοῦ: em. Blass ‖ 27 χοροὶ δ᾽ Fuhr:
χοροὶ S πολλοὶ δὲ Υ ‖ 28 ὑβρίζοντες S

4 BT Plut. vit. I 2 ed. Ziegler [1673]

8 πράγματα τοῖς πολεμίοις. ἐπεφύετο δὲ καὶ Κλέων ἤδη, διὰ
τῆς πρὸς ἐκεῖνον ὀργῆς τῶν πολιτῶν πορευόμενος ἐπὶ τὴν
δημαγωγίαν, ὡς τὰ ἀνάπαιστα ταῦτα δηλοῖ ποιήσαντος
Ἑρμίππου (fr. 46 CAF I 236)·

e   βασιλεῦ σατύρων, τί ποτ᾽ οὐκ ἐθέλεις   5
    δόρυ βαστάζειν, ἀλλὰ λόγους μὲν
    περὶ τοῦ πολέμου δεινοὺς παρέχεις,
    ψυχὴ δὲ Τέλητος ὕπεστιν;

    κἀγχειριδίου δ᾽ ἀκόνῃ σκληρᾷ
    παραθηγομένης βρύχεις κοπίδος,   45 L
    δηχθεὶς αἴθωνι Κλέωνι.   11

34. Πλὴν ὑπ᾽ οὐδενὸς ἐκινήθη τῶν τοιούτων ὁ Περικλῆς, ἀλλὰ πράως καὶ σιωπῇ τὴν ἀδοξίαν καὶ τὴν ἀπέ-
χθειαν ὑφιστάμενος, καὶ νεῶν ἑκατὸν ἐπὶ τὴν Πελοπόννησον στόλον ἐκπέμπων, αὐτὸς οὐ συνεξέπλευσεν, ἀλλ᾽ 15
ἔμεινεν οἰκουρῶν καὶ διὰ χειρὸς ἔχων τὴν πόλιν, ἕως
2 ἀπηλλάγησαν οἱ Πελοποννήσιοι. θεραπεύων δὲ τοὺς πολλοὺς [ὅμως] ἀσχάλλοντας ἐπὶ τῷ πολέμῳ, διανομαῖς τε
f χρημάτων ἀνελάμβανε καὶ κληρουχίας ἔγραφεν· Αἰγινήτας
γὰρ ἐξελάσας ἅπαντας, διένειμε τὴν νῆσον Ἀθηναίων τοῖς 20
3 λαχοῦσιν. ἦν δέ τις παρηγορία καὶ ἀφ᾽ ὧν ἔπασχον οἱ
πολέμιοι. καὶ γὰρ οἱ περιπλέοντες τὴν Πελοπόννησον 335 S
χώραν τε πολλὴν κώμας τε καὶ πόλεις μικρὰς διεπόρθη-
171 σαν, καὶ κατὰ γῆν αὐτὸς ἐμβαλὼν εἰς τὴν Μεγαρικὴν
4 ἔφθειρε πᾶσαν. ᾗ καὶ δῆλον ἦν, ὅτι πολλὰ μὲν δρῶντες 25
κατὰ γῆν κακὰ τοὺς Ἀθηναίους, πολλὰ δὲ πάσχοντες

19 Thuc. 2, 27, 1 ‖ 22 Thuc. 2, 25. 31 Diod. 12, 43. 44

[S(UMA =)Υ] 1 κλέων ἤδη E: κλεωνίδη SΥ ‖ 2 ἐπὶ s. s. S
(m. 1) ‖ 3 δηλοποιήσαντος: em. Salvinius ‖ 5 τί π᾽ οὐκ U ‖ 7 παρέχῃ Υ ‖ 8 ψυχὴ–ὕπεστιν Emp.: ψυχὴν–ὑπέστης S ψυχὴν–ὑπέστη
Υ ‖ 10 παραθηγομένην S -μένη Υ: em. Dacerius | βραχεῖ S
βρύχει Υ: em. Anon. | κοπίδας: em. Cor. ‖ 16 ὅλην πόλιν S Zie. ‖
18 ὅμως del. Cor. ‖ 19 ἀνέγραφεν Υ ‖ 23 μικρὰς Υ: οὐ μικρὰς S ‖
25 ἦν om. Υ ‖ 26 κατὰ γῆν om. Υ

ὑπ᾽ ἐκείνων ἐκ θαλάττης, οὐκ ἂν εἰς μῆκος πολέμου
τοσοῦτο προὔβησαν, ἀλλὰ ταχέως ἀπεῖπον, ὥσπερ ἐξ
ἀρχῆς ὁ Περικλῆς προηγόρευσεν, εἰ μή τι δαιμόνιον ὑπη-
ναντιώθη τοῖς ἀνθρωπίνοις λογισμοῖς. νῦν δὲ πρῶτον 5
5 μὲν ἡ λοιμώδης ἐνέπεσε φθορὰ καὶ κατενεμήθη τὴν ἀκμάζουσαν ἡλικίαν καὶ δύναμιν, ὑφ᾽ ἧς καὶ τὰ σώματα κακού-
46 L μενοι καὶ τὰς ψυχάς, παντάπασιν ἠγριώθησαν πρὸς τὸν
Περικλέα, καὶ καθάπερ [πρὸς] ἰατρὸν ἢ πατέρα τῇ νόσῳ
παραφρονήσαντες ἀδικεῖν ἐπεχείρησαν, ἀναπεισθέντες ὑπὸ b
10 τῶν ἐχθρῶν ὡς τὴν μὲν νόσον ἡ τοῦ χωρικοῦ πλήθους εἰς
τὸ ἄστυ συμφόρησις ἀπεργάζεται, θέρους ὥρᾳ πολλῶν
ὁμοῦ χύδην ἐν οἰκήμασι μικροῖς καὶ σκηνώμασι πνιγηροῖς ἀναγκαζομένων διαιτᾶσθαι δίαιταν οἰκουρὸν καὶ
ἀργὴν ἀντὶ καθαρᾶς καὶ ἀναπεπταμένης τῆς πρότερον,
15 τούτου δ᾽ αἴτιος ὁ τῷ πολέμῳ τὸν ἀπὸ τῆς χώρας ὄχλον c
εἰς τὰ τείχη καταχεάμενος καὶ πρὸς οὐδὲν ἀνθρώποις
τοσούτοις χρώμενος, ἀλλ᾽ ἐῶν ὥσπερ βοσκήματα καθειρ-
γμένους ἀναπίμπλασθαι φθορᾶς ἀπ᾽ ἀλλήλων καὶ μηδε-
μίαν μεταβολὴν μηδ᾽ ἀναψυχὴν ἐκπορίζων.

20 **35.** Ταῦτα βουλόμενος ἰᾶσθαι καί τι παραλυπεῖν τοὺς c
πολεμίους, ἑκατὸν καὶ πεντήκοντα ναῦς ἐπλήρου, καὶ
πολλοὺς καὶ ἀγαθοὺς ὁπλίτας καὶ ἱππεῖς ἀναβιβασάμενος,
ἔμελλεν ἀνάγεσθαι, μεγάλην ἐλπίδα τοῖς πολίταις καὶ
φόβον οὐκ ἐλάττω τοῖς πολεμίοις ἀπὸ τοσαύτης ἰσχύος
25 παρασχών. ἤδη δὲ πεπληρωμένων τῶν νεῶν καὶ τοῦ Περι- 2
κλέους ἀναβεβηκότος ἐπὶ τὴν ἑαυτοῦ τριήρη, τὸν μὲν ἥλιον
ἐκλιπεῖν συνέβη καὶ γενέσθαι σκότος, ἐκπλαγῆναι δὲ πάν-
336 S τας ὡς πρὸς μέγα σημεῖον. ὁρῶν οὖν ὁ Περικλῆς περί-

---

4 Thuc. 2, 47–53 Diod. 12, 45, 2. 58 ‖ 10 Thuc. 2; 17 Aristoph.
eq. 792sq. Andoc. fr. 4 (= Suda s. v. σκάνδιξ) ‖ 20 Thuc. 2,
56, 1 Diod. 12, 45, 3 ‖ 25 Thuc. 2, 28 Cic. rep. 1, 16, 25

[S(UMA =)Υ] **1.** 2 τοσούτου πολέμου S ‖ 3 προσηγόρευεν S |
εἰς
ὑπεναντιωθείη S ‖ 4 ἀνθρώποις Υ ‖ 8 πρὸς S πρὸς Υ: del. Rei. ‖
9 [ἀνα]πεισθέντες Cob. ‖ 10 χωρικοῦ U χωρητικοῦ MA ‖
11 ἐργάζεται Υ ‖ 13 ἠναγκασμένων Υ ‖ 22 καὶ¹ om. UA | ἱπ-
πέας Υ ‖ 24 ἔλαττον Υ

4*

φοβον τὸν κυβερνήτην καὶ διηπορημένον, ἀνέσχε τὴν
d χλαμύδα πρὸ τῆς ὄψεως αὐτοῦ, καὶ παρακαλύψας ἠρώ-
τησε, μή τι δεινὸν ἢ δεινοῦ τινος οἴεται σημεῖον· ὡς
δ᾽ οὐκ ἔφη, „τί οὖν" εἶπεν „ἐκεῖνο τούτου διαφέρει, πλὴν 47 L
ὅτι μεῖζόν τι τῆς χλαμύδος ἐστὶ τὸ πεποιηκὸς τὴν ἐπι- 5
σκότησιν;" ταῦτα μὲν οὖν ἐν ταῖς σχολαῖς λέγεται τῶν
φιλοσόφων.

3 Ἐκπλεύσας δ᾽ οὖν ὁ Περικλῆς οὔτ᾽ ἄλλο τι δοκεῖ τῆς
παρασκευῆς ἄξιον δρᾶσαι, πολιορκήσας τε τὴν ἱερὰν Ἐπίδαυρον ἐλπίδα παρασχοῦσαν ὡς ἁλωσομένην, ἀπέτυχε 10
διὰ τὴν νόσον. ἐπιγενομένη γὰρ οὐκ αὐτοὺς μόνον, ἀλλὰ
καὶ τοὺς ὁπωσοῦν τῇ στρατιᾷ συμμείξαντας προσδιέφθει-
e ρεν. ἐκ τούτου χαλεπῶς διακειμένους τοὺς Ἀθηναίους
4 πρὸς αὐτὸν ἐπειρᾶτο παρηγορεῖν καὶ ἀναθαρρύνειν. οὐ
μὴν παρέλυσε τῆς ὀργῆς οὐδὲ μετέπεισε πρότερον, ἢ τὰς 15
ψήφους λαβόντας ἐπ᾽ αὐτὸν εἰς τὰς χεῖρας καὶ γενομένους
κυρίους ἀφελέσθαι τὴν στρατηγίαν καὶ ζημιῶσαι χρήμασιν,
ὧν ἀριθμὸν οἱ τὸν ἐλάχιστον πεντεκαίδεκα τάλαντα, πεν-
5 τήκοντα δ᾽ οἱ τὸν πλεῖστον γράφουσιν. ἐπεγράφη δὲ τῇ δίκῃ
κατήγορος, ὡς μὲν Ἰδομενεὺς (FGrH 338 F 9) λέγει, Κλέων, 20
ὡς δὲ Θεόφραστος, Σιμμίας· ὁ δὲ Ποντικὸς Ἡρακλείδης
(fr. 47 Wehrli) Λακρατείδην εἴρηκε.

36. Τὰ μὲν οὖν δημόσια ταχέως ἔμελλε παύσεσθαι,
f καθάπερ κέντρον εἰς τοῦτον ἅμα ⟨τῇ⟩ πληγῇ τὸν θυμὸν
ἀφεικότων τῶν πολλῶν· τὰ δ᾽ οἰκεῖα μοχθηρῶς εἶχεν 25
αὐτῷ, κατὰ τὸν λοιμὸν οὐκ ὀλίγους ἀποβαλόντι τῶν ἐπι-
2 τηδείων, καὶ στάσει διατεταραγμένα πόρρωθεν. ὁ γὰρ

8 Thuc. 2, 56, 4 || 15 Thuc. 2, 65, 3 Diod. 12, 45, 5 [Demosth.]
26, 6 (802)

[S(UMA =)Υ] 2 χαλμύδα U | πρὸ τῶν ὄψεων S | 5 τι om. S ||
11 ἐπιγενομένης S || 12 συμπήξαντας Υ || 14 ἐπειρᾶτο U (ἐπ s. s.
m. 2) || 15 παρέλυσε SMA (sed π in ras. A): γὰρ ἔλυσε U | τῆς
ὀργῆς Blass (cf. Thuc. 2, 65, 1): τὴν ὀργὴν | μετέπεισε] γρ κατέ-
παυσε Sᵐ (m. 1) || 18 ὧν τὸν ἀριθμὸν S || 22 λακρατίδαν: em.
Kaiser || 23 παύεσθαι Υ || 24 τοῦτο Blass ταὐτὸν Orelli | τῇ
add. Cor. || 26 κατά τε τὸν Υ || 27 διατεταραγμένω S -μένων Υ:
em. Sauppe

48 L πρεσβύτερος αὐτοῦ τῶν γνησίων υἱῶν Ξάνθιππος, φύσει
τε δαπανηρὸς ὢν καὶ γυναικὶ νέᾳ καὶ πολυτελεῖ συνοικῶν,
Τεισάνδρου θυγατρὶ τοῦ Ἐπιλύκου, χαλεπῶς ἔφερε τὴν
τοῦ πατρὸς ἀκρίβειαν, γλίσχρα καὶ κατὰ μικρὸν αὐτῷ
5 χορηγοῦντος. πέμψας οὖν πρός τινα τῶν φίλων ἔλαβεν 3 172
337 8 ἀργύριον ὡς τοῦ Περικλέους κελεύσαντος. ἐκείνου δ᾽ ὕστε- 4
ρον ἀπαιτοῦντος, ὁ μὲν Περικλῆς καὶ δίκην αὐτῷ προσέλαχε, τὸ δὲ μειράκιον ὁ Ξάνθιππος ἐπὶ τούτῳ χαλεπῶς
διατεθεὶς ἐλοιδόρει τὸν πατέρα, πρῶτον μὲν ἐκφέρων ἐπὶ
10 γέλωτι τὰς οἴκοι διατριβὰς αὐτοῦ καὶ τοὺς λόγους οὓς
ἐποιεῖτο μετὰ τῶν σοφιστῶν. πεντάθλου γάρ τινος ἀκοντίῳ 5
πατάξαντος Ἐπίτιμον τὸν Φαρσάλιον ἀκουσίως καὶ κτείναντος, ἡμέραν ὅλην ἀναλῶσαι μετὰ Πρωταγόρου διαποροῦντα, πότερον τὸ ἀκόντιον ἢ τὸν βαλόντα μᾶλλον ἢ τοὺς
15 ἀγωνοθέτας κατὰ τὸν ὀρθότατον λόγον αἰτίους χρὴ τοῦ
πάθους ἡγεῖσθαι. πρὸς δὲ τούτοις καὶ τὴν περὶ τῆς γυναι- 6 b
κὸς διαβολὴν ὑπὸ τοῦ Ξανθίππου φησὶν ὁ Στησίμβροτος
(FGrH 107 F 11) εἰς τοὺς πολλοὺς διασπαρῆναι, καὶ ὅλως
ἀνήκεστον ἄχρι τῆς τελευτῆς τῷ νεανίσκῳ πρὸς τὸν
20 πατέρα διαμεῖναι τὴν διαφοράν· ἀπέθανε γὰρ ὁ Ξάνθιππος
ἐν τῷ λοιμῷ νοσήσας. ἀπέβαλε δὲ καὶ τὴν ἀδελφὴν ὁ 7
Περικλῆς τότε καὶ τῶν κηδεστῶν καὶ φίλων τοὺς πλείστους καὶ χρησιμωτάτους πρὸς τὴν πολιτείαν. οὐ μὴν 8
ἀπεῖπεν οὐδὲ προὔδωκε τὸ φρόνημα καὶ τὸ μέγεθος τῆς
25 ψυχῆς ὑπὸ τῶν συμφορῶν, ἀλλ᾽ οὐδὲ κλαίων οὔτε κηδεύων
οὔτε πρὸς τάφῳ τινὸς ὤφθη τῶν ἀναγκαίων, πρίν γε δὴ c
49 L καὶ τὸν περίλοιπον αὐτοῦ τῶν γνησίων υἱῶν ἀποβαλεῖν
Πάραλον. ἐπὶ τούτῳ δὲ καμφθείς, ἐπειρᾶτο μὲν ἐγκαρ- 9
τερεῖν τῷ ἤθει καὶ διαφυλάττειν τὸ μεγαλόψυχον, ἐπι-
30 φέρων δὲ τῷ νεκρῷ στέφανον ἡττήθη τοῦ πάθους πρὸς

[S(UMA =)Υ] 1 πρεσβύτατος: em. Blass ‖ 3 οἰσανδρου S
ἰσάιδρου Υ: em. Sint. cf. Andoc. 1, 117. 3, 29 ‖ 4 γλίσχρως C ‖
8 ὁ Ξάνθ. del. Cob. ‖ 11 ἐποίει Υ | τινος S: ἵππον Υ ‖ 12 ἐπιτιμίου
τοῦ φαρσαλίου Υ ‖ 14 μᾶλλον om. Υ ‖ 16 ἡγεῖσθαι Υ: γενέσθαι S
(num λέγεσθαι? Fuhr) ‖ 20 παραμεῖναι Υ ‖ 25. 26 οὔτε ... οὔτε
Blass: οὐδὲ ... οὐδὲ ‖ 27 υἱῶν om. Υ

τὴν ὄψιν, ὥστε κλαυθμόν τε ῥῆξαι καὶ πλῆθος ἐκχέαι δακρύων, οὐδέποτε τοιοῦτον οὐδὲν ἐν τῷ λοιπῷ βίῳ πεποιηκώς.

37. Τῆς δὲ πόλεως πειρωμένης τῶν ἄλλων στρατηγῶν εἰς τὸν πόλεμον καὶ ῥητόρων, οὐδεὶς βάρος ἔχων ἰσόρροπον οὐδ᾽ ἀξίωμα πρὸς τοσαύτην ἐχέγγυον ἡγεμονίαν 5 ἐφαίνετο· ποθούσης δ᾽ ἐκεῖνον καὶ καλούσης ἐπὶ τὸ βῆμα 338 S
d καὶ τὸ στρατήγιον, ἀθυμῶν καὶ κείμενος οἴκοι διὰ τὸ πένθος ὑπ᾽ Ἀλκιβιάδου καὶ τῶν ἄλλων ἐπείσθη φίλων
2 προελθεῖν. ἀπολογησαμένου δὲ τοῦ δήμου τὴν ἀγνωμο-
a. 430 σύνην τὴν πρὸς αὐτόν, ὑποδεξάμενος αὖθις τὰ πράγματα 10 καὶ στρατηγὸς αἱρεθείς, ᾐτήσατο λυθῆναι τὸν περὶ τῶν νόθων νόμον, ὃν αὐτὸς εἰσενηνόχει πρότερον, ὡς μὴ παντάπασιν ἐρημίᾳ διαδοχῆς [τὸν οἶκον] ἐκλίποι τοὔνομα καὶ
3 a. 451 τὸ γένος. εἶχε δ᾽ οὕτω τὰ περὶ τὸν νόμον. ἀκμάζων ὁ Περικλῆς ἐν τῇ πολιτείᾳ πρὸ πάνυ πολλῶν χρόνων καὶ 15 παῖδας ἔχων ὥσπερ εἴρηται γνησίους, νόμον ἔγραψε, μόνους Ἀθηναίους εἶναι τοὺς ἐκ δυεῖν Ἀθηναίων γεγονότας.
4 ἐπεὶ δὲ τοῦ βασιλέως τῶν Αἰγυπτίων δωρεὰν τῷ δήμῳ
e πέμψαντος τετρακισμυρίους πυρῶν μεδίμνους ἔδει διανέμεσθαι τοὺς πολίτας, πολλαὶ μὲν ἀνεφύοντο δίκαι τοῖς 20 νόθοις ἐκ τοῦ γράμματος ἐκείνου τέως διαλανθάνουσι καὶ 50 L παρορωμένοις, πολλοὶ δὲ καὶ συκοφαντήμασι περιέπιπτον. ἀπεκρίθησαν οὖν ἁλόντες ὀλίγῳ πεντακισχιλίων ἐλάττους, οἱ δὲ μείναντες ἐν τῇ πολιτείᾳ καὶ κριθέντες Ἀθηναῖοι μύριοι καὶ τετρακισχίλιοι καὶ τεσσαράκοντα τὸ πλῆθος 25
5 ἐξητάσθησαν. ὄντος οὖν δεινοῦ τὸν κατὰ τοσούτων ἰσχύ-

cap. 37 Thuc. 2, 65, 4 ‖ 11 Aristot. Ἀθπ. 26, 4. 42, 1. pol. 3, 5 p. 1278 a 30 sq. ‖ 18 schol. Aristoph. vesp. 716

[S(UMA =)Υ] 4 οὐδεὶς S: ὡς οὐδεὶς Υ ‖ 6 δ᾽ om. S ‖ 7 καί² Υ: δὲ καί S | κείμενος] καθήμενος Cob. ‖ 9 προσελθεῖν Υ ‖ 10 τὴν om. Υ ‖ 11 ᾐτήσατο S: εἰσηγήσατο Υ | ἀπολυθῆναι S ‖ 13 τὸν οἶκον del. Madvig | ἐκλείποι S ‖ 18 δωρεάς: em. Rei. ‖ 21. 22 διαλανθάνουσαι καὶ παρορώμεναι: em. Sauppe ‖ 23 ἀπεκρίθησαν Cor.: ἐπράθησαν Υ ἐπράχθησαν S (ἀπηλάθησαν Cob.) | δ᾽ οὖν S ‖ 26 τὸν S: τοῦ Υ | τοσοῦτον Υ

σαντα νόμον ὑπ' αὐτοῦ πάλιν λυθῆναι τοῦ γράψαντος, ἡ
παροῦσα δυστυχία τῷ Περικλεῖ περὶ τὸν οἶκον, ὡς δίκην
τινὰ δεδωκότι τῆς ὑπεροψίας καὶ τῆς μεγαλαυχίας ἐκεί- f
νης, ἐπέκλασε τοὺς Ἀθηναίους, καὶ δόξαντες αὐτὸν νεμε-
5 σητά τε παθεῖν ἀνθρωπίνων τε δεῖσθαι, συνεχώρησαν
ἀπογράψασθαι τὸν νόθον εἰς τοὺς φράτορας, ὄνομα θέμενον τὸ αὐτοῦ. καὶ τοῦτον μὲν ὕστερον ἐν Ἀργινούσαις 6
καταναυμαχήσαντα Πελοποννησίους ἀπέκτεινεν ὁ δῆμος
μετὰ τῶν συστρατήγων.

10 38. Τότε δὲ τοῦ Περικλέους ἔοικεν ὁ λοιμὸς λαβέσθαι 173
339 S λαβὴν οὐκ ὀξεῖαν ὥσπερ ἄλλων οὐδὲ σύντονον, ἀλλὰ βλη- a.429
χρᾷ τινι νόσῳ καὶ μῆκος ἐν ποικίλαις ἐχούσῃ μεταβολαῖς
διαχρωμένην τὸ σῶμα σχολαίως καὶ ὑπερείπουσαν τὸ
φρόνημα τῆς ψυχῆς. ὁ γοῦν Θεόφραστος (fr. 146 W.) ἐν 2
15 τοῖς Ἠθικοῖς διαπορήσας, εἰ πρὸς τὰς τύχας τρέπεται τὰ
ἤθη καὶ κινούμενα τοῖς τῶν σωμάτων πάθεσιν ἐξίσταται
τῆς ἀρετῆς, ἱστόρηκεν ὅτι νοσῶν ὁ Περικλῆς ἐπισκοπουμένῳ τινὶ τῶν φίλων δείξειε περίαπτον ὑπὸ τῶν γυναικῶν
τῷ τραχήλῳ περιηρτημένον, ὡς σφόδρα κακῶς ἔχων ὁπότε
20 καὶ ταύτην ὑπομένοι τὴν ἀβελτερίαν. ἤδη δὲ πρὸς τῷ τελευ- 3
51 L τᾶν ὄντος αὐτοῦ, περικαθήμενοι τῶν πολιτῶν οἱ βέλτιστοι b
καὶ τῶν φίλων οἱ περιόντες λόγον ἐποιοῦντο τῆς ἀρετῆς
καὶ τῆς δυνάμεως, ὅση γένοιτο, καὶ τὰς πράξεις ἀνεμε-
τροῦντο καὶ τῶν τροπαίων τὸ πλῆθος· ἐννέα γὰρ ἦν ἃ στρα-
25 τηγῶν καὶ νικῶν ἔστησεν ὑπὲρ τῆς πόλεως. ταῦθ' ὡς οὐκέτι 4
συνιέντος, ἀλλὰ καθῃρημένου τὴν αἴσθησιν αὐτοῦ, διελέ-
γοντο πρὸς ἀλλήλους· ὁ δὲ πᾶσιν ἐτύγχανε τὸν νοῦν προσ-
εσχηκώς, καὶ φθεγξάμενος εἰς μέσον ἔφη θαυμάζειν ὅτι
ταῦτα μὲν ἐπαινοῦσιν αὐτοῦ καὶ μνημονεύουσιν, ἃ καὶ

7 Xen. hell. 1, 5, 16. 6, 29. 7, 2–34 Schol. Ar. ran. 1196 ‖
10 Thuc. 2, 65, 6 Diod. 12, 46, 1 Athen. 5, 217e Max. Tyr. 7, 4 ‖
25 mor. 186d 543c Iulian. or. 3 p. 128 c. d. app. V. II 132 Ars. 318

[S(U M A ⸗) Υ] 1 +++ νόμον S: τὸν νόμον Υ ‖ ὑπ'] ὑπὲρ Holzapfel ‖ διαλυθῆναι Υ ‖ 3 τινὰ] ἱκανὴν Cob. ‖ 4 ἀνεμέσητα Rei. ‖
5 ἀνθρωπίνως Υ ‖ 7 τὸ S: τοῦ Υ (sed τὸ s. s. A) ‖ ἀργικνούσαις
S ‖ 10 δὲ ⟨καὶ⟩ Rei. ‖ 20 ὑπομένον U ‖ 21 παρακαθήμενοι C ‖
22 ⟨περὶ⟩ τῆς Cob. ‖ 26 καθημένου S

45

πρὸς τύχης ἐστὶ κοινὰ καὶ γέγονεν ἤδη πολλοῖς στρατη-
c γοῖς, τὸ δὲ κάλλιστον καὶ μέγιστον οὐ λέγουσιν. „οὐδεὶς
γάρ" ἔφη „δι᾽ ἐμὲ τῶν πολιτῶν [Ἀθηναίων] μέλαν ἱμάτιον
περιεβάλετο."

39. Θαυμαστὸς οὖν ὁ ἀνὴρ οὐ μόνον τῆς ἐπιεικείας καὶ 5
πραότητος, ἣν ἐν πράγμασι πολλοῖς καὶ μεγάλαις ἀπεχθείαις διετήρησεν, ἀλλὰ καὶ τοῦ φρονήματος, εἰ τῶν αὑτοῦ
καλῶν ἡγεῖτο βέλτιστον εἶναι τὸ μήτε φθόνῳ μήτε θυμῷ
χαρίσασθαι μηδὲν ἀπὸ τηλικαύτης δυνάμεως, μηδὲ χρή-
2 σασθαί τινι τῶν ἐχθρῶν ὡς ἀνηκέστῳ. καί μοι δοκεῖ τὴν 10
μειρακιώδη καὶ σοβαρὰν ἐκείνην προσωνυμίαν ἐν τοῦτο
ποιεῖν ἀνεπίφθονον καὶ πρέπουσαν, οὕτως εὐμενὲς ἦθος
καὶ βίον ἐν ἐξουσίᾳ καθαρὸν καὶ ἀμίαντον Ὀλύμπιον προσ- 340 S
d αγορεύεσθαι, καθάπερ τὸ τῶν θεῶν γένος ἀξιοῦμεν αἴτιον μὲν ἀγαθῶν, ἀναίτιον δὲ κακῶν πεφυκὸς ἄρχειν καὶ 15
βασιλεύειν τῶν ὄντων, οὐχ ὥσπερ οἱ ποιηταὶ συνταράτ-
τοντες ἡμᾶς ἀμαθεστάταις δόξαις ἁλίσκονται τοῖς αὑτῶν 52 L
μυθεύμασι, τὸν μὲν τόπον, ἐν ᾧ τοὺς θεοὺς κατοικεῖν
λέγουσιν, ἀσφαλὲς ἕδος καὶ ἀσάλευτον καλοῦντες, οὐ πνεύ-
μασιν, οὐ νέφεσι χρώμενον, ἀλλ᾽ αἴθρᾳ μαλακῇ καὶ φωτὶ 20
καθαρωτάτῳ τὸν ἅπαντα χρόνον ὁμαλῶς περιλαμπόμενον,
ὡς τοιαύτης τινὸς τῷ μακαρίῳ καὶ ἀθανάτῳ διαγωγῆς
μάλιστα πρεπούσης, αὐτοὺς δὲ τοὺς θεοὺς ταραχῆς καὶ
δυσμενείας καὶ ὀργῆς ἄλλων τε μεστοὺς παθῶν ἀποφαί-
e 3 νοντες, οὐδ᾽ ἀνθρώποις νοῦν ἔχουσι προσηκόντων. ἀλλὰ 25
ταῦτα μὲν ἴσως ἑτέρας δόξει πραγματείας εἶναι.

Τοῦ δὲ Περικλέους ταχεῖαν αἴσθησιν καὶ σαφῆ πόθον
Ἀθηναίοις ἐνειργάζετο τὰ πράγματα. καὶ γὰρ οἱ ζῶντος
βαρυνόμενοι τὴν δύναμιν ὡς ἀμαυροῦσαν αὐτούς, εὐθὺς

[S(UMA=)Υ] 1 τύχην: em. Ha. || 3 πολιτῶν Cob. Wil.:
ὄντων | Ἀθηναίων del. Cob. Wil. || 4 περιεβάλλετο U || 7.8 εἰ . . .
ἡγεῖτο Υ: εἰπὼν ὡς . . . ἡγοῖτο S || 10 ἀνηκέστων S || 11 σοβαρὰν
καὶ μειρακιώδη S | ἐν τούτῳ S || 13 Ὀλύμπιον προσαγορεύεσθαι del.
Rei || 18 μυθεύμασι S: ποιήμασι Υ || 19 οὐ Υ: οὔτε ⁎S || 20 αἴθραι
S: αἰθρίᾳ Υ || 20 μαλακῇ] μάλα Herw. cl. Hom. Od. 6, 44 ||
21 καθαρῷ Υ || 22 τινὸς om. Υ | τῷ | καρίῳ U || 28 ζῶντες S ||
29 αὐτοῖς Υ

ἐκποδὼν γενομένου πειρώμενοι ῥητόρων καὶ δημαγωγῶν ἑτέρων, ἀνωμολογοῦντο μετριώτερον ἐν ὄγκῳ καὶ σεμνότερον ἐν πραότητι μὴ φῦναι τρόπον. ἡ δ᾽ ἐπίφθονος ἰσχὺς 4 ἐκείνη, μοναρχία λεγομένη καὶ τυραννὶς πρότερον, ἐφάνη 5 τότε σωτήριον ἔρυμα τῆς πολιτείας γενομένη· τοσαύτη φορὰ καὶ πλῆθος ἐπέκειτο κακίας τοῖς πράγμασιν, ἣν ἐκεῖνος ἀσθενῆ καὶ ταπεινὴν ποιῶν ἀπέκρυπτε καὶ κατεκώλυεν ἀνήκεστον ἐν ἐξουσίᾳ γενέσθαι.

Comparison of Pericles and Fabius

28 (1). Οἱ μὲν οὖν βίοι τῶν ἀνδρῶν τοιαύτην ἔχου- [Σύγ-κρισις] σιν ἱστορίαν· ἐπεὶ δὲ καὶ πολιτικῆς καὶ πολεμικῆς ἀρετῆς πολλὰ καὶ καλὰ παραδείγματα καταλελοίπασιν ἀμφότε-
20 ροι, φέρε τῶν πολεμικῶν ἐκεῖνο πρῶτον λάβωμεν, ὅτι Περικλῆς μὲν ἄριστα πράττοντι τῷ δήμῳ καὶ μεγίστῳ b καθ᾽ αὑτὸν ὄντι καὶ μάλιστα πρὸς δύναμιν ἀκμάζοντι
373 S χρώμενος ὑπὸ κοινῆς ἂν δόξειεν εὐτυχίας καὶ ῥώμης πραγμάτων ἀσφαλὴς διαγενέσθαι καὶ ἄπταιστος, αἱ δὲ Φαβίου
25 πράξεις ἐν αἰσχίστοις καὶ δυσποτμοτάτοις καιροῖς ἀναδεξαμένου τὴν πόλιν οὐκ ἐπ᾽ ἀγαθοῖς ἀσφαλῆ διετήρησαν, ἀλλ᾽ ἐκ κακῶν εἰς βελτίω μετέστησαν. καὶ Περικλεῖ μὲν 2 αἱ Κίμωνος εὐπραξίαι καὶ τὰ Μυρωνίδου καὶ τὰ Λεωκράτους τρόπαια καὶ πολλὰ καὶ μεγάλα Τολμίδης κατορθῶν

[S(UMA =)Υ] 2 ἀνωμολόγουν A ‖ 4 λεγομένη Υ: γενομένη S ‖ 6 φθορά: em. Br. Sch. ‖ 8 ἐν om. Υ ‖

[(UMA =)Υ] 25 αἰσχίστοις] ἐσχάτοις Naber | δυσποτμωτάτοις M

⟨ἐν⟩εορτάσαι μᾶλλον καὶ ἐμπανηγυρίσαι στρατηγοῦντι
τὴν πόλιν ἢ κτήσασθαι πολέμῳ καὶ φυλάξαι παρέδωκε·
c 3 Φάβιος δ᾽ ὁρῶν πολλὰς μὲν φυγὰς καὶ ἥττας, πολλοὺς δὲ 92 L
θανάτους καὶ σφαγὰς αὐτοκρατόρων καὶ στρατηγῶν, λίμνας δὲ καὶ πεδία καὶ δρυμοὺς νεκρῶν στρατοπέδων πλή- 5
θοντας, αἵματι δὲ καὶ φόνῳ ποταμοὺς ἄχρι θαλάττης
ῥέοντας, [ἐν] τῷ καθ᾽ ἑαυτὸν ἐρρωμένῳ καὶ βεβηκότι τὴν
πόλιν ἀντιλαμβανόμενος καὶ ὑπερείδων οὐκ εἴασε τοῖς
4 ἐκείνων ὑποφερομένην πταίσμασι τελέως ἐκχυθῆναι. καίτοι δόξειεν ἂν οὐχ οὕτω χαλεπὸν εἶναι πόλιν ἐν συμφοραῖς 10
μεταχειρίσασθαι ταπεινὴν καὶ τοῦ φρονοῦντος ὑπ᾽ ἀνάγ-
d κης κατήκοον γενομένην, ὡς δι᾽ εὐτυχίαν ἐπηρμένῳ καὶ
σπαργῶντι [τῷ] δήμῳ χαλινὸν ἐμβαλεῖν ὕβρεως καὶ θρα-
5 σύτητος· ᾧ δὴ μάλιστα φαίνεται τρόπῳ Περικλῆς Ἀθηναίων περιγενόμενος. ἀλλὰ τῶν Ῥωμαίοις συμπεσόντων 15
τότε κακῶν τὸ μέγεθος καὶ τὸ πλῆθος ἰσχυρόν τινα γνώμην καὶ μέγαν ἔδειξεν ἄνδρα τὸν μὴ συγχυθέντα μηδὲ
προέμενον τοὺς αὑτοῦ λογισμούς.

29 (2). Καὶ Σάμῳ μὲν ὑπὸ Περικλέους ἁλούσῃ τὴν
Τάραντος ἔστι κατάληψιν ἀντιθεῖναι, καὶ νὴ Δί᾽ Εὐβοίᾳ 20
τὰς περὶ Καμπανίαν πόλεις· ἐπεὶ αὐτήν γε Καπύην οἱ περὶ
Φούλβιον καὶ Ἄππιον ὕπατοι κατέσχον. ἐκ δὲ παρατάξεως
a.233 e Φάβιος οὐ φαίνεται μάχῃ νενικηκώς, πλὴν ἀφ᾽ ἧς τὸν
πρότερον εἰσήλασε θρίαμβον, Περικλῆς δ᾽ ἐννέα τρόπαια 374 S
κατὰ γῆν καὶ κατὰ θάλατταν ἔστησεν ἀπὸ τῶν πολεμίων. 25
2 οὐ μὴν λέγεται τοιαύτη πρᾶξις Περικλέους οἵαν ἔπραξε
Φάβιος Μινούκιον ἐξαρπάσας Ἀννίβου καὶ διασώσας ἐντε-
λὲς στρατόπεδον Ῥωμαίων· καλὸν γὰρ τὸ ἔργον καὶ κοι-

---

23 cf. ad p. 48, 25

[UMA(= Υ)] 1 ἑορτάσαι: em. Steph. ‖ 2 φυλάξασθαι: em.
Rei. | παρέδωκε UA: παρέδωκαν M ‖ 5 στρατοπέδων del. Herw. ‖
7 ἐν del. Zie., ex correctura ἐρ ad ὁρμωμένῳ exstitisse ratus |
ἐρρωμένῳ Rei.: ὁρμωμένῳ libri ἡρμοσμένῳ Cor. ὡρμισμένῳ Sch. ‖
9 ἐκλυθῆναι Cor. cl. p. 69, 29 ‖ 13 τῷ del. Cor. ‖ 16 τινα] τὴν
Rei. τινα τὴν Cor. cl. p. 32, 9 ‖ 21 ἐπειδὴ τήν γε Li. ‖ 22 Φούλβιον Xy.: φούριον UA φρούριον M

νὸν ἀνδρείας ὁμοῦ καὶ φρονήσεως καὶ χρηστότητος· ὥσπερ
93 L αὖ πάλιν οὐδὲ σφάλμα λέγεται Περικλέους οἷον ἐσφάλη
Φάβιος διὰ τῶν βοῶν καταστρατηγηθεὶς ὑπ' Ἀννίβου,
λαβὼν μὲν αὐτομάτως καὶ κατὰ τύχην ὑπελθόντα τοῖς
5 στενοῖς τὸν πολέμιον, προέμενος δὲ νυκτὸς λαθόντα καὶ
μεθ' ἡμέραν βιασάμενον καὶ φθάσαντα μέλλοντος καὶ κρα- f
τήσαντα συλλαβόντος. εἰ δὲ δεῖ μὴ μόνον χρῆσθαι τοῖς 3
παροῦσιν, ἀλλὰ καὶ τεκμαίρεσθαι περὶ τοῦ μέλλοντος
ὀρθῶς τὸν ἀγαθὸν στρατηγόν, Ἀθηναίοις μὲν ὡς Περι-
10 κλῆς προέγνω καὶ προεῖπεν ἐτελεύτησεν ὁ πόλεμος· πολυπραγμονοῦντες γὰρ ἀπώλεσαν τὴν δύναμιν· Ῥωμαῖοι δὲ
παρὰ τοὺς Φαβίου λογισμοὺς ἐκπέμψαντες ἐπὶ Καρχηδονί-
ους Σκιπίωνα πάντων ἐκράτησαν, οὐ τύχῃ, σοφίᾳ δὲ τοῦ
στρατηγοῦ καὶ ἀνδρείᾳ κατὰ κράτος νικήσαντος τοὺς πολε-
15 μίους· ὥστε τῷ μὲν τὰ πταίσματα τῆς πατρίδος μαρτυ- 4 191
ρεῖν ὅτι καλῶς ἔγνω, τὸν δ' ὑπὸ τῶν κατορθωμάτων ἐλέγ-
χεσθαι τοῦ παντὸς ἐσφαλμένον. ἴση δ' ἁμαρτία στρατηγοῦ κακῷ περιπεσεῖν μὴ προσδοκήσαντα, καὶ κατορθώ-
ματος καιρὸν ἀπιστίᾳ προέσθαι· μία γὰρ ὡς ἔοικεν ἀπει-
20 ρία καὶ θράσος γεννᾷ καὶ θάρσος ἀφαιρεῖται. ταῦτα περὶ
τῶν πολεμικῶν.

30 (3). Τῆς δὲ πολιτείας μέγα μὲν ἔγκλημα τοῦ Περικλέους ὁ πόλεμος. λέγεται γὰρ ἐπακτὸς ὑπ' ἐκείνου γενέσθαι, Λακεδαιμονίοις ἐρίσαντος μὴ ἐνδοῦναι. δοκῶ δὲ μηδ'
25 ἂν Φάβιον Μάξιμον ἐνδοῦναί τι Καρχηδονίοις, ἀλλ' εὐγε-
νῶς ὑποστῆναι τὸν ὑπὲρ τῆς ἡγεμονίας κίνδυνον. ἡ μέντοι 2 b
375 8 πρὸς Μινούκιον ἐπιείκεια τοῦ Φαβίου καὶ πρᾳότης ἐλέγχει τὸν πρὸς Κίμωνα καὶ Θουκυδίδην στασιασμόν, ἄνδρας
ἀγαθοὺς καὶ ἀριστοκρατικοὺς εἰς φυγὴν ὑπ' αὐτοῦ καὶ
94 L τοὔστρακον ἐκπεσόντας. ἀλλ' ἤ γε δύναμις μείζων ἢ τοῦ
31 Περικλέους καὶ τὸ κράτος. ὅθεν οὐδ' ἄλλον εἴασεν ἐνδυσ- 3
τυχῆσαι τῇ πόλει κακῶς βουλευσάμενον στρατηγόν, ἀλλ'

[UMA(= Υ)] 2 οὐδὲ] οὐδὲν Cob. ‖ 14 κατὰ κράτος om. Μ ‖
15 μαρτυρεῖν Μ: μαρτυρεῖ UA ‖ 20 θάρσος UM: θράσος Α ‖
22 τοῦ] τῆς Rei. ⟨τῆς⟩ τοῦ Zie. cl. v. 30 ‖ 28 τὸν ⟨Περικλέους⟩
Rei. ⟨ἐκείνου⟩ Zie.

ἢ μόνος αὐτὸν ἐκφυγὼν Τολμίδης καὶ διωσάμενος βίᾳ
προσέπταισε Βοιωτοῖς· οἱ δ' ἄλλοι προσετίθεντο καὶ κατε-
κοσμοῦντο πάντες εἰς τὴν ἐκείνου γνώμην ὑπὸ μεγέθους
c 4 αὐτοῦ τῆς δυνάμεως. Φάβιος δὲ τὸ καθ' ἑαυτὸν ἀσφαλὴς
ὢν καὶ ἀναμάρτητος, τῷ πρὸς τὸ κωλύειν ἑτέρους ἀδυνάτῳ 5
φαίνεται λειπόμενος. οὐ γὰρ ἂν τοσαύταις συμφοραῖς
ἐχρήσαντο Ῥωμαῖοι Φαβίου παρ' αὐτοῖς ὅσον Ἀθήνησι
Περικλέους δυνηθέντος.

5 Καὶ μὴν τήν γε πρὸς χρήματα μεγαλοφροσύνην ὁ μὲν
τῷ μηδὲν λαβεῖν παρὰ τῶν διδόντων, ὁ δὲ τῷ προέσθαι 10
πολλὰ· τοῖς δεομένοις ἐπεδείξατο, λυσάμενος τοῖς ἰδίοις
6 χρήμασι τοὺς αἰχμαλώτους· πλὴν τούτων μὲν οὐ πολὺς
ἦν ἀριθμός, ἀλλ' ὅσον ἐξ τάλαντα. Περικλῆς δ' οὐκ ἂν
ἴσως εἴποι τις ὅσα καὶ παρὰ συμμάχων καὶ βασιλέων
d ὠφελεῖσθαι καὶ θεραπεύεσθαι παρόν, τῆς δυνάμεως διδού- 15
σης, ἀδωρότατον ἑαυτὸν καὶ καθαρώτατον ἐφύλαξεν.

7 Ἔργων γε μὴν μεγέθεσι καὶ ναῶν καὶ κατασκευαῖς
οἰκοδομημάτων, ἐξ ὧν ἐκόσμησεν ὁ Περικλῆς τὰς Ἀθήνας, οὐκ ἄξιον ὁμοῦ πάντα τὰ πρὸ τῶν Καισάρων φιλοτιμήματα τῆς Ῥώμης παραβαλεῖν, ἀλλ' ἔξοχόν τι πρὸς ἐκεῖ- 20
να καὶ ἀσύγκριτον ἡ τούτων ἔσχε μεγαλουργία καὶ μεγα-
λοπρέπεια τὸ πρωτεῖον.

[UMA(= Υ)] 1 ἢ] ὁ Rei. Cor. ‖ 2 μετεκοσμοῦντο Parisinus
1677 ‖ 4 καθ' αὑτὸν MA ‖ 12 τούτῳ: em. Rei. ‖ 16 καθαρὸν M ‖
22 τὸ del. Zie.

COMMENTARY

1.1–2.5

An elaborate introduction and justification for writing lives, ending with a specific application to Pericles and Fabius (2.5). The purpose is ethical: we must διώκειν τὸ βέλτιστον (1.2). Observing τὰ ἀπ' ἀρετῆς ἔργα stimulates us to imitation (1.4). (The digression in 1.4–2.2 demonstrates that other *erga* do not.) What is excellent *(τὸ καλόν)* molds character; an account of a fine deed furnishes a choice of conduct *(προαίρεσις)*. On the importance of this statement of purpose for an understanding of the *Pericles* see the Introduction, 2.1 and 2.5. On P.'s idea of mimesis here, especially the different values he assigns to the written and plastic arts, see Wardman 1974, 21–25. Plato's influence is strong: cf., e.g., *Rep.* 395Bff. The sentences are in P.'s richest style. On P.'s use of proems, see Stadter 1988.

1.1

ἔκγονα: an early emendation for the τέκνα of the manuscripts, which was considered unsuitable for animals. In fact P. uses both words of both humans and animals, most noticeably in *De am. prol.*, the incomplete declamation in which he urges humans to learn from animals to love their offspring (493A–497E). Ziegler rightly remarks, however, that ἔκγονα is made more likely by the intrusive note κυνῶν τε καὶ πιθήκων ἔκγονα found in line 8. The reading τ' ἔκγονα given by Blass might explain the origin of τέκνα, coming from τεκγονα, but P. does not seem to use τε in this position.

ἐν τοῖς κόλποις: used generally to refer to being held in the arms or lap: see *De tranq.* 472C, Herodas 6.102. Note that Alcibiades held a quail ἐν τῷ ἱματίῳ, *Alc.* 10.1. For apes as pets in Rome cf. Cic. *De div.* 1.34.76.

ἀγαπῶντας: here, "show affection for, pet."

ὁ Καῖσαρ: Probably Augustus, who passed laws encouraging fertility and was given to such comments (cf. Suetonius *Aug.* 34, 42). In the Egyptian papyri, Augustus is regularly called simply Καῖσαρ, less frequently Καῖσαρ θεός, Καῖσαρ θεοῦ υἱός, or other forms: see Preisigke 1931, 41–42 and Bureth 1964, 21–23. On the thought, cf. *Sol.* 7.3–4. A similar anecdote is ascribed to Masinissa, the king of Numidia (Athen. 12.518F–519A, citing Ptolemy Euergetes, *FGrHist* 234 F8); cf. for the thought Eubulus in his *Charites* (F115 K., *CAF* vol. 2). This sort of *chreia*, or apophthegm, is one of the techniques Plutarch uses to begin a life: see also *Pelopidas*, *Phocion*, and *Dio*. General *gnomai* also serve the same function, as in *Demosthenes*, *Pompey*, and *Aratus*. P. moves from the scene that Augustus confronted *(ἰδὼν)*, to his question *(ἠρώτησεν)*, to his purpose *(νουθετήσας)*. The object of *νουθετήσας* is τοὺς . . . καταναλίσκοντας.

φιλόστοργον: "affection," here especially toward children. Cf. *De am. prol.* and the comments at *Sol.* 7.3.

1.2

Ἆρ᾿ οὖν: introduces an affirmative inference in the form of a rhetorical question expecting an affirmative answer (Denniston, 46–51). It is particularly suitable for dialogue, and is found some 342 times in Plato. Plutarch uses it 46 times, but only here and at *Comp. Sol.–Publ.* 1.1 in the *Lives*. The emphatic position of φύσει ties the thought to τὸ φύσει φιλητικόν of the preceding sentence, making the progression from φιλητικὸν καὶ φιλόστοργον to φιλομαθὲς καὶ φιλοθέαμον.

φιλοθέαμον: "loving contemplation." Cf. *Symp.* 673B, τὸ φύσει φιλοθέαμον ἐν ἑκάστῳ καὶ φιλόσοφον τῆς ψυχῆς ἰδίαν χάριν ζητεῖ καὶ τέρψιν (the pleasure has earlier been defined as λόγοις . . . καὶ μαθήμασι καὶ ἱστορίαις καὶ τῷ ζητεῖν τι τῶν περιττῶν (673A).

λόγον ἔχει + inf. as subject = "it is reasonable to." Note the parallelism in καταναλίσκοντας and καταχρωμένους, and the chiastic position of καταχρωμένους and παραμελοῦντας before and after the cases they govern.

γάρ introduces an explanation of the difference between αἴσθησις (μὲν) and νοῦς (δὲ). The verb is implied in ἀνάγκη (ἐστὶ) τῇ αἰσθήσει θεωρεῖν πᾶν. For the idea see also *Demetr.* 1.2.

κατὰ πάθος: "passively," as κατὰ φύσιν means 'naturally.' See LSJ s.v. κατά VIII. The clause κατὰ πάθος κτλ. brings out the passive nature of sense perception.

τὴν πληγήν: Ziegler accepts this reading, taking τὴν πληγήν as object of ἀντιλαμβομένη, with the mss.; Flacelière prefers the emendation τῆς πληγῆς (dependent on πάθος). Ἀντιλαμβάνομαι is used in the technical sense, "apprehend, perceive."

ἄν τε = ἐάν τε.

With τῷ νῷ the construction shifts: ἕκαστος πέφυκεν χρῆσθαι τῷ νῷ καὶ τρέπειν ἑαυτὸν καὶ μεταβάλλειν πρὸς τὸ δοκοῦν. Note that the datives αἰσθήσει and νῷ are not syntactically parallel.

μεταβάλλειν: "change direction or purpose."

1.3

An explanatory parallel: the eye is excited and nourished by colors as the mind is by θεάματα. Again the construction shifts between the two parts: ὡς χρόα (ἐστὶ) πρόσφορος ὀφθαλμῷ / οὕτω δεῖ ἐπάγειν τὴν διάνοιαν θεάμασιν. The asymmetric parallel is continued in the relative clauses. The theory of sight implied here is similar to that described in Plato's *Timaeus* 45B–E, where the fire in the eye emits a stream, which is strengthened when it is reinforced by the light outside, so as to form a perception of an object. Plutarch defends the Platonic theory at *Symp.* 626C (the whole passage on presbyopia, 625C–E, and another on the evil eye, 681A–C, are interesting for Plutarch's thinking on sight) and employs it at *De E* 390B, *De def. or.* 433D–E, 436D, and *De facie* 921C–D. Plato's theory is rejected by Arist. *De sensu* 437a20–438b16; cf. *De anima* 2.418b9ff. Here Plato's notion is particularly appropriate because both Plato and Plutarch use vision as a parallel for the activity of the mind: see Plato *Rep.* 507B–508D and the account of the divided line that follows, 509A–511E, and other passages in the *Phaedrus* 251A–C and *Symposium* 219A. Cf. Malten 1961, 36–39. Sight was one of the most fascinating problems of perception for the philosopher: see the views summarized by Siegel 1970, 16–40, and Beare 1906, 9–

92. P. frequently refers to sight in similes: see Fuhrmann 1964, 104–5, 140n. 1.

χρόα: here as usually in discussions of sight, not "skin" but "color, surface appearance." Cf., e.g., Plato *Rep.* 507E.

ἀναζωπυρεῖ: "rekindle." Cf. Plato *Tim.* 45C, ὅτου τε ἂν αὐτό ποτε ἐφάπτηται, and similar expressions in P., *De def. or.* 433D *(συνεξάπτοντος)* and 433E *(ἐξάπτει)*. Plato uses the word ἀναζωπυρέω to describe the mind's excitement by astronomy at *Rep.* 527D, a passage that might also have been in P.'s mind.

1.4

ἱστορήσασιν: "to those who examine them."

τῶν γ' ἄλλων: a genitive of connection, "in other cases" (Smyth 1381). *Τὸ πραχθέν* is object of *θαυμάσαι*.

The opposition in χαίροντες . . . καταφρονοῦμεν is emphasised by chiasmus.

βαφεῖς: "dyers."

ἀνελευθέρους . . . βαναύσους: the word order is common in P.: see the Introduction, 2.8. The perfumer's trade had been forbidden to men by Solon: Athen. 13.612A, 15.687A. P.'s social bias is apparent. See also Dio Chrysostom 7.117, who criticizes dyers and perfumers, along with other occupations, for falsifying nature, an opinion already found in Hdt. 3.22.

1.5

Antisthenes: the follower of Socrates and author of Socratic dialogues; see the Introduction, 3.3.c. This is fragment 158 in Caizzi's edition.

Ismenias: a Theban, famous for his skill on the αὐλός, a reed flute, more similar to the oboe than to a modern flute. Plutarch refers to him also at *Demetr.* 1.6, *Reg. et imp. apophtheg.* 174E–F (repeated at *De Alex. fort. aut virt.* 334B and *Non posse* 1095F), and *Symp.* 632C.

The latter passage shows that he was a gentleman, though he played better than a hired performer. Two statesmen of this name are known in this period, one very wealthy (cf. *De tranq.* 472D, *De cup. div.* 527B, *Praec. ger. rep.* 823E; Plato *Meno* 90A) and a lifelong opponent of the Spartans, who was killed after the capture of the Cadmeia in 382 (*De gen. Socr.* 576A, *Pel.* 5.1, 3); the other probably his son, a friend of Pelopidas, captured with him in Thessaly in 368 (*Pel.* 27.1, 29.12; Diod. 15.71), and ambassador with him to Susa in 367 (*Artax.* 22.8). According to the anecdote of *Reg. et imp. apophtheg.* 174E–F, the fluteplayer was captured by Anteas, king of the Scythians, presumably in Philip II's campaign against Anteas in 339. Thus he could be the friend of Pelopidas, his son, or another person altogether. The fact that P. always identifies him as "the fluteplayer," however, suggests that he was not the friend of Pelopidas. Antisthenes criticized not fluteplaying as such, but serious work at it. The stricture would have been particularly appropriate for a member of a leading family of Thebes. Epaminondas, perhaps P.'s favorite hero, played the flute as a youth (cf. Nepos *Epam.* 2.1), but P. never mentions this in referring to him, stressing rather his philosophical studies. P. does not add that Ismenias introduced the habit of performing in outlandish costume and that his tunes were sung on triremes and at the fountains (cf. Pliny *NH* 37.6–7; Diog. Laert. 4.22).

1.6

Philip: king of Macedon and father of Alexander the Great. P. thinks a βασιλεύς should be a spectator, not a performer. Cf. also the anecdote of Pyrrhus, *Pyrrh.* 8.7: when asked which of two fluteplayers was the better, the king replied, "Polyperchon is the better general"; and the frequently quoted anecdote of Philip and the lyre-player (*De adul. et amic.* 67F, *Reg. et imp. apophtheg.* 179B, *De Alex. fort. aut virt.* 334C–D, *Symp.* 634 C–D): when the king argued with the musician on musical theory, the man replied, "I hope that you won't be in such a bad way, king, that you would know more about this than I do." The Roman emperors were also called βασιλεύς, so it is relevant to quote here an interesting comment on the emperor Nero's reputation as a musical performer in the myth in *De ser. num. vind.* 567F: Nero is about to be punished for his crimes by reincarnation as a viper, when by divine command he is made a frog instead, ᾠδικόν τι . . . περὶ ἕλη καὶ λίμνας ζῷον, since he had freed Greece. His good deeds permitted him to continue singing, though in a lower state!

2.1–4

P. contrasts the effects of attention to the fine arts and attention to virtue. For an overview of P.'s views on art see Svoboda 1934. Plutarch clearly enjoyed the arts of music, poetry, painting, and sculpture (cf., e.g., *Symp.* 673C–674C), but subordinated them to moral values (*De tranq.* 470A, 477C, *An seni* 786B–C). P. has no doubt that philosophy and virtue are more important than works of art, because the latter are simply enjoyed by the senses, whereas the former move one to virtuous action: cf. *Max. cum princ.* 776C–D: οὐκ "ἀνδριαντοποιός" ἐστιν ὁ τῆς φιλοσοφίας λόγος, "ὥστ' ἐλινύοντα ποιεῖν ἀγάλματ' ἐπ' αὐτᾶς βαθμίδος ἑσταότα," κατὰ Πίνδαρον· ἀλλ' ἐνεργὰ βούλεται ποιεῖν ὧν ἂν ἅψηται καὶ πρακτικὰ καὶ ἔμψυχα καὶ κινητικὰς ὁρμὰς ἐντίθησι καὶ κρίσεις ἀγωγοὺς ἐπὶ τὰ ὠφέλιμα καὶ προαιρέσεις φιλοκάλους καὶ φρόνημα καὶ μέγεθος μετὰ πραότητος καὶ ἀσφαλείας. . . . In this case he is being purposely provocative, using the example of the most famous Greek sculptors to make his point more effectively.

2.1

The chiastic order of the genitives renders the sentence more artful: ἡ αὐτουργία τῶν ταπεινῶν παρέχεται τὸν πόνον (ὡς) μάρτυρα τῆς ῥαθυμίας. Note the use of pejorative words to characterize the arts (ταπεινῶν, ἀχρήστοις) and the exclusion of physical objects from τὰ καλά.

εὐφυής: "of a temperament naturally noble, given to virtue." Cf. *De aud.* 47A and *Galb.* 23.2. The word is a favorite of Plato's, where it combines both the senses of "clever, quick to learn" (cf. *Phaedr.* 270A, quoted at 8.2) and "noble, fine."

τὸν ἐν Πίσῃ . . . Πολύκλειτος: The statue of Zeus at Olympia (in the district of Pisa) by Phidias and that of Hera at Argos by Polyclitus were considered masterpieces of the art (cf. Aemilius Paullus' remark, "Phidias has sculpted the Zeus of Homer," *Aem.* 28.5). Dio Chrysostom, P.'s contemporary, suggested that the plastic arts, and especially the Zeus of Phidias, could lift man to higher things and give him an idea of the divine (12.44–46), and much of the speech is given to a praise of Phidias' art. On Phidias see below at 13.6. Polyclitus of Argos, his contemporary, was famous also for his Doryphoros and Diadoumenos. Sculptors in antiquity were considered craftsmen and not essentially different from stonecutters. Cf. 3.4, τεχνιτῶν, and Lucian *Somnium* 14. Note that Plato would have excluded all who work with their hands from citizen rights in his republic, and Aristotle thought artisans incapable of virtue (*Pol.* 1319a28). Cf. Schweitzer 1963, esp. 27–40. Seneca (*Ep.* 88.18) excluded painters and sculptors from the liberal arts as *luxuriae ministri*, an attitude that P. must have shared to some extent. Cf. Brunt 1973.

Anacreon: the sixth-century lyric poet, cited at 27.4 and *Amat.* 751A and named along with Sappho at *Mul. virt.* 243B. His reputation as an erotic poet led Dio Chrysostom to eliminate him, along with Sappho, from the education of a king (*Or.* 2.28). Plutarch's very limited references to him seem to indicate less a lack of knowledge of his works, which were frequently quoted at dinner parties (cf. the citation of one of the Anacreonteia in Gellius, *NA* 19.9), than the sense that their content was inappropriate to his own writings. Cf. Schläpfer 1950, 32.

Philemon: the writer of New Comedy, third and second century. When he had mocked Magas, the stepson of Ptolemy I, in a play, Magas threatened him with execution but then sent him a ball and dice as if he were a child (*De coh. ira* 458A; cf. *De virt. mor.* 449E). Apuleius considered him rather risqué and biting. Some editors have found his name out of place here and have suggested instead Philetas, a Hellenistic poet, or Hipponax, the iambic writer of the sixth century, but neither seems an improvement.

Archilochus: the seventh-century elegiac and iambic poet, famous for his biting invective, and frequently quoted by P., although he criticizes his license and puerility (*Cat. Min.* 7.2). Cf. Schläpfer 1950, 30–31. All three of these poets were known for lascivious or satiric content, and this is probably the reason for their inclusion here. Rather tendentiously, P. does not compare the sculptors with more serious poets.

2.2

ὅθεν: "for which reason"; cf. 3.4, 13.4.

μιμητικὸς . . . ζῆλος: repeats 1.4, ζῆλον . . . εἰς μίμησιν, summing up the point of the digression.

ἀνάδοσις: "a sprouting up, or bursting forth" (not digestion, as LSJ explains this passage).

ἀλλ’ ἥ γ’ ἀρετή returns to the main subject. ἀλλὰ . . . γε is frequent, especially in Plato, to define more sharply the idea introduced (Denniston, 119).

ταῖς πράξεσιν is dative of means with διατίθησιν, "disposes (one)." P. gives us in his *Lives* examples of men admiring and wishing to emulate the ἀρετή of others: Theseus and Heracles (*Thes.* 6.8–9), Themistocles and Miltiades (*Them.* 3.3–5). Cf. Sallust, *Bell. Jug.* 4.5.

2.3

Another comparison: τὰ μὲν ἐκ τύχης ἀγαθά and τὰ δ’ ἀπ’ ἀρετῆς are appreciated and used in different ways. Cf. on this contrast P.'s declamations *On the Luck of the Romans* and *On the Luck and Virtue of Alexander*, as well as frequent comments in the *Lives*.

2.4

Note the stress on πρακτικῶς, πρακτικήν, "active," continuing the previous πράξεσιν, πράξεις.

ἠθοποιοῦν: the neut. part., modifying καλόν.

προαίρεσιν παρεχόμενον: τὸ καλόν does more than invite to imitation; it produces a moral decision or purpose (cf. *Max. cum princ.* 776C–D, quoted at the head of this chapter).

ἠθοποιοῦν οὐ τῇ μιμήσει, ἀλλὰ τῇ ἱστορίᾳ παρεχόμενον: "not affecting character in the observer by an imitation, but by furnishing a moral purpose by the investigation of an action." On the meaning of προαίρεσις for P. see Wardman 1974, 107–15. P. sees the element of conscious choice as central to the life of virtue, both for his subjects and for his readers.

2.5

οὖν introduces the conclusion: because of the foregoing, P. writes *Lives*, in which one can behold ἀρετή in action.

τῇ περὶ τοὺς βίους ἀναγραφῇ: as regularly, P. speaks of himself as a writer, not a speaker. Cf. below, ἐκ τῶν γραφομένων, and 24.12, κατὰ τὴν γραφήν.

βιβλίον: the *Lives* were written in pairs, each pair composing a book. On the notion of combining lives in this way, and specifically on the comparison of Pericles and Fabius, the virtues of πραότης and δικαιοσύνη seen in the two heroes, and the position of this book in the collection of *Lives*, see the Introduction, 1.3, 2.2.

δέκατον: predicate. The fifth pair was *Demosthenes–Cicero*, the twelfth *Dion–Brutus*.

συντετάχαμεν: "compose."

Fabius: that P. identifies Fabius as the one who fought with Hannibal is an indication that he thought that his chief audience would be Greek.

περιέχον: "encompassing," modifying βιβλίον.

κατά τε: correlative with καὶ τῷ δύνασθαι . . . γενομένων.

πραότητα: not meekness, but the ability to control one's emotions, self-restraint.

δήμων: refers to both the Athenian and the Roman populace; συναρχόντων especially to Minucius Felix, Fabius' impatient *magister equitum* when he was dictator.

3.1–7

Family, birth, and physical appearance.

3.1

γάρ: explanatory γάρ, after γραφομένων, cf. Denniston, 59; here introducing the body of the *Life*.

φυλῶν, δήμων: Athenian citizens after the reforms of Clisthenes at the end of the sixth century were distributed among ten tribes (φυλαί) made up from about 139 demes (δῆμοι), small local districts (villages or city wards) that were the basis of many aspects of political life. Cf. Arist. *Ath. pol.* 21; Traill 1975, esp. 73–81 (on demes).

Ἀκαμαντίδης: the adjective for the tribe Ἀκαμαντίς, named for the legendary Acamas, son of Theseus.

Χολαργεύς: the deme was Cholargus, on the northwest outskirts of Athens, near the modern Kato Liosia (Traill 1975, 47).

οἴκου: the immediate family, with an implication of wealth.

γένους: family in the sense of ancestors.

κατ' ἀμφοτέρους: sc. γονέας, "on both sides."

3.2

Xanthippus: at the battle against the Persians at Mycale in 479 (Hdt. 9.96–101), Xanthippus was *stratēgos* of the Athenians (Hdt. 7.33, 8.131, Diod. 11.34.2), although Leotychidas the Spartan was admiral of the fleet (Hdt. 9.90.1). Xanthippus was chief prosecutor of Miltiades in 489 (Hdt. 6.136), but five years later was himself ostracized (Arist. *Ath. pol.* 22). A number of ostraka with his name have been found, including an elegiac couplet: Χσάνθ[ιππον τόδε] φεσὶν ἀλειτερὸν πρυτάνειον / τὄστρακ[ον 'Αρρί]φρονος παῖδα μά[λ]ιστ' ἀδικεῖν, which perhaps means, "This ostrakon says that Xanthippus son of Arriphron does most wrong of all the damned leaders," although its interpretation has been disputed. Cf. Raubitschek 1947; Wilhelm 1949; ML, p. 42; Figueira 1986; and Merkelbach 1986. He returned with Aristides and others before the battle of Salamis, was elected a general for 479, and participated in an embassy to Sparta. After the victory of Mycale he took Sestos for the Athenians, and then disappears from the record. He and his experiences in politics would certainly have had a major influence on Pericles. See in general *RE* s.v. Xanthippos 6, IXA, 2 (1967) 1343–46. On Pericles' family see Davies, *APF* 455–60 and his table I. Xanthippus would have married Agariste shortly after 500 B.C. There may already have been a marriage relation between the two families: see Davies, addenda.

ἔγγονον: "granddaughter or descendant." (From ἐκ-γονος, but later distinguished from it: see Allen 1974, 36–37. Note ἔκγονα at 1.1 in the sense of "offspring." But our mss. are unreliable.) P. is in error here, since she was in fact Clisthenes' niece. It is through her that Pericles can be called an Alcmeonid (cf. Hdt. 6.131). See the simplified family tree in figure 1.

ὃς ἐξήλασε: Herodotus (5.62–64) credits the expulsion of the tyrant Hippias in 510 to the Alcmeonids generally, not solely to Clisthenes, but Clisthenes was the leader in the strife that followed with the partisans of Isagoras, who were supported by King Cleomenes of Sparta. When Cleomenes and Isagoras were defeated, Clisthenes introduced a series of reforms that laid the basis for the fifth-century democracy, although their exact nature and purpose is much disputed: see Hdt. 5.69 and Arist. *Ath. pol.* 20–21 with Rhodes, *CAAP* ad loc.; Forrest 1966, 191–203; Hignett, *HAC* 124–58; Traill 1975; Andrewes 1977.

The late antique rhetor Sopatros, in preparing a specimen defense of Alcibiades, misread this sentence and attached the relative clause to Xanthippus, making him a tyrant-slayer and legal reformer: see Russell 1983, 127. He provides an interesting example of the reading public of P. in later centuries.

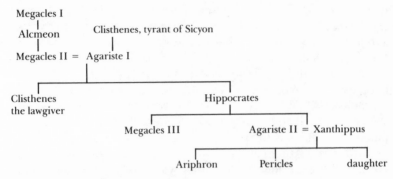

Figure 1. Pericles' Alcmeonid ancestry.

ἔθετο: "to make laws," LSJ s.v., A.V. The middle voice is used when the lawgiver himself is subject to the law.

ἄριστα κεκραμένην: κεράννυμι, used of blending wine, is figuratively applied to climate, personality, or, as here, constitution, in the sense "temperate, well-balanced." Cf. von Fritz 1954, 76–95.

σωτηρίαν: referring, of course, to the victory in the Persian Wars. Clisthenes' constitution was much admired in later years: see e.g. Arist. *Ath. pol.* 29.3.

3.3

P. found this dream in Hdt. 6.131.2: [᾽Αγαρίστη] ἔγκυος ἐοῦσα εἶδε ὄψιν ἐν τῷ ὕπνῳ, ἐδόκεε δὲ λέοντα τεκεῖν· καὶ μετ᾽ ὀλίγας ἡμέρας τίκτει Περικλέα Ξανθίππῳ. The lion is an image for a tyrant or strong man in the city: cf. Hdt. 5.92.3 (Cypselus of Corinth); Ar. *Knights* 1037 (Cleon), *Frogs* 1431 (Alcibiades). Val. Max. 7.2.ext. 7 mistakenly has the *Frogs* passage spoken by Pericles rather than by Aeschylus. The passage in Herodotus is clearly portentous, although scholars disagree as to whether it is favorable or hostile: Herodotus probably wanted it that way. Cf. Fornara 1971b, 53–54.

Pericles was born ca. 498–94, as he was choregus (producer) of Aeschylus' *Persians* in 473/72 and prosecuted Cimon ca. 463 (cf.

note to 10.6 and Arist. *Ath. pol.* 27.1, ἔτι νέος ὤν) but took no part in the Persian Wars. He would have been at least thirty when as *stratēgos* he took a fleet of fifty ships beyond the Chelidonian islands (*Cim.* 13.4), after the peace of Callias (which I place in the 460s; cf. note to 12.2).

τὰ μὲν ἄλλα τὴν ἰδέαν: two successive accusatives of respect, a general and a particular (Smyth 1601b,c).

προμήκη δὲ τῇ κεφαλῇ: "with an elongated head." Dat. of respect (Smyth 1516). Note the ABA word order, adj.-noun-adj. P. and the authors he quotes here are our only evidence for anything unusual in Pericles' appearance.

3.4

εἰκόνες: there survive only several marble busts, copies of the bronze statue by Cresilas, a contemporary. The head in fact wears a helmet, which from its angle might be thought to conceal an oddly shaped head. See frontispiece of this volume; Richter 1965, 102–4 and plates 429–47; Robertson 1975b, 1:335–37; Boardman 1985, 206. It is uncertain whether statues at this time were actually considered portraits. The general with helmet was a common type, and P.'s inference that it was purposely chosen because of Pericles' head shape is otherwise unsupported. There is a close parallel in the fifth-century bronze statues from Riace: both heads show notable elongation. Apparently it was a standard feature of helmeted bronze statues, making it easier to support the helmet. Cf. Cohen 1985. Cresilas' statue perhaps was nude, like the Riace statues, and held a spear. The inscription on the base of the statue is still partially preserved: . . . Περ]ικλέος / . . . Κρεσ]ίλας ἐποίε (*IG* I^2 528). Raubitschek (1973–74) suggests that the name Xanthippus be restored in the first line, and that the inscription indicates that Pericles' son erected the statue during Pericles' lifetime. Pausanias (1.25.1, 28.2) saw a statue of Pericles on the Acropolis, near the Propylaea, which may have been the one known to P. On the importance of its location see Hoelscher 1975.

τεχνιτῶν: used even of famous sculptors: cf. 2.1.

οἱ δ' Ἀττικοὶ ποιηταί: here, only the comic poets.

σχινοκέφαλον: σχῖνος = σκίλλα, the squill or sea onion. This plant, *Urginea maritima*, is notable for its bulb, which is ovoid, very large—up to 6 inches (15 cm) in diameter—and protrudes from the ground. The bulb may weigh up to 15 pounds (7 kg). "Onion-head" was perhaps just a general term of abuse, like "egghead," and with as much anatomical accuracy. The word is used by Cratinus F71 K. = 73 K.A., quoted by P. at 13.10.

3.5

Cratinus (F240 K. = 258 K.A., F111 K. = 118 K.A.): see the Introduction, 3.1.e. Both the *Chirons* and the *Nemesis* concerned Pericles and contemporary politics under mythological guise. In both cases Pericles is Zeus (cf. also 13.10): in the *Chirons* he is the son of Cronus by Faction (instead of Rhea) and a tyrant. Tyranny became a standard political slogan against Pericles' influence in Athens: see 16.1. The *Chirons* passage is from a chorus, and in a dactylo-epitrite meter, which was occasionally used in Old Comedy (see Dale 1968, 178–194, and, e.g., *Knights* 1264–73 = 1290–99). *PCG* analyzes it as: iamb choriamb / paroemiac / bacchiac cretic bacchiac / prosodiac (or -D) / incertus. It apparently was followed by the fragment quoted at 24.9.

κεφαληγερέταν: a comic distortion of νεφεληγερέτα, "the cloud-gatherer," a Homeric epithet of Zeus (e.g., *Il.* 1.511). Ὅν . . . θεοὶ καλέουσιν is also Homeric (e.g., *Il.* 1.403).

μόλ': for μόλε in invocations of the gods; cf. Ar. *Lys.* 1263, 1298; Eurip. *Bacch.* 553, 583.

ξένιε: a regular epithet of Zeus (e.g., *Od.* 9.271): "protector of guest-friends, visitors."

καραϊέ: Meineke's emendation, accepted by Ziegler and *PCG*. (S has κάριε, Y has μακάριε.) Zeus Karaios was worshiped in Boeotia (see *RE* XA, 1 [1972] 319 and suppl. XV [1978] 1459; Roesch 1982, 112–17), but here Cratinus would be making a pun on κάρα. Flacelière accepts Kock's suggestion καράνιε, a distortion of κεραύνιος, "of the thunderbolt"; for this epithet see *RE* XA, 1 (1972) 322–23 and suppl. XV (1978) 1461. The word κάριε, instead, would remind the audience of Zeus Karius, who was worshiped by the family of Isagoras at Athens, according to Herodotus (5.66.1). The verse is part of an iambic trimeter. Webster 1949, 114–15 argues that the actor of Zeus-Pericles wore a portrait mask of Pericles in these plays, so that the joke would be clear; the difficulties in this theory are explored by Dover 1967.

3.6

Teleclides (F44 K.): see the Introduction, 3.1.g. P. quotes two passages, introducing them by ποτὲ μὲν . . . , ποτὲ δὲ . . . (cf. the same method of introducing two passages at *De aud.* 24F). Ziegler's text (followed by Flacelière), which makes the two phrases part of the quotation, should be corrected. We cannot be certain of the exact form of the citations, as P. has placed them in indirect discourse. Cf. the change to indirect discourse at 8.4 (Ar. *Ach.* 531). However, καρηβαροῦντα and μόνον . . . ἐξανατέλλειν seem to reflect the original words, if not the original forms. For a restoration cf. Magnien 1907.

ἐν τῇ πόλει: "on the acropolis"; cf. LSJ s.v. I.1.

καρηβαροῦντα: "with a heavy head, with a headache." P. sees an allusion to Pericles' outsize head. Sauppe 1863 suggested that the parallel is to Zeus giving birth to Athena. Cf. Lucian *Dial. deor.* 13 (8) (Zeus to Hephaistos), ἀπόλλυμαι γὰρ ὑπὸ τῶν ὠδίνων, αἵ μοι τὸν ἐγκέφαλον ἀναστρέφουσιν. The form of the word is iambic and cannot fit the anapests of the following citation, unless it is emended to καρηβαριῶντα, from καρηβαριάω, found in Ar. frag. 792 K. = 832 K.A.

μόνον . . . ἐξανατέλλειν is anapestic, probably the last two dimeter lines of an anapestic run such as are frequent in Aristophanes (e.g., *Knights* 834–35, which also uses indirect discourse, as Plutarch's quotation does).

ἑνδεκακλίνου: "large enough to hold eleven couches." Rooms were measured by the number of couches they could contain. Xenophon speaks of δεκάκλινος στέγη (*Oec.* 8.13). Cf. *Symp.* 679B (thirty-couch rooms!) and Athen. 2.47F–48A. The line compares Pericles, who gives birth to a tumult (presumably the Peloponnesian War), to Zeus, who gave birth to Athena from his head.

ἐξανατέλλειν: "cause to spring up from."

3.7

Eupolis (F93 K., F115 K.A.): see the Introduction, 3.1.h. Someone (Pyronides? cf. 24.10 and note to F115 K.A.) is commenting on those who have been brought back from the dead. The line is iambic trimeter.

δημαγωγῶν: apparently not pejorative: "leaders of the people."

ὅ τί περ κεφάλαιον: "that man who is the true head of those below." Ὅ τί περ intensifies the following word: see Ar. *Eccl.* 53, ὅ τί πέρ ἐστι ὄφελος. P. thinks Eupolis is again mocking Pericles' head.

4–6

Chapters 4–6 treat the conventional topic of education, with some remarks on character, as is customary. Note, however, that Damon (4.1–4) apparently influenced Pericles only in the 440s and 430s; that Zeno (4.5) came to Athens ca. 450, when Pericles was about forty-five; and that Anaxagoras might well not have come to Athens until the mid- or late 470s, when Pericles was already twenty years old. That is, P. is here speaking of cultural influences on the mature Pericles, rather than of his boyhood teachers (contrast, e.g., *Alc.* 2–7; *Alex.* 5.7–8.5). Moreover, the men do not seem to be treated in chronological order. The names of the teachers derive from several passages in Plato. Wardman 1974, 211–20, discusses the recurrent theme of the philosopher advising the statesman in the *Lives*. Cf. also the fragment of P.'s treatise *Philosophers and Princes* (*Max. cum princ.* 776A–779C).

P. does not here report the story he mentions elsewhere, that Pericles met with Socrates in the house of Simon the shoemaker (*Max. cum princ.* 776B; cf. D. B. Thompson 1960 and Hock 1976).

The notion that Pericles was a special patron of the Sophists, and chiefly responsible for the intellectual climate of Athens, seen most recently in Kerferd 1981, 18–22, goes far beyond the evidence of P. and our other sources. For other references to Pericles' ties with philosophers see 8.1, 16.7–9, 24.5, 32.2, 32.5, 35.2, 36.5.

4.1

τῶν μουσικῶν: τὰ μουσικά was an essential part of ancient Athenian education: see Marrou 1964, 69–70, and in general W. D. Anderson 1966 as well as P.'s account in *Them.* 2.4–5. Note that Alexander the Great had learned to play the lyre (*Per.* 1.6), as had Alcibiades (*Alc.* 2.5–6). The work *De musica* ascribed to P. is not by him.

Damon: the son of Damonides, frequently cited from Plato on as a musical theorist (fragments in *FVS* 1:381–84, no. 37; cf. Lasserre 1954, 74ff.; Guthrie, *HGP* 3:35n.1). His theories, however, had strong ethical and political implications: see Plato *Rep.* 3.400A, 4.424B–C; *Lach.* 180D; W. D. Anderson 1966, 74–81. He is presented as teacher or companion of Pericles in [Plato] *Alc. I*, 118C; Isoc. 15.235; cf. Plut. *Arist.* 1.7. The statements made here as to his political interests and ostracism have been supported by the discovery of two ostraka, later than ca. 450 and apparently written by the same hand, reading Δάμον Δαμονίδο (*MDAI(A)* 40 [1915] 20–21, *IG* I²:912; F. W. Hamdorf, in Hoepfner 1976, 210, no. K100). See figure 2, this volume. He was active in the latter half of the fifth century, apparently only associating with Pericles when the latter was an old man, if we can trust *Alc. I*, 118C: (Alcibiades on Pericles' knowledge of politics) λέγεταί γέ τοι, ὦ Σώκρατες, οὐκ ἀπὸ τοῦ αὐτομάτου σοφὸς γεγονέναι, ἀλλὰ πολλοῖς καὶ σοφοῖς συγγεγονέναι, καὶ Πυθοκλείδῃ καὶ Ἀναξαγόρᾳ· καὶ νῦν ἔτι τηλικοῦτος ὢν Δάμωνι σύνεστιν αὐτοῦ τούτου ἕνεκα. His father, Damonides, was also an advisor to Pericles (9.2, Arist. *Ath. pol.* 27.4). According to *Ath. pol.*, Damonides also was ostracized. Many scholars consider two ostracisms in the same family highly unlikely and argue that only one politician, Damon, is meant in both cases (see Rhodes, *CAAP* on 27.4). More likely, Aristotle has made a mistake in referring the son's ostracism to the father, and both father and son were advisors. If Damon was the man mentioned by Andocides (1.16) as a husband of a certain Agariste, whose name reveals her as an Alcmeonid, he was a relative by marriage of Pericles. See Mooren 1948, 87–108; Raubitschek 1955a; Davies, *APF* 383; Schachermeyr 1969; Meister 1973.

βραχύνοντας: i.e., Δάμων from δαμάω, not Δᾶμων, a Doric form for Δήμων, related to δῆμος. The explanation may come from a comic scholion or a book of κωμῳδούμενοι: cf. the references in 4.4. P. considers the quantity of syllables the special sphere of the γραμματικός, or literature teacher: cf. 474A, 947E. The name itself is not unusual.

ἐκφέρειν: "pronounce"; cf. LSJ s.v. II.9.

παρά: "in the school of, with (as a student)."

Pythoclides: named together with Damon in Plato *Alc. I* 118C as an associate of Pericles. The work of Aristotle referred to by Plutarch is unknown (we now know that it is not *Ath. pol.*, to which the citation was assigned by Rose 1886, fr. 401). Many works of Aristotle have been lost, but it is possible that P. has simply confused his source here, and he is thinking of the Platonic passage. About all we know of Pythoclides of Ceos is that he was a musician and a Pythagorean (Plato *Prot.* 316E; schol. to *Alc. I* 118C).

4.2

σοφιστής: the word still had a general sense in Pericles' day, applying to knowledgeable men and to professional teachers, especially those who considered ethical or political matters. See Guthrie, *HGP* 3:27–34. P. uses the term regularly to refer to orators or political advisors who are not true philosophers, apparently the sense here. For his understanding of the fifth-century term see *Them.* 2.6, on Mnesiphilus, who was not a ῥήτωρ or one of the "physical philosophers," ἀλλὰ τὴν τότε καλουμένην σοφίαν, οὖσαν δὲ δεινότητα πολιτικὴν καὶ δραστήριον σύνεσιν, ἐπιτήδευμα πεποιημένου . . . ἣν οἱ μετὰ ταῦτα δικανικαῖς μείξαντες τέχναις καὶ μεταγαγόντες ἀπὸ τῶν πράξεων τὴν ἄσκησιν ἐπὶ τοὺς λόγους, σοφισταὶ προσηγορεύθησαν. At 36.4 he refers generally to the mid-fifth-century sophists, and particularly to Protagoras.

καταδύεσθαι: the concept derives from Plato *Protag.* 316E, where Protagoras, upon being questioned about his profession of sophist, replies that it is very old, but that most early wise men were afraid to declare themselves as such and hid under other names. After giving examples of teachers of poetry and gymnastics, he continues: μουσικὴν δὲ ᾽Αγαθοκλῆς τε ὁ ὑμέτερος πρόσχημα ἐποιήσατο, μέγας ὢν σοφιστής, καὶ Πυθοκλείδης ὁ Κεῖος καὶ ἄλλοι πολλοί. P. takes ἄλλοι πολλοί to include Damon.

ἐπικρυπτόμενος: the present participle replaces the conative imperfect, representing the attempt, not the actual fact.

ἀλείπτης: "trainer." For P.'s references to the gymnasium, cf. Fuhrmann 1964, 245.

4.3

φιλοτύραννος: another indication that Pericles was accused by his enemies of tyrannical ideas (cf. 3.5). Damon's marriage to an Alcmeonid would not have helped.

ἐξωστρακίσθη: the Clisthenic law on ostracism permitted a citizen to be ostracized, that is banished for ten years without loss of rights or property, by a vote of 6,000 citizens at a special *ostrakophoria*. The original idea apparently had been to limit attempts at tyranny and factional strife. Pericles himself engineered the ostracisms of Cimon and Thucydides: see below 9.5, 14.3. The name comes from the ostraka (potsherds) used to vote, of which some 11,000 have now been found, an extraordinarily rich supplement to the literary tradition (4,662 of these bear the name of Pericles' uncle Megacles!). See ML 40–47 (no. 21); Vanderpool 1970; Thomsen 1972; Rhodes, *CAAP* 267–71 (on 22.3–4); D. J. Phillips 1982. Cf. Plut. *Arist.* 7.2–8, *Nic.* 11; Arist. *Ath. pol.* 22.

τοῖς κωμικοῖς: we do not know that he was mentioned by anyone except Plato Comicus.

4.4

Plato the comic poet (F191 K.): See the Introduction, 3.1.j. Damon is called Chiron ("you . . . as Chiron") because the centaur was the legendary teacher of Achilles and other heroes. Those who believe that only Damon and not his father was advisor to Pericles cite this as evidence that Damon was older than Pericles, as Chiron was older than Achilles. We do not know what Damon is being asked, by whom, or in what play.

ἀντιβολῶ: "please," a common word in comedy, often with σε: LSJ s.v. I.5; cf., e.g., Ar. *Clouds* 110, *Plutus* 103, 444.

4.5

διήκουσε: "was a hearer or disciple of," LSJ s.v.

Zeno . . . Parmenides: Zeno of Elea, born ca. 490, was a pupil of Parmenides, and about twenty-five years younger. Parmenides in his hexameter didactic poem had argued for an extreme view of reality, "what is," as one, timeless, and unchanging. (See Kirk, Raven, and Schofield 1983, 239–62; Guthrie, *HGP* 2:1–80; Taran 1965. The fragments are in *FVS* no. 28.) Zeno used his great gifts as dialectician to defend Parmenides' views by showing the contradictions implicit in his opponents' opinions, using such famous paradoxes as that of Achilles and the tortoise (Lee 1936; Kirk, Raven, and Schofield 1983, 263–79; Guthrie, *HGP* 2:80–101; K. von Fritz, *RE* s.v. Zenon 1, XA, 1 [1972] 53–83). Testimonia and fragments are in *FVS* no. 29. The citation from Timon is given at greater length as 29A1 (= Diog. Laert. 9.25). Plato *Parmenides* 127A tells of the visit of the two philosophers to Athens, probably ca. 450–445. They met Socrates, and Zeno taught two prominent Athenians, Pythodorus and Callias (Plato *Alc. I* 119A). Only P. suggests that Pericles heard Zeno's lectures.

ἀντιλογίας: Zeno was considered by Aristotle (quoted in Diog. Laert. 8.57) to be the founder of dialectic, or the ability to reveal contradictions in an argument. Cf. Plato *Phaedr.* 261D.

ἕξιν: "a trained habit or skill," LSJ II.3. Ἕξιν is object of ἐξασκήσαντος and modified by ἐλεγκτικήν τινα and κατακλείουσαν.

Timon of Phlius: a Skeptic philosopher and follower of Pyrrhus, who lived ca. 320–230. (Phlius is a small polis in northeastern

Peloponnesus, about 20 miles from Corinth). He wrote many works, including some thirty-two comedies, but was most famous for his *Silloi*, three books of satirical hexameters directed against philosophers. This passage from the *Silloi* seems to be one of many from a kind of Homeric visit to the Underworld, and is cited as well in ancient commentaries to Aristotle and Plato. P. cites three other passages from the *Silloi* in his works, and perhaps paraphrases him at 4.6 with reference to Anaxagoras. His life is found in Diog. Laert. 9.109–16; the fragments are collected in Diels 1901 (this is no. 45), and in Lloyd-Jones and Parsons 1983, 368–95 (this is no. 819). See also Brochard 1923, 79–91; Long 1978.

ἀμφοτερογλώσσου: "with a two-edged tongue, able to argue on both sides of the question." The word is one of Timon's many comic neologisms.

σθένος οὐκ ἀλαπαδνόν: a Homeric reminiscence (e.g., *Il.* 7.257), as is the periphrasis of the type σθένος Ζήνωνος for Ζήνων.

ἐπιλήπτορος: "corrector, attacker," from ἐπιλαμβάνομαι (found only here). Long 1978, 71, translates "who trapped everyone."

4.6

Anaxagoras: from Clazomenae in Asia Minor, a philosopher in the tradition of the Ionian φυσικοί, with an original theory of the structure of matter: see Guthrie, *HGP* 2:266–338; Kirk, Raven, and Schofield 1983, 352–84; *FVS* no. 59; Lanza 1966; Sider 1981. The facts about his life (ca. 500–428) and especially his sojourn in Athens are controversial. The anecdote of the one-horned ram (*Per.* 6), if it reflects a real incident, occurred after Cimon's departure for Cyprus and before the ostracism of Thucydides in 443. There was a tradition that Anaxagoras remained thirty years in Athens (Diog. Laert. 2.7). Taylor 1917 argued that Anaxagoras was in Athens ca. 480–450 and thus influenced Pericles in his youth (so also Schofield 1980; Woodbury 1981. More commonly, his stay is placed later: Davison 1953, followed by Meiggs, *AE* 435–36, argues that he was expelled from Athens twice, ca. 456/55 and ca. 433/30 (the latter is referred to in *Per.* 32.2), which seems a desperate attempt to reconcile contradictory accounts. The problem is tied to the date of the trial of Phidias: see Mansfeld 1979 and 1980 and my discussions at 31.2–32.6 and 32.2.

Anaxagoras is famous for his ideas of νοῦς as the initial mover and of "seeds" of everything in everything. His study of a recently fallen meteorite and other calculations may have led him to state that the sun was "a piece of molten metal, bigger than the Peloponnese," and gave him a reputation as a freethinker and atheist. The influence on Pericles indicated by P. does not reflect specifically ethical teaching, but is P.'s interpretation of Plato *Phaedrus* 270A (see note to 5.1). Anaxagoras' influence is stated again in chapters 8 and 16; after Plato it had become a commonplace: cf., e.g., [Plato] *Ep.* 2, 311A, [Dem.] 61.45, Cic. *De or.* 3.138. For a listing of ancient traditions about him see Gershenson and Greenberg 1964; for his importance to Plato and thus indirectly to P. see Babut 1978. For P.'s knowledge of his book and his presentation of him as philosopher adviser to Pericles in the Platonic mold see Hershbell 1982. Hershbell argues that there is no conclusive evidence that P. knew Anaxagoras' book directly, although we know that it was still extant, and suggests Theophrastus' *Physikon doxai* as the source. I consider it more likely that at one time he had read the book (it was not long) and taken notes, but that his approach and interpretations would have derived from criticisms in Plato, Aristotle, and later philosophers. P. quotes opinions of Anaxagoras rather frequently (see Helmbold and O'Neill 1959, 3, but note that 874D–911C, the *De placitis philosophorum*, was not written by Plutarch).

ὄγκον: "weight, dignity," or in a bad sense, "pride, self-importance." P. here uses it in a positive sense, but in 7.6 it is ambiguous. The resolution occurs at 39.3, where Pericles is found to be μέτριος ἐν ὄγκῳ. P. notes the importance of ὄγκος in the speeches of a statesman at *Praec. ger. rep.* 803B, but is also aware that some rulers try to counterfeit it (καὶ γὰρ οὗτοι βαρύτητι φῶνης καὶ βλέμματος τραχύτητι καὶ δυσκολίᾳ τρόπων καὶ ἀμιξίᾳ διαίτης ὄγκον ἡγεμονίας καὶ σεμνότητα μιμεῖσθαι δοκοῦσιν) rather than relying on the real weight of philosophical knowledge (*Ad princ. inerud.* 780A). Anaxagoras' influence gives Pericles a true inner dignity. Early in the *Fabius* (4.3) P. notes that Fabius asserts the ὄγκος of the dictator-

ship, suggesting one (in this case rather flimsy) of the parallels
between the two lives.

φρόνημα: a fundamental attribute of the Plutarchean Pericles.
Μέγα φρονεῖν is to have high thoughts or large plans (LSJ s.v.
φρονέω II.2.b); φρόνημα is the noun, and as such it is used very
frequently in the life (5.1, 8.1, 10.7, 17.4, 31.1, 36.8, 39.1); another form is μεγαλοφροσύνη (14.2, 16.7, 17.4). Although it can
have a bad connotation ("presumption"), here it is always a desirable quality. For the complex of words associated with φρόνημα,
including ὄγκος, σεμνότης, etc., see Bucher-Isler 1972, 15–17.

δημαγωγίας ἐμβριθέστερον: "more weighty than simple demagoguery." On the varied meanings of ἐμβριθής see Holden's note, and
for this passage esp. Brut. 1.3: οὑτοσὶ δ' ὑπὲρ οὗ γράφεται ταῦτα,
παιδείᾳ καὶ λόγῳ διὰ φιλοσοφίας καταμείξας τὸ ἦθος, καὶ τὴν φύσιν
ἐμβριθῆ καὶ πραεῖαν οὖσαν.

ὅλως τε: "and in general"; cf. LSJ s.v. ὅλος III.2.

Νοῦν προσηγόρευον: The same comment appears in Harpocration
and Diog. Laert. 2.6, who quotes Timon of Phlius (F24, Lloyd-
Jones and Parsons 1983, no. 798), καί που Ἀναξαγόρην φασ' ἔμμε-
ναι, ἄλκιμον ἥρω Νοῦν. The nickname could originally be from
comedy.

φυσιολογίαν: the study of φύσις, inquiring into natural causes.

τοῖς ὅλοις . . . νοῦν ἐπέστησε: a summary of Anaxagoras' most
important doctrine. Τὰ ὅλα here = the world (more usually τὸ
ὅλον: see LSJ s.v. ὅλος II.1) or the πάντα χρήματα of frag. B1.
The words in this passage show P.'s familiarity with Anaxago-
rean thought as known in antiquity. See Kirk, Raven, and Schofield 1983, 362–66; Hershbell 1982. Διακοσμέω is the usual word
for the activity of the mind in this theory (e.g., B12 [p. 38, l. 11]);
for καθαρόν cf. B12 (p. 38, l. 2), ἔστι γὰρ λεπτότατόν τε πάντων καὶ
καθαρώτατον; for ἄκρατον cf. B12 (p. 37, l.19), μέμεικται οὐδενὶ
χρήματι. One might translate, "But he established Mind as some-

thing pure and unmixed among all the other things, which was separating out the homogeneous items."

ἐν μεμειγμένοις πᾶσι τοῖς ἄλλοις: all other things except mind are mixed. Note the use of συμμεμειγμένα in B12. The phrase modifies νοῦν, as in B 14, ὁ δὲ νοῦς . . . καὶ νῦν ἐστιν ἵνα καὶ τὰ ἄλλα πάντα ἐν τῷ πολλὰ [sic mss., Sider 1981; πολλῷ Diels] περιέχοντι καὶ ἐν τοῖς προκριθεῖσι καὶ ἐν τοῖς ἀποκριμένοις. Τοῖς ἄλλοις is to be preferred to ὅλοις, a correction found in S and accepted by Flacelière. Cf. B14, τὰ ἄλλα πάντα.

ἀποκρίνοντα: a word regularly used of the function of νοῦς: see B6, 9, 12, 14.

ὁμοιομερείας: a word for Anaxagoras' "seeds" (cf. Aristotle Phys. 1.5.187a23, τὰ ὁμοιομερῆ), used especially by Diogenes Laertius, pseudo-Plutarch De Placitis, and the commentators to Aristotle. Anaxagoras uses simply μοῖρα or "portion." See Guthrie, HGP 2:325–26.

5–6

P. moves easily from education to character, describing the effect of Anaxagoras' teaching on Pericles' behavior (already suggested by the reference to his ὄγκον and φρόνημα in 4.6). There is no indication of the sources for the two anecdotes in 5.2 and 6.2–3.

5.1

The artful construction of this sentence is noteworthy, especially the position of adjectives and participles. The first verb has two objects (φρόνημα, λόγον), the second five subjects (σύστασις, πραότης, καταστολή, πλάσμα, ὅσα τοιαῦτα). This chapter piles up a rich variety of words describing Pericles' seriousness and measured calm. The picture recalls Aristotle's description of the μεγαλόψυχος, Eth. Nic. 4.3.1125a12–14: καὶ κίνησις δὲ βραδεία τοῦ μεγαλοψύχου δοκεῖ εἶναι, καὶ φωνὴ βαρεῖα, καὶ λέξις στάσιμος. Some of the same qualities appear in the description of Fabius' calmness after Cannae, Fab. 17.7: μόνος ἐφοίτα διὰ τῆς πόλεως πρᾴῳ βαδίσματι καὶ προσώπῳ καθεστῶτι καὶ φιλανθρώπῳ προσαγορεύσει.

τῆς λεγομένης μετεωρολογίας καὶ μεταρσιολεσχίας: cf. Plato *Phaedrus* 270A, where Socrates speaks rather ironically of the good effects of Anaxagoras on Pericles, noting that all great arts need ἀδολεσχίας καὶ μετεωρολογίας φύσεως πέρι, and later, that Pericles was μετεωρολογίας ἐμπλήσθεις by Anaxagoras (the full passage is quoted below in the note to 8.2). Plato did not mean to praise Pericles (cf. most recently Rowe 1986, 204–5). Μεταρσιολεσχία is an Ionic form of μετεωρολογία (τὰ μεταρσία = heavenly things, τὰ μετέωρα). These words were frequently given a mocking connotation, most notably in Aristophanes' *Clouds*, cf. Plut. *Nic.* 23.4. Plato's connection of μετεωρολογία with ἀδολεσχία ("prattling") is also ironic: cf. as well the use of ἀδολέσχης and μετεωρολέσχης of the helmsman in *Rep.* 489A, C. Note also the reference in [Plato] *Sisyphus* 389A, οὐκοῦν καὶ περὶ τοῦ ἀέρος Ἀναξαγόραν τε καὶ Ἐμπεδοκλέα καὶ τοὺς ἄλλους τοὺς μεταρσιολέσχας ἅπαντας.

σοβαρόν: not "pompous, insolent," as usually, but "dignified."

τὸν λόγον ὑψηλόν: cf. Plato *Phaedr.* 270A, τὸ ὑψηλόνουν.

ὀχλικῆς: "vulgar, suited to the mob (ὄχλος)." The word occurs only five times in P., twice (*Conj. praec.* 142A, *Symp.* 719B) in a quite different sense, to characterize the "arithmetical" notion of democracy—one man, one vote.

βωμολοχίας: "clownishness, vulgarity." Aristides was also free from it (*Arist.* 2.2); Cleon was not (*Nic.* 3.2, *Demetr.* 11.2). P. found it unsuitable for a politician; cf. *Praec. ger. rep.* 803C, 810D, 822C. Aristotle defines it as an excess with regard to good humor *Eth. Nic.* 4.7, 1128a4–7.

προσώπου σύστασις: "facial composure." His teacher Anaxagoras was said never to have been seen smiling: Aelian *VH* 8.13.

ἄθρυπτος εἰς γέλωτα: "never breaking into a laugh." Ἄθρυπτος, from θρύπτω, "shatter," or, figuratively, "enervate, corrupt," is always favorable in P., implying a rejection of flattery or other corruption: cf. the λέξις ἄθρυπτος of the Spartan, *Lyc.* 21.1; ἔρως ἄθρυπτος, *Amat.* 751A; ὦτα . . . ἄθρυπτα κολακείᾳ, *De rect. aud.* 38B. Pericles rejects ὑποθρυπτομένης δημαγωγίας at 15.1. Fabius acts ἀθρύπτως at *Fab.* 3.7.

πρᾳότης: one of Pericles' distinguishing characteristics: see 2.5. P. frequently uses the term in describing physical movement: see H. Martin 1960, 66–67.

καταστολὴ . . . λέγειν: "an arrangement of his garment (the *himation*) that was never disturbed by any emotion as he was speaking." The opposite was true of Cleon (cf. *Nic.* 8.6). The whole sentence indicates how Pericles' φρόνημα was apparent in his appearance.

πλάσμα: "tone, modulation," literally "shaping."

ἐξέπληττε: the emphatic word completes the period and encapsules the thought.

5.2

γοῦν introduces an example confirming the previous statement (cf. 4.4, 38.2). The anecdote itself is timeless, belonging to any part of Pericles' career, but demonstrates Pericles' control of his feelings. Cf. *De cap. util.* 90D, οὔτι μὴν τούτου σεμνότερον καὶ κάλλιόν ἐστι, τοῦ, λοιδοροῦντος ἐχθροῦ, τὴν ἡσυχίαν ἄγειν.

κακῶς ἀκούων: the passive of κακῶς λέγων.

βδελυρῶν: "crude, vulgar, disgusting," used by P. especially of Cleon (*Nic.* 2.2, *Demetr.* 11.2) and Clodius (*Pomp.* 46.4, *Caes.* 9.3, *Ant.* 2.6). The notion is of one who does not know where to draw the line: see the examples in Theophrastus *Characters* 11, or the exasperation of Thrasymachus with Socrates at *Rep.* 338D.

τι τῶν ἐπειγόντων: "some pressing business."

βλασφημία: "slander, abuse," as often.

φῶς λαβόντι: it was late, and there were no street lights.

καταστῆσαι: here in the not uncommon sense of "take (someone) back."

5.3

Ion of Chios (*FGrHist* 392 F15): see the Introduction, 3.1.b. In characteristic fashion P. cites an authority that contradicts his viewpoint, then responds with his own comments. The poet liked good company and found Pericles' sobriety a sign of boorishness, not highmindedness.

μοθωνικήν: a μόθων or μόθαξ at Sparta was the free son of a Spartiate and a helot mother, raised with the legitimate children. Cf. *Cleom.* 8.1; Athen. 6.271E–F (= Phylarchus, 81 F43); Busolt and Swoboda 2:657–58; Lotze 1962; Toynbee 1969, 343–46. The word came to be used of those who were vulgar, presumptuous, or impudent (cf. Ar. *Plut.* 279). The adjective is very rare, and perhaps Ion's own word.

ὑπότυφον: "rather arrogant, self-important." Another rare word, not otherwise found in P.

μεγαλαυχίαις: note that the plural avoids hiatus; cf. also *Alex.* 23.7, *De laude ipsius* 540D. The singular is more frequent in other cases (e.g., *Per.* 37.5, *Fab.* 8.3, *De aud.* 19D, and, for the dative, *De laude ipsius* 539B, 541B, 545B).

ὑπεροψίαν: "disdain." Although P. rejects the notion here, he is aware that this was the perception of some, cf. 37.5.

περιφρόνησιν: "contempt." P. uses this twice as often as the more classical καταφρόνησις (cf. Hamilton to *Alex.* 75.2), although καταφρονέω is much more frequent than περιφρονέω.

Cimon: the political leader opposed to Pericles (see note to 7.3) and a friend of Ion. P. reports several of Ion's references to him in *Cimon* (5.3, 9.1–6, 16.10 = 392 F12–14).

ἐμμελές καὶ ὑγρόν: "harmonious," and hence "tactful, easy, and smooth." But P. also sees Pericles as acting ἐμμελῶς (15.2).

⟨συμ⟩περιφοραῖς: "social contacts, drinking parties." The emendation is necessary because περιφοραί refers almost exclusively to the movements of the heavenly bodies, whereas the compound is frequent in P. referring to convivial drinking. P. himself counseled moderation on such occasions but was aware of the potential for being considered antisocial: see esp. *De tu. san.* 123E–124D on the problems of social entertaining in his own day.

ἀλλ' Ἴωνα κτλ.: "However, let us leave Ion to one side, who thinks that *aretē*, like a tragic production, should always have a satyric portion." Three tragedies and one satyr play were presented together by an author at the fifth-century dramatic festivals, the satyr play usually mocking the theme of the tragedies. P. suggests that Ion, who wrote tragedies, thought some lightheartedness was essential in even the most virtuous person, and invites the reader to join him in ignoring Ion *(ἐῶμεν)*.

δοξοκοπίαν: "thirst for popularity"; cf. κόπτω, "beat, pester," and δοξοκοπεῖν, "court popularity," just below. Plato speaks of the δημοκοπικὸς βίος (*Phaedr.* 248E).

τῦφον: "arrogance"; cf. ὑπότυφον just above.

Zeno: usually identified as Zeno of Elea, just mentioned in 4.5 (this sentence is *FVS* 29A17), but it is more likely Zeno of Citium, the founder of Stoicism (d. 262/61), to whom many apophthegms of this sort are attributed, although most concern contemporaries. See Meinhardt, 28n. 64; and on Zeno of Citium, von Arnim 1903, 1:63–71; K. von Fritz, *RE* s.v. Zenon 2, XA (1972) 83–121; Long 1974, 109–13; Sandbach 1975, 20–27. Both Zenos are cited elsewhere by P., but the founder of Stoicism much more often, especially in P.'s works against the Stoics (*De stoicorum repugnantiis* and *De communibus notitiis adversus Stoicos*). Recently an Arabic collection of his sayings has been discovered: see Altheim and Stiehl 1962, 12–14, 372–75.

προσποιήσεως: "pretense."

ὑποποιούσης: "produce unconsciously," the prefix suggesting the hidden action.

τῶν καλῶν: take with ζῆλον καὶ συνήθειαν.

λεληθότως: "imperceptibly."

6.1

A transition to the ram anecdote. Pericles' lack of superstition (not irreligion) is referred to again at 35.2 and 38.2.

δεισιδαιμονίας: "superstition"; cf. the definition in *On superstition* 165B: δόξαν ἐμπαθῆ καὶ δέους ποιητικὴν ὑπόληψιν οὖσαν ἐκταπεινοῦντος καὶ συντρίβοντος τὸν ἄνθρωπον, οἰόμενον μὲν εἶναι θεούς, εἶναι δὲ λυπηροὺς καὶ βλαβερούς, "an emotional opinion and concept productive of a fear that humiliates and crushes a man, since he thinks that gods exist, but that they cause pain and harm." P. believed that such superstition was as bad as, if not worse than, atheism. Cf. Erbse 1952; Moellering 1963; Smith 1975, who presents (insufficient) arguments against its authenticity; and the edition of Lozza 1980. On P.'s religious thinking in general see Brenk 1977, and the perceptive short account in Russell, *Plutarch*, 63–83. The proper attitude toward the gods was a significant element of the good statesman: see Wardman 1974, 86–93.

καθυπέρτερος: commonly figurative = "superior to."

θάμβος: "amazement," a poetic word, but used by Plato in the myth in *Phaedrus* 254C and by Plutarch sixteen times in the *Lives*.

αἰτίας: P. believes that a knowledge of physical phenomena protects one from excessive fear and strengthens true religious feeling (εὐσέβεια).

περὶ τὰ θεῖα δαιμονῶσι: "go crazy when they consider divine action." The verb δαιμονάω is poetic (cf. Aesch. *Choeph.* 566, *Sept.* 1001; Eur. *Phoen.* 888). P. uses it only three times, once in the sense "be harassed by *daimones*" (*Marc.* 20.9) and twice punningly of the superstitious, here and at *De superst.* 169D: those who think wrongly about the *daimones* "are crazy" or "are possessed by *daimones*." The wordplay is already found in Xen. *Mem.* 1.1.9, where Socrates says that men δαιμονᾶν who think that nothing is δαιμόνιον.

ὁ φυσικὸς λόγος: "a reasoned account of nature, natural philosophy," rather than "science" in our sense.

φοβερᾶς: "fearful."

φλεγμαινούσης: "inflamed," a medical term. Plato uses it of a sick polis (*Rep.* 372E); P. of emotions here and at *Pomp.* 21.1.

6.2

Another timeless anecdote (ποτε), but necessarily belonging after the death of Cimon and before the ostracism of Thucydides son of Melesias (on which see note to 14.3). The anecdote does not actually show Pericles rising above superstition, or the superiority of Anaxagoras' science, as Pericles seems to remain on good terms with Lampon (who after all has his prediction confirmed), but does indicate that Pericles balanced religious interpretation with scientific investigation. It is also more evidence of Pericles' contact with Anaxagoras, and an occasion for P. to suggest that Pericles' ascendance was favored by the gods and to digress on the action of the gods in the world, a favorite subject (cf., e.g., *On the Pythian Oracle* and the debate in *On the Daimon of Socrates*). By noting that a full world view combines both natural science and teleology, as Plato did, he corrects what he considers Anaxagoras' too narrowly scientific viewpoint. The anecdote also foreshadows the struggle for power that is a central feature of the life.

Omens are frequently mentioned at the beginning of a career in the *Lives*, although in this case P. has had to take one from Pericles' mature years. Fabius' reaction to prodigies is rather different, although P. makes the same distinction between superstition and piety (*Fab.* 4.4–6). For omens and portents in P., and especially their importance in the dramatic structure of the *Lives*, see Brenk 1977, 184–213; cf. also von Arnim 1921.

Lampon: Although he appears only here in the *Pericles*, Lampon was a well-known public figure, perhaps the son of Olympiodorus the son of Lampon, a hero at Plataea (Hdt. 9.21.3). He was most famous as one of the founders of Thurii (Diod. Sic. 12.10.3–4; schol. Ar. *Clouds* 332; Hesychius, Photius, and Suda s.v. θουριο-μάντεις). He made a substantial amendment to a decree regarding the giving of first fruits to the sanctuary at Eleusis, ca. 422 (*IG* I² 76 = ML 73, ll. 47–61, *IG* I³ 78), among other things making himself a committee of one to draft a law concerning the first fruits of olive oil. Thucydides (5.19.2, 5.24.1) lists him as the first signer of the treaties of April and May 421. Comic writers mock him as a *mantis* and a great eater (because he had the right to eat in the *prytaneion* at public expense): Ar. *Clouds* 332, *Birds* 521, 987–88, Cratinus F62 K. = 66 K.A., and the passages quoted in Athenaeus 8.344E.

Thurii may have been a Periclean project (cf. 11.5), and P. elsewhere states that Pericles in sending Lampon was following his normal practice of using friends to accomplish his projects rather than take credit directly (*Praec. ger. rep.* 812D). Much has been made of the possible implications of Pericles' friendship with Lampon, although these references in fact tell us almost nothing: see, e.g., Schachermeyr 1968, 25–32. A *mantis* was someone recognized as able to interpret signs from the gods (Lampon's interpretation of the ram prodigy here is a good example), but had no official position. Cf. *RE* s.v. μάντις 1, XIV, 2 (1930) 1345–55. We do not know why he was awarded meals in the *prytaneion*, an unusual honor (on which see Osborne 1981). Perhaps he was also an official *exēgētēs*, or interpreter of religious law, as suggested by a fragment of Eupolis (F297 K. = 319 K.A.). See Jacoby 1949, 18–23; Kett 1966. A cross-examination of Lampon by Pericles concerning knowledge of the mysteries is recorded by Aristotle (*Rhet.*

3.1419A). Pericles seems to be trying to discredit Lampon, and if so, this would suggest that they were not always friends, if they ever were. Interestingly enough, the interrogation hinges on the fact that Lampon was not an initiate in the Eleusinian mysteries, as one might naturally expect.

τὸ κέρας . . . πεφυκός: anomalies of nature were considered prodigies that might signal the gods' wishes or intentions. The ram was frequently taken as a symbol of power and leadership: see Korres 1970, with illustrations of ram's-head helmets on statues of generals (there are none on those of Pericles, however). For a similar prodigy, interpreted in different ways by seer and philosopher, cf. *Sept. sap. conv.* 149C–E (where the philosopher's explanation is quite wrong).

δυναστειῶν: "dominating powers," expressing the political power concentrated in the hands of the two leaders. Cf. *Cic.* 23.4: νόμος ὑπ' αὐτῶν εἰσήγετο καλεῖν Πομπήιον μετὰ τῆς στρατιᾶς, ὡς δὴ καταλύσοντα τὴν Κικέρωνος δυναστείαν.

Thucydides: see note to 11.1.

περιστήσεται: note the future indicative here, though the optative appears immediately after in the relative clause. P. tends to avoid the future optative. A search of sigma futures yields twenty-four examples in P., of which eighteen are in the *Lives* and twelve are represented by ἔσοιτο. For the others see *Them.* 25.2 (twice), *Luc.* 41.6, *Cat. Min.* 70.4, *Cam.* 39.4, *Tim.* 9.4, *Phil.* 3.3, *Sull.* 6.16, *Caes.* 28.7, *Brut.* 10.3, *De Pyth. or.* 399D, 403B. For other optatives in the *Pericles* see 8.4, 18.2, 20.1, 31.2, 32.3.

παρ' ᾧ: "on whose land, property."

τὸν δ' Ἀναξαγόραν . . . ἀρχήν: "But Anaxagoras cut open the head and demonstrated that the brain had not filled the pan, but had collected together, pointed like an egg, from the whole cavity to the place from which the root of the horn began." Ἐπιδεῖξαι is the regular word for scientific (and rhetorical) demonstration.

The notion of dissection is very interesting. For a roughly contemporary example, cf. Hippocrates *Sacred Disease* 14, ἢν διακόψῃς τὴν κεφαλήν [of a goat with epilepsy], εὑρήσεις τὸν ἐγκέφαλον ὑγρὸν ἐόντα, with a conclusion similar to that of Anaxagoras: καὶ ἐν τούτῳ δηλονότι γνώσει ὅτι οὐχ ὁ θεὸς τὸ σῶμα λυμαίνεται, ἀλλ᾽ ἡ νοῦσος. Alcmaeon of Croton also is said to have practiced dissection in the fifth century: see *FVS* 24 A10 and E. D. Phillips 1973, 20–22. However, P.'s description cannot be accurate. An animal so deformed would not have lived long enough to grow its "strong, solid" horn, nor is there in fact any relation between the horn and the skull (much less the brain). The *processus cornus* grows not from the skull but upon the skin, and only fuses to the skull later. Because these centers can change position or be damaged, it is possible that a ram might have one horn, but not for the reason given here. Aristotle knew that the horn grew from the skin, not the skull (*Hist. an.* 3.9, 517A). See Sisson and Grossman 1953, 136–37, and Dove 1936 ("Artificial Production of the Fabulous Unicorn"). In 1985 and 1986 the Ringling Brothers circus was exhibiting a "unicorn," actually a goat with one central horn, caused by the surgical removal of one *processus* and the movement of the other to the center of the forehead.

οὐ πεπληρωκότα: after verbs of showing or proving P. rarely admits the general postclassical tendency to use μή rather than οὐ with the participle. Cf. for ἐπιδείκνυμι *Cim.* 18.5, ἐπιδεικνύμενος αὐτῷ τὸν λοβὸν οὐκ ἔχοντα κεφαλήν, *Aem.* 26.11, *Pyrrh.* 16.11, *Dion* 17.6, against *Cleom.* 39.1 ἐπέδειξε τὴν ἀρετὴν ὑβρισθῆναι μὴ δυναμένην. Cf. also *Per.* 13.12, ἐμήνυσε . . . οὐκ ἀποστατοῦσαν, and two examples of ἐδήλωσε with οὐ, *Rom.* 9.2, *Caes.* 69.6. On the tendency to use μή see Blass and Debrunner 1961, nos. 426, 430. In general P. is not far from the classical ratios in the use of μή and οὐ: using the LEX program, I count a total for μή of 4,720 as against 10,453 for οὐ, οὐκ, οὐχ, a ratio of 1:2.2. Compare Xenophon, a ratio of 1:1.6; Plato, a ratio of 1:1.9; but Pausanias, a ratio of 1:8.7.

ὀξὺν ὥσπερ ᾠόν: cf. Arist. *Gen. An.* 752a16, τοῦ ᾠοῦ τὸ ὀξύ.

6.3

καταλυθέντος: "defeated, deposed," more commonly used of political systems (cf. 7.8, 25.2; LSJ s.v. 2) than of individuals, but cf. 33.1 and Thuc. 1.18.

6.4

P.'s personal comments on the issue of divination versus science. A major interest of Plutarch, both as philosopher and as priest at Delphi, was the role of the gods in human affairs, and he commented on the matter on a number of occasions. The question of divination and prophecy is discussed at length in *On the decline of oracles*, and 434F–437C considers especially the relation of divine to natural causes. Note 435 E–F: "[Plato (*Phaedo* 97B–99D)] criticized the ancient Anaxagoras because he was too much attached to physical causes and always pursued and sought out that which was produced necessarily by the contacts of bodies, and ignored the better causes and origins, that is, the final and efficient causes." Anaxagoras' science is more narrow-minded than Plato's larger view, with its strong teleological sense. This view of Anaxagoras recurs in P.'s writings: see Hershbell 1982, 141–46. In our passage, P. adduces the analogy of human signals, which also have both a physical mechanism and a signification. Cf. also *De Pyth. or.* 397B–C, 404B, *De gen. Socr.* 593A–C, and *Cor.* 38.

τὸν φυσικόν: the regular Aristotelian expression for a natural philosopher, especially a pre-Socratic: cf. Arist. *De an.* 403a29, *Phys.* 184b17, etc.; and Plut. *Alex.* 44.2, τοὺς φυσικοὺς ἄνδρας, used of the early geographers.

ἐπιτυγχάνειν: "hit the mark, be correct," used absolutely; cf. *De def. or.* 438A, *Brut.* 16.2.

ἐκλαμβάνοντος: "choosing for interpretation."

ὑπέκειτο: "it was the role (or assignment) of," with the dative.

πρὸς τί: "for what purpose?"

6.5

τῆς αἰτίας . . . σημεῖον: note the chiastic order and the rhyming word play. ᾿Αναίρεσιν: "denial, direct confutation." Σημεῖον, which could have been translated "prodigy" at 6.2, is now given its most general meaning of "sign, signifier, signal."

ἐπινοοῦσιν: with the supplementary participle in indirect discourse, like οἶδα.

ἀθετοῦντες: "do away with, set at naught," is used regularly of skeptical rejection of divine signs: De def. or. 420C, Cor. 38.5.

τεχνητά: "artificial," made by τεχνή.

ψόφους τε δίσκων: hanging metal disks were regularly used as bells to announce the end of lectures (Cic. De or. 2.21) or as a signal in astronomical observations (Sextus Empiricus Math. 5.2.8 [68–69]).

πυρσῶν: "beacon-fires."

γνωμόνων ἀποσκιασμούς: "shadows thrown by the pointers of sundials." By introducing examples of signs or signals made by men, P. implies by analogy that the gods make natural phenomena function as signs also.

μὲν οὖν marks the return from the digression: cf. 28.3.

πραγματεία: "essay, literary work," as regularly in postclassical Greek: cf. 39.3. This may be a forward reference to *On the Decline of Oracles*.

7–8

After treating Pericles' philosophical training, P. turns to his political career, the direction it takes, and the qualities he brings to it. As in the preceding section, the particular incidents range over most of Pericles' career, from his first activity as a young man (7.1) to the reform of the Areopagus in 462 (7.8), the struggle for leadership with Thucydides (8.5), and the Samian and Peloponnesian wars (8.9, 8.7). As in the previous chapters, P. moves easily from specific events to general character traits and underlying philosophical questions. The precise information on Pericles' early career is very limited (note the absence of any specific offices or campaigns), indicating the absence of a fuller tradition. P. creates a sense of Pericles' activity by combining stray notices from *Ath. pol.* and the rhetorical tradition with his own ideas based on Pericles' later activity: see Meinhardt, 29–32. For an analysis of these years suggesting that Pericles might not have been hostile to Cimon at this time see Sealey 1956.

7.1

νέος . . . ὤν: Pericles was born ca. 498–494 (see note to 3.3). P. seems to be thinking of the period between his coming of age ca. 478 and the more active role described in 7.3. *Νέος* can be used up to the age of forty (cf. Plato *Leg.* 2.666B, 12.951E, 12.961B; Plut. *Reg. et imp. apophtheg.* 200A, of Scipio Minor at Carthage, when he was about thirty-six; *Apophtheg. Lac.* 211A of Artaxerxes, who became king at thirty-two; and *Praec. ger. rep.* 804B, a man older than Alexander in ca. 324, when he was thirty-two). According to *Ath. pol.* 27.1, Pericles was *νέος* when he prosecuted Cimon ca. 463 (cf. Rhodes, *CAAP* 325, and note to 10.6). Pericles would not have become prominent until his father died, sometime between his campaign at Sestos in 479/78 (Hdt. 9.114.2) and Pericles' choregia for the *Persians* in 472 (see below, note to 7.2).

τὸν δῆμον εὐλαβεῖτο: "was wary of the demos." He had reason: his maternal uncle Megacles had been ostracized in 486, his father Xanthippus in 484 (cf. note to 3.2). Xanthippus' recall and victory at Mycale would not have obscured Pericles' awareness of the political infighting at this time, as members of prominent families and relative newcomers like Themistocles and Aristides tried to win support for their own ambitions and policies.

καὶ γάρ: introduces the corroborative statement *ἐδόκει . . . ὁμοιότητα*. Cf. 24.4, 24.5, 24.9, 26.4, 34.3, 39.3; Denniston, 108.

Pisistratus: tyrant of Athens, ruling in three periods between 561/60 and his death in 528/27, when he was succeeded by his sons Hippias and Hipparchus. Hipparchus was assassinated in 514/13; Hippias was expelled by the Spartans led by Cleomenes in 511/10. See Hdt. 1.59.4–64, 5.55–61; *Ath. pol.* 14–19; Thuc. 6.54–59; Andrewes 1963, 100–115. Pericles was related to Pisistratus through his mother: Herodotus (1.61.1) reports that the tyrant married a daughter of Megacles the grandfather of Agariste. Thus Pisistratus would have been Pericles' great-uncle by marriage.

The resemblance to Pisistratus recalls the charge that Pericles became a tyrant, which surfaces occasionally throughout the life and acts as foil to P.'s presentation of him as an "aristocratic" statesman: see note to 16.1.

ἐξεπλήττοντο: here takes both an accusative expressing the object of amazement *(φωνὴν, γλῶτταν*; cf. *Cleom.* 16.3, *Dion* 32.1) and πρὸς τὴν ὁμοιότητα giving the reason (cf. 35.2; *Thes.* 19.6) On Pisistratus' fame as an orator, cf. Cic. *Brut.* 27. P.'s story clearly derives from the same source as Val. Max. 8.9.ext. 2: *Fertur quidam, cum admodum senex primae contioni Periclis adulescentuli interesset idemque iuvenis Pisistratum decrepitum iam contionantem audisset, non temperasse sibi quominus exclamaret, caveri illum civem oportere, quod Pisistrati orationi simillima eius esset oratio.* Such men would have been old indeed: Pisistratus died at least thirty years before Pericles was born, and the listeners would have to be in their eighties. Valerius adds: *Nec hominem aut aestimatio eloqui aut morum augurium fefellit. Quid enim inter Pisistratum et Periclen interfuit, nisi quod ille armatus, hic sine armis tyrannidem gessit.* The source is probably Theopompus (cf. note to 8.3); P. has removed the open hostility toward Pericles. The variation between singular and plural is insignificant in this kind of anecdote, but note that P. has been more specific in describing the style of oratory.

7.2

πλοῦτον: the wealth of a member of the old elite (cf. Davies, *APF* 459), joined naturally with γένους . . . λαμπροῦ (cf. note to 3.1–2). Aristotle noted that the upper class was distinguished by its wealth, good birth, *aretē*, and education (e.g., *Pol.* 1291b28–29).

φίλων: powerful friends (usually made through family connections) were a major source of political power; cf. Connor 1971, 30–32, 36–43. Φοβούμενος ἐξοστρακισθῆναι: cf. note to 7.1. The fate of Themistocles, ostracized ca. 472, would have been a warning, but in fact Pericles would seem to be too young to have such worries at least for another decade. P. is projecting these fears earlier to create an explanation for the decision to turn to the demos for support. For the infinitive after φοβοῦμαι see MT 373.

ἐν δὲ ταῖς στρατείαις: nothing is known of his service on the various campaigns of the 470s. P. is simply inventing a probable detail. Cf. the revealing case of the *Coriolanus*: Russell 1963, esp. 23–24.

P. does not mention the only sure information that we have from this period, his choregia of Aeschylus' *Persians* in 472: cf. *IG* II^2 2318, l. 10; Hyp. to Aesch. *Pers.*; Pickard-Cambridge 1968, 90, 104. This fact confirms that Pericles' family was wealthy and indicates that Xanthippus had died and Pericles had come into control of his share of the inheritance; it cannot be used as evidence for his support of whatever political ideas might be found in the *Persians*. For the manner of selection of dramatic choregoi, and the expense involved, cf. Pickard-Cambridge 1968, 86–90; Rhodes, *CAAP* 622–23. Unlike earlier leaders, Pericles' generation (e.g., Cimon, Ephialtes, Thucydides) did not seek the archonship.

7.3

Pericles' entry into politics is seen in terms of the opposition of *dēmos* and *oligoi* that is regularly found in both Greek and Roman lives (cf. esp. Pelling 1986a, on P.'s imposition of the *dēmos-boulē* dichotomy on Roman political history). P. would have found this fundamental division between the many and poor on the one hand and the few and rich on the other in *Ath. pol.* and other Aristotelian works as well as in many other writers: see the Introduction, 3.2.c. When Athenian politics is seen in these terms, as here and in *Ath. pol.* 28.2 (cf. also schol. to Aristid. 46.118, 3:446 Dindorf), the demos is championed successively by Themistocles and Pericles (Aristotle includes Ephialtes between them) against Aristides, Cimon, and finally Thucydides son of Melesias (11.1) as leader of the *oligoi* (on this and similar lists see Rhodes, *CAAP* on 28.2). Pericles opposes Cimon in chapters 9–10, Thucydides in

11–14 (cf. τὴν Κίμωνος δόξαν ἀντιταττόμενος 9.2; and for Thucydides, ἀντιπολιτεύσατο τῷ Περικλεῖ 8.5, τὸν πρὸς αὐτὸν ἀντιτασσόμενον and ἀνέστησαν ἐναντιωσόμενον 11.1). The opposition is resolved when Thucydides is ostracized and Pericles dissolves τὴν ἀντιτεταγμένην ἑταιρείαν (14.3). For this antithetical pairing of leaders cf. *Arist.* 2.1, *Them.* 3.1, *Nic.* 2.2. P. cites Aristotle's list of opposed champions (*Ath. pol.* 28) at *Nic.* 2.1. On *dēmos* and *dēmokratia* in the fifth century see Sealey 1973.

There are many difficulties with applying this scheme so rigidly to fifth-century politics. Note, however, that to P. a popular leader is not per se desirous of resolving all issues according to the will of the majority, but rather is a supporter of the demos, the common people, against a limited number of powerful men—often as a means of acquiring power for himself.

For Aristotle the ideal forms of government were kingship, aristocracy, or polity, in which government was by one, a few, or many good men for the good of the whole polis (*Pol.* 1279a32–1279b10). Both oligarchy and democracy were declinations from the ideal, the former from aristocracy, the latter from polity. (The collection of Aristotelian constitutions that included *Ath. pol.* was apparently divided by form of government: see Diog. Laert. 5.27, πολιτεῖαι πόλεων δυοῖν δεούσαν ρξ΄· κατ᾽ εἴδη· δημοκρατικαί, ὀλιγαρχικαί, τυραννικαί, ἀριστοκρατικαί.) Any constitution that aimed toward virtue, however, could loosely be called an aristocracy. Furthermore, mixed constitutions tending toward oligarchy were commonly termed aristocracies, Aristotle noted, because of the association of the marks of the oligarchic καλὸς κἀγαθός—wealth, education, and birth—with virtue (*Pol.* 1293b34–42). For P. as well, ἀριστοκρατικός is not simply a synonym for ὀλιγαρχικός (although 10.8 may be an exception), but emphasizes the virtue of the statesman. Thus his references to Pericles' ἀριστοκρατικὴν πολιτείαν at 9.1 and to his ἀριστοκρατικὴν καὶ βασιλικὴν πολιτείαν at 15.1 are strong praise, indicating that Pericles was indeed establishing an ideal constitution, marked by rule of the best man. Cf. the theoretical notion of the man preeminent in *aretē*, whose rule is accepted and acceptable because of his superiority, Arist. *Pol.* 1288a15–29. The exact source of Plutarch's knowledge of Aristotelian political concepts is uncertain: cf. the Introduction, 3.2.c.

Aristides: son of Lysimachus, called "the Just." He led the Athenian hoplites at Salamis and Plataea, and played a major role in
the establishment of the Delian League. In the tradition he was a
conservative opponent of Themistocles (cf., e.g., Hdt. 8.79.2; *Ath.
pol.* 23.4), but he could also be described as a democrat and ally of
Themistocles (*Ath. pol.* 23.3–4, 41.2, etc.; cf. Rhodes, *CAAP* ad
loc.). P. wrote his life, as well as those of Themistocles and Cimon.
The place and date of his death were uncertain. According to
Arist. 26, some said he died in Pontus on the Black Sea, others in
Athens, and Craterus that he died in Ionia after being fined for
taking bribes, sometime after the ostracism of Themistocles. We
know nothing for certain of his political activity after 477.

Themistocles: the son of Neocles, the man responsible for building the Athenian fleet into Greece's largest navy and the Athenian
commander at Salamis. He was ostracized and then pursued on a
charge of treason as far as Epirus. Finally he fled to the king of
Persia, under whose protection he died. For his later years see esp.
Thuc. 1.135–38; Plut. *Them.* 22–32. The dates of his ostracism
and subsequent flight represent one of the more puzzling problems of fifth-century chronology: cf. Gomme, *HCT* 1:397–401;
Lenardon 1959; Rhodes 1970; Frost 1980, 187–92. Ca. 472 B.C. is
a reasonable guess.

Cimon: the son of Miltiades and Hegesipyle, of the ancient and
influential Philiad *genos* (cf. Davies, *APF* 302). His father, Miltiades, had been prosecuted by Pericles' father, Xanthippus, in 489
and fined 50 talents, an immense sum. After Miltiades died in
prison, Cimon gave his sister Elpinice in marriage to Callias, the
richest man in Athens, and the fine was paid. Cimon was related to
Pericles by marriage, for his wife, Isodice, was an Alcmeonid, as
was Pericles' mother, Agariste. He emerged as the leading figure
of Athenian politics thanks to his family connections, good temperament, and success as fleet-commander in a number of campaigns in the early period of the Delian League. He recovered the
bones of Theseus from Scyros, inflicted a major defeat on the
Persians at the Eurymedon River on the southern coast of Asia
Minor, and put down the revolt of Thasos. His generosity was
responsible for a number of buildings and public works at Athens,

including the Stoa Poikile and the planting of trees in the Agora and the Academy. Like many aristocrats Cimon was pro-Spartan, not only serving as *proxenos* of Sparta but naming one son Lacedaemonius. Cf. Meiggs, *AE* 68–91; Kagan, *OPW* 59–68; Mosley 1971; Podlecki 1971.

αἱ στρατεῖαι: as usual, P. shuns exactness, and our own estimates are uncertain as well. His life of Cimon (7.1–17.3) treats the expeditions he may be thinking of: Eion, Scyros (which he dates to the archonship of Apsephion, 469/68), one or more expeditions collecting tribute, the battle of the Eurymedon, the operations in the Chersonese, the siege of Thasos, and an unspecified naval expedition during which Ephialtes reformed the Areopagus. Others, such as the expedition to aid Sparta after the earthquake, and a second to help at Ithome, are excluded by τῆς Ἑλλάδος ἔξω, as perhaps are those to Thasos and Scyros. This list is very difficult to reconcile with Thucydides' summary account (1.98–102), Diodorus (11.60–70), or our other sources. Despite valiant efforts the precise dates remain uncertain: see the discussion of Meiggs, *AE* 68–91. P. probably has no specific occasion in mind, but thinks that Cimon's frequent absences made Pericles' rise to power easier. In a similar way he states that Ephialtes was able to make his reforms when Cimon sailed out on campaign (ὡς δὲ πάλιν ἐπὶ στρατείαν ἐξέπλευσε), although we know of no sea campaign at this time (cf. note to 9.5). Contrast Pericles' difficulties when his rival was Thucydides, who did not leave the city (11.1). P. does not mention in this context Pericles' prosecution of Cimon after the siege of Thasos (10.6; *Cim.* 14.3–5).

οὕτω δή: "in these circumstances." For οὕτως or οὕτω δή in the apodosis after a temporal clause or participle see LSJ s.v. οὕτως I.7. The use is classical.

φέρων: "enthusiastically, at full tilt, wholeheartedly." This sense is especially common with verbs of giving or entrusting: cf. 12.5, *Fab.* 6.2, *Them.* 24.3, *Luc.* 6.5, *Pomp.* 27.6; LSJ s.v. φέρω A.X.2.b; *MT* 837.

προσένειμεν ἑαυτόν: "took the part of, attached himself to." This postclassical development from "assigned himself to" is already found in [Dem.] *Ep.* 3.2 ταῖς τοῦ δήμου προαιρέσεσιν προσένειμεν ἑαυτόν; cf. also *Pomp.* 21.7, τῷ δήμῳ προσνεμεῖ μᾶλλον ἑαυτὸν ἢ τῇ βουλῇ; *Pel.* 26.1, *Cat. Mai.* 3.4, *Mar.* 41.5, *Sert.* 4.7, *Eum.* 3.1, *Sull.* 4.3 and Holden's note ad loc.

παρὰ τὴν αὐτοῦ φύσιν: P. is careful to point out that Pericles is not by nature a populist but takes this course only in view of the political circumstances. This warning prepares us for the "aristocratic" Pericles of 9.1 and 15.1. Such comments on actions παρὰ φύσιν are valuable indications of P.'s opinion of his subject's underlying character, that is, his natural tendency or disposition. Cf. *Luc.* 6.2, *Mar.* 28.1, *Tim.* 14.4, in each case indicating an uncharacteristic action made under the pressure of circumstances; and *Nic.* 18.11 and *Crass.* 16.1, uncharacteristic confidence and boastfulness preceding disaster. See further on this passage the note to 9.1; Connor 1968, 179n. 32; Breebaart 1971, 262; Wardman 1974, 138; and in general Gill 1983.

δημοτικήν: The adjective is difficult to translate. Its fundamental meaning is "of, relating to, for the demos." Since the demos often means the mass of the people, and not the economic and social elite, it can mean "ordinary, used by the people," as of a wine, or "of the common people, not wealthy," like Tellus the Athenian in Solon's story (*Sol.* 27.6) or Aristides (*Arist.* 6.2, ἀνὴρ πένης καὶ δημοτικός). Politically, it means "favoring, taking the side of the demos" against the wealthy or few. Of course, the word in this sense is ideal for political labeling: cf. Aeschines 3.168–70, where Aeschines argues that Demosthenes is far from being δημοτικός. It is frequently used as the adjective for the noun "democracy," therefore "democratic, favoring the rule of the people" (cf. *Ath. pol.* 9.1, 22.1, with Rhodes, *CAAP* ad loc.; de Ste. Croix 1954–55, 22–24), and is often found in the comparative. But it also means "respecting the rights of the demos, not lording it over the demos," as at *Praec. ger. rep.* 817C, δημοτικὸν δὲ [ἐστι] καὶ βλασφημίαν ἐνεγκεῖν καὶ ὀργὴν ἄρχοντος, or *Nic.* 2.6, and can be opposed to σεμνός, with its implications of elitism and arrogance (cf. 813C, οὐ γὰρ σεμνὸν οὐδὲ δημοτικὸν ἡ φιλαρχία). Here P. has several meanings in mind: his birth and wealth meant that Pericles was not one of the people, his φρόνημα σοβαρόν (5.1) and σεμνότης (5.3) that he was not "ordinary." The narrative will demonstrate his "aristocratic" policy.

7.4

ὑποψίᾳ . . . τυραννίδος: cf. 7.1. We have no other evidence that Pericles would be considered a potential tyrant at the beginning of his career. The phrase, however, echoes Ath. pol. 22.3: ὀστρακισμόν, ὃς ἐτέθη διὰ τὴν ὑποψίαν τῶν ἐν ταῖς δυνάμεσιν, ὅτι Πεισίστρατος δημαγωγὸς καὶ στρατηγὸς ὢν τύραννος κατέστη. P. is probably making an inference from Aristotle, supported by the later attacks on Pericles' "tyranny." Fear of ostracism made Pericles first wary of the demos (7.1), then attached to it. On the relation of ostracism to popular fear of tyranny see Rhodes, CAAP on Ath. pol. 22.3, pp. 269–70: the ancient sources agree that the institution was originally aimed at those who became too powerful, especially the friends of the tyrants. Tyranny might emerge either from democracy or oligarchy: see Arist. Pol. 1305a7–28, 37–41. The reaction against Alcibiades at the time of the Hermocopidae (Thuc. 6.15.4, 60.1) demonstrates that the fear of tyranny was a very real undercurrent in Athenian politics.

περιπεσεῖν: again the infinitive after a verb of fearing: see 7.2, φοβούμενος ἐξοστρακισθῆναι.

ἀριστοκρατικόν: on the term see note to 7.3. Cimon had a φύσις ἀριστοκρατική (cf. Comp. Cim.–Luc. 2.7); his aristocratic policy was tied to his philo-Laconism (Cim. 10.8, προαιρέσεως ἀριστοκρατικῆς καὶ Λακωνικῆς οὔσης).

τῶν καλῶν κἀγαθῶν: a common classical term for a gentleman, one of the upper class in terms of family and social position: here another name for the πλούσιοι καὶ ὀλίγοι. In P., more often written separately, καλὸς καὶ ἀγαθός: cf. 8.5 (of Thucydides son of Melesias) and 11.2 (his supporters), Nic. 2.2 (Thucydides' supporters), and Ath. pol. 28.5 (Thucydides and Nicias as καλοὺς κἀγαθούς). P. used the term also of the Roman optimates (e.g., Cic. 11.2).

ὑπῆλθε . . . παρασκευαζόμενος: This statement has been considered hostile to Pericles (e.g. by Siefert and Blass 1909 ad loc.), but P. takes no exception to Pericles' reasons. ὑπῆλθε is not "insinuate oneself into the good graces of" as Holden and LSJ, but simply "win over": see *Dion* 14.5, *Luc.* 6.4, *Pyrrh.* 4.6, *Cat. Min.* 50.2. Thus also ὑπεποιεῖτο at 9.2. The invidious meaning derives from the means used in certain cases: e.g., δώροις καὶ κολακείαις in *Luc.* 6.4.

7.5

τοῖς περὶ τὴν δίαιταν: his way of life; cf. *Praec. ger. rep.* 800B. The use at 16.4 is similar but applies more to regular expenses than to habits. On this passage see Connor 1971, 121–28, noting how Pericles' new habits established him as an expert in public business and free of corrupting obligations to friends: his attention was given exclusively to public business in agora and council chamber, and he did not attend the usual upper-class dinner parties. Both represent a marked shift from earlier practice, including Cimon's (cf. the contrast noted by Ion, 5.3). The conduct described here and in 5.1–3 is held up as an example to the politician in the *Praecepta* (800B–C).

ἀγοράν: not only the marketplace, but the center of civic life and government, where courts and commissions met, magistrates did business, and new proposals to the assembly were posted. See Wycherley 1968 and 1978, 27–40; H. A. Thompson and Wycherley 1972; H. A. Thompson et al. 1976; Camp 1986. The continuing excavations there have become an extraordinary source for our knowledge of classical Athens, thanks to the uncovering of buildings and the discovery of inscriptions and every kind of artifact. One of the buildings in the southwest corner, erected in the mid-fifth century, may be the *stratēgeion*, or office for the board of generals (H. A. Thompson et al. 1976, 113–14; Wycherley 1978, 46; Camp 1986, 116–18). P.'s phrase is slightly different in *Praec. ger. rep.* 800C: μίαν ὁδὸν πορεύεσθαι τὴν ἐπὶ τὸ βῆμα καὶ τὸ βουλευτήριον.

τὸ βουλευτήριον: the meeting house of the boule, which handled much of the daily business of the city as well as planning legislation for the assembly: see *Ath. pol.* 43–49; Rhodes 1972, 30–48. Its remains have been excavated in the southwest corner of the Agora (the "old bouleterion"); cf. Wycherley 1978, 33–34; H. A. Thompson et al. 1976, 49–50; Camp 1986, 52–53. On the close cooperation between *stratēgoi* and the boule see Rhodes 1972, 43–46.

κλήσεις τε δείπνων: "invitations to dinners." Cf. the dinners with Cimon and Sophocles described by Ion of Chios (392 F13, F6), and the dinner party for which Bdelycleon prepares Philocleon (Ar. *Wasps* 1208–52).

φιλοφροσύνην: "friendliness, familiarity."

συνήθειαν: "regular contact."

ἐν . . . γενομένοις: note that P. is here speaking of Pericles' whole career, not just the early years. For the length of his career cf. 16.3.

ὡς . . . ἐλθεῖν: ὡς for the more usual ὥστε; see Smyth 2252; *MT* 608–609.

Euryptolemus: This cousin of Pericles is otherwise unknown, since he cannot be identified either with the son of Megacles and father of Cimon's wife, Isodice (*Cim.* 4.10, 16.1), or the son of Pisanax and cousin of Alcibiades (Xen. *Hell.* 1.4.19, etc.), although like them he would have been an Alcmeonid, related to Pericles through his mother, Agariste, perhaps Isodice's brother or son: see Davies, *APF* 376–78; W. E. Thompson 1969. The anecdote indicates the strength of Pericles' ties with the Alcmeonids.

γαμοῦντος: a banquet was given by the father of the bride before she was taken to the groom's house; Pericles left after the libations to the gods (σπονδαὶ) at the end of the meal, before the festive drinking. For the wedding ceremony see Erdmann 1934, 250–61; Flacelière 1965, 61–64, 173–75. For the importance of the feast see *Symp.* 666D-667B.

ἐξανέστη: "rose and left"; cf. Plato *Rep.* 328A, ἐξαναστησόμεθα γὰρ μετὰ τὸ δεῖπνον; Isoc. 1.32, ἐξανίστασο πρὸ μέθης.

7.6

δειναὶ γὰρ . . . ἐστι: The word order, alliteration, generalizing plural, and postponement of the verb give the statement a sententious ring and augment the contrast between φιλοφροσύνη, συνήθεια and ὄγκος, τὸ σεμνόν. The best modern example of a politician who used this device might be Charles de Gaulle.

τῆς ἀληθινῆς δ' ἀρετῆς: in contrast to τὸ πρὸς δόξαν σεμνόν. Pericles' aloofness is an ambiguous quality, to P. as well as to Ion (cf. 5.3). Some distance from the populace is good, but aloofness from friends suggests a need to conceal one's true qualities: real virtue is most appreciated when best known. P., as so often, thinks of his own friends and social world, the easy intercourse of the *Table Talk*, or his close relations with the young men in his house: cf. Barrow 1967, 18–19. The original model, however, was Socrates: cf. *An seni* 796D–E, describing Socrates as "philosophizing" whether joking, drinking, serving on campaign, or talking in the Agora, πρῶτος ἀποδείξας τὸν βίον ἅπαντι μέρει, καὶ πάθεσι καὶ πράγμασιν ἁπλῶς ἅπασι, φιλοσοφίαν δεχόμενον.

τὰ μάλιστα φαινόμενα: "the aspects that are most manifest."

τοῖς ἐκτός: "strangers, the outside world."

ὁ καθ' ἡμέραν βίος: "ordinary, day-by-day life." The virtuous man's intimates, who know him best, will be most impressed by his virtue.

7.7

καὶ τῷ δήμῳ: i.e., not only to his (wealthy) friends. Πλῆθος below is a stylistic variation for δῆμος.

τὸ συνεχές: the neut. sing. adj. for an abstract noun: "constant exposure."

οἷον ἐκ διαλειμμάτων: "as if at intervals." The οἷον excuses his use of the medical term for intermittent treatment: see Sansone 1988.

Σαλαμινίαν: The Salaminia and the Paralus were two sacred triremes with elite crews, used for special state business, such as fetching Alcibiades from Sicily in 415 (*Alc.* 21.7, Thuc. 6.53.1).

P. uses this example in *Praec. ger. rep.* 811C in the context of contemporary politics. First he praises those who, like the elder Cato, Epaminondas, and himself, are willing to undertake any work for the city, however humble. Then he writes: ἕτεροι δὲ σεμνότερον οἴονται καὶ μεγαλοπρεπέστερον εἶναι τὸ τοῦ Περικλέους, ὧν καὶ Κριτόλαός ἐστιν ὁ Περιπατητικός, ἀξιοῦντος [ἀξιῶν mss.], ὥσπερ ἡ Σαλαμινία ναῦς Ἀθήνησι καὶ ἡ Πάραλος οὐκ ἐπὶ πᾶν ἔργον ἀλλ᾽ ἐπὶ τὰς ἀναγκαίας καὶ μεγάλας κατεσπῶντο πράξεις, οὕτως ἑαυτῷ πρὸς τὰ κυριώτατα καὶ μέγιστα χρῆσθαι. He then notes the error of attempting to do everything in a city, citing especially the case of Metiochus, a friend of Pericles, who was mocked by a comic poet for just that. There follow examples of other statesmen: on the one hand, Scipio Africanus, who avoided envy by retiring for long periods to the country; on the other, Timesias of Clazomenae and Themistocles, who suffered from the hatred and envy of the citizens they served. Finally, he concludes that the statesman must keep an eye on everything, but not necessarily do it all himself, using the analogy of the helmsman who does some things himself, others through the ship's crew. This was the method of Pericles, he concludes. The hand's division into fingers does not weaken it but strengthens it and makes it more useful. Clearly P., although he is aware of the dangers of being too reserved, thinks Pericles' practice the best to follow on most occasions. The eagerness to control everything is more dangerous than the fear of overexposure.

Critolaus: a head of the Peripatetic School in the second century B.C. and one of the ambassadors of Athens to Rome in 155 (with Carneades the Academic and Diogenes the Stoic). See Wehrli 1959, 49–74. There are some forty fragments of his works: this is no. 37 (p. 58). He may also be the author of historical works, *FGrHist* 823.

7.8

Ephialtes: for Ephialtes and his role in the Areopagus reform see note to 9.3–5. P. singles out the most important action done (as he sees it) through an intermediary. There is no chronological difficulty: in 7.5–7 he has been describing Pericles' character as a politician, which leads naturally to the example of Ephialtes and the effect on the demos. The aside diverts our attention from Pericles' behavior to the effect of his decision to support the demos, which will become the subject of chapters 9–14.

Plato: *Rep.* 562C (describing the change from a democratic polis to a tyranny), Ὅταν οἶμαι δημοκρατουμένη πόλις ἐλευθερίας διψήσασα κακῶν οἰνοχόων προστατούντων τύχῃ, καὶ πορρωτέρω τοῦ δέοντος ἀκράτου αὐτῆς μεθυσθῇ, . . . The passage is also echoed in *Cim.* 15.2, referring to Ephialtes' ἄκρατον δημοκρατίαν, and quoted in *Qu. Gr.* 295C–D, describing the outrageous behavior of the Megarian demos after the expulsion of the tyrant Theagenes.

οἱ κωμῳδοποιοί: adespota F41 K., *CAF* 3:406. The fragment seems to refer to the Euboean expedition of 446 (cf. 23.3), although Meiggs (*AE* 120) prefers a time in the late 450s. The image presents the demos as an unruly and sexually aroused horse, as P. explains. The verse is anapestic tetrameter. The infinitives of P.'s quotation may be those of the original, as such charges are often attributed to others in comedy. Cf. also 3.6. Ar. *Clouds* 211–13 also makes a joke of Pericles' treatment of Euboea.

ἐξυβρίσαντα: "breaking out in insolence," which for animals is sexual; cf. the ὑβριστὴς ἵππος of Plato *Phaedrus* 254C, E.

πειθαρχεῖν: "obey the reins."

τολμᾶν: "endure, have patience."

ἀλλ᾽ ⟨ἐν⟩δάκνειν: Ziegler's emendation, moved from the apparatus to the text of the third edition, is unsatisfactory, as it requires lengthening the vowel before mute plus liquid, which is anomalous for comedy, and would mean "bite Euboea like a bit," which is not appropriate here. The mss. ἀλλὰ δάκνειν expresses the typical behavior of an undisciplined stallion: cf. Xen. *Cyr.* 7.5.62, οἵ τε ὑβρισταὶ ἵπποι ἐκτεμνόμενοι τοῦ μὲν δάκνειν καὶ ὑβρίζειν ἀποπαύονται; *Eq.* 5.3, ὁ γὰρ κημὸς [halter] ἀναπνεῖν μὲν οὐ κωλύει, δάκνειν δὲ οὐκ ἐᾷ.

ταῖς νήσοις ἐπιπηδᾶν: "mount upon the islands," referring to the mistreatment of the allies, perhaps the cleruchies mentioned in 11.5 or the appropriation of money for Athenian buildings, 12.1–2. Again the image is sexual: cf. Plato *Phaedr.* 254A; Arist. *Hist. an.* 5.539b.

8

Oratory was the chief instrument of Pericles' political success; P. sees it both as demagogic rhetoric (esp. 8.5) and an instrument of philosophy. On Pericles' ability see also Thuc. 1.139.4 *(λέγειν . . . δυνατώτατος)* and 2.65.8–9. One branch of the tradition about his skill, probably originating with Theopompus, is analyzed by Connor 1962b. See also Meinhardt, 86–88, and Blass 1887, 1.2:34–39. P. returns to the subject in 15.2–3.

8.1

τῇ μέντοι . . . ὑποχεόμενος: "However, tuning his oratory, like an instrument, in harmony with his way of life and the greatness of his conceptions, he often stretched Anaxagoras among the strings, pouring out natural philosophy like a dye on his rhetoric." The richness of the shifting metaphors causes some difficulty in comprehension.

τῇ . . . περὶ τὸν βίον κατασκευῇ: roughly equivalent to τοῖς περὶ τὴν δίαιταν at 7.5.

τῷ μεγέθει τοῦ φρονήματος: cf. note to 4.6.

ὥσπερ ὄργανον: cf. *Cic.* 4.4, ὥσπερ ὄργανον ἐξηρτύετο τὸν ῥητορικὸν λόγον; *Comp. Arist.–Cat. Mai.* 2.5, πρόβλημα τοῦ βίου καὶ δραστήριον ὄργανον ἔχων τὸν λόγον; *Cat. Min.* 4.3, ἤσκει δὲ καὶ τὸν ὀργανικὸν εἰς πλήθη λόγον. P. treats at length the importance of oratory in politics and gives advice on speechmaking in *Praec. ger. rep.* 801C–

804D. According to 802B, the statesman adorns the city, as an architect a building, ἐνὶ χρώμενος ὀργάνῳ τῷ λόγῳ. The example of Pericles, who ruled the city διὰ λόγου δύναμιν, confirms the statement. Although ὄργανον is a general word, the image here is of a musical instrument, tuned in harmony with his life and plans. Cf. Fuhrmann 1964, 129n. 3, 196.

ἐξαρτυόμενος: especially appropriate for a musical instrument ("tuned"): cf. De def. or. 437D, ὄργανον ἐξηρτυμένον καὶ εὐηχές.

παρενέτεινε: continues the metaphor. A. is "strung on as an extra string" on Pericles' instrument. Cf. Sol. 3.4, γνώμας ἐνέτεινε φιλοσόφους . . . τοῖς ποιήμασιν; De prof. in virt. 84A, Φρῦνιν μὲν γὰρ οἱ ἔφοροι ταῖς ἑπτὰ χορδαῖς δύο παρεντεινάμενον ἠρώτων πότερον τὰς ἄνωθεν ἢ τὰς κάτωθεν ἐκτεμεῖν αὐτοῖς ἐθέλει παρασχεῖν. Ziegler's conjecture παρενέσπειρε ("sowed"; cf. Dion 11.1, [τοῦ Δίωνος] τῶν λόγων τοῦ Πλάτωνος ἔστιν οὕστινας ὑποσπείροντος) is not convincing, and he abandons it in his third edition. It changes the metaphor unnecessarily and employs a very rare word. Ὑποσπείρω occurs several times in P. (Per. 24.4, Lys. 5.3, De adul. et amic. 65C), but neither ἐνσπείρω nor παρενσπείρω. P.'s preferred form of σπείρω in this context would be ἐγκατασπείρω (cf. Thes. 3.2, De Is. 380A, Plat. quaest. 1001B).

οἷον βαφὴν . . . ὑποχεόμενος: the metaphor shifts to dyeing (cf. Fuhrmann 1964, 186 and n. 3). Although βαφή can mean the temper of a sword, I do not see how one can use ὑποχέομαι βαφήν in that sense. For Anaxagoras' teaching and φυσιολογίαν see 4.6.

8.2

Plato: a free quotation from Phaedr. 270A, already echoed in 5.1: πᾶσαι ὅσαι μεγάλαι τῶν τεχνῶν προσδέονται ἀδολεσχίας καὶ μετεωρολογίας φύσεως πέρι· τὸ γὰρ ὑψηλόνουν τοῦτο καὶ πάντῃ τελεσιουργὸν ἔοικεν ἐντεῦθέν ποθεν εἰσιέναι. ὃ καὶ Περικλῆς πρὸς τῷ εὐφυὴς εἶναι ἐκτήσατο· προσπεσὼν γὰρ οἶμαι τοιούτῳ ὄντι ᾿Αναξαγόρᾳ, μετεωρολογίας ἐμπλησθεὶς καὶ ἐπὶ φύσιν νοῦ τε καὶ διανοίας ἀφικόμενος, ὧν δὴ πέρι τὸν πολὺν λόγον ἐποιεῖτο ᾿Αναξαγόρας, ἐντεῦθεν εἵλκυσεν ἐπὶ τὴν τῶν λόγων τέχνην τὸ πρόσφορον αὐτῇ. Both P.'s precision in paraphrasing and his freedom (omissions, finite verbs changed to participles, etc.) are typical of his method and are indicative for passages where his source cannot be checked. ʿΟ θεῖος is used as an epithet for Plato also at *De cap. util.* 90C.

τελεσιουργόν: "effective, accomplishing its purpose."

τὸ πρόσφορον: that which is suitable to the τέχνη.

8.3

ἀναθημάτων: this word, inserted by Ziegler, avoids a construction that is extremely rare in P., the relative following upon the article. Scanning the Teubner text, I find τῶν οἷος (*Lys.* 24.5), τοῦ δ (*De comm. not.* 1070E), τὸ οὗ ἕνεκα (*De def. or.* 435F and *Symp.* 698B), [τὸ] οὗ (*Aquane an ignis* 957E), and τὸ ὃ (*De lib. et aegrit.* 8). The ἀναθήματα are the Acropolis buildings (see 12.1 and the account in chapters 12–13).

διὸ καὶ τὴν ἐπίκλησιν: Plutarch lists three reasons for the epithet: the buildings he built for the city, his political and military power, and his oratorical ability. His own thoughts will be given at 39.2.

δυνάμεως: cf. Diod. 13.98.3, τοῦ προσαγορευθέντος κατὰ τὴν δύναμιν Ὀλυμπίου.

Ὀλύμπιον: the earliest known use of the name is part of Dicaeopolis' explanation of the cause of the Peloponnesian War in Ar. *Ach.* 530–31: ἐντεῦθεν ὀργῇ Περικλέης οὐλύμπιος / ἤστραπτ᾽, ἐβρόντα, ξυνεκύκα τὴν Ἑλλάδα. These lines became part of a standard tradition about Pericles' oratory found in both Latin and Greek writers (Cic. *Or.* 29, *De or.* 3.138, *Brutus* 38, 44, 59; Val. Max. 8.9.ext. 2; Pliny *Ep.* 1.20.17–19; Quint. 12.2.22, 12.10.24–25, 12.10.64–65; Diod. 12.40.5–6; Aristid. 46.128–130 [2:173–75 Dindorf]) that has been traced by Connor 1962b. Plutarch uses this tradition, which perhaps derives from Theopompus (cf. also notes to 7.1, 16.3), alongside Plato and other sources. Another tradition connected the epithet with Pericles' calmness: cf. Val. Max. 5.10.ext. 1 and below, 39.2.

συνδραμεῖν . . . ἀπὸ πολλῶν προσόντων: "was the combined result of many of (his) qualities." Πρόσοντα, "the qualities attaching to a person."

οὐδὲν ἀπέοικεν: "it is not at all unlikely."

8.4

διδασκάλων: poets, as the author of a play trained the chorus and actors.

σπουδῇ: "seriously."

ἀφεικότων . . . εἰς αὐτόν: "letting fly at him." Ἀφίημι is regularly used of missiles.

προσωνυμίαν: "nickname, epithet."

βροντᾶν . . . ἀστράπτειν: both taken from Ar. Ach. 531 (quoted in note to 8.3) with the indicatives changed to infinitives to fit the construction of the sentence.

δεινὸν . . . φέρειν: the author of this verse (adespota F10 K., CAF 3:399) is unknown. Note that it does not come from the same play as the words quoted immediately before, although we would have been tempted to say so if the Acharnians were not preserved. Cf. 3.5. Δέ belongs to P.'s sentence, not the verse, so that the iambic trimeter lacks the third and fourth elements of the first metron. The reference to a thunderbolt implies a comparison or identification of Pericles with Zeus, as in the Acharnians passage. Cf. also note to 3.5–7. Plutarch passes over other passages on Pericles' oratory that do not help explain Ὀλύμπιος, including one from Eupolis that was part of the Theopompan tradition (F94 K. = 102 K.A.):

(Α.) κράτιστος οὗτος ἐγένετ' ἀνθρώπων λέγειν·
ὁπότε παρέλθοι ⟨δ'⟩, ὥσπερ ἀγαθοὶ δρομῆς,
ἐκ δέκα ποδῶν ᾕρει λέγων τοὺς ῥήτορας.
(Β.) ταχὺν λέγεις δε. (Α.) πρὸς δέ ⟨γ'⟩ αὐτοῦ τῷ τάχει
πειθώ τις ἐπεκάθιζεν ἐπὶ τοῖς χείλεσιν,

οὕτως ἐκήλει καὶ μόνος τῶν ῥητόρων
τὸ κέντρον ἐγκατέλειπε τοῖς ἀκροωμένοις.

Cf. also the phrase of Cratinus quoted by Aristides 45.19, 2:23 Dindorf (F293 K. = 324 K.A.): ὦ μεγίστη σὺ γλῶττα τῶν Ἑλληνίδων.

8.5

διαμνημονεύεται: a common verb introducing an anecdote (cf., e.g., *Sol.* 18.7), and not necessarily indicative that the source was the memoirs of Ion of Chios. This would be a good story in rhetorical schools (cf. Meinhardt, 28), but the use of ἀντιπολιτεύσατο is a strong indication that P. derived it from Theopompus: see Ruschenbusch 1980. The anecdote supplies additional confirmation for Pericles' ability as speaker. A slightly different version is told at *Praec. ger. rep.* 802C, illustrating the value for a politician of oratorical skill (cf. note to 8.1).

Thucydides: already mentioned at 6.2–3: see note to 11.1.

Archidamus: the Eurypontid king of Sparta, 469–427, who rallied the Spartans after the great earthquake (*Cim.* 16.4–7) and led the invasion of Attica in 431 (Thuc. 2.10–12, 18–20). He was a guest-friend of Pericles (33.3). The time and occasion of the encounter (if it ever took place) are unknown: the two may have met at a major festival during the 440s, or after Thucydides' ostracism. As Pericles' example shows (and later that of Alcibiades; cf. Thuc. 5.43), upper-class Athenians maintained ties with Sparta; moreover, Thucydides was closely related to Cimon, who had brought help to Sparta after the earthquake. For Archidamus' influence cf. Lewis 1977, 45–48; de Ste. Croix, *OPW* 141–43; Westlake 1968, 122–35.

παλαίει: the metaphor is particularly appropriate because Thucydides belonged to a family of wrestlers; see note to 11.1.

καταβάλω: a technical term, "throw for a fall"; the passive is πίπτω. See Plato *Hipp. Min.* 374A, αἴσχιον ἐν πάλῃ τὸ πίπτειν ἢ τὸ καταβάλλειν; *Euthyd.* 277D, etc.

μεταπείθει: "persuades to a different opinion." For a similar wrestling joke cf. Ar. *Knights* 571–73.

8.6

οὐ μὴν ἀλλά: "nonetheless"; despite his skill, Pericles was always careful.

οὕτως ὁ Περικλῆς: *sic* Holzapfel, *Philologus* 51 (1892) 276, accepted by Ziegler and Flacelière. However, αὐτός (mss.) rightly emphasizes the contrast between Thucydides' characterization of Pericles and the man's actual performance and seems supported by *Praec. ger. rep.* 803F (καὶ Περικλῆς ἐκεῖνος, "even the great Pericles") and by *Fab.* 4.3 (οὐ μὴν ἀλλὰ καὶ αὐτὸς ὁ Φάβιος). Although οὐ μὴν ἀλλὰ καὶ is common in P., it is nowhere else followed by οὕτως, and only at *Fab.* 4.3 by αὐτός.

τὸ βῆμα: the speaker's platform, especially the one on the Pnyx where the assembly met.

ηὔχετο: the same prayer is reported in *Praec. ger. rep.* 803F, exemplifying the statesman's need for preparation. See also Quint. 12.9.13, *nec immerito Pericles solebat optare, ne quid sibi verbum in mentem veniret quo populus offenderetur*; Aelian *VH* 4.10, ὁσάκις ἔμελλεν [ὁ Περικλῆς] ἐς τὴν ἐκκλησίαν παριέναι, ηὔχετο μηδὲν αὐτῷ ῥῆμα ἐπιπολάσαι τοιοῦτον, ὅπερ οὖν ἔμελλεν ἐκτραχύνειν τὸν δῆμον, πρόσαντες αὐτῷ γενόμενον καὶ ἀβούλητον δόξαν. Both these versions make Pericles afraid of the demos, an idea absent from the two in Plutarch. The ultimate source is unknown.

Another example of caution in speaking, not recorded by Plutarch, is found in the Suda, s.v. Περικλῆς Π1180: ὅστις πρῶτος γραπτὸν λόγον ἐν δικαστηρίῳ εἶπε, τῶν πρὸ αὐτοῦ σχεδιαζόντων. Cf. also *Praec. ger. rep.* 813D, quoted in note to 18.1.

[μηδὲ] ῥῆμα μηδέν: Ziegler brackets μηδέ unnecessarily, as the use of the adverb to intensify, though rare, occurs several times in P., including the version of the same anecdote at *Praec. ger. rep.* 803F as well as *Phoc.* 37.3.

πρὸς τὴν προκειμένην χρείαν: "to the present need"; cf. Thuc. 2.60.5, γνῶναί τε τὰ δέοντα καὶ ἑρμηνεῦσαι ταῦτα.

8.7

ἔγγραφον . . . οὐδέν: for a general treatment of Pericles' speeches and the extant fragments see Blass 1887, 1.2:34–39. Cicero refers to extant speeches (*Brut.* 27, *De or.* 2.93), but his stylistic judgments are based on those in Thucydides (see Douglas 1966, xlv–xlvi). Quintilian expressly denies the genuineness of speeches attributed to him (3.1.12; cf. 12.2.22, 12.10.49). Plutarch does not consider the speeches in Thucydides evidence for Pericles' oratory (cf. Stadter 1973b, 118–23).

πλὴν τῶν ψηφισμάτων: Attic decrees found on inscriptions regularly record the mover as part of the preamble (e.g., ML 58, l. 2: Καλλίας εἶπε). None of Pericles' are preserved on stone. Craterus, however, made a collection of decrees, which must have included some of Pericles' (see the Introduction, 3.1.l), and others may have been recorded in other sources (see Frost 1961). A Περικλέους γνώμη[ν], which might be a decree moved by Pericles, often referred to as the "papyrus decree," is mentioned in a fragment of a commentary to Demosthenes 22 (P. Stras. 84), but restoration and interpretation are disputed (cf. Meiggs, *AE* 515–18, and below, note to 12.1). Plutarch refers explicitly to Pericles' decrees often in this life: 10.4, 20.2, 25.1, 30.2–3, 32.2–3, 37.3, and esp.17.1–3.

ὀλίγα: of the eight fragments known, three are quoted here (the Sophocles anecdote should not be counted, as it is not from a speech), another at 33.5, and the remaining four in Aristotle's *Rhetoric*. Aristotle's quotations indicate that distinctive phrases or figures were recalled in rhetorical circles. He cites two as examples of the use of similes at 3.1407a1–5: καὶ ἡ Περικλέους εἰς Σαμίους, ἐοικέναι αὐτοὺς τοῖς παιδίοις ἃ τὸν ψωμὸν δέχεται μέν, κλαίοντα δέ. καὶ εἰς Βοιωτούς, ὅτι ὅμοιοι τοῖς πρίνοις· τούς τε γὰρ πρίνους ὑφ' αὐτῶν κατακόπτεσθαι, καὶ τοὺς Βοιωτοὺς πρὸς ἀλλήλους μαχομένους. Two others he cites as examples of metaphor, at 3.1411a2–4, ὥσπερ Περικλῆς ἔφη τὴν νεότητα τὴν ἀπολομένην ἐν τῷ πολέμῳ οὕτως ἠφανίσθαι ἐκ τῆς πόλεως ὥσπερ εἴ τις τὸ ἔαρ ἐκ τοῦ ἐνιαυτοῦ ἐξέλοι (from the Samian funeral oration: see *Rhet.* 1.1365a31–33 and below, note to 8.9) and 3.1411a15–16, καὶ Περικλῆς τὴν Αἴγιναν ἀφελεῖν ἐκέλευσε τὴν λήμην τοῦ Πειραιέως (repeated by P. in this passage). A fifth citation, recalling a trick of Pericles in his cross-examination of Lampon (3.1419a2–6; cf. note to 6.2), may be from a judicial speech.

οἷον τὸ . . . κελεῦσαι: this example and the following are compressed into a single articular infinitive.

τὴν Αἴγιναν . . . ἀφελεῖν: "to remove Aegina, the pus in the eye of the Piraeus." Aegina probably did not join the Delian League at its foundation but in ca. 459 was made tributary after being defeated by Athens in a major sea battle and losing seventy ships (Thuc. 1.105.2, 108.4; cf. ML 33). After the peace treaty of 446 she remained in the empire, but her continuing complaints to Sparta supplied one of the motives for the war (Thuc. 1.67.2, 139.1). In 431, after the Spartan invasion, the Athenians removed the Aeginetans from the island and settled their own citizens there (*Per.* 34.2; Thuc. 2.27.1). These words probably belong to the latter occasion, as they seem similar to Thucydides' explanation: τὴν Αἴγιναν ἀσφαλέστερον ἐφαίνετο τῇ Πελοποννήσῳ ἐπικειμένην αὐτῶν πέμψαντας ἐποίκους ἔχειν. The phrase was recalled for its forceful image: conjunctivitis was a common ancient disease, marked by a purulent discharge of the eye, sticking the eyelids together and impairing or blocking vision. The offending matter needed to be cleaned out (cf. *Non posse* 1101C, δεῖ μὲν γὰρ ἀμέλει τῆς περὶ θεῶν δόξης ὥσπερ ὄψεως λήμην ἀφαιρεῖν τὴν δεισιδαιμονίαν). Aegina similarly inhibited the use of the Piraeus. Plutarch quotes the phrase also at *Dem.* 1.2, and *Reg. et imp. apophtheg.* 186C and *Praec. ger. rep.* 803A, perhaps from Arist. *Rhet.* 3.10.7.1411a15–16. Our "eyesore" is now trite, and in any case has a different meaning, referring to an obvious blight external to the viewer. The expression is attributed to Demades in Athen. 3.99D; Strabo (9.1.14 [395]) says some applied it to the island of Psyttalia.

τὸν πόλεμον . . . προσφερόμενον: "he said he descried the war approaching from the Peloponnese." The occasion is not known, perhaps the debate on sending help to Corcyra (cf. 29.1 and Thuc. 1.44.2, ἐδόκει γὰρ ὁ πρὸς Πελοποννησίους πόλεμος καὶ ὣς ἔσεσθαι αὐτοῖς). Although not cited elsewhere, the phrase was no doubt remembered for the image, apparently of a ship approaching over the sea. Such an approach would often be dangerous and undesired: cf. *Thes.* 19.10, *Per.* 26.1, etc. Siefert and Blass 1909 think rather of a cloud coming; cf. Dem. 18.188, τὸν κίνδυνον παρελθεῖν ὥσπερ νέφος.

8.8

καί ποτε τοῦ Σοφοκλέους: Sophocles the tragedian also held political positions, although his tenure of some is disputed. Most certain are the offices of *Hellēnotamias* in 443/42 (*IG* I^2 202 = I^3 269) and general in 441/40 with Pericles at the time of the Samian War (Androtion, *FGrHist* 324 F38; cf. Aristodemus 15.4; schol. Ar. *Peace* 697; Strabo 14.1.18 [638]). The *Vita Sophoclis* 9 gives him a generalship against the Ananians (the Samian exiles) "seven years before the Peloponnesian War." He probably served as *proboulos* in 411 (Arist. *Rhet.* 3.1419a25–30): see Jameson 1971; Calder 1971, 172–74; Karavites 1976. The notice of P. (*Nic.* 15.2) that Sophocles was a colleague of Nicias in the 420s is rejected by Woodbury 1970; Avery 1973 errs in rejecting all offices except the generalship of 441/40. We have no way of judging his actual or perceived competence for these offices. P.'s anecdote is also found in Cic. *De off.* 1.144 and Val. Max. 4.3.ext. 1 and is probably to be dated to 440 and the Samian campaign, when the two were generals together. In [Plut.] *Vitae dec. or.* 839A a similar admonition to Sophocles is ascribed to Isocrates; in *Arist.* 24.7 Aristides speaks in like manner to Themistocles. In an anecdote of Ion of Chios, Sophocles notes his own generalship in snatching a kiss from a pretty wine-pourer (*FGrHist* 392 F6 = Athen. 13.603E–604D); this story could be from the same source, or another. Sophocles' erotic feelings were well known: cf. e.g. Plato *Rep.* 329B–C. The relation between Pericles and Sophocles is explored in a highly speculative manner by Ehrenberg 1954. Note that in this period there was another Sophocles, general in 426/25 and 425/24 in Sicily, exiled for not subduing the island (Thuc. 4.65.3), probably identical with the Sophocles who was one of the thirty tyrants (Xen. *Hell.* 2.3.2).

8.9

ὁ δὲ Στησίμβροτός φησιν: *FGrHist* 107 F9; on Stesimbrotus see the Introduction 3.1.c. Pericles' Funeral Oration after the Samian War was famous (cf. 28.4–7); another striking phrase was cited by Aristotle *Rhet*. 1.7.1365a31–33: οἷον Περικλῆς τὸν ἐπιτάφιον λέγων, τὴν νεότητα ἐκ τῆς πόλεως ἀνῃρῆσθαι ὥσπερ τὸ ἔαρ ἐκ τοῦ ἐνιαυτοῦ εἰ ἐξαιρεθείη (cf. 3.10.1411a2–4; Hdt. 7.162.1). Treves 1941 discusses the influence Pericles' expression may have had on Herodotus; cf. also Fornara 1971b, 83–84. For speculation on the content of the oration see Weber 1922.

οὐδὲ γάρ: the negative of καὶ γάρ, cf. Denniston, 111. The argument is in the form of an enthymeme, or rhetorical syllogism: we know (although we cannot see them) that the gods are immortal because of the honors they receive and the benefits they bestow; the fallen also receive honors and bestow benefits; therefore, the fallen, although we no longer see them, are immortal. As usual, the enthymeme suppresses one of the premises. One notes the use of sophistic logic and especially the rationalization of our understanding of the gods. The undying fame of the fallen became a topos of Athenian funeral orations, but only Lysias makes a direct comparison with the gods: ὑμνοῦνται δὲ ὡς ἀθάνατοι διὰ τὴν ἀρετήν. καὶ γάρ τοι θάπτονται δημοσίᾳ, καὶ ἀγῶνες τίθενται ἐπ' αὐτοῖς ῥώμης καὶ σοφίας καὶ πλούτου, ὡς ἀξίους ὄντας τοὺς ἐν τῷ πολέμῳ τετελευτηκότας ταῖς αὐταῖς τιμαῖς καὶ τοὺς ἀθανάτους τιμᾶσθαι (2.80).

9.1

Plutarch poses the problem of Pericles' political character in terms of the opposition between Thucydides' praise of his control of the people and Plato's criticism of his pandering to them. For the account of the struggle with Cimon and the reform of the Areopagus, our best source, however inadequate, is *Ath. pol.* 25–27, for which Rhodes's discussion, *CAAP* 309–44, is invaluable. P. also treats Cimon's life in his *Cimon*, but with a different focus and selection of incident: see the Introduction, 2.6. *Cim.* 10–19 covers the same period as *Per.* 9–10.

Thucydides: a direct quote from 2.65.9, part of his evaluation of Pericles, cited also at *Praec. ger. rep.* 802C.

ἄλλοι δὲ πολλοί: especially Plato. Cf., e.g., *Gorg.* 515E, on whether Pericles made the Athenians better, or corrupted them: ταυτὶ γὰρ ἔγωγε ἀκούω, Περικλέα πεποιηκέναι Ἀθηναίους ἀργοὺς καὶ δειλοὺς καὶ λάλους καὶ φιλαργύρους, εἰς μισθοφορίαν πρῶτον καταστήσαντα. Cf. also *Gorg.* 518E.

κληρουχίας: see 11.5–6.

θεωρικὰ καὶ μισθῶν διανομάς: "festival funds and wage distributions." This general statement is particularized in what follows: see 9.3, 11.4, 12.4–5 and commentary.

πολυτελῆ: "extravagant," not "expensive." The order of the adjectives is chiastic, σώφρονος responding to ἀκόλαστον and αὐτουργοῦ to πολυτελῆ. Cf. *Cat. Mai.* 2.3, ἐπέτεινε τὴν αὐτουργίαν καὶ περιέκοπτε τὴν πολυτέλειαν. As in that passage, αὐτουργία refers most often to working one's own land (Cato had just observed Manius Curius, who τὸ χωρίδιον αὐτὸς ἔσκαπτε) but also in general to any manual occupation by which one earns one's living. One thinks of men like Dicaeopolis in the *Acharnians* or Euphiletus in Lysias *Or.* 1, farmers who either lived on their land, or lived in the city or their deme and went out to their farms. *Autourgia* was still a question in P.'s day: cf. Dio Chrysostom's admiration for the rustics of Euboea and his advice on suitable pursuits for urban workers in *Or.* 7, *Euboicus.* For the combination of πολυτέλεια and ἀκολασία cf. *Praec. ger. rep.* 800D (of Alcibiades), and for the adjectives *Ant.* 2.4, *Symp.* 709B.

θεωρείσθω: for similar third-person commands cf. *Lyc.* 17.5, *Mar.* 2.4, *Sert.* 9.10, *Dion* 2.6, *Brut.* 16.3, *Arat.* 10.5, 38.6.

διὰ τῶν πραγμάτων: the fundamental idea of Plutarchean biography, to learn from a man's actions his character, but usually stated at the beginning of a life: cf. *Mar.* 2.4, *Cim.* 3.3, *Agis* 2.9; but also *Arat.* 10.5.

τῆς μεταβολῆς: the change in Pericles, from a demagogue to the good monarch. See Breebaart 1971. The change to be examined here is not one in character but, as often in Plutarch, of political policy, from demagoguery to "aristocratic" government. As Connor (1968, 179n. 32) has remarked, P. had already noted a change of policy in Pericles, toward the demos, in 7.3–4. Similar changes are noted in Theseus and Romulus (*Comp. Thes.–Rom.* 2.1) from monarch to *dēmotikos* and *tyrannos* respectively, in Crassus (πολλὰς μεταβολὰς ἐν τῇ πολιτείᾳ μεταβαλλόμενος; cf. *Comp. Nic.–Crass.* 2.2) and in Antony (*Cic.* 43.4, [it was rumored that] μεταβεβλῆσθαι μὲν Ἀντώνιον θαυμαστὴν μεταβολήν; cf. *Brut.* 21.1). Alcibiades, like a chameleon, changed his ethos and with it his policies, but never his nature (cf. *Alc.* 2.1, 23.5). On such changes see Russell 1966, 146. These changes should be distinguished from major changes in character, which might suggest a change in nature (*physis*), as in the cases of Philip V (cf. *Arat.* 51.4) and Sulla (cf. *Sull.* 30.5), on which see Gill 1983, esp. 478–79. For *metabolē* as a change in behavior cf. *Them.* 3.4, *Tim.* 14.4, *Pel.* 1.4, *Cat. Mai.* 24.11, *Mar.* 3.2, *Sull.* 2.3, *Luc.* 38.3, *Pomp.* 18.2, *Dion* 11.4; as change in fortune, see *Aem.–Tim.* and *Demetr.–Ant.*, passim. Cf. also P.'s examination of the change in the frequency of oracles, *De def. or.* 412B, ὥστε τὴν αἰτίαν ἄξιον εἶναι παρὰ τῷ Πυθίῳ διαπορῆσαι τῆς μεταβολῆς.

9.2

ἐν ἀρχῇ: In 9.2–10.8 we see Pericles winning control of the city from Cimon in two stages. First, despite Cimon's generosity in distributing his wealth, Pericles wins the favor of the demos by distributing public funds. He then uses the demos to restrict the Areopagus and to ostracize Cimon. Later, when Cimon's conduct at Tanagra and the demos' desire for peace weaken Pericles' position, he recalls Cimon, but with a secret agreement that he retain power at home while Cimon fights abroad. Cimon dies on campaign (10.8). The struggle for control is renewed in the conflict with Thucydides son of Melesias (11–14), until he is ostracized (14.3). The sources are mixed, but Theopompus and *Ath. pol.* are prominent. See below and Meinhardt, 33–35.

Our information on the political activity of this period, and especially on the reforms of the Areopagus, which introduced a new stage in Athenian government, is very thin and often contradictory. We do not know that P.'s was much better. Note that Nepos' *Cimon* hardly mentions Cimon's political activity, omitting any notice of the Areopagus reform, Pericles, or Ephialtes, and ascribing his ostracism purely to the *invidia* that the Athenians regularly showed toward their leaders. Diodorus knows Cimon as a commander but omits his ostracism and recall. The reforms are ascribed to Ephialtes alone (11.77.6). Theopompus recorded Cimon's generosity (F89) and his recall from ostracism after only five years (F88), but the fragments do not reveal how much else he might have said. Nevertheless some historians have seen him as the major source for both P. and Nepos. Cf., however, the Introduction, 3.2.b.

Outside of the *Pericles* P. occasionally marks Cimon as a political rival of Pericles (*Pel.* 4.3, *Praec. ger. rep.* 812F) but more frequently of Themistocles—a role for which he was trained by Aristides (*Cim.* 5.6; *Them.* 5.4, 20.4, 24.6; *An seni* 791A, 795C)—and, after Themistocles' ostracism, of Ephialtes (*Cim.* 10.8, 15.2, 16.9; cf. *Ath. pol.* 28.2).

P.'s *Cimon* makes Ephialtes the central figure of the reform, with Pericles only a useful ally: cf. 10.8, πρὸς Ἐφιάλτην ὕστερον χάριτι τοῦ δήμου καταλύοντα τὴν ἐξ Ἀρείου πάγου βουλὴν διηνέχθη and 15.2, ἤδη καὶ Περικλέους δυναμένου καὶ τὰ τῶν πολλῶν φρονοῦντος (quoted at greater length in note to 9.5). The earlier life's depreciation of Pericles follows the tendency found in *Ath. pol.* 25.1–2, which focuses on Ephialtes and Cimon. In the *Pericles*, as regularly in the *Lives*, P. highlights and even exaggerates the activities of his hero, helped by the focus on Pericles' competition with Cimon in *Ath. pol.* 27 (cf. also Arist. *Pol.* 3.1274a7–9). The actual roles of the three in the events preceding and at the time of the reform cannot be stated with any certainty. Themistocles, who is associated with Ephialtes in a trick to discredit the Areopagus in *Ath. pol.* 25.2–4 (cf. Hypothesis to Isoc. 7), probably had challenged the Areopagus in some way before his ostracism, or in connection with his trial for treason. Archestratus, named at *Ath. pol.* 35.2, presumably moved some of the legislation.

ὥσπερ εἴρηται: refers back to 7.3–4, after the digression of 7.5–8.9.

ὑπεποιεῖτο: "curried their favor"; cf. Dem. 19.76; Arist. *Pol.* 5.1303b24; *Ath. pol.* 6.3.

ἐλαττούμενος . . . χρήμασιν: Cimon's lavish use of his wealth, especially the enormous sums derived from the booty of his campaigns, is described in more detail in the *Cimon* (10.1–3). P. derives his knowledge from *Ath. pol.* 27.3–4 and Theopompus (cf. *FGrHist* 115 F89 = Athen. 12.533A–C). See Wade-Gery 1938, 133–34 (= 1958, 236–38); Connor 1968, 30–38. Note that in the *Cimon* the notice is fuller and provokes a panegyric on Cimon's generosity (10.6–8) that has no place here. See the Introduction, 2.6.

ἀνελάμβανε: "win the favor of"; cf. 34.2 and Holden's note to this passage.

τῷ δεομένῳ: cf. Theopompus F89, *ἐθεράπευεν δὲ τοὺς . . . δεομένους*. *Ath. pol.* says he helped only those of his deme, Laciadae.

τοὺς πρεσβυτέρους ἀμφιεννύων: According to Theopompus, when Cimon encountered someone poorly clothed, he would have one of his retinue exchange clothes with him. That those poorly dressed were old is an addition by P.

ὀπωρίζωσιν: "pick and eat fruit"; cf. *ὀπωρίζονται* in Theopompus, *τῆς ὀπώρας ἀπολαύειν* in *Ath. pol.* That the verb is found only here in P. suggests that he took it from Theopompus, but it is found also in Herodotus and Plato. For the distinction between picking fruit for immediate consumption and carrying it off for future use or sale cf. Plato *Laws* 844D–845D and Matthew 12:1.

καταδημαγωγούμενος: Theopompus concludes, *ἐκ τούτων ἁπάντων ηὐδοκίμει* [Cimon] *καὶ πρῶτος ἦν τῶν πολιτῶν*. *Ath. pol.* notes that Pericles had to *ἀντιδημαγωγεῖν* (27.3). Both imply, like P., that Cimon had played the demagogue. In the *Cimon* P. acknowledges that there were those who charged that Cimon's distribution of money was "truckling to the mob and demagoguery" but argues that the accusations were disproved by Cimon's aristocratic and Laconian leanings (10.8).

τρέπεται: the historical present appears eight times in the *Pericles*. Five times it is used of decrees: γράφει ψήφισμα (17.1, 30.2, 30.3; cf. also *Them.* 10.4, 11.1, *Arist.* 22.1, *Phoc.* 26.3); ψηφίζεται (24.1, cf. *Mar.* 29.9, *Caes.* 33.6, *Ti. Gracch.* 21.4, *Dem.* 27.6, *Ant.* 60.1; also καταψηφίζεται, *Sull.* 10.1); and κυροῦται ψήφισμα (32.3). Other examples are 31.2, καθίζουσιν (cf. *Luc.* 9.2, *Cat. Min.* 27.7, *Arat.* 21.6) and 33.4 ἐμβάλλουσιν (cf. *Fab.* 6.2 and twelve other examples in the *Lives*). The present adds vividness, but P.'s criterion for choosing to use it also seems to depend on the usage patterns of certain verbs and stylistic precedent. Cf. Schwyzer and Debrunner 1959, 2:271–73; Eriksson 1943. Eriksson notes (p. 55) that Dionysius of Halicarnassus, for instance, regularly uses the present for decrees or resolutions of the senate, a usage already found in the orator Lycurgus (*contra Leocrates* 113, καὶ ψηφίζεται ὁ δῆμος); this stylistic habit certainly explains the frequency of P.'s usage of the historical present for similar expressions in the *Pericles*. Τρέπεται appears as a historical present some twenty-four times in the *Lives*, most often referring to battle, but also, as here, to taking a new course of action. Cf. Eriksson (p. 66) on its use in Dionysius.

Damonides: not to be confused with his son Damon (see 4.1–4), as he was in *Ath. pol.* 27.4, the passage to which P. refers: πρὸς δὴ ταύτην τὴν χορηγίαν ἐπιλειπόμενος ὁ Περικλῆς τῇ οὐσίᾳ, συμβουλεύσαντος αὐτῷ Δαμωνίδου τοῦ Οἴηθεν (ὃς ἐδόκει τῶν πολλῶν εἰσηγητὴς εἶναι τῷ Περικλεῖ· διὸ καὶ ὠστράκισαν αὐτὸν ὕστερον), ἐπεὶ τοῖς ἰδίοις ἡττᾶτο, διδόναι τοῖς πολλοῖς τὰ αὐτῶν, κατεσκεύασε μισθοφορὰν τοῖς δικαστηρίοις. Damonides was Pericles' advisor in the 460s, Damon in the 430s: see note to 4.1–4 and Raubitschek 1955a, 82–83. Damonides' deme was Oe (Οἴηθεν), not Oa (Ὄαθεν) as in Stephanus of Byzantium: see Dow 1963, 180–81 (but contrast Rhodes, *CAAP* 341). Dow and some other scholars prefer the properispomenon accent, Οἶηθεν. Ziegler's text, with the addition of ⟨Δάμωνος τοῦ⟩, unwarrantedly presumes that the son was the only advisor of Pericles.

9.3

καὶ ταχύ: The exact dates and sequence of the measures by which Pericles won over the people are uncertain; P. slides smoothly over the problem. The following list is an expansion of δημοσίων διανομήν in 9.2, but P. omits the details that would allow us to judge the value of his statement and specify his sources. In stressing the personal factor, he neglects whatever larger political aims or principles Pericles may have had in allowing the demos to share in public monies.

θεωρικοῖς: "festival monies." The theoric fund (τὸ θεωρικόν or τὰ θεωρικά [sc. χρήματα]) provided funds for the festivals (θεωρίαι). In Demosthenes' day it probably paid two obols a day for citizens to attend dramatic festivals: see Pickard-Cambridge 1968, 265–68; Van Ooteghem 1932; Buchanan 1962 (with the review by de Ste. Croix 1964); Rhodes, *CAAP* 514. Pericles had no connection with this fund: Ruschenbusch 1979 has argued convincingly that the fund was established in the fourth century by Eubulus. The indications in our ancient sources are contradictory. Most place its origin in the mid-fourth century, but some refer the fund to Pericles, and others to Agyrrhius, the demagogue who introduced in 395 payment for attendance at the assembly (cf. Harpocration s.v. θεωρικά). It is uncertain whether in fact P. means to allude to this two-obol payment or is thinking simply of increased public support of festivals, which would naturally please the demos. P. refers at 11.4 to Pericles' generosity in supplying festivals and theatrical performances, the frequency of which were also noted by Thucydides (2.38.1) and pseudo-Xenophon (*Ath. pol.* 2.9). But although it is possible that P. is using the generalizing plural θεωρικὰ in this vague sense of support for festivals, it is more likely that he is following an old tradition found, e.g., in Ulpian's note to Demosthenes 1.1 (p. 33 Dindorf = p. 16 Dilts) cited by Pickard-Cambridge 1968, 266n. 12: "Note that these public funds were originally made theoric by Pericles for this reason: since many wanted to see the show and were fighting for places, both strangers and citizens, and in the end the rich used to buy up the places, (Pericles), desiring to please the demos and the poor people, wrote a law that money coming in to the city should be theoric money for the citizens." (Cf. also schol. Aeschin. 3.24). Wade-Gery 1938, 133–34 (= 1958, 236–38), argues that P. continues to follow Theopompus here; Meinhardt thinks of Philochorus (cf. 328 F33, cited by Pickard-Cambridge 1968, 266n. 12), but other sources are possible as well. In *Arist.* 24.5 P. associates the growth of *theō-*

rika and other distributions with the demagogues who succeeded Pericles.

δικαστικοῖς λήμμασιν: Aristotle specified that pay for jury duty was the first innovation of Pericles (*Ath. pol.* 27.3, ἐποίησε δὲ καὶ μισθοφόρα τὰ δικαστήρια Περικλῆς πρῶτος, ἀντιδημαγωγῶν πρὸς τὴν Κίμωνος εὐπορίαν; 27.4, quoted in note to 9.2; and *Pol.* 2.1274a9). P. could have deduced from Aristotle that this move preceded the reforms of Ephialtes and the ostracism of Cimon, but he may have found the notion already in Theopompus or another source. Dating the introduction of jury pay before the reforms suits P.'s belief in the importance of Pericles' political role in the 460s; those who question this argue that jury pay was introduced only after the reforms (e.g., Rhodes, *CAAP* 339–40). The evidence is reviewed by Hignett, *HAC* 216–21, 342–43; Rhodes, *CAAP* 338–40. Pay for service in the popular courts would have been desirable for those seeking popular support, not only to respond to the generosity of Cimon—although that undoubtedly would have been a factor—but because it permitted the demos both to take an active part in this aspect of government and to profit from the wealth coming into the Athenian treasury. The original payment of two obols a day was raised to three obols by Cleon (schol. Ar. *Wasps.* 88, 300). Such payments were of course criticized by Plato for encouraging the populace to be lazy and talkative (cf. note to 9.1).

ἄλλαις μισθοφοραῖς: P. is distressingly imprecise, so that we cannot be certain what other payments, if any, he thought that Pericles introduced. *Ath. pol.* 24.3 lists many categories of citizens who were supported by revenues from the Delian League: judges, bowmen, cavalrymen, councilmen, Acropolis guards, state officials, and hoplites and sailors. Not all of these would have been introduced at the same time. P. is probably counting all payments from public funds, but especially the navy (11.4), army (12.5), and public works (12.5–6). Although the date of origin and the amounts paid are disputed, the evidence seems to support military and naval payments before the Peloponnesian War: Ulpian on Dem. 13 (p. 222 Dindorf = p. 167 Dilts), πρῶτος γὰρ ἐκεῖνος [Pericles] ἔταξε μισθοφορὰν καὶ ἔδωκε τῷ δήμῳ στρατευομένῳ, is supported by *Ath.*

pol. 27.2, stating that when the Peloponnesian War began the Athenians were already accustomed to being paid for military service (συνεθισθεὶς ἐν ταῖς στρατείαις μισθοφορεῖν), and by ps.-Xen. *Ath. pol.* 1.13. See the discussion by Pritchett 1974, pt. 1, 7–14.

χορηγίαις: frequently used in the general sense of "largess" (cf. Holden on *Them.* 5.1).

συνδεκάσας: "bribe wholesale, in a body" (cf. Holden on this passage). Note that both χορηγία and δεκάζειν appear in *Ath. pol.* 27.4–5, which probably influenced P.'s choice of vocabulary.

ἐχρῆτο: sc. τῷ πλήθει.

τῆς ἐξ Ἀρείου πάγου βουλῆς: the council of the Areopagus was the most traditional body in the state, composed of those who had passed their εὔθυνα after serving as one of the nine archons listed by P.: the eponymous archon, king, polemarch, and six thesmothetae. See *Ath. pol.* 3.6 and, for the duties of the archons, 3.1–5, 55–59. The duties of the Areopagus both before and after the reform of Ephialtes are highly controversial. Until 462 the council, among other duties, judged cases of homicide and apparently oversaw official cults and infractions against them and could punish magistrates for misuse of office (see Hignett, *HAC* 89–91, and, for a recent discussion of the multiple problems involved, Ostwald 1986, 7–47). It was thought to have been influential in organizing the Athenians at the time of the Persian Wars (cf. *Ath. pol.* 23.1), but in the 460s was seen as opposing the plans and careers of men like Ephialtes and Pericles. Once the archons were chosen by lot, the influence of the Areopagus undoubtedly lessened, but there were other factors at work as well, such as a desire for stricter control of public monies: cf. W. G. Forrest 1966, 209–20; Davies 1978b, 63–75. Aeschylus presents the mythical foundation of the council by Athena in the *Eumenides*, produced in 458.

9.4

κληρωταί τ' ἦσαν ἐκ παλαιοῦ: according to *Ath. pol.* 8.2, from the time of Solon. *Ath. pol.* 22.5 adds that the procedure was changed

by Pisistratus and that choice by lot from a select group was rein-
troduced in 487/6, although Herodotus (6.109.2) states that Callimachus, the polemarch at Marathon, had been selected by lot. On
this question and the contrast with Arist. *Pol.* 2.21.1273b41–74a3,
according to which Solon made no change, see Rhodes, *CAAP*
272–74.

οἱ δοκιμασθέντες: "those who had been approved." *Δοκιμασία* at
Athens was the process of examining a candidate for the magistracy, described at length in *Ath. pol.* 55.2–4. There is no other
evidence for such a procedure before one entered the Areopagus.
P. uses δοκιμάζω frequently, but apparently never in the Athenian
technical sense. (He uses δοκιμασία only once, also not in this
sense: *Cleom.* 10.11; cf. [Plut.] *De lib. ed.* 9D.) P. is probably thinking
of the εὔθυνα, the examination of a magistrate's administration at
the end of his term in office (Hignett, *HAC* 203). It is unlikely that
he is referring to the examination before the archonship, which
would imply that the current archons were also members of the
Areopagus. Such a practice seems contradicted by *Ath. pol.* 60.3
and other passages (see Rhodes, *CAAP* 107 and ad loc.), although
Forrest 1966 and Forrest and Stockton 1987 argue for it.

ἀνέβαινον: a technical word for becoming a member of the council
of the Areopagus; cf. *Ath. pol.* 60.3.

9.5

μᾶλλον ἰσχύσας: P. takes Pericles' attack on the Areopagus as an
effect, not the cause, of his strength with the demos. Most historians think P. is anachronistic in attributing so much power to Pericles so early in his career and prefer to think of Ephialtes as the
dominant figure in the attack. See below at δι' Ἐφιάλτου.

κατεστασίασε: "defeated in factional rivalry." *Στάσις* is the term for
political strife within the polis. P. uses κατεστασίαζω to describe
the defeat of a political opponent, both in Greece (esp. Themistocles' ostracism of Aristides, *Them.* 5.7, 11.1, *Comp. Arist.–Cato* 2.4;
but cf. also *Thes.* 35.5, *Phil.* 13.8, 15.11, *Dion* 37.6) and in late
Republican Rome (*Mar.* 28.8, *Comp. Lys.–Sull.* 5.2, *Sert.* 4.6, *Pomp.*
47.2, *Caes.* 14.17, *Cat. Min.* 29.5, *Cic.* 45.4, *Brut.* 22.3). The word

may have been used by Theopompus (cf. 115 F240), but appears in other fourth-century writers as well. P. sees two results of Pericles' attack: (1) (μέν), the restriction of the jurisdiction of the Areopagus; (2) (δὲ), the ostracism of Cimon, who, although not known to be a member of the council, attempted to reverse this action (*Cim.* 15.3).

ἀφαιρεθῆναι τὰς πλείστας κρίσεις: the exact scope of the reforms made by Ephialtes in 462/61 is disputed. Cf. *Cim.* 15.2, τελέως ἀνεθέντες οἱ πολλοὶ καὶ συγχέαντες τὸν καθεστῶτα τῆς πολιτείας κόσμον τά ⟨τε⟩ πάτρια νόμιμα οἷς ἐχρῶντο πρότερον, Ἐφιάλτου προεστῶτος ἀφείλοντο τῆς ἐξ Ἀρείου πάγου βουλῆς τὰς κρίσεις πλὴν ὀλίγων ἁπάσας, καὶ τῶν δικαστηρίων κυρίους ἑαυτοὺς ποιήσαντες, εἰς ἄκρατον δημοκρατίαν ἐνέβαλον τὴν πόλιν, ἤδη καὶ Περικλέους δυναμένου καὶ τὰ τῶν πολλῶν φρονοῦντος. In both the *Cimon* and the *Pericles* P. gives as the major change the transfer of legal jurisdiction to the Council of the Five Hundred and the other courts: cf. *Ath. pol.* 25.2. According to Philochorus (328 F64), Ephialtes left the Areopagus only homicide cases; cf. Dem. 23.22, 65–66. Lysias (*Or.* 7.22) notes that it was also responsible for the sacred olives. It may have been at the time of the reform that Ephialtes installed the axones with the laws of Solon in the Agora (cf. Anaximenes, *FGrHist* 72 F13; Immerwahr 1985; Rhodes, *CAAP* 134–35). For discussions of the reforms see Hignett, *HAC* 193–213; Sealey 1964; Ruschenbusch 1966; Rhodes, *CAAP* 314–19; Ostwald 1986, 28–83.

δι' Ἐφιάλτου: Here, at 7.8, and at *Praec. ger. rep.* 812D, P. speaks of Ephialtes as an agent of Pericles, although in *Cim.* 15.2 and *Ath. pol.* 25.1–2 Ephialtes is portrayed as acting on his own. (The alleged association of Themistocles and Ephialtes in *Ath. pol.* 25.3–4 is most unlikely, unless we are to refer it to a separate occasion at a much earlier date, in the 470s.) The present statement is consistent with P.'s figure of forty years at 16.3, which would have Pericles πρωτεύων as early as 468. The focus throughout this chapter is on Pericles' defeat of Cimon by winning over the demos. Contrary to P., modern historians presume that Ephialtes was the older and more influential at this time. However, we know practically nothing about Ephialtes. His father, Sophonides, is unknown, so he may not have belonged to the elite class of old and wealthy land-owners, which could explain Ephialtes' reputation for poverty (Aelian *VH* 2.43, 11.9, 13.39). As a general he led a naval expedition beyond the Chelidonian islands off the south coast of Asia Minor, south of Phaselis (*Cim.* 13.4, citing Callisthenes, *FGrHist* 124 F16). He must have had political support. However, it is quite possible that Pericles, with his wealth and family connections, was the more influential if not the more active of the two. Ephialtes is paired with Cimon: this may indicate that he was older than Pericles, or simply that, like Cimon, he left the political scene long before Pericles. It is possible that Ephialtes began the attacks on the Areopagus and that Pericles associated himself only later. Ephialtes' one other known political stand was his opposition to Cimon's support of Sparta (*Cim.* 16.9). For a recent review of the evidence, see Piccirilli 1989.

ἐξοστρακισθῆναι: in P.'s mind, Pericles' major goal. The charges made against Cimon are more specific in *Cim.* 15.3–5, which adds an incestuous relation with his sister Elpinice. (That Elpinice was a factor at least in some Athenians' minds is confirmed by an ostrakon of Cimon found in the Keramaikos, with the comment "let him get out and take his sister with him"; cf. Mattingly 1971–72, 284.) For his Spartan sympathies see note to 7.3, and *Cim.* 16.1–17.3; he was μισόδημος because he tried to restore the privileges of the Areopagus, which according to P. had been curtailed in his absence (*Cim.* 15.3). P. does not consider here Cimon's expedition to Mount Ithome in Messenia to help the Spartans (Thuc. 1.101–2, *Cim.* 16.4–10, 17.3), the date and circumstances of which are much debated: see Busolt, *Gr. Gesch.* 2:453–55; Meiggs, *AE* 88–89; Gomme, *HCT* on 1.101.2–102.4 and p. 411n. 1; Cole 1974; Kagan, *OPW* 71–74; de Ste. Croix, *OPW* 179.

The ostracism probably fell immediately after Ephialtes' reforms, in spring 461, five years before the battle of Tanagra (see Theopompus 115 F88), although Unz 1986, 79, argues for 459. There are more than five hundred ostraka naming Cimon now known: see Thomsen 1972, 76, 83n. 207; and figure 3, this volume. One of them, interestingly enough, is a sherd from the same pot as ostraka naming Megacles and Themistocles (p. 95), indicating that Cimon was already an important political figure in the

480s, or that this ostrakon is naming an older relative. On the institution of ostracism see note to 4.3.

νίκας: esp. at Eion (Thuc. 1.98.1; Diod. 11.60.1–2; *Cim.* 7) and the Eurymedon (Thuc. 1.100.1; Diod. 11. 60–62; *Cim.* 12–13).

ὡς ἐν τοῖς περὶ ἐκείνου γέγραπται: see *Cim.* 10, 13.5–7. P. not infrequently gives such cross-references, especially to works written at about the same time. Attempts to analyze these cross-references to establish the chronology of the *Lives* are made more problematic by the existence of citations between some pairs in both directions: see Mewaldt 1907 and Stoltz 1929. Mewaldt is certainly right in arguing that some pairs were published together, although his precise groups cannot be accepted. See Hamilton 1969, xxxiv–xxxvii. However, the *Pericles*, which belongs to the tenth pair, would be later than the pair *Cimon–Lucullus*, which was among the first written: cf. Jones 1966b, 66–68; and see the Introduction, 1.3.

τοσοῦτον . . . Περικλέους: the ostracism is evidence of Pericles' power, although not until Thucydides' ostracism (14.3) will he be completely free to act.

10.1

νόμῳ: dat. of means with *ὡρισμένην*, in this position to avoid the hiatus of *νόμῳ εἶχε* or *νόμῳ ὡρισμένην*.

φεύγουσιν: the normal word for exiles; for the ostracized, *μεθεστῶτες* is more common (cf. *Arist.* 8.1, etc.).

τῷ διὰ μέσου: sc. *χρόνῳ*. The Tanagra campaign is usually dated to summer 457. The campaign is described in Thuc. 1.107.2–108.1 and Diod. 11.80; cf. *Cimon* 17.4–9 and modern discussions by Gomme, *HCT* ad loc.; Reece 1950; de Ste. Croix, *OPW* 190–91; Meiggs, *AE* 417–18. The Spartans had helped Doris against the Phocians and were returning home through Boeotia when they were attacked by the Athenians at Tanagra. Both sides suffered heavy casualties. The two accounts in Plutarch reveal how he adjusts his narrative to fit the purpose of each life: see the Introduction, 2.6.

P. is silent here on Thucydides' references to oligarchic encouragement to the Spartan army: τὸ δέ τι καὶ ἄνδρες τῶν Ἀθηναίων ἐπῆγον αὐτοὺς κρύφα, ἐλπίσαντες δῆμόν τε καταπαύσειν καὶ τὰ μακρὰ τείχη οἰκοδομούμενα (1.107.4); cf. καί τι καὶ τοῦ δήμου καταλύσεως ὑποψίᾳ (1.107.6). In the *Cimon* (17.5) Cimon is sent away not as an exile, but from fear of conspiracy, τῶν ἐχθρῶν αὐτοῦ καταβοώντων ὡς συνταράξαι τὴν φάλαγγα βουλομένου καὶ τῇ πόλει Λακεδαιμονίους ἐπαγαγεῖν. The accusation of conspiracy would not fit P.'s picture here of the gentle and reasonable Pericles.

Κίμων: his appearance on the battlefield is found only here and in *Cim.* 17.4–5.

ἔθετο . . . τὰ ὅπλα: "took his position."

φυλετῶν: the phyle was Oineis, *Cim.* 17.4.

φίλοι τοῦ Περικλέους: according to *Cim.* 17.5, the Council of Five Hundred, on the grounds that Cimon wanted to confuse the soldiers and help the Spartans (Rhodes 1972, 36, notes that the involvement of the boule is most unlikely). Thucydides (1.107.4) says that some of the Athenian oligarchs had led the Spartans to this part of Boeotia.

10.2

Περικλῆς: This is our only evidence for Pericles' participation in the battle. It may have been invented by P. to improve the story and emphasize the contrast of Pericles and Cimon. On the other hand, Pericles could easily have been a soldier, officer, or even general at this time.

10.3

ἔπεσον: about one hundred fell, according to *Cim.* 17.7.

ἡττημένους: thus Thuc. 1.108.1, although Plato *Menex.* 242A and Diod. 11.80.2 call it a draw. This and προσδοκοῦντας modify Ἀθηναίους and explain the reason for their change of heart.

ἐπὶ τῶν ὅρων: Tanagra is in the valley of the Asopus, in eastern Boeotia, and rather close to Attica. This was the first time Sparta and Athens had fought in open battle.

εἰς ἔτους ὥραν: "for the fine season of the year," i.e., for next spring. Cf. *Cim.* 17.8, προσδοκῶντες εἰς ὥραν ἔτους στρατίαν Πελοποννησίων ἐπ' αὐτούς. In fact the Athenians within two months defeated the Boeotians at Oinophyta and won temporary control of Boeotia (Thuc. 1.108.2–3).

10.4

γράψας αὐτός: One of the many decrees attributed to Pericles in this life, which P. may have seen in Craterus (see the Introduction, 3.1.1). P. respects Pericles' flexibility in responding to circumstances.

κἀκεῖνος ἐπανελθών: Ἐπανελθών is an emendation of Coraes accepted by Ziegler for the mss.' ἀπελθών, which is meaningless here. P. more likely wrote κατελθών, suggested by Sintenis and accepted by Flacelière. Ἐπανέρχομαι occurs frequently in the sense of "return," and would be possible here, but the term usually used by P. for return from ostracism is κατέρχομαι (*Them.* 11.1, *Alc.* 25.6, 27.1, 32.2), the word used in the parallel passage in the *Cimon* (18.1, ὁ Κίμων κατελθών).

The fact and the date of Cimon's recall are much disputed, largely because P. here and at *Cim.* 17.8–18.1 seems to conflict with Thuc. 1.112.1, who speaks of a five-year treaty between Sparta and Athens usually dated to 451 by modern scholars. Plutarch may be using Theopompus: cf. 115 F88, οὐδέπω δὲ πέντε ἐτῶν παρεληλυθότων πολέμου συμβάντος πρὸς Λακεδαιμονίους ὁ δῆμος μετεπέμψατο τὸν Κίμωνα, νομίζων διὰ τὴν προξενίαν ταχίστην ἂν αὐτὸν εἰρήνην ποιήσασθαι. ὁ δὲ παραγενόμενος τῇ πόλει τὸν πόλεμον κατέλυσε. Gomme, *HCT* 1:326–27, on the basis of Theopompus, accepts the early return of Cimon but places the treaty in 451;

Meiggs, *AE* 111, 422–23, accepts a special recall not after Tanagra, but after the Egyptian defeat, ca. 452; some, following Beloch, *Gr. Gesch.* 2.2:210–11, reject any recall, supposing that Cimon returned only in 451 after his ten years were up. Raubitschek 1954–55 and 1966 accepts the recall and places the five-year treaty of Thuc. 1.112.1 in 458/57; Kagan, *OPW* 91–92, accepts a recall after Tanagra and thinks the peace referred to by P. is the four-months' peace mentioned in Diod. 11.80.6; Unz 1986, 76–82, argues strongly for Cimon's recall in 454 (after five years of exile) in response to the Egyptian disaster. Andoc. 3.3 mentions the recall of a Miltiades son of Cimon and a fifty-year peace; Nepos (*Cim.* 3.3) follows Theopompus in placing the recall in the fifth year of Cimon's ostracism. Plato *Gorg.* 516D ("Didn't [the Athenians] ostracize him, so that they wouldn't hear his voice for ten years?"), despite the reference to ten years, cannot be used as evidence that he actually remained in exile for the whole period of the ostracism. Connor 1968, 24–30, is perhaps correct in suggesting that Theopompus, like P., is telescoping events, presenting the sequence Tanagra–recall–peace–Cyprus without further chronological precision. Probably neither writer wished to imply a fixed framework. Note that Thuc. 1.112.1 speaks of a two-year pause in hostilities before the formal peace. P.'s emphasis here is on Pericles' ability to make a politic arrangement, as the following sentences indicate. In the process, chronology is collapsed: cf. the clearer case of compression at 24.1.

οἰκείως . . . εἶχον: This feeling hardly seems to fit with the Spartans' dismissal of his troops at Ithome or his conduct at Tanagra, but they may have trusted him more than other Athenian leaders.

10.5

ἔνιοι δέ φασιν: The source of this account is unknown; it may be a modified version of an anecdote by Antisthenes, the founder of the Cynic school and author of Socratic dialogues, who along with other tidbits on Pericles' sex life said that the recall of Cimon was arranged at the price of Elpinice's lying with Pericles (Athen. 13.589E). P. introduces the story here (though not in the *Cimon*) because it gives a better idea of Pericles' gift for compromise. The arrangement with Cimon is given as a model for the statesman in

Praec. ger. rep. 812F. In *Cim.* 18.1 Cimon goes on expeditions of his own accord, to avoid war among the Greek states. The figure of two hundred ships also appears in Thuc. 1.112.2; *Cim.* 18.1 gives three hundred. Connor 1971, 58–64, suggests that Cimon's marriage with Isodice, an Alcmeonid, might have been part of this agreement (cf. *Cim.* 4.10, 16.1).

καταστρεφόμενον: The suggestion in this anecdote of campaigns against Persia sufficiently disposes of Cimon. It is only necessary for P. to mention his death on Cyprus (10.8). Βασιλεύς without the article regularly means the king of Persia.

10.6

ἐδόκει δὲ καὶ πρότερον: a flashback to an earlier incident, which also demonstrates Pericles' politic behavior, an aspect of his πρᾳότης. The parallel account in *Cim.* 14.3–5, giving Stesimbrotus as the source of the story (107 F5; see the Introduction, 3.1.c), states that Cimon was prosecuted by his enemies after the reduction of Thasos (463/62?) for having accepted bribes not to attack Macedonia. Schol. Aristid. 46 (3:446 Dindorf) connects the prosecution with Λανίκη [sc. Ἐλπινίκη] ἡ ἀδελφή and the expedition to Scyros (476/75?). Ephialtes was responsible for a series of trials of leading figures before the reform of the Areopagus (10.8; *Ath. pol.* 25.2). This trial may have arisen from the standard εὔθυνα στρατηγῶν, held at the end of a general's term; cf. *Ath. pol.* 27.1, [Pericles] κατηγόρησε τὰς εὐθύνας Κίμωνος στρατηγοῦντος νέος ὤν; Rhodes, *CAAP* 335–36. We cannot be sure of the nature of *euthynai* in the period before the Ephialtic reforms (cf. Rhodes, *CAAP* 316–18). For their later use to ensure responsible performance of duties see Harrison, *Law* 1:208–11; Roberts 1982, 17–18, 24–26, and passim (on this case, 56–57). Rhodes, *CAAP* 335–36, considers that Cimon was tried before the Areopagus. But the words προβεβλημένος and προβολήν (which appears in this sense only here in P.) suggest that P. is thinking of the procedure of *probolē*. This procedure, which is not otherwise mentioned for the period prior to the reforms of 462/61, is instead well documented in fourth-century authors, referring to the initiation of judicial proceedings by securing a preliminary vote of the assembly. See, e.g., Xen. *Hell.* 1.7.35; Isoc. 15.313–14; Dem. 21.1–2, 8–11; *Ath.*

pol. 43.5; Harrison, *Law*, 2:59–64; MacDowell, *Law*, 194–97; Rhodes, *CAAP* 526–27, 659–60. We cannot be sure whether the procedure was the same in the fifth century or whether P.'s term accurately reflects the usage of his source. P. implies a procedure whereby the demos voted to have several persons prosecute a case in its name, which would be different from the later procedure. See Carawan 1987, esp. 179–81, 202–5. Ostwald 1986, 40–41, argues rather for εὔθυναι before the Areopagus, followed by a trial before the people.

πρᾳότερον: cf. note to 2.5.

τὴν θανατικὴν δίκην ἔφευγεν: "was a defendant on a capital charge." A useful reminder that politics was a serious business. Presumably Cimon would have fled into exile if he had lost.

προβεβλημένος: προβάλλεσθαι here = "to be put forward, chosen (as one of the prosecutors)"; cf. *Sol.* 18.7, *Dem.* 14.4, *Sept. sap. conv.* 154E; LSJ s.v. B.IV.

γραῦς εἶ . . . διαπράσσειν: The sexual implication is manifest: Elpinice is too old to charm Pericles (or offer herself to him? see note to 10.5). Cf. also 28.7, where the line of Archilochus is an example of the stereotypical scorn for old women. The remark is an interesting example of upper-class Athenian conversation between the sexes, and perhaps of male rejection of female interference in politics. We would like to know the context in which Stesimbrotus told the story. Note that schol. Aristid. 3:446 also connects Elpinice with this incident. Elpinice had a reputation, not only for incest with her brother but also for an affair with Polygnotus while he was painting the Stoa Poikile (*Cim.* 4.6). If P. is correct in saying that she was an unmarried girl in 489 (*Cim.* 4.4), she would at this point be in her forties. On the construction of ὡς (usually ὥστε) plus infinitive to supplement an adjective see *MT* 588, 758.

οὐ μὴν ἀλλά: "nevertheless," adversative, answering μέν; cf. Denniston, 28–29.

πρὸς τὸν λόγον: cf. *Cim.* 14.5, πρὸς τὴν κατηγορίαν.

τὴν προβολὴν ἀφοσιούμενος: "meeting the obligation of his appointment." Cf. *Cim.* 14.5, ὥσπερ ἀφοσιούμενον. Sealey 1956 explains Pericles' forbearance by postulating that in his early career Pericles was closer to Cimon than P. and other ancient writers suggest. But P. may be right to conclude that Pericles was reluctant to pursue the political rivalry to an extreme, at least at this time. Death or exile was considerably more severe than ostracism.

10.7

An indignant defense of Pericles' character against a charge by the third-century writer Idomeneus (*FGrHist* 338 F8; see the Introduction, 3.3.e).

πῶς ἂν οὖν: introduces a rhetorical question. For this sort of argument from character in P., cf. Wardman 1974, 167.

τῆς . . . προαιρέσεως: "his political position."

δολοφονήσαντος: modifies Περικλέους.

ζηλοτυπίαν . . . δόξης: Idomeneus sees Pericles as so dominated by ambition that he would kill his collaborator to further it, a view quite different from P.'s.

οὐκ οἶδ' ὅθεν: one phrase, "from somewhere or other."

ὥσπερ χολήν: to be taken with συναγαγὼν: "gathering these accusations as if he were gathering bile."

προσβέβληκε: Reiske's emendation ("he attacked") seems more satisfactory than mss. προβέβληκε, "throw up to one, confront with," but cf. *Brut.* 29.7, Βρούτῳ δὲ λέγουσι μηδὲ τοὺς ἐχθροὺς προβαλεῖν τοιαύτην διαβολήν (προβάλλειν P, προσβάλλειν cet., em. Ziegler).

ἀνεπιλήπτῳ: "without fault."

φρόνημα: cf. 5.1.

10.8

The digression at 10.7 leads to another on the true cause of Ephialtes' death, based on *Ath. pol.* 25.2, 4.

καί: connects *φοβερὸν ὄντα* and *ἀπαραίτητον*.

εὐθύνας: see 9.4.

διώξεις: "prosecutions"; *διώκειν*, "prosecute," is the opposite of *φεύγειν*, "be a defendant."

Aristodicus: Cf. *Ath. pol.* 25.4, the passage P. is citing: *ἀνῃρέθη δὲ καὶ ὁ Ἐφιάλτης δολοφονηθεὶς μετ᾽ οὐ πολὺν χρόνον δι᾽ Ἀριστοδίκου τοῦ Ταναγραίου*. He is not otherwise heard of; cf. Rhodes, *CAAP* 321–22. The killer is unknown to Antiphon (5.68) and Diodorus (11.77.6). The murder is dated to 462/61 (cf. *Ath. pol.* 26.2). Stockton 1982 reminds us how uncertain is our knowledge by suggesting that he may have died of natural causes, such as a heart attack. Nevertheless, some historians accept Idomeneus' statement: see R. W. Wallace 1974, 269 and Piccirilli 1987; 1989, 71–78.

ἐτελεύτησε: the end of Cimon's opposition to Pericles. Although the expedition to Cyprus is mentioned by several sources (cf. Thuc. 1.112.2–4; Diod. 12.3–4; *Cim.* 18–19.1), the date of his death is variously set in 451, 450, and 449. See Meiggs, *AE* 124–26, 456–57, arguing for 451 against 449, the date given by Diodorus and accepted, e.g., by Gomme, *HCT* 1:410. P. (*Cim.* 19.1) reports that most say he died of an illness, but some of a wound.

Note that in concentrating on Pericles' struggle with Cimon, P. has passed over most of the events of the 450s, including the Athenian expedition to Egypt, the transfer of the league treasury to Athens (cf. 12.1), Pericles' expedition to the Corinthian Gulf (cf. 19.2–3), and his citizenship law (cf. 37.3).

11–14

After Cimon's death a new rival, Thucydides son of Melesias, forced Pericles to continue his struggle to win security and power. Because of Thucydides' stronger political organization Pericles had to take new initiatives, the chief of which was the building program, which could give him the strength finally to ostracize Thucydides.

As far as we can see, the content of these chapters is the result of P.'s own synthesis, combining information from disparate sources, some of which shared his overall vision. In the process he has greatly expanded some items (the polarization of politics, the debate on the building program, the list of construction projects) and omitted others (the effect of foreign affairs on domestic politics, the positive policies of Thucydides or other opponents of Pericles, the tightening of the imperial administration; cf., e.g., ML 46 on the tribute and ML 45 on weights and measures). No chronological sequence is set: these are simply the policies by which Pericles finally won ascendancy in the city. We know that the building program had hardly begun when Thucydides was ostracized (ca. 443; see note to 14.3), and most of the campaigns of chapters 18–23 precede that date. Andrewes 1978 argues that the whole passage is "worthless" and "has seriously distorted our picture of this period." The origin of this harsh opinion lies with those modern scholars who have thought that P. reproduced exactly an early and supposedly more reliable source, such as Theopompus. Andrewes's arguments are really directed not against P. but against imaginative reconstructions of the political climate by Wade-Gery (1932) and other scholars, extrapolating from P.'s account. Ameling 1985 concludes that most of these chapters are a rhetorical elaboration of well-known themes from Thucydides and Isocrates, written to encourage similar programs in the cities of his own day, an *adhortatio* rather than a "historischen Bericht." This is closer to the truth but sets up a false dichotomy between historical accuracy and rhetorical goals.

We cannot establish P.'s sources for the information presented: Ephorus, Aristotle, and Theopompus seem important, as well as the buildings themselves and writers who described them. P. ascribes supplementary material to Plato, the comic poets, and

Stesimbrotus. Cf. Meinhardt, 37–45. P.'s elaborations are especially apparent in 11.1–3 and 12.1–13.5, but the whole has been composed for maximum effect (cf. the Introduction, 2.5). Although P. deplores such political infighting (cf. *Comp. Per.–Fab.* 3.2), he nevertheless considers Pericles' response to Thucydides' challenge as unusually enlightened and responsible, not only securing his own political position but caring for his country, especially the poorer citizens, and creating a lasting monument of Greece's greatness. As was suggested in 9.1, τὰ πράγματα αὐτά allow us to see the relation between the demagogue and the aristocratic monarch. The struggle for δύναμις (cf. 11.1) gravely divided the polis, but Pericles' weapons were not vulgar ones.

11.1

οἱ δ᾽ ἀριστοκρατικοί: P. continues his division of the city into two political tendencies, the popular and the aristocratic or oligarchic (see note to 7.1–4). For ἀριστοκρατικός see note to 7.3.

ἤδη . . . καὶ πρόσθεν: Pericles once more as before (at the time of Cimon's ostracism, 9.5) becomes the most powerful of the citizens.

εἶναί τινα τὸν . . . ἀντιτασσόμενον: for the idea of opposing pairs of statesmen cf. 7.3–4, 9.2. The participle is used substantively; see *MT* 825. The usage requires the articles, otherwise unusual with τινα: "they wanted someone to oppose him."

κομιδῇ μοναρχίαν: "entirely the rule of one man." The use of κομιδῇ, "out and out, downright," implies that Pericles' power would be superior in any case, but that Thucydides' opposition would limit it somewhat. The reference to monarchy relates back to the citation from Thucydides at 9.1 and forward to chapter 15 and the final statement at 39.4.

Thucydides: Although he was clearly an important figure in the politics of the 440s, we know little that is certain about this man, in part because he was regularly confused with the historian and others of the same name. His father was Melesias (*Per.* 8.5; schol. Aristid. 3:446 Dindorf; schol. Ar. *Wasps* 947), who can be identified with the distinguished wrestling coach mentioned several times by Pindar (*Ol.* 8, *Nem.* 4, 6). Thucydides was the father of two sons, Melesias and Stephanus, also known for their wrestling (Plato *Meno* 94C), and was a relative by marriage of Cimon. On the family see Wade-Gery 1932, 208–11 (= 1958, 243–47); Davies, *APF* 230–37. The only sure facts of his political career are that he opposed Pericles (*Ath. pol.* 28.2) and was ostracized (for ostraka see figure 2 and ML 21; for the probable date, 443, see note to 14.3). The anonymous life of Thucydides (the historian) contains a few sentences (in 6–7) probably referring to the son of Melesias, stating that he successfully defended Pyrilampes (see note to 13.15) on a charge of murder when Pericles was accuser, that he was elected general and became *prostatēs* of the demos but later, after a visit to Sybaris, was prosecuted by Xenocritus and found guilty, and finally that after his ostracism he retired to Aegina. The prosecution of Xenocritus could be that mentioned by the scholiast to *Wasps* 947. Diogenes Laertius (2.12) quotes Satyrus the biographer for the information that Thucydides brought a case against Anaxagoras for impiety and Medism, as part of his rivalry with Pericles (cf. note to 32.3). Much has been written on the policies and activities of Thucydides, attempting to fill the gaps in our sources, especially by Wade-Gery 1932. Most of it is unsubstantiated, as Andrewes 1978 points out. Cf. also Rhodes, *CAAP* 349–51; Molitor 1986.

Thucydides' deme, Alopeke (the deme of Aristides, Callias the son of Hipponicus, and Socrates) is given only by P. and the first scholiast to Ar. *Wasps* 947. From *Ath. pol.* 28.2 P. knew that he was κηδεστὴν Κίμωνος (any relative by marriage, but here probably either son-in-law or brother-in-law; cf. schol. Aristid. 3:446 Dindorf, γαμβρός; Davies, *APF* 232; Wade-Gery 1932, 211 [= 1958, 247]). P.'s other sources are unknown, although schol. *Wasps* 947 cites Philochorus (328 F120), Ammonius (350 F1), Theopompus (115 F91), and Androtion (324 F37). Raubitschek 1960b traces most of the tradition on Thucydides to Theopompus, but see Connor 1968, 37, and Frost 1964b, esp. n. 1.

ἄνδρα . . . κατέστησεν: The description of Thucydides is not paralleled in any other source and no doubt represents P.'s free elaboration of his source material. See Meinhardt, 37–38, and, for the technique of expansion, Pelling 1980, 129–30. Σώφρονα is regularly used of conservatives and oligarchs; cf. North 1966, 44, 102. Only P. says that Thucydides was "put forward" (ἀνέστησαν) by a group of ἀριστοκρατικοί. The future participle, ἐναντιωσόμενον, expresses purpose; see *MT* 840. The following clauses contrast Cimon, who won his fame in war, with Thucydides, who frequented the Agora and was engaged in civic affairs. Ἀγοραῖος, originally of one who frequented the marketplace, can mean "vulgar, popular" (*Fab.* 1.8, *Nic.* 4.1, etc.), "connected with business" (*Symp.* 710D), or "effective in public or forensic speaking" (*De. vit. pud.* 532B); frequently two senses combine, as at *Aem.* 38.4, "effective speakers with the common people." P. usually contrasts the *politikos* and the *agoraios*: cf. *An seni* 785D. In this case he combines the two. The distinction between καλὸς κἀγαθός (landed gentry) and ἀγοραῖος (manufacturers or traders) suggested by Connor 1971, 154–58, is not appropriate here. Πολιτικός, "engaged in politics, civic life," is opposed to πολεμικός. Thucydides' skill in the political arena makes him a dangerous opponent for Pericles.

συμπλεκόμενος: like ἀντίπαλον, a wrestling term and hence appropriate to the son of Melesias (cf. 8.5), though both words are regularly used figuratively. Cf. for the former, e.g., *Fab.* 8.1, 11.5, 25.1; for the latter, *Them.* 20.4 (Cimon ἀντίπαλον ἐν τῇ πολιτείᾳ to Themistocles), and *Cim.* 16.9 (Athens vs. Sparta).

πολιτείαν: the word can refer to the city (39.4), the citizen body (37.4), a particular form of government (3.2), or frequently the political activity, policy, and administration of a particular individual or group (8.3, 9.1, 10.7, 13.2, 15.1, 16.3, 16.8, 36.7, 37.3, and regularly in *Praec. ger. rep.*). Thus Thucydides "swiftly made his political action and policy a rival (to that of Pericles)."

11.2

τοὺς καλοὺς καὶ ἀγαθούς: cf. note to 7.4.

ἐνδιεσπάρθαι: Verbs with a double prepositional prefix occur several times in P.; here the ἐν adds a sense of "among" (the people) to the simple "scatter, disperse." Note also the accumulation of verbs to express the same ideas (ἐνδιεσπάρθαι, συμμεμεῖχθαι, ἠμαυρωμένους and διακρίνας, συναγαγών), usually a sign of elaboration by P.

χωρὶς . . . εἰς ταὐτό: it is not clear what action Thucydides took to bring his supporters together physically. He may have urged them to band together in the Agora, in the assembly, or on other public occasions. Interest groups regularly sat together in the assembly for mutual support and to impress others: cf. Ar. *Eccl.* 298–99 (the women who wish to take over the government) and Thuc. 6.13.1 (ἐνθάδε τῷ αὐτῷ ἀνδρὶ παρακελευστοὺς καθημένους), so much so that in 410/9 a law was passed requiring that the members of the boule take their seats by lot (Philochorus 328 F140). Cf. Rhodes 1986, esp. 139.

ἐμβριθῆ: "weighty." P. plays on the literal sense, appropriate for the following metaphor, and the more common figurative sense, "dignified, grave" (cf. 4.6).

ἐπὶ ζυγοῦ ῥοπήν: "he made, so to speak, a counterweight on the scale." The image of a balance is a favorite of P.'s; cf. 37.1, *Fab.* 3.7, *Phoc.* 14.6 (ὃ μεγίστην ῥοπὴν ἐποίησε), Arist. 5.2, *Cleom.* 13.1, *Dion* 33.3, *Artax.* 30.9, and frequently in the *Moralia*. See also Fuhrmann 1964, 75n. 4.

11.3

διπλόη: "flaw" or weak spot in metal, a sure correction for mss. διαπλοκή. Cf. *Praec. ger. rep.* 802B, διπλόας ἐν σιδήρῳ μαλάσσων καὶ καταλεαίνων; *Symp.* 715F, τὸ ὕπουλον, ὥσπερ τινὰς διπλόας ἀναπτύσσει τῆς ψυχῆς (with the same combination of medical and metallurgical images). Plato uses this word only once, making a pun with διπλοῦς, *Soph.* 267E. Ὕπουλος, which is used by Plato in the context of his criticism of Pericles at *Gorg.* 518E, is also common in P.: cf. Hamilton 1969 to *Alex.* 47.11. For images derived from metalworking see Fuhrmann 1964, 86n. 1.

ὑποσημαίνουσα: "signaling": the verb is used of trumpet signals in battle (*Comp. Marc.–Pel.* 3.2; Thuc. 6.32). The prefix carries no weight (the original meaning was perhaps "signal in reply").

δημοτικῆς . . . προαιρέσεως: "of popular and aristocratic preferences." Προαίρεσις is P.'s regular word for free conscious choice in politics: cf. 2.4, 10.7, *Praec. ger. rep.* 798C, 802C, etc. For δημοτική see note to 7.3; for ἀριστοκρατική, note to 7.4. Cf. *Aem.* 38.2, σπουδαζόμενον ὑπὸ τοῦ δήμου καὶ τιμώμενον διαφερόντως ἐπὶ τῆς ἀριστοκρατικῆς μεῖναι προαιρέσεως.

ἐκείνων: with τῶν ἀνδρῶν.

τομὴν τεμοῦσα: The figure emphasizes the division. P. states that Thucydides' action in setting apart the ἀριστοκρατικοί and Pericles' response formalized and made obvious a division only latent before. This seems unlikely, as there were already strong divisions in the late 460s (cf. note to 9.2–5), and after the ostracism of Thucydides Pericles (at least according to P.) was able to bring the whole city under his control (15.1–3). It is possible, however, that Thucydides' action gave a new self-awareness to his supporters and his opponents alike.

P.'s account has been alternately accepted uncritically and rejected. Contrast Wade-Gery 1932, 208 (= 1958, 243), "The rivalry had one profound and disastrous result: it created the Class War. . . . The method which the son of Melesias invented is comparable to the modern caucus, or the Whip system: the Opposition was instructed to vote, not on the merits of the case, but as it bore on the question of breaking Pericles; not by their private judgement, but as the party decreed," and Andrewes 1978, 1, "Plutarch's account of the conflict of Thucydides and Pericles is worthless." However, one can recognize the special role of Thucydides in organizing the opposition to Pericles' policies without accepting either P.'s neat division into *demos* and *oligoi* or a scheme derived from modern political parties. Especially one must accept that P.'s account is not a transparent reproduction of a source but his own presentation of what he thought important in that source for this life.

11.4

Pericles responds to Thucydides with new actions to win the favor of the demos: more sumptuous religious celebrations, naval expeditions, cleruchies, and colonies. We do not know P.'s source for any of these acts.

διὸ καί: a favorite combination of P.'s (cf. 8.2, 9.5, 10.2, 27.3, 33.3; διὸ alone at 1.5).

τὰς ἡνίας ἀνείς: "relaxing the reins" (ἀνίημι); cf. also 15.1, ἀνειμένης . . . δημαγωγίας. For the demos as horse see 7.8; for the bridle as image of control see Fuhrmann 1964, 141n. 2.

ἐπολιτεύετο πρὸς χάριν: "shaped his policy toward gratification (of the people)." Contrast *Them.* 3.3 on Aristides: πολιτευόμενος οὐ πρὸς χάριν οὐδὲ πρὸς δόξαν, ἀλλ' ἀπὸ τοῦ βελτίστου (note that in 15.1, after Thucydides' ostracism, Pericles' policy is aimed πρὸς τὸ βέλτιστον).

In *Praec. ger. rep.* 818A–E, P. discusses the question of yielding to *hoi polloi* and notes that yielding can give the statesman credit in more important matters, according to a πολιτικώτερον precept: τὸ τὰ μικρὰ τοῖς πολλοῖς προΐεσθαι χαριζόμενον, ἐπὶ τῷ τοῖς μείζοσιν ἐνίστασθαι καὶ κωλύειν ἐξαμαρτάνοντας (818A). A statesman will yield as little as possible on major matters—violence, confiscation of property, distribution of public funds—ἐὰν δ' ἑορτὴν πάτριον οἱ πολλοὶ καὶ θεοῦ τιμὴν πρόφασιν λαβόντες ὁρμήσωσι πρός τινα θέαν ἢ νέμησιν ἐλαφρὰν ἢ χάριν τινὰ φιλάνθρωπον ἢ φιλοτιμίαν, he will allow them to enjoy it. Pericles, Demetrius (of Phaleron), Cimon, and Cato the Younger did this (818C–D). The important thing is not yielding per se but the statesman's overall policy. Cf. 15.1, of the "aristocratic" Pericles: κατὰ καιρὸν μὲν ἡδονὰς ἀβλαβεῖς . . . προσφέροντα. On the dangers of yielding in all things to the crowd cf., e.g., *Agis* 2.6.

θέαν . . . πομπήν: Θέαν is a general term for any spectacle, especially athletic or poetic contests (cf. *Thes.* 25.5, *Pyrrh.* 22.12, *Arat.* 17.3; in the Roman lives it translates *ludi*); πανηγυρικήν is especially used of festivals open to all, citizens and noncitizens, as were most of the major Athenian festivals. Ἑστίασις is a public feast, sponsored either by the state or an individual, in connection with sacrifices to the gods (Arist. *Pol.* 1321a35–42 notes the wisdom of giving such a feast for the demos when entering upon a magistracy). Πομπαί, such as the Panathenaic procession depicted on the Parthenon frieze, were a regular means of honoring the gods; the account of Nicias' arrangements for the procession and festival at Delos (*Nic.* 3.5–7) gives an idea of how extra expense could be incurred. Democratic Athens became famous for the number and extravagance of its festivals, as Pericles is made to boast (καὶ μὴν καὶ τῶν πόνων πλείστας ἀναπαύλας τῇ γνώμῃ ἐπορισάμεθα, ἀγῶσι μέν γε καὶ θυσίαις διετησίοις νομίζοντες, Thuc. 2.38.1) and the "Old Oligarch" laments (ἑορτάσαι ἑορτὰς ὅσας οὐδεμία τῶν Ἑλληνίδων πόλεων, ps.-Xen. *Ath. pol.* 3.2; cf. 2.9, 3.8). The festivals would be set by the religious calendar, but the amount spent and the number of days of celebration could be determined by the assembly, magistrates, or individual holders of liturgies. Note the progressive expansion of the Panathenaea described by Parke 1977, 33–50. Using evidence from several centuries, Mikalson 1975, 201, concludes that almost half of the days of the year were regular festive days at Athens. A very prosperous economy would be required to support such a program, much fuller than that of most other states. Note also that under Pericles there was an increasing centralization of public cult, indicated by the publication of building records and temple accounts (cf. ML 54 and 58–60), while the demos expected more and more from wealthy citizens (cf. Humphreys 1978, 145–46).

διαπαιδαγωγῶν: not "entertaining, amusing" as Holden argues, but a more general word covering a gamut of activities by which the pedagogue controls his charge: instructing (*Sert.* 16.11, *Crass.* 22.5), occupying his time and keeping him under control (*Ant.* 29.1, *Pel.* 10.4, *De gen. Socr.* 596F), disciplining (*Cic.* 8.5). Entertainment, such as Cleopatra gives to Antony (*Ant.* 29.1, ἀεί τινα καινὴν ἡδονὴν ἐπιφέρουσα καὶ χάριν) is only a means of exercising control. Although Pericles relaxes the reins, he does not release them completely. For Pericles as a teacher cf. 15.1, διδάσκων τὸν δῆμον.

οὐκ ἀμούσοις ἡδοναῖς: cf. Plato *Phaedr.* 240B, ἡδονήν τινα οὐκ ἄμουσον.

ἑξήκοντα δὲ τριήρεις: a unique notice on the normal activity of the navy, but one difficult to accept as stated. The number of ships and the length of time (eight months, the full sailing season) are both large, and taken together would be very expensive. In 415 B.C., 60 talents would pay for sixty ships for a month (Thuc. 6.8.1); eight months would cost 480 talents. However, the rate of pay in the 440s may have been lower, and the whole fleet probably was

not out for eight months. See Meiggs, *AE* 427. Eddy 1968 demonstrates the financial difficulty, but his proposal to emend 60 to 16
is unconvincing palaeographically and logically. Amit 1965, 51,
and Jordan 1975, 105, on the other hand, see no difficulty. According to *Ath. pol.* 27.1, Pericles μάλιστα προύτρεψεν τὴν πόλιν ἐπὶ
τὴν ναυτικὴν δύναμιν, and other sources stress the importance of
naval power (see Rhodes, *CAAP* ad loc.), but the exact nature of his
initiative is not stated. P. speaks of particular expeditions before
the Samian War at 19–23.

ἔμμισθοι: Service in the navy was a major means by which the
Athenians profited from the empire. *Ath. pol.* 24.3 speaks of service on twenty patrol ships (νῆες φρουρίδες), as well as on other
ships used to bring in tribute, as one of the advantages of empire
(see Rhodes, *CAAP* ad loc.). P. speaks of other payments at 9.3 and
12.4–6.

μελετῶντες: On the necessity of practice for naval expertise see ps.-
Xen. *Ath. pol.* 1.19–20; Thuc. 1.142.5–9. Training was not the
primary purpose but a valuable by-product (ἄμα) of fleet activity.
On the expertise of the Athenian navy see, e.g., Thuc. 2.83–84,
90–92.

11.5

This list of cleruchies and colonies is partial, but the fullest we
have, and is especially useful for giving the number of settlers. It
may derive from Ephorus, who had a particular interest in new
settlements (Polyb. 9.1.4 = 70 T18b), since four of the five items
have some correspondence in Diodorus. P. presents the sending
out of these settlements as a response to Thucydides' political
initiatives, but it is unwise to rely on this fact for precise chronological limits, as is evident from the account of buildings that
follows, which goes far beyond Thucydides' ostracism. Modern
dates for settlements attempt to reconcile P., Diodorus, and other
writers with our inferences from changes in the tribute quotas
from the cities and districts involved: see, e.g., Gomme, *HCT*
1:376–80; *ATL* 3:286–300; Meiggs, *AE* 159–60. Ancient terminology is frequently imprecise, but it is useful to distinguish between a cleruchy, in which lot-holders (κληροῦχοι) from Athens

were assigned lands in conquered or recently rebellious territory but did not form a new polis, and a colony (ἀποικία), in which the settlers created a new polis either ex nihilo or by combination with earlier settlers, using new founders and often a new name. See Ehrenberg 1948, 1952; Graham 1964; Brunt 1966; Gauthier 1973; Meiggs, *AE* 261-62.

P.'s list does not include those sent to Chalcis and Hestiaea after the revolt in Euboea (cf. 23.4), to Sinope and Amisos on the Black Sea (cf. 20.2, *Luc.* 19.6–7), to Aegina (33.2), to Astakos on the Propontis, or to others known from inscriptions. For the colony sent to Brea (ML 49) see the note to "Bisaltae" below.

Chersonese: cf. 19.1; Diod. 11.88.3 (for the archon year of Lysicrates, 453/52): [Pericles], ἐλθὼν εἰς Χερρόνησον, χιλίοις τῶν πολιτῶν κατεκληρούχησε τὴν χώραν; cf. also Andoc. 3.9, Aeschin. 2.175. Dated by Meiggs, *AE* 160, to 447. In *De glor. Ath.* 349C–D P. lists δήμων ἀποικισμοὶ μυρίανδροι, and specifically the Chersonese and Amphipolis, as prizes of Athenian victories.

The Thracian Chersonese (the modern Gallipoli peninsula) was a large area of fertile land, essential for the control of the grain supply coming to Athens from the Black Sea. In the sixth century it had been held as a personal fief by an Athenian, the elder Miltiades, and his family. After the Persian Wars at least Sestos was recovered, but Persians were still in the Chersonese to be expelled by Cimon ca. 465 (*Cim.*14.1). This cleruchy accompanied Pericles' action against incursions from Thrace (cf. 19.1). In 453 the tribute assessment for the Chersonese was 18 talents; in 446 the cities paid separately, but the total was less than 3 talents, a reduction that must be at least partially the result of the cleruchy (Meiggs, *AE* 160).

κληρούχους: The Chersonesan settlers, like those on Naxos and Andros, were cleruchs, as defined above, although at 19.1 they are called ἔποικοι. An Athenian inscription, *IG* I^3 417, apparently listing land to be sold in the Chersonese, probably should be connected with this settlement.

Naxos: cf. Diod. 11.88.3, ἅμα δὲ τούτοις πραττομένοις [sc. the Chersonesan cleruchy] Τολμίδης ὁ ἕτερος στρατηγὸς εἰς τὴν Εὔβοιαν παρελθὼν ἄλλοις χιλίοις πολίταις [lacuna] τὴν τῶν Ναξίων γῆν διένειμε; also Andoc. 3.9; Aeschin. 2.175; Paus. 1.27.5. Meiggs, *AE* 123, sets the date at 450. P. does not mention the Euboean cleruchy found in the other sources, which on the other hand credit Tolmides with the cleruchy on Naxos.

Naxos, the richest island of the Cyclades and one of the original members of the Delian League, revolted in the early 460s (Thuc. 1.98.4) and after a siege was forced to remain a tributary member. The cleruchies to Naxos, Andros, and Euboea, all apparently sent at the same time, may reflect further unrest among the allies as well as Pericles' domestic struggle with Thucydides (Meiggs, *AE* 121–24). The passage of the citizenship law in 451 (cf. 37.3) may imply overpopulation at Athens as an additional reason for the move.

Andros: The cleruchy is not mentioned elsewhere. The date 450 seems indicated by the reduction in the tribute quota: 12 talents in 450, 6 in 449 (cf. Meiggs, *AE* 123, 530). Andros, the northernmost of the Cyclades, was probably also a founding member of the Delian League.

⟨τοὺς⟩ ἡμίσεις: Cobet's addition of τοὺς (1878, 155), accepted by Ziegler, is unnecessary: note the absence of the article at *Ant.* 50.2, *Dion* 29.4.

Bisaltae: these were a Thracian people living along the Strymon River and in the territory to the west. The area was important for timber and silver, and Athens had long had an interest in it. Neighboring Argilos was perhaps an original member of the Delian League (*ATL* 3:221–23). In 476 Cimon took Eion from the Persians and occupied it. Later, when Thasos revolted, Athens sent ten thousand settlers, citizens and allies, to Ennea Hodoi on the Strymon; the colonists were annihilated by the Thracians (Thuc. 4.102.2). Berge, a small city among the Bisaltae, is on the tribute quota list for 451. Finally, in 437/36 the Athenians founded the colony of Amphipolis on the Strymon at the site of Ennea Hodoi (Thuc. 4.102). See *RE* s.v. Bisaltai, III (1899) 499–500; Hammond and Griffith 1979, 2:117–22.

The settlement mentioned by P. is usually identified with Brea, a colony in Thrace whose foundation is described in an extant decree (*IG* I² 45 = I³ 46; ML 49) and which is mentioned by the comic poet Cratinus (F395 K.). The date most frequently suggested is ca. 446–45 (Meiggs, *AE* 159; ML, pp. 132–33). However, there are serious difficulties with this identification. The location of Brea is uncertain (ML 49, l. 17 refers only to [πολέ]ον τὸν ἐπὶ Θράικες); the only literary source to mention it is Theopompus (*FGrHist* 115 F145 = Steph. Byz. s.v.); Thucydides' silence on this colony of one thousand Athenians is particularly disturbing, as he reviewed rather carefully activity in this area, which he knew well (4.104); and the decree does not speak, as P. does, of synoecism with the natives. See Woodhead 1952; Kagan, *OPW* 389–90; Asheri 1969.

It is much more probable that P. is here thinking of the foundation of Amphipolis, although this occurred in 437/36, after the ostracism of Thucydides son of Melesias. Thucydides (4.104.3) notes that some of the neighboring Argilii were co-settlers of Amphipolis with the Athenians. Argilos was set among the Bisaltae (Hdt. 7.115.1), so that P.'s words Βισάλταις συνοικήσαντας fit Thucydides' description, as well as Diod. 12.32.3, τῶν οἰκητόρων οὓς μὲν ἐκ τῶν πολιτῶν κατέλεξαν, οὓς δ' ἐκ τῶν σύνεγγυς φρουρίων. In addition, P.'s silence in this life on the foundation of a colony as well known to the literary sources as Amphipolis would be noteworthy (cf. his own reference at *De glor. Ath.* 349D). The name of the colony is secondary in P.'s mind to its general location, as immediately below with Thurii. But the most reasonable assumption is that it was in fact Amphipolis, founded by Hagnon on the site of the older Ennea Hodoi to control trade routes and the mineral and timber resources of Thrace. The colony was lost to Brasidas in 424, when the native Argilii invited him to take the town (Thuc. 4.103.4). Cf. Meiggs, *AE* 195–96; Kagan, *OPW* 186–89.

⟨ἀν⟩οικιζομένης: Ἀνοικίζω means to "rebuild, resettle," and is more appropriate here than the simple οἰκίζω. The prefix may have been lost by haplography with the preceding -αν of Ἰταλίαν.

Sybaris: one of the wealthiest of the Greek states of southern Italy, destroyed in 510 by Croton, its neighbor on the Gulf of Taranto.

In 452 some citizens attempted to refound the city but were driven out again (Diod. 11.90.3–4, 12.10.2).

Thurii: After their second expulsion, the Sybarites sent a request for settlers to Sparta and Athens (Diod. 12.10.3, for 446/45). The ensuing conflicts between Sybarites and new settlers are unclear, as our sources (chiefly Diod. 12.10.3–11.3 and Strabo 6.1.3 [263]) disagree, but in 444/43 the new city of Thurii was established by a committee of ten from Athens headed by Lampon the seer (cf. note to 6.2) and Xenocritus, who led settlers from Athens and other Greek cities (including Herodotus and the future orator Lysias; Protagoras is named as a lawgiver, Hippodamus of Miletus as town planner). The implications of this endeavor for Athenian politics and western ambitions are much disputed: does it reveal Athenian military or economic imperialism, Periclean Panhellenism, or simply the appeal of new fields to land-hungry Greece? Note that only P. connects this settlement directly with Pericles; hence Wade-Gery 1932, 217–19 (= 1958, 255–57) could argue that the leading politician behind it was in fact Thucydides son of Melesias. Our sources in general speak only of "the Athenians" or "the polis." See Ehrenberg 1948; Kagan, *OPW* 154–69, 382–84; de Ste. Croix, *OPW* 381; Meiggs, *AE* 185–86; Rutter 1973; Brandhofer 1971, 22–53; Andrewes 1978, 5–8. The sources are listed in Hill, *Sources*, 345.

11.6

The three reasons given for sending out settlers are all statesmanlike rather than demagogic: reducing the inactive throng in the city, relieving poverty, and establishing garrisons among the allies. None seems to involve simple pandering to the urban demos. For an analysis of the strategic value of these settlements for control of the grain routes of the empire see Brunt 1966.

ἀποκουφίζων . . . τὴν πόλιν: P. seems to imagine a large urban proletariat, more suitable to second-century A.D. metropolitan centers than to fifth-century Athens. But he is really arguing against those who thought Pericles made the Athenians lazy (cf. 9.1; Plato *Gorg.* 515E, Περικλέα πεποιηκέναι Ἀθηναίους ἀργοὺς καὶ δειλοὺς καὶ λάλους καὶ φιλαργύρους). Κουφίζω and its compounds are frequent in medical and figurative senses (relief of a disease or emotion); ἀποκουφίζω is found in P. only here and *Cleom.* 18.3 (Aetolia had done Sparta a good turn, lightening her of fifty thousand slaves), but cf. κουφίζειν καὶ καθαίρειν (of menstruation) at *De am. prol.* 495E. Πολυπράγμων and related compounds are usually pejorative in P.: "restless, busybody."

ἐπανορθούμενος . . . ἀπορίας: ἐπανορθοῦμαι, like the active, "correct, improve, put right." Cf. *Cleom.* 16.7, ἀναίρεσιν πλούτου καὶ πενίας ἐπανόρθωσιν. For the plural ἀπορίας, "difficulties," and in particular, "poverty," see Dem. 19.146, εὐπορίας, κτήματα, πλοῦτον ἀντὶ τῶν ἐσχάτων ἀποριῶν. This and the preceding clause fit well with the amendment to the decree establishing Brea: ἐς δὲ Βρέαν ἐχ θετῶν καὶ ζευγιτῶν ἰέναι τὸς ἀποίκος (ML 49, ll. 39–42). The thetes and zeugites were the two lowest classes; as settlers they became landowners and potential hoplites. Thus Athens' public interests were strengthened as well. The restrictions on citizenship passed in 451 (cf. 37.3) suggest other pressures on the growth of the citizen population that these settlements would relieve. Isocrates (5.120, 8.24) also thought new colonies could ease poverty and social unrest in Greece.

φόβον . . . τοῖς συμμάχοις: P. stresses the use of settlements to reinforce the empire against internal dissension, not external threats (as for example, in the Chersonese, 19.1); cf. Isoc. 4.107, εἰς τὰς ἐρημουμένας τῶν πόλεων φυλακῆς ἕνεκα τῶν χωρίων ἀλλ᾿ οὐ διὰ πλεονεξίαν ἐξεπέμπομεν. Amphipolis and the cleruchies at Naxos and Andros would fit into this category. See Gomme, *HCT* 1:373–76; *ATL* 3:284–97; Kagan, *OPW* 119; Brunt 1966, 71–73, 81.

τοῦ μὴ νεωτερίζειν: the infinitive to express purpose (*MT* 798); less probably, after an expression of hindering (φρουράν), see *MT* 807d.

παρακατοικίζων: the compound, meaning "settle (someone) beside (someone else)," is rare, but already in Isoc. 6.28 and 87. Here φόβον and φρουράν should be taken as appositives to an implied personal object.

12–14.2

The Building Program. P. concludes with Pericles' major weapon against Thucydides son of Melesias, the building program. Although P. lists it as an act of demagoguery, following ἐπολιτεύετο πρὸς χάριν (11.4), he shares none of the strictures of Plato but rather presents the building program as one of Pericles' greatest accomplishments. Plato mentions only the middle wall promoted by Pericles (*Gorg.* 455E; cf. 13.7 below) and is silent on the other works listed by P., although he does praise the work of Phidias (*Men.* 91D, Φειδίαν τε, ὃς οὕτω περιφανῶς καλὰ ἔργα ἠργάζετο). The expense of the Propylaea was criticized by Demetrius of Phaleron (Cic. *De off.* 2.60 = 228 F8). Ameling 1985 provides an analysis and brief commentary to these chapters.

The program is introduced in the most laudatory fashion: it was a pleasure and ornament to Athens, a cause of astonishment to non-Athenians, and the only physical witness in P.'s day of Greece's ancient power and wealth. Cf. also the encomiastic comments at the end of the *Comparison* (3.7). The tradition of public building for personal glory, family prestige, and political power was at least as early as Pisistratus and continued through the Hellenistic kings and Roman dynasts into the imperial period. Not only emperors but notables in cities throughout the Roman empire vied to display their generosity through lavish building programs, sometimes bankrupting themselves or their cities in the process. Cf. Veyne 1976, 185–273 ("euergetism" in Greece); Jones 1978, 104–14 (the benefactions of Dio Chrysostom); Kleiner 1983 (the distinctive monument built by P.'s friend King Philopappus on the hill of the Muses). In such a climate P. could only admire the grandeur of Pericles' program and the efficiency of its administration. He himself had no doubt contributed to the repair or construction of buildings in Chaeronea and perhaps elsewhere. Toward the end of his life he would see the extraordinary effect of Hadrian's benefactions at Delphi and Athens.

The Acropolis—especially the Propylaea and the Parthenon—was often the object of admiration: see, e.g., Isoc. 7.66, 15.234; Dem. 22.13, 76.

P.'s list of works built under Pericles in 13.7–14 is far from complete: see especially the surveys in Boersma, *Building Policy*, 65–81; Knell 1979; and Corso 1986.

12.1

The sentences in chapter 12 are very elaborate, running seventeen, thirteen, nine, and twelve lines respectively in our modern text. In the first sentence, the words ὅ . . . ὄλβον, with the appositive phrase, ἡ τῶν ἀναθημάτων κατασκευή, are the antecedent of τοῦτο, the object of ἐβάσκαινον and διέβαλλον. The rest of the sentence is indirect discourse after βοῶντες, divided into two parts at 12.2, καὶ δοκεῖ, and thick with participial phrases (μεταγαγών, δείσαντα, ὁρῶσα, καταχρυσοῦντας, καλλωπίζοντας, περιαπτομένην) and the relative clause ἣ δ' ἔνεστιν . . . τὰ κοινά. This structure is typical of P.'s rich style and an indication that the whole chapter is his embellishment of Pericles' defense, not a simple extract from Theopompus.

ἡδονήν: on the delight derived from sight cf. 1.3, and 2.1 on the sculpture of Phidias and Polyclitus. The works were beautiful (cf. 13.5), and beauty gives pleasure. Cf. Plato *Hipp. Mai.* 298A, *Gorg.* 474D–E, *Phil.* 51C. At *Publ.* 15.4 P. speaks of the beautiful proportions of the columns cut at Athens for the Capitoline temple in Rome, later altered for the worse. Plato also stressed the importance of measure and proportion in beauty (cf. *Phil.* 56B, 64E).

κόσμον: cf. *Comp. Per.–Fab.* 3.7, ἐκόσμησεν.

ἤνεγκε: cf. 18.3, δόξαν ἤνεγκεν.

ἔκπληξιν: "astonishment, awe." Cf. Isoc. 15.234, [Pericles] οὕτως ἐκόσμησε τὴν πόλιν καὶ τοῖς ἱεροῖς καὶ τοῖς ἀναθήμασι καὶ τοῖς ἄλλοις ἅπασιν ὥστ' ἔτι καὶ νῦν τοὺς εἰσαφικνουμένους εἰς αὐτὴν νομίζειν μὴ μόνον ἄρχειν ἀξίαν εἶναι τῶν Ἑλλήνων ἀλλὰ καὶ τῶν ἄλλων ἁπάντων (a repetition, slightly changed, of Isoc. 7.66).

μαρτυρεῖ: Thucydides had already considered the buildings of Athens as evidence of power to future ages but noted that it would be unreliable because grander that the actual city: 1.10.2, Ἀθηναίων δὲ τὸ αὐτὸ τοῦτο παθόντων [sc. the city being abandoned] διπλασίαν ἂν τὴν δύναμιν εἰκάζεσθαι ἀπὸ τῆς φανερᾶς ὄψεως τῆς πόλεως ἢ ἔστιν. Cf. Thuc. 2.41.4.

ἡ τῶν ἀναθημάτων κατασκευή: the Acropolis buildings, including the Propylaea, were dedications to Athena: cf. 14.1 and Dem. 22.76, τὰ δὲ τῶν ἀναθημάτων τῶν ἐπ' ἐκείνοις σταθέντων τὸ κάλλος, προπύλαια ταῦθ', ὁ παρθενὼν . . . .

μὴ ψεύδεσθαι: "is not misrepresented," passive.

πολιτευμάτων: "political schemes"; cf. 9.1 and ἐπολιτεύετο in 11.4. A common word in P.

In this passage P. seems to think of repeated attacks in a number of assemblies (ἐν ταῖς ἐκκλησίαις), not a single debate on the building program. The objections that follow would be a summary of items mentioned over months or years, rather than a précis of a speech. Note the iterative imperfects ἐβάσκαινον, διέβαλλον, and for Pericles' reply, ἐδίδασκεν. P.'s choice of verbs implies condemnation of Pericles' opponents. The vocabulary and style are P.'s.

On the basis of this passage and 14.1 the notion of a "building debate" has grown up, in which Pericles and Thucydides faced off before the Athenian demos. It is not certain what actual indication there was in his source that led P. to present the opposition (identified at 14.1 as led by Thucydides) as charging Pericles with spending money contrary to the purposes for which it was collected from the allies. There is no reason to think that Thucydides or other oligarchs opposed the empire or the wealth it brought Athens (see H. D. Meyer 1967), although they may indeed have thought it useful to oppose Pericles on the construction of the Parthenon or other buildings. Andrewes 1978, 4, refers to P.'s source as the composition of a postclassical schoolboy on the theme of the morality of using the tribute to beautify Athens; rather P. is exercising the freedom of the biographer to make vivid Pericles' struggle with Thucydides, perhaps on not much more evidence than his knowledge of Thucydides' opposition to Pericles, of the criticism of extravagance in later authors such as Demetrius of Phaleron, and of similar debates over public spending in his own day. Cf. Ameling 1985, 50–55.

P. Stras. 84, the "anonymous Argentinensis" or "papyrus decree," has sometimes entered the discussion of the building program. It is a fragment of a commentary to Dem. 22.13–17, including a note to the lemma ὅτι ᾠκοδόμησαν τὰ Προπύλαια καὶ τὸν

Παρθενῶνα, referring to (1) a Περικλέους γνώμη[ν], (2) τὰ ἐν δημοσί⟨ωι⟩ ἀποκείμενα τάλαν[τα, and (3) πε]ντακισχείλια [talents?] κατὰ τὴν 'Αριστεί[δου τάξιν as well as other matters. It is possible that a decree of Pericles authorizing the expenditure of money for the Parthenon or Propylaea is meant. The reference to a Εὐ]θυδήμου may mean the archon of 431/30 (thus Wilcken 1907) or the archon of 450/49, called Euthynus in the inscriptions but Euthydemus in the literary record (thus *ATL* 1:572, 3:281; Wade-Gery and Meritt 1957). However, even this evidence is inconclusive, as in this period archon dates were not recorded on decrees and the date would have been assigned by the scholiast on other grounds. Not only the date but the interpretation of this fragment is extremely controversial, because much must hang on the restorations proposed: see the text, review of arguments, and bibliography in Meiggs, *AE* 515–18, and the skepticism of, e.g., Sealey 1958 and de Ste. Croix, *OPW* 310–11. I consider the text to be too fragmentary to suppose more than that Pericles made a proposal to spend money, perhaps from the league tribute, for the Parthenon and/or Propylaea. If this is the case, it might refer to the debate envisioned by P.

ἐβάσκαινον: "to malign"; cf. *Cam.* 36.1, *Ages.* 22.4, *Pomp.* 21.4, 29.1, *Caes.* 59.6, *Dem.* 16.4, *De cap. util.* 91B; Dem. 18. 189.

ἀδοξεῖ: "is held in low esteem, is losing its reputation"; cf. *Fab.* 9.3; Dem. 19.103. 'Αδοξέω, ἀδοξία, and ἄδοξος are all common words in P. Pericles himself endures ἀδοξία at 34.1.

κακῶς ἀκούει: the passive of κακῶς λέγει; cf. 5.2, 29.3.

τὰ κοινὰ . . . μεταγαγών: referring to the transfer of the treasury of the Delian League to Athens from its original location on Delos. (From the beginning, it had been controlled by an Athenian commission, the Hellenotamiae; see Thuc. 1.96.2.) Although the literary record does not give a specific date, this probably took place in 454, as from 454/53 the Athenians began to set up inscriptions recording on stone the first fruits (ἀπαρχαί) that were given to Athena, of which a great number are preserved. Of course the treasury might have been on the Acropolis previously, but no *aparchai* paid, or recorded. Concerning the heading of the first list see the new fragment published by Meritt 1972, the new edition of the first list in *IG* I³ 259, and Raubitschek 1984 (arguing against restoration of συμμαχικοῦ and for the phrase ἀπὸ τῶν πόλεων). In 454 the Athenians would have been motivated by the disaster in Egypt (Thuc. 1.109–110; cf. below, δείσαντα τοὺς βαρβάρους), as well as the opportunity to strengthen their control over the league money. The allies, who were already restive (not much later Miletus and Erythrae caused problems; cf. Meiggs, *AE* 112–116), might well have complained about the transfer. On the other hand, if the treasury was already in Athens, the Egyptian disaster might have led the Athenians for religious reasons to initiate or revise the *aparchai* to Athena, and record them carefully and publicly on stone. P. elsewhere reports a story that when the Samians had suggested moving the treasury to Athens, Aristides replied that this would be οὐ δίκαιον μέν, συμφέρον δέ (*Arist.* 25.3). This might date the transfer to Aristides' lifetime, but the story is probably apocryphal (cf. the similar punchline at *Them.* 20.3), and even the role of the Samians or the time of their proposal is uncertain. Justin (3.6) instead connects the transfer with the tension between Sparta and Athens after the Athenian force under Cimon was sent back from Messene, which might imply a date ca. 461. For objections to the 454 date see esp. Pritchett 1969. For arguments in favor see Busolt, *Gr. Gesch.* 3.1:204, 332; *ATL* 3:262–64; Meiggs *AE* 109. Diodorus, presumably depending on Ephorus, speaks of the sum of 8,000 (12.38.2) or 10,000 talents (12.40.1, 54.3; 13.21.3) being moved. Cf. also Aristodemus, *FGrHist* 104 F1.7; Nepos *Arist.* 3.1. There is no reason to connect closely in time the transfer of the treasury and the proposal of the building program. In P.'s mind the excuse for this transfer was the security of the fund; if the fund were misused, the excuse would be nullified.

ἔνεστιν: "was available."

τοὺς ἐγκαλοῦντας: "the detractors" (of the demos); cf. 29.3, 29.5.

12.2

ὕβριν . . . ὑβρίζεσθαι: cf. *Sept. sap. conv.* 148F, οἵαν ὕβριν . . . εἰς ἡμᾶς Περίανδρος ὕβρικεν. The cognate accusative is frequent especially in tragedy and Demosthenes; see LSJ s.v. ὑβρίζω II.2. Dem. 22.68 gives the flavor of demagogic address similar to the occasion here.

τυραννεῖσθαι: another word from impassioned debate; cf., e.g., Dem. 20.161. The word returns in 16.1, applied to Pericles. Cf. the characterization of the Athenian empire as a τυραννίς, put in Pericles' mouth by Thucydides (2.63.2).

ὁρῶσα: followed by the accusative *(ἡμᾶς)* and two participles, καταχρυσοῦντας and καλλωπίζοντας.

τοῖς εἰσφερομένοις ὑπ' αὐτῆς ἀναγκαίως πρὸς τὸν πόλεμον: τὰ εἰσφερόμενα, or the φόρος, the contributions to the Delian League treasury originally paid voluntarily by the allies to support the war against Persia. As cities became reluctant to continue their contributions, Athens and other allies forced them to do so (thus ἀναγκαίως). Cf. *Cim.* 11; Thuc. 1.98.4–99; Meiggs, *AE* 90–91.

πρὸς τὸν πόλεμον: This phrase (here and at 12.4) raises a difficult question: how can the reference to a war at the time of the building debate be reconciled with other evidence for a peace with Persia, the so-called Peace of Callias? The phrase has been used either as evidence that P.'s account is worthless, as it does not show an awareness of the peace (e.g., Andrewes 1978, 1); or to prove that the peace never existed (e.g., Stockton 1959). Neither conclusion is necessary.

As stated before, we have no way of knowing what specific information P. had on the debate. The phrasing and probably many if not all the arguments are P.'s. We do not know P.'s source and certainly cannot presume that he accurately reflects an unimpeachable source. In writing, P. seems to have imagined a continuing state of hostility between Athens and Persia, as evidence for which in this life we find Cimon's expedition to Cyprus (10.8), the Athenian plans against Egypt (20.3), Pissouthnes' aid to the Samians (25.3), and the threat of Phoenician intervention (26.1). Nevertheless, ancient sources, including P. (*Cim.* 13.4–5), speak of a peace made by Callias Λακκόπλουτος at Susa, which set a boundary for Persian action in the Aegean area: to quote the *Cimon*, the Persians agreed "not to allow a bronze-beaked warship to sail west of the Cyanaean and Chelidonian islands," that is, of the Bosporus in the north and Phaselis in the south. Unfortunately, references are inconsistent and the exact terms are recorded variously in our sources: see Bengtson 1962, no. 152. The existence, terms, and effects of the peace have been endlessly debated: for the older literature see Busolt, *Gr. Gesch.* 3.1:444–49; for more recent discussions, the review of evidence by Meiggs, *AE* 129–51, 487–95, 598.

The authenticity of the peace was challenged in the fourth century by Theopompus, who saw an inscribed stele with the peace, but recognized that the Ionic alphabet in which it was written came into general use in Athens only in 403/2 (*FGrHist* 115 F153–55). It is not mentioned by Thucydides, as might have been expected. These and other points, including this phrase in *Per.* 12.2, have led some modern scholars to reject the treaty as a forgery: see Stockton 1959; Sealey 1976, 278–82, 295–96; Meister 1982.

On the whole, however, modern scholars have tended to accept the peace, and the argument has focused on its historical context and effect. For some time a degree of consensus was established around the arguments (Wade-Gery 1940; developed in *ATL* 3:279–80 and Meiggs, *AE*) that the peace was concluded in 449, after the death of Cimon in Cyprus and before the beginning of the Parthenon building program. One result of the peace would have been the temporary cessation of tribute payments by the Athenian allies, marked by the absence of a tribute quota list for 448; another the Congress Decree described in *Per.* 17, with its intention to discuss the rebuilding of the temples burnt by the Persians and means to "keep the peace."

There has always been some dissatisfaction with this reconstruction; cf. e.g. Raubitschek's arguments (1976) for setting the peace in 457. Recently, however, scholars have once again focused on *Cim.* 13.4–5, which seems to set the peace immediately after Cimon's victory at the Eurymedon ca. 468 (cf. also Lycurg. *contra*

Leocr. 72–73) and have found new arguments for placing the peace in this context. See the review of Meiggs by Sordi 1973; Walsh 1981, 31–49; and esp. Badian 1987. I find the arguments for this early date more convincing. Note also that this would explain why P., who had defended the authenticity of the peace in the *Cimon*, noting that it had been recorded by Craterus in his collection of decrees (cf. the Introduction, 3.1.1), did not think it desirable to include it in the *Pericles*. He considered it an example of Cimonian action, not Periclean.

However, many problems are left concerning Greco-Persian relations after the peace, which clearly were seldom without tension and sometimes involved armed combat. Any agreement between the Athenian League and Persia was likely to be more of an armed truce than a real peace. Whether a formal peace was signed or not, it was necessary for Athens to maintain a large force both to protect the Aegean from the Persians and to insure the stability of her own financial and political power. Not only Thucydides (5.25.3, 26.2–3) would have realized that a state of "cold war" might continue even after a peace was signed. The course of events since the Second World War has led historians to speak of different levels of war and peace: cf. e.g. Eddy 1973 ("cold war") and Holladay 1986 ("detente") and, in general, the illuminating discussion in Lewis 1977. I conclude that a peace had been made after Eurymedon, but that the atmosphere of tension continued and even erupted into war with the Athenian intervention in Egypt and Cyprus in the 450s. Tensions relaxed somewhat after Cimon's death (Badian 1987 suggests a second or renewed peace). In any case Pericles and his opponents could quite reasonably have spoken of money collected πρὸς τὸν πόλεμον, even in the context of the building debate.

The actual phrase, however, is most likely P.'s own. It appears fifty-one times in the *Lives*, nine times in *Pericles–Fabius*, four times in this life (12.2, 4; 25.4; 26.3). One of its two appearances in the *Moralia, De aere al.* 828B, is particularly interesting because P. is paraphrasing Thucydides' report (2.13.5) that the gold on the Parthenos statue could be used if necessary. Thucydides writes χρησαμένους τε ἐπὶ σωτηρίᾳ, P. rephrases τὸ χρησάμενοι πρὸς τὸν πόλεμον.

ἡμᾶς: more vivid than ὁ δῆμος of 12.1, but not a proof that P. is actually reporting the words of his source.

καταχρυσοῦντας: "gilding"; cf. the criticism of those gilding couches, *De superst.* 166B.

καλλωπίζοντας: frequently used pejoratively by P. (e.g., *Symp.* 693C) of ornamentation beyond what is fitting; but favorably at *Cim.* 13.7.

ἀλαζόνα γυναῖκα: an unusual expression. The ἀλαζών is vain, boastful, pretentious, but usually a man; here, not a harlot but a vain and pretentious woman.

περιαπτομένην: middle voice, "wearing, putting on herself." The verb frequently is used figuratively in a derogatory sense, which is perceptible here: cf. Plato *Apol.* 35A, αἰσχύνην τῇ πόλει περιάπτειν; Dem. 20.10, οὗτος ὁ νόμος ταύτην [δόξαν] ἀντὶ καλῆς αἰσχρὰν τῇ πόλει περιάπτει.

λίθους πολυτελεῖς: as applied to women, these would be jewels, but with reference to the Acropolis, expensive marble. The ambiguity eases the shift to the following words, applicable only to the Acropolis.

ἀγάλματα: a rhetorical plural, referring to the Parthenos statue.

ναοὺς χιλιοταλάντους: a noteworthy exaggeration; cf. Stanier 1953 (who comes up with a cost of ca. 469 talents); Gomme, *HCT* 2:22–26; Burford 1965. However, the Parthenos statue would have been an additional 700 to 900 talents, the gold alone costing 616 talents: cf. Donnay 1967; Eddy 1977. There was a tradition of incredible expense: one later writer, Heliodorus, set the cost of the Propylaea at 2,012 talents (Harpocration s.v. προπύλαια ταῦτα); Isocrates (7.66) set the whole at 1,000 talents.

12.3–6

ἐδίδασκεν, κτλ.: the justification for the building program that P. here assigns to Pericles is extraordinary. The first part responds to the objection that it is a misuse of funds: Pericles replies that the allies are getting what they paid for and the Athenians were not accountable for the surplus (εὐπορία) that remained. The second gives the positive purposes: to gain glory for the city and to distribute the money to the city by giving work to every trade. Nowhere else in antiquity do we find the latter justification: building programs are either castigated as devices of a tyrant to burden the people (e.g. *Mul. virt.* 262B; Arist. *Pol.* 5.11.1313b21–25) or praised as munificent gifts and a beautification of the city (*Cim.* 13.5–7; Suet. *Caes.* 44, *Aug.* 28–29; Pliny *Paneg.* 51, etc.).

Did P. draw this idea from a fifth-century source (even if through an intermediary), or does it reflect his own notion of good reasons for such a program, based on the opinion of his own day? The absence of parallels and P.'s stylistic elaboration render judgment difficult, but the conception fits the fifth century at least as well as the empire. P. does not describe an anachronistic "full employment policy," but an effort to distribute a monetary surplus to as many people as possible while getting something of value from it. The idea is the same as that of pay for the navy or dicasts: state money is used to achieve a purpose (temples, defense, juries) while enriching the people. In this sense it is democratic and based on "sharing the wealth" rather than a paternalistic care for the poor. Cf. ἀπὸ τῶν δημοσίων ὠφελεῖσθαι καὶ μεταλαμβάνειν, 12.5. It was well known that cities were more prosperous when the craftsmen were fully occupied: see the examples of the feverish military preparations at Ephesus under Lysander (*Lys.* 3.3–4) and Agesilaus (Xen. *Hell.* 3.4.16–17). Thucydides in the Funeral Oration refers to work or action as a means to escape poverty: ἄλλα μὴ διαφεύγειν [sc. τὸ πένεσθαι] ἔργῳ αἴσχιον (2.40.1). On the other hand, there is no evidence from antiquity for conceiving public works programs simply as a means of feeding the urban poor, except perhaps Josephus *AJ* 20.219–22. Public works were undertaken when there was a monetary surplus on hand, and for reasons similiar to those of private benefactors. See Giglioni 1974, who has shown that the analogy with modern "full employment" programs is false and that public works in antiquity generally were the result of a sudden influx of capital, not a desire to feed the masses; and cf. Veyne 1976. For recent discussions of the question see Frost 1964b, 389–92; Brunt 1980, 81–100; de Ste. Croix 1981, 188–95. Ferguson 1904 is still valuable.

The style matches the nobility of Pericles' ideas. The twelve-line sentence (12.3–4) introduced by ἐδίδασκεν is divided into two major clauses, χρημάτων μὲν οὐκ ὀφείλουσι . . . λόγον and δεῖ δὲ . . . τὴν εὐπορίαν τρέπειν, which in their turn are elaborated by participial phrases, genitive absolutes, and relative clauses. Note the hyperbaton of χρημάτων . . . λόγον, the chiasmus of προπολεμοῦντες . . . ανείργοντες, and the antithesis and paronomasia of ἃ . . . λαμβάνουσι. In the second part of the sentence τῆς πόλεως . . . πόλεμον is a genitive absolute; the movement of this part then flows from εἰς ταῦτα to ἀφ' ὧν and the chiasmus and paronomasia of δόξα . . . ἑτοίμη, which with a kind of stylistic εὐπορία overflows into the genitive absolute, relative clause, and participles of the last lines.

12.3

ἐδίδασκεν: To P., Pericles, even when he is struggling for power against Thucydides, is a superior person, guiding and instructing the demos (cf. 11.4, διαπαιδαγωγῶν, and 15.3). The image of the rhetor as teacher is common, however, in Greek rhetoric.

προπολεμοῦντες αὐτῶν: "fighting in their defense"; cf. *Aem.* 8.9, *Flam.* 13.3; Isoc. 14.33; Plato *Rep.* 423A, etc. Hands 1975 notes that προπολεμοῦντες can be used of those in the front line of defense even if not currently fighting.

ανείργοντες: "keeping under control, holding back"; cf. 21.1, on controlling the Spartans, and *Fab.* 20.1.

οὐχ ἵππον . . . τελούντων: the tricolon with οὐ rather than οὔτε is a favorite device of P.'s: cf. *Fab.* 17.3, οὐ πόλιν, οὐκ ἐμπόριον, οὐ λίμενα; *Sol.* 7.1, οὐ πλοῦτον, οὐ δόξαν, οὐ σοφίαν; *Per.* 39.2. Holden counted twenty-one similar passages in the *Lives*, twenty-six in the *Moralia*.

The statement is false, at least for the 450s, when allies assisted Athens at sea against Aegina (Thuc. 1.105.2) and Egypt (1.110.4) and on land at Tanagra (1.107.5). But our specific information on contributions other than money is meager. It is possible that there were no contributions in kind by those who paid tribute at the time of the debate (no allies are mentioned, e.g., in the suppression of the Euboean revolt of 446, Thuc. 1.114); more likely P.'s rhetoric leads him into error. Cf. the review of the evidence by Blackman 1969.

ἄν = ἐάν.

12.4

πρὸς τὸν πόλεμον: cf. note to 12.2.

τρέπειν: "to direct, apply."

αὐτῆς: i.e., of the city (as with ἐξ αὐτῆς four lines below).

δόξα . . . ἀίδιος: cf. Thuc. 2.41.4, μνημεῖα κακῶν τε κἀγαθῶν ἀίδια.

εὐπορία . . . ἑτοίμη: "immediate prosperity." The repetition of εὐπορία, just one line after its previous use, is unusual. If our text is sound here, P. is playing on the term, which occurs again in 12.5 and 12.6. Wealth or abundance can be used to create wealth.

γενομένων . . . γινομένων: these forms are reversed in the mss., but the correction seems to be necessary: fame for what has happened, prosperity from what is happening. "(It is necessary to apply the surplus to those enterprises) which when completed will bring eternal renown, and which while in progress will provide immediate prosperity."

ἐργασίας: productive labor, opp. ἀργία (Xen. Mem. 2.7.7).

χρειῶν: "needs," rather than "occupations," since it is further explained by the relative clause αἵ . . . τρεφομένην.

ἔμμισθον: cf. 11.4.

12.5

γάρ: Note the shift of subject between the μὲν and δὲ clauses: αἱ στρατεῖαι and Pericles. Again it is uncertain whether the explanation introduced here (5–6) is P.'s own or his source's. There has been a shift from the explanation ascribed to Pericles (ἐδίδασκεν . . . τρεφομένην) and that describing his actions.

αἱ στρατεῖαι: cf. 11.4. For an ancient calculation of all those employed by Athens in the fifth century see Ath. pol. 24.

τὸν ἀσύντακτον καὶ βάναυσον ὄχλον: "the crowd of disorganized artisans." Ἀσύντακτος is usually applied to a disordered army; here P. thinks of the lack of organization before the craftsmen are arranged into "armies" (cf. 12.6, end). Oliver 1960, 72n. 9, suggests, too precisely I think, that P. is opposing those who were not enrolled in military service to the gennētai of the levy.

λημμάτων: "payments"; cf. 9.3. Λήμματα must also be supplied as object of λαμβάνειν.

ἀργὸν καὶ σχολάζοντα: Again P. stresses against Plato that Pericles did not simply institute a dole that made the people lazy; cf. 11.6 and Gorg. 515E.

μεγάλας . . . ἐχόντων: the words are as grand as the projects. Note the multiple abstract nouns: κατασκευασμάτων, "constructions" (cf. κατασκευή at 12.1); ἐπιβολὰς "projects"; ὑποθέσεις "undertakings"; and the rare compound adjective πολυτέχνους, "requiring many skills."

διατριβὴν ἐχόντων: "requiring a long time (to complete)." For other examples of ἔχω = "involve, carry with itself" cf. 18.1, 28.8, 38.1, and LSJ s.v. ἔχω A.I.11.

ἐνέβαλε φέρων εἰς τὸν δῆμον: "introduced wholeheartedly to the assembly," or "proposed enthusiastically to the people." For a similar though not identical use of ἐμβάλλω cf. Nic. 10.5, ἐμβαλὼν αὐτοὺς εἰς τὸν δῆμον. For φέρων see note to 7.3.

ἵνα: The clause states more fully the purpose stated in the preceding participial phrases.

τῶν πλεόντων . . . στρατευομένων: the three standard kinds of military service—with the navy, on garrison duty, or on campaign.

12.6

This is one of the most detailed ancient descriptions of the work behind Greek temple building. We can supplement it with the inscribed building accounts erected in Athens and elsewhere. Those for the Parthenon (*IG* I³ 436–51), the Parthenos statue (*IG* I³ 453–60), the doors of the Parthenon (*IG* I³ 461), and the Propylaea (*IG* I³ 462–66) are directly relevant, though those of the Erechtheum (*IG* I³ 474–79) and the sanctuary of Aesculapius at Epidaurus (*IG* IV².1 102–20 and *ABSA* 61 [1966] 254–339) are much fuller. See the selections and commentary in ML 54, 59, 60. For an analysis of the process of temple building see Burford 1963, 1969. For the work on the Parthenos statue see Leipen 1971 and Pausanias' detailed description (5.11.1–9) of Phidias' chryselephantine statue of Zeus at Olympia. On raw materials see Orlandos 1966, with chapters on woods, metals, ivory, and transport. P. divides his account into three categories: raw materials, craftsmen at the site, and those involved in supplying and transporting the materials.

ὅπου: "since, inasmuch as"; cf. 13.16. It governs the clauses connected by μὲν . . . δὲ . . . δὲ . . . δὲ as far as γινόμενον; the main clause follows in εἰς πᾶσαν . . . εὐπορίαν.

ὕλη: raw material.

ἐλέφας, χρυσός: the Parthenon building accounts report the sale of surplus gold and ivory (*IG* I³ 436–51, ll. 389–94), although one thinks especially of the chryselephantine Parthenos statue for which large quantities of both were necessary, as is clear from the accounts (*IG* I³ 453–60). According to Eddy 1977 the gold was obtained from the coin paid as tribute.

ἔβενος: Ebony was an exotic wood, imported from India or Africa. Phidias used it on the throne of the statue of Zeus at Olympia (Paus. 5.11.2). There is no evidence for how it was used on the Acropolis, but like ivory it was often used decoratively with other woods. On the wood used in the Acropolis building program see Meiggs, *Trees*, 196–202 and (for ebony) 282–86.

κυπάρισσος: another imported wood, brought from Crete and other Mediterranean areas, appreciated because rot resistant and able to take a high polish (Pliny *NH* 16.212–15; Theophr. *Hist. pl.* 5.4.2; cf. Meiggs, *Trees*, 78–81, 292–94). Long cypress timbers might have been employed as ridgepoles and other major timbers. The inscribed account of the Parthenon doors (*IG* I^3 461) refers to cypress wood (l. 35) as well as elm (ll. 33, 37). The doors of the temple of Artemis at Ephesus were of cypress. Elm was especially useful for frameworks, posts, and lintels; see Meiggs, *Trees*, 426. The building accounts of the Parthenon list pinewood (πεύκινα, *IG* I^3 436–51, l. 107), perhaps for secondary timbers or scaffolding; cf. Meiggs, *Trees*, 202.

τέχναι: "trades," specified in the following unusually full list of artisans. Many of these trades are referred to in the Parthenon or Propylaea accounts (*IG* I^3 436–51, 462–66).

τέκτονες: workers with wood, "carpenters, joiners," although occasionally other skilled craftsmen are included: cf. *IG* I^3 436–51, l. 26; 462–66, l. 155. Cf. also the item for ξυλουργίας (436–51, l. 269).

πλάσται: "modelers," usually in terra-cotta, although because of the importance of making the form when casting bronze and chryselephantine statues, the word was applied to artists working in metal, and then even to those working with stone (cf. 31.2, *Φειδίας ὁ πλάστης* and *Aem.* 28.5, *τὸν Ὁμήρου Δία Φειδίας ἀποπλά-σαιτο*). Phidias used terra-cotta forms for the gold drapery of the chryselephantine statue; such forms have been found in Phidias' workshop at Olympia (photographs in Mallwitz 1972a, 56–57, figs. 63–66, and 1972b, 261). On the Parthenon accounts, the word for a sculptor of the pedimental figures is ἀγαλματοποιός (*IG* I³ 436–51, ll. 310, 338, 360, 403).

χαλκοτύποι: "bronze- or coppersmiths." These are not mentioned in the preserved accounts, but they would have been needed for a variety of tasks, including the bronze accessories on the marble statues and the gilded bronze parts of the Parthenos statue (cf. Leipen 1971, 20).

λιθουργοί: "masons, stoneworkers, sculptors," the usual word for any craftsmen with stone. The Parthenon accounts refer to λιθουργίας, *IG* I³ 436–51, l. 273.

βαφεῖς χρυσοῦ: "gilders." The gold is the material added, not what is colored; cf. the gilded slippers, χρυσοβαφεῖς ἐμβάδας, of Demetrius Poliorcetes (Plut. *Demetr.* 41.6) or the words such as πορφυρό-βαπτος, "dyed in purple." Βάπτω and βαφεύς normally refer to dyeing but are applied to gilding by the authors on alchemy, e.g., pseudo-Democritus, in Berthelot 1888, 46–47. The bronze of items such as the snake of Athena and the trimming of the sculpture would have been gilded. Blümner 1887, 4:318, on the other hand, thinks of experts in making colored gold alloys. Plut. *De glor. Ath.* 348E speaks of ἐγκαυσταὶ καὶ χρυσωταὶ καὶ βαφεῖς who decorate statues: "painters, gilders, and colorers."

μαλακτῆρες ἐλέφαντος: "ivory softeners." P. elsewhere tells us (*An vitiositas suff.* 499E) that ivory could be shaped and bent after being soaked in beer: τὸν ἐλέφαντα τῷ ζύθει μαλακὸν γενόμενον καὶ χαλῶντα κάμπτουσι καὶ διασχηματίζουσιν, ἄλλως δ' οὐ δύνανται; cf. Sen. *Ep.* 90.33. Pausanias (5.12.2) says that it could be shaped by fire. For many uses, including the flesh parts of the Parthenos statue, the ivory laminae would need to be flattened out of their natural curve. Philostratus speaks of "unrolling" or "unfolding" ivory (*Vit. Apoll.* 2.13). Some have wrongly connected μαλακτῆρες with χρυσοῦ, either by inserting καί before ἐλέφαντος (Reiske) or by punctuating βαφεῖς, χρυσοῦ μαλακτῆρες, ἐλέφαντος ζωγράφοι. See references in *RE* s.v. Elfenbein, V (1905) 2363–65.

ζωγράφοι: "painters," especially for the sculpture, although other architectural elements were painted as well.

ποικιλταί: the meaning is uncertain. The word usually means "embroiderers" or "workers in colored cloth," by which P. would refer to the making of the tapestries, hangings, furniture coverings and so on. But since he is talking of hard materials—stone, bronze, gold and wood—he may be thinking of enamelwork, or the kind of decoration with glass and other materials reported to have been used on the Zeus at Olympia (Paus. 5.11.1–2) and now confirmed by the discoveries in the workshop of Phidias there (Mallwitz 1972a, 56, 58).

τορευταί: men who do ornamental metal work, whether engraving or embossing, especially with precious metal. See Milne 1941. P. might be thinking of the craftsmen who made the gilded silver shield of the Parthenos statue. The Parthenon accounts mention χρυσοχοῖς, "goldsmiths" (IG I³ 436–51, l. 74).

κατὰ θάλατταν: The bronze, ivory, gold, ebony, and cypress all come from overseas, as well as unnamed items such as the "Egyptian blue" pigment of the metopes (on which see Brommer 1967, 161). Note the chiasmus with οἱ κατὰ γῆν. Ἔμποροι are precisely merchants engaged in overseas trade.

ἁμαξοπηγοί: "wagonmakers." See the accounts from Eleusis for making a special wagon for carting stone in 327/26 (IG II² 1673, ll. 11–43, translated by Burford 1969, 252–53). The Parthenon and Propylaea accounts speak of τὰ κύκλα, special wheels or heavy carriages (bogies) for transporting stone (IG I³ 436–51, ll. 306–7, 333–34, 357–58, 399–401; 462–66, l. 50). See also R. Martin 1965, 167–68, with diagrams of the τετράκυκλοι ἅμαξαι used at Eleusis in the fourth century. Normal farm carts would not have been sufficient, although they were undoubtedly used.

ζευγοτρόφοι: "keepers of ox-pairs." For the word cf. IG II² 1576, ll. 73–74, Σκάμανδρος ζευγοτρόφος ἐμ Πειραι(εῖ) οἰκῶν. Tod 1901–2, 211, thinks the animals might be horses, but this seems unlikely for this context. On their use cf. ζεύγεσι τοὺς λίθους ἄγουσι μισθός in *IG* II² 1656.

ἡνίοχοι: "muleteers." P. does not mention in this life a story he knew concerning a mule that wished to continue to accompany others carting stone for the Parthenon, even after it had been retired from service: *Cat. Mai.* 5.3, *De soll. anim.* 970A–B (cf. also Arist. *Hist. an.* 577b34; Aelian *Nat. an.* 6.49; Pliny *NH* 8.175).

καλωστρόφοι: "rope-makers." The importance of rope in the carting and hoisting of marble is apparent from the Eleusinian building inscription, *IG* II² 1673: note the references to skeins of rope, rope for a winch, and the need to split ropes and retwist broken cables.

λινουργοί: "linen-weavers," an emendation of Xylander accepted by Ziegler and Flacelière, here would have to mean "makers of linen ropes." I suggest rather λιθουλκοί, "stone-draggers or -hoisters." The mss.' λιθουργοί is a mistaken repetition from four lines before. LSJ cites λιθουλκός as a name for a tool, but the agent noun would also be a regular formation. Note, moreover, the reference to λιθολκία πρὸς τὰ ἐργαστέρια in the Parthenon accounts, *IG* I³ 436–51, ll. 24, 272, 309, 336, 359. Another possible correction is λιθαγωγοί, "stone-haulers." The expense of λιθαγωγία is frequently listed on the Parthenon and Propylaea accounts (*IG* I³ 436–51, ll. 23, 271, 308, 335, 356; 462–66, ll. 87, 151, 153); cf. also the λιθαγωγοί of *SIG*³ 241A, l. 47, 244B, l. 38.

σκυτοτόμοι: "leatherworkers, saddlers." Here not "cobblers," as usually, but makers of the harnesses and other gear, especially for the multiple teams of oxen needed to draw the heavily loaded wagons. Cf. σκυτῶν περιτμημάτων of the Propylaea accounts (*IG* I³ 462–66, l. 26).

ὁδοποιοί: "roadmakers," necessary both for new roads from the quarries and to repair old roads for the heavy wagon traffic. Cf. the ὑπουργοὶ Πεντελῆθεν ὁδοποιοῦντες, assistants making the roads from the deme, Pentele, on Mount Pentelikon, in the Parthenon and Propylaea accounts (*IG* I³ 436–51, ll. 28, 164, 398; 462–66, l. 49).

μεταλλεῖς: "miner." Here probably used of quarrymen as well (cf. (μαρμάρου μέταλλα in Strabo 9.1.23 [399], of the quarries on Mount Hymettus and Mount Pentelikon). The silver mines at Laurion were worked chiefly by slaves with free overseers, but quarrymen seem to have been citizens; see Burford 1972, 72–77. There are frequent payments to λιθοτόμοι in the Parthenon and Propylaea accounts (*IG* I³ 436–51, ll. 23, 270, 304, 331, 355; 462–66, ll. 84–86, 150, 152).

P. does not mention more specialized work listed on the accounts, such as rough hewing the stone (πελεκητὴς τῶν λίθων) and loading it (λίθους ἀνατιθεὶς ἐπὶ τὰ κύκλα).

ἑκάστη δὲ . . . γινόμενον: P. uses images to explain how these *technai* give jobs even to the mass of unskilled laborers. Each skill had its work crews, as a general has an army, or a workman his tools, or a soul its body.

τὸν θητικὸν ὄχλον καὶ ἰδιώτην: the unskilled hired laborers. Aristotle (*Pol.* 4.4.1290b39–1291a8; cf. 6.7.1321a5–6) distinguished four parts of the πλῆθος: γεωργικὸν, βάναυσον, ἀγοραῖον, θητικόν, that is, food producers, craftsmen, traders, and hired workers. Ἰδιώτης here is adjectival and refers to the unskilled worker as opposed to the skilled craftsman under whom he serves: cf. Plato *Soph.* 221C, πότερον ἰδιώτην ἤ τινα τέχνην ἔχοντα θετέον εἶναι τὸν ἀσπαλιευτήν [fisherman]. P. seems to think of the unskilled workers as a subset of the βάναυσον ὄχλον of 12.5. Several of the trades listed by P. appear among those of new freedmen in the "Catalogi paterarum argentearum," *IG* II² 1553–78; cf. Tod 1901–2.

συντεταγμένον: "organized, ordered"; contrast ἀσύντακτον in 12.5. Pericles has organized the lowest class of citizens into a useful troop, benefiting both the polis and themselves.

ὄργανον . . . γινόμενον: "the instrument and physical means of the service (which the craftsmen render)." Ὑπηρεσία is a very general word for service: see LSJ s.v. II. P. is drawing on one of his favorite images, that of the body as instrument of the soul: cf. *Sept. sap. conv.* 163E, ψυχῆς γὰρ ὄργανον τὸ σῶμα, θεοῦ δ' ἡ ψυχή, and *De Pyth. or.* 404B. We use the affective sense of the body ὥσπερ ὀργανικῆς ὑπηρεσίας ἐπὶ τὸ πρακτικόν (*De virt. mor.* 444D). Thus Pericles, far from pandering to the masses, is organizing the disordered parts of the state under the rule of reason as the soul does the body, or as the god does the heavenly bodies (cf. also *Plat. quaest.* 1002D, 1006D, etc.). Cf. also *Cat. Mai.* 1.5, τὸν δὲ λόγον ὥσπερ δεύτερον σῶμα καὶ τῶν καλῶν μονονοὺκ ἀναγκαῖον ὄργανον.

εἰς πᾶσαν . . . εὐπορίαν: The sentence sums up the effect of the building program in distributing the wealth of the empire. Ὡς ἔπος εἰπεῖν: "so to speak." The absolute infinitive limits the exaggeration of πᾶσαν; cf. *MT* 777; Smyth 2012.

13.1–5

P. praises the incomparable beauty of the Parthenon buildings in a fulsome passage, clearly expressing his own admiration for Pericles' achievement. Rhetorical figures abound; translation is sometimes difficult.

13.1

ἀναβαινόντων κτλ.: "As the buildings were rising, overwhelming in size and inimitable in shapeliness and grace, as the craftsmen were striving to surpass their craft with fine workmanship, the speed of the work was especially surprising." For ἀναβαίνω with impersonal subjects cf. *Pel.* 30.2 (fame); Hdt. 2.13 (a river); Xen. *Symp.* 4.23 (hair). ὑπερηφάνων . . . χάριτι: note the chiasm, varied slightly by the addition of χάριτι in emphatic position.

Ὑπερήφανος is almost always pejorative. The only other positive example in P. is *Fab.* 26.3, πράξεις ὑπερήφανοι τὸ μέγεθος καὶ τὸ κάλλος; cf. the ὑπερηφάνως at *Phil.* 14.6, *Ages.* 34.6. The examples cited from Plato in LSJ as positive are either pejorative or ironic. Thus P. creates a tension between the two parts of the sentence: the buildings are overwhelming, "arrogant," in their size, but redeemed by their beauty.

μορφῇ: "beauty of form," as often, from Homer on.

τῶν δημιουργῶν . . . δημιουργίαν: "as the craftsmen were striving to surpass their craft"; the paronomasia emphasizes both the effort and the following word καλλιτεχνία, itself a rare compound (note its emphatic position also in *Lyc.* 9.9, ἀπηλλαγμένοι γὰρ οἱ δημιουργοὶ τῶν ἀχρήστων, ἐν τοῖς ἀναγκαίοις ἐπεδείκνυντο τὴν καλλιτεχνίαν).

13.2

ὧν γὰρ . . . συντέλειαν: "All these works, each one of which men expected would come to completion only in many successive generations, had their conclusion in the prime of a single administration." Διαδοχαῖς: "successions," used in hendiadys with ἡλικίαις, "generations." Note the double contrast: one item, slowly, versus all, rapidly. Most sacred areas in Greece grew slowly, like P.'s own Delphi.

13.3

καίτοι: introduces a potential objection; cf. Denniston, 558.

Agatharchus: a fifth-century painter from Samos, credited with being the first to use perspective: see Overbeck, *Schriftquellen*, 1118–25; Pollitt, *Sources*, 109–10. According to P. *Alc.* 16.5 and [Andoc.] 4.17, Alcibiades locked him in his house until he had painted it, then gave him a gift and let him go. The genitive Ἀγαθάρχου is dependent on ἀκούσαντα.

τὰ ζῷα: not only animals, but also "figures" in general.

Zeuxis: also a painter, from Heraclea in southern Italy, famous for the subtlety of his shading, which gave his work an extraordinary realism: see Pliny *NH* 35.61–65; Overbeck, *Schriftquellen*, 1647–91; Pollitt, *Sources*, 154–58. P.'s anecdote presumes that the two painters are contemporaries, although Pliny expressly prefers a date of 397 for the beginning of Zeuxis' career against those who prefer 424 as his prime.

ἐγὼ δ' ἐν πολλῷ χρόνῳ: Zeuxis was proud of his care, for the reasons P. gives in the following sentence. The point is expressed explicitly in another version of the anecdote, *De am. mult.* 94E, "ὁμολογῶ," εἶπεν, "ἐν πολλῷ χρόνῳ γράφειν, καὶ γὰρ εἰς πολύν."

13.4

βάρος . . . ἀκρίβειαν: note the chiasmus. Βάρος μόνιμον, like μέγα φρονοῦντος in the previous sentence, reminds us of Periclean virtues. Agatharchus is proud of his speed but does not have the sureness of Zeuxis, or of Pericles (cf. βάρος at 37.1).

ὁ δ᾽ εἰς τὴν γένεσιν . . . ἀποδίδωσιν: "The time advanced by effort toward the production (of the work of art) pays in return the strength (apparent) in the durability of the object." Προδανεισθείς: "lent beforehand, advanced." Ἐν is used in the sense "by, by means of," found occasionally in classical Greek (cf. LSJ, s.v. III) and commonly in koine. For ἀποδίδωμι as "pay in return, repay," see *De E* 388C, *Symp.* 637A, *An seni* 796B.

τὰ Περικλέους ἔργα: the phrase is usually used of accomplishments or deeds, rather than buildings; cf. *Flam.* 11.6, τὰ πρὸς Εὐρυμέδοντι καὶ τὰ περὶ Κύπρον Κίμωνος ἔργα; *Pel.* 25.7, αὔξων τὰ τοῦ Χάρωνος ἔργα, καὶ τὰς στρατηγίας τὰς ἐκείνου καὶ τὰς νίκας ἐγκωμιάζων. But for buildings see, besides 13.1, 5, 6, 15, *Luc.* 39.3, τὰ δ᾽ ἐν τοῖς παραλίοις καὶ περὶ Νέαν πόλιν ἔργα. In this they seem more like those of a Hellenistic monarch or Roman dynast than a democratic leader. Cf. Augustus' *Monumentum Ancyranum* 18.20, ἔργα καίνα (= Lat. *opera nova*) and *Comp. Per.–Fab.* 3.7, τὰ πρὸ τῶν Καισάρων φιλοτιμήματα.

13.5

κάλλει . . . ἐχόντων: "For in beauty each one was ancient from the first, but in freshness each is recent and new-wrought even today: thus a kind of newness always flowers on them, preserving their appearance untouched by time, as if the monuments had mingled in them an ever-living breath and unaging soul." The first two cola neatly balance, with opposition of the then-now, old-new. For ἀρχαῖος as "classic" cf. Demetrius *De eloc.* 15 and 67. Ἀειθαλής is poetic when not literally "evergreen." Πνεῦμα and ψυχή both imply a life within the buildings themselves. On the grandeur of the buildings see also *Comp. Per.–Fab.* 3.7; Strabo 9.1.16 (396).

13.6

πάντα δὲ διεῖπε . . . Φειδίας: Phidias gained his reputation as one of the greatest sculptors of the ancient world chiefly for his two colossal chryselephantine statues of Athena Parthenos at Athens and of Zeus at Olympia. The Parthenos was completed in 438/37 (see note to 13.14), the Zeus in the following years. The alternate theory, that the Zeus preceded the Parthenos, has been disproved by the discovery of Phidias' studio at Olympia, with material clearly dating to the 430s: see Kunze 1959, 277–91; Mallwitz and Schiering 1964, 174–75, 272–77; Prees 1967, 171–73. Two other famous works were the bronze Athena Promachos, a monument of the victory at Marathon erected on the Acropolis, and the Lemnian Athena, both preceding the Parthenos. P. presents Phidias as a friend of Pericles (13.14, *διὰ φιλίαν Περικλέους*; cf. 31.2 and Dio *Or.* 12.55). He was accused of embezzlement of material upon completion of the Parthenos and convicted. The circumstances of his death are not clear, but P. is wrong in not leaving time for his sojourn in Olympia (cf. notes to 31.2–5). For his life and work see Richter 1970, 167–78; Becatti 1951; M. Robertson 1975a, 1:292–322; Ridgeway 1981, 159–171; Linfert 1982, 57–77. Ancient references are collected in Overbeck, *Schriftquellen*, 113–44, and Pollitt, *Sources*, 66–76.

Only here and at 13.14 is Phidias given any larger role in the Periclean building program than that of sculptor of the Parthenos statue. We cannot identify P.'s sources or know how far he can be trusted, but it is certainly mistaken to take his words at face value and make Phidias Pericles' chief architect, master sculptor, and head of public works. Neither *διεῖπε* nor *ἐπίσκοπος* are technical words in Attic or in P.'s usage. The redoubling of *πάντα . . . πάντων* is typical of P.'s style (cf. note to 29.4), and the statement is probably a rhetorical exaggeration of P.'s, perhaps based on nothing more than the fame of Phidias, the story of Pericles' involvement with the sculptor at the time of his trial (cf. 31), and passages in Old Comedy such as Ar. *Peace* 605ff. Nor can we be sure of Pericles' friendship with the sculptor, which may be built on similar evidence, although the example of Socrates, the son of the sculptor (λιθουργός; cf. Diog. Laert. 2.18) who could circulate with the most aristocratic men of Athens, indicates that such a relationship would be possible. In fifth-century Athens direct financial supervision of individual projects was entrusted to a board of *epistatai*, which usually if not always changed annually. Technical aspects were under the supervision of the *architectōn*, a master builder. (Cf. *IG* I³ 474, giving the *epistatai*, the *architectōn*, and the board secretary for the Erechtheum. For the term *architectōn* see Burford 1969, 138–45.) The board and the architect would work according to *syngraphai*, a written description of the building, which had been approved by the demos (cf. ML 44 = *IG* I³ 35, ll. 12–13, καθότι ἂν Καλλικράτης χσυγγράφσει, and Coulton 1977, 51–55). As has been convincingly argued by Himmelmann 1977, there is no position in this procedure for an official supervisor independent of the board; for a contrary view see Donnay 1967 and Boersma, *Building Policy*, 69. Schweitzer 1940 argued that Phidias had a more limited role: master sculptor of the Parthenon, and as such responsible for the unity of execution and design he saw in the metopes and friezes, as well as for the Parthenos statue. Continued study, however, has questioned that unity and thus Phidias' special role. The only certain part that Phidias played in the building program was as sculptor of the Parthenos. It is possible of course that as a friend of Pericles, he advised the statesman on the design and progress of the city's projects, but P.'s evidence is a weak reed to lean on. Ameling 1985, 57, follows Himmelmann in thinking that P. has been influenced by contemporary habits—for example, the relation of Trajan and the architect Apollodorus.

διεῖπε: from διέπω, "manage, administer." Found in Homer and Herodotus but rare in good Attic. Common in P. with the sense of "manage" (a war, a province), "perform the duties of" (an officer). But cf. also διέπων τὰ πράγματα (*Pomp.* 77.2); τὰς θέας διεῖπεν ἐν τῷ θεάτρῳ (*Cat. Min.* 46.4).

ἐπίσκοπος: "supervisor, overseer." The word, which is frequent in P., usually refers not to an official office but to a responsibility or protectorship (cf. *Reg. et imp. apophtheg.* 200E, *Qu. Rom.* 272C, etc.) and should not be confused with the official Athenian inspector in some allied cities, e.g., ML 40, l. 13 (= *IG* I³ 14).

καίτοι: for καίπερ, as commonly in P. with the participle. The separation of ἐχόντων and ἔργων is noteworthy.

13.7

τὸν μὲν γὰρ ἑκατόμπεδον . . . Ἰκτῖνος: the chief glory of Athens, the Parthenon, built between 447 and 432. Fragments of the inscribed building accounts are preserved (*IG* I³ 436–51). On the term *hekatompedos*, "hundred-foot long," see Herington 1955, 13, who notes that in the inscribed inventories of the fifth and fourth centuries, the word is used for the large eastern cella containing the Parthenos, whereas by the end of the fourth century it is used occasionally for the whole building. In *Cat. Mai.* 5.3 ἑκατόμπεδος alone is used for the Parthenon; at *De glor. Ath.* 349D (speaking generally) παρθενῶνες ἑκατόμπεδοι, 351A τοὺς ἑκατομπέδους, at *De soll. anim.* 970A τὸν γὰρ ἑκατόμπεδον νέων . . . ἐν ἀκροπόλει (*Dion* 45.6 refers to a building in Syracuse). P. uses the term Parthenon only in *Demetr.* 23.5, 26.5, *Comp. Demetr.–Ant.* 4.4, and *De exil.* 607A. In the *Demetrius* he perhaps wants to emphasize the scandal of Demetrius' conduct in the temple of the virgin goddess.

The architect Callicrates is known to have worked also on the long walls (see below) and may have done the designs for the temple of Athena Nike (ML 44 = *IG* I³ 35): see I. M. Shear 1963. P. connects Ictinus as well with the telesterion at Eleusis (below); he may also have been architect of the temple of Apollo at Bassae: see Paus. 8.41.9 and Knell 1968. At *Praec. ger. rep.* 802A Ictinus is cited as an example of a craftsman good at his work but unable to speak well, and so losing a commission. According to Vitruvius 7 pref. 12, however, Ictinus wrote an account of the building of the Parthenon (with a third architect, Carpion, otherwise unknown). We do not know the relation of the three men to the work done. P.'s source may have been one of the periegetical works on the Acropolis: see the Introduction, 3.4. For the architects and other craftsmen working on the building see Burford 1963; Wesenberg 1982 (arguing that Ictinus built the predecessor to the Parthenon). For general descriptions and bibliography on the Parthenon see Dinsmoor, *Architecture*, 159–79; Travlos, *Pictorial Dictionary*, 444–59; Orlandos 1977–78; Berger 1984. Carpenter 1970 attempted a full reevaluation of the evidence, according to which an original plan by Callicrates, prepared under the patronage of

Cimon, was drastically revised by Ictinus, but his arguments have not been widely accepted. See, e.g., Bundgaard 1976.

τὸ δ' ἐν Ἐλευσῖνι τελεστήριον: Eleusis, a large city in Attica on the road betwen Corinth and Athens, was the center of the most popular Greek mystery cult, sacred to the goddesses Demeter and Persephone. The cult was state-supported, and the hall of the mysteries (telesterion, from τελέω, "to make perfect, to initiate"; cf. τελετή, "rite of initiation") was successively enlarged and rebuilt in the sixth century (esp. by Pisistratus), in the early fifth (before 480) by the restored democracy, and by Pericles. On the site, the buildings, and the mysteries see Mylonas 1961, with many plates. P. himself, like most Athenians and many famous Romans, was an initiate: cf. *Cons. ad uxor.* 611D, τὰ μυστικὰ σύμβολα τῶν περὶ τὸν Διόνυσον ὀργιασμῶν, ἃ σύνισμεν ἀλλήλοις οἱ κοινωνοῦντες, and his generalizing account in his work *On the Soul* (frag. 178 Sandbach).

ἤρξατο μὲν Κόροιβος . . . ἐκορύφωσε: P.'s is the most explicit statement on the confused architectural history of the telesterion, but it does not name Ictinus, who is given as architect by Vitruvius (7 pref. 16, *cellam immani magnitudine Ictinos dorico more sine exterioribus columnis . . . pertexit*) and Strabo (9.1.12 [395]). P.'s source is unknown: perhaps a guide book or antiquarian study of the sanctuary, or a knowledgeable friend (see the Introduction, 3.5). The building was remarkable for its size, ca. 51 meters square, designed to accommodate the crowds of initiates. Excavations reveal that an original fifth-century design, requiring a forest of 7 × 7 columns, was replaced by a design for 5 × 4 columns, and finally by a 7 × 6 design. However, despite excavations and P.'s description, much remains uncertain about the design and chronology of the building. See especially Noack 1927, 139–201; Dinsmoor, *Architecture*, 195–96; Travlos 1950–51, 1–16; Mylonas 1961, 77–88, 111–24 and plates; T. L. Shear, Jr. 1966, 147a–214, and 1982; and Boersma, *Building Policy*, 185–87. Mylonas connects the first design with Ictinus, the second with Coroebus (in contrast, e.g., to Dinsmoor, who gives the first design to Coroebus, the second to Ictinus, and the third to Metagenes). Coroebus' participation is confirmed by an inscription, *IG* I³ 32 (= Hill, *Sources*, B41), ca. 450/49, setting up a board of *epistatai* for a building at Eleusis and naming (l. 26) τὸν ἀρχιτέκτονα Κόροιβον. The date 450/49 is defended by Meritt and Wade-Gery 1963, 111–14. P. associates Coroebus with the first level of columns and the architraves (ἐπιστύλια) that joined them. Metagenes added the balcony and the upper columns; Xenocles designed the roof opening. The time required for construction is quite uncertain: Noack 1927, 198–200, thought it was completed in the late 420s; T. L. Shear, Jr. 1966, 203–10, reaffirms the argument of Cavaignac that it was still incomplete in 408/7, as an inventory of that date (*IG* I^2 313–14, I^3 386–87) contains construction materials suitable for the telesterion.

Metagenes: Otherwise unknown. The deme name (an emendation of Ξυπέτιος, which is otherwise unattested) might show that this information was derived by P. or his source from a public document, as with Xenocles just below. It also distinguishes this Metagenes from the general ἐκ Κοίλης, who was sent to Corcyra in 433/32 (*IG* I^3 364, l. 20 = ML 61).

τὸ διάζωσμα κτλ.: A διάζωσμα or διάζωμα should be a girdle or band around or across something; here, however, the meaning is disputed. I take it to mean a frieze (perhaps a cornice) as in Theophrastus *Lapid.* 7. There is evidence for a Doric frieze of triglyphs and metopes running around the outside of the building at the top of the wall, as on the Propylaea or the arsenal of Philo in the Piraeus. See Jeppesen 1958, 106–8; T. L. Shear, Jr. 1966, 179. The frieze could also have been on the inside wall, but not around the central cella, as was the case of the ζώνη in the temple of Zeus at Olympia mentioned in Paus. 5.10.5, as the multiple rows of columns would not have left an open area in the center as at Olympia. The scholion that explains τὸ τοὺς κίονας ἄνωθεν συνέχον ὃ καὶ γεισίον φασὶ τὸ νῦν κοσμητάριον mistakenly places the cornice directly above the columns (Manfredini 1979, 99).

τοὺς ἄνω κίονας: a second tier of columns, presumably only in the center, to support the clerestory. Noack was wrong to postulate a balcony, as there is no evidence of stairs.

τὸ δ' ὀπαῖον: literally, an "opening"; cf. ὀπή, "hole," of a smokehole or window. Noack thought of a large opening in the roof, covered by shutters; Dinsmoor, *Architecture*, 196, rather of a lantern, a raised central part of the roof, with windows for light. In a monograph on *opaia* and lanterns Spuler 1973, 12–16, argues that it was simply a square opening in the roof, similar to that of the Erechtheum north porch.

ἐπὶ τοῦ ἀνακτόρου: the *opaion* would have been above the *anaktoron*, a small shrine structure within the larger hall, on which see esp. Travlos 1950–51. (For the word cf. Hdt. 9.65; Mylonas 1961, 120–21.)

Xenocles of Cholargos: Otherwise unknown. He comes from Pericles' deme, cf. 3.1. Hoepfner 1976, 119, 132–34, suggests that he was also the architect of the classical Pompeion, built ca. 410–393.

ἐκορύφωσε: "crowned," not "roofed," particularly appropriate for the highest part of a peaked roof.

τὸ δὲ μακρὸν τεῖχος: The long walls that united Athens to her harbor city, Piraeus, assured Athens of access to her fleet and grain supply at all times and were a major feature in Athenian strategy in the Peloponnesian War. The wall in question here is the "middle" or "southern" wall that ran directly to the Piraeus, parallel to the northern wall, replacing the outer wall that ran to the harbor of Phaleron, as P. specifically states at *De glor. Ath.* 351A when quoting this same passage from Cratinus: περὶ τοῦ διὰ μέσου τείχους. See Thuc. 1.107.1, 108.3; Judeich 1931, 155–57; Boersma, *Building Policy*, 74, 156–57; bibliography and map in Travlos, *Pictorial Dictionary*, 163–64. According to P., the earlier long wall had been partially built or strengthened with the spoils from the Eurymedon by Cimon (*Cim.* 13.6), which seems contrary to Thucydides. Our best evidence for the date of Pericles' middle wall (ca. 445–443) is Plato *Gorg.* 455E, Περικλέους δὲ καὶ αὐτὸς ἤκουον ὅτε συνεβούλευεν ἡμῖν περὶ τοῦ διὰ μέσου τείχους, cited by P., and an inscription (*IG* I² 343, l. 90, I³ 436–451, line 127) recording transfers from a wall project ([π]αρὰ τειχ[οποιῶν]) to Parthenon funds in 443/42. (*ATL* 3:341n. 64; Judeich 1931, 76n. 1).

ἠργολάβησε: "contracted to build"; cf. ἐργολάβος, 31.2.

Callicrates: made responsible for the wall though busy at the same time with the Parthenon. In a decree dated ca. 447/46 he was given a commission to do (wall building?) work on the Acropolis: see *IG* I² 44, I³ 45; Boersma, *Building Policy*, 162.

13.8

Cratinus: See the Introduction, 3.1.e. This is F300 K. = F326 K.A. P. made effective use of the same quote in *De glor. Ath.* 351A, comparing Isocrates' slowness of composition with Pericles' activity; here it provides evidence for his building program. Φησί, of course, does not belong to the quote: for other similar insertions in comic citations see *Per.* 3.5, *Alc.* 1.8. For γὰρ αὐτό at the end of a line cf. Ar. *Knights* 890, ἐγὼ γὰρ αὐτόν. The play is not known, nor why P. thinks this applies to the building of the wall. The meter is iambic tetrameter catalectic.

13.9

᾽Ωιδεῖον: As its name implies, a music hall, called the Odeion of Pericles to distinguish it from the Odeion of Herodes Atticus still visible on the slopes of the Acropolis and the Odeion of Agrippa in the Agora. Pericles' Odeion was on the south slope of the Acropolis, east of the theater of Dionysus. P. knew only a reconstruction of the building, which had been burned by the Athenians in 86 B.C., to prevent its wood from being used by Sulla to besiege the Acropolis (Appian *Mithr.* 38; cf. Vitr. 5.9.1; Paus. 1.20.4). Both the date and the politician responsible for the Odeion are in question. P. credits it to Pericles, Vitruvius to Themistocles: *quod Themistocles columnis lapideis dispositis navium malis et antemnis spoliis Persicis pertextit.* The citation from Cratinus suggests that the Odeion was near completion or completed shortly before an ostracism, which might be that of 443, when Thucydides was expelled. However, it has been argued that the *Thracian Women* was produced some years later than this, between 435 and 430, in which case another ostracism may be meant. Could such an enormous building have been constructed simultaneously with the Parthenon? Robkin 1979, 10–11, argues rather that it was planned for earlier, and already in place by 446. (Her suggestion that it was built to hold the planned Panhellenic congress [cf. *Per.* 17] does not sufficiently explain the construction of such an enormous building, requiring work over a long period.)

Excavations have revealed that the Odeion was a very large building, 62.4 × 68.6 meters, with ten rows of nine columns (cf. P.'s πολύστυλον). The forest of columns would have been similar to the telesterion at Eleusis but covered an even larger area. The shape of the building might indeed have been inspired by Xerxes' royal tent, captured at Plataea (cf. Paus. 1.20.4; Hdt. 9.70.3, 82.1), with its multiple internal supports and peaked roof. But we do not know that Xerxes' tent was ever reerected at Athens, as some have suggested. According to Vitruvius the masts and spars of the Persian ships (from Salamis) were used to construct the roof. Meiggs, *Trees*, 474, notes that the roof beams would have been enormous, more than 70 feet (21.3 meters) long. Could they have been preserved for some thirty-five or forty years before being used? Simply put, we do not know enough to interpret our sources on the building's history, and the excavations made so far have not resolved the question. The Odeion was used not only for musical contests but as a court (cf. Ar. *Wasps* 1108–9); the Thirty used it as an assembly point when they were defending their rule in winter 404/3 (Xen. *Hell.* 2.4.9, 24). See Dinsmoor, *Architecture*, 211; Travlos, *Pictorial Dictionary*, 387–91; Boersma, *Building Policy*, 72, 206; Robkin 1979; von Gall 1979; Meinel 1980, 135–50. On *Per.* 13.9–11 as a whole see Davison 1958, 33–36 (= 1968, 48–54).

πολύεδρον: "with many seats, benches." Only here in P.

περικλινὲς καὶ κάταντες: "steep and sloping downward." P. looks at the roof from its peak down. Apparently the roof was pyramidal, sloping on four sides. Περικλινὲς, however, is probably not "sloping on all sides," as given by LSJ, but "steep," as is apparent from P.'s usage elsewhere: cf. *Pel.* 32.3, λόφων περικλινῶν καὶ ὑψηλῶν; *Marc.* 29.4; *Mar.* 20.5.

βασιλέως: the Persian king; cf. 10.5.

ἐπιστατοῦντος καὶ τούτῳ: On *epistatai* see note to 13.6. Pericles is not listed on the extant inscriptions that preserve the names of members of the boards of *epistatai* of the Parthenon, of the chryselephantine statue of Athena, and of the Propylaea. P. uses the words ἐπιστάτης and ἐπιστατέω regularly for "overseer" and "to oversee." The only time he seems to refer to an actual office is *Them.* 31.1 (Themistocles was τῶν ᾿Αθήνησιν ὑδάτων ἐπιστάτης), but our fourth-century evidence for the title is that it was ἐπιμελητὴς τῶν κρηνῶν (*Ath. pol.* 43.1; cf. Rhodes, *CAAP* ad loc.). P. here, as in speaking of Phidias at 13.14, is probably using the word in this nonspecific sense. Other writers call Pericles the *epistatēs* of the Parthenon and the telesterion (Strabo 9.1.12 [395]), of the Athena statue (Philochorus, *FGrHist* 328 F121; cf. Diod. 12.39.1; Aristodemus 16.1), and of the Lyceum (Harpocration s.v. Λύκειον, citing Philochorus 328 F37); see Boersma, *Building Policy*, 73. Philochorus is the most reliable for technical matters, so Pericles probably was legally only *epistatēs* of the statue and the Lyceum. He was called to account as *epistatēs* of the statue: cf. note to 32.3.

13.10

Cratinus: F71 K. = 73 K.A. See the Introduction, 3.1.e. The *Thracian Women* cannot be dated accurately: if the ostracism mentioned is that of 443, the play may have been produced shortly afterwards; but this is not certain, and some scholars argue for ca. 435–430; see Davison 1958, 35 (= 1968, 52); Meiggs, *AE* 289n. 3. The correct division of lines is more likely that of Meineke in *FCG*, followed by Kassel and Austin (*PCG*), dividing after προσέρχεται and retaining Περικλέης; Cobet 1873a, 371, followed by Ziegler and Flacelière, breaks after ὅδε, deleting Περικλέης. The meter is iambic trimeter.

σχινοκέφαλος: see note to 3.4. Pericles seems to be wearing the Odeion (or its pointed roof) as he did the helmet in the Cresilaus portrait: perhaps Cratinus thought that the pyramidal roof of the Odeion, with its sharp peak, would be suitable for Pericles' head. If the joke for Cratinus was the shape of the roof, there is no need to think the Odeion just completed, although that is possible.

ὅδε: Meineke (*FCG*) and Kassel and Austin (*PCG*) prefer Bekker's ὁδί to the mss.' ὅδε. The former is frequent in comedy and required by the meter, if the line ends with προσέρχεται. In comic dialogue, πϱ does not normally make position: see MacDowell 1971, 21. For ὁδὶ προσέρχεται at the end of a verse see Ar. *Knights* 146, *Plut.* 1038; cf. also *Wasps* 1324, *Lys.* 77. However, P. may have written ὅδε: there are only three instances of ὁδί in his works, all concentrated in the *De gen. Socr.*, two at 575F, one at 582D.

Περικλέης: Cobet 1873a, 371, deleted this word as not belonging to the quote. It might have been added by P. himself, using this form in -έης to fit the meter, rather than by a glossator, who would have supplied the usual contracted form.

τοὔστρακον: for ὀστρακισμός, the occasion of ostracism. See note to 9.5.

παροίχεται: absolute; the ostracism has passed by.

13.11

φιλοτιμούμενος: Although the whole building program is seen in the context of political rivalry (cf. 12.1), the reference to the ostrakophoria in the citation from Cratinus recalls the subject to P.'s attention, so that here the decree on the Panathenaea is explicitly presented as an act of political ambition (φιλοτιμία).

τότε πρῶτον ἐψηφίσατο: Another reference to a decree of Pericles, although P. need not have seen it himself. Τότε gives no real indication of date, but a certain Phrynis δοκεῖ πρῶτος κιθαρίσαι παρ' Ἀθηναίοις καὶ νικῆσαι Παναθηναίοις ἐπὶ Καλλι[μαχ]ου ἄρχοντος (446 B.C.) in schol. Ar. *Clouds* 969. Thus Pericles' law would belong shortly before 446. See Davison 1958, 40–41 (= 1968, 63–64); Rhodes, *CAAP* 670–71. The mss.' Καλλίου would place the date earlier (456). Πρῶτον is an error: musical competitions at the Panathenaea in the sixth century are known from a prize amphora (Davison 1958, 36–37 (= 1968, 54–62), but they probably were discontinued. Davison suggests that Pericles revived them at the time of construction of the Odeion.

The Panathenaea were the yearly festival in honor of Athena, held on 28 Hekatombaion, but celebrated with special pomp every fourth year (the Greater Panathenaea). See Mommsen 1898, 41–159; Deubner 1956, 22–35; H. A. Thompson 1961, 224–31;

Parke 1977, 33–50; N. Robertson 1985. Besides the contests in music listed here, there were gymnastic contests and horse races. See Arist. *Ath. pol.* 60.1, 3, and *IG* II² 2311, a fourth-century list of the prizes for each contest.

ἀθλοθέτης: The duties of the *athlothetai* are described in *Ath. pol.* 60; cf. Rhodes, *CAAP* ad loc. Their principal responsibility was the Greater Panathenaea, organizing the procession, the athletic and musical contests, and related matters. They appear on inscriptions as early as 415/14, on a list of payments, ML 77 (= *IG* I² 302, I³ 370), 67.

13.12

τὰ δὲ Προπύλαια: the Propylaea, the monumental gateway to the Acropolis and the most famous Periclean building after the Parthenon, constructed 437/36–433/32. See Travlos, *Pictorial Dictionary*, 482–93; Dinsmoor, *Architecture*, 199–205; Lawrence 1957, 161–64; Boersma, *Building Policy*, 70, 200–201; Bundgaard 1957. Mnesicles is mentioned as an architect also by Philochorus (*FGrHist* 328 F36). For the Propylaea building accounts see ML 60; *IG* I³ 462–66; for the earlier entrances see W. B. Dinsmoor, Jr. 1980. Pericles is also given as the builder at *De glor. Ath.* 351A.

τὴν θεόν: Athena, as goddess of the Acropolis.

13.13

ἄγαλμα τῆς Ὑγιείας Ἀθηνᾶς: A semicircular statue base has been found beside the southeast wall of the Propylaea, inscribed Ἀθεναῖοι τεῖ Ἀθεναίαι τεῖ Ὑγείαι. Πύρρος ἐποίησεν Ἀθεναῖος (*IG* I² 395; photographs in Raubitschek 1949, 185–88; Travlos, *Pictorial Dictionary*, 126, fig. 170). On the sanctuary of Athena Hygeia, dating at least from the early fifth century, see Judeich 1931, 242–44; Travlos, *Pictorial Dictionary*, 124. Pliny *NH* 22.44 gives a more elaborate version of the story, naming the herb revealed to Pericles. Another version of the story reveals how historical or pseudo-historical anecdotes were used in the philosophical schools: according to Diog. Laert. 9.82, the Skeptic Pyrrho used as a philosophical example "the slave of Pericles, sleepwalking on the top of the roof"; cf. also Hieronymus F19 Wehrli. Some modern scholars (e.g., Raubitschek, Judeich) reasonably associate the dedication with the plague of 429 rather than an injury to a workman. P. considers the Propylaea so famous as not to need comment, but prefers through this anecdote to indicate the goddess's approval of the work. Although the inscription speaks only of the Athenians, P. considers the statue an initiative of Pericles, another example of substituting his hero for a less specific agent.

13.14

Phidias: P., having enumerated the other architects (13.6–13), now returns to Pericles' head architect.

εἰργάζετο μέν: made himself, as opposed to the supervising described in the next clause (πάντα δ' ἦν . . .).

τὸ χρυσοῦν ἕδος: the gold and ivory statue inside the Parthenon, which with the similar statue of Zeus in Olympia (see note to 2.1) was the masterwork of the sculptor. For descriptions and reconstructions see Ridgeway 1981, 161–67; M. Robertson 1975b, 1:311–16; Leipen 1971; Richter 1970, 217–20, figs. 632–45; Stevens 1957, 350–61; Herington 1955. According to Philochorus, *FGrHist* 328 F121, the statue was set up in 438/37, with Pericles *epistatēs* (i.e., one of the commission: see note to 32.2).

τῇ στήλῃ: Which stele? Perhaps the one recording the indictment against him (cf. 31 and the indictment against Alcibiades at *Alc.* 22.4), or one marking the dedication of the statue. It is unlikely that his name would appear on the honorary decree for Menon (31.5) or the accounts of the statue, fragments of which have been found (ML 54; *IG* I³ 453–60). Orlandos 1977–78, 1:423, suggests that it might be the bronze stele with the inventory of the statue, referred to in an inscription of 303 B.C. (see *Hesperia* 40 [1971] 449, ll. 13–14).

13.15

τῷ μέν: Phidias.

βλασφημίαν: slander.

εἰς ταὐτὸ φοιτώσας: "visiting the same place, meeting." However, the reading of the mss., εἰς τὰ ἔργα, "visiting the buildings under construction," is acceptable. There is no need for Ziegler's emendation (accepted by Flacelière) εἰς ταὐτό, although that phrase is regularly used as a euphemism for sexual intercourse; cf. 32.1. Φοιτάω is often found with εἰς plus a location: cf. 32.1 and *Lyc.* 12.6, *Cam.* 10.1, *Sert.* 14.4, *Ages.* 20.5, *Demetr.* 24.4, *Mul. virt.* 253F, *Symp.* 643C, *Amat.* 771A. There must have been much gossip about Pericles' real or imagined sexual activity: besides the women mentioned here and Aspasia (cf. chapter 24), he is associated with Elpinice (cf. note to 10.5) and Chrysilla of Corinth (cf. Athen. 10.436F, quoting Teleclides). Both seduction of a free woman and procuring were offenses prosecutable under Athenian law: cf. MacDowell, *Law*, 124–25. Note that Elpinice was also thought to have been attracted by an artist working on a building (*Cim.* 4.6).

ὑποδεχομένου: the regular word for entertaining, but since it is used also in 32.1 of Aspasia, it may have a suggestive sense. The Acropolis was a sacred area, with severe restrictions on what could be done there: cf. the fragments of regulations in *IG* I³ 4 and P.'s indignation at the behavior of Demetrius Poliorcetes, ὁ δ' ἐν αὐτῷ τῷ Παρθενῶνι ταῖς τε πόρναις συνῆν καὶ τῶν ἀστῶν κατεπόρνευσε πολλάς (*Comp. Demetr.–Ant.* 4.4).

δεξάμενοι: "accepting" the story; cf. 32.3.

οἱ κωμικοί: adespota F59 K., *CAF* 3:410. See the Introduction, 3.1.d, k.

πόλλην ἀσέλγειαν αὐτοῦ κατεσκέδασαν: "poured over him much abuse." For the expression cf. *Thes.* 16.3, οἱ τραγικοὶ . . . ἀδοξίαν αὐτοῦ κατεσκέδασαν; Dem. *De Corona* 50.

εἰς: "with regard to"; cf. 8.5, 13.16, and 29.2, προσδιαβληθείη . . . εἰς τὸν λακωνισμόν.

Menippus: unknown except for *Praec. ger. rep.* 812C, Περικλῆς Μενίππῳ μὲν ἐχρῆτο πρὸς τὰς στρατηγίας. P.'s source in both places is probably the same comic passage. Because there was no official ὑποστράτηγος at Athens, Menippus may have been a fellow general of Pericles but under his influence, as Metiochus was (*Praec. ger. rep.* 811E), or an assistant used by him (thus in Xen. *Anab.* 5.6.36, [Neon,] ὃς Χειρισόφῳ ὑπεστρατήγει; cf. 3.1.32). Cobet's emendation συστρατηγοῦντος (1873a, 136) is unnecessary. P. uses the word also at *Cras.* 9.5 and *Comp. Demetr.–Ant.* 1.3 (= legate) and at *Arat.* 29.7.

Pyrilampes: a wealthy man, who on return from an embassy to Persia in the 440s brought back peacocks, a gift from the king. The birds were an attraction to visitors for at least thirty years, although Aristophanes' Dicaeopolis was not impressed (*Ach.* 62–63): ἄχθομαι 'γὼ πρέσβεσιν / καὶ τοῖς ταῶσι τοῖς τ' ἀλαζονεύμασιν. He was with Socrates at the battle of Delium in 424. Cf. Plato *Charm.* 158A; Athen. 9.397C–D, Plut. *De gen. Socr.* 581D; Meiggs, *AE* 146; Davies, *APF* 329–30, 335. His son Demos was also a famous beauty (cf. Ar. *Wasps* 98 and schol.; Plato *Gorg.* 481D; Lys. 19.25). Pyrilampes' second wife was Perictione, his niece and the mother of Plato. The Pyrilampes prosecuted by Pericles for the killing of his lover (anon. vit. Thuc. 6) may be identical, although it seems more probable that he is a relative.

ὑφιέναι: "provide secretly," either as temptation to or reward for favors. An ordinary cock was a regular love-gift to a boy: see Dover 1978, 92. For the verb cf. *Mul. virt.* 256E, ταύτην ὑφῆκε τἀδελφῷ τοῦ τυράννου δέλεαρ, and *Pomp.* 20.4, δέλεαρ αὐτῷ δέκα σπείρας ὑφῆκεν.

ἐπλησίαζε: another euphemism. See 24.4, *Cim.* 4.6.

13.16

καὶ τί ἄν τις . . . θαυμάσειεν: an indignant rhetorical question. The initial καὶ expresses emotion; cf. Denniston, 310–11.

σατυρικούς: given to debauchery, like satyrs; cf. *Galb.* 16.3, of actors and wrestlers: ἐφήμεροι καὶ σατυρικοὶ τοῖς βίοις ἄνθρωποι.

τάς . . . ἀποθύοντας: "always offering their slanders against their betters in sacrifice to the envy of the multitude, as if to an evil spirit." The attacks on Pericles, according to P., arose chiefly from envy for his influence and achievements.

ἑκάστοτε: with ἀποθύοντας.

ὅπου καί: "when even."

Stesimbrotus: *FGrHist* 107 F10b. See the Introduction, 3.1.c.

μυσῶδες: "abominable, disgusting." For this word, much preferable to μυθῶδες (mss.), see *Tim.* 5.2, λοιδοροῦντες ὡς ἀσεβὲς ἐξειργασμένον καὶ μυσῶδες ἔργον, referring to Timoleon's participation in the assassination of his tyrant brother.

ἐξενεγκεῖν: "publish, spread abroad"; cf. 36.4, *Them.* 23.3, *Nic.* 5.4.

τὴν γυναῖκα τοῦ υἱοῦ: the story appears more fully at 36.6 (cf. also Athen. 13.589D–E), where it seems that the son, Xanthippus, is himself responsible for the accusation. P. is horrified by the idea of such an incestuous relationship, especially because it conflicted with his conception of Pericles' self-control. (Contrast the tolerant presentation of Cimon's relation with his sister Elpinice as well as with other women, *Cim.* 4.6–10.)

οὕτως ἔοικε πάντῃ χαλεπὸν κτλ.: The feeling of dissatisfaction with sources must have been particularly strong in writing the *Pericles*, for much of which there were no satisfactory narrative accounts, and other sources clearly were written for other purposes than historical accuracy. The difficulty of writing accurately about the past because of the intervening time was already clear to Thucydides (1.1.3, 1.20.1, 1.21.1). P. speaks most explicitly of the difficulty at *Thes.* 1.1–4. Tacitus expresses epigrammatically the difficulty with contemporary historians' writing about the emperors: *res florentibus ipsis ob metum falsae, postquam occiderant recentibus odiis compositae sunt.* He, of course, will write *sine ira et studio* (*Ann.* 1.1; cf. *Hist.* 1.1; Arrian *Anab.* pref. 2; Lucian *De hist. conscr.* 39). Despite these problems P. generally preferred to use contemporary authors: see the Introduction, 3.

δυσθήρατον ἱστορίᾳ: "hard to track down by research"; cf. *Pomp.* 38.6, τὸν Μιθριδάτην ἑώρα δυσθήρατον ὄντα τοῖς ὅπλοις.

ἐπιπροσθοῦντα τῇ γνώσει: "obstructing knowledge."

ἡλικιῶτις: "contemporary" (to the events).

τὰ μὲν . . . τὰ δέ: coordinating the datives of manner and circumstantial participles.

14.1

τῶν δὲ περὶ τὸν Θουκυδίδην ῥητόρων: The personal attacks on Pericles lead back to the political division set out in chapter 11 and the attacks on the building program in 12.1–2. The idiom οἱ περί with a proper name, which is very common in P., frequently refers to just one person (cf. *Cic.* 42.3, νεῖμαι δὲ τοῖς περὶ Κάσσιον καὶ Βροῦτον ἐπαρχίας; *Phoc.* 17.2, *Arat.* 3.4, 41.3, *Pyrrh.* 20.1; and see Radt 1980). Here, however, several speakers probably are intended: "Thucydides and his supporters."

σπαθῶντος . . . ἀπολλύντος: note the chiasmus. Σπαθάω, lit. "strike down the woof," that is, to tamp it firmly into place when weaving, early came to mean "squander, waste money," because tamping too hard would use more wool for a given length of cloth. Cf. Strepsiades' complaint to his wife, λίαν σπαθᾷς (Ar. *Clouds* 55). The nouns should be taken together, "tribute money." These complaints are a restatement of the debate at 12.1–3, altered by P. to form an introduction to the following anecdote.

ἐμοὶ δεδαπανήσθω: "let the cost be put to my account." The anecdote, apocryphal as it sounds—Pericles' private fortune could not have paid for even one of the major buildings—may have a basis in fact. A fragmentary decree, *IG* I³ 49 (the "springhouse decree"), concerning expenses for the water supply, has been restored to read (ll. 14–16) [ἐπαινέσαι δὲ καὶ Περικλεῖ καὶ Παρ]άλοι καὶ Χσανθίπποι καὶ τοῖς ὑέ[σιν· ἀπαναλίσκεν δὲ ἀπὸ τὸν χρεμάτον] hόσα ἐς τὸν φόρον τὸν Ἀθεναίον τελ[εῖται, ἐπειδὰν hε θεὸς ἐχς αὐτὸν λαμ]βάνει τὰ νομιζόμενα. That is, Pericles, his sons Paralus and Xanthippus, and other unspecified sons had offered to pay for something, but the demos decided to use the money from the tribute instead. Note, however, that Hiller's restoration of Pericles' name (1919, 666) has been inspired by P.'s notion of Pericles as a general supervisor of monuments, and in fact neither Hiller's ἐπαινέσαι and Περικλεῖ nor ἀναλίσκειν (restored by Meritt 1937, 18–19) appear on the stone, although the presence of Pericles' sons is sure enough. For other suggested restorations and interpretations of the inscription cf. Mattingly 1961, 164n. 73 (restoring τοῖς ὑέ[σιν Κλενίο: χρέσθαι δὲ τοῖς χρέμασιν]); W. E. Thompson 1971, 329–32 (putting the date at ca. 430); Woodhead 1973–74 (arguing for ca. 435/34).

Whatever the truth of the story, P. is impressed both by Pericles' μεγαλοφροσύνη (cf. 14.2) and his ability to overcome his opponents and win over the demos. Pericles' challenge also reminded the demos of the major change brought about since the 460s, the substitution of the expenditure of public money according to a vote of the assembly for private largess (such as Cimon's embellishment of the Academy and gift of shade trees for the Agora); cf. Kagan, *OPW* 145–46.

τῶν ἀναθημάτων: the buildings dedicated to the gods, as at 12.1.

τὴν ἐπιγραφήν: "the dedicatory inscription." For a reverse case cf. Pausanias' dedication of serpent column and tripod at Delphi in his own name, and the subsequent reinscription in the name of the cities that fought at Plataea (Thuc. 1.132.2; cf. Plut. *De malig Her.* 873C). Buildings, like other dedications, carried the name of the dedicator, whether city, group, or individual. P. refers to many, including that on the Acanthian treasury, Βρασίδας καὶ Ἀκάνθιοι ἀπ' Ἀθηναίων (*Lys.* 1.1; cf. *Them.* 5.5, *Alc.* 21.4, *Arist.* 1.3, *Alex.* 16.18, *De Pyth. or.* 401C, *De malig. Her.* 867F, 870F, 871B). Normally, of course, only tyrants and monarchs had the resources to do this: cf. Alexander's dedication of the temple of Athena at Priene, Βασιλεὺς Ἀλέξανδρος ἀνέθηκε τὸν ναὸν Ἀθηναίηι Πολιάδι (Tod, *GHI* 2:184). Strabo (14.1.22 [641]) quotes Artemidorus of Ephesus for the story that Alexander was refused permission to pay for the rebuilding of the temple of Artemis at Ephesus, ἐφ' ᾧ τε τὴν ἐπιγραφὴν αὐτὸν ἔχειν, "since it was not suitable for a god to make dedications to a god"! Ameling 1985 is wrong in arguing that it would have been impossible for Pericles' name to appear on one of the Acropolis buildings. He is right, however, to note that P. would have also been familiar with the practice from contemporary monuments, erected not least to win honor for the donor: cf., e.g., the inscription of M. Agrippa on the Pantheon, a notable example from an earlier generation at Rome.

14.2

κελεύοντες: sc. τὸν Περικλέα.

χορηγεῖν: cf. 36.2 and 9.3, χορηγίαις; 16.5, χορηγός.

14.3

τέλος δέ: "finally"; the conclusion of the rivalry begun at 11.1. P. makes no direct connection between the debate on the building program (which in any case would have been a matter of continuous discussion) and the ostracism of Thucydides, nor does he assign any date to the ostracism. The notice merely completes the story and prepares for the next section on Pericles' monarchical power: compare the abrupt notice on Cimon's death at 10.8, omitting the Cyprian campaign. Thus although it is possible that the ostracism was a reaction to Thucydides' criticism of the building program (thus Meiggs, AE 186–87; Kagan, OPW 145), P.'s account does not rule out other factors, such as the prosecution of Xenocritus (anon. vit. Thuc. 7); it simply ignores them.

The date of this ostracism is usually given as 443 on the basis of Per. 16.3, μετὰ δὲ τὴν Θουκυδίδου κατάλυσιν καὶ τὸν ὀστρακισμὸν οὐκ ἐλάττω τῶν πεντεκαίδεκα ἐτῶν διηνεκῆ καὶ μίαν οὖσαν ἐν ταῖς ἐνιαυσίοις στρατηγίαις ἀρχὴν καὶ δυναστείαν κτησάμενος, counting fifteen terms from 443/32 to 429/28, the year of his death, and including 430/29 even though he was removed from office before its completion (Per. 35.4; cf., e.g., Wade-Gery 1932, 206 [= 1958, 240]). However, the numbers could be rounded, or the count ended at 431/30, or both. P.'s statement would not exclude a date between 445 and 442 and there is no other evidence; cf. Busolt, Gr. Gesch. 3.1:495n. 1 (442 B.C.); Beloch, Gr. Gesch. 2.1:185 (445 B.C.); Andrewes 1978, 7 (444 or 443). P., of course, could be mistaken, if not in his count of fifteen consecutive years, perhaps in believing that they must have started *after* the ostracism of Thucydides. Krentz 1984 argues that Thucydides Melesiou is in fact the general of 440/39 named by Thucydides (1.117.2), and that the ostracism must have taken place only later, perhaps in 437 or 436, after the attacks on Pericles' friends treated by P. in chapters 31–32. This reconstruction is not impossible.

A number of ostraka bearing Thucydides' name have been found: see figure 2 and cf. Thomsen 1972, 80, 82, 93, 100; Vanderpool 1974, 193; ML 45, 47. Note that others were apparently ostracized in the same decade, such as Damon (cf. note to 4.3) and Callias son of Didymus, an Olympic victor in 472; see Vanderpool 1970, 25–26. Of course, ostraka were also cast for Pericles himself, though only two have been found: see figure 3 and T. L. Shear 1941, 2–3 and fig. 2; H. A. Thompson 1952, 113; Boulter 1953, 99; Vanderpool 1970, fig. 33. Historians are only beginning to sort out the implications of our new finds of ostraka. One thing is clear, however: both P. and the historian Thucydides present an immensely simplified picture of the political scene at Athens in this period.

With his ostracism, Thucydides disappears from the *Pericles*, although he is usually thought to have returned after ten years (if not before) and perhaps led the opposition to Pericles in the late 430s (see note to 31–32).

εἰς ἀγῶνα . . . καταστάς: for the expression cf. Plat. *Apol.* 24C, *Rep.* 494E. It is more a legal than a wrestling term (but cf. Connor 1971, 63).

περὶ τοῦ ὀστράκου: ὄστρακον is P.'s usual word for ostracism, both the voting procedure and the resulting banishment; cf. *Comp. Per.–Fab.* 3.2, *Arist.* 1.2, 7, *Nic.* 11.1, 3, 4, 9 (τὸν περὶ τοῦ ὀστράκου κίνδυνον), *Alc.* 13.6; Cratinus, cited at *Per.* 13.10.

κατέλυσε . . . ἑταιρείαν: P. thinks of the grouping described in 11.1–2. The term ἑταιρεία was used from the fifth century (e.g., Thuc. 3.82.5) for associations or clubs, more or less formally organized, of citizens (usually wealthy) with some political interests. As P. suggests here, they were regularly formed around one leading

Figure 2. Ostraka of Damon and Thucydides son of Melesias (see *Per.* 4.1, 14.3): (a) *ΔAMON ΔAMONIΔO*; (b) *ΘOKYΔIΔH MEΛHΣIO*; (c) *ΘΩKYΔIΔE MEΛEΣIΩ*; (d) *ΘOKYΔIΔEΣ MEΛEΣIO*. Deutsches Archäologisches Institut Athen, neg. nos. Ker 510, 517.

Figure 3. Ostraka of Pericles and Cimon (see *Per.* 9.5, 14.3): (a) . . *]PIKΛΗ ΞΑΝΘΙΠΠΟ* (P21527); (b) *ΠΕΡΙΚΛΕΣ ΧΣΑΝΘΙΠΠΟ* (P16755); (c) *KIMON ΜΙΛΤΙΑΔΟ* (P18555). American School of Classical Studies Agora Excavations.

individual: cf. Connor 1971, 25–29, 66–79. In the *Comparison* the ostracisms of Cimon and Thucydides are seen as bad in themselves but justified because they established Pericles securely in power (3.2–3).

15–16

Overview of Pericles' "Monarchic" Rule. The ostracism of Thucydides gives occasion for P. to present the real, "aristocratic" Pericles. These are transition chapters, both completing the inquiry into Pericles' *metabolē* begun at 9.1 and preparing for the presentation of his principal virtues in chapters 17–23 (see the Introduction, 2.4). The chronological references are ambiguous: Pericles' monarchical period can begin only after Thucydides' ostracism removes the divisions in the city; yet his influence and virtuous activity had already been in evidence for years and was revealed in the actions described in chapters 17–23. The major topical division comes not at 16.1 but 15.3, with the move from rhetorical ability to integrity in handling money, the subject of 15.3–16.9. The qualities that define Pericles' leadership thus are oratorical skill (15.1–2), honesty (15.3–16.9), *megalophrosynē* (17), and generalship, including caution (18–23).

15.1

P. introduces the "aristocratic" Pericles with a twenty-line sentence in his most elaborate style. A temporal clause, ὡς . . . περιήνεγκεν . . . τὰς Ἀθήνας καὶ τὰ . . . πράγματα, is enriched with two genitive absolutes in chiastic order (παντάπασι λυθείσης . . . γενομένης) and appositive lists (φόρους . . . δυναστῶν). The three main clauses (οὐκεθ' ὁ αὐτὸς ἦν, ἀλλ' . . . τὰ μὲν πολλὰ . . . ἦγε, ἦν δ' ὅτε . . . ἐχειροῦτο), the latter two paired by μὲν . . . δὲ, are expanded with participial phrases that reinforce through images the portrait of Pericles.

διαφορᾶς: the one noted in 11.3 between the aristocrats and the demos.

ὁμαλῆς: "smooth, even," without the dividing flaw of 11.3. Cf. 6.3, ὁμαλῶς.

περιήνεγκεν εἰς ἑαυτόν: "drew to himself," less invidious than "subjected to himself." Cf. *Galb.* 8.1, πάντα πράγματα . . . περιήνεγκεν εἰς ἑαυτόν.

φόρους . . . δυναστῶν: the list provides a rhetorical *auxēsis* of Pericles' power. Note the polysyndeton in the first part, the epanaphora with πολλὴν μὲν . . . πολλὴν δὲ, and the participial clause expanding ἡγεμονίαν with a triplet of two-word phrases. The variety of classes of items in the list (φόρους, θάλασσαν, ἡγεμονίαν) also contributes to the effect.

δι' Ἑλλήνων . . . διὰ βαρβάρων ἤκουσαν: "penetrating, pervading Greeks and barbarians." P. borrows the notion from Plato *Alc. I* 104B: [Pericles], ὃς οὐ μόνον ἐν τῇδε τῇ πόλει δύναται πράττειν ὅτι ἂν βούληται, ἀλλ' ἐν πάσῃ τῇ Ἑλλάδι καὶ τῶν βαρβάρων ἐν πολλοῖς καὶ μεγάλοις γένεσιν. P. is thinking of peoples either subject to Athens or in its sphere of influence.

ἔθνεσι: cf. γένεσιν in the Plato passage, and *Per.* 20.1.

χειροήθης: "submissive, tame." Often in a good sense, e.g., *An seni* 795C, [an older man should prepare a young man going into politics,] παρέχων, ὥσπερ οἱ διδάσκοντες ἱππεύειν, ἐν ἀρχῇ χειροήθη καὶ πρᾷον ἐπιβῆναι τὸν δῆμον. Cf. *Praec. ger. rep.* 821B.

συνενδιδόναι: "go along with, yield to with (the crowd)." Cf. *Caes.* 31.2, *De tranq.* 468D, and Plut. fr. 200, l. 42 Sandbach.

ἐκ . . . πολιτείαν: "Instead of that lax and sometimes spineless demagoguery—a florid and effeminate scale, as it were—he tuned an aristocratic and kingly government." The musical image (cf. 8.1) is elliptically presented.

ἐκ indicates succession and replacement: LSJ s.v. I.3; cf. 15.3, 24.6.

ὑποθρυπτομένης: the compound only here in P., although θρύπτω is common. Ἔνια is adverbial, "on some occasions, in some cases."

ἀνθηρᾶς: "flowery," therefore "florid, exuberant, excessive."

ἀριστοκρατικὴν . . . πολιτείαν: Aristotelian terminology; cf. note to 7.3. The same is true of ὀρθῇ καὶ ἀνεγκλίτῳ below: according to Arist. *Pol.* 4.2.1289a26–b26, there are three ὀρθαὶ πολιτεῖαι (βασιλεία, ἀριστοκρατία, and πολιτεία) and three παρεκβάσεις or deviations (τυραννίς, ὀλιγαρχία, and δημοκρατία). Note that P. uses ὀρθή with πολιτεία only here. Ἀνέγκλιτος, which here describes the *politeia* that has not deviated, occurs otherwise in P. only at *De E* 393A, in a nonpolitical context.

ἦγε πείθων: cf. Thuc. 2.65.8, οὐκ ἤγετο μᾶλλον ὑπ' αὐτοῦ ἢ αὐτὸς ἦγε.

διδάσκων: again Pericles is presented as teacher; cf. 12.3. The theme is developed at length by Aristides *On the Four* 15–16.

κατατείνων: "reining in," as if the demos were a wild horse (cf. 7.8, 11.4). For the verb cf. *Publ.* 13.4. The application to control of the emotions (e.g., *De virt. mor.* 445C, *De garr.* 503C) echoes the image in Plato *Phaedr.* 253Cff.

προσβιβάζων . . . συμφέροντι: "bringing them over, he subdued them to what was advantageous." For προσβιβάζω, the causal form of προσβαίνω, see *Cat. Min.* 36.4; Ar. *Knights* 35. The dative after χειρόω usually expresses means, but here seems to give the end.

ἰατρόν: Plato (*Phaedr.* 270B–D) also had compared the true rhetorician to a doctor. The true statesman is analogous to the doctor who uses φάρμακα, καύσεις, and τομαί (*Rep.* 425A–426B). For P.'s use of medical imagery with respect to statesmanship cf. Fuhrmann 1964, 238–40.

ποικίλῳ νοσήματι: "a complicated disease," or one with many symptoms. For the phrase cf. *Symp.* 732E, ποικίλα νοσημάτων εἴδη, and Plato *Rep.* 426A, ποικιλώτερα ποιεῖν τὰ νοσήματα. Ποικίλος is a standard medical term. P. often speaks metaphorically of disease in the state: cf. *Lyc.* 5.3, [Lycurgus tried to completely remake the state,] ὥσπερ σώματι πονηρῷ καὶ γέμοντι παντοδαπῶν νοσημάτων τὴν ὑπάρχουσαν ἐκτήξας καὶ μεταβαλὼν κρᾶσιν ὑπὸ φαρμάκων καὶ καθαρμῶν, ἑτέρας ἄρξεται καινῆς διαίτης, and *Lyc.* 8.3, *Aem.* 8.10, *Sull.* 4.6, 13.2, etc.

δηγμούς: "bites"; in hendiadys with φάρμακα, "biting drugs." Cf. *De rect. aud.* 46D, ὥσπερ φαρμάκῳ δάκνοντι λόγῳ χρωμένης, and *De adul. et amic.* 55C, *An seni* 796B. P. shifts his image because he is thinking of the healing value of sharp criticism as similar to that of medicine: cf. *Alc.*4.2, *De rect. aud.* 47A, *De adul. et amic.* 56A, 68F, *Praec. ger. rep.* 810C, and esp. *De ser. num. vind.* 553A, ἐνίοις δηγμοῦ δεομένοις καὶ κολάσεως ἐμβαλὼν ὁ θεὸς πικρίαν τινὰ τυράννου δυσμείλικτον . . . οὐ πρότερον ἐξεῖλε τὸ λυποῦν καὶ ταράττον ἢ τὸ νοσοῦν ἀπαλλάξαι καὶ καθᾶραι. τοιοῦτο καὶ Φάλαρις ἦν Ἀκραγαντίνοις φάρμακον καὶ Ῥωμαίοις Μάριος, and for politics, *Phoc.* 2.3, πολλάκις οἱ ἀληθινοὶ καὶ νοῦν ἔχοντες λόγοι δάκνουσι καὶ παροξύνουσι τοὺς κακῶς πράττοντας. P. never uses δηγμός in a strictly medical sense ("caustics"), as suggested by Holden. Δηκτικόν is paired with πικρόν at *De adul. et amic.* 74D, *De prof. in virt.* 81C.

15.2

τὸ μέγεθος: a cognate acc. with τοσαύτην; cf. Smyth 1565.

μάλιστα . . . παραμυθούμενος: P. elaborates with simile and metaphor the analysis in Thuc. 2.65.9, ὁπότε γοῦν αἴσθοιτό τι αὐτοὺς παρὰ καιρὸν ὕβρει θαρσοῦντας, λέγων κατέπληξεν ἐπὶ τὸ φοβεῖσθαι, καὶ δεδιότας αὖ ἀλόγως ἀντικαθίστη πάλιν ἐπὶ τὸ θαρσεῖν.

ὥσπερ οἴαξι: "as if with rudders"; fear helps him control the direction of the people. This image is frequent in P. to express wise control, often with a parallel reference to a χαλινός. Thus in connection with Alexander's education he quotes Sophocles fr. 785, πολλῶν χαλινῶν ἔργον οἰάκων θ᾽ ἅμα (*Alex.* 7.2; cf. *Amat.* 767E). Cf. *De Is.* 369C, *An seni* 788D. When applied to politics, it recalls the ship of state: cf. *Cleom.* 15.1, ἐν χειμῶνι πραγμάτων μείζονι μεθεὶς ἑτέρῳ τὸν οἴακα; also *Phoc.* 3.4, *Arat.* 38.5, *An seni* 790E, *Praec. ger. rep.* 801D (quoting Plato *Critias* 109C); Fuhrmann 1964, 236.

συστέλλων: "constricting, hemming in"; common in P., both in the military sense and figuratively, as at *Cim.* 12.1, συνέστειλε τὸ φρόνημα [τοῦ βασιλέως]; 15.1, παρὼν μὲν ἐκράτει καὶ συνέστειλε τὸν δῆμον; *Alc.* 6.5, πιέζων τῷ λόγῳ καὶ συστέλλων ταπεινὸν ἐποίει [τὸν Ἀ.] καὶ ἄτολμον. The mss.' προσστέλλων occurs only once in P., in a quite different sense than needed (*Sull.* 19.1), although it is a variant for προσαναστέλλω at *Alex.* 6.7.

ἀνιείς: "relieving, relaxing." This, like συστέλλων, could be a nautical term, (describing "taking in" and "letting out" sail), but the precise nautical sense does not seem appropriate with οἴαξι. The image would rather be equestrian, from the relaxing of the reins.

ἔδειξε . . . ψυχαγωγίαν οὖσαν: Plato *Phaedr.* 261A, ἡ ῥητορικὴ ἂν εἴη τέχνη ψυχαγωγία τις διὰ λόγων; 271C, ἐπειδὴ λόγου δύναμις τυγχάνει ψυχαγωγία οὖσα, τὸν μέλλοντα ῥητορικὸν ἔσεσθαι ἀνάγκη εἰδέναι ψυχὴ ὅσα εἴδη ἔχει. P. uses Plato's own ideas to defend Pericles against Plato's attack.

τὴν περὶ τὰ ἤθη καὶ πάθη μέθοδον: another echo of the *Phaedrus* passage: cf. 270C, ἄνευ τῆς μεθόδης ταύτης; 270D, ἡ γοῦν ἄνευ τούτων μεθόδος ἐοίκοι ἂν ὥσπερ τυφλοῦ πορείᾳ; 271B, διαταξάμενος τὰ λόγων τε καὶ ψυχῆς γένη καὶ τὰ τούτων παθήματα.

ὥσπερ τινὰς τόνους . . . δεομένους: "as if they were some pitches and notes of the soul that needed an especially musical touch and stroke." Both ἁφῆς and κρούσεως refer to lyre-playing and are modified by ἐμμελοῦς. The musical image emphasizes the Platonic notion of knowledge leading to harmonious control. The sequence of images in 15.1–2, music, medicine, seamanship, and back to music, reflects a range of rational procedures and skills to create harmony and order. For musical harmony as an image of concord in the state cf. Fuhrmann 1964, 241. Cf. also the comparison of the governance of the state with the movements of the sun and with harmonious blendings at *Phoc.* 2.6–9.

15.3

In 15.3–16.9 P. presents Pericles' attitude toward money as both a cause for his ascendancy over the demos and evidence for his "aristocratic" rule.

ἡ τοῦ λόγου ψιλῶς δύναμις: P. refers back to *Phaedrus* 271C to correct it.

Thucydides: a close paraphrase of 2.65.8, αἴτιον δ' ἦν ὅτι ἐκεῖνος μέν δυνατὸς ὢν τῷ τε ἀξιώματι καὶ τῇ γνώμῃ, χρημάτων τε διαφανῶς ἀδωρότατος γενόμενος, with a number of verbal echoes. The topic of Pericles' foresight lies behind much of chapters 18–35 and is mentioned explicitly at *Comp. Per.–Fab.* 2.3, εἰ δὲ δεῖ μὴ μόνον χρῆσθαι τοῖς παροῦσιν, ἀλλὰ καὶ τεκμαίρεσθαι περὶ τοῦ μέλλοντος ὀρθῶς τὸν ἀγαθὸν στρατηγόν, Ἀθηναίοις μὲν ὡς Περικλῆς προέγνω καὶ προεῖπεν ἐτελεύτησεν ὁ πόλεμος· πολυπραγμονοῦντες γὰρ ἀπώλεσαν τὴν δύναμιν (cf. Thuc. 2.65.7, 13). For the implications of P.'s differences from Thucydides, see de Romilly 1988, 23–26.

ὅς . . . κατέλιπε: *auxēsis* of the theme of honesty, stressing the opportunities that his power gave Pericles for accumulating wealth. Cf. the similar passage in Isoc. *Peace* 126.

ἐκ μεγάλης μεγίστην: cf. Thuc. 2.65.5, ἐγένετο ἐπ' ἐκείνου μεγίστη and *Comp. Per.–Fab.* 1.2.

ὧν ἔνιοι . . . ἐκείνου: a difficult passage, probably corrupt, and with no editorial consensus. Ziegler accepts the emendation ⟨τοῖς⟩ ἐκείνου. I prefer the text of the mss., but with the deletion of ἐκεῖνος as a gloss marking the resumption of the clause begun with ὅς: ὧν ἔνιοι καὶ ἐπὶ τοῖς υἱέσι διέθεντο. I translate "of whom some even left [their power] to their sons." There are several difficulties with the text: (1) the use of ἐκεῖνος to repeat ὅς, not elsewhere found, except perhaps Xen. *Cyr.* 1.4.19; (2) διέθεντο without an object; (3) ἐπί with διέθεντο. Flacelière keeps the manuscript text, with a comma after διέθεντο. Madvig's ἐπί⟨τροπον⟩ τοῖς υἱέσι διέθεντο ἐκεῖνον (1871, 574) addresses all three difficulties but introduces a new idea not elsewhere mentioned in our sources.

Weissert 1975, responding to (2), suggests reading καὶ ἐπιτόκια τοῖς υἱέσι, but ἐπιτόκιον does not occur elsewhere in P. The chief point is Pericles' honesty when he had so much opportunity for gain: cf. *Comp. Per.–Fab.* 3.6, Περικλῆς δ' οὐκ ἂν ἴσως εἴποι τις ὅσα καὶ παρὰ συμμάχων καὶ βασιλέων ὠφελεῖσθαι καὶ θεραπεύεσθαι παρόν, τῆς δυνάμεως διδούσης, ἀδωρότατον ἑαυτὸν καὶ καθαρώτατον ἐφύλαξεν.

μιᾷ δραχμῇ . . . κατέλιπε: "he did not make his property one drachma greater than what his father had left him." Isocrates (8.126) says that he left even less: οὐκ ἐπὶ τὸν ἴδιον χρηματισμὸν ὥρμησεν, ἀλλὰ τὸν μὲν οἶκον ἐλάττω τὸν αὑτοῦ κατέλιπεν ἢ παρὰ τοῦ πατρὸς παρέλαβεν. P. approves of not increasing wealth: note his praise of Aemilius Paulus, ἐκεῖνο μέντοι τοῦ Αἰμιλίου θαυμαστόν, ὅτι τηλικαύτην βασιλείαν καταστρεψάμενος οὐδὲ δραχμῇ μείζονα τὴν οὐσίαν ἐποίησεν οὐδ' εἶδεν οὐδ' ἥψατο τῶν χρημάτων, καίτοι πολλὰ δοὺς ἑτέροις καὶ δωρησάμενος. . . . οὐ γὰρ τὸ λαβεῖν ἐκ τοιούτων αἰσχρόν, ἀλλὰ τὸ μὴ λαβεῖν κρεῖττον, καὶ περιουσία τις ἀρετῆς ἐν οἷς ἔξεστιν ἐπιδεικνυμένης τὸ μὴ δεόμενον (*Comp. Aem.–Tim.* 2.8–9; cf. *Aem.* 4.4). Cf. also Cephalus in Plato's *Republic* (330B), who is not passionate for money, but pleased that he can leave not less than he inherited, and even perhaps a bit more. But P. chooses not to follow Isocrates' lead in making Pericles actually diminish his family estate.

16.1

καίτοι κτλ.: "and indeed (he did have great power, for) Thucydides gives a clear account of his power, and the comic poets suggest it maliciously." The particle introduces a response to a possible objection, that Pericles was honest because his power was negligible. It is continuative (cf. Denniston, 559–61), but with some adversative force.

Thucydides: referring to the whole narrative, but especially 2.65.8–10. Take σαφῶς . . . διηγεῖται in antithesis to παρεμφαίνουσιν, "to intimate, suggest." Cf. *Cat. Mai.* 1.4, ὡς ὁ ποιήσας τὸ ἐπιγραμμάτιον οὐκ εὐμενῶς παρεμφαίνει, and *Symp.* 617B, ἡ δ'

Ἀθηνᾶ φαίνεται τὸν πλησίον ἀεὶ τοῦ Διὸς τόπον ἐξαίρετον ἔχουσα καὶ τοῦτο παρεμφαίνει μὲν ὁ ποιητὴς δι' ὧν ἐπὶ τῆς Θέτιδός φησιν.

οἱ κωμικοί: the comic poets; cf. the Introduction, 3.1.d, k. This citation is *CAF* 3:411, adespota F60. Pericles was compared to the tyrant Pisistratus (cf. 7.1). To compare him and his associates with the sons of Pisistratus who continued the tyranny, Hippias and Hipparchus, was a natural variation of the same theme. (Οἱ περὶ αὐτὸν ἑταῖροι, like the simple expression οἱ περὶ αὐτὸν, means Pericles and his coterie; cf. note to 14.1.) For other references to Pericles' "tyranny" in the comic poets cf. 3.5. For the use of νέους cf. 24.9, Ὀμφάλη νέα. In both cases the term is probably P.'s and not the comic poet's. This use of νέος only became common in Hellenistic times: cf. the examples cited by Headlam 1966 to Herodas 4.57; Nock 1928, 35n. 73; Raubitschek 1954, 317–19; Lampe 1961 s.v. III.B.2.

ἀπομόσαι μή: "to swear that he would not." For μή after the verb of swearing see *MT* 685.

ὡς ἀσυμμέτρου . . . ὑπεροχῆς: "since there was a superiority to him that was oppressive and not appropriate to a democracy." Περὶ αὐτόν replaces a genitive; cf. 2.3 etc.

16.2

Teleclides (F42 K.): see the Introduction, 3.1.g. The meter is anapestic tetrameter catalectic, the content an excellent statement of P.'s thesis that Pericles held total power, a list of everything that the Athenians had entrusted to him. The two pairs of infinitives of purpose (*MT* 770) strengthen the point even more.

τὰς μὲν . . . ἀναλύειν: "some to be enslaved, others freed," lit. "to be put in fetters, to be unbound." Not to be taken in the general sense often associated with the similar expression in Matt. 16:19, 18:18.

τὰ μὲν . . . καταβάλλειν: building walls could refer to the long wall at Athens, but tearing down must refer to the removal of walls in the allied cities, especially after revolts. Cf. Meiggs, *AE* 149–51.

16.3

καιρὸς . . . πολιτείας: all three expressions indicate a fleeting moment and are reinforced by the image of flowering. Cf. *Max. cum princ.* 778A, οὐδ' οἷς ὥρα καὶ χάρις συνέπεται καὶ ἄνθος δεδίττεται τὸν φιλόσοφον, with reference to the brief flowering of sexual beauty and charm. Χάρις: here, "popularity, favor." Πολιτεία: "a given administration or policy."

τεσσαράκοντα μὲν ἔτη πρωτεύων: The number is traditional: cf. Cic. *De or.* 3.138, *itaque hic doctrina consilio, eloquentia excellens quadraginta annis praefuit Athenis et urbanis eodem tempore et bellicis rebus.* Both references derive from the same tradition on Pericles' oratory, probably originating with Theopompus. See note to 8.1–4, and Connor 1962b. The figure is notable because it places the beginning of Pericles' ascendancy very early: ca. 468 if measured to his death in 429. Cf. P.'s references to his early career in 7.3–4, 9.2–4, 10.6. This contrasts with the standard modern view that he became prominent only after Ephialtes' death.

ἐν Ἐφιάλταις κτλ.: The plural establishes a class: "among men like Ephialtes . . ."; cf. Smyth 1000. For Ephialtes see note to 9.5; for Cimon, notes to 9.2ff.; for Tolmides, note to 18.2; for Thucydides, notes to 8.5, 11.1–2. Leocrates son of Stroebus was a general at Plataea (Plut. *Arist.* 20.1; cf. *IG* I² 821; Bicknell 1972, 101–3) and at the siege of Aegina in the early 450s (Thuc. 1.105.2; Diod. 11.78.4). Myronides was also a general at Plataea (Plut. *Arist.* 20.1) and a member of the embassy to Sparta with Cimon and Xanthippus (*Arist.* 10.10), the general at Megara who defeated the Corinthians in the Megarid ca. 458 (Thuc. 1.105.3–106.2; Diod. 11.79.3), the victor over the Boeotians at Oenophyta (Thuc. 1.108.2–3; Diod. 11.81.4–83.1), and commander of an expedition to Thessaly (Thuc. 1.111.1; Diod. 11.83.3–4). For his actions he achieved an outstanding reputation: cf. Ar. *Lys.* 801–804, *Eccl.* 303–306. Cf. *Comp. Per.–Fab.* 1.2, naming Cimon, Myronides, Leocrates, and Tolmides, and the similar list, giving generals celebrated by Thucydides (including Pericles, Phormio, Nicias, Demosthenes, Cleon, Tolmides, and Myronides) in *De glor. Ath.* 345C–D.

οὐκ ἐλάττω τῶν πεντεκαίδεκα ἐτῶν: for the calculation see note to 14.3. The article indicates that the fifteen years are a subset of the forty: cf. Smyth 1125a.

διηνεκῆ . . . δυναστείαν: this is our only evidence for Pericles' having held the generalship for fifteen consecutive years after the ostracism of Thucydides. It seems to be of a piece with the allusion to forty years of preeminence and may be no more reliable. We have explicit confirmation for his generalship in six of these years: the two years of the Samian revolt, 441/40 and 440/39 (cf. 25.2 and note), 432/31 (Thuc. 2.13.1), 431/30 (33.7; Thuc. 2.31.1), 430/29 (35.4; Thuc. 2.59.3), and 429/28 (37.2; Thuc. 2.65.4). His name is also reasonably restored in ML 56, ll. 29–30, a list of the generals for 439/38. If the Pontic expedition belongs to the early 430s (cf. note to 20.1–2), this might be evidence for another year. The sequences 441–439 and 432–429 lend credibility to P.'s statement.

Pericles was one of the board of ten generals. Although he would have had exceptional influence because of his political strength and continuing presence on the board, it is wrong to consider him as a chairman or head of the board: cf. Dover 1960, correcting the prevailing opinion (found, e.g., in Hignett, *HAC* 348–54, and more strongly stated in Bloedow 1987). Both *Ath. pol.* (22.2, 61.1; cf. Rhodes, *CAAP* 264–66, 676–77) and inscriptional and literary evidence indicate that each tribe usually had a representative on the board. However, inscriptions have steadily revealed more instances when one or more tribes had more than one representative and others none. See Lewis 1961; Fornara 1971a; Bicknell 1972, 101–12. Various procedures have been suggested to permit multiple representation, of which the simplest and most convincing is that of Ruschenbusch 1975. He suggests that during the fifth century each tribe presented two candidates, and the ten candidates who received the most votes from the assembly were elected. Cf. also Piérart 1974. The argument that Pericles was elected in a preliminary ballot *ἐξ ἁπάντων*, and the other generals in a second ballot (see, e.g., Jameson 1955), seems contrary to normal Athenian practice for elections and has no basis in the ancient evidence. The fact that Pericles was frequently elected as one of two from his tribe, Acamantis, indicates his popularity.

The responsibilities of the generals extended to every area of military action, including strategic planning, calling up of the levy, signing of armistices and treaties, and recommendations for military preparations. They were in close contact with the boule, although it is not clear that they were ex-officio members (see Rhodes 1972, 43–47). Even in peacetime they would have had much to do with the machinery of empire, in terms of maintaining and deploying the navy and garrisons in the cities, and of collecting tribute from delinquents. It was an ideal office for influencing the long-range plans of the city and for remaining constantly before the people. See in general Busolt and Swoboda 2:1121–28; Hignett, *HAC* 244–51.

ἀνάλωτον ὑπὸ χρημάτων: "impregnable to money." The image was probably still felt by Plutarch: cf. *Phoc.* 21.5, αὐτὸν μὲν ὡς ἔρυμα παντόχθεν ἀνάλωτον ὑπὸ τοῦ χρυσίου, and the self-conscious comparison with τείχη ἀνάλωτα in Xen. *Ages.* 8.8. Other examples occur in *Lyc.* 30.1, *Phil.* 15.9, *Dem.* 14.2.

ἀργῶς ἔχων πρὸς χρηματισμόν: P. employs ἔχω πρός τι (τινα) with an adverb frequently: cf. 10.4, *Lyc.* 23.2, and Holden's note here. The idiom is found already in Demosthenes (9.45, 63). P. did not consider making money generally desirable in a statesman, as he presumed that the statesman would be wealthy already and that business was vulgar and undignified (cf. *An seni* 785C–D). He mocks Chrysippus for saying the sage will make money (*De Stoic. repug.* 1043D–E). However, farming was δικαιότατος τῶν χρηματισμῶν (*Phil.* 4.5), and Pericles' methods made it even more acceptable.

δίκαιον: P. considers inherited wealth legitimate.

ἀμελούμενος ἐκφύγοι: sc. ὁ πλοῦτος. Cf. Soph. *Oed. Tyr.* 111, ἐκφεύγει δὲ τἀμελούμενον, quoted at *De fortun.* 98A.

συνέταξεν εἰς οἰκονομίαν: "organized into an administration." P. describes, in the context of Pericles' honesty in handling money, his management of his property. The source of his information cannot be determined: Meinhardt, 46–47, suggested Stesimbrotus, who certainly recorded the hostility of Xanthippus toward his father (16.5; cf. 13.16, 36.6 = 107 F10b, 11); others think of Theopompus or Theophrastus. The miserly distribution of daily expenses to a spendthrift son might also be from comedy, where the domestic scene could serve as an analogy to the political situation, mocking Pericles' careful management of public finances. Alternatively, the references to Anaxagoras at 16.7–8 suggest a philosophical source, perhaps a Socratic dialogue.

Pericles' arrangement was to set his property under a specially trained bailiff, his slave Evangelus, who was responsible for a precise accounting (note ἀκριβεστάτην, ἀκριβέστατον, ἀκριβείαν) of the expenses and receipts of the estate, by number and measure. (The use of a bailiff is also recommended in Xenophon's *Oeconomicus* although in that case the bailiff is responsible chiefly for the direction of the slaves.) Accurate recording of expenses and receipts in money and in kind is best documented in the Zeno archive from Ptolemaic Egypt. Unlike modern farm management, this did not involve an analysis of the rate of return for different crops or methods; cf. Mickwitz 1937. The most notable feature, however, is that all crops were sold in a group (presumably as each crop came in), then all necessary purchases made in the market. Although not uncommon on a modern one-crop farm, this method seems quite uneconomic for fifth-century Athens. Both Xenophon's Ischomachus and Phaenippus (ps.-Dem. 42) keep significant stores on the farm, although the latter is constantly engaged in selling as well. The focus on sale, however, does reflect the increasing monetization of Athenian agriculture in the fifth and fourth centuries. While small farmers like Diceaopolis lived off their land and bought as little as possible (Ar. *Ach.* 32–36), larger landowners could grow for sale, as is apparent in the case of Phaenippus (cf. Heichelheim 1964, 113–15; Pečírka 1973; Jameson 1977–78). Cf. also ps.-Arist. *Oec.* 1.6.2.1344b28–35, 1.6.6.1345a18–24. Either Pericles had made a radical shift to raising crops solely for market, or he was a poor businessman: the practice as described would result in selling cheap, at the height of the harvest, and buying dear. I suspect that P. has overinterpreted his source or, more likely, that the source itself was a philosophical work more interested in the theory than in the practical realities of farm management.

Pericles' family estate or estates (at least one of which was threatened in the Spartan invasion of 431; cf. 33.3) would have been his chief source of wealth. Apparently he was trying to put his relatively unpredictable domestic income on the same regulated basis he was using for the polis, as known to us from many inscribed accounts and decrees, of which perhaps the most elaborate are the Callias decrees, ML 58 (*IG* I³ 52). The effect was to limit closely the expenditures of the household, disgruntling his sons and daughters-in-law, who expected the generous allowances and free spending habits associated with wealthy households. See the example of Critobulus' spending habits in Xen. *Oec.* 2.5–8.

16.4

τὰ περὶ τὴν δίαιταν: cf. 7.5.

16.5

ἐνηλίκοις: "full grown, adult." The children remained under the father's economic control even after marriage. For the problems caused cf. 36.2–4 and notes.

δαψιλὴς χορηγός: "a generous provider"; cf. 9.3, 14.2, 36.2. The situation P. envisions carries the notion of strict accounting much farther than simply a money economy: Pericles insists upon daily allowances or accounting, strictly limited (συνηγμένην) spending, and none of the conspicuous liberality normally displayed by noble and powerful houses. In personal as in public finance, Pericles went against established tradition.

ἀναλώματος . . . λήμματος: "expenditure and income," both in cash and kind.

16.6

Evangelus: not otherwise known.

κατεσκευασμένος: "trained"; cf. Xen. *Cyr.* 8.1.43, οὓς δ' αὖ κατεσκεύαζεν εἰς τὸ δουλεύειν.

16.7

ἀπᾴδοντα: "out of tune with," Valckenaer's emendation for mss. ἅπαντα. Though it captures the sense, the use of a participle with ἦν understood is unusual. A correction is necessary, as P. does not use ἅπαντα with ταῦτα (except perhaps fr. 22 Sandbach), whereas ταῦτα, and the sentence, need a verb, or a suitable adjective with ἦν understood. Coraes emended to ἀπεναντία, which however does not occur elsewhere in P.

εἴγε: "if it is really true that"; cf. Denniston, 142. On Anaxagoras' relation to Pericles see notes to 4.6 and 5.1. This is *FVS* 59A13. Cf. *De aere al.* 831F, Ἀναξαγόρας δὲ τὴν χώραν κατέλιπε μηλόβοτον, and Plato *Hipp. Mai.* 283A, τοὐναντίον γὰρ Ἀναξαγόρᾳ φασὶ συμβῆναι ἢ ὑμῖν [sc. Hippias]˙ καταλειφθέντων γὰρ αὐτῷ πολλῶν χρημάτων καταμελῆσαι καὶ ἀπολέσαι πάντα, with 281C and the anecdote in Diog. Laert. 2.6–7. Diels and Kranz, *FVS*, suggest Ion as the source; Meinhardt, 47, more probably thinks of the philosophical schools. It would be an example of philosophical otherworldliness. See Jaeger 1948, 426–61 (appendix 2, "On the Origin and Cycle of the Philosophic Ideal of Life"), esp. 427–29.

τὴν χώραν . . . μηλόβοτον: cf. *Lys.* 15.3, τὴν δὲ χώραν ἀνεῖναι μηλόβοτον (echoing Isoc. 14.31).

οὐ ταὐτὸν δ᾽ ἐστὶν οἶμαι: P.'s own view of the difference in way of life between philosopher and statesman: because the latter is involved with human needs, wealth can be not only a necessity but also a good.

ἀνόργανον: "without instruments"; cf. *De Is.* 381A, χρωμένην κινήσεσιν ἀνοργάνοις, of the asp.

ἀπροσδεῆ . . . ὕλης: "with no need for external materials."

τῷ δ᾽: sc. πολιτικῷ.

16.8

καὶ μέντοι γε: "And in fact," adding a confirming example: cf. Denniston, 413–14. The combination of the three particles is unique for Plutarch, and quite rare: Denniston, 410, notes only Ar. *Th.* 709. The anecdote (again from the philosophical schools?) is *FVS* 59A32. It would be useful for any philosopher looking for a patron's support.

συγκεκαλυμμένον: "wrapped up," in his himation, either to warm his weak body, or in anticipation of death (cf. Dem. 29.4; Plat. *Phd.* 118A; Xen. *Cyr.* 8.7.28).

ἀποκαρτεροῦντα: "starving himself to death." Cf. *Lyc.* 29.8, *Num.* 21.5, *Symp.* 690A, *De comm. not.* 1069D.

προσπεσόντος: "came to his ears"; cf. LSJ s.v. προσπίπτω II.5.

δεῖσθαι πᾶσαν δέησιν: "make every entreaty." For the cognate accusative cf. 9.5, 11.3.

16.9

ἐκκαλυψάμενον: cf. Socrates saying a last word before dying, ἐκκαλυψάμενος (*Phd.* 118A).

17

The Congress Decree. This passage of P. is our only source for this important document, whose authenticity, date, and nature are subjects of continuing controversy. P.'s sole indication of time, ἀρχομένων δὲ τῶν Λακεδαιμονίων ἄχθεσθαι τῇ αὐξήσει τῶν Ἀθηναίων, is too vague to be helpful and suggests that P. himself had no more precise date or did not consider added precision desirable (cf. the similar phrase at 29.1). Attic decrees of the mid-fifth century usually did not have archon dates. The Spartans had long been distressed with the growth of Athenian power: Hdt. 5.91 has them worried already at the end of the sixth century. They were disturbed when they agreed to help the revolting

Thasians ca. 465 (Thuc. 1.101), but on that occasion they were stopped by the earthquake and helot revolt. Cimon preferred helping Sparta in its trouble to τὴν τῆς πατρίδος αὔξησιν (*Cim.* 16.9). From P.'s phrase the decree could be placed anytime from the 460s to the beginning of the Peloponnesian War. Morever, since this is meant as an example of Pericles' lofty thinking, cited here (παρεθέμην) to document one aspect of his forty-year leadership, the decree's position in the *Life* is no indication of chronology, least of all that it must have occurred after the ostracism of Thucydides.

A *terminus ante quem* is provided by the beginning of work on the Parthenon in 447, after which the temples that had been burnt by the Persians would no longer be a subject of discussion.

The reference to "the peace" in the third clause most probably (although not necessarily) applies to the Peace of Callias, which thus provides a terminus post quem: the 460s for some, 449 for others. (See the discussion of the peace in note to 12.2.) This decree should probably be dated not long after the peace, but P.'s vague dating formula does not permit us to go beyond that. It would not be necessary for Cimon to be dead, or even ostracized, before it could have been moved.

This decree, like the others reported by P., most probably derives from Craterus' *Synagoge*, which provided in addition to the text some commentary (cf. *Arist.* 26.4), sufficient to contain evidence for the dating phrase of 17.1 and the notice of the failure of the invitation to the congress in 17.4 (see note to 17.1). Seager argued in 1967 that the decree was an anti-Macedonian forgery from the period after the peace of Philocrates of 346; soon after, Bosworth (1971) suggested that it should rather be understood as a pro-Macedonian forgery produced after Chaeronea. Seager's objections do not bear close scrutiny, as they presume that the terms of the decree must reflect the precise words of the source, rather than what we would expect, a paraphrase by P. Moreover, as Meiggs notes, *AE* 514, "Even the best of orators would not be able to make much capital from a rejected scheme, and if the decree was invented for the benefit of the anti-Macedonian orators why do we hear nothing about it in the orators?" See also Balcer 1974, 35–39; Perlman 1976, 7–13; Griffith 1978; Walsh 1981, 59–63; and MacDonald 1982.

The question of fourth-century forgeries of fifth-century decrees has been especially stimulated by the discovery of the "Themistocles decree" at Troizen. The difficulty has been stated most forcefully by Habicht 1961, who considers the decrees purportedly contemporary with the Persian Wars forgeries. A different view is introduced by N. Robertson 1982, noting that there is a third alternative for explaining difference from the fifth century: not only forgery and scribal error, but adaptation to suit the contemporary situation or purpose of inscribing. In fact our criteria for rejecting decrees is unreliable, and no effective case has been made against the Congress Decree.

The decree as reported by P. calls for an assembly of Greeks to discuss three points: (1) the temples that had been burnt by the Persians, (2) the sacrifices that were owed, and (3) how all might sail safely on the sea and keep the peace. According to Wade-Gery 1945, 222–24 (cf. also *ATL* 3:279–80), the decree is principally a financial document, aimed at raising money from the Greeks to rebuild the Parthenon at Athens, celebrate festivals, and finance the Athenian fleet in peacetime. The emphasis in P., however, is broader and I believe more correct: Athens wished to lead Greece in common action ($\varkappa o\iota vo\pi\varrho\alpha\gamma\iota\alpha$) and was asserting for herself a hegemonic role that Sparta could not accept. Cf. MacDonald 1982, 121: "Athens was making a claim for leadership of all the Greeks." The decree was at the same time imperial and Panhellenic, extending an invitation to all Greeks. The financial obligations of the Delian League were already established, and the evidence that the peace with Persia called them into question is problematic at best, chiefly tied to the difficult question of the missing quota list of 449/48. Despite the argument of *ATL* (3:279–80) that the Congress Decree was an attempt to persuade the allies to resume tribute payments after they had stopped them, there is no real reason to see it in this light. One could argue that Athens hoped to gain from the Greek cities neither members of the league nor tribute money but recognition of her role as leader against the barbarian and as unifier of Greece. It is no surprise that Sparta blocked this daring initiative to replace her in mainland Greece as she had already been replaced in the islands and Asian cities.

Despite its lack of success, P. rightly introduces the decree as an example of Pericles' lofty conceptions. The effect of its inclusion in the life parallels that of the Funeral Oration in Thucydides' *History* (cf. Stadter 1973b, 121), but as a decree P. found it a more reliable index of Pericles' thinking.

17.1

ἀρχομένων . . . Ἀθηναίων: such vaguely temporal introductions to anecdotes illustrating character are common in P.: cf. *Them.* 22.1, ἤδη δὲ καὶ τῶν πολιτῶν διὰ τὸ φθονεῖν ἡδέως τὰς διαβολὰς προσιεμένων.

ἐπαίρων . . . μέγα φρονεῖν καὶ μεγάλων αὐτὸν ἀξιοῦν πραγμάτων: "so as to excite them to . . . think big and consider themselves equal to large projects," recalled again at 17.4. Μεγαλοφροσύνη and cognate terms are hallmarks of Pericles' character; cf. note to 5.1.

γράφει ψήφισμα: one of several known to P. and quoted in the *Pericles* (see note to 8.7), probably from Craterus' collection; cf. Cobet 1873a, 112–14; Meinhardt, 47–48; and the Introduction, 3.1.1. Meiggs's suggestion, *AE* 512, that there might have been a separate collection of Pericles' decrees is improbable. The historical present is frequent in referring to decrees; see note to 9.2. As elsewhere in P., the decree is paraphrased, not quoted (cf., e.g., *Them.* 10.4 and the Themistocles decree, ML 23).

πάντας Ἕλληνας: The western Greeks of Sicily and Italy were excluded (though not the Peloponnesians, *pace* Balcer 1974, 37).

ὁποίποτε: "wherever," not otherwise found in P., but classical; cf. Soph. *Phil.* 780; Plato *Lach.* 197E, *Resp.* 568D; and the similar phrase in the decree on the Eleusinian first fruits, ML 73 (= *IG* I³ 78), ll. 30–31, ἐπαγγέλλεν δὲ τὲν βολὲν καὶ τέσι ἄλλεσι πόλεσιν τέσι ἑλλενικέσιν ἁπάσεσι, ὅποι ἂν δοκεῖ αὐτέι δυνατὸν ἔναι.

καὶ μικρὰν πόλιν καὶ μεγάλην: this sort of opposition is common in P., but note especially *Pomp.* 57.1, καὶ μικρὰ καὶ μεγάλη πόλις . . . ἑώρταζε, and cf. Hdt. 1.5.3, ὁμοίως σμικρὰ καὶ μεγάλα ἄστεα ἀνθρώπων ἐπεξιών. Seager 1967, while noting similar phrases in

Thucydides (1.125.1, 5.77.5), questions its suitability in a fifth-century document: it may well be P.'s own phrase.

περὶ τῶν Ἑλληνικῶν ἱερῶν, ἃ κατέπρησαν οἱ βάρβαροι: Although most of the Greeks on Xerxes' route surrendered to the Persians and were not sacked, Phocis, Attica, and the Boeotian cities of Thespiae and Plataea all suffered sacking and burning (Hdt. 8.32–33, 35, 50, 53; Paus. 10.35.2). For archaeological evidence of destruction of temples in Attica see Meiggs 1963, 39, and *AE* 505–6. Pericles may also have thought of those destroyed after the Ionian revolt and in the Marathon campaign: Miletus and Didyma (Hdt. 6.19), the islands (6.32), the Hellespont (6.33), Naxos (6.96), and Eretria (6.101.3). Given the size of the Persian army, we may also imagine wanton destruction even in Medizing territory.

The so-called Oath of Plataea, which according to fourth-century orators and later writers was sworn by the Greeks before Plataea, included the clause τῶν ἱερῶν τῶν ἐμπρησθέντων καὶ καταβληθέντων οὐδὲν ἀνοικοδομήσω, ἀλλ᾽ ὑπόμνημα τοῖς ἐπιγινομένοις καταλείψω τῆς τῶν βαρβάρων ἀσεβείας (Diod. 11.29.3; cf. Lycurg. *contra Leocr.* 81; Paus. 10.35.2; the inscribed version, Tod, *GHI* 204, does not have this clause). The existence of this oath seems the best explanation for the lack of temple construction at Athens before midcentury. See Meiggs, *AE* 504–7; Boersma, *Building Policy*, 43–44. This clause in P. indicates that one reason for calling the congress was to reconsider that resolution concerning the temples. Pericles may have had various ideas in mind: rebuilding, new construction, or financial contributions to support new building. If the decree is not placed in the early 440s, it is not necessary to think that he already had planned to use league money to construct the Parthenon. Seager 1967 thinks this clause would be offensive to those who had Medized in 480. But force and betrayal (cf. the Theban argument in Thuc. 3.62.3–5) were sufficient excuse to these states, and they may have been eager now to participate in a common Greek cause.

The Oath of Plataea, like the Peace of Callias, was considered a fabrication by Theopompus (115 F153), a view accepted by many: see especially Habicht 1961. But even if there were not the oath to consider, the question of the ruined temples would remain.

κατέπρησαν: as Holden noted, not a classical word, though common in P., and therefore good evidence for P.'s paraphrase of the original text.

οἱ βάρβαροι: the singular and plural are used for the Persian invader in the Themistocles decree, the Oath of Plataea, Herodotus, and Thucydides.

τῶν θυσιῶν, ἃς ὀφείλουσιν: we do not know what sacrifices are meant, although it is certain that the Greeks made many promises to the gods while fighting the Persians, both during the invasion and after (e.g., before Eurymedon). A Covenant of Plataea, distinct from the Oath, is cited by P. (*Arist.* 21.1–2). It calls for a regular festival, the Eleutheria, at Plataea and for the Plataeans to offer sacrifice ὑπὲρ τῆς Ἑλλάδος. When put on trial by the Spartans in 428 they insisted that they had done so (Thuc. 3.58.4–5). Pericles probably thought of other sacrifices as well, no doubt centering on Athens. On the covenant cf. Meiggs, *AE* 507–8; Habicht 1961 (against); Raubitschek 1960a (for).

εὐξάμενοι τοῖς θεοῖς: cf. the similar phrases at Thuc. 2.74.2, 3.58.5.

τῆς θαλάττης . . . ἄγωσιν: The third clause concerns peaceful commerce upon the sea. The implied threat would be raiding of ships and piracy, such as the Dolopes on Scyros conducted before being put down by Cimon (*Cim.* 8.3–5). Thessalian merchants who had been attacked appealed for help to the Amphictyonic League, but it refused to contribute money, leading Cimon, the Athenian commander, to act on his own. Cf. also the Hestiaea decree (*IG* I³ 41, l. 39) and in general Ziebarth 1929, 9–11; Amit 1965, 119–21. Pericles hoped to create a better defense against the pirates, while strengthening Athens' influence. He may also have wished to raise money from those participating in the congress and to legitimize a new role for the Delian League, as suggested in *ATL* 3:279–80, but the main purpose more likely was assertion of leadership— money and power, as with the Delian League, could follow later. Seager's (1967) criticism that this clause reflects the fourth-century international situation is not convincing.

τὴν εἰρήνην ἄγωσιν: "keep the existing peace." The phrase is not otherwise found in P. Without the article, εἰρήνην ἄγειν means "keep quiet, remain at peace" (*Comp. Sert.–Eum.* 2.2, *Ant.* 24.2, *Apophtheg. Lac.* 216E, *De gen. Socr.* 579A). When used with other verbs, τὴν εἰρήνην usually refers to a specific peace agreement (e.g., *Alc.* 14.4, *Pyrrh.* 6.8), although not always (cf. *Per.* 23.2, οὐ τὴν εἰρήνην ὠνούμενος, where the sense is somewhat ambiguous). This is normally thought to be the Peace of Callias, but the phrase itself could refer to an agreement among the Greeks, such as the five-year truce of Thuc. 1.112.1. It is only the earlier reference to decisions on temples destroyed and sacrifices promised during the Persian Wars that suggests that a peace with Persia might be meant.

17.2

ἄνδρες . . . γεγονότων: This phrase and the following list of routes are our best indication that P.'s source was an official decree, because it reflects fifth-century epigraphical formulae not likely to be found in a literary work. This age restriction on envoys was rare (cf. ML 65, ll. 16–17, π[ρέσβες δ]ὲ τρὲς πέμφσαι hυπὲρ πεντέκοτα ἔτε γεγον[ότας]). But the specification of numbers of envoys, as here, is frequent: see Griffith 1978; Mosley 1973, 46, 55–56.

ὧν πέντε μὲν κτλ.: For similar routes to cities of the Delian League see ML 45, clause 9; 46, 22–28; 69, 4–6. The first two routes recall the districts of the league after 442: Ionia, Caria (later joined with Ionia), the Hellespont, the Thracian region, and the islands. The precise composition of the list of those invited, its origin, and purpose have been much discussed. It now seems agreed that it was meant to include members of the Delian League (especially routes 1 and 2), the members of the Hellenic alliance against Persia (*ATL* 3:279n. 20 observes that all the cities of the serpent column erected in 479 could be included in P.'s list of routes, except Leukas), and members of the Delphic amphictyony (route 4; cf. *ATL* 3:105). Finally, it is notable that states that had Medized in 480–79, such as Thessaly and the cities of Boeotia, were included, indicating the Panhellenic rather than purely anti-Persian aspect of Pericles' initiative.

Ἴωνας καὶ Δωριεῖς: Athenian inscriptions also regularly omit the Aeolians.

ἄχρι Λέσβου καὶ Ῥόδου: If P. can be relied on here, then presumably Lemnos and Imbros were included on the Hellespontine circuit, unlike the tribute districts, which placed them with the islands. Rhodes usually was part of the Carian district.

εἰς Βοιωτίαν . . . Ἀμβρακίας: The route seems unusually long: one wonders whether the envoys expected to attend a meeting of the Peloponnesian League to facilitate their work.

Λοκρῶν: the western Locrians, on the Corinthian Gulf.

ἕως: "as far as." This local sense is not classical, beginning only with Aristotle, and is quite rare in P. (elsewhere only *Demetr.* 43.5, ἕως ἀκροστολίου; *Apophtheg. Lac.* 223C, ἀπὸ τῶν σφύρων ἕως ἐπὶ τοὺς καιρίους τόπους). For a parallel cf. Acts 11:19, διῆλθον ἕως Φοινίκης καὶ Κύπρου καὶ Ἀντιοχείας.

17.3

Οἰταίους . . . Θεσσαλούς: Compare the list of states belonging to the Delphic amphictyony in Aeschin. 2.116: Thessalians, Boeotians, Dorians, Ionians, Perrhaebeans, Magnesians, Locrians, Oitaeans, Phthiotians, Malians, and Phocians. Eastern Locris, Oitaea, Malis, and Achaea Phthiotis surrounded the Gulf of Malis. The Athenians made an alliance with the Thessalians after their rejection by the Spartans ca. 462 (Thuc. 1.102.4) and at an uncertain date (perhaps after Oenophyta) an alliance with the Amphictyonic League (*IG* I² 26 = *IG* I³ 9; cf. Meiggs, *AE* 175, 418–20).

κοινοπραγία: "common action." The word is Hellenistic (cf. Polyb. 5.95.2, etc.). The noun form is unique to P. here, but cf. κοινοπραγεῖν at *Galb.* 6.4, *De Is.* 380A.

17.4

ὡς λέγεται: The rejection of the invitation, of course, would not be found in the decree itself but would have been given by Craterus or whoever else recorded it.

τῆς πείρας ἐλεγχθείσης: "the effort was challenged." The Spartan opposition to Athens' hegemonic ambitions led finally to the Peloponnesian War.

παρεθέμην: "I have provided as evidence." The word is used frequently in P. for citing evidence or verbal citations. Cf. *Arist.* 26.4: Craterus usually cites a judgment or decree, καὶ παρατίθεσθαι τοὺς ἱστοροῦντας; *Arist.* 26.5, *Cic.* 38.3, *An seni* 784E, ἀλλὰ μὴν ἅ γε Ξενοφῶν περὶ Ἀγησιλάου γέγραφεν, αὐτοῖς ὀνόμασιν ἄξιόν ἐστι παραθέσθαι, followed by a direct quote of *Ages.* 11.15; and esp. *De Stoic. repug.* 1035A, 1036D, 1046D, 1047E, 1051E, 1054E. The decree demonstrated a major feature of Pericles' character.

18.1

ἐν δὲ ταῖς στρατηγίαις: P. here takes up a new aspect of Pericles' life, his military leadership as *stratēgos*. Along with a number of minor campaigns (18–23), this includes the Samian War (24–28) and the Peloponnesian War (29–35, 37) and therefore dominates the rest of the life, with only occasional digressions (on Aspasia, 24.2–12; on Pericles' reasons for refusing to repeal the Megarian decree, 30–32; and on his family life, 36). P. only rarely explicitly states that Pericles was general on a specific occasion: in the Chersonese (19.1), in 446 (23.1), with Sophocles (at Samos, 8.8; cf. 25.2, etc.), in 431 (33.7), 430 (35.4), and 429 (37.2). For other evidence, and discussions of his role as general, see note to 16.3.

The order of events for chapters 18–28 is by topics: (1) Pericles' caution as a general in contrast to Tolmides, whose recklessness led to his defeat and death at Coronea; (2) his successful expeditions (to the Chersonese, Corinthian Gulf, and Black Sea); (3) his restraint of the demos and concentration on opposing Sparta, exemplified by the restoration of the Delphians; and (4) his effectiveness dealing with revolts in Euboea, Megara, and Samos. As a result the campaigns do not follow a simple chronological order: Coronea (447 or 446), Chersonese (447?), Peloponnese (454 or 455), Pontus and Sinope (430s), Sacred War (448), Euboea and Megara (446), Samos (440).

Note that P. does not include any of the examples of *stratēgēmata* or special tricks of warfare ascribed to Pericles by Frontinus (1.3.7, 1.5.10, 1.11.10, 1.12.10, 3.9.5, 3.9.9).

ἀσφάλειαν: seen by P. as a leading characteristic of Pericles' leadership (cf. 19.3, 20.3–4, 21, 38.4) and one basis for the comparison with Fabius Maximus.

P. could have referred here to the habit of Pericles that he recalls elsewhere: when putting on his general's cloak, he would say to himself, πρόσεχε, Περίκλεις· ἐλευθέρων ἄρχεις, Ἑλλήνων ἄρχεις, πολιτῶν Ἀθηναίων (*Praec. ger. rep.* 813D; cf. *Reg. et imp. apophtheg.* 186C, *Symp.* 620C–D). However, this anecdote would have illustrated more Pericles' self-restraint than his caution in strategy.

οὔτε μάχης . . . στρατηγούς: an expansion of the notion of ἀσφάλεια. P. has no specific instances in mind beyond the example of Tolmides that follows, which was chosen precisely for this purpose.

ἐκ τοῦ παραβαλέσθαι: "at the risk of their lives"; cf. *Alex.* 19.4, 40.4, *Caes.* 37.7; LSJ s.v. παραβάλλω II.1. Ἐκ with the articular infinitive expresses the underlying circumstance: cf. *Cat. Min.* 18.4, ταῖς ἐκ τοῦ μὴ χαρίζεσθαι τὰ δημόσια μηδὲ κρίνειν κακῶς ἀπεχθείαις.

λέγων: the saying is not recorded elsewhere.

18.2

Tolmides: an active general, famous for his expedition around the Peloponnese (456/55), when he burned the Spartan shipyards at Gythium, won over the cities of Cephallenia, took Naupactus and Chalcis on the Gulf of Corinth, and raided the territory of Sicyon (Thuc. 1.108.5; Diod. 11.84; schol. Aeschin. 2.75). He may also have been at Oenophyta (457?), although Myronides was the hero of the battle (Aristodemus 12.2; Thuc. 1.108.2–3; Diod. 11.81.4–83.4). He led cleruchies to Euboea and Naxos (Diod. 11.88.3; cf. *Per.*11.5). Diodorus' account of the Peloponnesian adventure stresses his rivalry with Myronides and the trick he used to recruit at Athens a large and carefully selected force.

διὰ τὰς πρότερον εὐτυχίας: cf. Flaminius in *Fab.* 2.3, μεγάλαις ἐπαιρόμενον εὐτυχίαις. Like Flaminius, Tolmides in his recklessness demonstrates the value of caution and self-control. His name and patronymic, both using the root τολμ-, make him especially suitable as an object lesson on rash daring.

ἐκ τῶν πολεμικῶν: "on account of his military activities."

πεπεικότα . . . δυνάμεως: cf. Thuc. 1.113.1: ἐστράτευσαν ἑαυτῶν μὲν χιλίοις ὁπλίταις, τῶν δὲ ξυμμάχων ὡς ἑκάστοις ἐπὶ τὰ χωρία ταῦτα πολέμια ὄντα, Τολμίδου τοῦ Τολμαίου στρατηγοῦντος. However, the idea of the select volunteer force seems suspect, as it duplicates Diodorus' notion of Tolmides' force for the Peloponnesian expedition, composed of one thousand τῶν νέων τοὺς ἀκμάζοντας ταῖς ἡλικίαις καὶ τοῖς σώμασιν εὐρωστοτάτους, plus another three thousand volunteers, from men τῇ ῥώμῃ διαφερόντων (Diod. 11.84.4). Diodorus' source, and probably P.'s, would be Ephorus: either Diodorus shifted the anecdote of the volunteers to Tolmides' earlier campaign, to make a pair with Myronides' thousand "eager beavers" (Diod. 11.81.4–5; cf. Plut. *Reg. et imp. apophtheg.* 185E), or, as seems more likely, P., working from memory, has unconsciously shifted the volunteer story to the Coronea campaign.

ἐθελοντὰς στρατεύεσθαι: "serve as volunteers." Cobet's emendation (1873a, 137) fits P.'s usage (cf. 20.2; the ἐθελοντὶ of the mss. is not found elsewhere in P.) and recalls Diodorus' ἐθελοντὴν στρατεύειν.

κατέχειν ἐπειρᾶτο: a frequent activity of Pericles as leader, reflecting his caution, even temper, and sobriety; cf. the same verb at 21.1, 27.2. Contrast Tolmides, confident in his fortune (εὐτυχίας) and setting out σὺν οὐδενὶ καιρῷ. The parallel to Fabius instructing Minucius (*Fab.* 8.1) is evident.

If it could be trusted, this would be a valuable indication of Pericles' policy in the 450s. Many historians ascribe the aggressive attempt to create a "land empire" to Pericles, but in fact we have no evidence of his policy or of his participation in the campaigns of the 450s following Tanagra (cf. 10.1–2) except for that on the Corinthian Gulf, 19.2–3 (cf. de Ste. Croix, *OPW* 315–17).

τὸ μνημονευόμενον: This word is fairly common in P. and not an indication that the apophthegm derives from Ion's *Epidemiai* as suggested by Meinhardt, 49. The apophthegm is not recorded elsewhere. It is not apparent what Pericles' strategy would have been: P. thinks only in terms of the moral situation, in which a cool head is better, and finds confirmation in the event.

οὐχ ἁμαρτήσεται . . . ἀναμείνας: The future indicative after the optative πείθοιτο is not uncommon in a quotation; cf. *MT* 670. Ἀναμείνας is a supplementary participle, "he will not be wrong to wait for . . ."; cf. Smyth 2101.

18.3

Κορώνειαν: the defeat at Coronea (in 447 or 446), as Tolmides was returning from capturing Chaeronea, caused Athens to lose the control of Boeotia that it had won at Oenophyta (Thuc. 1.113; Diod. 12.6.1–2). P. knows more of the battle than he tells here: both that Alcibiades' father Clinias died there (*Alc.* 1.1, probably from Plato *Alc. mai.* 112C, but cf. also Isoc. 16.28) and that the Boeotians, under their Spartan general, had erected a trophy in front of the temple of Athena Itonia (*Ages.* 19.2). Coronea was about 10 miles from P.'s home at Chaeronea, and the temple was just beyond, on the road to Alalcomenae (Paus. 9.34.1); P. undoubtedly had seen it. Despite the defeat Tolmides was not disgraced, for he was honored with a statue seen by Pausanias (1.27.5). The epitaph for the fallen has been discovered: *SEG* 10:410; Hill, *Sources*, B50, p. 301; cf. Bowra 1938. Only P. mentions Pericles' opposition or the Athenians' subsequent esteem for him (cf. also *Comp. Per.–Fab.* 3.3, and especially the similar account of Fabius after Cannae, *Fab.* 17.5). For the background of the Coronea campaign see Meiggs, *AE* 176–77; Kagan, *OPW* 122–24; Buck 1970; Amit 1971.

φιλοπολίτῃ: "loving one's fellow citizens" (cf. also *Lyc.* 20.7, *Flam.* 13.8, *Arat.* 15.2). More appropriate here, because of the emphasis on saving lives, than φιλόπολις.

19.1

τῶν δὲ στρατηγιῶν: The list of Pericles' campaigns as general begins with two selected as outstanding examples: ἠγαπήθη μὲν . . . μάλιστα . . . ἐθαυμάσθη δὲ. Chronology does not influence the order either of these two or of those in chapters 20–21.

ἡ περὶ Χερρόνησον: The campaign, like the cleruchy (cf. 11.5) is perhaps to be dated to 447, on the basis of the tribute lists (see *ATL* 3:59, 289–90). The campaign is not mentioned elsewhere but is apparently confirmed by an inscription (ML 48 = *IG* I² 943) with an epigram beginning hoíδε παρ' hελλέσποντον ἀπόλεσαν, listing Athenian casualties ἐγ Χερρονέσοι (l. 1), ἐμ Βυζαντίοι (l. 49) and ἐν τοῖς ἄλλοις πολέμοις (ll. 41–42). A general and twenty-seven men died in the Chersonese, twelve others at Byzantium. See comments to ML 48 and Meiggs, *AE* 159–61. For Athenian interests in the Chersonese see the note on the Chersonesan cleruchy at 11.5.

τὸν αὐχένα διαζώσας: the Chersonese is less than four miles wide at its narrowest point. Διαζώννυμι here is not "gird round," but "run a belt across"; cf. *Phoc.* 13.7, διάζωμα τῆς νήσου σφιγγομένης ἑκατέρωθεν ταῖς θαλάσσαις, where διάζωμα is the narrow "waist" of an island. Αὐχένα, "neck," is quite suitable for a peninsula like the Chersonese (cf. Hdt. 6.37.1). Pericles repeated the project of Miltiades: cf. Hdt. 6.36.2, ὁ δὲ [Μιλτιάδης] πρῶτον μὲν ἀπετείχισε τὸν ἰσθμὸν τῆς Χερσονήσου ἐκ Καρδίης πόλιος ἐς Πακτύην, ἵνα μὴ ἔχοιέν σφεας οἱ Ἀψίνθιοι δηλέεσθαι ἐσβάλλοντες ἐς τὴν χώρην. εἰσὶ δὲ οὗτοι στάδιοι ἕξ τε καὶ τριήκοντα τοῦ ἰσθμοῦ. In 398 the Spartan Dercyllidas again built a wall to protect the Chersonesan cities from the Thracians (Xen. *Hell.* 3.2.10).

περικεχυμένων: "crowded about," a regular meaning of περιχέομαι; cf. *Aem.* 39.4, *Flam.* 11.1; Plat. *Rep.* 488C.

ἐνδελεχῆ: "continuous, constant."

συνείχετο: "was oppressed."

βαρβαρικαῖς . . . συνοίκων: "having close relations with barbarian districts and being full of brigands, both on the borders and within." Cimon earlier had attacked a center of piracy at Scyros (*Cim.* 8.3, λῃζόμενοι δὲ τὴν θάλασσαν ἐκ παλαιοῦ; Thuc. 1.98.2).

19.2

πρὸς τοὺς ἐκτὸς ἀνθρώπους: "among strangers, foreigners." The expression, with or without the noun, occurs some nine times in P. Cf. *Rom.* 23.6, ἐθαύμαζον δὲ πολλοὶ καὶ τῶν ἐκτὸς ἀνθρώπων, and *Lys.* 23.13, δέομαι δέ σου καὶ διὰ τοὺς ἐκτὸς ἀνθρώπους, οἳ πρὸς ἡμᾶς ἀποβλέπουσιν. It appears as early as Plato *Leg.* 629D.

περιπλεύσας Πελοπόννησον: Pericles' expedition along the Corinthian Gulf was not actually a circuit of the Peloponnesus, as he left from and returned to Pegae on the gulf. Perhaps a year earlier Tolmides had in fact brought a fleet around the Peloponnesus into the Corinthian Gulf (Thuc. 1.108.5; Diod. 11.84; schol. Aristid. 2.75). This is the first of Pericles' actions to be reported by Thucydides (1.111.2–3), who notes explicitly that he was *strategos* and took one thousand hoplites. The date is three years before the five-year treaty that ended the first Peloponnesian War, thus in 454 or perhaps 455. Diodorus divides the expedition between two years (11.85.1–2, 455/54, and 88.1–2, 453/52). Although Thucydides implies that it was inconclusive (ἐς Οἰνιάδας ἐστράτευσαν καὶ ἐπολιόρκουν, οὐ μέντοι εἷλόν γε, ἀλλ᾿ ἀπεχώρησαν ἐπ᾿ οἴκου), Diodorus is more positive and Plutarch sees it as a major success. If Pericles was responsible for winning over Achaea, this would indeed have been a major accomplishment. Plutarch's sources are probably Ephorus and Thucydides.

ἐκ Πηγῶν: the harbor of Pegae on the Corinthian Gulf was one of the most important gains for Athens after the alliance with Megara in the early 450s (Thuc. 1.103.4), because it gave direct access to the gulf, which otherwise could be reached only by a long and hazardous journey around the Peloponnese (cf. Gomme, *HCT* on 1.103.4; de St. Croix, *OPW* 190–95). Athens surrendered it by the terms of the peace treaty of 446 (Thuc. 1.115.1).

ἑκατόν: Fifty, according to Diodorus (11.85.1).

οὐ γαϱ . . . τὴν ἔφοδον: These phrases are a rhetorical preparation for the facts that follow and give no independent information.

τῆς παραλίας πολλήν: cf. Diod. 11.85.2, τῆς Πελοποννήσου πόλλην ἐπόρθησεν. For Tolmides see note to 18.2.

συνέστειλε: "drove back," lit. "compressed"; cf. Pyrrh. 25.7, βιασθεὶς καὶ συσταλεὶς πρὸς τὸ στρατόπεδον.

Nemea: an open valley in the territory of Cleonae, site of the sanctuary of Nemean Zeus and the Nemean games. Although P. is thinking of an inland engagement (note πόρρω θαλάττης πρόελθων), this seems too far inland (ca. 12 miles) for a sea-based force, and P. may have confused a reference in his source to the river Nemea, which flows into the gulf, with the sanctuary. According to Diodorus (11.88.2) the Sicyonians opposed the Athenians as they were ravaging the land, but were defeated and driven back into the city.

19.3

᾿Αχαίας φίλης οὔσης: Apparently it became an ally as a result of the expedition: cf. Thuc. 1.111.3, παραλαβόντες ᾿Αχαιούς. Athens surrendered Achaea (had there been a garrison there?) in 446 (Thuc. 1.115.1). Cleon claimed its return in 425 (Thuc. 4.21.3). In 431 all Achaea except Pellene was neutral, but later it joined the Peloponnesians (Thuc. 2.9.2–3). Φίλος is rare in the sense of "friendly, allied" but not unknown: cf. Tim. 10.1, Pel. 29.7; Lys. 12.38; Isoc. 16.21. For the history of Achaea in this period see J. K. Anderson 1954, esp. 80–83.

τὴν ἀντιπέρας ἤπειρον: that is, to the north shore of the gulf.

παραπλεύσας τὸν ᾿Αχελῷον: "sailing past the mouth of the Achelous," the largest river in Greece and the border between Aetolia and Acarnania.

᾿Ακαρνανίαν κατέδραμε: according to Diod. 11.85.2, πλὴν Οἰνιαδῶν ἁπάσας τὰς πόλεις προσηγάγετο. Thucydides mentions only

Oeniadae, and credits Phormio with allying Acarnania with Athens at an unknown date (2.68.7). Most of Acarnania supported Athens in 431 (2.9.4).

Οἰνιάδας: the city, built on a hill on the west of the Achelous and protected from the sea by the islands and alluvial deposits of the river mouth, was consistently hostile to Athens (Thuc. 2.102.2, *αἰεί ποτε πολεμίους ὄντας μόνους Ἀκαρνάνων*; the site is described, 2.102.2–5; cf. Gomme, *HCT* ad loc. and *Princeton Encyclopedia of Classical Sites* [Stillwell 1976] s.v.). It finally joined Athens in 424 (Thuc. 4.77.2).

ἀπῆρεν ἐπ' οἴκου: cf. Thuc. 1.111.3, *ἀπεχώρησαν ἐπ' οἴκου*. Aelius Aristides *Or*. 30.387 (1:585 Dindorf) defends Nicias by citing Pericles' abandonment of this siege.

ἀσφαλὴς δὲ καὶ δραστήριος: the combination is unusual, but cf. *Phoc*. 6.3, *ἀσφαλὴς οὖν ἅμα καὶ δραστήριος ὁ Φωκίων φαινόμενος*. Fabius, on the other hand, is the complete opposite of Marcellus, the "man of action" (*Fab*. 19.1–2).

οὐδὲν γὰρ . . . στρατευομένους: "For no difficulty arose, not even by chance, with regard to the men on the expedition." A *πρόσκρουσμα* is an obstacle, annoyance, or cause of offense (cf., e.g., *Conj. praec*. 141B, *καθημερινὰ προσκρούσματα*). *Περί* suggests a more general sense than the simple dative.

20.1

Εἰς δὲ τὸν Πόντον εἰσπλεύσας: The probable date of this expedition, mentioned only by Plutarch, is between the Samian War and the beginning of the Peloponnesian War, 438–432, as can be deduced by the role played by Lamachus. The date 450, argued for in *ATL* 3:114–17, already improbable in terms of Lamachus' career, is excluded by the discovery of a new fragment of the casualty list, *IG* I² 944, confirming the reading *ἐν [Σιν]όπει* for one of the sites of Athenian losses. See Clairmont 1979, 123–26; the new fragment also excludes the restoration [*ἐν Ἀλ*]*όπει* based on Thuc.

2.26.2, 431 B.C., accepted by Bradeen 1974, 20–21. The lettering of the inscription suits the 430s much better than the 450s.

The purpose and scope of the expedition are less clear. Plutarch speaks of care for the Greek cities and a demonstration of power to the barbarian tribes, kings, and dynasts, but this might represent in large part a rhetorical elaboration of the Sinope affair rather than independent information (cf. the expansion of Thucydides and Ephorus in 19.2–3). However, after the defeat in Egypt supplies of grain from the Euxine would have become more important, and there would be a natural temptation to demonstrate the power of the Athenian navy to the Greek cities there. At any rate, in the tribute assessment of 425 the Athenians listed a Euxine district containing at least forty cities, including not only Heracleia and Apollonia but probably towns on the north shore such as Tyras, Nikonia, Karkinitis, Tamyrake, Patrasys, and the Cimmerians and on the south shore Karousa and Kerasous (*ATL* 2:A9; ML 69, *IG* I^3 71). This list and Plutarch's words suggest that Pericles visited more than the south coast. According to Diodorus (12.31.1) a new king, Spartacus, had taken power in the Bosporan kingdom in southern Russia in 438/37; Pericles may have wished to demonstrate Athenian power and assure continued goodwill in the area after the accession of the new dynasty. However, no cities were added to the league at that time; Black Sea cities do not appear on the quota lists. Besides Sinope, Amisos received colonists from Athens (and was renamed Piraeus), perhaps at this time (Plut. *Luc.* 19.7; Theopomp. *FGrHist* 115 F389).

Perhaps Pericles should be credited with an extraordinary initiative in the Black Sea, which because of the silence of Thucydides and Diodorus remains quite obscure. Plutarch's source is unknown, but despite Diodorus' silence, may be Ephorus (thus Meinhardt, 50). See Rostovtzeff 1922, 66–68; Gomme, *HCT* 1:367–68; Meiggs, *AE* 197–99; Kagan, *OPW* 180, 387–89; *ATL* 3:114–17. For Athenian pottery and silverware on the northeast and east coast of the Black Sea cf. *ArchReports* 1983–84, 91, 92, 93. Brasinskij 1958, 110–21, argues that Pericles did not reach the north shore of the Euxine and places the expedition in 439, before the accession of Spartacus. Ferrarese 1974, 7–19, argues unconvincingly that the whole expedition is a fabrication of the anti-Macedonian propaganda of the fourth century. Karamoutsos 1979, 9–36, reviews and rejects previous suggestions and opts for a date of 447, at the time of the Chersonesan expedition. However, his argument that P. would have had to place this incident after chapter 28 if it took place after the Samian War is incorrect, and he does not consider the new fragment of *IG* I² 944.

στόλῳ μεγάλῳ καὶ κεκοσμημένῳ λαμπρῶς: The size is left vague, but the fact that thirteen ships were left with Lamachus suggests that the whole fleet was about fifty. The latter two words recall the Sicilian expedition of 415 (cf. Thuc. 6.31, esp. 31.6, ὄψεως λαμπρότητι). The entire sentence is marked by generalizations whose factual background is impossible to establish.

ταῖς Ἑλληνίσι πόλεσιν: For the Greek settlements of the Black Sea see C. M. Danoff, *RE* s.v. Pontos Euxeinos, suppl. IX (1962) 866–1175, 1911–20; Boardman 1980, 238–64; A. J. Graham, *CAH*² 3.3 (1982) 122–30; and the archaeological update by Hind 1983–84. However, the only polis actually mentioned by P. is Sinope.

ὧν ἐδέοντο διεπράξατο: The suggestion is that Pericles helped them against the barbarians surrounding them. For διαπράττομαι τινί τι cf. *De gen. Socr.* 577E, *Amat.* 760B, *Cic.* 24.7.

προσηνέχθη φιλανθρώπως: "treated kindly"; cf. *Cleom.* 13.2 and, for φιλανθρώπως, note to 30.3.

ἔθνεσι . . . δυνάσταις: referring to the non-Greek peoples.

ἐπεδείξατο . . . τὸ μέγεθος: cf. again the Sicilian expedition, Thuc. 6.31.4, ἐς τοὺς ἄλλους Ἕλληνας ἐπίδειξιν μᾶλλον εἰκασθῆναι τῆς δυνάμεως καὶ ἐξουσίας.

ᾗ βούλοιντο . . . θάλασσαν: a genitive absolute, with the Athenians as the implied subject.

Σινωπεῦσι: Sinope was a major trading center (modern Sinop), excellently situated in the middle of the south shore, founded by

Miletus in the seventh century; see Strabo 12 (545); Roebuck 1959, 117–22. On the importance of Sinope see Leaf 1916. This incident is undocumented except for the casualty list mentioned above. Timesilaus, however, has recently been recognized on an inscription from Olbia: [Δόγμ]α ['Ολβιο]πολιτέ[ων: Τι]μησίλ[εων, Θεο]πρόπο[ν . . . α]γόρεω Σ[ινωπέ]ας πολιήτ[ας ἔ]ναι καὶ ἀτε[λέ καὶ γῆς [ἔγκ]τ[ησιν ἔναι αὐτοῖς. See Vinogradov 1981, no. 156, 65–90, with summary in German; J. and L. Robert 1982 no. 235 (REG 95 [1982] 356–57). Apparently the tyrant and his brother fled Sinope and were given citizenship and ateleia at Olbia, on the north coast of the Black Sea.

Lamachus: Probably the same man as the general who lost ten ships while collecting tribute in the Euxine in 424 (Thuc. 4.75.1–2) and served on the Sicilian expedition in 415/14. He was mocked by Aristophanes (Acharnians, 425 B.C.) as a blustering soldier. At the time of this expedition he was probably a general with Pericles and hence was at least thirty years old. If the expedition took place in 436, he would have been at least fifty-one in 415. On the other hand, a date as early as 450, as argued in ATL 3:114–17, seems highly unlikely.

20.2

ἐκπεσόντος: banished; cf. 7.3.

ἐψηφίσατο . . . Σινωπεῦσι: apparently these colonists sailed separately, after the return of the expedition, although Lamachus' squadron may still have been in Sinope. For such a decree cf. the Brea inscription, IG I² 45, I³ 46, ML 49. The colony is not included in the list at 11.5. ἐψηφίσατο: "got a decree passed"; cf. 13.11, 24.1; he may not have moved the decree himself.

νειμαμένους: "distributing"; cf. 34.2, the Aegina cleruchy, and the establishment of ten γεωνόμοι to divide the land at Brea, ML 49, ll. 6–8.

οἱ τύραννοι: Timesilaus and his ἑταῖροι.

20.3

After listing these three campaigns, P. once more emphasizes the careful control that Pericles exercised over the citizens (cf. 2.5, 15.1–2, etc.), lest we think that he pursued activity or glory without considering the consequences. It is possible that the following examples of Egypt, the Persian coastal provinces, and Delphi were suggested by Thuc. 1.112 (or did Ephorus expand Thucydides, keeping the same order?).

τἆλλα: acc. of respect.

συνεχώρει: "go along with, yield to."

συνεξέπιπτεν: "fall in with, be carried along with."

ὑπὸ ῥώμης . . . τοσαύτης: cf. Comp. Per.–Fab. 1.1, ὑπὸ κοινῆς . . . εὐτυχίας καὶ ῥώμης πραγμάτων; Pyrrh. 23.3, εὐτυχία δὲ καὶ ῥύμη [Ziegler, mss. ῥώμη] τῶν παρόντων ἐπαιρόμενος; Nic. 18.11.

ἐπαιρομένων: cf. 17.1; Pericles both stirs up the people and calms them, as necessary.

Αἰγύπτου τε πάλιν ἀντιλαμβάνεσθαι: Athens mounted a major campaign, eventually running six years, to aid Inaros, who was trying to establish Egypt as a kingdom separate from Persia. They were crushingly defeated, losing as many as two hundred ships in 454; cf. Thuc. 1.104, 109–110; Diod. 11.71.2–3, 74.1–75.4, 77.1–5; Meiggs, AE 101–108. However, a few years later Cimon led his expedition to Cyprus (cf. 10.8, Cim. 18–19.1) and dispatched sixty of his two hundred ships to Egypt to help Amyrtaeus. These were then recalled after his death (Thuc. 1.112.3–4; Cim. 18.5–6). This second (πάλιν) expedition may be the one referred to here; no later effort is known.

κινεῖν . . . θαλάσσῃ: This again seems to refer to the recall of Cimon's expedition, which had fought against naval forces from Cyprus, Cilicia, and Phoenicia (Thuc. 1.112.3–4; Diod. 12.3–4; Cim. 18–19.1). Pericles would have opposed those who after Cimon's death wished to continue the expedition. Κινεῖν here means "trouble, stir to rebellion." On the interpretation of Cimon's last expedition, the purpose and success of which are both uncertain, see Meiggs, *AE* 126–28, and note to 10.8 above. For Athenian concentration on the Aegean after the Egyptian campaign see *AE* 118. Note that Plutarch does not connect Pericles' restraint with the Peace of Callias.

20.4

Σικελίας: Athens' interest in Sicily and southern Italy long preceded its first expedition there in 427–424 (Thuc. 3.86, 88, 90, 99, 103; 4.1–2, 25, 48.6, 65) and the great armada of 415–13 (Thuc. 6–7). Themistocles named two of his daughters Italia and Sybaris (*Them.* 32.2) and fled to Corcyra—Stesimbrotus says he went as far as the court of Hieron in Sicily—before going to Asia (*Them.* 24.7). A treaty was made with Egesta in the 450s (ML 37) and sometime later others with Rhegium and Leontini, which were renewed in 433/32 (ML 63, 64). Thurii was founded 444/43 (cf. note to 11.5). The Athenian commander Diotimus, probably the same one who participated in the expedition to Corcyra in 433/32, also visited Naples while on a command in Sicily (Timaeus 566 F98; Tzetzes to Lycophron *Alex.* 732–33). The Corcyreans noted and the Athenians remembered the importance of their island for the voyage to Sicily (Thuc. 1.36.2, 44.2). Pericles therefore may indeed have had to restrain the Athenians. But from the lack of precision of Plutarch's note here and at *Alc.* 17.1 (Σικελίας δὲ καὶ Περικλέους ἔτι ζῶντος ἐπεθύμουν Ἀθηναῖοι), he would seem to be merely building upon Thucydides' comments in 2.65.11–12 (ἡμαρτήθη καὶ ὁ ἐς Σικελίαν πλοῦς, etc.). Ephorus may have expanded Thucydides in the same way: cf. Diod. 12.54.1, Ἀθηναῖοι δὲ καὶ πάλαι μὲν ἦσαν ἐπιθυμηταὶ τῆς Σικελίας διὰ τὴν ἀρετὴν τῆς χώρας. Meinhardt's suggestion, 51, of a Sicilian source (Philistus or Timaeus) seems unnecessary. The language of these two sentences is in Plutarch's rich style. For a general review of Athenian relations with the West in this period see Brandhofer 1971.

δύσερως . . . καὶ δύσποτμος ἔρως: note the double figure, playing on both δυς- and ἔρως. For the latter cf. Euripides, δυσφήμους φήμας, *Hec.* 194; γάμους δυσγάμους, *Phoen.* 1047; δύσνοστον νόστον, *Troad.* 75. Plutarch quotes Euripides' δυσέρωτες δὴ φαινόμεθ' ὄντες (*Hipp.* 193) at *Amat.* 764E and *Non posse* 1105B, and several times compares his heroes to οἱ δυσέρωτες (*Cic.* 32.5 *Dion* 16.3, *Arat.* 33.5), but only here is it used to qualify another noun: "that madly loving love." The inspiration may be Nicias' μηδ' . . . δυσέρωτας εἶναι τῶν ἀπόντων (Thuc. 6.13.1); for ἔρως cf. Thuc. 6.24.3, καὶ ἔρως ἐνέπεσε τοῖς πᾶσιν ὁμοίως ἐκπλεῦσαι.

Δύσποτμος, another poetic word, seems to occur otherwise in Plutarch only at *Fab.* 18.4 and *Comp. Per.–Fab.* 1.1, referring to the disaster at Cannae. Plutarch uses more than two hundred words with the prefix δυς-, many only once. However, examples of pairs of two adjectives in δυς- are few in the *Lives*: see *Rom.* 28.9, *Num.* 4.8, *Fab.* 26.3, *Arist.* 14.6, *Nic.* 5.2, *Cat. Min.* 1.5, *Comp. Dem.–Cic.* 1.6, *Dion* 8.3, 17.10, *Brut.* 13.2.

ἐξέκαυσαν: the same image is found at 33.6; cf. also *Alc.* 17.2, τὸν ἔρωτα τοῦτον ἀναφλέξας.

οἱ περὶ τὸν Ἀλκιβιάδην ῥήτορες: Plutarch probably means only Alcibiades himself: cf. note to 14.1. For Alcibiades' role in urging the Sicilian expedition of 415–413, which was to end so disastrously, see esp. Thuc. 6.15–19.1; *Alc.* 17.1–18.3.

Τυρρηνία καὶ Καρχηδὼν: probably based on Alcibiades' words at Sparta in Thuc. 6.90.2, ἐπλεύσαμεν ἐς Σικελίαν πρῶτον μὲν, εἰ δυναίμεθα, Σικελιώτας καταστρεψόμενοι, μετὰ δ' ἐκείνους αὖθις καὶ Ἰταλιώτας, ἔπειτα καὶ τῆς Καρχηδονίων ἀρχῆς καὶ αὐτῶν ἀποπειρά-σοντες ; cf. also *Alc.* 17.3, Καρχηδόνα καὶ Λιβύην ὀνειροπολῶν; *Nic.* 12.2.

οὐκ ἀπ' ἐλπίδος: "not without hope, not unlikely." For this use of ἀπὸ see LSJ s.v. I.3.

ὑποκειμένης: "existing, present," equivalent to ὑπάρχω; cf. *Alex.* 47.7, οὐκ ἀνάρμοστα τοῖς ὑποκειμένοις εἶναι πράγμασιν; *Comp. Sol.–Popl.* 4.4, *Cam.* 19.4, *Pel.* 8.5, *Cat. Min.* 59.9; LSJ s.v. II.8.b.

εὔροιαν: "smooth flow, prosperous course." Frequent in Polybius, but already in Plato (*Laws* 784B).

21.1

ἀλλ': Plutarch continues his own interpretation of Pericles' policy. Ἀλλ' . . . κατεῖχε responds to οὐ συνεχώρει of 20.3.

κατεῖχε: cf. 18.2, 27.2.

ἐκδρομήν: "charge, sally." The metaphor of a general restraining the impetuosity of his troops is not found elsewhere in the *Lives*. Cf., however, *De prof. in virt.* 77A, ὅσοι τὸ πρῶτον μεγάλαις ἐκδρομαῖς ἐχρήσαντο πρὸς φιλοσοφίαν, and *De Is.* 371B, *De cur.* 520F. It well fits the running comparison with Fabius.

περιέκοπτε: "kept trimming, pruning"; cf. *Cat. Mai.* 2.3, περιέκοπτε τὴν πολυτέλειαν.

ἔτρεπεν . . . τῶν ὑπαρχόντων: For this aspect of Pericles' policy see Thuc. 1.144.4, τούς τε ἐχθροὺς παντὶ τρόπῳ ἀμύνεσθαι καὶ τοῖς ἐπιγιγνομένοις πειρᾶσθαι αὐτὰ μὴ ἐλάσσω παραδοῦναι. Cf. Thuc. 2.65.7.

ὑπεναντιούμενος: "opposing"; cf. 17.4, 34.4. Here, as often, ὑπο- means not "secretly" or "gradually" but "in response" to another action; cf. Buttrey 1977.

τὸν ἱερὸν . . . πόλεμον: The war, called the Sacred War because it concerned control of the sanctuary at Delphi, is mentioned by Thuc. 1.112.5, Λακεδαιμόνιοι δὲ μετὰ ταῦτα [Cimon's last expedition] τὸν ἱερὸν καλούμενον πόλεμον ἐστράτευσαν, καὶ κρατήσαντες τοῦ ἐν Δελφοῖς, καὶ αὖθις ὕστερον Ἀθηναῖοι ἀποχωρησάντων αὐτῶν στρατεύσαντες καὶ κρατήσαντες παρέδοσαν Φωκεῦσιν. Slightly different versions are reflected in schol. Ar. *Birds* 556 (with references to Philochorus 328 F34, Theopompus 115 F156, and Eratosthenes 241 F38) and the Suda s.v. ἱερὸς πόλεμος. Philochorus says the Athenian action came two years (τρίτῳ ἔτει) after the Spartan campaign, but Thucydides surely is right in suggesting that it followed immediately, in the same campaign season, which would probably be 448. See Meiggs, *AE* 175, 423; Gomme, *HCT* 1:337–38, 409. The authors of *ATL* (3:178) and Kagan, *OPW* 120–22, accept Philochorus and date the two campaigns in 449 and 447. The Spartan and Athenian armies did not fight each other and thus avoided violating their thirty-five-year treaty (Thuc. 1.112.1). P. seems to derive from Thucydides, but adds the *promanteia* and the wolf. This is the second Sacred War; the first was ca. 590, the third ca. 356–346, the fourth 340–338.

21.2

ὁ Περικλῆς: As regularly, P. substitutes "Pericles" for the "Athenians" of Thucydides (it is unlikely that another source was more precise). See the Introduction, 2.6. Thus we cannot with confidence use this passage as evidence for Pericles' foreign policy at this time.

21.3

προμαντείαν: the right of first consultation of the oracle, awarded to benefactors of the god. Cf. Hdt. 1.54.2 (Croesus) and K. Latte, *RE* suppl. IX (1962) 1237–39. P. could have found the notice on the *promanteia* in Philochorus F34, or perhaps in Theopompus, who was interested in the oracle (cf. *De Pyth. or.* 403E–F = 115 F336, Θεόπομπος οὐδενὸς ἧττον ἀνθρώπων ἐσπουδακὼς περὶ τὸ χρηστήριον).

ἐγκολαψάντων: "having inscribed, carved."

τοῦ χαλκοῦ λύκου: Pausanias (10.14.7) saw the wolf near the great altar and tells us why it was originally dedicated by the Delphians. Plutarch, a priest of Delphi and curious about everything connected with the sanctuary, would have seen the wolf and the inscriptions himself. The main altar is still visible directly before the temple; the wolf was probably just north of it, beside the column of Eumenes II (see Daux 1936, 157). If there was also a written source for the inscriptions, it has not survived. One thinks of a detail added by P. to fill out Thucydides' bare notice. For the practice of putting new inscriptions on old dedications see, e.g., Hdt. 1.51.3.

ἐνεχάραξεν: "engraved," *variatio* from ἐγκολαψάντων above.

22–23

The Revolts of Euboea and Megara and the Peloponnesian Invasion of Attica. P. continues to follow Thucydides (1.114), supplementing him from Ephorus and Theophrastus and changing the emphasis of the narrative. The introductory sentence on the value of Pericles' restraint and the stories of the bribery of Cleandridas and Gylippus remind us of Pericles' caution and prudence. The two episodes are treated separately: 22.1–23.2, the invasion, and 23.3–4, the pacification of Euboea.

22.1

ὅτι δ' ὀρθῶς . . . τὰ γενόμενα: P. resumes the thought of 20.3–4, on the dangers of entanglements outside Greece. He seems to have in mind Pericles' advice in Thuc. 2.65.7 against attempting to extend the Athenian *archē*, recalled also in *Comp. Per.–Fab.* 2.3. Ἐν τῇ Ἑλλάδι is emphatically placed next to ὀρθῶς: "He was right to confine Athens' forces to Hellas. . . ."

τὰ γενόμενα: "events," i.e., the revolts of Megara, Euboea, and Samos.

πρῶτον μὲν γὰρ κτλ.: This sentence is very close in thought and diction to Thuc. 1.114.1 but with significant omissions. Like Thucydides, P. does not consider the causes of the revolts, or their importance to Athens. On Euboea see note to 23.3.

The two revolts took place in summer 446, between the battle of Coronea (18.3) and the thirty-year treaty of late autumn 446 (24.1). On the background see Gomme, *HCT* 1:340–41 (for the date, 1:409); Meiggs, *AE* 177–78; Kagan, *OPW* 124–25; de Ste. Croix, *OPW* 196–200; Legon 1981, 194–99. Megara had allied itself with Athens in 461 to protect itself from Corinth (Thuc. 1.103.4), and received garrisons at Nisaea and Pegae. P. suppresses the violence of the revolt, in which some of the Athenians were killed, and the support the Megarians received from Corinth, Sicyon, and Epidaurus (Thuc. 1.114.1). Diod. 12.5 (448/47) describes an Athenian invasion immediately after the revolt, which pinned the Megarians to the city. If this is true, both Thucydides and P. have compressed events. P. focuses not on the loss of Megara (he clearly never considered either Boeotia or Megara rightfully subject to Athens) but on Pericles' resourcefulness in turning back the Spartans. In a different context, P. can speak of the Megarian victory over the Athenians (*De Pyth. or.* 402A, [ἡ μάχη] ἦν Ἀθηναίους μετὰ τὰ Περσικὰ τὴν πόλιν ἔχοντας αὐτῶν νικήσαντες ἐξέβαλον). Cf. also ML 51 and Gomme, *HCT* 1:340–41, on an Athenian force retreating from Pegae to Athens.

ἐκπεπολεμωμένοι: "had gone to war" (cf. 29.1, *Phoc.* 16.1; Thuc. 8.57). The word occurs ten times in P. Here it replaces Thucydides' ἀφέστηκε for *variatio* of the previous ἀπέστησαν.

Plistonax: This son of the regent and victor of Plataea, Pausanias, became Agiad king in 458 but had been too young to lead in the Tanagra campaign (Thuc. 1.107.2). His father was killed for treason before Themistocles' exile, probably in the late 470s, although the date is uncertain (Thuc. 1.134). Because Pausanias had two sons younger than Plistonax, the king would have been at least twenty-five in 446, and probably older. White 1964, 140–41, argues from P.'s phrase διὰ τὴν ἡλικίαν that he must have been under thirty, probably by several years. However, the phrase may only represent P.'s interpretation of Cleandridas' role, and not a documented fact. There is no other confirmation of Plistonax' age, except that his son Pausanias was not of age (i.e., twenty) in 427 (Thuc. 3.26.2). P.'s phrase is taken from Thuc. 1.114.2, although he uses the contracted form of the name, as on every other occasion he mentions him, and omits the patronymic.

22.2

πάλιν οὖν κτλ.: cf. Thuc. 1.114.3.

ἀνεκομίζετο: passive, with the intransitive sense "returned." The imperfect, here as in Thucydides, suggests the time involved in the move (cf. *MT* 35).

συνάψαι μὲν εἰς χεῖρας: "join in hand to hand battle"; cf. *Phil.* 18.11 and συμβαλόντων εἰς χεῖρας, *Fab.* 3.2.

Cleandridas: Thucydides at 1.114.3 mentions neither Cleandridas nor the charge of bribery. The Spartan kings were absolute commanders in the field but were regularly accompanied by two ephors (Xen. *Hell.* 2.4.36, *Lac. pol.* 13.5). On special occasions the Spartans might send extra advisors to other commanders (Thuc. 2.85.1, 3.69.1, 8.39.2) but the ten advisors sent with King Agis in 418 were considered a novelty by Thucydides (5.63.4). Cleandridas was presumably an ephor (cf. Suda, s.v. ἔφοροι) with special influence because of the king's youth. The description of his role seems to be in P.'s words, not those of his source: cf. *Lyc.* 3.3, εἰσέπεμψε παρέδρους . . . καὶ φύλακας; *Cat. Min.* 48.2, παρεκάλει σύμβουλον αὐτῷ καὶ πάρεδρον εἶναι τῆς ἀρχῆς. We do not know why the other king, Archidamus, did not lead the army instead. For the later career of Cleandridas see below, 22.3.

διαφθείρας χρήμασιν: found in Ephorus F193 (quoted in note to 23.1) and Diod. 13.106.10. The trial and charge is alluded to by Thucydides (2.21.2, 5.16.3). The Spartan withdrawal with so little accomplished, when the Athenians were in a very weak position, is difficult to explain: Thucydides says they got no further than Eleusis and the road to Thria, perhaps 10 miles inside Attica, although Diodorus (12.6.1) says they ravaged much territory and besieged some forts. The Spartans obeyed but were obviously angry: the closest parallel is the withdrawal of Agis from contact with the Argives in 418 (Thuc. 5.60–63). At that time the infuriated Spartans almost destroyed the king's house and fined him 100,000 drachmas. In both cases the kings may have had their own aims, which they thought could be achieved without the risk of a battle. Plistonax and Cleandridas may have felt that the loss of Megara and Boeotia was sufficient damage to Athens and the invasion itself only a means to insure that Athens did not try to reconquer them, rather than an attempt to bring her to her knees. Some (e.g., Meiggs, *AE* 181–82) have thought that the terms of the thirty-year peace, concluded in the following fall (cf. 24.1), were tentatively agreed to at this time (compare the negotiations with Agis that preceded his retreat, Thuc. 5.59.4–5). Philippides 1985 has suggested that there was a solar eclipse visible in Attica on 2 September 446, which would have given Plistonax a reason for retiring, as with Cleombrotus at the Isthmus in 480 (Hdt. 9.10).

Spartan kings, far from being immune to criticism, frequently were called to account, fined, and exiled. See Andrewes 1966; de Ste. Croix, *OPW* 350–53; Lewis 1977, 43–48. Bribery, or some other illegal way to increase one's fortune, was a common problem for the Spartans, especially when out of their country: cf. Lewis 1977, 33–34. Aristotle (*Pol.* 1270b10–13) noted that poor ephors were especially susceptible. P. has narrated the story, probably from Ephorus, so as to enhance Pericles' reputation for honesty and for protecting the lives of citizens. On the episode see Kagan, *OPW* 124–26; de Ste. Croix, *OPW* 196–200. For more on Spartan acceptance of bribes cf. 23.2.

22.3

βαρέως φέροντες οἱ Λακεδαιμόνιοι: Plistonax took up residence at the sanctuary of Zeus Lycaeus on the Arcadian border, apparently seeking the god's protection from the Spartans. Finally he was permitted to return and be king again in late 427. Thucydides (5.16.1–3) considered him the chief Spartan supporter of the Peace of Nicias of 421. He continued as king until his death in 408. P.'s vague οἱ Λακεδαιμόνιοι does not give us any help in discovering before whom he actually was tried. It may have been the *gerousia* and ephors, not the full citizen body: cf. de Ste. Croix, *OPW* 199.

φεύγοντος: he spent his exile in Thurii, where he became famous as a general: cf. Diod. 13.106.10; Antiochus, *FGrHist* 555 F11 = Strabo 6.1.14 (264); Polyaenus 2.10.

22.4

Γυλίππου . . . καταπολεμήσαντος: in 414–413; cf. Thuc. 7. While at Syracuse he was accused of avarice (*Nic.* 28.4); later, after the surrender of Athens in 404, he was entrusted by Lysander with carrying some of the booty to Sparta. He tried to keep some for himself but was caught and exiled (*Lys.* 16.1–17.1; Diod. 13.106.8–9). P. probably got this story too from Ephorus: cf. the reference to Ephorus in this context in the *Lysander* (17.3 = 70 F205) and the notice in Diodorus. However, Theopompus, who is also cited in *Lys.* 17.3 (115 F332), is a possibility. On the story see Alessandrì 1985.

συγγενικὸν . . . νόσημα: cf. *Nic.* 28.4, ἀρρώστημα πατρῷον. P. is interested in the possibility (ἔοικε) of hereditary weaknesses of character in the φύσις. Cf. *De ser. num. vind.* 561C–562D for a parallel between hereditary predisposition to sickness (νόσημα) and to vice (κακίας δ' ὁμοιότητα συγγενικὴν ἐν νέῳ βλαστάνουσαν ἤθει). The question of congenital disease is treated by Galen, *Commentaria in Hippocratis Epidemiarum Librum Tertium* (*Corp. Med. Gr.* 5:10.2.1).

συγγενικόν: "congenital," like συγγενής.

προστρίψασθαι: "impart," often implying a bad effect, "inflict upon," as in *Nic.* 8.5.

ἐν τοῖς περὶ Λυσάνδρου: *Lys.* 16. *Lysander–Sulla* shortly preceded the *Pericles*: see Jones 1966b, 66–68, and the Introduction, 1.3.

23.1

ἐν τῷ τῆς στρατηγίας ἀπολογισμῷ: "in his defense of his generalship." Ἀπολογισμός is a quite general term, applied, e.g., to Solon's poems (*Sol.* 3.4) and to Sulla's account of his actions ἐν ἐκκλησίᾳ (*Sull.* 34.3); cf. also *Dem.* 8.1, *Symp.* 726B, *Praec. ger. rep.* 822E. However, P. seems to be thinking of the year-end review of each magistracy, which involved both accounting for money spent before the ten auditors (λόγος) and justification of action (εὔθυνα). If any suspicion arose generals were brought before the ecclesia for trial (*Ath. pol.* 48.4–5, 54.2, with Rhodes, *CAAP* ad loc.). P.'s reference to ὁ δῆμος here implies that such was the case in 446/45, but this detail may be only narrative color supplied by him. Ostwald 1986, 436n. 104, thinks rather of Pericles' responding to questions in the assembly. There is no reason to put this accounting before the return to Euboea: P. is simply completing the story of the bribe, before going on to the next point.

εἰς τὸ δέον: "for what was needed." The expression caught the Athenian imagination, and was recalled by Aristophanes in the

Clouds (858–59) twenty years later: when Phidippides asks his father, "What happened to your slippers?" Strepsiades replies, ὥσπερ Περικλέης, εἰς τὸ δέον ἀπώλεσα. The sum was 20 talents according to schol. Ar. *Clouds* 859 (Ephorus 70 F193): φασὶ δὲ, ὅτι καὶ λογισμοὺς διδοὺς τάλαντα εἴκοσιν ἁπλῶς εἶπεν εἰς τὸ δέον ἀνηλωκέναι. φησὶ δὲ Ἔφορος ὅτι μετὰ ταῦτα μαθόντες οἱ Λακεδαιμόνιοι Κλεανδρίδην μὲν ἐδήμευσαν, Πλειστοάνακτα δὲ ιε' ταλάντοις ἐζημίωσαν, ὑπολαβόντες δωροδοκήσαντας αὐτοὺς διὰ τὸ φείσασθαι τῆς λοιπῆς Ἀθηναίων γῆς ὑπὸ τῶν περὶ τὸν Περικλέα, μὴ θελήσαντα γυμνῶς εἰπεῖν ὅτι "δέδωκα τοῖς Λακεδαιμονίων βασιλεῦσι τὸ ἐνδεές." Cf. also Suda s.v. δέον (50 talents, and a 5-talent fine).

μὴ πολυπραγμονήσας: on μή with the participle cf. note to 6.2. Here it avoids hiatus. The reaction of the assembly demonstrates their confidence in Pericles. Later, when shaken by war and plague, they would be more ready to condemn him (32.3–4, 35.4). It may never have been precisely known how the money was spent: Thucydides, at least, avoids making a positive statement on the subject of Pleistonax' bribe (2.21.1, 5.16.3).

23.2

ἔνιοι . . . ὁ φιλόσοφος: for Theophrastus see the Introduction, 3.2.d. Despite the plural ἔνιοι, P. may in fact be thinking only of Theophrastus for this story, which is not found elsewhere. The source might be the πολιτικὰ πρὸς τοὺς καιρούς, which treated the statesman's response to particular situations and gave historical examples. The attention given by the Spartans to the bribery of Plistonax and Cleandridas argues against Theophrastus' report of regular payments every year.

ἐφοίτα: regularly used of repeated trips or visits.

τοὺς ἐν τέλει: "those in authority," as opposed to ordinary citizens: cf. Andrewes in Gomme, *HCT* 4:23, on Thuc. 5.27.2.

παρῃτεῖτο: "averted (by persuading with bribes)." Here the accusative gives the thing avoided; in 25.3, παραιτούμενος τὴν πόλιν, the people spared.

οὐ τὴν εἰρήνην . . . βέλτιον: a justification for Pericles' unusual action—by Theophrastus or by P.?

23.3

εὐθὺς οὖν κτλ: cf. Thuc. 1.114.3, καὶ Ἀθηναῖοι πάλιν ἐς Εὔβοιαν διαβάντες Περικλέους στρατηγοῦντος κατεστρέψαντο πᾶσαν, καὶ τὴν μὲν ἄλλην ὁμολογίᾳ κατεστήσαντο . . . ; also Diod. 12.7; Ar. Clouds 211–13 and schol. (= Philochorus 328 F118). Οὖν resumes after the digression on bribery, 22.3–23.2. Only P. gives the size of the force (cf. Diod. 12.7, μετὰ δυνάμεως ἀξιολόγου). In the Comparison he parallels this victory to Fabius' victory in Campania (2.1). Flacelière accepts the emendation αὖθις, perhaps influenced by Thucydides' πάλιν. However εὐθύς also makes good sense here, and εὐθὺς οὖν is far more common in P. than αὖθις οὖν (thirty-five times to four in the Lives).

Euboea had been in the Athenian sphere of influence at least since Athens had defeated Chalcis and established a cleruchy there in 506. The cities of Euboea were members of the Delian League, although Carystus had to be forced to join by Cimon (Thuc. 1.98.3). The establishment of a cleruchy in Euboea by Tolmides shortly before this revolt (Diod. 11.88.3) suggests that there had been recent unrest there, although the tribute lists record payment of the quota for spring 446. The island was vital to Athenian interests because of its size, fertility, and proximity to Athens. Loss of Euboea would have been a major blow to Athens, much more than the secession of Boeotia and Megara, which had only recently joined her alliance. Cf. Thuc. 8.96.1–2 and Westlake 1948 on the Athenians' reaction to its loss in 411. The comic poets mention Athens' treatment of the island: cf. Per. 7.8; Ar. Clouds 211–13. See in general Gomme, HCT 1:342–47; Meiggs, AE 565–70. The Athenian cleruchies there present a variety of problems: see Brunt 1966, esp. 87–89; Green and Sinclair 1970; and the bibliography on cleruchies cited above at 11.5. P. again supplements Thucydides from another source, perhaps Ephorus, but ignores the report of Theopompus (115 F387; see note to 23.4).

23.4

Χαλκιδέων: The hippobotai or "horse-raisers" of Chalcis had already lost at least part of their land to Athenian cleruchs in 506

(Hdt. 5.77.2, identifying them as παχέες τῶν Χαλκιδέων). As the wealthy class, they would have led the revolt against Athens and tried to establish an oligarchy, and now were expelled. Neither P. nor Thucydides mention a second cleruchy to Chalcis at this time. Aelian *VH* 6.1, sometimes cited for a new cleruchy (e.g., *ATL* 3:295), fits better the events of 506. Manfredini 1968 unconvincingly argues that P.'s notice is a mistaken version of Herodotus' account of the events of 506. It seems better to see two stages of Athenian control: the cleruchy of 506 and the expulsion of the die-hard oligarchs in 446.

An inscription (ML 52, *IG* I³ 40) preserves a decree regulating relations between Chalcis and Athens, probably passed in 446/45 as part of the pacification of the island: see Balcer 1978. A fragment of a similar treaty with Eretria has also been found (*IG* I³ 39).

Ἑστιεῖς: cf. Thuc. 1.114.3, Ἑστιαᾶς δὲ ἐξοικίσαντες αὐτοὶ τὴν γῆν ἔσχον; 7.57.2, Ἑστιαιῆς οἱ ἐν Εὐβοίᾳ Ἑστίαιαν οἰκοῦντες ἄποικοι ὄντες. The expulsion and subsequent cleruchy is mentioned by Philochorus (328 F118 = schol. Ar. *Clouds* 213) and Diodorus (12.7, 12.22), though only P. gives the reason for this extreme measure. The Hestiaeans were settled in Macedonia, and the new Athenian settlement was named Oreus (Theopompus 115 F387; cf. Thuc. 8.95.7). A fragmentary inscription (*IG* I³ 41) that contained detailed instructions for legal procedures, ferry tariffs to the mainland, and so on may be connected with the foundation of the Athenian settlement: see McGregor 1982, with a new edition of the text, and Graham 1964, 17–72. This, like the later settlement in Aegina (cf. 34.2), would have been a cleruchy.

24.1

σπονδῶν: in winter 445/44. Cf. Thuc. 1.115.1. The Athenians had to surrender Nisaea and Pegae in the Megarid, and Troizen and Achaea in the Peloponnese. P. ignores what should be regarded as a substantial setback to Athens. Cf. also Diod. 12.7; Paus. 5.23.3; Andoc. 3.6.

ψηφίζεται τὸν εἰς Σάμον πλοῦν: According to Thucydides, there was a five-year interval between the treaty and the outbreak of the war (1.115.2, ἑκτῷ δὲ ἔτει). P. follows Thucydides in jumping this gap but, unlike him, does not indicate any lapse of time. In the meantime Thurii was founded and Thucydides son of Melesias ostracized. For Samos' quarrel with Miletus, and the Samian war, see note to 25.1. For the historical present see note to 9.2. The article designates "the famous" expedition to Samos.

αἰτίαν ποιησάμενος: = αἰτιασάμενος, "having charged against them"; cf. 30.2. For similar constructions with abstract nouns see 31.2, 36.4, 38.3; LSJ s.v. ποιέω A.II.5.

24.2

Ἀσπασίᾳ χαριζόμενος: P.'s source probably is Duris of Samos; cf. Harpocration s.v. Ἀσπασία (= FGrHist 76 F65), δοκεῖ δὲ δνοῖν πολέμων αἰτία γεγονέναι, τοῦ τε Σαμιακοῦ καὶ τοῦ Πελοποννησια-κοῦ, ὡς ἔστι μαθεῖν παρά τε Δούριδος τοῦ Σαμίου καὶ Θεοφράστου ἐκ τοῦ δ' τῶν Πολιτικῶν καὶ ἐκ τῶν Ἀριστοφάνους Ἀχαρνέων. P. used Duris for the Samian War: cf. notes to 26.4, 28.2; and the Introduction, 3.2.e. Ar. Acharnians (523ff.; cf. 30.4) refers only to the Peloponnesian War, as probably also Theophrastus. It is in fact not unlikely that Aspasia had some role in Pericles' decision, but many other factors were involved. The idea of women causing wars is as old as Homer and Helen, and lists were regularly made: cf. Hdt. 1.1–4 and Athen. 13.560B–F, which does not include Aspasia.

δοκεῖ: "is generally considered"; cf. 10.2 and LSJ s.v. II.5.

καιρὸς διαπορῆσαι μάλιστα περὶ τῆς ἀνθρώπου: "an excellent time to raise the question about this woman." Ἡ ἄνθρωπος is not derisive or patronizing; P. uses the expression of queens and heroines. See Lyc. 3.4 (the wife of a Spartan king), Nic. 13.6 (a priestess of Athena), Alex. 2.5 (Olympias), Thes. 27.6 (Antiope), Mul. virt. 260D (Timoclea), Amat. 768B (Camma).

The problem is the extraordinary role this woman was said to have held in Athenian society, and which makes her one of the Greek women best known to us. Nevertheless the information is slight and of dubious reliability; most is assembled by P. in this passage (24.3–10). Wilamowitz's suggestion, 1893, 263n. 7, that P. and other late writers depended on a Hellenistic biography is improbable. The chief sources were comedy and the Socratic dialogues, especially the two *Aspasias* of Aeschines the Socratic and of Antisthenes and the *Menexenus* of Plato (cf. the Introduction, 3.3.b, c, a.) The scholion to *Menex.* 235E, unfortunately rather garbled in our tradition, gives an indication of the standard later picture: Ἀσπασίαν: αὕτη Ἀξιόχου, Μιλησία, γυνὴ Περικλέους, παρὰ Σωκράτει πεφιλοσοφηκυῖα, ὡς Διόδωρος ἐν τῷ περὶ Μιλήτου συγγράμματί φησιν (*FGrHist* 372 F40). ἐπεγήματο δὲ μετὰ τὸν Περικλέους θάνατον Λυσικλεῖ τῷ προβατοκαπήλῳ, καὶ ἐξ αὐτοῦ ἔσχεν υἱὸν ὀνόματι Ποριστήν, καὶ τὸν Λυσικλέα ῥήτορα δεινότατον κατεσκευάσατο, καθάπερ καὶ Περικλέα δημηγορεῖν παρεσκεύασεν, ὡς Αἰσχίνης ὁ Σωκρατικὸς ἐν διαλόγῳ Καλλίᾳ καὶ Πλάτων ὁμοίως Πεδήταις. [Read ἐν διαλόγῳ Ἀσπασίᾳ καὶ Καλλίας ὁμοίως Πεδήταις (F15 K.) with Bergk and Dindorf or ἐν διαλόγῳ Ἀσπασίᾳ καὶ Πλάτων καὶ Καλλίας ὁμοίως Πεδήταις with Immisch.] Κρατῖνος δὲ Ὀμφάλῃ τύραννον αὐτὴν καλεῖ χείρων, Ὀμφάλην Εὔπολις Φίλοις (F274 K.): [Read τύραννον αὐτὴν καλεῖ Χείρωσιν, Ὀμφάλην Εὔπολις Φίλοις (Bergk) or Ὀμφάλην αὐτὴν καλεῖ Χείρωσιν, τύραννον δὲ Εὔπολις Φίλοις (Meineke).] ἐν δὲ Προσπαλτίοις Ἑλένην αὐτὴν καλεῖ (F249 K.): ὁ δὲ Κρατῖνος καὶ Ἥραν (F241 K. = 259 K.A.), ἴσως ὅτι καὶ Περικλῆς Ὀλύμπιος προσηγορεύετο. ἔσχε δὲ ἐξ αὐτῆς ὁ Περικλῆς νόθον υἱόν, ἐφ᾽ ᾧ καὶ ἐτελεύτα τῶν γνησίων προαποθανόντων, ὡς Εὔπολις Δήμοις (F98 K.). For a biographical sketch, giving the ancient references, see W. Judeich, *RE* s.v. Aspasia 1, II (1896) 1716–21. Women in Athens were not expected to have a public role: cf. Thuc. 2.45.2; Gould 1980, 38–59, with bibliography; Pomeroy 1975, 56–92. Drinking and conversing with men is cited as evidence for a woman's status as a prostitute in [Dem.] 59, *In Neaeram* 28, 48, etc. Keuls 1985 draws a vivid picture of the role of women in a male-dominated society: see esp. chapters 6–10, pp. 153–273, on prostitutes and concubines.

24.3

Μιλησία γένος, Ἀξιόχου θυγάτηρ: cf. schol. Plato *Menex.* 235E; Plato, *Menex.* 249D; Harpocration s.v. Ἀσπασία. Wilamowitz (1893, 263n. 7) suggested that these words might have appeared on her gravestone, whence they were recorded by a certain Diodorus, cited in schol. *Menex.* 235E (*FGrHist* 372 F40; both the author's name and the title of the work are uncertain), but the father's name would have been a normal means of identification.

Thargelia: a famous Milesian courtesan who helped win Thessaly over to the Persians at the time of Xerxes' invasion. P.'s notice seems to be from Aeschines' *Aspasia*: cf. Philostratus *Epist.* 73 quoting Aeschines (F10, p. 44 Krauss), Θαργηλία Μιλησία ἐλθοῦσα εἰς Θετταλίαν ξυνῆν Ἀντιόχῳ Θετταλῷ βασιλεύοντι πάντων Θετταλῶν; Athen. 12.608F–609A (Hippias, *FVS* 86 F4); and *Anon. de mulieribus* (Westermann 1963, 217, no. 3).

Ἰάδων: Ionian women. Cf. Athen. 5.220B, ἐν δὲ τῇ Ἀσπασίᾳ . . . [Aeschines calls] τὰς δ' ἐκ τῆς Ἰωνίας γυναῖκας συλλήβδην μοιχάδας καὶ κερδαλέας.

ἐπιθέσθαι: "to win over, seduce." The literal meaning here is "to make a campaign against, to attack"; cf. ἐχειρώσατο, at 24.2.

24.5

σοφήν τινα καὶ πολιτικήν: P. divides his treatment into two parts, Aspasia's reputation for political astuteness (οἱ μέν, 5–7) and her erotic appeal (φαίνεται μεντοί, 7–10), apparently emphasizing the first but unwilling to pass over the second. For her political wisdom he cites Plato and Aeschines, both of whom have Socrates meeting with Aspasia and learning from her. Cf. also Xen. *Mem.* 2.6.36, *Oec.* 3.14; Harpocration, etc.

οὐ κοσμίου . . . τρέφουσαν: P. clearly accepts the notion that Aspasia supported herself by running a brothel. Προεστῶσαν ἐργασίας : "to direct a business." The ambiguity of παιδίσκας, which most often means simply "young girl" (either free or slave) is removed by ἑταιρούσας, used by P. to refer to prostitutes or call-girls: cf. *Rom.* 4.4, τῶν γυναικῶν τὰς ἑταιρούσας, equivalent to Latin *lupas*; *Luc.* 6.2, *De adul. et amic.* 62E. For a description of the activity of procuresses see [Dem.] 59.18 (Nicarete, a freedwoman in Corinth, buys girls, trains them as prostitutes, and lives off them); Hyperides *In Athenogenem* 3 (a retired prostitute who now has become a procuress). Williams 1983, 92–106, suggests that several vases usually thought to depict matrons in fact depict *hetairai* primping or conversing while waiting in a brothel.

The social status of Aspasia is much disputed, but the evidence indicates that she must have been a *hetaira*, that is, an independent woman, free to give her favors to whomever she wanted and unrestricted by the traditional customs of Athenian married women. The later legitimatization of her son by Pericles indicates that she must have been a free woman (cf. Davies, *APF* 458–59). As a noncitizen, she could not have legitimate Athenian children after the passage of the citizenship law of 451 (cf. 37.3), but she could have led, and did not, the life of the normal Athenian wife. This is apparent from the manner in which she is named by Aristophanes (*Ach.* 527, in the same context as the Megarian harlot Simaitha). The comic poet, although harsh against men, does not name real living women unless they are *hetairai* or other women of no reputation, or a public figure like the priestess Lysimache. See Sommerstein 1980, 393–409. (On the general reluctance to name respectable women cf. Schaps 1977 and Bremmer 1981.) In the same passage Aristophanes speaks of her πόρνα δύο, indicating that she kept women for hire; in the *Knights* (765) her husband Lysicles is associated with two prostitutes. Note that she is named, most unusually, by both Plato (*Menex.* 235E–236C) and Xenophon (*Mem.* 2.6.36, *Oec.* 3.14). Xenophon confirms that she prepared women for association with men: in the former passage she is an expert on matchmaking (or rather, pandering), in the second on training women. Other comic writers call her παλλακή or πόρνη; cf. below, 24.9–10. The difference in names can be a reflection both of actual fact and of the feeling or opinion of the speaker (cf. Dover 1978, 21) but in any case refers to a woman who supported herself by her body. The speech against Neaera ([Dem.] 59), although reflecting different circumstances, is informative on the question of status. Neaera is accused of being an ex-slave and prostitute who associates with an Athenian citizen. He has pretended that she is his wife and her children his, so that if condemned he would pay a fine and she would be sold into slavery. See esp. [Dem.] 59.18–48, the alleged history of Neaera, and 107–126, the impassioned peroration. Aspasia probably had a similar history as *he-*

taira and owner of *hetairai* before and perhaps during her liaison with Pericles. Cf. Keuls 1985, 198–99, 272.

24.6

Aeschines: in his dialogue *Aspasia* (F8, p. 46 Krauss). See the Introduction, 3.3.b.

Lysicles: cf. schol. Plato *Menex.* 235E, quoted above in a note to 24.2, and Harpocration and Suda s.v. Ἀσπασία. In Ar. *Knights* 132 "the sheep-merchant" is listed as one of the pre-Cleonian demagogues; cf. schol. ad loc. and Photius s.v. προβατοκάπηλον. Lysicles was mocked for his connection with trade, as was Cleon "the tanner," though both were wealthy men. He may be identical with the general who died in action in Caria in 428/27 (Thuc. 3.19.1; cf. Gomme, *HCT* ad loc.; *PA* 9417). If so, it raises the question when Aspasia began to associate with him, as Pericles had died only shortly before. Was it while Pericles was still alive? Aspasia's relation to Lysicles, like that to Pericles, furnished material for the comic poets and philosophers. The name of his son, Poristes ("Supplier"), is extraordinary and may be a comedian's joke. Aspasia could not have been his legal wife any more than Pericles'.

τὴν φύσιν: acc. of specification, here contrasting "nature" (e.g., being lowborn) with his training in rhetoric by Aspasia.

24.7

Plato: The *Menexenus* consists almost entirely of the text of a funeral speech for the dead of the Corinthian War composed by Aspasia and recited by Socrates. Cf. 235E, [Socrates] ᾧ τυγχάνει διδάσκαλος οὖσα οὐ πάνυ φαύλη περὶ ῥητορικῆς, ἀλλ᾽ ἥπερ καὶ ἄλλους πόλλους καὶ ἀγαθοὺς πεποίηκε ῥήτορας, ἕνα δὲ καὶ διαφέροντα τῶν Ἑλλήνων, Περικλέα τὸν Ξανθίππου. MEN. Τίς αὕτη; ἢ δῆλον ὅτι Ἀσπασίαν λέγεις; and 236A–B, αὐτὸς μὲν παρ᾽ ἐμαυτοῦ ἴσως οὐδέν, Ἀσπασίας δὲ καὶ χθὲς ἠκροώμην περαινούσης ἐπιτάφιον λόγον περὶ αὐτῶν τούτων. The whole introduction to the dialogue, 234A–236D, is what P. calls τὰ πρῶτα. The humor (παιδιά) is found not only in the anachronism of Socrates' delivering a speech for a war that began four years after his death, but also in his mockery of the orators (cf. 235C, ἀεὶ σὺ προσπαίζεις, ὦ Σώκρατες, τοὺς ῥήτορας) and his description of the speech itself as παίζειν (236C). P., however, although aware of Plato's irony here, believes that there still may be some truth in Plato's notice, and that Athenians actually came to her to discuss rhetoric. Note that he does not treat as fact that Socrates (or Pericles) had learned the funeral speech from her. Other ancient writers also took the *Menexenus* seriously: cf., e.g., Dionysius of Halicarnassus *Demosthenes* 23–30, who quotes extensively from the *Menexenus* in order to compare Plato's political course with that of Demosthenes. On Plato as source for P. see the Introduction, 3.3.a.

εἰ καί: "even though." Cf. *Tim.* 7.7, etc.

ἀγάπησις: "affection, warm feeling," e.g., of parents toward children (*De am. prol.* 495C, *Non posse* 1100D), or citizens toward their fellows (*Comp. Thes.–Rom.* 6.2, *Cor.* 37.3), etc.

24.8

γυνή: This wife remains unidentified, and her relation to Pericles uncertain. Davies prefers to keep this wife "irritatingly anonymous" (*APF* 18n. 1; cf. also W. E. Thompson 1970, 31), but others have argued that she is Dinomache, mother of Alcibiades and wife of Clinias (who would then be the third man): see most recently Cromey 1984. Dinomache was Pericles' first cousin, the daughter of his mother's brother, Megacles. The order of her marriages given by P. (Hipponicus, Pericles, a third man) is difficult because of the chronology of the children's births. On the reasoning of Beloch, *Gr. Gesch.* 2:35, and Davies, *APF* 262–63, P. must be mistaken, and Pericles the woman's first husband, with Hipponicus the second, and no third. P.'s order, however, is defended by Bicknell 1982 and Cromey 1982; the latter notes especially that Hipparete, child of Hipponicus and wife of Alcibiades, need not be child of this woman, and that her brother Callias, who was, could indeed have been in his eighties when on embassy to Sparta in 371. For this woman's children Xanthippus and Paralus see chapter 36.

συνῳκηκυῖα: a normal word for "married to"; cf. 36.2, *Caes.* 10.6.

Hipponicus: "the richest man in Greece," according to later writers. On his family and its wealth see Davies, *APF* 254–70. His father, Callias, was ambassador to Susa and responsible for the peace that bore his name, as well as ambassador to Sparta in 446; his mother, Elpinice, was the sister of Cimon (*Cim.* 4.8). The wealth of the family was based on mining but did not survive the Peloponnesian War. His son Callias was said by Plato to have spent more on sophists than everyone else in Athens put together (*Apol.* 20A); his home is the setting of the dialogue *Protagoras*. The family was very active in politics in the fifth century, and their marriage connections to Cimon and Pericles were obviously of major importance, although given the state of our evidence we cannot interpret their precise significance. On the family's relation with Alcibiades, who married Hipponicus' daughter Hipparete, see *Alc.* 8.1–6.

τὸν πλούσιον: cf. *Arist.* 25.6, πλουσιώτατος Ἀθηναίων, and *De cup. div.* 527B.

τῆς συμβιώσεως οὐκ . . . ἀρεστῆς: For divorce by mutual consent see Harrison, *Law*, 1:39–44; W. E. Thompson 1972; and Hipparete's attempt to divorce Alcibiades, *Alc.* 8.4–6.

συνεξέδωκεν: Pericles, who as her husband was her *kurios*, gave her in marriage in conjunction with the *kurios* (father or brother) she would have when divorced. P.'s picture is one of complete harmony: contrast Athen. 12.533C–D, Περικλέα δὲ τὸν Ὀλύμπιόν φησιν Ἡρακλείδης ὁ Ποντικὸς ἐν τῷ περὶ Ἡδονῆς ὡς ἀπήλλαξεν ἐκ τῆς οἰκίας τὴν γυναῖκα καὶ τὸν μεθ' ἡδονῆς βίον προείλετο ᾤκει τε μετ' Ἀσπασίας τῆς ἐκ Μεγάρων ἑταίρας καὶ τὸ πολὺ μέρος τῆς οὐσίας εἰς ταύτην κατανάλωσε.

Ἀσπασίαν λαβών: The date is uncertain, as is the nature of their legal relationship. Their son Pericles must have been born after the citizenship law of 451/50 (unless it was retroactive, as argued by Humphreys 1974; see below, note to 37.2–5) but by 440 (because he must have been thirty to serve as Hellenotamias in 410/9). Cf. Davies, *APF* 458. She would then have been young, as she was able to bear a child to Lysicles ca. 428. She could not have entered a normal marriage, whose purpose was the birth of citizen children, so she probably lived as a concubine (παλλακὴ) "for the birth of free children" in his house (cf. Busolt, *Gr. Gesch.* 3.1:505–8), unless she kept her own home. On the normality of such concubinage cf. Ehrenberg 1951, 197–98.

24.9

ὥς φασι: Antisthenes (F1 Dittmar); cf. Athen. 13.589E, Ἀντισθένης δ᾽ ὁ Σωκρατικὸς ἐρασθέντα φησὶν αὐτὸν Ἀσπασίας δὶς τῆς ἡμέρας εἰσιόντα καὶ ἐξιόντα ἀπ᾽ αὐτῆς ἀσπάζεσθαι τὴν ἄνθρωπον. The anecdote plays on Aspasia's name.

καταφιλεῖν: "to kiss or embrace warmly." P. is being unusually reserved in not criticizing such a public display of affection: cf. *Conj. praec.* 139E, εἰ δ᾽ αἰσχρόν ἐστιν, ὥσπερ ἐστίν, ἑτέρων παρόντων ἀσπάζεσθαι καὶ φιλεῖν καὶ περιβάλλειν ἀλλήλους. Rather φιλοφρόσυναι should be ἀπόρρητοι. Note the decorum of Xenophon's Panthea, who salutes her beloved husband by kissing—his chariot (*Cyr.* 6.4.10), and the license of Antony's kissing Fulvia and Cleopatra (*Ant.* 10.9, 74.5).

ἐν δὲ ταῖς κωμῳδίαις: *CAF* 3:411, adespota F63 K.; cf. Schwarze 1971, 165. Omphale and Deianira were respectively the Lydian queen who owned Heracles as a slave for a year (*An seni* 785E; Soph. *Trach.* 248–53) and his long-suffering wife (Soph. *Trach.* passim). Aspasia was called Omphale either by Cratinus or Eupolis (schol. Plat. *Menex.* 235E, quoted above in a note to 24.2); Pericles would have been Heracles. According to the same scholion, Eupolis also called her Helen in the *Prospaltoi* (= F249 K.). Cf. also the hypothesis to Cratinus' *Dionysalexandros* (P. Oxy. 663; *CGFP* F70; *PCG* p. 140), which identifies Dionysus/Paris as Pericles.

Hera: as wife of "the Olympian."

Cratinus: F241 K. = 259 K.A.; cf. the Introduction, 3.1.e. This seems to follow directly on F240, quoted at 3.5, and thus comes from the *Chirons*. The genealogy of the gods continues: Lechery begets (Aspasia-)Hera to Cronus. The meter is still dactylo-epitrite (analyzed by *PCG* as: prosod prosod/lec, or · D – D e - e. Cobet

1878, 156, may be right to delete "Aspasia" from the quote as a gloss; as it stands it would be an epithet for Hera. Καταπύγων, "bugger," and its abstract, καταπυγοσύνη, are standard terms of abuse on vases and in comedy, deriving from πυγή, "buttocks," and referring originally to anal intercourse. Cf. Ar. *Lys.* 137, ὦ παγκατάπυγον θἠμέτερον ἅπαν γένος, of women, and *Clouds* 529 with Dover's note. For vases see Milne and von Bothmer 1953; Fraenkel 1955, 42–45. Cratinus' κυνώπιδα, "dog-eyed, shameless," is Homeric, an alteration on the standard βοῶπις πότνια Ἥρη of *Il.* 1.551, etc. For κυνῶπις cf. *Od.* 4.145, of Helen; *Il.* 18.396, of Hera.

24.10

τὸν νόθον: the younger Pericles; cf. note to 37.2–5. Note that this passage from Eupolis is the only evidence cited in antiquity for Aspasia's being the mother of the younger Pericles. P.'s own hesitation is suggested by δοκεῖ.

Eupolis: F98 K. = F110 K.A.; cf. the Introduction, 3.1.h.

Myronides: this reading, accepted by Ziegler and Flacelière, seems to be a Byzantine conjecture, found in only one manuscript. Pyronides, the reading of the best manuscripts, should be preferred. The name also appears as the name of a speaker in P. Oxy. 1240 (Eupolis F100 K.A.). Pyronides is unknown; Myronides would be the well-known mid-fifth-century general (cf. note to 16.3). On this question see Wilamowitz 1919, 69, and the note to F100 K.A.

πόρνης ὑπωρρώδει: Eupolis' use of the term πόρνη, "whore," like the reference in Aristophanes, indicates that Aspasia was never a legal wife. Cf. note to 24.5. Ὑπωρρώδει, "be somewhat afraid," is a compound of ὀρρωδέω: "unless he is put off by the misfortune of the whore," that is, of being the son of Aspasia. The exact allusion is unclear, as the younger Pericles was given citizenship rights before Pericles' death (cf. 37.5). It may be that he was not presenting himself for office, even though his age would have permitted it; the first known position held by him is Hellenotamias in 410/9. The younger Pericles was probably also called *nothos* in Eupolis' *Marikas*, produced in 421. See the fragments of a commentary published in Austin, *CGFP* F95, ll. 166–69 = *PCG* F192, P. Oxy. 2741 fr. 4, ll. 9–12.

24.11

Cyrus: the younger son of Darius II, whose disastrous expedition to unseat his reigning brother Artaxerxes in 401 is described by Xenophon in the first book of his *Anabasis*. This Aspasia was captured at the battle of Cunaxa (*Anab.* 1.10.2, where she is called simply ἡ Φωκαῖς). For her role in the Persian court see *Artax.* 26.5–27.5; Justin 10.2.1–4. Athen. 13.576D quotes a certain Zenophanes for the change of name; Aelian *VH* 12.1 says that Aspasia was her original name, and Milto the new one. Cf. W. Judeich, *RE* s.v. Aspasia 2, II (1896) 1721–22; Fogazza 1970.

24.12

ταῦτα . . . ἀπάνθρωπον ἦν: a vivid reminder of the importance of memory for P.'s method of composition, and of his relaxed relationship with his audience. He mentions the younger Aspasia because he thought of it, and to pass it over would be "misanthropic" or "cold." (For the adjective cf., e.g., *Alc.* 8.6, *Cat. Min.* 5.4, *Dion* 7.5.) Her beauty and influence reinforce P.'s point about Aspasia's power in the preceding sections and recall the figure of Thargelia. P. is trying to put Pericles' Aspasia into a context of influential courtesans. The notice itself may come directly from Xenophon and Ctesias (both used by P. for the *Artaxerxes*) or from scholarly notes or books on κωμῳδούμενοι or ὁμώνυμοι (such as that of Demetrius of Magnesia; cf. *Dem.* 15.4, 27.7; [Plut.] *Vitae dec. or.* 847A).

25–28

The Samian War. Cf. Thuc. 1.115.2–117.3; Diod. 12.27–28; schol. Ar. *Wasps* 283.

The open break and subsequent full-scale war with Samos (440–439), because of the wealth and power of the island, represents a major episode in the history of the Athenian League. Samos had fought at Lade in 494 with sixty triremes (Hdt. 6.8.2). Together with Chios and Lesbos, it had helped form the league and still continued at this time to supply ships rather than tribute. The successful defection of such a power would almost certainly have meant the rapid end of Athenian domination of the Aegean. P., however, concentrates on Pericles' actions, passing over the larger implications both for Athens and for Pericles' domestic and foreign policy. The war is another example of Pericles' wisdom in avoiding foreign adventures (cf. 21.1). Thucydides, on the other hand, reports it as one more instance of Athenian energy and imperialism. For general accounts see Meiggs, *AE* 188–94, 428, 562–65; Kagan, *OPW* 170–78; Legon 1972; Fornara 1979; Quinn 1981, 10–17; Shipley 1987, 113–22. P. follows the general outline of Thucydides, but probably could have derived this from Ephorus, who used Thucydides, as well as from Thucydides himself. He cites in addition Aristotle (the *Constitution of the Samians*), as well as minor writers. It is a useful exercise to read Thucydides' account alongside P.'s, noting where the latter compresses and where he expands with new details (25.2–3, 4; 26.1, 3, 4).

25.1

Ἀσπασίας δεηθείσης: repeating the charge, still unrefuted, of 24.2.

αἱ γὰρ πόλεις . . . πόλεμον: Miletus had had an Athenian garrison imposed ca. 450–449 (cf. the decree, *ATL* 2:D11; *IG* I^3 21) but may have had internal difficulties later. See Meiggs, *AE* 188, 562–65; Barron 1962. Samos controlled territory on the mainland, which was separated from Miletus by the territory of Priene. Samos may have taken advantage of Miletus' weakness to grab more land at Priene's expense (cf. Meiggs, *AE* 428, and note that there had been fighting between Samos and Priene in the sixth century: *Qu. Gr.* 296A = Arist. F576 Rose). Cf. Thuc. 1.115.2, οἱ Μιλήσιοι ἐλασσούμενοι τῷ πολέμῳ παρ' Ἀθηναίους ἐλθόντες κατεβόων τῶν Σαμίων. Aspasia may well have added her voice on behalf of her native city, but Thucydides would not have thought it worth mentioning.

παύσασθαι . . . κελευόντων: The Athenians insisted that the cities of the league have the same allies as they did, so the war was contrary to their treaty with Samos.

δίκας λαβεῖν καὶ δοῦναι: the normal expression for submitting a dispute to arbitration; cf., e.g., Hdt. 5.83.1; Thuc. 5.59.5. The Athenians would have been the arbitrators (παρ' αὐτοῖς). On the necessity of the allies' coming to Athens to try certain types of cases see Thuc. 1.77.1–4; [Xen.] Ath. pol. 1.16–18; Meiggs, AE 220–33, although these all seem to refer to private cases. On other means of imperial control see Meiggs, AE 205–19.

25.2

ὁ Περικλῆς: Thus also Diodorus 12.27.1. Forty ships sailed, according to Diodorus and Thucydides 1.115.3.

τὴν . . . ὀλιγαρχίαν . . . κατέλυσεν: Thucydides explains that some Samians supported the Milesian appeal, hoping for a change of government.

ἐν Σάμῳ: with οὖσαν, but displaced to avoid hiatus.

Λῆμνον: The Athenians considered Lemnos particularly reliable; they may also have placed a cleruchy on the island ca. 451–449. Cf. Meiggs, AE 424–25.

τῶν πρώτων: the leading citizens, now deposed from power.

ὁμήρους: the numbers are those of Thuc. 1.115.3. Hostages were regularly taken to guarantee the good behavior of a suspect city. Athens took hostages from Chalcis and Eretria in 446/45: see ML 52, ll. 47–50 (IG I³ 40); Hesychius s.v. Ἐρετρικὸς κατάλογος; Amit 1970. For children as hostages cf. Thuc. 5.77.1. The addition of ⟨ἄνδρας⟩ (van Herwerden 1880, 462) makes more explicit the contrast with the children but is not strictly necessary, as οἱ πρῶτοι are naturally adults.

καίτοι κτλ.: introduces a supplement to Thucydides. It would have been normal to attempt to pay cash instead of giving hostages, but P. treats this as a bribe, which Pericles, unlike Plistonax (22.2), wholly resists. The oligarchs were probably taken off guard by Athens' rapid response and wished to restore, even at the cost of an indemnity (or bribe), the *status quo ante*. Diod. 12.27.2., [Pericles] *πραξάμενος δὲ παρὰ τῶν Σαμίων ὀγδοήκοντα τάλαντα*, seems a variant of the same story (from Ephorus?), but with the Athenians fining the Samians (or alternatively, with Pericles personally exacting money). P. prefers a version that shows Pericles above the attractions of money.

25.3

Pissouthnes: the satrap of Lydia, with his palace in Sardis, was also involved in Greek affairs at the time of the Mytilenean revolt thirteen years later (cf. Thuc. 3.31.1, 34.2). Without open hostilities he supported opposition to Athens, pursuing a policy of "cold war." As a son of a Hystaspes he would have been closely related to the Persian king, but he revolted at some point (cf. Ctesias, *FGrHist* 688 F15.53) as did his son Amorges (Thuc. 8.5.5). P. understands as simple goodwill (*εὔνοια*) what must have been a conscious policy of disruption. Cf. Lewis 1977, 59–60.

μυρίους χρυσοῦς: sc. *στατῆρας*. If these were Persian darics, they were worth 20 drachmas each, or three hundred to the talent (cf. Xen. *Anab.* 1.7.18), hence a total of 33⅓ talents, an extraordinary sum.

παραιτούμενος: "interceding for"; cf. *Marc.* 20.11, *παρῃτεῖτο τοὺς πολίτας*.

καταστήσας δημοκρατίαν: cf. Thuc. 1.115.3, *δημοκράτιαν κατέστησαν*. According to Fornara 1979, 12–13, this would be in June–July 441.

25.4

οἱ δ' εὐθὺς ἀπέστησαν: The major phase of the war begins with open revolt against the Athenian settlement. P.'s brevity suggests that the democracy revolted, but Thucydides (1.115.4–5) and Diodorus (12.27.3) explain that some of the *δυνατώτατοι* in the city combined with Pissouthnes and with other oligarchs who had escaped to the mainland, to lead seven hundred mercenaries to Samos and overthrow the demos, then rescue the hostages from Lemnos. The oligarchs turned the Athenian garrison and magistrates over to Pissouthnes and prepared to resume the war against

Miletus. The last step is puzzling: how could they not have expected an immediate Athenian reaction? Did Pissouthnes have aims on Miletus? In any case the new revolt was a serious mistake. The oligarchs looked to Persia and to Sparta for help but none came, despite a rumor of Phoenician ships (see 26.1) and discussion by the Peloponnesian League (cf. Thuc. 1.40.4). The threat of Persian or Spartan intervention no doubt made Athens desperate to crush the revolt; cf. her reaction in the case of Mytilene in 428. Thucydides (1.117.3) adds that Byzantium also revolted at this time, but it apparently caused the Athenians no trouble and soon returned to allied status.

ἐκκλέψαντος . . . Πισσούθνου: P. uses the same word, *ἐκκλέπτω*, as Thucydides and Diodorus but makes Pissouthnes the agent instead of the Samian oligarchs.

πρὸς τὸν πόλεμον: apparently against Athens, as in Diod. 12.27.3, rather than against Miletus, as Thuc. 1.115.5.

Περικλῆς ἐξέπλευσεν: Thuc. 1.116.1 notes that Pericles was just one of the ten generals (*δέκατος αὐτός*; cf. Dover 1960) and that the whole force was sixty ships, but sixteen had been sent off, some to Caria to watch for Phoenician ships, some to get aid from Chios and Lesbos. This may have been the regular fleet of sixty sent out each year; cf. 11.4.

οὐχ ἡσυχάζοντας . . . τῆς θαλάττης: added by P. to give importance to the battle, although Thucydides (8.76.4) also speaks of control of the sea.

ἐγνωκότας: echoes the *ἐγνώκει* used immediately above of Pericles. Both sides are resolute, and this will make the war more bitter.

25.5

Τραγίας: Thuc. 1.116.1, *Τραγία*; cf. Strabo 14.1.7 (635): modern Agathonisi, some 12 miles south of Samos and 16 west of Miletus. The Samian ships were returning from Miletus.

λαμπρῶς: "brilliantly," therefore "decisively." The numbers are those of Thucydides.

στρατιώτιδες: "troop-carriers," and therefore not as maneuverable in battle.

26.1

ἁμῶς γέ πως: "somehow or other." The phrase is Platonic, occurring a total of seventeen times in the Dialogues, twelve in the *Laws*, but not in Thucydides, Xenophon, or Demosthenes, once in Lysias (13.7), and twice in Aristotle (*Metaphys.* 1022a2, *Phys.* 196a16). The distribution in P. is unusual: twenty-three times in the *Parallel Lives*, twice in the *Galba*, but never in the *Moralia*. It occurs only six times in the first ten pairs of *Lives* (for these see the Introduction, 1.3), but six times in the *Pompey*.

τοῦ λιμένος κρατήσας: "gained control of the harbor (of Samos)"; cf. Thuc. 7.36.5, *τοῦ λιμένος . . . κρατήσειν*. This intermediate stage and the reference to the daring of the Samians is not found in Thucydides or Diodorus.

μείζων στόλος: forty Athenian ships and twenty-five from Lesbos and Chios: the total was now 125.

ἔπλευσεν εἰς τὸν ἔξω πόντον: out of the Aegean into the Mediterranean. Ὁ ἔξω πόντος only here in P.: ἡ ἔξω θάλασσα is always the ocean. Thuc. 1.116.3: *ἐπὶ Καύνου καὶ Καρίας* (Caunus is on the southwestern corner of Anatolia, in Caria, near the strait between Rhodes and the mainland).

οἱ πλεῖστοι: including Thucydides and Diodorus.

Φοινισσῶν νεῶν: Because of Pissouthnes, the Athenians had a real fear of a Persian attempt to take advantage of the revolt of Samos to weaken their control of the Aegean. It was necessary to take precautions even if the Peace of Callias forbade such intervention. Thucydides adds that a Samian, Stesagoras, had gone with five ships to fetch the Phoenicians, the Persians' chief naval force that might threaten the Aegean: they had been defeated at the Eurymedon (1.100.1) and off Salamis in Cyprus (1.112.4) and later, after 412, played an important part in Tissaphernes' policy (Thuc. 8.46.1, 58.3–4, 87–88, 108–9). See Lewis 1977, 60; cf. also Corbetta 1977, 166n. 4, who notes that it is most unlikely that the Phoenician fleet could have been mobilized so quickly and that reports of its arrival were simply rumors. He also makes the reasonable suggestion (n. 68) that this was the occasion when Pericles sailed with fifty ships beyond the Chelidonian islands, off the coast of Lycia (Callisthenes, *FGrHist* 124 F16 at Plut. *Cim.* 13.4).

Stesimbrotus: *FGrHist* 107 F8; cf. the Introduction, 3.1.c.

ἐπὶ Κύπρον: There probably is no real contradiction. Pericles sailed to the south coast of Anatolia to waylay the Phoenician fleet; this is the route to Cyprus. P. does not think Pericles would have sailed so far, and Stesimbrotus may have exaggerated to put Pericles in a bad light. Corbetta 1977 argues that he must have gone well beyond Caunus toward Cyprus.

26.2

ἁμαρτεῖν ἔδοξε: a pragmatic judgment: it was a mistake to go.

Melissus: one of the last of the Eleatic school, who wrote a book περὶ φύσεως. Cf. *FVS* no. 30. He is frequently cited as an example of a philosopher with practical skills. For his battle against Pericles cf. *Them.* 2.5; Suda s.v. Μέλητος. Thucydides and Diodorus do not mention him.

καταφρονήσας . . . στρατηγῶν: There would have been sixty-five ships, a good-sized fleet, since forty-four had been sufficient to win at Tragia. Androtion, *FGrHist* 324 F38, names eight generals of the year (441/40), including Sophocles the poet (cf. *Per.* 8.8).

26.3

μάχης: Thuc. 1.117.1, οἱ Σάμιοι ἐξαπιναίως ἔκπλουν ποιησάμενοι ἀφάρκτῳ τῷ στρατοπέδῳ ἐπιπεσόντες τάς τε προφυλακίδας ναῦς διέφθειραν καὶ ναυμαχοῦντες τὰς ἀνταναγομένας ἐνίκησαν.

ἐχρῶντο τῇ θαλάσσῃ: according to Thucydides, they controlled the sea for fourteen days.

παρετίθεντο τῶν ἀναγκαίων: "they were busy laying in supplies"; cf. Thuc. 1.117.1, ἐσεκομίσαντο καὶ ἐξεκομίσαντο ἃ ἐβούλοντο. This would have been a fine occasion for Pissouthnes to cause more trouble by furnishing supplies.

Aristotle: this is F577 Rose, probably from *The Constitution of the Samians*. See the Introduction, 3.2.c. Samian sources may have thought the battle at Tragia a victory, as the Samians were able to return safely from Miletus to Samos.

26.4

ἔστιζον: "tattooed," not "branded," as frequently translated. Runaway or difficult slaves were regularly tattooed with a mark or even whole sentences: cf. Herodas 5.27–28, 65–66, 78–79, esp. 65–66, κέλευσον ἐλθεῖν τὸν στίκτην ἔχοντα ῥαφίδας καὶ μέλαν (needles and ink), and the references in comedy: Ar. *Birds* 760, δραπέτης ἐστιγμένος; Eupolis (F259 K.), ἐγὼ δέ γε στίξω σε βελόναισιν τρισίν, etc. Aeschines 2.79 calls Demosthenes ἀνδραποδώδης, καὶ μόνον οὐκ ἐστιγμένος αὐτόμολος; schol. to 2.83 (pp. 56–57 Dindorf) explains that some had written κάτεχέ με. φεύγω. Cf. also Hesychius s.v. Γράμματα ἑπτά. ΔΡΑΠΕΤΑ. Other slaves were marked simply for safekeeping; cf. Xen. *Vect.* 4.21, suggesting that public slaves, σεσημασμένα τῷ δημοσίῳ σημάντρῳ, be let out for hire. Cf. Andocides fr. 5; Bion at Diog. Laert. 4.46.

By Xerxes' order, the Persians ἔστιξαν στίγματα βασιλήια the Thebans who had offered earth and water but then fought against him at Thermopylae (Hdt. 7.233.2; cf. Hdt. 7.35, a similar desire to tattoo the Hellespont). Although frequently described as branding, this is clearly the practice of tattooing a runaway. If the story is true, the Samians would have been considered Athenian property and therefore could be marked with the state emblem—but at the same time reminded of their similarity to runaway slaves, a remarkable assimilation of Athenian methods to Persian. The Samians retaliated in kind. Similarly, Athenian prisoners at Syracuse were tattooed with a horse, a Syracusan symbol (*Nic.* 29.2). Aristotle's *Constitution of the Samians*, instead, explained that the tattooed Samians were slaves who had been enrolled as citizens (F575 Rose). Cf. Jones 1987; and the references collected by Headlam 1966 in his notes on Herodas 5.

According to P.'s version (also found in Photius s.v. τὰ Σαμίων ὑποπτεύεις), the Athenians mocked the Samian prisoners by marking them with a Samian symbol, and the Samians retaliated. P. has certainly erred here, reversing the truth. The correct version (Photius and Suda s.v. Σαμίων ὁ δῆμος; Aelian VH 2.9) says that the Athenians marked the Samians with an Athenian owl, and the Samians used the samaina. This story, like that at 28.2, is from Duris (FGrHist 76 F66: a πλάσμα Δούριδος, according to Photius). Both stories attest to the bitterness of feeling generated by the war (cf. Busolt, Gr. Gesch. 2.1:548n. 4). The examples cited suggest that the story is at least partially true, though many historians are skeptical, as most recently Karavites 1985, 54–56. Jacoby (FGrHist ad loc.) thinks that P. did not use Duris directly here, but that Duris may have quoted the verse from Aristophanes. On the other hand, P. may have found the citation to Duris in a grammarian's commentary to Aristophanes. But other combinations are possible.

γλαῦκας: the standard symbol of Athens, found on coins of all periods: cf. Ar. Birds 1106–8, speaking of "owls from Laurion."

σάμαινα ναῦς: the typical Samian ship. P.'s description is our fullest, but cf. also Choerilus of Samos, νηῦς δὲ τις ὠκυπόρος Σαμίη, ὑὸς εἶδος ἔχουσα (F6, p. 269 Kinkel 1877); Hesychius s.v. Σαμιακὸς τρόπος; Photius and Suda s.v. Σαμίων ὁ δῆμος. The pig-nosed prow (ὑόπρωρος) with its ram is clearly seen on tetradrachms made by the Samian exiles at Zankle ca. 494–489 (Barron 1966, 6 and plates VI–VII; Morrison and Willams 1968, 111 and plate 20e) and probably is the same as that of the pirate ship illustrated in Casson 1958, plates V–VI. The mark used would presumably be the prow of the ship only, as on the coins.

τὸ σίμωμα: "the upturned part, the bow." The word is rare, and found in P. only here. In schol. Pindar Olym. 7.35 it is given as a word for a ship's ram.

φορτοφορεῖν: Coraes' emendation ("carry freight"), a word otherwise unattested and, although accepted by Ziegler and Flacelière, unnecessary. Read with mss. *ποντοπορεῖν*: "to sail across the sea, rather than coasting"; cf. *Dion* 25.2. It was usual for a fast ship, like a trireme, to put into land every evening. The word is poetic: cf. *Od.* 11.11, etc.

Polycrates: tyrant of Samos, ca. 540–522, exceedingly prosperous until killed by the Persian satrap Oroetes. Cf. the "Samian stories" in Hdt. 3.39–60, 120–25.

λέγουσι: that is, grammarians and scholiasts, such as those used by Photius and the Suda. This verse in iambic trimeter (F64 K. = 71 K.A.) comes from Aristophanes' *Babylonians*, produced in 426. It was spoken as the Babylonians emerged from work in a mill, and clearly compared the Samians to slaves. The line is cited, with various explanations, by Hesychius, Photius, and the Suda. On this line and its meaning in the context of the play see Welsh 1983, esp. 138–44.

ἠνίχθαι: "referred to indirectly" (*αἰνίσσομαι*).

πολυγράμματος: literally "many-lettered." Elsewhere used by P. to mean (ironically) "well-read, learned" (*Symp.* 676E, *Adv. Colot.* 1121F), but here apparently "much written-on, with many designs." Photius reports other interpretations: a reference to enrolling slaves as citizens at Samos, or to the Samian alphabet of twenty-four letters, which later replaced the old Attic twenty-one-letter alphabet.

27.1

δ'οὖν: resumptive after the digression (cf. 26.2).

ἐβοήθει: Thuc. 1.117.2 reports that before the battle another forty ships from Athens under Thucydides, Hagnon, and Phormio, twenty more under Tlepolemus and Anticles, and thirty from

Chios and Lesbos had arrived, making the total 160 Athenian and 55 allied ships—an overwhelming force—although some may have been reassigned or returned home.

περιετείχιζε: for the second time; the Samians had already been besieged with a three-part wall before Pericles left (Thuc. 1.116.2).

δαπάνη . . . βουλόμενος: P.'s own explanation, to emphasize the themes of Pericles' ἀσφάλεια and control of the citizens (κατασχεῖν in 27.2; cf. 21.1). Diodorus however, has Pericles συνεχεῖς ποιού-μενος προσβολάς (12.28.2).

27.2

ἔργον ἦν: "it was a difficult task"; cf. Alc. 15.2, Ant. 40.4, Thes. 27.2.

⟨εἰς⟩ ὀκτὼ μέρη διελών: "dividing (the whole army) into eight parts." Although the Greek idiom can take a double object, seeing διαιρεῖν as separating the (preexisting) parts (as in Plato Polit. 283D, διέλωμεν αὐτὴν δύο μέρη; Dem. 14.17, ἑκάστην διελεῖν κελεύω πέντε μέρη), P. regularly uses εἰς. Cf. Num. 16.6, Sol. 13.1, Cam. 7.3, etc. Athenian armies were occasionally divided by lot among commanders (e.g., Thuc. 6.42.1, 6.62.1, 8.30.1), but this reference to rotating duty during a siege is unusual. (Cf., however, the reference to rotating work crews at Plataea, Thuc. 2.75.3.) In this case, each day one group of the eight would take a day off, their λευκὴ ἡμέρα. The anecdote may be invented, but such a regular system would in fact have made the siege more effective. The white bean drawn from among the black ones was the regular means of sortition at Athens: e.g., Hdt. 6.109.2; IG I² 41.19 (= IG I³ 41.105, the Hestiaea decree); Ar. Birds 1022; Thuc. 8.66.1; And. 1.96; ML 40, ll. 9, 13 (= IG I³ 14, Athenian democracy at Erythrae). Of the precise mechanism no more is known than P. tells us. Cf. the late statement in Lexicon Cantabrigiense 671, κυαμεύονται. κληροῦνται. ἐχρῶντο γὰρ κυάμοις οἱ Ἀττικοὶ ἐν ταῖς κληρώσεσι τῶν ἀρχῶν μέλασι καὶ λευκοῖς. καὶ ὁ τὸν λευκὸν ἀναρπάσας ἦρχεν; Gilbert 1895, 218; Rhodes, CAAP 149.

τρυχομένων: "were exhausted, consumed (with effort)." A poetic word, but cf. Thuc. 1.126.8, *τρυχόμενοι τῇ προσεδρίᾳ*. P. usually employs the compounds with *ἀπό* and *κατά*.

27.3

λευκὴν ἡμέραν: a proverbial expression for a lucky day. Cf. Photius s.v.: *ἡ ἀγαθὴ καὶ ἐπ' εὐφροσύνῃ [ἡμέρᾳ]· Εὔπολις Κόλαξι* (F174 K. = 182 K.A.). The expression also occurred in Menander's *Leucadia* (F315 K.) and elsewhere. Cf. Pearson 1917 and Radt 1977 on Sophocles F6. In various collections of proverbs (cf. Leutsch and Schneidewin 1839) it is explained by the custom of marking good days and bad with white and black pebbles, variously attributed to the Thracians (Pliny *NH* 7.131), the Scythians (Phylarchus, *FGrHist* 81 F83), and even the Athenians (*Mantissa Proverbiorum* 2.19). P. is the only writer to give the explanation found here: is it his own deduction, or taken over from a scholiast, perhaps one to Eupolis F174 K. = 182 K.A., or from Ephorus? The expression was also used of one day of the Choes festival at Athens, which was unlucky for citizens but lucky for slaves: cf. Pfeiffer's note to Callimachus F178.2. Compare the Latin expression *dies candidiore nota*, Catullus 68.148, 107.6; cf. Horace *Carm.* 1.36.10 with the note of Nisbet and Hubbard 1970.

Ephorus: *FGrHist* 70 F194. Cf. Diod. 12.28.3, *κατεσκεύασε δὲ καὶ μηχανὰς πρῶτος τῶν πρὸ αὐτοῦ τούς τε ὀνομαζομένους κριοὺς καὶ χελώνας, Ἀρτέμωνος τοῦ Κλαζομενίου κατασκευάσαντος*. Ephorus was especially interested in inventions, as here of siege equipment (*μηχαναῖς*). Cf. F12, 54, 59, 115. P. is more interested in the story of Artemon than in the details of the machines. Despite Thucydides' silence, special devices probably were used (such as the "tortoises" attributed to Artemon), as later at Potidaea (Thuc. 2.76.4) and elsewhere.

Artemon: an engineer from Clazomenae who invented the "tortoise" to cover a ram (Diod. 12.28.3; Pliny *NH* 7.202) and perhaps the *artemon* mentioned by Vitruvius (10.2.9), variously made contemporary to Pericles (Diod. 12.28.3; Leutsch and Schneidewin 1839, 1:441) and to Aristides (schol. Ar. *Ach.* 850). The latter two sources, like P., say he was lame and needed to be carried about to sites, whence his nickname. However, the nickname had already been given by the poet Anacreon, a contemporary of Polycrates of Samos (F27; cf. F43 Page 1962), to another Artemon, whose soft living is described by Heraclides (see below, 27.4) and Chamaeleon (Athen. 12.533E). Most probably a confusion in the tradition has given the nickname also to the later Artemon. If not, the later Artemon would have been given his nickname on the basis of his earlier namesake. Pliny (*NH* 34.56) mentions a statue of the later Artemon by Polyclitus.

παρ⟨ασχ⟩όντος: Ziegler's emendation for πάροντος, which does not explain Artemon's presence. Other verbs are possible: D. A. Russell in a personal note suggests παρασκευάζοντος, which would fit the sense well (cf. Diod. 12.28.3). Conomis 1975, 85, defends πάροντος.

τά κατεπείγοντα: "pressing matters." Cf. *Alex.* 72.1, *Brut.* 36.1, *Pel.* 27.1.

27.4

Heraclides: an academic philosopher from Heraclea on the Black Sea, who hoped to succeed Speusippus in 339 as head of the Academy but was rejected and returned to Heraclea. His writings reveal wide interests: see Diog. Laert. 5.86–93; Wehrli 1953; *RE* suppl. XI (1968) 675–86; Gottschalk 1980. This is Wehrli F60, assigned to the περὶ ἡδονῆς. Heraclides is interested in the luxury of the earlier Artemon.

τοῖς Ἀνακρέοντος ποιήμασιν: The lines are quoted by Athenaeus (12.533E) via Chamaeleon (F27 Page 1962):

ξανθῇ δ' Εὐρυπύλῃ μέλει
ὁ περιφόρητος Ἀρτέμων.

The phrase was well known in the scholiastic tradition, as Aristophanes puns on it at *Ach.* 850 with περιπόνηρος Ἀρτέμων: cf. schol. ad loc. and references in Page.

ἡλικίαις: "generations."

τῷ βίῳ: dat. of respect; cf. note to 3.3.

φησι: sc. Heraclides.

ὑπερεχόντων: cf. Ar. *Birds* 1508, τουτὶ λαβών μου τὸ σκιάδειον ὑπέρεχε.

ἐν κλινιδίῳ κρεμαστῷ: "in a hanging litter." What was unusual was not the litter per se, but its being hung from the poles so that it was as low as possible. On the virtue of a hanging litter (as opposed to an ordinary stretcher) cf. the medical writer Oribasius at 6.23.6, quoting Antyllus: τὸ διὰ τοῦ κρεμαστοῦ κλινιδίου καὶ πρὸ τροφῆς καὶ ἐπὶ τροφῇ χρήσιμον. He recommends for a fever a nice outing, either before or after eating.

παρὰ τὴν γῆν αὐτήν: "close to the ground."

28.1

ἐνάτῳ . . . μηνί: cf. Thuc. 1.117.3, ἐξεπολιορκήθησαν ἐνάτῳ μηνί. According to the chronology of Fornara 1979, this would be ca. January 439, eight months after the battle of Tragia and the beginning of the siege. Meritt 1984, 129–30, places it in midsummer 439. The victory was unusually rapid: the sieges of Thasos and Potidaea each took more than two years. Pericles must have prosecuted it energetically (the rotation scheme and siege machines would have helped). No mention is made of help from the democrats within the walls, a common reason for winning a city. But the Samians would also have been hindered by the lack of planning for the revolt. At *Comp. Per.–Fab.* 2.1 P. compares the defeat of Samos with Fabius' capture of Tarentum.

παραστάντων: "surrender, come to terms"; LSJ s.v. παρίστημι B.III.

τὰ τείχη καθεῖλε κτλ: cf. Thuc. 1.117.3, τεῖχός τε καθελόντες καὶ ὁμήρους δόντες καὶ ναῦς παραδόντες καὶ χρήματα τὰ ἀναλωθέντα ταξάμενοι κατὰ χρόνους ἀποδοῦναι. The Athenians regularly removed the walls of cities that had revolted or that they distrusted: cf. the cases of Thasos (Thuc. 1.101.3), Mytilene (3.50.1), and Chios (4.51); cf. also the order to Potidaea, Thuc. 1.56.2; Gomme, *HCT* 1:18. The Ionian cities were generally unwalled (Thuc. 3.33.2), presumably as a result of Athenian policy: cf. the verse of Teleclides in *Per.* 16.2; Meiggs, *AE* 149–51; Andrewes in Gomme, *HCT* 5:35–36. Thasos and Mytilene likewise lost their ships after revolts, and Thucydides (1.99.3) suggests that it was the usual practice, either after a defeat or by agreement. Neither the size of the reparations paid by the Samians, nor the time they were given to pay, is known. The literary sources are discordant but can be emended to agree on 1,200 talents as the cost of the war: Isoc. 15.111, ἐπὶ Σάμον στρατεύσας, ἣν Περικλῆς . . . ἀπὸ διακοσίων [νεῶν] καὶ χιλίων ταλάντων κατεπολέμησε; Diod. 12.28.3, ἐπράξατο τοὺς Σαμίους τὰς εἰς τὴν πολιορκίαν γεγενημένας δαπάνας, τιμησάμενος αὐτὰς ταλάντων ⟨χιλίων⟩ διακοσίων; Nepos *Timotheus* 1, *Athenienses mille et ducenta talenta consumpserant.* A fragmentary inscription, *IG* I³ 363 (= *IG* I² 293, ML 55), preserves a summary of the accounts for the war with sums for three years—128 + , 368 + , and 908 + talents—and a grand total of 1,400 + talents (on which see most recently Fornara 1979, 7–19). The fact that the literary figure, even if restored correctly, is less than that in the inscribed account shows that there were different ways of calculating the cost, even in antiquity. P.'s words suggest that a large sum was paid at once and the rest over a number of years, contrary to the suggestion in *ATL* (3:4–35) of a 50-talent annual payment for twenty-six years, to 413. It seems most unlikely that the reparation payments would be stretched out so long or be so small. Thasos and Aegina were regularly assessed 30 talents' tribute. Moreover, we do not know whether the Athenians asked the full cost of the war, or how they calculated it. Thasos may also have paid reparations after surrendering: cf. Thuc. 1.101.3, χρήματά τε ὅσα ἔδει ἀποδοῦναι αὐτίκα ταξάμενοι καὶ τὸ λοιπὸν φέρειν, which suggests a special heavy payment at first, together with the loss of mainland territories and the mines. Until 447/46 Thasos' quota was only three talents per year. Cf. also Nicias' offer to pay reparation to Syracuse, Thuc. 7.83.2.

ταξάμενοι κατοίσειν: "having been assessed to pay"; cf. Thuc. 1.99.3, χρήματα ἐτάξαντο ἀντὶ τῶν νεῶν τὸ ἱκνούμενον ἀνάλωμα φέρειν, 1.101.3 (cited above), and 3.50.2. For καταφέρειν, the compound for the simple φέρειν, cf. Aem. 29.2, προσέταξεν αὐτοῖς . . . ἡμέρᾳ ῥητῇ καταφέρειν; Polyb. 1.62.9, 33.11.6. The Samians did not pay tribute in the period for which quota lists are extant. The future infinitive is used as with verbs of swearing or promising: cf. Polybius 18.7.7, ταξάμενοι . . . πάλιν ἀπαντήσειν; MT 136.

ὁμήρους: on the taking of hostages cf. note to 25.2.

Fragments of an alliance with Samos have been preserved, ML 56 (IG I² 50, I³ 48); cf. Fornara 1979, 14–18; Breslin 1980; Bridges 1980; Meritt 1984. Diodorus 12.28.4 says that Pericles restored the democracy, which is what one would expect. Some of the wealthy fled to the mainland, where they established a base at Anaea (Thuc. 3.19.2, 3.33.2, 4.75.1, 8.19.1). Nevertheless a bloody revolution deposed an oligarchic government and set up a democracy in summer 412 (Thuc. 8.21). Diodorus may therefore be wrong, and the Athenians permitted an oligarchic arrangement in 439, or there was a change in constitution over the years, perhaps after the disaster in Sicily (cf. Diod. 13.34.2). Andrewes reviews the question thoroughly in Gomme, HCT 5:44–47.

28.2

Duris: FGrHist 76 F67. See the Introduction, 3.2.e. His enmity toward Athens (28.3) was a result of the hostility that had existed between the two cities for generations. Timotheus had captured Samos in 365, and the Samians were exiled from their city from 365 to 321. See Habicht 1957; Shipley 1987, 138, 175–81.

τούτοις ἐπιτραγῳδεῖ: "adds to this in tragic style." Cf. Artax. 18.7, ἀλλὰ ταῦτα μὲν οὐκ ἄδηλον ὡς ἐπιτραγῳδεῖ [sc. Ctesias] τῇ Κλεάρχου μνήμῃ, and for the simple verb Dem. 21.2, ὡς γράφει καὶ τραγῳδεῖ Θεόπομπος. Duris' work was an outstanding example of "tragic history," which aimed, as here, to rouse the reader to pity and fear; see the Introduction, 3.2.

ὠμότητα: "savagery, brutal cruelty."

οὔτε Θουκυδίδης κτλ.: cf. the similar criticism of a story of Duris in *Alc.* 32.2, *οὔτε Θεόπομπος οὔτ' Ἔφορος οὔτε Ξενοφῶν γέγραφεν.* This kind of negative statement indicates that P. has read these authors. In referring to Aristotle he must be thinking of the *Constitution of the Samians* (this is F578 Rose).

ἀλλ' οὐδὲ ἀληθεύειν ἔοικεν: "Besides, he does not even give the appearance of telling the truth." P. finds the tale not only exaggerated but implausible. At 36.8 *ἀλλ' οὐδὲ* follows *οὐ μὴν*: "Indeed, he did not . . . , nor yet. . . ." Cf. Denniston, 21–22, 338.

ὡς ἄρα: introduces a reported statement with scepticism, or at least disclaiming responsibility; cf. Denniston, 38–39.

τοὺς τριηράρχους καὶ τοὺς ἐπιβάτας: Both the trierarchs and the hoplite soldiers on shipboard would have belonged to the wealthier class and thus have been either actual or potential oligarchs.

σανίσι προσδήσας: "binding to planks." The punishment itself, harsh though it is, fits a standard procedure. The Athenian name apparently was *ἀποτυμπανισμός*, once explained as beating with sticks (on the basis of Bekker 1814, 1:438, ll. 12–15) but now reinterpreted on the basis of seventeen skeletons found at Phalerum (see Keramopoullos 1923). The skeletons, still strapped to wood with iron collars and irons around wrists and ankles, had been buried in a common grave, presumably after death by exposure or strangulation. Although these date to the seventh century, the punishment is similar to the exposure of the Persian Artayctes (Hdt. 7.33, 9.120), of Prometheus, and of Mnesilochus in Aristophanes' *Thesmophoriazusae.* The punishment was painful and quite possibly of long duration, as the victim endured exposure to weather, birds, and insects if he were not suspended in such a way that he died of suffocation or strangulation first. It was the normal punishment for traitors and a wide class of *κακοῦργοι*, including thieves caught red-handed. See Gernet 1981, 252–76 (originally Gernet 1924); R. J. Bonner and G. Smith 1938, 2:279–87. This explanation of *apotympanismos* and its association with this passage of P. is rejected by K. Latte, *RE* s.v. Todesstrafe, suppl. VII (1940) 1606–7, wrongly, I believe. The existence of this punishment makes it likely that Duris' story is at least partially true. The men might have survived some time, if not actually ten days, if they were not hung by the arms, and this final killing may have been considered an act of mercy. The exact judicial basis for *apotympanismos* in this case is uncertain (treason?), nor is it clear why they would have been exposed at Miletus, unless they had been captured in the battle of Tragia, while returning from an attack on that city. Such selective punishment was certainly less harsh than that voted against Mytilene a decade later, at the time of the Mytilenean revolt (Thuc. 3.36.2, 50.1). Execution of captives was not uncommon after a particularly harsh siege; see Ducrey 1968, 208–15. P., on the other hand, finds such cruelty incompatible with his notion of Pericles' philosophic calm, or common humanity. Karavites 1985, 48–53, argues unconvincingly that Duris misreports an action taken against the Samians in 412.

συγκόψαντας: refers to the Athenians implied as the subject of ἀνελεῖν and προβαλεῖν.

προβαλεῖν: cf. *Them.* 22.2, οὖ νῦν τὰ σώματα τῶν θανατουμένων οἱ δήμιοι προβάλλουσι. The ἀκήδευτα need not mean "unburied," but rather "lacking in proper rites and honors." The bodies at Phalerum (see above) had been thrown in a mass grave, still attached to their planks. Cf. Joseph. *AJ* 6.14.8 (375).

28.3

μὲν οὖν: summing up the topic of Duris, before moving back with δὲ in 28.4 to Pericles. Cf. Denniston, 471–72. P. firmly rejects Duris' authority, on the basis of his habits of exaggeration.

κρατεῖν . . . ἀληθείας: "to keep his narrative based on truth, to maintain a true narrative." For κρατέω with the accusative in this sense of control cf. *De tu. san.* 125F, τὰ γὰρ εὐτελῆ κρατεῖ τὴν ὄρεξιν ἐπὶ τῶν φυσικῶν μέτρων. Here ἐπὶ = "with regard to, within the limits of"; cf. LSJ s.v. A.III.3 and Dem. 18.17, οὔτε δικαίως οὔτ' ἐπ ἀληθείας οὐδεμιᾶς εἰρημένα.

μάλλον . . . ἐνταῦθα: "on this occasion all the more," as he does have an ἴδιον πάθος, the Athenian defeat of his native Samos.

δεινῶσαι: "make more terrible, exaggerate"; cf. Thuc. 8.74.3, ἐπὶ τὸ μεῖζον πάντα δεινώσας. The verb is found only here in P., as in Thucydides, but δείνωσις is a technical rhetorical term for exaggeration: cf. LSJ s.v.; Ant. 14.7 (Antony's speech over Caesar's body), ἐνέμειξε τοῖς ἐπαίνοις οἶκτον ἅμα καὶ δείνωσιν ἐπὶ τῷ πάθει; Flam. 18.10, Ti. Gracch. 2.3.

28.4

ταφάς: for the Athenian custom of public burial of the ashes of those fallen in war see Thuc. 2.34 and Jacoby 1944. Stelai were also set up with the names of the dead. ML 48 (= *IG* I² 943) has been thought to belong to 440/39 (e.g., Tod, *GHI* 1:48), as it mentions casualties from Byzantium, which revolted with Samos (Thuc. 1.115.5, 117.3), but the casualty list for that year certainly would have included those from Samos. It is better to associate it with Pericles' Chersonesan campaign; cf. 19.1.

τὸν λόγον: The funeral speech required of the ceremony became a standard genre, of which other specimens are Hyperides' (or. 6) and those attributed to Lysias (or. 2) and Demosthenes (or. 60). Plato's *Menexenus* reports at length one supposed to have been composed by Aspasia. The Samian funeral oration was the one connected with Pericles in antiquity (cf. note to 8.9), though Thucydides (2.35–46) credits him with a brilliant oration in 431, now simply called "Pericles' Funeral Oration." Pericles probably delivered others as well. For the genre cf. Soffel 1974, Loraux 1986.

28.5

στεφάνοις ἀνέδουν κτλ.: Both crowns and fillets of red wool were signs of victory, bound on the victor by the president of the games or by his admirers: cf. Paus. 6.20.19, a statue of Hippodameia, ταινίαν τε ἔχουσα καὶ ἀναδεῖν τὸν Πέλοπα μέλλουσα ἐπὶ τῇ νίκῃ, and Plat. *Symp.* 212E, Alcibiades arrives at Agathon's house ἐστεφανωμένον αὐτὸν κιττοῦ τέ τινι στεφάνῳ δασεῖ καὶ ταινίας ἔχοντα ἐπὶ τῆς κεφαλῆς πάνυ πολλάς, and says ἥκω ἐπὶ τῇ κεφαλῇ ἔχων τὰς ταινίας, ἵνα ἀπὸ τῆς ἐμῆς κεφαλῆς τὴν τοῦ σοφωτάτου καὶ καλλίστου κεφαλὴν ἐὰν εἴπω οὑτωσὶ ἀναδήσω. See also two red-figure vases, plates 56 and 58 in Yalouris 1976, and his description of the awards, pp. 134–41.

For this sort of welcome for a general cf. Thuc. 4.121.1 (Brasidas at Scione), τὰ τ' ἄλλα καλῶς ἐδέξαντο καὶ δημοσίᾳ μὲν χρυσῷ στεφάνῳ ἀνέδησαν ὡς ἐλευθεροῦντα τὴν Ἑλλάδα, ἰδίᾳ δὲ ἐταινίουν τε καὶ προσήρχοντο ὥσπερ ἀθλητῇ, and as an omen, Plut. *Tim.* 8.3.

28.6

Elpinice: cf. note to 10.6. The source of the anecdote is unknown, perhaps Stesimbrotus.

ὅς: refers to Pericles. It is unusual to have a vocative as the antecedent for the relative. For this reason Ziegler added ⟨σου⟩ after θαυμαστά. Sansone 1988 suggests instead ⟨τὰ σὰ⟩, citing examples of relatives referring back to pronouns. The emendation might be supported by 320F, also in a quotation: λαμπρὰ μὲν τὰ σὰ ἔργα καὶ μεγάλα. But no emendation is necessary: for examples of relatives referring to vocatives see, e.g., Ar. *Clouds* 264; Eur. *Andr.* 1186–87. The lack of expressed antecedent is found with relatives having causal force, as here: cf. the passages cited by Jebb on *Oed. Col.* 263.

συγγενῆ: The Athenians considered that the Ionians, including the Samians, were their kin, descendants of the Athenian king Ion, and immigrants from Attica. On the other hand Pericles might have noted that the Samians were receiving help from the Persians (cf. 25.3, 26.1).

28.7

ἀτρέμα: "without being disturbed, calmly," with μειδιάσας. Common in P., the word here accents the πρᾳότης of his response. Cf. the same phrase at *Alex.* 46.4.

Archilochus: F27 Diehl, 205 West, quoted also by Athenaeus 15.688E. Archilochus, from Paros, lived in the mid-seventh century and wrote iambic and elegiac poetry with a strong personal note, describing love affairs, wars, etc. P. was quite familiar with his work: see Schlaepfer 1950, 30–31. Helmbold and O'Neill 1959 list some twenty-five citations of twenty-two passages. The iambic trimeters, like this one, are frequently abusive. The protasis seems to be omitted: "(If you had sense,) you would not perfume yourself, since you are an old woman." Originally addressed to a woman whom the person scorns, in the Periclean context it implies that (1) Elpinice does not understand her proper position (that is, to keep quiet on such matters; cf. Thuc. 2.45.2; Ar. *Lys.* 507–16) and (2) she can no longer use her beauty as a political weapon (cf. the same point, made in an anecdote set more than twenty years earlier, at 10.2). For a similar poetic quotation to insult an older woman cf. Ar. *Plutus* 1002, πάλαι ποτ' ἦσαν ἄλκιμοι Μιλήσιοι, from Anacreon or Timocreon (cf. Page 1962, 426, 733).

γραῦς: Archilochus would have said γρηῦς.

ἠλείφεο: Athenaeus has ἠλείφετο.

θαυμαστὸν δέ τι καὶ μέγα φρονῆσαι: "in fact he was extraordinarily elated." Θαυμαστὸν, like μέγα, is adverbial; τι weakens its force somewhat; cf. 24.5, σοφήν τινα; 27.4, τρυφερόν τινα.

Ion: *FGrHist* 392 F16; cf. the Introduction, 3.1.b. Jacoby 1947, 13–15, notes that this anecdote could illustrate the ὑπεροψίαν καὶ περιφρόνησιν τῶν ἄλλων ascribed to Pericles by Ion (cf. *Per.* 5.3) but suggests that this is a distortion of a comparison from Pericles' funeral speech, where he would have been praising the Athenians, not himself.

Ἀγαμέμνονος: The comparison of contemporary victories with the Trojan War was not unusual: cf. Herodotus' suggestion (1.3–4) that the Trojan War is parallel to, and even a cause of, the Persian Wars; Thucydides' analysis of the Trojan War (1.9–12), showing it less important than the Peloponnesian War; and Agesilaus' attempt to sacrifice at Aulis before sailing to Asia (Xen. *Hell.* 3.4.3; Plut. *Ages.* 6.6–11). One of the epigrams on the herms set up by Cimon after the fall of Eion compared the Athenian leader at Troy, Menestheus, with contemporary Athenians (*Cim.* 7.6). Note that P. already knew this anecdote when he wrote *De gloria Atheniensium*, usually considered an early work (cf. *De glor. Ath.* 350E, καὶ Περικλῆς ἐννέα μησὶ Σαμίους καταστρεψάμενος ἐφρόνει τοῦ Ἀγαμέμνονος μεῖζον ἔτει δεκάτῳ τὴν Τροίαν ἑλόντος). Understand ἑλόντος with Ἀγαμέμνονος as well.

28.8

οὐκ ἦν ἄδικος ἡ ἀξίωσις: "the evaluation was not unfair," a Thucydidean expression (3.9.2, καὶ οὐκ ἄδικος αὕτη ἡ ἀξίωσίς ἐστιν), but used to express P.'s own judgment on the Samian campaign.

ἀδηλότητα: "uncertainty"; cf. 18.1, πόλλην ἀδηλότητα καὶ κίνδυνον.

Thucydides: 8.76.4, [Samos] ἤ παρ' ἐλάχιστον δὴ ἦλθε τὸ Ἀθηναίων κράτος τῆς θαλάσσης, ὅτε ἐπολέμησαν, ἀφελέσθαι. P. reinforces his opinion with a Thucydidean quote far removed from the historian's account of the Samian War—presumably remembered or jotted down because a striking sentiment, without direct relation to the *Pericles*. Perhaps another historian, Duris or Ephorus, had already quoted Thucydides in this context, but noting such phrases would be standard practice in rhetorical training.

παρ' ἐλάχιστον ἦλθε: "came within an ace of"; cf. LSJ s.v. παρὰ C.III.5.b.

29–32

Pericles and the Responsibility for the Peloponnesian War. The subject of this section is not the causes of the war in general, but Pericles' personal role, so that Thucydides' analysis is for the most part beside the issue. There are two main divisions: 29.1–30.1, the antecedents of the war and Pericles' decision not to revoke the Megarian decree; and 30.2–32.6, alternative explanations for Pericles' intransigence concerning the Megarian decree. In the first part, the Corcyrean alliance leads to the complaints of the Spartan allies, of which the most important is the Megarian decree (because the Spartans demanded its revocation as the price of peace). The second part contains three versions of the antecedents of the Megarian decree. The sequences of the three versions clearly overlap, but P. does not fix the beginning or end of any.

The selection and disposition of this section is P.'s, using Thucydides, Ephorus, Stesimbrotus, and others not named, probably including Craterus' *Collection of Decrees*. The narrative frame is Thucydidean, from the decision to aid Corcyra to the repulse of the Spartan ultimatum, with insertions on Pericles' hostility to Cimon's sons (29.1–2), the antecedents of the Megarian decree (30.1–4), and the trials (31.1–32.6). P. considered Pericles responsible for the war (29.8, 31.1, 32.6) and saw this as a charge against him (*Comp.* 3.1), but not so great as to negate his other good actions. The bibliography on the causes of the war, especially the Megarian decree, is enormous. Besides the articles on particular points cited in these notes, the following general studies are useful for bibliography or presentation of overall problems: Busolt, *Gr. Gesch.* 3.2:758–853; Andrewes 1959; Kagan, *OPW* 205–374; de Ste. Croix, *OPW* passim; Sealey 1975.

29.1–3

The Alliance with Corcyra. The prehistory of the quarrel between Corinth and Corcyra over Epidamnus is narrated by Thucydides (1.24.1–31.1; cf. Diod. 12.30.2–5, 31.2–3, 32.1–3, for the years 439/38–437/36). The Corcyrean embassy and Corinthian counterproposal, the Athenian decision, and the battle of Sybota are found in Thuc. 1.31.2–55.2 and Diod. 12.33.1–4 (436/35). Because Thucydides gives no dates and Diodorus' are unreliable, our chronology is a construct based on the known date for the dispatch of Lacedaemonius' ten ships, ca. 10 July 433 (cf. note to 29.1), and the probable date of Sybota in late August or early September 433. The debate in Athens thus would be in May or June 433. The full treatment given the conflict by Thucydides and, based on him, by Diodorus (through Ephorus) contrasts markedly with the silence of the comic writers and orators. Apparently only Thucydides saw the importance of the Corcyrean alliance as an example of the Athenian imperialism that terrified Sparta. P. ignores one of Thucydides' main concerns: the Athenian desire to avoid breaking the treaty, and how the pressure of the situation led the Athenian commanders, against their will, to fight with the Corinthians. See in general Busolt, *Gr. Gesch.* 3.2:761–91; Kagan, *OPW* 223–50; Gomme, *HCT* 1:157–99; Meiggs, *AE* 199–201.

29.1

μετὰ ταῦτα: six years later, in May–June 433.

κυμαίνοντος κτλ.: "as the Peloponnesian War was already beginning to heave and swell." The metaphor refers to the turmoil of waves at sea in a storm; cf. *Ant.* 65.1, *μεγάλῳ πνεύματι κυμαθὲν τὸ πέλαγος*, and *Plat. quaest.* 1005E. P. applies it variously to a wild party (*Symp.* 713E), to the turmoil of a new marriage (*Amat.* 754C), to a battle line (*Pomp.* 69.6), a polis (*Pomp.* 53.7), or the demos (*Num.* 2.5). The general expression permits him to avoid precise dates (cf. 17.1), but Thucydides also states (1.33.3, 44.2) that there was a lively expectation of war even before Sybota. P. frequently uses sea imagery for political affairs: see Fuhrmann 1964, 234–37. However, as the parallels above suggest, here he is thinking more of a gathering storm than of the very common image of the ship of state (on which see Nisbet and Hubbard 1970, 179–80, on Horace *Odes* 1.14).

τοῦ Πελοποννησιακοῦ πολέμου: The term first appears in the first century B.C., used by Cicero, Diodorus, Strabo, etc. Thucydides speaks of "the war of the Peloponnesians and the Athenians" (1.1.1, 2.1.1). The later usage reflects the Athenian viewpoint; cf. de Ste. Croix, *OPW* 294–95.

ἔπεισε: Only P. ascribes the initiative explicitly to Pericles. As often, he credits a collective action to the statesman whose life he is writing (cf. note to 21.2). The Athenians decided specifically for a defensive alliance (*ἐπιμαχία*) rather than a full alliance (*συμμαχία*) in the hope that this would keep Corcyra out of the Peloponnesian sphere without breaking the treaty (Thuc. 1.44). The two Corcyrean ambassadors to Athens, whose graves, marked by stele and epigram, are found in the Kerameikos, may have belonged to this embassy: see *IG* II² 5224, with Knigge 1972.

ἀποστεῖλαι βοηθείαν: cf. Thuc. 1.45.1, *ἀπέστειλαν βοηθούς*.

προσλαβεῖν . . . νῆσον: "bring into their camp an island furnished with a strong naval force." The vocabulary echoes the debate in

Thucydides: cf. 1.33.3, προκαταλαμβάνοντας; 36.1, προσλαβεῖν; 36.3, προκαταλήψονται; 44.2, ναυτικὸν ἔχουσαν τοσοῦτον. The Corcyrean fleet was the second in Greece, after the Athenian, with 120 triremes (Thuc. 1.25.4).

ὅσον οὐδέπω: "very little short of, almost." The expression ὅσον οὐ (οὔπω, οὐδέπω) is common in P. with an infinitive or participle (cf. Alc. 14.3, 25.4, etc.) but here echoes Thuc. 1.36.1, τὸν μέλλοντα καὶ ὅσον οὐ παρόντα πόλεμον.

ἐκπεπολεμωμένων: cf. note to 22.1.

ἀπέστειλε . . . Λακεδαιμόνιον: cf. Thuc. 1.45.1–2, δέκα ναῦς αὐτοῖς ἀπέστειλαν βοηθούς· ἐστρατήγει δὲ αὐτῶν Λακεδαιμόνιός τε ὁ Κίμωνος καὶ ὁ Διότιμος ὁ Στρομβίχου καὶ Πρωτέας ὁ Ἐπικλέους. An inscription records the payments made by the treasurers of Athena for this and the following squadron (ML 61 = IG I³ 364). The record for the first squadron uses demotics rather than patronymics, but also names Lacedaemonius first: παρέδοσα]ν στρατεγοῖς ἐς Κόρκυραν τοῖς / [πρότοις ἐκ]πλέοσι Λακεδαιμονίοι Λακιά/[δει, Προτέαι] Αἰχσονεῖ, Διοτίμοι Εὐονυμεῖ (ll. 7–9). Lacedaemonius was one of the hipparchs when an equestrian statue group was dedicated on the Acropolis from spoils of the enemy (IG I² 400; cf. Raubitschek 1949, no. 135), but nothing else is known of him, not even whether he continued his father's rivalry with Pericles.

οἷον ἐφυβρίζων: "as if mocking him," that is, by using his power to put Lacedaemonius in an awkward position. The phrase is common in the Lives for this sort of insulting behavior: cf. Cam. 28.6, Cat. Mai. 18.1, Phil. 16.6, Mar. 8.6, Lys. 5.1, 23.7, and (with ὥσπερ) Agis 13.4. Thucydides stresses the Athenians' fear of breaking the treaty (1.45.3); they may have felt that Lacedaemonius would be least likely to do so. However, P.'s version, emphasizing the personal element, reveals another facet of the incident: Lacedaemonius did not wish to go (μὴ βουλόμενον). P. derived his knowledge of Cimon's children from Stesimbrotus (see below, note to 29.2). Whether this interpretation is also from him, or P.'s own inference, is uncertain. Unlike modern apologists P. did not con-

sider it unnatural for Pericles, or he would have said so, or suppressed the incident entirely. He includes it to give additional
insight into Pericles' character, reminding us of the importance of
personal rivalry. On possible Athenian (Periclean?) motivation for
the weak support of Corcyra see Stadter 1983.

29.2

ὡς ἄν: for this usage with the optative, combining potential and
final (purpose) constructions, see *MT* 329 and p. 401, and cf.
Aem. 32.5, *Pel.* 34.2, *Cim.* 12.2. It is common in Herodotus and
Xenophon.

προσδιαβληθείη κτλ.: "the family would be criticized even more for
its Laconism"; προς-, "in addition." For εἰς with διαβάλλω cf. 13.15,
Cic. 25.4; Thuc. 8.88. The subject seems to waver between Lacedaemonius, just mentioned, and οἶκος, which fits better with the
plurals in the following sentence.

κολούων: "humiliate, discredit, put down." Initially of curtailing
something, in P. the word especially means curtailing someone's
ambition or pride: cf. *Alc.* 34.5, κομιδῇ κολούσειν καὶ ταπεινώσειν
τὸν Ἆγιν; *Nic.* 6.1, κολούοντα τὸ φρόνημα καὶ τὴν δόξαν; and the
examples given in Holden's note here. For the object, understand
τοὺς Κίμωνος υἱούς.

μηδὲ τοῖς ὀνόμασι κτλ.: "not even their names were legitimate,"
e.g., fully Athenian. After 451 it was necessary for a child to be
born of two citizens to be legitimate (cf. 37.3). All of Cimon's
children were born before this law and were full citizens. But their
foreign mother and foreign names left them vulnerable to insult,
probably not in the 430s, as P. implies, but when Cimon was a rival.

Cimon's marriages and children are difficult to sort out. P. notes
in the *Cimon* (16.1) that according to Stesimbrotus (*FGrHist* 107
F6) he had twins, Lacedaemonius and Eleius, ἐκ γυναικὸς . . .
Κλειτορίας, and adds, διὸ πολλάκις Περικλέα τὸ μητρῷον αὐτοῖς γένος ὀνειδίζειν. However, P. adds, Diodorus the Periegete (*FGrHist*
372 F37) says that these two and a third, Thettalus, were children
of Isodice, a daughter of Euryptolemus and an Alcmeonid. Diodorus wrote about monuments and may have seen grave stelai—

or simply reported what he was told when he visited the family tombs. Cimon did marry Isodice (cf. *Cim.* 4.10) but apparently had other relationships (*Cim.* 4.6–9), and it is reasonable to accept Stesimbrotus' testimony despite the general unreliability of his judgments. Cf. Piccirilli 1982. The woman of Clitor in Arcadia could at that time have been a legitimate wife. (Raubitschek's suggestion, *RE* XVIII, 2, 1942, 2000, that ἐκ γυναικὸς Κλειτορίας is meant obscenely, as a reproach to Isodice, seems to me improbable.) P. is using Stesimbrotus here as in the *Cimon*, but it is not clear that Stesimbrotus considered all three sons children of the Arcadian. Three other sons are ascribed to Isodice—Cimon, Miltiades, and Pisanax (schol. Aristid. 3:515 Dindorf)—of whom P. seems to know nothing. If they existed, they may have died young. All, of course, had good Athenian names.

In 415 Thettalus indicted Alcibiades for profanation of the mysteries (*Alc.* 19.3, 22.4), but he is otherwise unattested. The name perhaps reflects Cimon's connection with Menon of Pharsalus in Thessaly at the time of the Athenian campaign at Eion in 477; cf. Raubitschek 1955b, 288n. 13. According to schol. Aristid. 3:515 Dindorf, Cimon was a proxenus of Thessaly as well as Sparta. On the other hand, Connor 1967 argues that the Thessalian connection came later, suggesting that Thettalus was the son of Isodice, born after Cimon's recall in the later 450s, and that the proxeny belongs to that period. Ἠλεῖος is a corruption found in all our literary texts for Οὔλιος, preserved in fourth-century inscriptions (*IG* II² 1388, ll. 81–82; 1400, l. 66; 1447, l. 16; 1451, l. 16). P. may have found the corruption already in his text of Stesimbrotus. The point of the attack depends on the presence of foreign names in the family, but Thettalus and Lacedaemonius would be sufficient for that. The inclusion of Oulius-Eleius may come from P. or an earlier account. Οὔλιος appears as a name in the early stemma of Cimon's family, the Philiadae, in the genealogy of Pherecydes (*FGrHist* 3 F2) and is a cult name for Apollo (interpreted as "healer"), so that it may have had symbolic associations. On the problem of the name see Jacoby, commentary to *FGrHist* 107 F6; Raubitschek, *RE* s.v. Oulios, XVIII, 2 (1942) 1999–2000. For a full discussion of Cimon's children see Davies, *APF* 304–7.

29.3

κακῶς οὖν ἀκούων: "when he was attacked for this"; cf. 5.2. Thucydides (1.50.5) says that the Athenians sent the additional ships δείσαντες . . . μὴ νικηθῶσιν οἱ Κερκυραῖοι καὶ αἱ σφέτεραι δεκὰ ναῦς ὀλίγαι ἀμύνειν ὦσιν. Diodorus (12.33.2) writes that they had planned from the beginning to send more if necessary.

πρόφασιν τοῖς ἐγκαλοῦσι: "an excuse for those (enemies) who wished to complain," thinking of the Corinthian accusations at Sparta (29.4).

πλείονας: twenty ships, which arrived just as the Corcyreans were retreating and forced the Corinthians to retreat in their turn, according to Thuc. 1.50.5–51.3. For the battle off Corcyra near the Sybota islands see Thuc. 1.48–51; Diod. 12.33.4. The commanders of this second squadron were Glaucon and Andocides according to Thucydides, but Glaucon, Metagenes, and Dracon or Dracontides according to the treasurer's accounts, ML 61, ll. 19–21. We do not know the explanation for the discrepancy: see ML and Gomme, HCT 1:188–90. Apparently Thucydides was mistaken, or an error has entered our manuscripts.

29.4

χαλεπαίνουσι: On this meeting at Sparta in 432 see Thuc. 1.67. P. follows closely Thucydides' list of the allies' complaints. Corinth argued specifically that Athens had broken the treaty. See also their speech before the Spartans, Thuc. 1.68–71. For the Megarians cf. 1.67.4, Μεγαρῆς, δηλοῦντες μὲν καὶ ἕτερα οὐκ ὀλίγα διάφορα, μάλιστα δὲ λιμένων τε εἴργεσθαι τῶν ἐν τῇ Ἀθηναίων ἀρχῇ καὶ τῆς Ἀττικῆς ἀγορᾶς παρὰ τὰς σπονδάς; cf. Diod. 12.39.4. P. has reinforced the complaint with parallelism and doubling: πάσης . . . πάντων; εἴργεσθαι καὶ ἀπελαύνεσθαι; δίκαια καὶ ὅρκους. Cf. de Ste. Croix, OPW 388–91. For another instance of πᾶς used for rhetorical emphasis see 34.3. On the Megarian decree itself see notes to 30.2–4. P. has reordered Thucydides to put the Megarians first after the Corinthians, matching the greater emphasis he gives to the decree as cause of the war.

29.5

Aeginetans: cf. Thuc. 1.67.2, Αἰγινῆται τε φανερῶς μὲν οὐ πρεσβευόμενοι, δεδιότες τοὺς Ἀθηναίους, κρύφα δὲ οὐχ ἥκιστα μετ' αὐτῶν ἐνῆγον τὸν πόλεμον, λέγοντες οὐκ εἶναι αὐτόνομοι κατὰ τὰς σπονδάς. Aegina, a Dorian city, had become a tribute-paying member of the league in the 450s (Thuc. 1.108.4; Diod. 11.78.4) but remained hostile toward Athens: cf. Kagan, OPW 258–59; de Ste. Croix, OPW 333–35; Meiggs, AE 183–84.

ἐποτνιῶντο: "cry ὢ πότνια," in horror, indignation, or entreaty. Although listed as Attic by the grammarian Moeris, the verb is now found only in postclassical prose. P. uses it often, usually in the mouths of women: cf. Caes. 63.9, Cat. Min. 27.2, Ant. 35.3, Artax. 3.6, De adul. et amic. 62D, De Pyth. or. 408A, De garr. 507C.

29.6

Potidaea: see Thuc. 1.56–66; Diod. 12.34.2–5, 37.1. A member of the league that maintained strong ties to Corinth, its mother city, it revolted in 433 when Athens ordered it, after Sybota, to dismantle its walls. The complaint was brought by Corinth (Thuc. 1.67.1, 68.4). See Kagan, OPW 273–85; de Ste. Croix, OPW 79–85; Meiggs, AE 309–10.

ἀποστᾶσα καὶ πολιορκουμένη: translate as "the revolt and siege of Potidaea," as with Latin Caesar mortuus; cf. MT 829b.

29.7

οὐ μὴν ἀλλά: cf. 8.6. Despite the complaints, the Spartans were willing to treat. P. ignores the statement of Thucydides (1.126.1) that they had already decided on war but considered that the embassies would establish a better justification for their decision.

πρεσβειῶν: P. does not distinguish their missions. Thucydides speaks of three (although there may have been more): the first demanding the removal of the "Cylonian curse" (1.126.1–2, 127.1–3), treated by P. at 33.1–2; the second stating a series of complaints but focusing particularly on the Megarian decree as the one obstacle to peace (1.139.1–2); and the third, an ultimatum demanding that the Greek cities be left αὐτόνομοι (1.139.3), not mentioned by Plutarch. Cf. also Diod. 12.39.4 and Ar. *Ach.* 536–37 on the Spartan requests to repeal the Megarian decree. On the diplomatic exchanges see Nesselhauf 1934; Adcock and Mosley 1975, 42–43.

Archidamus: see note to 8.5. Thucydides calls him ξυνετὸς (1.79.2) and portrays him as cautious and wishing to avoid war: cf. esp. Thuc. 1.80–85, 2.12; Westlake 1968, 122–135.

εἰς διαλύσεις ἄγοντος: "trying to resolve, compromise." Cf. *Sull.* 28.2, *Agis* 43.9, *Ant.* 19.1.

πραΰνοντος: "calming," from πρᾶος. The verb and its compound καταπραΰνω are used by Plato and are common in P. in political contexts. Cf. 33.5, of Pericles.

οὐκ ἄν: with συμπεσεῖν, "would not, it seems, have come about from the other causes."

καθελεῖν: "repeal." Cf. Thuc. 1.139.1, μάλιστά γε πάντων καὶ ἐνδηλότατα προύλεγον τὸ περὶ Μεγαρέων ψήφισμα καθελοῦσι μὴ ἂν γίγνεσθαι πόλεμον, and Diod. 12.39.4. P.'s words echo Thucydides.

29.8

ἐναντιωθείς: cf. Thuc. 1.127.3, [Pericles] ἠναντιοῦτο πάντα τοῖς Λακεδαιμονίοις; 139.4–144 (his speech); Diod. 12.39.5–40.6.

παροξύνας: The word is used by Thucydides of the Corinthians at Sparta (1.67.5, 84.2), but not of Pericles. The idea that Pericles urged the Athenians to war is Thucydidean, however: cf. 1.127.3, ἐς τὸν πόλεμον ὥρμα τοὺς Ἀθηναίους, with 1.144.3, 1.145, 2.59.2, 2.60.4–5 (and Diod. 12.40.5, παρορμήσας). Παροξύνω is a favorite of P.'s, appearing more than seventy times in the *Lives*, though only here in *Pericles*. P. sees Pericles as uncharacteristically violent, in contrast to the calming influence of Archidamus and the Spartans. His attempt to understand Pericles' strong feelings leads to the treatment of causes at 30.2–32.6. Note, however, that he does not refer here to the power of Pericles' oratory, as do Aristophanes and Diodorus.

φιλονικία: "rivalry," a pejorative word in P.; cf. 31.1.

μόνος . . . τὴν αἰτίαν: "he alone was responsible"; cf. 31.1, 32.6, Comp. 3.1, Nic. 9.9, Alc. 14.2. The view is already found in Ar. Ach. 515–39, Peace 606–11. Αἰτίαν ἔχειν has a wide variety of meanings, referring both to legal charges and personal attacks or rumor. The context here suggests "was responsible for" (cf. Alc. 16.6, τοὺς Μηλίους ἡβηδὸν ἀποσφαγῆναι τὴν πλείστην αἰτίαν ἔσχε, τῷ ψηφίσματι συνειπών, and Cor. 24.1, 35.8, Brut. 20.2), though "was held responsible for" is also possible. Cf. Comp. Per.–Fab. 3.1, τῆς δὲ πολιτείας μέγα μὲν ἔγκλημα τοῦ Περικλέους ὁ πόλεμος. λέγεται γὰρ ἐπακτὸς ὑπ' ἐκείνου γενέσθαι, Λακεδαιμονίοις ἐρίσαντος μὴ ἐνδοῦναι . Thucydides' broader understanding did not affect the standard opinion. The charge is a serious one, for P. deplored war between Greeks: cf. Comp. Per.–Fab. 3.1, Cim. 19.3–4, Tim. 29.6, Flam. 11.3–6, De Pyth. or. 401C–D, 408B; the peace of Nicias, in contrast, is a ἑλληνικώτατον πολίτευμα, Comp. Nic.–Crass. 2.7. Note that Pausanias (8.52.3) also explicitly excludes all the leading men of the Peloponnesian War from his list of benefactors of Greece, calling them αὐτόχειρας καὶ ὅτι ἐγγύτατα καταποντιστὰς τῆς Ἑλλάδος; cf. Habicht 1985, 113–14.

30.1

πρεσβείας: probably not a special embassy following those of 29.7 (as, e.g., de Ste. Croix, OPW 248), but Thucydides' second embassy. P. is enlarging upon Thucydides to dramatize Pericles' stubbornness. The source of the anecdote is unknown; its accuracy cannot be verified.

νόμον τινά: The words suggest an earlier law forbidding removal of publicly posted decrees (and perhaps other notices), except by authorized magistrates or after a fixed time. We have no evidence for such a law, though it would seem to be necessary. For regular erasure of rosters, records of contracts, etc., cf. *Ath. pol.* 36.2, 47.5, 49.2, but these were temporary documents by nature. Removal of the stele recording a law or decree was tantamount to annulling it, as when the Thirty removed the stelai with the laws of Ephialtes and Archestratus from the Areopagus, and perhaps some of the laws of Solon as well (*Ath. pol.* 35.2). But this was not a legal procedure, so that, e.g., the decree to reinscribe a proxeny decree destroyed under the Thirty did not require a new vote of proxeny (*IG* II² 6 = Tod, *GHI* 98). Care was taken to remove published decrees when the assembly revoked them for some reason: cf. Andoc. 1.79, 103 (the decree of Patroclides of 405) and *IG* II² 43 = Tod, *GHI* 123, ll. 31–35. In 340/39 Demosthenes carried a decree ordering the removal of the stele recording the peace and alliance with Philip of Macedon (Philochorus 328 F55). A law of 375/74 charges the secretary of the boule to remove any *psēphisma* written on a stele that is contrary to the new law: see Stroud 1974, esp. ll. 55–56 with pp. 184–85. (For other references see Triantaphyllopoulos 1985, 74; on the duties of the secretary see Rhodes 1972, 134–41.)

Perhaps, however, Pericles refers to a clause of the decree that forbade change or repeal: cf. ML 49, ll. 20–25 (= *IG* I² 45, I³ 46), "If any one moves a decree contrary to the stele or a rhetor speaks or tries to encourage to remove or dissolve any of what has been decreed, he shall lose citizen rights, and his children also, and his money should be confiscated and a tenth given to the goddess." Well-known examples of this sort of clause may be found in the second Callias decree (ML 58B, ll. 17–19 = *IG* I² 92, I³ 52B) and the decree establishing the second Athenian confederacy (Tod, *GHI* 123, ll. 51–63 = *IG* II² 43). See Lewis 1974.

P. seems to use the terms νόμος and ψήφισμα indiscriminately (e.g., the citizen law of 451 is called a νόμος, 37.2, 3, 5). From the end of the fifth century through the middle of the fourth, Athenian law and practice distinguished between νόμος, a written statute, part of the law code, and ψήφισμα, a decree of the council or people (cf. Ostwald 1969, 1–3). But P.'s use of the term here should not be forced into this pattern.

προβαλομένον: "having put forward as an excuse"—not necessarily a pretext.

τὸ πινάκιον: the wooden tablet, painted white, on which a decree could be temporarily displayed. More commonly used of accounts or other temporary records (*IG* I² 66, ll. 30–31 = I³ 34, ML 46, ll. 44–45; I² 76, l. 27 = I³ 78; I² 127, l. 10 = I³ 133; II² 1237, ll. 61–62; *Ath. pol.* 48.4, *εἰς πινάκιον λελευκωμένον*). A synonym was *σανίς*: *IG* I² 75, l. 5 = I³ 59; I² 65 = I³ 68, l. 18. One would expect, however, that this like other important decrees would have been inscribed on a bronze or stone stele. Honorary decrees were often recorded on a *sanis* in the bouleuterion (*IG* I³ 27, 56, 155, 165). Posting a decree at the enclosure of the eponymous heroes or in another prominent place was the standard method of publication; erasure or, as here, turning the face would indicate that the decree need no longer be observed. On publication and archiving of decrees see Boeghold 1972; for *pinakes* and similar objects see Wilhelm 1909, 239–49.

Polyalces: not otherwise known.

στρέψον εἴσω: "turn to face the wall." Cf. the similar expression in Ar. *Ach.* 536–37: *τὸ ψήφισμ' ὅπως / μεταστραφείη*. Polyalces' response, if not itself from a comedy, may have been created or preserved to explain Aristophanes. The parallel does not authenticate the story (*pace* Lewis 1977, 49n. 157).

κομψοῦ: "witty, sophisticated."

30.2–3

The Diplomatic Antecedents of the Megarian Decree. These sentences are troublesome because they are not easily reconciled with Thucydides' narrative, or indeed with the preceding section, 29.4–30.1. Thucydides speaks of a decree in effect in 432, which excluded the Megarians from "the harbors in the Athenian sway and the Athenian agora" (1.67.4, 139.1, 144.2; cf. *Per.* 29.4). The Spartans asked that it be repealed and were refused, unless they gave up their own exclusion of strangers, *ξενηλασία* (1.139.1–2, 4; 144). The provisions are mocked by Aristophanes for sounding like a drinking song: ὡς χρὴ Μεγαρέας μήτε γῇ μήτ᾽ ἐν ἀγορᾷ / μήτ᾽ ἐν θαλάττῃ μήτ᾽ ἐν ἠπείρῳ μένειν, *Ach.* 533–34; for the original song of Timocreon (which does not have the phrase μήτ᾽ ἐν ἀγορᾷ) see schol. *Ach.* 532. The reasons given for the decree vary: ἐπεργασίαν Μεγαρεῦσι τῆς γῆς τῆς ἱερᾶς καὶ τῆς ἀορίστου, καὶ ἀνδραπόδων ὑποδοχὴν τῶν ἀφισταμένων (Thuc. 1.139.2; cf. schol. *Ach.* 532, schol. *Peace* 605); or the theft of two of Aspasia's harlots (Ar. *Ach.* 523–34); or the prosecution of Phidias for theft (Ar. *Peace* 605–18; cf. schol. *Peace* 605; Diod. 12.38.1–39.3, 40.6). The date, purpose, provisions, and effect of the Megarian decree have been endlessly debated (bibliography in de Ste. Croix, *OPW* 381–83). The date is usually put in 432, just before the Megarian complaint (Meiggs, *AE* 202–3, 430–31; Kagan, *OPW* 260), but Brunt 1951 has shown that Thucydides does not require this and argued, rightly, I think, for an earlier date. Most writers think that it was a deliberate act of imperialism against Megara and that the effect on Megara was disastrous; de Ste. Croix, *OPW* 225–89, thinks the cause was indeed religious but that the effect was negligible. On the other hand, for MacDonald (1983), the decree hides behind a religious cloak political maneuvers intended to block Megarian intervention in Megarian colonies in the Athenian empire. I take it as a genuine religious action with clearly perceived imperial consequences.

The events of *Per.* 30.2–3 are regularly squeezed into 432–431 between the first Spartan embassy and the first months of the war (Gomme, *HCT* 1:450), although some place Charinus' decree after the outbreak of hostilities. Connor (1962a), noting the problems involved with these dates (on which see below), thought P. had misplaced Anthemocritus and the Charinus decree and that they really belonged to another dispute over the *orgas* in the 350s; cf. also de Ste. Croix, *OPW* 246–51. But this drastic solution is not convincing: see Dover 1966. Cawkwell 1969 presents a spirited defense of the traditional view that there were three decrees—the decree excluding the Megarians (Thuc. 1.139.4; *Per.* 29.7), the decree sending out Anthemocritus, and the decree of Charinus— but suggests that the latter two belong between spring 431, the time of the usual dispatch of Eleusinian heralds, and the beginning of hostilities. The better solution, as argued by Fornara 1975, is that 30.2–3 is a flashback, in which P. goes back in time to give the antecedents to the Megarian decree, which in turn serve to explain Pericles' stubbornness and unusually strong feeling.

The sequence P. gives is, as Fornara has shown, (1) the Megarians take over for their own use the sacred land, (2) Pericles moves the "reasonable" decree, (3) Anthemocritus goes out and is killed (or thought to be), (4) the Charinus decree. Fornara dismisses the Charinus decree as an irrelevant aside by P. (1975, 220). However, because the Charinus decree is the final element in the series, the item for which the series of events provides the explanation, it must in fact—at least in P.'s mind—be identical to the "Megarian" decree, which he is trying to explain. The list of items associated with Charinus' proposal indicates that the Megarian decree contained terms much broader than Thucydides states. The complete Megarian decree, as reported by P., was moved by Charinus and included clauses declaring a hostility to Megara "without truce or herald," establishing the penalty of death for any Megarian found on Attic soil, requiring an oath from the generals to invade Megara twice a year, and authorizing the public burial of Anthemocritus. The identity of the Megarian decree and the Charinus decree in P.'s narrative is confirmed by the Megarian explanation (30.4), which rejects the killing of Anthemocritus as cause of the Megarian decree, giving instead the story of Aspasia's harlots. Finally, at 31.1, P. concludes that it is difficult to know the ἀρχὴν, the origin of the Megarian decree. For a fuller presentation of this reading of P.'s account see Stadter 1984 and cf. the notes on the individual phrases below.

30.2

ὑπῆν . . . ἀπεχθεία: "He (Pericles) certainly had an antipathy of some sort." Ὑπῆν is not "there lurked" but simply "there was present, pre-existing": cf. Dem. 18.36, διὰ τὴν τόθ' ὑπουσαν ἀπεχθείαν πρὸς τοὺς Θηβαίους; Hdt. 1.31.6; Thuc. 6.87.4, 8.36.1, etc. Take μὲν with the following δὲ, οὖν as the logical connective: cf. 8.7, 32.5. Ἀπεχθεία may refer to previous experience (e.g., the Megarian revolt, 22.1–2) or to the Aspasia story (cf. 30.4).

κοινὴν καὶ φανεράν: "public," opp. to ἰδία.

ποιησάμενος αἰτίαν: cf. 24.1. The nominative picks up the dative of interest (αὐτῷ) of the μὲν clause.

ἀποτέμνεσθαι . . . ὀργάδα: "that they were appropriating the sacred *orgas*." Ἀποτέμνομαι is the regular word for taking land over for one's own use: cf. *Qu. Rom.* 267C, *Lyc.* 2.1, *Cor.* 30.7, *Pel.* 24.9; Hdt. 1.82; Isoc. 5.122. Thucydides gives a similar accusation: 1.139.2, ἐπεργασίαν Μεγαρεῦσι τῆς γῆς τῆς ἱερᾶς καὶ τῆς ἀορίστου; cf. also schol. Ar. *Ach.* 532, *Peace* 605. The *orgas* was fertile but uncultivated territory, sacred to the Eleusinian goddesses, but on the border with Megara. (Kahrstedt 1932, 9–10, with fig. 2, suggests a small plain ringed by hills, which drains into the Megarid but is separated from it by a ridge. Ober 1984, appendix, argues that it was an area on the Megarian side of the Kerata range.) Cleomenes of Sparta apparently had once violated it (cf. Hdt. 6.75; Paus. 3.4.2), but our chief information comes from another dispute with Megara ca. 350, when it is mentioned by Demosthenes 13.32 and Didymus' scholion, citing Philochorus (*FGrHist* 328 F155) and Androtion (324 F30), and is the subject of a long inscription, *IG* II^2 204 = Ziehen 1906, 2.1:28; Sokolowski 1969, 32. Cf. Foucart 1889; Cawkwell 1969, 328–32. The accusation is also in schol. Ar. *Ach.* 532, *Peace* 605. Violation of the sacred land was a serious offense: cf. the heavy penalty assessed at Corcyra for taking vine stakes (Thuc. 3.70.4, with Gomme, *HCT* ad loc.), the penalties prescribed for removing wood or even fallen leaves from a sacred area (*IG* II^2 1362 = Ziehen 1906, 2.1:23; Sokolowski 1969, 37) and the Theban denunciation of the cultivation of the sacred plain at Delphi, which was the immediate cause of the Sacred War of the 350s.

γράφει ψήφισμα: this "courteous" decree is expressly attributed to Pericles; cf. 8.7 and note. For the present tense cf. note to 9.2, and for the same tense in another flashback, 31.2, καθίζουσιν; 32.3, κυροῦται. The decree is not mentioned elsewhere. In de Ste. Croix's reconstruction, *OPW* 250, this is the first of the Megarian decrees but has no connection with Anthemocritus.

30.3

μὲν οὖν: cf. 30.2.

εὐγνώμονος . . . ἐχόμενον: "presenting a reasonable and courteous claim for justice." For ἔχομαι + gen. as "presenting, laying claim to" cf. *C. Gracch.* 9.1, νόμους ἔγραψεν, οὔτε τῶν καλῶν τινος οὔτε τῶν λυσιτελῶν ἐχόμενος; Plato *Rep.* 496A, 568A; LSJ s.v. ἔχω (A), C.I.2. P. wishes to stress that Pericles' response to the offense was restrained and in character. Cf. Ptolemy's εὐγνώμονα καὶ φιλάνθρωπον λόγον to Demetrius (*Demetr.* 5.4) and the contrast between Tiberius Gracchus' first agrarian proposal, than which μηδέποτε πραότερος γραφῆναι (*Ti. Gracch.* 9.2), inasmuch as it was sensible and fair (τῆς ἐπανορθώσεως οὔσης εὐγνώμονος, 9.3), and later when Tiberius παροξυνθεὶς . . . τὸν μὲν φιλάνθρωπον ἐπανείλετο νόμον . . . (10.4). For P.'s admiration for φιλανθρωπία see Martin 1961 and Aalders 1982, 46. For this sense of δικαιολογία cf. δικαιολογέομαι at *De adul. et amic.* 61A, *Apophtheg. Lac.* 230C. Raubitschek 1973, 33–34, has suggested that the Athenians at the Peloponnesian conference at Sparta in 433 were precisely the embassy bringing this claim.

Anthemocritus: not mentioned by Thucydides, but in pseudo-Demosthenes and the lexicographers: Harpocration s.v., Ἰσαῖος ἐν τῷ πρὸς Καλυδῶνα, "τό τε βαλανεῖον τὸ παρ' Ἀνθεμοκρίτου ἀνδριάντα." τουτέστι πρὸς ταῖς Θριασίαις πύλαις. οὗτος ἦν Ἀθηναίων μὲν κῆρυξ, ὑπὸ Μεγαρέων δ' ἀπεσφάγη ἀπαγορεύων αὐτοῖς τὴν ἱερὰν ταῖν θεαῖν ὀργάδα μὴ ἐπεργάζεσθαι; Suda s.v.; ps.-Dem. 12.4 (Philip complaining of the Athenian treatment of his embassy), Μεγαρέων γοῦν Ἀνθεμόκριτον ἀνελόντων εἰς τοῦτ' ἐλήλυθεν ὁ δῆμος ὥστε μυστηρίων μὲν εἶργον αὐτούς, ὑπομνήματα δὲ τῆς ἀδικίας ἔστησαν ἀνδριάντα πρὸ τῶν πυλῶν; Paus. 1.36.3, ἰοῦσι δὲ ἐπ' Ἐλευσῖνα ἐξ Ἀθηνῶν ἥν Ἀθηναῖοι καλοῦσιν ὁδὸν ἱεράν, Ἀνθεμοκρίτου πεποίηται μνῆμα. ἐς τοῦτον Μεγαρεῦσίν ἐστιν ἀνοσιώτατον ἔργον, οἳ κήρυκα ἐλθόντα, ὡς μὴ τοῦ λοιποῦ τὴν χώραν ἐπεργάζοιντο, κτείνουσιν Ἀνθεμόκριτον· καὶ σφισι ταῦτα δράσασι παραμένει καὶ ἐς τόδε μήνιμα ἐκ τοῖν θεοῖν, οἷς οὐδὲ Ἀδριανὸς ὁ βασιλεὺς ὥστε καὶ ἐπαυξηθῆναι μόνοις ἐπήρεσκεν Ἑλλήνων. Anthemocritus' statue was a well-known landmark already in Isaeus' day (ca. 380–350). The Megarian offense still was not forgotten in the second century A.D., as Pausanias' last sentence shows. The bath mentioned by Isaeus has been discovered outside the Dipylon gate: see Travlos, *Pictorial Dictionary*, 180.

ἀποθανεῖν: "was killed," as often. Killing a herald was a serious wrong, which might bring down the wrath of the gods: cf. the story of the "wrath of Talthybius" aroused by the murder of Persian heralds, Hdt. 7.133–137; Wéry 1966 (with bibliography in n. 1); Parker 1983, 188.

ἔδοξε: P. does not commit himself to the truth of the story.

γράφει . . . Χαρῖνος: this decree, enacted in response to the Megarian *asebeia* in working the sacred land and killing the herald, is identified by P. with the "Megarian" decree: cf. the only other sure reference to Charinus, *Praec. ger. rep.* 812D, [Pericles] διὰ δὲ Χαρίνου τὸ κατὰ Μεγαρέων ἐκύρωσε ψήφισμα; and note schol. Ar. *Peace* 246, Χαρίνου [Wilamowitz; mss. χάριν τοῦ] τὸ πινάκιον συνθέντος τὸ κατ' αὐτῶν [the Megarians] εἰς τὴν Περικλέους χάριν, ὥστε μήτε γῆς μήτε λιμένων Ἀττικῶν ἐπιβαίνειν τοὺς Μεγαρέας. Aristophanes' ascription of the law to Pericles (*Ach.* 532) is a comic simplification; Thucydides and Diodorus do not name the mover.

   Apparently using a documentary source, as for other decrees (cf. the Introduction 3.1.l), P. gives the provisions in more detail than Thucydides, who emphasizes the complaints of the Megarians.

ἄσπονδον . . . ἔχθραν: "a hostility without truce or use of heralds." Cf. Xen. *Anab.* 3.3.5 for a πόλεμον ἀκήρυκτον after a herald had been slain. The usual phrase has πόλεμος, not ἔχθρα: cf. Aeschin. 2.80; Dem. 18.262; and in P., *Arist.* 1.5, οὐ γάρ ἐστι τοῖς ἀγαθοῖς ἀκήρυκτος καὶ ἄσπονδος πρὸς τὰς παρὰ τῶν φίλων δωρεὰς πόλεμος, and *Non posse* 1095F. For πόλεμος ἀκήρυκτος alone cf. Hdt. 5.81; Aeschin. 2.37; Plato *Laws* 626A; Plut. *Mul. virt.* 253F.

ὃς δ' ἂν . . . ζημιοῦσθαι: cf. schol. Ar. *Peace* 246 (quoted above) and 609, μήτε γῆς μήτε λιμένων αὐτοὺς ἐπιβαίνειν Ἀττικῶν, εἰ δὲ μή, τὸν ληφθέντα ἀγώγιμον εἶναι; schol. *Ach.* 527 (= Suda s.v. Ἀσπασία), ἀπαγορεῦον δέχεσθαι αὐτοὺς εἰς τὰς Ἀθήνας. The law's penalty is similar to others prescribed or assigned for serious crimes. A citizen might suffer permanent exile under pain of death, with confiscation of property (the regular punishment for serious *asebeia*: cf. Harrison, *Law*, 2:59, 62–63, 185–86; MacDowell, *Law*,

149). For a noncitizen the only penalty could be exclusion from Attica on pain of death (cf. Plato *Laws* 854D). The reference to harbors of the empire in 29.4, Thucydides, and others, shows that the exclusion was from the allied states as well, the normal Athenian procedure. Cf. the Erythrae decree, ML 40 (= *IG* I² 10, I³ 14), ll. 29–32: if someone kills an Erythraean and is condemned to exile, he is to be exiled from all the Athenian alliance. Cf. also Tod, *GHI* 123 (= *IG* II² 43), ll. 51–63: if someone tries to change the law, he will be outlawed, his money confiscated, and he will be punished with death or exile "from wherever the Athenians or the allies rule"; if he is executed, he is not to be buried "in Attica or in the land of the allies." For the mention of market and harbors (as important public gathering places) in exclusion penalties see de Ste. Croix, *OPW* 281–84, 397–98. At least the Agora must have been mentioned in the decree, as this is added by Aristophanes to Timocreon's song (*Ach.* 533; cf. schol. to 532). [Dem.] 12.4, quoted above, specifies exclusion from the Eleusinian mysteries. For somewhat comparable cases cf. the exclusion of the Spartans from the sanctuary at Olympia (Thuc. 5.49.1) and the expulsion of the Delians from Delos (Thuc. 5.1). The extent of this exclusion suits well Pericles' offer to repeal the decree if the Spartans would repeal their exclusion of foreigners, ξενηλασία, for the Athenians and their allies (Thuc. 1.144.2). Once the war began, the Spartans exacted the death penalty from all found sailing the Aegean, whether merchants or military, whether Athenians and their allies or third parties (Thuc. 2.67.4; cf. 3.32.1).

τὸν πάτριον ὅρκον: the oath of office sworn by the generals, similar to that of other magistrates (cf. *Ath. pol.* 7.1, 55.5). It included promises to enroll in the army those who had not yet served (Lys. 9.15) and not to be bribed (Dinarchus 3.2). Cf. the oath of the ephebes, cited by the orators and discovered on stone, Tod, *GHI* 204, ll. 5–20; for a recent discussion see Siewart 1977.

ἐπομνύειν: "swear in addition." The prefix here, exceptionally, carries weight and is not simply used for *variatio*.

καὶ δὶς . . . εἰσβαλοῦσι: The sworn twice-yearly invasion of Megarian territory was a religious act, though with obvious political effect; cf. Raubitschek 1973, 34. Ἀνὰ πᾶν ἔτος for "annually" occurs only here and at *De def. or.* 421A in P. and seems inspired by Herodotus, where it is common (1.136.1, etc.). It is not used in fifth-century inscribed decrees. The invasions are confirmed, at least for the period of the war, by Thuc. 4.66.1 (cf. 2.31.3).

The difficulty of imagining invasions prior to the war, which neither were such an obvious violation of the treaty as to provoke war at once, nor were considered important enough to be mentioned by Thucydides, is the chief reason for denying the identity of the Megarian decree and the Charinus decree and for dating the Charinus decree after the outbreak of the war: see Busolt, *Gr. Gesch.* 2:814n. 4; Connor 1962a, 227. However, a formal invasion need not have been excessively damaging, especially if it were recognized as a reprisal for alleged offenses: cf. Phillipson 1911, 2:349–66; Dareste 1902. Moreover, raids did not always break treaties: cf. the Spartan response to Athenian raids from Pylos (Thuc. 5.115.2). They did not consider the treaty as broken at that time, but when they did decide to fight, they considered these raids as justification (7.18.3). The parallel with Megara seems clear.

ταφῆναι . . . πύλας: This clause, if found in the decree and not invented by P. or his source, confirms the link between the Charinus decree and the mission of Anthemocritus. Only P. joins the two. The Thriasian gate, leading to Thria on the Eleusinian plain, Eleusis, and Megara, was the most important city gate; in the fourth century it was rebuilt and took the name Dipylon from its double passage (the name first appears in *IG* II^2 673, 278/77 B.C.). See Judeich 1931, 135–38; Travlos, *Pictorial Dictionary*, 159 and fig. 602. The bath mentioned by Isaeus has been identified outside the gate (Travlos, 180 and fig. 391). From the Dipylon gate and the nearby Sacred Gate roads fanned out to Piraeus, Eleusis, and the Academy (Travlos, fig. 417). The road to Eleusis and Megara was particularly appropriate for Anthemocritus' tomb. As Pausanias (1.36.3) says that the tomb was on the Sacred Way, it must have been in the area immediately outside the wall, between the two gates. The Kerameikos excavations continue to reveal tombs of all sorts in this area (cf. Travlos, 299–322). Connor 1962a, 243–46, argues that P. is in error, as a statue would have been unusual in the 430s, when in general monuments were simple; but in fact conspicuous public burials of individuals seem to have started about this time. See Stupperich 1977, esp. 26n. 4, 200, who thinks the ἀνδριάς must have been a relief stele: one might compare that of Eupherus (*MDAI(A)* 79 [1964] 93–95, 99–104, plates 48.1, 49, 51.1), dated to ca. 430. For classical Athenian tombs in general see Kurtz and Boardman 1971, 91–141.

30.4

Megarians: P. could mean Megarian historians, of whom a few are known but who are more often cited as a group. See Piccirilli 1975 and Jacoby, *FGrHist* 484–87 (this is Piccirilli 5 F23, *FGrHist* 487 F13), and the Introduction, 3.2.f. Equally probably, P. could be referring to his contemporary friends as citing Aristophanes or a standard account; Paus. 1.36.3 demonstrates current interest in the question. Cf., e.g., his friend Heracleon of Megara (Ziegler, *RE* 676). For historians see Piccirilli 1975, 138–40 (with full discussion of the question) and Dover 1966; against, see Jacoby, commentary to 487 F13; Connor 1970, 305; de Ste. Croix, *OPW* 387.

τὰς αἰτίας: i.e., of the Megarian decree.

Aspasia: Aristophanes' parody of Hdt. 1.1–4 in *Ach.* 523–39 became a serious explanation in the scholiastic tradition (schol. *Peace* 609, *Ach.* 527; Harpocration and Suda s.v. Ἀσπασία; cf. also Syncellus 489.3 for the year 432/31). P. accepted as historical the description of Aspasia as the owner of *hetairai* (cf. 24.5). According to Harpocration, the explanation was found also in Duris of Samos (76 F65) and Theophrastus. The story is exaggerated by Athenaeus (13.569F–570A), who introduces *Ach.* 524–29 with ἐπλήθυνεν ἀπὸ τῶν ταύτης [Aspasia] ἑταιρίδων ἡ Ἑλλάς. Aristodemus 16 quotes *Ach.* 524–34 without explanation; Diodorus 12.40.6, on the other hand, cites only the verses on Pericles' eloquence, *Ach.* 530–31. According to schol. *Ach.* 527 and Suda, Pericles himself was enamored of one of the harlots. Cf. also note to 24.5.

τοῖς . . . στιχιδίοις: Ar. *Ach.* 524–27, in trimeter. Dicaeopolis, the speaker, tries to convince the angry Acharnians that the fault is not all on the Spartan side. Δημώδεσι: "hackneyed, commonly cited." Cf. *Sol.* 8.4, τὰ μὲν οὖν δημώδη τῶν λεγομένων, citing a story with which he does not agree (the only other use of the word in P.). Στιχιδίοις: a somewhat disparaging diminutive of στίχος, "verse": cf. *De adul. et amic.* 60A, *De glor. Ath.* 347F, *De E* 384D, *Symp.* 668A. P. apparently thought little of this explanation. Note that he does not quote the famous description of Pericles' thundering and writing laws like drinking songs (*Ach.* 530–34), although he refers to the thundering at 8.3–4. Unlike Diodorus, he prefers to separate Pericles' powerful eloquence from the causes of the war (cf. Diod. 12.39.5, 40.5–6).

Simaetha: unknown. Schol. Ar. *Ach.* 524, which notes that Alcibiades loved her and urged the business, is improbable.

μεθυσοκότταβοι: a comic compound of μέθυσος, "drunk," with κότταβος, a party game of tossing wine with a flick of the wrist into a dish set up as a target. The game was often associated with erotic play as well; cf. Sparkes 1960.

πεφυσιγγωμένοι: "garlic-stung," that is, excited by garlic, a prime export of Megara (cf. *Ach.* 521, 761–63). Φῦσιγξ is the outer skin of the garlic, but there is also a pun on πεφυσημένοι, "inflated." Eating garlic was thought to make one ὀξύτερος and a better fighter: cf. Xen. *Symp.* 4.9; Ar. *Knights* 494; schol. Ar. *Ach.* 166.

31.1

τὴν μὲν οὖν ἀρχήν: sc., of the Megarian decree, although the word ἀρχὴν may have been suggested by the line following the passage just quoted from the *Acharnians*: κἀντεῦθεν ἀρχὴ τοῦ πολέμου κατερράγη. Here μὲν οὖν is transitional and resumptive, with the μέν clause summarizing the previous paragraph before leading on to the next idea (Denniston, 472).

οἱ μέν: This clause is a paraphrase of the words ascribed to Pericles at Thuc. 1.140.4–5: τὸ γὰρ βραχύ τι τοῦτο πᾶσαν ὑμῶν ἔχει

τὴν βεβαίωσιν καὶ πεῖραν τῆς γνώμης. οἷς εἰ ξυγχωρήσετε, καὶ ἄλλο
τι μεῖζον εὐθὺς ἐπιταχθήσεσθε ὡς φόβῳ καὶ τοῦτο ὑπακούσαντες·
ἀπισχυρισάμενοι δὲ σαφὲς ἂν καταστήσαιτε αὐτοῖς ἀπὸ τοῦ ἴσου
ὑμῖν μᾶλλον προσφέρεσθαι. Note πεῖραν τῆς γνώμης, ξυγχωρήσετε,
ἀπισχυρισάμενοι.

ἐκ φρονήματος κτλ.: These are all words of praise to P. For φρόνημα
μέγα see note to 5.1; for γνώμη see 33.6; for τὸ βέλτιστον see note
to 15.1.

πεῖραν . . . ἀσθενείας: chiastic order, with the two predicates
πεῖραν and ἐξομολόγησιν surrounding the two nouns they explain.
Note the frequency of abstract nouns in this paragraph. For
ἐνδόσεως cf. 30.1 (ἐνέδωκεν), 32.6, 33.3, Comp. Per.–Fab. 3.1; for
ἐξομολόγησις ("admission, confession") cf. Alex. 62.5, ἐξομολόγησιν
ἥττης τιθέμενος τὴν ἀναχώρησιν; Luc. 21.5, ἐξομολόγησις . . . δου-
λείας. Both these words are postclassical; συγχώρησις appears already in Plato, ἔνδειξις in Andocides.

οἱ δέ: sc. φασιν αὐτόν. No extant ancient writer seems to present
precisely this appraisal. Something similar, combined with elements of the first explanation, is found at De malig. Her. 856A,
quoted below in note to 31.2. The words here are pejorative:
αὐθαδεία (cf. Cor. 15.4, Cat. Min. 55.6, Dion 8.1, Praec. ger. rep.
808D), φιλονικία (cf. 29.8), περιφρονῆσαι.

31.2–32.6

The Trials of Pericles' Friends. The trials of Pericles' friends, and
especially of Phidias, are the center of controversy. They are
clearly essential to our understanding both of the internal politics
of Athens in the crucial period of Pericles' ascendancy and of
the underlying causes of the Peloponnesian War, yet the sources
are few, difficult to interpret, and contradictory. Of the many who
have written on the subject see especially Busolt, *Gr. Gesch.*
3.2:825–29; Adcock, *CAH* 5:477–80; Gomme, *HCT* 2:184–89;
Jacoby, commentary to *FGrHist* 328 F121; Kienast 1953; Frost
1964a, 1964b; Donnay 1968; Kagan, *OPW* 194–201; Prandi 1977;
Klein 1979; Mansfeld 1980 (of which pp. 24–33 form a short
commentary to *Per.* 31–32); Ameling 1986.

P. includes these attacks partially for completeness—after all, they represented the most common explanation for the war—and partially to indicate the kind of political opposition that Pericles had to withstand as leader, parallel to the pressure upon Fabius Maximus (see Stadter 1975, 84–85). Despite the space given to this "worst reason" P. does not say that he accepts it, but leaves the question of Pericles' motivation moot (32.6). Phidias' trial was a familiar subject in P.'s day: note the use made of the story of the sculptor in Dio Chrysostom *Or.* 12.

Like 30.2–3 and 30.4, these chapters represent a flashback from 29.8, Pericles' refusal to rescind the Megarian decree. They give an explanation of his action by noting the effect of the preceding threats to his friends and himself, but they assign no date to them. It is certainly wrong to associate Dracontides' motion with the deposition of Pericles in 430, as has often been assumed (e.g., Busolt, *Gr. Gesch.* 3.2:950; Gomme, *HCT* 2:187). Frost 1964a, 71–72, has argued convincingly that it must rather be connected with the attack on Phidias because of the emphasis on accounts and religious obligations and because of the presence of Hagnon in the assembly. Cf. also Mansfeld 1980, 48–51. P.'s words at 32.6, ὡς δὲ διὰ Φειδίου προσέπταισε τῷ δήμῳ, . . . τὸν πόλεμον . . . ἐξέκαυσεν, indicate that he thought that the attacks on Aspasia and Anaxagoras had preceded that against Phidias, and that the latter was not too distant from his opposition to repealing the decree in 432. Note that περὶ τοῦτον τὸν χρόνον at 32.1 is an imprecise indication of time, which cannot bear the weight sometimes placed on it (e.g., by Frost 1964b, 396–97 arguing for 438/37, precisely in the same year as he assigns Phidias' trial). It is typical of P.'s method to combine items from different years that have a common theme: e.g., chapters 19–20, describing expeditions of 447, 453, and the 430s. From P. we cannot tell that the attacks on Aspasia and Anaxagoras do not go back into the 440s, although it seems reasonable to put them later. Moreover, P. sometimes compresses time to make a point (cf. Pelling 1980, 127–28, and the Introduction, 2.6). Although he associates Phidias' trial with the rejection of Spartan demands in 432, there may have been an interval of several years between.

Our one sure datum is the relative chronology of the career of Phidias, known from Philochorus (as quoted in schol. Ar. *Peace*

605, *FGrHist* 328 F121) and the excavations at Olympia. Philochorus tells us that the Parthenos statue was dedicated in 438/37. The Olympia excavations have uncovered the workshop of Phidias for the statue of Zeus, firmly set by pottery in a context of the 430s–420s and even revealing a cup with the graffito Φειδίο εἰμί, thus putting to rest suggestions that Phidias may have created the Zeus before the Parthenos. See Mallwitz and Schiering 1964, 174–75, and Kunze 1959, 277–91, with Heilmeyer 1981, 447–48. Philochorus mentions in the same notice that Phidias was tried for stealing gold and ivory destined for the statue, but fled to Elis, where he made the statue of Zeus and was later tried for theft and executed. It is now orthodox to use this notice to date the trial to 438/37 (see Frost 1964b, 392–99; Donnay 1968; Kagan, *OPW* 194–98; cf. Eusebius' date of 440/39). However, Philochorus clearly is giving a sketch of Phidias' subsequent history in connection with the dedication of the statue, and his notice cannot be taken as evidence for the date of the trial (cf. Jacoby, commentary to F121, *FrGrHist* 3B suppl., 1:490). We cannot in fact be certain that Phidias was not accused *before* the completion of the statue, or even two or three years later, when the political situation seemed ripe. Alcibiades' accusers waited until he was out of town to press charges in 415. Recently Triebel-Schubert (1983) has argued from the inscribed Parthenos accounts that Philochorus is incorrect and that the statue was only completed in 435/34. Under this hypothesis the trial would not have taken place before spring or summer 434.

Philochorus' account is one of the two basic traditions related to Phidias. The second begins with Ar. *Peace* 605–11 and continues in Ephorus (cf. Diod. 12.39) and later writers, stating that Pericles took fright at the attack on Phidias and began the war to distract the attention of his enemies. (The passage from Aristophanes has recently been discussed in the context of the whole speech of Hermes by Cassio 1982, esp. 26–27.)

P.'s "worst charge" combines the Ephoran account of attacks on Phidias with new material: a decree honoring Phidias' accuser and stories of the death of Phidias (31.5)—clearly incorrect—and of accusations against Aspasia, Anaxagoras (the latter also in Diodorus), and Pericles himself. Most valuable are P.'s reports of the decrees of Glaucon, Diopithes, and Dracontides, which are not otherwise mentioned in our sources but must derive from a documentary source, most probably Craterus (see the Introduction, 3.1.l). P. does not identify the political position of Pericles' attackers. Although he suggests that Pericles' enemies were trying to turn the demos against him, it is not clear whether these were the *oligoi* or impatient radicals of Cleon's type; modern scholars have argued for both sides. Although the basis for P.'s narrative is Ephorus, his individual treatment should be recognized. Ephorus' account as known to us from Diodorus is organized as follows (Diod. 12.38–40 = *FGrHist* 70 F196):

1. Pericles' accounts (not from Ephorus, according to Jacoby, commentary to 70 F196)
   a. Pericles is given responsibility for the league monies, but has trouble with his accounts (38.2)
   b. Alcibiades' advice (38.3)
   c. Pericles looks for war (38.4)
2. The trials
   a. Phidias' accusation and trial, accusation of Pericles (39.1–2)
   b. Attack on Anaxagoras (39.2)
   c. Pericles decides to start war (39.3)
3. Pericles refuses to repeal the Megarian decree, citing the resources of Athens (39.4–40.5, from Thucydides)
4. Reasons for persuasiveness
   a. His oratorical ability (40.5):
   b. As seen in *Peace* 603–11 and
   c. *Ach.* 530–31 and
   d. Eupolis (40.6).

P. has ignored item 1, despite the witty anecdote of Alcibiades (included in *Alc.* 7.3; cf. also *Reg. et imp. apophtheg.* 186E), and suppressed the charge of *hierosylia* against Pericles. He has already treated Thucydides' account of the Megarian decree in a different context, in chapter 29, and mentioned the brilliance of Pericles' oratory at the beginning of his career, in chapter 8. Now he supplements the Ephoran base with the references to Hermippus' attack on Aspasia and to the decrees of Glaucon, Diopithes, Dracontides, and Hagnon, none of which are otherwise known. Aeschines the Socratic furnishes the detail of Pericles' weeping at Aspasia's trial. In addition P. now describes the two groups behind

Menon's accusation, accounts for Phidias' condemnation by supplying the reference to the self-portrait on the shield, and tells of
Phidias' imprisonment and death. Finally, he sets this narrative as
one of several possible explanations, after a summary of better
reasons (31.1), and characterizes it as the "worst reason." As so
often in P., we find a combination of historical sources (Ephorus),
documentary evidence (the decrees), and personal information
blended into a not altogether consistent whole.

An outline will clarify P.'s mode of presentation:

1. The case of Phidias
   a. Menon's accusation
   b. Trial and condemnation
      (1) Theft not proven: gold removable
      (2) Envy: the portraits on the shield
   c. Phidias in prison
      (1) Died of sickness
      (2) Died of poison
   d. Glaucon's decree honoring Menon
2. Other trials
   a. Aspasia indicted for *asebeia*
   b. Diopithes' decree threatening Anaxagoras
   c. Dracontides' decree on Pericles' accounts
      (1) Special procedure
      (2) Hagnon's amendment
   d. Aspasia freed by Pericles' oratory
   e. Anaxagoras forced to leave Athens
   f. Pericles fears a trial and inflames the war
3. Conclusion

The three other cases are subordinate to the case of Phidias. Each
is presented in two halves, the accusation and the reaction.

The historical situation, as far as we can reconstruct it, is that
despite Pericles' preeminence after the ostracism of Thucydides,
stressed in chapters 15–16, he continued to be under attack. As
before, when Ephialtes and Pericles had attacked the Areopagus,
a major weapon was indictment for misuse of funds, but now there
was added the theme of *asebeia*, used alone against Aspasia and
Anaxagoras but also present, at least implicitly, in the accusations
against Phidias and Pericles for misuse of sacred monies. These

religious factors were still present at the outbreak of the war, in the religious background of the Megarian decree and in the Spartan call to drive out those under curse. Apparently despite the attacks Pericles' financial probity was never seriously compromised: cf. Thuc. 2.60.5, 65.8. For the charge of impiety against Phidias cf. note to 31.3; for the other defendants, notes to 32.1–3.

31.2

ἡ δὲ χειρίστη μὲν αἰτία: The worst reason—worst because Pericles would have substituted personal goals for public ones—was that Pericles had refused to repeal the decree so that the need for his leadership in the war would reestablish his influence, which had been shaken by the attacks on his friends. At *De malig. Her.* 856A P. notes that this is a malicious explanation of Pericles' action and ascribes it specifically to the comic poets: ὥσπερ οἱ κωμικοὶ τὸν πόλεμον ὑπο τοῦ Περικλέους ἐκκεκαῦσθαι δι' Ἀσπασίαν ἢ διὰ Φειδίαν ἀποφαίνοντες, οὐ φιλοτιμίᾳ τινὶ καὶ φιλονεικίᾳ μᾶλλον στορέσαι τὸ φρόνημα Πελοποννησίων καὶ μηδενός ὑφεῖσθαι Λακεδαιμονίοις ἐθελήσαντος. Examples of comic explanations are Ar. *Ach.* 523–39 (cf. *Per.* 30.4), *Peace* 605–11, and Cratinus' *Dionysalexandros*, the hypothesis of which concludes, κωμῳδεῖται δ' ἐν τῷ δράματι Περικλῆς μάλα πιθανῶς δι' ἐμφάσεως ὡς ἐπαγειοχὼς τοῖς Ἀθηναίοις τὸν πόλεμον (P. Oxy. 4.663; cf. the Introduction, 3.1.d, note). In *De malig. Her.* 856A ἐκκεκαῦσθαι suggests that P. is thinking of Ar. *Peace* 605–11, which uses the same image of enkindling, and which he uses in this life at 32.6.

πλείστους μάρτυρας: presumably Aristophanes, Ephorus, and the authors who followed them. Aspasia's role in causing the war was mentioned by Duris and Theophrastus, but connected to the theft of her whores, not to her indictment: see note to 30.4. For such counting of authorities cf., e.g., *Thes.* 31.2, *Rom.* 3.1, *Sol.* 19.3, 27.1, *Aquane an ignis* 955E. P.'s weakness is that he does not realize that many authors may derive from a single source, so that numbers do not strengthen the case.

οὕτω πως λέγεται: a clear indication that P. is retelling the story in his own words, putting together various sources.

ὥσπερ εἴρηται: at 13.6 and 14.

πλάστης: "sculptor"; cf. 12.6. The syntax of the sentence begins simply, but rapidly becomes complex, with several main verbs, six participles, and an indirect question.

ἐργολάβος: "contractor"; cf. 13.7, ἠργολάβησε. With γενόμενος the initial antithesis becomes subordinate to that which follows.

οἱ δέ: P. shifts construction: there were two groups attacking Phidias, those who were jealous of his influence with Pericles (τοὺς μὲν, object of ἔσχεν), and those enemies of Pericles who were testing the feelings of the demos (οἱ δὲ), both of which united in suborning Menon. P. is more subtle in the presentation of motivation than Diodorus (see below). These comments are no doubt his own rather than derived from a superior source. The sentence imitates the gradual accumulation of enemies leading to the final denunciation, ἐπὶ μηνύσει καὶ κατηγορίᾳ, while circling back to the initial subject with τοῦ Φειδίου.

Μένωνα . . . καθίζουσιν: This Menon is otherwise unknown. Although the name appears in prominent families in Athens (e.g., the archon of 473/72), this man is probably not a citizen: see note to 31.5. Diodorus (12.39.1) speaks of several men, but gives no names: τῶν δὲ συνεργασαμένων τῷ Φειδίᾳ τινὲς διενεχθέντες ὑπὸ τῶν ἐχθρῶν τοῦ Περικλέους ἐκάθισαν ἐπὶ τὸν τῶν θεῶν βωμὸν· διὰ δὲ τὸ παράδοξον προσκαλούμενοι ἔφασαν πολλὰ τῶν ἱερῶν χρημάτων ἔχοντα Φειδίαν δείξειν, ἐπισταμένου καὶ συνεργοῦντος τοῦ ἐπιμελητοῦ Περικλέους. P. has gotten the name from Glaucon's decree (cf. 31.5). The altar was that of the Twelve Gods, built in the center of the Agora by the younger Pisistratus and regularly used by suppliants (e.g., the Plataeans; Hdt. 6.108.4). For the remains see Travlos, *Pictorial Dictionary*, 458–61; H. A. Thompson and Wycherley 1972, 129–36; for the testimonia see Wycherley 1957, 119–22.

καθίζουσιν: for the historical present see note to 9.2.

ἄδειαν: "immunity from prosecution," as in the case of the Hermocopidae; cf. Thuc. 6.27.2, μηνύειν ἀδεῶς τὸν βουλόμενον, and Andoc. 1.11–12 with MacDowell's commentary (1962). Menon apparently was either an accomplice in the theft or afraid of being charged as a thief himself. If an offender gave information he could be given ἄδεια, but if the accusation was not true, the penalty was death: εἰ μὲν τἀληθῆ μηνύσειέ τις, εἶναι τὴν ἄδειαν, εἰ δὲ τὰ ψευδῆ, τεθνάναι (Andoc. 1.20). A different sort of ἄδεια was involved in the restrictions on spending found in the Callias decrees (ML 58 [= IG I³ 52], B16 and p. 160; cf. ML 77, 15).

μηνύσει: the offering of information to the boule or ecclesia, without necessarily bringing a charge. The assembly could then decide on the proper course of action, whether referral to a court or to the boule, or consideration by the ecclesia itself. See MacDowell, Law, 181–83; Ostwald 1986, 54n. 210. A famous instance was the profanation of the mysteries in 415: cf. Andoc. 1.11–28, Thuc. 6.27.2–28.1, 53.1, 60; Plut. Alc. 19.1–3.

31.3

ἐν ἐκκλησίᾳ διώξεως: P. envisages the prosecution before the assembly, rather than a lesser court. Cf. also Diod. 12.39.2, διόπερ ἐκκλησίας συνελθούσης περὶ τούτων, οἱ μὲν ἐχθροὶ τοῦ Περικλέους ἔπεισαν τὸν δῆμον συλλαβεῖν τὸν Φειδίαν, καὶ αὐτοῦ τοῦ Περικλέους κατηγόρουν ἱεροσυλίαν. Diodorus adds the charge against Pericles himself, which P. treats at 32.3–4. This type of prosecution before the assembly was called εἰσαγγελία, a name also applied to other procedures: see MacDowell, Law, 183–86, and Harrison, Law, 2:50–59; and with a different classification, Hansen 1975. The details of the procedure are disputed: see Rhodes 1979 and Hansen 1980. We know a number of cases from the fifth century, including the prosecution of the profaners of the mysteries and of famous politicians such as Miltiades and Themistocles. Some hesitate to see εἰσαγγελία as the procedure in Phidias' case (Hansen does not include it in his catalogue of cases, 1975, 69–111, and MacDowell writes, p. 149, "it is not clear whether [Phidias] . . . was prosecuted for impiety or temple-robbery or both, nor which legal procedure was used"). But there is every reason to accept that the assembly heard the case directly, for theft of material destined for the chryselephantine statue was certainly of major concern to the Athenians, even without the obvious political implications, and could easily have been classified as impiety (*asebeia*) or temple-robbery (*hierosylia*, Diodorus' word). P. describes the charge as theft, using the less serious term to avoid connecting Phidias and Pericles with *hierosylia*. But the charge represents a frontal attack on Pericles' famous incorruptibility and care in public accounts as well as on the reverence for the gods implied in the construction of the Parthenon and other buildings. The danger to Pericles of such a charge should not be underestimated.

κλοπαὶ μὲν οὐχ ἠλέγχοντο: "theft was not proven." This does not necessarily mean that Phidias was acquitted, as often understood. The following ἡ δὲ δόξα τῶν ἔργων ἔπιεζε φθόνῳ τὸν Φειδίαν should probably be taken as a comment on the same trial, rather than a reference to a second trial for *asebeia*, and P.'s meaning would be "although the charge was not proven, factors such as envy and his self-portrait resulted in his condemnation."

τὸ γὰρ χρύσιον κτλ.: Cf. Thuc. 2.13.5, ἀπέφαινε δ᾽ ἔχον τὸ ἄγαλμα τεσσαράκοντα τάλαντα σταθμὸν χρυσίου ἀπέφθου, καὶ περιαιρετὸν εἶναι ἅπαν. χρησαμένους τε ἐπὶ σωτηρίᾳ ἔφη χρῆναι μὴ ἐλάσσω ἀντικαταστῆσαι πάλιν. (This passage is freely quoted by P. at *De aere al.* 828B.) For the design of the statue, by which plates—gold for Athena's garments and ivory for the flesh—were affixed to an inner wooden core, see the bibliography cited at 13.14. There is no certain evidence that the gold was ever removed for any purpose, although Lachares, the third-century tyrant of Athens, was said to have done so to pay his mercenaries: cf. *De Is.* 379C; Paus. 1.25.7; and the skeptical note of Gomme, *HCT* 2:25n. 1.

Figures for the quantity of gold vary: Diod. 12.40.3 says 50 talents, Philochorus F121 gives 44, and Thucydides 2.13.5 reports 40. In a note to *IG* I^3 460, the summation of expenses for the statue, D. M. Lewis calculates that 44 gold talents equal 616 silver talents at 14:1 and that the minimum total costs extant on the annual records were almost 354 silver talents, whereas the *epistatai* received in all between 700 and 1,000 silver talents. See also Gomme, *HCT* 2:24–25; Donnay 1967; Eddy 1977. There was ample opportunity for theft! Philochorus F121 speaks of the ivory plaques on the statue: *Φειδίας ὁ ποιήσας, δόξας παραλογίζεσθαι τὸν ἐλέφαντα τὸν εἰς τὰς φολίδας, ἐκρίθη*, although a paraphrase mentions gold, *ὑφείλετο τὸ χρυσίον ἐκ τῶν δρακόντων τῆς χρυσελεφαντίνης Ἀθηνᾶς*. Gold was much more valuable than ivory and easier to steal. Kunze 1959 notes that many scraps of ivory were found in Phidias' workshop at Olympia, but only traces of gold. It would not have been a trivial matter to accept Pericles' challenge and dismantle the statue to weigh the gold (cf. Mansfeld 1980, 28–29).

γνώμη τοῦ Περικλέους: P. grants to Pericles the foresight elsewhere ascribed to him (cf. 18.1, 21.1, 33.3, 6). More likely, it was the most practical way of making the statue.

ἐκέλευσε: a rhetorical challenge, as at 14.1. P. does not say that the gold was actually removed.

τὴν πρὸς Ἀμαζόνας μάχην: The great shield of the Parthenos statue was decorated with a complex relief composition representing the battle of Theseus and the Athenians against the invading Amazons. The figures would have been at least a meter high. For the story of the battle cf. Plut. *Thes.* 26–28. The battle with the Amazons was a favorite subject of Greek art, especially at Athens (e.g., on the Athenian treasury at Delphi, the Stoa Poikile, and the Theseion): see von Bothmar 1957; Boardman 1982. It appears also as part of the sculptural program of the Parthenon, on the west metopes. For attempts to reconstruct the design of the shield, on the basis of late copies and imitations of the Parthenos statue or of the shield, see E. Harrison 1966, 1981; Strocka 1967, 1984; Leipen 1971, 41–47; Hoelscher and Simon 1976.

πρεσβύτου . . . χειρῶν: The figure is clearly visible on copies, e.g., the Lenormant Athena (E. Harrison 1966, plate 36a); on the Strangford copy he holds an axe. See Harrison's no. 15; Hoelscher and Simon 1976, no. 16.

τοῦ Περικλέους εἰκόνα: Although in some versions the face is not covered, Plutarch's testimony and the Strangford copy (see E.

Harrison 1966, plate 37a) would indicate that on the original it was. The figure is no. 2 in Harrison and in Hoelscher and Simon 1976.

31.4

σχῆμα: "position, pose."

οἷον . . . ἑκατέρωθεν: "as if it were meant to hide the resemblance that could be glimpsed from either side." For βούλεται with an impersonal subject cf. *Sol.* 20.1, *Sull.* 34.3, *De glor. Ath.* 348A, etc.; LSJ s.v. βούλομαι III.

The gold and ivory statue soon became a wonder in popular legend, and Phidias, its sculptor, a new Daedalus who combined technical skill and magic. The self-portrait is not mentioned in fifth- or fourth-century sources, and surely is invented. Cicero speaks of a portrait of Phidias on the shield, which he considers a kind of artistic signature (*Tusc.* 1.34). Only Plutarch and Dio Chrysostom (*Or.* 12.6) mention the portrait of Pericles as well as that of Phidias. All three references to portraits probably depend on a single post-classical tradition with no basis in fact. Cf. the similar story of Polygnotus painting a portrait of Elpinice in the Stoa Poikile, *Cim.* 4.6. There is always a desire to make such personal connections with works of art. Other late authors, however, connect Phidias' portrait with a hidden mechanism to destroy the statue if the portrait were removed, clearly a fantastic reference to the actual possibility of removing the gold panels. See Val. Max. 8.14.6, ps.-Arist. *De mir. ausc.* 846a, *De Mundo* 399b; Apuleius *De Mundo* 32; Ampelius *Lib. mem.* 8.10 (where Phidias is replaced by Daedalus), with the analysis of Preisshofen 1974.

31.5

εἰς τὸ δεσμώτηριον . . . ἐτελεύτησε: Only P. and Philochorus F121 trace Phidias' fate beyond his trial, P. having him die in prison at Athens whereas Philochorus reports that he fled or was exiled, went to Olympia, and there was charged with theft and died in prison. Schol. *Peace* 605 gives two slightly different paraphrases of Philochorus: φυγὼν εἰς Ἦλιν ἐργολαβῆσαι τὸ ἄγαλμα τοῦ Διὸς τοῦ ἐν Ὀλυμπίᾳ λέγεται, τοῦτο δὲ ἐξεργασάμενος ἀποθανεῖν ὑπὸ Ἠλείων

and καταγνωσθεὶς ζημιώθη φυγῇ· γενόμενος δὲ εἰς Ἧλιν καὶ ἐργο-
λαβήσας παρὰ τῶν Ἠλείων τὸ ἄγαλμα τοῦ Διὸς τοῦ Ὀλυμπίου καὶ
καταγνωσθεὶς ὑπ' αὐτῶν ὡς νοσφισάμενος ἀνῃρέθη. For the correct-
ness of Philochorus, at least in having Phidias work at Elis after
constructing the Parthenos statue, see note to 31.2–32.6 ("The
Trials of Pericles' Friends"). P.'s imprisonment story seems to be a
doublet of Philochorus' account, or simply a compression of his
source, like the union of the Epidaurus and Potidaea campaigns at
35.3. Both stories seem to be inventions, death narratives of the
sort favored by Hellenistic authors, although there is nothing improbable about Phidias' enriching himself from the materials for
the statue, or being suspected of it. Imprisonment was normal at
Athens for one who did not pay a fine owed to the state: see
Harrison, *Law*, 2:177, 241–44. Later tradition said that Miltiades
had been held in prison until he could pay his fine, and died there,
although Herodotus is silent on that part of the story, which may
be invented: cf. Hdt. 6.136.3; Nepos *Mil.* 7.6; Diod. 10.30.1; Val.
Max. 5.3.ext. 3; Plut. *Cim.* 4.4. The reference to poison in Phidias'
case is no doubt fictitious. According to Pausanias (5.14.4–5)
Phidias' descendants were honored at Elis, which argues against
his condemnation there. See the full discussion by Jacoby, commentary to *FGrHist* 328 F121, with the comments of Bloch 1959,
494–99. The papyrus fragment mentioning Phidias and Elis (see
Judeich 1925; Jacoby, *FGrHist* 3B suppl., 2:399n. 46a; Pack 1965,
no. 2532) is too mutilated to be useful.

We may conclude that Phidias was denounced by Menon, tried
by the ecclesia, and condemned despite Pericles' defense. He fled
from Athens to Elis (either before or after judgment), where he
made the great Zeus. He may have died there.

φασιν ἔνιοι: this version is otherwise unknown.

ἐπὶ διαβολῇ: "to discredit"; cf. 28.3. It is not clear, however, how
the poisoning or sudden death of Phidias would discredit Pericles:
was it that he could not help his friend, or that an apparent suicide
would seem a confession of guilt, or that Pericles had killed a
fellow criminal to preserve himself (cf. the charge that he had
killed Ephialtes, 10.7)? It all sounds rather like a declamation, as
in Hermogenes 56 Rabe: a general is convicted of treason, impris-

oned in a second general's house, then killed by the second general, who gives the explanation that the prisoner had seduced his wife. The second general is then suspected of being part of the same plot and of having removed his fellow conspirator to prevent his own exposure. Cf. Russell 1983, 51.

γράψαντος Γλαύκωνος: The naming of the mover indicates that P. knew a specific decree, his special contribution to the story of Phidias. Honorary decrees of this sort were regularly set up on stelai in a public place, where they would be accessible to a collector such as Craterus, P.'s probable source: see the Introduction, 3.1.1. Γλαύκωνος is Pareti's emendation (1909, 274) of Γλύκωνος, a name otherwise unknown in Attic prosopography. There were several politically important figures in fifth-century Athens named Glaucon, including the son of Leagros, who was general in 441/40, 439/38, and 433/32, when he led the reinforcing fleet to Corcyra (*RE* s.v. Glaucon 4, VII, 1 (1912) 1402; Davies, *APF* 90–92). If he is the mover, then Pericles had opponents even in the board of generals, a not unreasonable assumption. The Dracontides who attacked Pericles (cf. 32.2) was perhaps a general of the second squadron sent to Corcyra in 433; see note to 29.3.

ἀτέλειαν: "exemption from obligations," a valuable honor, given especially but not exclusively to noncitizens who had proved benefactors of the demos and were made πρόξενοι of Athens. Cf. M. B. Walbank 1978, 6; Henry 1983, 241–46; Rhodes, *CAAP* 509, 652–54. If this is a proxeny decree, then Menon was not a citizen. Perhaps he was an itinerant sculptor working on the building program. The grant would not have been made unless Phidias were condemned, and the decree is our best evidence that in fact he was. In an attempt to discredit this argument Gomme, *HCT* 2:185n. 1, suggested emending to ἄδειαν, making this the decree that gave Menon the immunity requested in 31.2. But P. without doubt is using the decree to close off his narrative of the trial, for which ἄδειαν does not make sense.

τοῖς στρατηγοῖς ἐπιμελεῖσθαι: another standard phrase in honorary decrees. Cf. M. B. Walbank 1978, 5–6; Henry 1983, 171–81; and, e.g., *IG* I³ 110 for Oiniades, ll. 15–19: καὶ ὅπως ἂν μὴ ἀδικῆται ἐπιμέλεσθαι τήν τε βολὴν τὴν ἀεὶ βολεύοσαν καὶ τοὺς στρατηγὸς. Ateleia is combined with this recommendation in only a few inscriptions (Walbank's nos. 37, 73, 77, 85, 93). This protection clause is not found after the fourth century (Henry, 186n. 42).

32.1

περὶ δὲ τοῦτον τὸν χρόνον: a very vague indication of date; cf. note to 31.2.

Aspasia: cf. note to chapter 24. The reality of this prosecution has frequently been doubted: that the accuser is a comic poet and that there is a reference to procuring suggest that the source was a scene from comedy (cf., e.g., Adcock, CAH 5, 478; Gomme, HCT 2:187; Donnay 1968, 29; Dover 1975, 28). However, Aeschines in his Aspasia (cf. 32.5 = p. 48 Krauss) gave Pericles' behavior at the trial as an instance of Aspasia's influence, and the argument would be without force if there were not a basis in fact. Its reality or probability is supported by Frost 1964b, 395–96; Schwarze, Beurteilung, 110–113; and Ehlers 1966, 68–69, 74–75. In Aeschines' dialogue there would have been a play between the roles of literal and philosophical procuress (cf. Socrates as matchmaker in Plat. Tht. 150A, etc.). Other references to the trial (Athen. 13.589E; schol. Ar. Knights 969; [Lucian] Amor. 30; and an anecdote preserved in Syriac, cf. Ehlers 1966, 77n. 158) all seem to derive from Aeschines, who is probably P.'s source as well. (Athenaeus may be citing Antisthenes' Aspasia to which he ascribes the sentence that immediately precedes the mention of the trial: thus Giannantoni 1983, 2:374. However, he is following Herodicus' collection of κωμῳδούμενοι and probably is here introducing without notice a citation to Aeschines instead. Cf. Dittmar 1912, 279; Ehlers 1966, 66n. 108.) Only P. gives the name of the accuser.

The charge, asebeia (cf. also Athen. 13.589E), is very general and not otherwise defined in our sources. Any number of offenses could be meant (cf. MacDowell, Law, 197–200) but the additional charge of procuring free women suggests that Aspasia was accused of entering sanctuaries or participating in sacred rites although as a prostitute or procuress she was excluded (cf. [Dem.]

59.113–14). There is no reason to think she was prosecuted for intellectual activity or for holding the "atheistic" views of which Anaxagoras was accused, nor for Medism, as argued by Montuori 1978 and 1981.

The time is uncertain. Hermippus won his first prize in 435; he would have been active before then. Exactly in 438/37 is overprecise. On this trial see Ehlers 1966, 68–71; Schwarze, *Beurteilung*, 110–13; Klein 1979, 509–10; Mansfeld 1980, 32–33, 77–78; Frost 1964b, 395–96.

For the theft of two of Aspasia's whores as the cause of the war see note to 30.4.

δίκην ἔφευγεν: "was prosecuted, was a defendant."

Hermippus: See the Introduction, 3.1.i. His opposition to Pericles is apparent in F46 K. = F47 K.A., quoted at 33.8.

ἐλευθέρας . . . ὑποδέχοιτο: A similar expression is used of Phidias at 13.15, where P. notes that the charge was taken up by the comic poets, along with other attacks on Pericles as a womanizer. Εἰς τὸ αὐτὸ φοιτώσας, "to visit together," seems to be P.'s euphemism for having sexual intercourse (see *Alex.* 48.7, *Pomp.* 35.6, *Brut. anim.* 990C; fr. 157, l. 93 Sandbach; and probably *Num.* 4.11, *Artax.* 19.3), and is not therefore a quotation from the comic poets.

32.2

Diopithes: a seer, often mocked by the comic poets as a fanatic and a thief; see Ar. *Knights* 1085, *Wasps* 380, *Birds* 988 with schol. He may be also the mover of the Methone decree (ML 65, ca. 430) and the seer who opposed Agesilaus' becoming king of Sparta in 397 (Xen. *Hell.* 3.3.3; Plut. *Ages.* 3.6–7, *Lys.* 22.10–12). Connor 1963 argues that he was not an oligarch, as usually thought, but a political opportunist; cf. also Frost 1964b, 396–99; Schachermeyr 1968, 61–65.

Only P., using his documentary source, mentions this decree, which seems especially aimed at Pericles. The imprisonment and trial of Anaxagoras, however, spawned a variety of stories. Diog. Laert. 2.12–14 cites four diverse accounts by name. According to Sotion, Anaxagoras was accused of *asebeia* by Cleon for having said that the sun was a mass of metal (μύδρος), was defended by Pericles, fined 5 talents, and exiled; according to Satyrus, he was prosecuted by Thucydides (as a way of opposing Pericles) for both impiety and Medism and was condemned to death in absentia. Hermippus has him in prison under a capital charge, and Hieronymus has a similar story that he was freed when Pericles brought him before the court, wasted with sickness. Thucydides and Cleon seem unlikely comrades in a trial, and probably one or the other, if not both, is erroneously named (*pace* Schachermeyr 1968, 57–59). A fifth account was given by Ephorus, who apparently put the trial in the context of the attack on Phidias and the beginning of the war (Diod. 12.39.2). P. refers to the prosecution at *Nic.* 23.4 as an indication of the hostile reception of scientific thinking at that time (οὐ γὰρ ἠνείχοντο τοὺς φυσικοὺς καὶ μετεωρολέσχας τότε καλουμένους, ὡς εἰς αἰτίας ἀλόγους καὶ δυνάμεις ἀπρονοήτους καὶ κατηναγκασμένα πάθη διατρίβοντας τὸ θεῖον, ἀλλὰ καὶ Πρωταγόρας ἔφυγε καὶ Ἀναξαγόραν εἰρχθέντα μόλις περιεποιήσατο ὁ Περικλῆς) and again at *De superst.* 169F, Ἀναξαγόρας δίκην ἔφυγεν ἀσεβείας ἐπὶ τῷ λίθον εἰπεῖν τὸν ἥλιον.

The date of the trial, like the whole chronology of Anaxagoras' life, has been the subject of furious controversy, with suggestions ranging between the 450s and 430. For a full study see Mansfeld 1980 (on the trial itself see 80–84). It is best to place it, as P. does, in proximity to Phidias' trial, but we cannot securely set it (as do Frost 1964b and Mansfeld) in 438/37. See also Derenne 1930, 13–41; Rudhardt 1960, 90–92; Schachermeyr 1968; Meiggs, *AE* 435–36; Marasco 1976, 116–19; Klein 1979, 510. Taylor's argument (1917) that Anaxagoras must have left Athens before 450 is untenable; Woodbury 1981 argues more persuasively for the early 440s. The compromise of Davison 1953 (followed by Meiggs, *AE* 283, 436), that there were two trials, one early and one late, seems unnecessary.

P. suggests in 32.5 that Anaxagoras never came to trial, because he was spirited out by Pericles beforehand, but other authors disagree; cf. Mansfeld 1980, 82–84. Dover 1975, 27–32, skeptically—but perhaps rightly—notes that of all our sources, "no one of them actually knew what happened to Anaxagoras," and that we have no real evidence for his trial. His doubts extend to Diopithes' decree (cf. pp. 39–41).

εἰσαγγέλλεσθαι: "be subject to εἰσαγγελία"; cf. note to 31.3. The usual procedure for *asebeia* was a *graphē*, as with Aspasia and Socrates. This is the earliest explicit example of an εἰσαγγελία proceeding, granted that P. is preserving the decree's technical language and not introducing his own. See Ostwald 1986, 196, 525.

τοὺς τὰ θεῖα μὴ νομίζοντας: cf. the accusation against Socrates, Plato *Apol.* 24B, θεοὺς οὓς ἡ πόλις νομίζει οὐ νομίζοντα. Νομίζω can mean "believe in, practice, observe." Diopithes was attacking new beliefs and practices concerning what was divine, such as Anaxagoras' argument that the sun was a physical object. In this sense the two clauses of the decree, on τὰ θεῖα and τὰ μετάρσια, refer to the same offense. For a full discussion see Derenne 1930, 217–24; Rudhardt 1960, 90–92; Ostwald 1986, 196–97, 528–36. Diod. 12.39.2 is more vague: Ἀναξαγόραν . . . ὡς ἀσεβοῦντα εἰς τοὺς θέους ἐσυκοφάντουν.

τῶν μεταρσίων: Ionic and poetic for τὰ μετέωρα, "things in the sky." Cf. note to 5.1, μεταρσιολεσχίας. The word is used by P. only here, except for a reference at *Qu. Gr.* 292C to Theophrastus' περὶ μεταρσίων (cf. Diog. Laert. 5.44, Μεταρσιολογικῶν α'β'). The use of the form is puzzling, as it reflects neither Attic prose usage nor P.'s own.

ἀπερειδόμενος . . . τὴν ὑπόνοιαν: "laying suspicion (of impiety) on Pericles through Anaxagoras."

32.3

δεχομένου: the receptivity of the demos toward the charges against Anaxagoras encouraged the opposition to move against Pericles. Προσιεμένου, "approving, welcoming," strengthens δεχομένου.

κυροῦται: "was passed"; cf. *Alc.* 33.1, τὸ μὲν οὖν ψήφισμα . . . ἐκεκύρωτο; *Ti. Gracch.* 13.1, κυροῦται μὲν ὁ περὶ τῆς χώρας νόμος. For the tense cf. note to 9.2.

Dracontides: This man and his decree demanding a review of Pericles' accounts are mentioned only by P., again using a documentary source. He probably is identical with the Dracontides who was *epistates* of the boule when a decree on Chalcis was passed in 446/45 (ML 52, l. 2 = *IG* I³ 40) and with one of the generals of the relief expedition to Corcyra in 433/32 with Glaucon (ML 61, l. 20 = *IG* I³ 364; cf. Thuc. 1.51, where the mss. have Andocides), but not with his namesake, who was one of the Thirty Tyrants (Xen. *Hell.* 2.3.2; cf. Arist. *Ath. pol.* 34.3). He may also be identical with the Dracontides mocked for escaping prosecution in Ar. *Wasps* 157 (cf. 438).

The decree demands a special accounting by Pericles to the prytany in office, with an extraordinary procedure to insure that they take their work seriously. As Frost has argued (1964a), this combination of financial review and religious obligation points to a scrutiny (εὔθυνα) in connection with the condemnation of Phidias for theft rather than the deposition described by Thucydides in 2.65.3 (cf. notes to 31.2 and 35.4). The decree itself, as usual at this time, would not have recorded the archon year. On the scrutiny of accounts cf. note to 23.1; and MacDowell, *Law*, 170–72; Roberts 1982, esp. 59–62. Diodorus must be referring to this accusation at 12.39.2, καὶ αὐτοῦ τοῦ Περικλέους κατηγόρουν ἱεροσυλίαν; cf. the Suda's notice (s.v. Φειδίας) that Pericles stole 50 talents. Harrison, *Law*, 2:57n. 4, suggests that Pericles' case would probably have been an εἰσαγγελία.

To this occasion should be ascribed the various anecdotes concerning Alcibiades' advice to Pericles, to consider how *not* to render an account: Diod. 12.38.3–4; Aristodemus 16.4; Val. Max. 3.1.ext. 1 (accounts for the Propylaea).

οἱ λόγοι τῶν χρημάτων: most probably his accounts as an *epistatēs* of the Parthenos statue, not as general. (For this position see note to 13.9.) These accounts would normally be examined by the *logistai* (*Ath. pol.* 54.2), not the *prytaneis*, that is, the fifty members of one tribe who sat as the executive committee of the boule for a tenth of the year. On their duties cf. Rhodes 1972, 21–23.

ἀποτεθεῖεν: "be set out for, be deposited with." Cf. *Ath. pol.* 54.2, λογιστὰς . . . πρὸς οὓς ἅπαντας ἀνάγκη τοὺς τὰς ἀρχὰς ἄρξαντας λόγον ἀπενεγκεῖν.

ἀπὸ τοῦ βωμοῦ: the great altar of Athena on the Acropolis, located near the east front of the Erechtheum, the goal of the Panathenaic procession. See Jahn and Michaelis 1901, at 26.20; Judeich 1931, 269–70; Herington 1955, 28–29; and for the probable location, Travlos, *Pictorial Dictionary*, plate 91, no. 121; Jahn and Michaelis 1901, plate E. It was here that the Cylonian conspirators had taken refuge, according to one version of the story (Thuc. 1.126.10; Heraclides' epitome of *Ath. pol.*, 2). Casting voting pebbles taken from an altar rendered the decision more solemn. For other examples of this practice see Hdt. 8.123.2 (cf. *Them.* 17.2) and Dem. 18.134.

φέρειν τὴν ψῆφον: "to cast one's vote"; cf. LSJ s.v. φέρω, A.IV.7.

τῇ πόλει: the Acropolis; cf. 3.6. P.'s word echoes his documentary source.

32.4

Hagnon: a leading figure in this period, general in 440/39 (when he participated in the Samian War; Thuc. 1.117), in 431/30 (when he besieged Potidaea; Thuc. 2.58), and in 429/28 (Thuc. 2.95.3). In 437/36 he led out the colony to Amphipolis, of which he was *oikistēs* (Thuc. 4.102.3, 5.11.1). Cratinus' *Ploutoi* made an issue of his wealth (cf. the new fragment in Page 1950, 201; *CGFP* 73; *PCG* F171, ll. 66–76). In later years he was a signer of the Peace of Nicias (Thuc. 5.19.2, 24.1) and chosen *proboulos* in 413 (Lys. 12.65). Cf. Davies, *APF* 227–28. The statesman Theramenes was his son. His amendment here indicates that he was a supporter of Pericles, softening Dracontides' attack (cf. Gomme, *HCT* 2:189), although some take him as another opponent.

τοῦτο μὲν ἀφεῖλε κτλ.: "he canceled this clause, and moved. . . ." Hagnon amended Dracontides' decree, changing the procedure to be used. Both original decree and amendment were recorded, as we often see in inscriptions, in the form Ἅγνων εἶπε· τὰ μὲν ἄλλα καθάπερ Δρακοντίδης· τὴν δὲ δίκην . . . (cf., e.g., ML 52, l. 70; 73, l. 47). The effect was to change the procedure to that of a normal trial, although with what probably was an unusually large jury. For other occasions when the ecclesia specified the size of a jury cf. ML

69, l. 16 (one thousand men), and Lysias 13.35 (two thousand). In the latter passage Lysias stresses that it was tyrannical of the Thirty to bring men to trial before the boule rather than before the court ordered by the demos. Cf. MacDowell, *Law*, 36–38; Rhodes 1972, 164–65.

εἴτε κλοπῆς . . . ἀδικίου: "whether for theft, bribery, or malversation." The three are listed as the possible charges resulting from examination by the *logistai* (*Ath. pol.* 54.2). The first two appear in Ar. *Clouds* 591 and Andoc. 1.74; the third, misuse of public monies, seems to be described in Andoc. 1.73 (cf. MacDowell's commentary, 1962, ad. loc.). Ἀδικίου, Reiske's emendation of ms. ἀδικίας or ἀδίκου, restores the technical word that would have been found in the original document, but that does not occur otherwise in P.

32.5

παρὰ τὴν δίκην: "during the trial," not "contrary to justice." Cf. *Pel.* 25.14, τὸν μὲν Χάρωνα παρὰ πᾶσαν τὴν δίκην ἐγκωμιάζων ἀφθόνως διετέλεσε; *Them.* 8.1, παρὰ τοὺς κινδύνους. Contrast *Cam.* 5.7, οὐ παρὰ δίκην ἀλλὰ κατ' ἀνάγκην.

Aeschines: the Socratic philosopher, in his dialogue *Aspasia* (F11, p. 48 Krauss). See the Introduction, 3.3.c, and notes to 24.6, 32.1. Cf. Athen. 13.589E, ὑπὲρ αὐτῆς πλείονα ἐδάκρυσεν ἢ ὅτε ὑπὲρ τοῦ βίου καὶ τῆς οὐσίας ἐκινδύνευε. Because she was a resident alien or metic, Pericles probably spoke as her *prostatēs*, and thus her *kyrios* as well: cf. schol. Ar. *Knights* 969 (an example of calling a case to court), Ἀσπασία καὶ κύριος, τούτεστιν Περικλέης; Clerc 1893, 264. But it is not certain that the relationship of *prostatēs* was permanent; see Whitehead 1977, 90–92.

φοβηθεὶς ⟨τὸ δικαστήριον⟩ ἐξέκλεψε καὶ προύπεμψεν: The text is uncertain. Ziegler accepts Madvig's (1878, 575) transfer of τὸ δικαστήριον after φοβηθεὶς and Emperius's emendation (1847) of ἐξέπεμψεν to ἐξέκλεψε. The problem lies in the mss.' repetitions of φοβηθεὶς and the two compounds of πέμπω, and the inappropriateness of προύπεμψεν, which in P. usually means "escort publicly." Φοβέομαι does not require an object, so Madvig's addition of δικαστήριον is unnecessary. He is right, however, to delete as a gloss φοβηθεὶς τὸ δικαστήριον in the next sentence. Ἐξέκλεψε is the *vox propria* for sneaking someone away from his enemies (cf. 25.4, *Them.* 24.6, *Pyrrh.* 2.1, etc.) but exactly for that reason is inappropriate here. Mansfeld 1980, 81, 86, notes that if Anaxagoras were a fugitive from Athenian justice he would not have been allowed to settle as he did in Lampsacus, a city of the Delian League, and even be honored there (cf. *Praec. ger. rep.* 820D). Pericles must have reached a compromise of some sort. In that case προύπεμψεν could stand, but it is best omitted as a doublet. Read with Flacelière φοβηθεὶς ἐξέπεμψεν.

P. thought that Anaxagoras had been imprisoned for a time (before or after trial?). Cf. *Nic.* 23.4, Ἀναξαγόραν εἰρχθέντα μόλις περιεποιήσατο Περικλῆς; *De prof. in virt.* 84F, *De exil.* 607F.

32.6

P. returns to the story found in Aristophanes and Ephorus. The sentence is made more weighty by the participles and the long genitive absolute τῆς πόλεως . . . ἀναθείσης ἑαυτήν.

προσέπταισε: "stumble over, be blocked by or clash with." Cf. *Comp. Per.–Fab.* 3.3, Τολμίδης . . . προσέπταισε Βοιωτοῖς; *Cat. Min.* 30.3, νομίζων οὐ μικρὰ προσπταίσειν τῷ Κάτωνι μὴ φίλῳ γενομένῳ.

φοβηθείς: cf. Ar. *Peace* 606–8, εἶτα Περικλέης φοβηθεὶς μὴ μετάσχοι τῆς τύχης, / τὰς φύσεις ὑμῶν δεδοικὼς καὶ τὸν αὐτοδὰξ τρόπον / πρὶν παθεῖν τι δεινὸν αὐτός. . . .

μέλλοντα τὸν πόλεμον καὶ ὑποτυφόμενον ἐξέκαυσεν: "he enflamed the war that was coming and smoldering." The second participle intensifies and elaborates the first. For this sense of μέλλω cf. *Aem.* 18.3, τοῦ μέλλοντος ἀγῶνος; *Alex.* 31.11; *Cim.* 16.6. P. frequently employs ἐκκαύω to refer to stirring up something already present: cf. 20.4, *Fab.* 7.4, *Pomp.* 30.6, etc.; and for wars, *Ages.* 31.4, ἐκκαύσας τὸν πόλεμον; *Comp. Ages.–Pomp.* 1.4, τὸν Βοιώτιον ἐκκαύσας πόλεμον. More examples of fire imagery in Fuhrmann 1964, 83n. 1, 254. The fire image is as early as Homer (cf. Whitman 1965, 129–44). But here P. probably was also thinking of Ar. *Peace*

608–10, ἐξέφλεξε τὴν πόλιν / ἢ 'μβαλὼν σπινθῆρα μικρὸν Μεγαρικοῦ ψηφίσματος, / ἐξεφύσησεν τοσοῦτον πόλεμον.

ἐν πράγμασι μεγάλοις: cf. Diod.12.39.3, ὁ δὲ Περικλῆς, εἰδὼς τὸν δῆμον ἐν μὲν τοῖς πολεμικοῖς ἔργοις θαυμάζοντα τοὺς ἀγαθοὺς ἄνδρας διὰ τὰς κατεπειγούσας χρείας, κατὰ δὲ τὴν εἰρήνην τοὺς αὐτοὺς συκοφαντοῦντα διὰ τὴν σχολὴν καὶ φθόνον, ἔκρινε συμφέρειν αὐτῷ τὴν πόλιν ἐμβαλεῖν εἰς μέγαν πόλεμον, ὅπως χρείαν ἔχουσα τῆς Περικλέους ἀρετῆς καὶ στρατηγίας μὴ προσδέχηται τὰς κατ' αὐτοῦ διαβολάς, μηδ' ἔχῃ σχολὴν καὶ χρόνον ἐξετάζειν ἀκριβῶς τὸν περὶ τῶν χρημάτων λόγον.

ἐκείνῳ: Pericles.

ἀναθείσης: "entrusting"; cf. *Mul. virt.* 263C, τῇ δὲ γυναικὶ τὴν ἀρχὴν καὶ τὴν πόλιν ἀναθεὶς ἅπασαν.

ἐνδοῦναι: cf. 30.1, ἐνέδωκεν; 31.1, ἐνδόσεως.

τὸ δ' ἀληθὲς ἄδηλον: P. refuses to commit himself. Cf. his comment at *De prim. frig.* 955C, τὸ ἐπέχειν ἐν τοῖς ἀδήλοις τοῦ συγκατατίθεσθαι φιλοσοφώτερον ἡγούμενος, and for historical questions, *Alc.* 35.1, *Alex.* 49.5, *Dem.* 10.5, 15.5. This is more cautious than his precept in *De malig. Her.* 855F, ὁ δ' ἱστορίαν γράφων ἅ μὲν οἶδε ἀληθῆ λέγων δίκαιός ἐστι, τῶν δ' ἀδήλων τὰ βελτίονα δοκεῖν ἀληθῶς λέγεσθαι μᾶλλον ἢ τὰ χείρονα. In any case P.'s admiration for Pericles and Thucydides prevents him from accepting the account of τοὺς πλείστους μάρτυρας.

33–35

From the Peloponnesian Invasion to Pericles' Condemnation (Spring 431–Fall 430). Once more Thucydides' narrative forms the basis for P., with only occasional additions (33.5, 35.2, 5: see Meinhardt, 61–64). P. of course omits historical actions not directly related to Pericles, such as the siege of Plataea (Thuc. 2.1–6) and the alliance with Sitalces (2.29–30). But he also omits much that Thucydides considered important about Pericles: his funeral oration and last speech (2.34–46, 60–64) and most of his evaluation of Athenian revenues (2.13.3–8), as well as his move to reject heralds while the Peloponnesians were on the march (2.12.2), the dispatch of the fleet to Locris (2.26, 32) and of Hagnon to Potidaea (2.58), the second Peloponnesian invasion (2.47.2, 55, 57) and the Athenian peace mission to Sparta (2.59.2). What remains is a simplified narrative emphasizing Pericles' efforts to control the Athenians, reinforced by P.'s own observations and deductions. That P. here can add only a few details to Thucydides' account indicates how much the historian's narrative dominated the tradition of these years.

The resulting portrait shows much less of Pericles the strategist and of his intellectual analysis of resources and military and political options, or even of Pericles the military commander, than Thucydides does. Intellectual capacity is not seen as a virtue (contrast Thucydides' emphasis on σύνεσις), and no effort is made to understand the military situation or nonpolitical needs.

References below show P.'s debt to Thucydides. For a justification of Pericles' policy of refusing to defend the Attic countryside against the Peloponnesian army (cf. Thuc. 1.143.5, 2.13.2, 2.62.2–3) see Cawkwell 1975, 53–70.

33.1

οἱ δὲ Λακεδαιμόνιοι κτλ.: P. backtracks to the embassies mentioned at 29.7, where his attention had become focused on Pericles' refusal to repeal the Megarian decree. This is the first embassy mentioned by Thucydides (1.126.1, 127.1). The Spartan demand links thematically with the previous chapter (as it increases Pericles' popularity) and begins the new account of Pericles' relations with the Athenians. P. does not report that the Spartans hoped thus to cause the Athenians to blame Pericles for the war (Thuc. 1.127.2). The return to this topic may have been suggested by Thucydides (2.13.1), who recalls the Spartan maneuver when he mentions Pericles' speech before the war and his guest-friendship with Archidamus.

καταλυθέντος: cf. note to 6.3.

μαλακωτέροις χρήσονται: "they will find them more compliant." *Χρῶμαι* is not found in this sense in LSJ s.v. *χράω* B., although C.IV., "treat as," is close, and Xen. *Cyr.* 3.2.4, cited there, has this sense. Holden's note cites a number of examples from P. For the thought cf. Thuc. 1.127.1, *νομίζοντες ἐκπεσόντος αὐτοῦ ῥᾷον ἂν σφίσι προχωρεῖν*; for *μαλακωτέροις* cf. Thuc. 2.18.3, *δοκῶν . . . μαλακὸς εἶναι*, of Archidamus.

τὸ ἄγος ἐλαύνειν: cf. Thuc. 1.127.1, *τοῦτο δὴ τὸ ἄγος οἱ Λακεδαιμόνιοι ἐκέλευον ἐλαύνειν*, and 2.13.1, *τὰ ἄγη ἐλαύνειν προεῖπον*. The call to exclude those accursed by murder of suppliants must have seemed a fitting reply to the Athenian exclusion of Megarians as sacrilegious.

το Κυλώνειον: probably not an intrusive gloss, as suspected by Ziegler; cf. *Sol.* 12.1. In the seventh century Cylon had attempted to make himself tyrant at Athens. When he failed, his supporters took refuge as suppliants at the statue of Athena. Nevertheless they were killed by the magistrates, led by the Alcmeonid Megacles. The killers were considered *ἐναγεῖς*, and they and their descendants were banished, either immediately or later under Solon. The Alcmeonids returned, but in 508 Clisthenes and the Alcmeonids were once more driven out as accursed by Cleomenes of Sparta. See Hdt. 5.70–72; Thuc. 1.126 with Gomme, *HCT* ad loc.; Plut. *Sol.* 12.1–2; Paus. 7.25.3; schol. Ar. *Knights* 445. Rhodes, *CAAP* 79–84, presents a succinct analysis of the problems of reconciling the conflicting accounts. Cities, families, and individuals all could suffer from pollution in this way, although the Alcmeonids were unusual in Athens in the way the curse was regularly revived. See Parker 1983, 16–17, 183–84, 204, 206, who notes both that the cry "accursed" was a useful political slogan (as the Spartans knew) and that the Greeks regularly suspected pollution, or an inadequate purification, when trouble struck. Note, e.g., the repeated purifications of Delos (Hdt. 1.64.2; Thuc. 3.104.1–2, 5.1), and cf. note to 34.2.

In *Sol.* 12 as throughout that life, which was written after the *Pericles*, P. followed Aristotle's *Ath. pol.*, using the sections that are now only partially preserved (cf. *Ath. pol.* chapter 1 and Heraclides' epitome 2). Here in the *Pericles* P. found Thucydides sufficient.

τὸ μητρόθεν γένος: his mother, Agariste, was an Alcmeonid; cf. 3.2.

Thucydides: 1.127.1, εἰδότες δὲ Περικλέα τὸν Ξανθίππου προσεχόμενον αὐτῷ [sc. τῷ ἄγει] κατὰ τὴν μητέρα.

33.2

ἡ δὲ πεῖρα περιέστη . . . εἰς τοὐναντίον: "The effort turned out the contrary of what the senders had expected." Cf. *Luc.* 19.5, ἐμὲ δὲ . . . τούτου [Sulla] ζηλωτὴν γενόμενον εἰς τὴν Μομμίου δόξαν ὁ δαίμων περιέστησεν; *Cor.* 14.4, *Tim.* 5.3. There is no direct parallel in Thucydides, but note the Athenian trust in Pericles at 1.145. P. draws his own conclusion, using parallel pairs of verbs and nouns. I see no echo of Ephorus (as does Busolt, *Gr. Gesch.* 3.2:728n. 2). The alliteration in the first words is noteworthy.

33.3

Archidamus: cf. note to 8.5.

προεῖπε: cf. Thuc. 2.13.1. In Justin 3.7.8–9 and Polyaenus 1.36.2 Pericles gives the land outright before the Spartans come. We do not hear that in fact Pericles' land was spared. Hannibal caused Fabius some difficulty with the Romans when he spared his land while ravaging the countryside (*Fab.* 7.2–3). Cf. the successful use of the same tactic by the Spartan Cleandridas against Tegea (Polyaenus 2.10.3).

ἐκείνου: used as reflexive, i.e., Pericles. Cf. 32.6; LSJ s.v. I.5; Smyth 1259.

ξενίαν: a formal relation of friendship between two persons of different states, often hereditary. Frequently mentioned in Homer, in historical times it is generally found between leaders in the cities. Spartan kings figure often: cf. Cleomenes and Isagoras of Athens (Hdt. 5.70.1), Demaratus and Xerxes (Hdt. 7.237.3), Agesilaus and Mausolus (Xen. *Ages.* 2.27), Agesilaus and the son of Pharnabazus (Xen. *Hell.* 4.1.39–40). Demosthenes (18.51–52) denies with bitter sarcasm that Aeschines could be a ξένος of Philip II or Alexander, for such men as he are not friends but hirelings. As Pericles shows, ξενία was usually subordinate to community obligations; cf. Xen. *Hell.* 4.1.34. *Xenia* should be distinguished from *proxenia*, the relationship between an individual and another polis, such as Cimon's to Sparta: see Herman 1987; Wallace 1970; Perlman 1958. Lewis 1977, 47, notes that Pericles' *xenia* probably began when Archidamus' grandfather Leotychidas and Pericles' father Xanthippus were joint commanders of the Greek fleet in 479 (cf. Hdt. 8.131.2–3). Cf. the *xenia* of Cleomenes and Isagoras, which began ἀπὸ τῆς Πεισιστρατιδέων πολιορκίης (Hdt. 5.70.1). Herman 1987, 143–45, suggests that the friendship with Pericles also explains Archidamus' reluctance to attack Athens in 431. It may have been a factor, but I doubt that it was a major one.

ἐπαύλεις: buildings; cf. Thuc. 2.13.1, οἰκίας. Pericles' deme of Cholargus was well inland toward Acharnae and thus vulnerable to the first attack.

33.4

ἐμβάλλουσιν: May 431; cf. Thuc. 2.19.1. P. omits the brief siege of the fort at Oinoe.

Ἀχαρνάς: the largest of the Attic demes, in the neighborhood of modern Menidi, in the northwest corner of the Attic plain, near the pass to the Thriasian plain, 7 miles north of Athens. Cf. Thuc. 2.19.2–23.1 and *Princeton Encyclopedia of Classical Sites* (Stillwell 1976) s.v. (which notes that no remains are now visible) and, on the size of the deme, Dow 1961, correcting Thuc. 2.20.4. P. omits both Archidamus' hope of fragmenting Athenian unity and the cavalry battle won by the Peloponnesians (Thuc. 2.20.4, 22.2). Acharnian charcoal burners, fiercely anti-Spartan, form the chorus of Aristophanes' *Acharnians*.

33.5

δεινὸν ἐφαίνετο: an echo of Thuc. 2.21.2, where, however, it is the Athenians who are outraged that their land is ravaged. Pericles' policy of not confronting the Peloponnesians runs throughout Thucydides' account; cf. also 2.55.2, on the second invasion, omitted by P.

ἑξακισμυρίους: The number (found elsewhere only at *An seni* 784E and in Aristides *On the Four*, 2:189 Dindorf) is impossibly large: 20,000 to 25,000 is more likely. Cf. Kagan, *AW* 19n. 19; Busolt, *Gr. Gesch.* 3.2:860; Gomme, *HCT* 2:13. Thucydides says only that each state furnished two-thirds of its force (2.10.2). The Atthidographer Androtion gave a number that could be restored as 60,000 or some other figure (*FGrHist* 324 F39, καὶ μυριάσι, where καί must be corrupt). P. marks the enormous number emphatically. Meinhardt, 61, suggests Ephorus as his source, but Diodorus (12.42.3, 6) gives no figures. Could P. or his ms. of Thucydides have confused the historian's τὸν στρατὸν ἑξήκοντα (= ξ') σταδίους τῆς πόλεως ἀπέχοντα (2.21.2) with an army of 60,000 (= ,ξ)? When the Athenians attacked Megara later in the year they could field only 13,000 hoplites (Thuc. 2.31.2; 10,000 citizens and 3,000 metics); another 3,000 were at Potidaea.

Βοιωτῶν: cf. Thuc. 2.12.5.

ὑπὲρ αὐτῆς τῆς πόλεως: because there would be no one to defend the city in case of defeat.

δυσπαθοῦντας: For the thought cf. Thuc. 2.21.2–3. For the word, which is postclassical, cf. *Aem.* 36.2, *Caes.* 38.7, *De prof. in virt.* 77E: "complaining, being impatient."

κατεπράυνε, λέγων: The calming action, typical of P.'s Pericles, leads into a saying not found in Thucydides, presumably one of those recalled in the rhetorical tradition (cf. *Per.* 8.7–9): "It is better for trees to be cut down than men." A similar thought does occur at Thuc. 1.143.5, Pericles' first speech. The saying emphasizes Pericles' ἀσφάλεια; cf. 18.1.

33.6

εἰς ἐκκλησίαν οὐ συνῆγε: cf. Thuc. 2.22.1. We have no evidence that the generals had the power to block the assembly from meeting, but only of their right to call the assembly. Pericles avoided calling a crisis meeting, which many must have desired, and perhaps was able to postpone the regular monthly meeting until the Peloponnesians retired. Cf. Hignett, *HAC* 246–47; Rhodes 1972, 44–45; Kagan, *AW* 55–56.

παρὰ γνώμην: cf. Thuc. 2.22.1, *τοῦ μὴ ὀργῇ τι μᾶλλον ἢ γνώμῃ ξυνελθόντας ἐξαμαρτεῖν*. But *βιάζεσθαι παρὰ γνώμην* is a phrase of P.'s: cf. *Nic.* 11.2, *Marc.* 25.1. See also de Romilly 1988, 26–27.

ὥσπερ νεὼς κυβερνήτης: The image is Platonic (cf. *Rep.* 488A–E) but rewritten to fit the present situation. Like the saying in 33.5, it is part of the *auxēsis* of Pericles' role as leader controlling his emotional people (cf. 2.5). In the process P. almost makes him appear Plato's philosopher-king. The helmsman image also appears at *Cat. Mai.* 19.7 and *Phil.* 17.2–3. P.'s images of the sea and sailing are listed by Fuhrmann 1964, 49–50, 69n. 3, 234–37. The image of the ship of state is as old as Alcaeus 6. At *An seni* 784E P. gives Pericles' ability to hold back the Athenians as an example that his power was at its height in his old age.

ἀνέμου κατιόντος: cf. Thuc. 2.25.4; *Cam.* 34.3, *Luc.* 10.3.

κατατείνας τὰ ὅπλα: "drawing the ropes and cordage taut." *Ὅπλα* in this sense is Homeric, but cf. Hdt. 7.36, *κατέτεινον . . . τὰ ὅπλα*, of the cables of the Hellespontine bridge.

ἐπιβατῶν: "passengers."

συγκλείσας: cf. *An seni* 784E, [Pericles] *μονονοὺ τὰ ὅπλα τοῦ δήμου καὶ τὰς κλεῖς τῶν πυλῶν ἀποσφραγισάμενος*.

φυλακαῖς: cf. Thuc. 2.22.1, *τήν τε πόλιν ἐφύλασσε*.

ἐχρῆτο . . . λογισμοῖς: parallel to χρῆται τῇ τέχνῃ in the simile. Cf. 26.2, and, of Fabius, τὸν μὴ . . . προέμενον τοὺς αὑτοῦ·λογισμούς, *Comp. Per.–Fab.* 1.5.

βραχέα φροντίζων: "paying little attention"; cf. *Alex.* 15.9, ἐλάχιστα φροντίζειν, etc.

33.7

τῶν φίλων: not mentioned in Thucydides, but a nice balance to ἐχθρῶν. In Thuc. 2.22.1 also Pericles rules alone, but P. does not imitate the details of his presentation.

προσέκειντο: "urged."

χοροί: the choruses of comic plays. P. adds to Thucydides the evidence of comedy, which he knew mocked Pericles (cf. the Introduction, 3.1.d, and *Per.* 3.4–7). Ἦιδον here refers to comic choruses but may have been brought to mind when P. read Thuc. 2.21.3, χρησμολόγοι τε ἦιδον χρησμούς.

ἄνανδρον: cf. Thuc. 2.21.3, ἐκάκιζον ὅτι στρατηγὸς ὢν οὐκ ἐπεξάγοι.

33.8

ἐπεφύετο: "latch onto, harass, attack"; used, e.g., of dogs holding close to their quarry (*Luc.* 1.3). It is particularly appropriate here in the light of δηχθεὶς . . . Κλέωνι below.

Cleon: One of the most influential successors of Pericles, attacked by Aristophanes, Thucydides, and P. as a notorious demagogue of low birth, emotional and greedy (cf. esp. Ar. *Knights*; Thuc. 3.36.6; Plut. *Nic.* 2.2–3; 7–8). He was intransigent in his opposition to the Spartans, until he fell at Amphipolis in 422. It is hard to see the real Cleon behind the animosity of our sources. See Woodhead 1960; Westlake 1968, 60–85; Connor 1971, passim; Davies, *APF* 318–20. He was said to be one of Pericles' accusers in 429; cf. 35.5.

Hermippus: F46 K. = F47 K.A.; see the Introduction, 3.1.i. For a thorough discussion of the corrupt text and disputed interpretation of these lines, probably from the *Moirai* of 430 B.C., see Schwarze, *Beurteilung*, 101–5, and the notes in *PCG* to F47 K.A. Pericles is mocked for his fine words but cowardly spirit. A possible translation: "King of satyrs, why do you not want to carry a spear, but rather supply clever speeches on the war, while the spirit you have is that of Teles? Whenever a small blade is sharpened on the hard whetstone, you gnash (your teeth), bitten by the fierce Cleon." Schwarze notes echoes of Cratinus' *Dionysalexandros*, produced at the Lenaea in 430, which also satirized Pericles' willingness to stir up the war but not to fight (cf. the Introduction, 3.1.d, note). The anapestic dimeters (the fourth and seventh of which are paroemiacs, that is, catalectic dimeters) are from a passage sung by a chorus.

βασιλεῦ: the king of satyrs was Dionysus, but the poet alludes to Pericles. The σάτυροι might be Pericles' supporters and hangers-on.

παρέχεις: thus Ziegler, following S, but note παρέχῃ UMA, accepted by Kassel and Austin, *PCG*.

ψυχὴ . . . ὕπεστιν: For various emendations of this problematic line cf. Schwarze, *Beurteilung*; Kassel and Austin, *PCG*.

Teles: unknown, but apparently a notorious coward, perhaps identical with Teleas (cf. Ar. *Peace* 1008, *Birds* 167–70 and schol.).

κἀγχειριδίου . . . κοπίδος: two nouns reinforcing each other: cf. Aesch. *Supp.* 21, ἐγχειριδίοις . . . κλάδοισιν, and Eur. *Cyc.* 241, κοπὶς μάχαιρα; though either could be considered adjectival. Cf. LSJ s.vv.

βρύχεις: "you gnash your teeth." This sense without ὀδόντας or στόμα, is unusual: Schwarze, *Beurteilung*, suggests "groan," as a by-form of βρυχάομαι.

Κλέωνι: The proper name provides a surprise twist at the end, after the epic reminiscence of *αἴθωνι*: cf. *αἴθωνι σιδήρῳ* (*Il.* 4.485, etc.). He is afraid when he hears the knife sharpened, for he has been bitten by the fiery—Cleon. Note also the play on *κύων*, as in Ar. *Wasps* 837–1008.

34.1

πρᾴως καὶ σιωπῇ: cf. his patience with the pest at 5.2, *σιωπῇ* . . . *κοσμίως*.

ὑφιστάμενος: "standing up to"; cf. *Them.* 3.1, *ὑφίστατο τὰς* . . . *ἀπεχθείας*, and Dio Chrys. 7.71, *σὺν ὑφίσταμαι*, said by a boy boasting of his skill as a hunter.

νεῶν . . . *ἐκπέμπων*: cf. Thuc. 2.23.2, who names the three comrades of the expedition, which had been planned even before the invasion (Thuc. 2.17.4). P.'s explanation of Pericles' reason for staying is his own deduction. Contrast Diod. 12.42.6–8, which presents the expedition as a simple way to force the invaders to leave without taking risks.

διὰ χειρὸς ἔχων: "keep under control"; cf. Thuc. 2.13.2, *τά τε τῶν ξυμμάχων διὰ χειρὸς ἔχειν*. P. often echoes words from the Thucydidean passages he is reading, putting them in the same or a different context. The idiom, however, is common: cf. LSJ s.v. *χείρ* II.6.c; Plut. *Cic.* 16.1, *Mar.* 10.4, *Demetr.* 5.6, *Sert.* 6.9, *Eum.* 4.1, *Num.* 6.4.

ἕως ἀπαλλάγησαν: They left after about a month, when their provisions were exhausted (Thuc. 2.23.1, 3).

34.2

θεραπεύων . . . *ἔγραφεν*: Again P. seems to be giving his own interpretation of Thucydides, who mentions only the one settlement on Aegina (2.27.1). We know of no other distributions of money by Pericles, but P. associates distributions and cleruchies at 9.1. Cf.

Meinhardt, 62. But the real reasons for the settlement certainly would have been to remove the threat of Aeginetan support for the Peloponnesians and to provide land and living space for those dispossessed by the invasion of Attica. Θεραπεύω appears already in Thucydides for "pay court to, win over" (cf. 1.9.2, 1.137.3), and frequently in P. (see Holden's note). Thucydides, in contrast, gives at this point an account of Athenian dispositions for the war (the reserve fund of 1,000 talents and the reserve fleet, 2.24.1–2).

[ὅμως]: unnecessarily deleted by Ziegler, following Coraes.

ἀσχάλλοντας: "distressed, impatient." Cf. Hdt. 3.152, 9.117; Dem. 21.125. The word is not usual in Attic prose.

Aeginetans: cf. note to 29.5. Thucydides (2.27.1) reports the incident very emphatically, noting that men, women, and children were evacuated, and explaining that they were removed both because of their responsibility in stirring up the war and for the better defense of Attica. Only P. ascribes the action directly to Pericles, so that we cannot be sure that that action was part of Pericles' policy. However, this may have been the occasion of Pericles' remark on Aegina quoted at 8.7. Hdt. 6.91 ascribes the Aeginetans' removal to a pollution (ἄγος) incurred when seven hundred citizens were killed in civil stasis in the first decades of the century, which they were not able to remove by sacrifices. This is a case where the actual disaster might have caused the Athenians to look for the cause in the earlier pollution; cf. Parker 1983, 184, 202.

Although Thucydides calls the new settlers ἐποίκους and οἰκή-τορας (2.27.1; cf. 8.69.3), they probably were cleruchs, as P. says (on the difference see note to 11.5). P. speaks quite precisely of distributing land, and is confirmed by Diod. 12.44.2; schol. Ar. Ach. 654; Theogenes (FGrHist 300 F2); and Diog. Laert. 3.3. These notices seem to represent three separate traditions, from Ephorus, comic scholia, and philosophical biography, and even if we question whether the families of Aristophanes and Plato were cleruchs on Aegina, the notices imply that the Aeginetan settlement was in fact a cleruchy. Cf. Ehrenberg 1952, 145–46; Graham 1964, 172–73.

The Spartans resettled the Aeginetans in Thyrea, on their border with Argos (Diod. 12.44.3; Thuc. 2.27.2, 4.56.2). P. omits the expedition to Locris reported in Thuc. 2.26, 30.

34.3

παρηγορία: "consolation," P.'s deduction.

οἱ περιπλέοντες . . . διεπόρθησαν: P. collapses into a single phrase the attempts on Methone and Pheia (Thuc. 2.25), the capture of Sollion and Astakos from the Corinthians, and the winning over of the Cephallenian tetrapolis (2.30). Justin considers this expedition immensely successful: 3.7.5–6, *multoque plura auferunt quam amiserant, prorsus ut in comparatione damnorum longe pluris fuerit ultio quam inuria. Clara quidem haec Pericli expeditio habita.* P., like Thucydides, was less sanguine.

αὐτὸς ἐμβαλών: cf. Thuc. 2.31.1–2. Interestingly, P. does not try to make anything special of this Periclean action, and in fact says less than Thucydides. Overall, P. does not attempt to present Pericles' generalship during the war.

πᾶσαν: a rhetorically motivated adjective, justified by the size of the force described by Thucydides, and his τὰ πολλὰ τῆς γῆς. Cf. *Per.* 29.4.

34.4

πολλὰ μὲν δρῶντες: the subject, of course, is the Peloponnesians. P. shifts to their feelings, to indicate the effectiveness of Pericles' policy.

προηγόρευσεν: cf. Thuc. 1.141.2–3, 7. Thucydides does not speak of a quick end, however.

τι δαιμόνιον: cf. Pericles' words at Thuc. 2.64.1: ἐπιγεγένηταί τε πέρα ὧν προσεδεχόμεθα ἡ νόσος ἥδε, πρᾶγμα μόνον δὴ τῶν πάντων ἐλπίδος κρεῖσσον γεγενημένον . . . φέρειν δὲ χρὴ τά τε δαιμόνια ἀναγκαίως τά τε ἀπὸ τῶν πολεμίων ἀνδρείως. P. picks up Thucydides' unique reference to τὰ δαιμόνια as an element that uncontrollably alters human plans.

34.5

From a simple beginning P. unfolds an extremely elaborate sentence describing the effect of the plague on the popular mood. The sentence falls into three parts: (1) the two short clauses νῦν δὲ . . . δύναμιν; (2) the relative clause ὑφ' ἧς . . . ἐπεχείρησαν, describing the Athenians, with the simile and progressively stronger verbs (κακούμενοι, ἠγριώθησαν, παραφρονήσαντες, ἀδικεῖν ἐπεχείρησαν); and (3) the participial phrase (ἀναπεισθέντες) introducing a description of the overcrowding that caused the plague (τὴν μὲν νόσον . . . πρότερον), including a three-line genitive absolute, and the accusation against Pericles (a series of four participles, τούτου δ' αἴτιος . . . ἐκπορίζων). P. wishes to rise to the occasion presented both by the plague and by the accusations, but not to challenge Thucydides directly (cf. his disclaimer of competition with Thucydides at Nic. 1.4: ἐμοὶ δ' ὅλως μὲν ἡ περὶ λέξιν ἅμιλλα καὶ ζηλοτυπία πρὸς ἑτέρους μικροπρεπὲς φαίνεται καὶ σοφιστικόν, ἂν δὲ πρὸς τὰ ἀμίμητα γίγνηται, καὶ τελέως ἀναίσθητον). The carefully constructed sentence, the use of similes, and borrowings from Thucydidean vocabulary all serve to raise the tone of the passage.

The plague struck Athens in spring 430, though P. does not mark the new year. Thucydides, who himself was infected, narrates its impact on Athens in one of the great descriptive passages of Greek literature (2.47–54). The identity of the disease is uncertain, despite many suggestions: see Gomme, HCT 2:150–53, and cf., e.g., McArthur 1954 (typhus); R. J. and M. L. Littman 1969 (smallpox); Wylie and Stubbs 1983 (tularaemia); Langmuir et al. 1985 (influenza complicated by staphylococcus). Especially important is the general treatment of Poole and Holladay 1979, who suggest that the problem is insoluble because of changes over time in virulency of diseases. The unhealthy conditions in the city would not have caused the disease but rather contributed to its virulence. Cf. also Nic. 6.3, τοῦ δὲ λοιμοῦ τὴν πλείσταν αἰτίαν ἔλαβε Περικλῆς, διὰ τὸν πόλεμον εἰς τὸ ἄστυ κατακλείσας τὸν ἀπὸ τῆς χώρας ὄχλον, ἐκ τῆς μεταβολῆς τῶν τόπων καὶ διαίτης ἀήθους γενομένου. P. himself seems to have associated such diseases with potent emanations or effluences: cf. De ser. num. vind. 558E, Max. cum princ. 776F.

ἡ λοιμώδης ἐνέπεσε φθορά: cf. Thuc. 2.47.3, λοιμὸς οὐδὲ φθορά; 1.23.3, φθείρασα ἡ λοιμώδης νόσος; 2.49.4, λύγξ . . . ἐνέπιπτε [or ἐνέπεσε] κενή; 2.48.2, ἐσέπεσε [mss. ἐνέπεσε].

κατενεμήθη: "overrun, spread over"; cf. Artax. 23.7, ἀλφοῦ [leprosy] κατανεμηθέντος αὐτῆς τὸ σῶμα; De ser. num. vind. 548F, νόσος κατανεμηθεῖσα τοῦ σώματος; Thuc. 2.54.5, ἡ νόσος . . . ἐπενείματο δὲ 'Αθήνας. By 426 the Athenians had lost 4,400 hoplites and 300 cavalrymen (Thuc. 3.87.3).

ἀκμάζουσαν ἡλικίαν: cf. Thuc. 2.20.2, 'Αθηναίους ἀκμάζοντας νεότητι πολλῇ.

τὰς ψύχας: cf. Thuc. 2.59.1, ἠλλοίωντο τὰς γνωμάς, and their ἀθυμία at 2.51.4.

ἠγριώθησαν: "became wild," a poetic word; cf. Pyrrh. 15.7, ἠγριωμένῳ πελάγει.

καθάπερ . . . παραφρονήσαντες: another simile illustrating the contrast between Pericles' calm and the popular frenzy; cf. 15.1, 33.6. The doctor is a common figure for the wise statesman in Plato; cf. Dodds 1959, 328, and above, note to 15.1. P. speaks of Pompey as a possible physician to the παραφροσύνη of the Roman late Republic (Caes. 28.5).

παραφρονήσαντες: "having gone mad." Used by Herodotus of Cambyses and Cleomenes (3.61.1, 6.75.2); cf. παραφροσύνη of Nero's folly, Plut. Ant. 87.9.

ἀναπεισθέντες: frequent in Thucydides (e.g., 2.14, 65.2).

τοῦ χωρικοῦ πλήθους: "the multitude from the country" (χώρα); cf. τὸν ἀπὸ χώρας ὄχλον later in this section and Nic. 6.3; Thuc. 2.14–17. Ziegler accepts χωρικοῦ of S, which is not found in literary authors. More likely is the reading of the other major mss., χωριτικοῦ (with the variant χωρητικοῦ), which would be unique in P., but appears adverbially at Xen. Cyr. 4.5.54. For P. cf. χωρίτης at Sull. 7.13.

συμφόρησις: "bringing together, piling up"; cf. *Oth.* 14.3 and Thuc. 2.52.1, ξυγκομιδή.

θέρους ὥρᾳ: ὥρᾳ ἔτους, Thuc. 2.52.2.

χύδην: "without order," lit. "poured out"; cf. Thuc. 2.52.2, οὐδενὶ κόσμῳ. The image is picked up below in καταχεάμενος.

ἐν οἰκήμασι μικροῖς καὶ σκηνώμασι πνιγηροῖς: cf. Thuc. 2.52.1, ἐν καλύβαις πνιγηραῖς. The word σκήνωμα is rare, used for the jingle with οἴκημα, but cf. Thuc. 2.34.2, πρότριτα σκήνην ποιήσαντες; 2.52.3, τὰ ἵερα ἐν οἷς ἐσκήνηντο; 1.133.1, σκηνησαμένου δίπλην διαφράγματι καλύβην. Πνιγηροῖς: "stifling."

διαιτᾶσθαι: Thuc. 2.52.2, διαιτωμένων.

ἀναπεπταμένης: "open to the outside air"; cf. *Amat.* 752C, τῆς ἐν ἡλίῳ καθαρᾶς καὶ ἀναπεπταμένης διατριβῆς; *Them.* 8.3.

τούτου δ᾽ αἴτιος: cf. Thuc. 2.59.2, τὸν μὲν Περικλέα ἐν αἰτίᾳ εἶχον.

ὥσπερ βοσκήματα: cf. Thuc. 2.51.4, ὥσπερ τὰ πρόβατα, though the sense is different.

ἀναπίμπλασθαι φθορᾶς ἀπ᾽ ἀλλήλων: cf. Thuc. 2.51.4, ἕτερος ἀφ᾽ ἑτέρου θεραπείας ἀναπιμπλάμενοι. P.'s construction with ἀναπίμπλασθαι ("to be infected") is again slightly different, here taking the genitive (φθορᾶς).

ἀναψυχήν: "relief, respite"; cf. Plato *Symp.* 176A.

35.1

ἰᾶσθαι: Pericles the doctor; cf. 34.5. But the verb is frequently used in this figurative sense: *Alc.* 25.9, *Comp. Alc.–Cor.* 2.7, *Dem.* 7.3.

παραλυπεῖν: "to harm in addition"; cf. Thuc. 2.51.1, ἄλλο παραλύπει . . . οὐδὲν τῶν εἰωθότων.

ἑκατὸν . . . ναῦς: cf. Thuc. 2.56.1–2: In spring 430, while the Peloponnesians were again ravaging Attica, Pericles led the largest force yet assembled: 100 ships, 4,000 hoplites, and 300 cavalry on special transports used for the first time. Fifty other ships were supplied by Chios and Lesbos. The purpose of this exceptionally large force is disputed; cf. Kagan, *AW* 71–78.

35.2

τὸν μὲν ἥλιον ἐκλιπεῖν: P. adds to the Thucydidean narrative this story, which he had heard in philosophers' lectures (σχολαῖς: cf. *De aud.* 25C, ταῦτα ἐν ταῖς σχολαῖς ἀκούομεν, etc.). This solar eclipse in fact occurred a year earlier (3 August 431; cf. Thuc. 2.28 and Gomme, *HCT* ad loc.). It was not total, but sufficient to allow at least planets (Venus and Mars) to be seen. P.'s story combines two incompatible elements: Pericles as commander of the fleet (in 430) and the eclipse (in 431). The error is difficult to explain, as P. is working so closely from Thucydides in this passage. The cause must lie not with simple negligence or ignorance but with his method, which can be imagined as follows. In focusing on the dramatic narrative of the plague, P. presumably forgot the earlier notice in Thucydides on the eclipse. He next moved to the anecdote of the eclipse, from a different source. He decided that it would be most effective if assigned to a specific occasion (unlike the versions in Cic. *Rep.* 1.16.25 and Val. Max. 8.11.ext. 1). The story P. knew may have associated it with the fleet. Thus when inserting it from memory or his notebook into his Thucydidean narrative he naturally assigned it to the expedition that Pericles led, without realizing that he was contradicting Thucydides' narrative. Apparently, P. when composing read a short section of Thucydides, thought about how he wished to present the material, then wrote it out without rechecking. This technique might also explain his conflation in 35.3.

The anecdote reminds us of the philosophical knowledge, gained from Anaxagoras, which according to P. lay behind Pericles' self-control (cf. 5.1–2) and his lack of superstition (cf. 6.1–3). The final λέγεται permits P. to distance himself from the truth of the anecdote. Cf. also the similar story of Pericles' explaining a lightning bolt by knocking two stones together: Suda s.v. *Περικλῆς* (*Π* 1179), Frontin. *Str.* 1.12.10.

P. knew that Anaxagoras had explained eclipses as shadows, but that it was not generally accepted in Pericles' time (*Nic.* 23.3–4; cf. Guthrie, *HGP* 2:306–8, and Hershbell 1982, 142–44). On P.'s understanding of solar eclipses such as this see *De facie* 931D–932C with Cherniss's discussion, 1957, 9–12, of the eclipses he might have seen; also Goergemanns 1970. For lunar eclipses see *Dion* 24.1 and Flacelière 1951.

σημεῖον: cf. 6.2–3.

παρακαλύψας: "when he had covered."

μή: introducing an indirect question with a negative answer expected, Latin *num*: cf. *MT* 369n. 1; *Cat. Mai.* 24.7, and other examples cited in Holden's note.

οὐκ ἔφη: "he said no."

35.3

P. presents the expedition as almost a complete failure; Thuc. 2.56.4–6 is much less negative. However, P. omits the attacks made on Troizen, Halieis, Hermione, and Prasiae after the unsuccessful attempt at Epidaurus (Thuc. 2.56.5–6). Note especially that he conflates the attack on Epidaurus with Hagnon's reinforcement of the siege at Potidaea and subsequent withdrawal because of the plague (Thuc. 2.58); the siege and plague at Potidaea are not otherwise mentioned in the *Pericles*. For such conflation when P. is summarizing see Pelling 1980, 127–28. As in 35.2, P. seems to be reading beforehand, then composing from memory, perhaps using brief notes. I do not see any literary purpose here in this conflation.

οὔτ' ἄλλο τι δοκεῖ τῆς παρασκευῆς ἄξιον δρᾶσαι: cf. Thuc. 2.58.2, *προυχώρει δὲ αὐτοῖς . . . οὔτε τἆλλα τῆς παρασκευῆς ἀξίως* (of Potidaea, not Epidaurus). Note *οὔτε . . . τε* for "both . . . not . . . and"; cf. 18.1.

πολιορκήσας: Thucydides says only πρὸς τὴν πόλιν προβαλόντες, but cf. 2.58.1, πολιορκουμένην, of Potidaea.

τὴν ἱερὰν Ἐπίδαυρον: Epidaurus, the second city after Argos in the Argolid, had furnished eight ships at Artemesium and ten at Salamis; because of its hostility to Argos it was pro-Spartan. It was famous for its sanctuary of Asclepius, about 5 miles from the town, now extensively excavated and a popular tourist site: cf. *Princeton Encyclopedia of Classical Sites* (Stillwell 1976) s.v. Epidauros, 311–14. The title ἱερὰ (used only here by P.) appears in inscriptions of the first century A.D.; cf. *IG* IV, 1²:83.15; 84.32, 36; 611; *SIG*³ 802A.20; and on later coins. The sanctuary flourished as a center of healing in P.'s day, and he must have been puzzled that Pericles attacked Epidaurus while the plague was raging rather than seek the god's help. Later, after the Peace of Nicias, the Athenians did just that, bringing the cult of Asclepius to Athens in 420/19 (cf. *Num.* 4.10 and the testimonia in Radt 1977, 57–58). P. makes no overt criticism, although the title may imply it.

ἐλπίδα παρασχοῦσαν ὡς ἁλωσομένην: cf. Thuc. 2.56.4, ἐς ἐλπίδα μὲν ἦλθον τοῦ ἑλεῖν.

ἐπιγενομένη . . . τοὺς συμμείξαντας προσδιέφθειρεν: cf. Thuc. 2.58.2, [at Potidaea] ἐπιγενομένη γὰρ ἡ νόσος ἐνταῦθα δὴ πάνυ ἐπίεσε τοὺς Ἀθηναίους, φθείρουσα τὴν στρατιάν, ὥστε καὶ τοὺς προτέρους στρατιώτας νοσῆσαι τῶν Ἀθηναίων ἀπὸ τῆς ξὺν Ἅγνωνι στρατιᾶς, ἐν τῷ πρὸ τοῦ χρόνῳ ὑγιαίνοντας. The infection by the army took place at Potidaea, where the men from the Peloponnesian expedition were sent upon their return. The collapse of Hagnon's effort against Potidaea was an additional frustration for the Athenians: cf. Kagan, *AW* 78–80.

χαλεπῶς διακειμένους: "exasperated"; cf. Thuc. 2.59.1–3.

ἐπειρᾶτο . . . ἀναθαρρύνειν: cf. Thuc. 2.59.3, θαρσῦναι; 2.65.1, ἐπειρᾶτο τοὺς Ἀθηναίους τῆς ἐς αὐτὸν ὀργῆς παραλύειν. P. is thinking, of course, of Pericles' third speech in Thucydides, 2.60–64.

35.4

Pericles' Removal from Office and Fine. Cf. Thuc. 2.65.3; Diod. 12.45.4. Pericles' rejection by the people proved for Plato that he was not making the citizens better: cf. *Gorg.* 516A, where the charge is κλοπή, theft of public money. Thucydides is distressingly brief: οὐ μέντοι πρότερόν γε οἱ ξύμπαντες ἐπαύσαντο ἐν ὀργῇ ἔχοντες αὐτὸν πρὶν ἐζημίωσαν χρήμασιν. ὕστερον δ' αὖθις οὐ πολλῷ, ὅπερ φιλεῖ ὁ δῆμος ποιεῖν, στρατηγὸν εἵλοντο καὶ πάντα τὰ πράγματα ἐπέτρεψαν.

Exactly how was Pericles removed from office? In the fourth century, an ἐπιχειροτονία, or vote on the satisfactory performance of generals and other magistrates, was held at the beginning of every prytany. If the general was voted down (ἀποχειροτονεῖσθαι), he would be judged in court. (This would be similar to, if not identical with, a trial begun by εἰσαγγελία). If he was condemned, the court set the penalty; if he was acquitted, he could hold office again (Arist. *Ath. pol.* 61.2). Cf. Roberts 1982, 15–17 and passim; Rhodes, *CAAP* on 61.2. On εἰσαγγελία in particular see Roberts; Rhodes 1979; Hansen 1975; and Harrison, *Law,* 2:50–59. Aristotle's description seems to fit our evidence: an angry assembly rejected Pericles after the failures of the Argolid and Potidaean expeditions, and a court voted not the worst penalty, death, but a substantial fine.

Pericles would have been elected in the spring (the seventh prytany) for the year to begin in July (*Ath. pol.* 44.4). The trial took place after the Argolid expedition and Hagnon's departure and return, therefore late summer 430. In the winter of the same year Hagnon and the other generals at Potidaea were charged and probably tried as well (Thuc. 2.70.4).

The charge, as Gomme notes, *HCT* 2:182, could be for embezzlement—κλοπή, as Plato says—for "deceiving the people," for mismanaging the Argolid expedition, or for some other incompetence (cf. Diod. 12.45.4, μικράς τινας ἀφορμὰς ἐγκλημάτων λαβόντες). In the absence of better evidence we can tentatively accept Plato's κλοπή. See Gomme, *HCT* 2:182–83; Kagan, *AW* 90–93; Roberts 1982, 30–34; and Busolt, *Gr. Gesch.* 3.2:949–57, who masterfully sets out the problems. However, Busolt (3.2:950–52, fol-

lowed by many modern scholars) assigns the decree of Dracontides with the amendment of Hagnon to this trial rather than to an
earlier one, as seems more correct (cf. note to 32.3).

For Pericles' reappointment see note to 37.1; for his accusers,
note to 35.5.

οὐ μὴν . . . χρήμασιν: a paraphrase of Thuc. 2.65.3. For παρέλυσε
τῆς ὀργῆς cf. Thuc. 2.65.1, ὀργῆς παραλύειν. P. seems to think that
the court's decision both deprived Pericles of office and fined him,
although this may just be a result of his striving for rhetorical
effect. He emphasizes the reversal as the judges take charge
(γενομένους κυρίους) against the man who had ruled as monarch.

ἀριθμόν: Diodorus (12.45.4) says eighty, which is incredibly high.
We have no way of recognizing which figure, if any, is correct.

35.5

Pericles' Accusers. The discrepancy of names is disconcerting, but
there may have been more than one (cf. the public prosecutors,
συνήγοροι, at 10.6, with *Ath. pol.* 54.2 and Rhodes, *CAAP* ad loc.,
and the three accusers of Socrates: Meletus, Anytus, and Lycon).
Meinhardt, 63, notes that P.'s sources here are not historians but
"philosophical authors," who would have been interested, like
Plato, in Pericles' rejection by the people. Cf. the lists of political
trials and other difficulties in *Nic.* 6.1, 3 and "those who write on
the wrongdoings of the people against their generals" (including
Pericles) at *Arist.* 26.5.

Idomeneus: *FGrHist* 338 F9; see the Introduction, 3.3.e. For
Cleon see note to 33.8. The Hermippus fragment there could be
the basis for Idomeneus' notice.

Theophrastus: This fragment of Theophrastus is not in Wimmer's (1862) collection; see the Introduction, 3.2.d. The very rar-
ity of the name Simmias at Athens may guarantee its authenticity.
In *Praec. ger. rep.* 805C, P. names him as an example of a man
attacking from envy an ἀνδρὶ χρηστῷ καὶ δι' ἀρετὴν πρωτεύοντι,
clearly thinking of this occasion.

Heraclides: F47 Wehrli; see the Introduction, 3.3.d. Lacratides, otherwise unknown, may have belonged to an old family: one man of that name was archon in the late sixth century, another hierophant in the fourth (Philochorus 328 F202; Isaeus 7.9). On the family see Davies, *APF* 43–47.

36

The Troubles in Pericles' Family. This chapter is inserted at a turning point in the life, between Pericles' dismissal and his return to power: cf. the similar passages in *Fab.* 24 (after the recapture of Tarentum) and *Cic.* 40–41 (after the reconciliation with Caesar). As in these, the chronology does not follow that of the main narrative: διατεταραγμένα πόρρωθεν introduces a flashback, and the deaths of sister and sons (36.7–9) could have preceded his dismissal. Cf., in *Fab.* 24.1, the reference to the younger Fabius' consulship in 213, although chapters 21–23 describe Tarentum's fall in 209. In some other lives a section of unchronological anecdotes has been inserted in a similar position: e.g., *Them.* 18, following the victory of Salamis. This insertion in the *Pericles* is connected to chapter 35 by references to the plague and the overlapping of political and domestic troubles, and to chapter 37 because it was the death of his sons that forced Pericles to legitimize his bastard son.

36.1

τὰ μὲν οὖν δημόσια . . . παύσεσθαι: "His troubles with public affairs would end soon." With τὰ δημόσια understand πράγματα or πάθη; cf. *Dem.* 22.5.

καθάπερ . . . τῶν πολλῶν: "For the populace had discharged its anger with its blow against him, as (a bee loses) its sting." Cf. Plato *Phaedo* 91C, ὥσπερ μέλιττα τὸ κέντρον ἐγκαταλιπὼν οἰχήσομαι. P. perhaps was influenced also by Ar. *Wasps*, where the waspish Athenian jurors wield their votes like stings; cf. ll. 422–32, 1112–13. Coraes's addition of τῇ is supported by *Pyrrh.* 30.10, ἅμα τῇ πληγῇ τοῦ δόρατος.

κατὰ τὸν λοιμὸν: "at the time of the plague."

στάσει . . . πόρρωθεν: "had been troubled by discord for some time." Πόρρωθεν is more often used of space than of time, but cf. Plato *Charm.* 155A; Plut. *Lyc.* 14.1, *Dion* 4.4, *De cur.* 520D, etc. Interestingly, P. does not include the relation with Aspasia when speaking of troubles in the family.

36.2

Xanthippus: the older child of Pericles' first wife (cf. 24.8), probably born by 457. As often, the eldest son was named after the paternal grandfather. According to Plato *Meno* 94B, their father gave both brothers an excellent education in horsemanship, music, and physical fitness, but he was not able to make them ἀγαθοί. Aeschines the Socratic also criticized them for the low company they kept (Athen. 5.220D). Plato includes both brothers among those listening to the sophist Protagoras at the home of their maternal half-brother Callias the son of Hipponicus (Plato *Prot.* 314E; cf. *Per.* 24.8), although he raises doubts about what this experience will accomplish (328 C–D).

Τεισάνδρου θυγατρὶ: Teisander the son of Epilycus belonged to the Philiad family, though to a different branch from that of Miltiades and Cimon. He was born ca. 490 and active enough in politics to be a candidate for ostracism in the 440s (cf. ML pp. 45–46). His son Epilycus was ambassador to Susa in 424. His three daughters all married into prominent families. On the family see Davies, *APF* 296–98. The reference to the expensive tastes of a woman of good family recalls Strepsiades' complaints about his wife, "a niece of Megacles son of Megacles, classy, expensive, a *grande dame*" (Ar. *Clouds* 46–48).

γλίσχρα . . . χορηγοῦντος: "giving him a meager allowance, a bit at a time." Cf. *Alc.* 35.5; Plato *Rep.* 553C, γλίσχρως καὶ κατὰ σμικρὸν φειδόμενος. For χορηγεῖν cf. 14.2. Even though Xanthippus was adult and had taken a wife, Pericles would retain control of the family property. It would be exceptional for a father to resign from headship of the *oikos* in favor of his son: cf. Lacey 1968, 106–7, 116–18, 125–30; Humphreys 1978, 164. Humphreys also notes, 202–3, the strong evidence for tension between father and adult son in the fifth century, apparent, e.g., in the reverse joke of Philocleon at Ar. *Wasps* 1352–55, ἐγώ σ' ἐπειδὰν οὑμὸς υἱὸς ἀποθάνῃ, / λυσάμενος ἔξω παλλακὴν ὦ χοιρίον. / νῦν δ' οὐ κρατῶ 'γὼ τῶν ἐμαυτοῦ χρημάτων: / νέος γάρ εἰμι καὶ φυλάττομαι σφόδρα. Cf. as well Reinhold 1976, 29–38. Aristophanes' Phidippides was not the only son who thought his father was out of date.

36.3

ἔλαβεν: "received as a loan." The lender probably was a fellow aristocrat rather than a banker, as banking had not developed except for limited commercial purposes. A wealthy landowner would borrow from a friend or acquaintance to meet the obligations of his status (e.g., for a liturgy). The lender would acquire prestige and status by the loan; normally he would be quite reluctant to ask for repayment, unless he in turn had a special expenditure expected of him. Pericles' parsimony, both in refusing to give his son money to live as befitted his status and in refusing to repay the creditor, went against the aristocratic norm. But note the same behavior on the part of Strepsiades, when dunned by his creditors (Ar. *Clouds* 1214–1302). Is our whole story here taken from a comic scene, in which Pericles or a surrogate drives off his creditors? The words of Aristophanes' second creditor would fit: μὴ σκῶπτέ μ', ὦ τᾶν, ἀλλά μοι τὰ χρήματα / τὸν υἱὸν ἀποδοῦναι κέλευσον ἅλαβεν (1267–68). Cf. Humphreys 1978, 152; Dover 1968, xxix–xxxii, and 1974, 177–78; Will 1972, 674–75.

36.4

ἀπαιτοῦντος: sc. from Pericles.

καὶ . . . προσέλαχε: "(He not only did not pay, but) even brought a suit against him besides." P.'s anecdote omits details, but apparently the creditor instituted a suit for the recovery of his money (cf. MacDowell, *Law*, 146–47) and Pericles made a countersuit, the exact nature of which is unknown. The law establishing the best-known type of countersuit, the παραγραφή, belongs to 403/2. This may be evidence for earlier suits of that nature, or an early example of ἀντιγραφή (cf. Harrison, *Law*, 2:107–8, 131–33). Δίκην λαγχάνειν is the technical expression for having a suit accepted for hearing by a magistrate (Harrison, 2:88–89). Προσλαγχάνω is very rare, but cf. Dem. 32.9, ἡμῖν δίκην προσείληχεν. The most likely source is Stesimbrotus or comedy, and the story may be distorted or false.

μειράκιον: not a precise term, but for P. usually meaning more than twenty years old. Cf. *Brut.* 27.3 of Octavian when he first held the consulship, οὔπω πάνυ μειράκιον ὤν, ἀλλ᾿ εἰκοστὸν ἄγων ἔτος; *Alc.* 7.3, *Aem.* 8.4, *Arat.* 46.2, *C. Gracch.* 1.2, *Caes.* 1.3, *Pomp.* 3.1. The use of the proper name in apposition is rare in P., but cf. *Luc.* 2.7, τὸ μειράκιον ὁ Πτολεμαῖος, *Comp. Gracch.–Agis–Cleom.* 5.7, τὸ μειράκιον Ἆγιν.

χαλεπῶς διατεθείς: "having become angry."

36.5

πεντάθλου: "a competitor in the pentathlon," which in ancient times consisted of footrace, broad jump, discus, javelin, and wrestling: cf. Gardiner 1910, 359–71; H. A. Harris 1964, 77–80; Patrucco 1972, 191–223. Epitimus is not otherwise known: he might have been killed at the Panathenaic games, which included the pentathlon.

ἀκουσίως καὶ κτείναντος: According to Athenian law, unintentional killing of an opponent during an athletic contest did not break the law; cf. *Ath. pol.* 57.3; Dem. 25.53; MacDowell 1963, 73–74; Rhodes, *CAAP* 644–45. The puzzle in this case is that the stricken man was not an opponent. In Antiphon *Tetralogies* 2 the model case concerns a boy killed by a javelin thrown in the gymnasium. The parallel warns us that we are dealing with a standard philosophical example, in which the names may be used for verisimilitude only. It is not good evidence for Pericles' contact with Protagoras.

μετὰ Πρωταγόρου . . . ἡγεῖσθαι: Protagoras of Abdera (ca. 490–420, *FVS* 80) perhaps the most famous of the sophists, visited Athens several times, perhaps twice during Pericles' lifetime, once before he prepared a law code for Thurii, ca. 444/43 (cf. 11.5; Diog. Laert. 9.50) and again on the visit recalled in Plato's *Protago-*

ras, ca. 432. Cf. Guthrie, *HGP* 2:262–69; Untersteiner 1954, 1–91.

διαποροῦντα: "inquiring, considering the question"; cf. 24.2. The questions of responsibility and law raised here can be related to Protagoras' teachings: cf. Untersteiner 1954, 30–32. However, Durić 1953 sees this only as an occasion for Protagoras to display his dialectic technique. For Pericles the matter was of practical concern both legally and rhetorically; how far it shows a general intellectual interest in topics raised by the sophists cannot be stated. Cf. notes to 4.1–5.1.

τὸ ἀκόντιον: Athenian law provided that animals or inanimate objects that killed a man should be tried and thrown out beyond the borders of Attica if found guilty; cf. MacDowell 1963, 85–89.

τοὺς ἀγωνοθέτας: P.'s usual word for those responsible for the games, although not the name of an official post at Athens until the late fourth century; cf. *Flam.* 12.5, *Symp.* 628A, 674F, *Plat. quaest.* 1000A. The official title for those managing the Panathenaea, ἀθλοθέται (cf. *Ath. pol.* 60.1–3), is found in P. only at *Per.* 13.11.

τὸν ὀρθότατον λόγον: "the truest argument." ὀρθός was a Protagorean word, referring to what can be established by reason as most probable; cf. Untersteiner 1954, 56. Plato plays with it in the *Protagoras*, using ὀρθῶς twenty-five times.

36.6

τὴν . . . διαβολήν: cf. 13.16.

Stesimbrotus: *FGrHist* 107 F11; cf. the Introduction, 3.1.c. It is not certain exactly how much of this chapter is derived from Stesimbrotus. Jacoby prints 36.1–6 as his text for F11; he thinks 36.2–5 may be from Stesimbrotus but only considers 36.6, πρὸς δὲ . . . διαφοράν, as certain.

36.7

τὴν ἀδελφήν: otherwise unknown.

36.8

προὔδωκε τὸ φρόνημα: "become a traitor to his nobility of mind"; cf. *Cleom.* 38.2, ἡ μὲν Κρατησίκλεια, καίπερ οὖσα γενναία γυνή, προὔδωκε τὸ φρόνημα πρὸς τὸ τῆς συμφορᾶς μέγεθος, καὶ . . . ὠλοφύρετο.

ἀλλ' οὐδὲ . . . ἀναγκαίων: "In fact he was not even seen weeping, either when preparing any one of his relatives for burial or at the tomb." For ἀλλ' οὐδὲ cf. note to 28.2. For P. control of grief indicated a philosophical self-control: cf., e.g., *Aem.* 36, *Cleom.* 22.2, and esp. *Cons. ad uxor.* (*Mor.* 608A–612B) for the death of their daughter Timoxena, recalling also the deaths of their two sons. P. does not include an anecdote ascribed to Pythagoras in [Plut.] *Cons. ad Apol.* 118E (*FVS* 80 B9), according to which Pericles, despite the loss of his two sons within seven days of each other, spoke to the assembly with garland and white robe. Cf. also Val. Max. 5.10.ext. 1; Aelian *VH* 9.6. P. reports instead the (more credible?) version that has Pericles finally yielding to tears.

Paralus: named, like one of the two Athenian sacred triremes, after the Athenian hero and patron of sailors, a son of Poseidon. The more common name is Paralius. He appears in *IG* I³ 49 and in Plato along with Xanthippus (cf. notes to 14.1 and 36.2), but nothing else is known of him.

36.9

καμφθείς: "was made to yield." Κάμπτομαι in the figurative sense means to soften, to yield to someone or something: e.g., Plato *Prot.* 320B. In P. it (and the opposite adjective ἄκαμπτος) frequently refer to the softening of an internal moral resolution: cf. *Mar.* 31.5, *De vit. pud.* 535B, *De gen. Socr.* 592B.

ἐγκαρτερεῖν τῷ ἤθει: "to hold true to his character." The dative after ἐγκαρτερεῖν usually refers to what is being endured, but here designates what he is holding on to with difficulty: cf. *Mar.* 29.8, ἐμμένων τῷ ἤθει καὶ πᾶν παθεῖν δεινὸν . . . παρεσκευασμένος; *Cat. Mai.* 4.3, ἐγκαρτεροῦντα τῇ τάξει τῆς ἀσκήσεως; fr. 204 Sandbach, οὕτως ἐνεκαρτέρησαν ἀμφότεροι τῷ πρέποντι.

στέφανον: The body was regularly crowned with a garland after washing, both as adornment and as a sign of consecration to the gods of the earth: cf. Kurtz and Boardman 1971, 143–44; Alexiou 1974, 5; Rohde 1966, 164 and n. 40.

πρὸς τὴν ὄψιν: "at the sight" of his dead son. Cf. *Sol.* 27.4, οὔτ᾽ ἔπαθεν οὐδὲν οὔτ᾽ εἶπε πρὸς τὴν ὄψιν; *Cor.* 34.3, συνταραχθεὶς πρὸς τὴν ὄψιν, etc.

37.1

P. resumes Pericles' political life after the digression on family. The sentence is carefully arranged, with two main clauses preceded by parallel genitive absolutes and elaborate disposition of nouns (e.g., στρατηγῶν εἰς τὸν πόλεμον καὶ ῥητόρων), but cannot conceal the paucity of information available to P. concerning Pericles' return to politics.

πειρωμένης κτλ.: suggested by Thuc. 2.65.8–10, although Thucydides is describing politicians after Pericles' death. Cf. P.'s similar phrase at 39.3.

βάρος . . . ἰσόρροπον οὐδ᾽ ἀξίωμα . . . ἐχέγγυον: Cf. the similar expression when Fabius Maximus is called to be dictator, *Fab.* 3.7: ἰσόρροπον ἔχοντα τῷ μεγέθει τῆς ἀρχῆς τὸ φρόνημα καὶ τὸ ἀξίωμα τοῦ ἤθους. Pericles and Fabius are similar in possessing this solidity, which makes them valuable in a crisis. Cf. Stadter 1975, 82–84. For the image of the balance cf. note to 11.2. Ἀξίωμα can refer to reputation, rank, or general worth and is used by both Thucydides and P. in all three senses. Here P. no doubt is influenced by Thuc. 2.65.8, ἐκεῖνος μὲν δυνατὸς ὢν τῷ τε ἀξιώματι καὶ τῇ γνώμῃ. For the relation of βάρος to ἀξίωμα and similar concepts see Bucher-Isler 1972, 28.

ἐχέγγυον: "sufficiently reliable," an extension of the original sense, "giving security for," used by P. with various constructions: cf. *Publ.* 4.4, *Aem.* 8.10, *De gen. Socr.* 595F, *De facie* 923C, *De Stoic. repug.* 1055B.

τὸ βῆμα καὶ τὸ στρατήγιον: e.g., as speaker and general. For βῆμα cf. note to 8.6; for στρατήγιον, note to 7.5.

ἀθυμῶν, κτλ.: otherwise unattested, and no doubt P.'s own invention.

Alcibiades: Pericles and his brother Ariphron became guardians of the young Alcibiades after his father Clinias' death at Coronea in 446. See *Alc.* 1.2, 3.1; Plato *Alc. I* 104B, *Prot.* 320A; Xen. *Mem.* 1.2.40; Isoc. 16.28; Davies, *APF* 18. One anecdote of a conversation between the two seems to have been part of Ephorus' account of the causes of the Peloponnesian War (*pace* Jacoby, commentary to 70 F196): cf. Diod. 12.38.3–4; Aristodemus 16.4; Val. Max. 3.1.ext. 1; Plut. *Alc.* 7.3, *Reg. et imp. apophtheg.* 186E. Another is found in Xen. *Mem.* 1.2.40–46. These might have induced P. to name Alcibiades here, or he may have known another anecdote not preserved. Alcibiades' exact relationship to Pericles is uncertain; both of their mothers, Dinomache and Agariste, were Alcmeonids. Dinomache's father, Megacles, was probably brother of Agariste, which would make Pericles first cousin to Dinomache; cf. Davies, *APF* 379. Others, like Cromey 1982, argue that Dinomache was Pericles' first wife: see note to 24.8.

37.2

ἀγνωμοσύνην: "foolishness"; cf. 2.5. Again P. fleshes out his sources. This Herodotean word is found only five times in P., twice in this life.

ὑποδεξάμενος . . . αἱρεθείς: cf. Thuc. 2.65.4, στρατηγὸν εἵλοντο καὶ πάντα τὰ πράγματα ἐπέτρεψαν; Diod. 12.45.5. The date of the reelection is disputed: Thucydides says only ὕστερον οὐ πολλῷ. There may have been a special election soon after his dismissal, or the Athenians may have waited until the regular annual election in spring 429, in which case Pericles would have taken office only in July 429. Cf. Gomme, *HCT* 2:183; Kagan, *AW*, 93, 101; F. Miltner, *RE* s.v. Perikles 1, XIX, 1 (1938) 743–90, at 787; Busolt, *Gr. Gesch.* 3.2:963n. 2. Busolt's arguments for the latter date are more persuasive. There is in fact no evidence that Pericles ever paid the fine ([Dem.] 26.6 is quite unreliable). The change of popular sentiment probably permitted it to be canceled. It is difficult to imagine a politician like Pericles paying an enormous fine simply to regain influence with the demos.

ἠτήσατο λυθῆναι τὸν . . . νόμον: Thucydides is totally silent on Pericles' activities after his recall. To fill the gap P. inserts this anecdote on legitimizing his bastard son (37.2–5). Whether bastards with two Athenian parents could be citizens is disputed: cf. (pro) Harrison, *Law*, 1:63–65; MacDowell 1976; and (contra) Lacey 1968, 282n. 15; Humphreys 1974, 88–95; Rhodes 1978, 89–92. This exemption must have been sought after the death of his legitimate sons in the plague, but we have no confirmation that Pericles requested it only after his trial and recall. P. combines in his account several elements not otherwise found together: Pericles' reelection, his request for exemption, the main clause of the law, a distribution of grain from Egypt and accompanying purging of the citizen rolls, the irony of Pericles' position, and details on the actual enrolling of his son as a citizen. The irony of the situation—a man who carried a harsh law must now beg for an exemption to it (note αὐτὸς εἰσενηνόχει, and 37.5)—would make this anecdote useful in schools of rhetoric, but P. provides more precise detail than usual in that context. Apparently he has assembled information from several sources to dramatize Pericles' situation more effectively. Of other versions, Aelian *VH* 6.10 stresses the element of nemesis; *VH* 13.24, the unexpected result; *VH* F68 (= Suda s.v. δημοποίητος), how Pericles demeaned himself in making the request. The ultimate source for the scene may be a comedy, perhaps Eupolis' *Demes* (cf. 24.10).

ἐρημία διαδοχῆς: cf. *Agis* 11.6, διαδοχῆς ἔρημον . . . τὴν βασιλείαν. Humphreys 1974, 94, notes that Pericles was more disturbed by the lack of an heir than by the noncitizen status of his son.

[τὸν οἶκον] ἐκλίποι: the verb is intransitive, "fail, die out"; τὸν οἶκον is an intrusive attempt to provide an object.

37.3

The Citizenship Law of 451/50. Cf. Ath. pol. 26.4, ἐπὶ Ἀντιδότου διὰ τὸ πλῆθος τῶν πολιτῶν Περικλέους εἰπόντος ἔγνωσαν μὴ μετέχειν τῆς πόλεως ὅς ἂν μὴ ἐξ ἀμφοῖν ἀστοῖν ᾖ γεγονώς. Cf. also Aelian, cited above in note to 37.2. Aristotle derived his notice from an Atthis, as is shown by the archon date and mover; P. probably used Aristotle, whom he cites elsewhere. His statement contradicts the Suda's date of only shortly before Pericles' appeal to exempt his son from the law. It is unlikely that the decree was recorded by Craterus; cf. Meinhardt, 64. This law has evoked considerable comment: cf. Patterson 1981; Walters 1983; Rhodes, *CAAP* on 26.2; Hignett, *HAC* 343–47; Jacoby, *FGrHist* 3B suppl., 1:471–82, etc. Our information on Athenian laws on mixed marriages and illegitimate children is conveniently gathered in Harrison, *Law*, 1:61–68. The importance of citizenship status at Athens, and the numerous laws and practices that protected and isolated the citizen group are analyzed by Davies 1978a.

Prior to Pericles' law the conditions for citizenship may not have been codified, as Athenian citizenship was based on enrollment in phratry and deme. When a male child came of age, the father presented his son as child of a legitimate wife, and the phratry (at sixteen) and the deme (at eighteen) accepted him, or rejected him as too young or illegitimate (cf. *Ath. pol.* 42.1; MacDowell, *Law*, 67–70). Children by women not wives were νόθοι and limited in their rights, but no objection was made to children of foreign wives, μητρόξενοι, such as Clisthenes, Themistocles, and Cimon. The new law did not define criteria for citizenship but set a more restricted minimum qualification: both parents must be Athenian. Aristophanes refers to this standard in *Birds* 1649–52. The law was reaffirmed in 403/2 (Eumelus, *FGrHist* 77 F2; cf. Dem. 57.30; Athen. 13.577B–C) and continued in force thereafter.

The impetus behind the law has been much debated: cf. the surveys in Rhodes, *CAAP* 333–34, and Patterson 1981, 97–104. Aristotle, the only ancient source to advance an explanation (*Ath. pol.* 26.4; cf. *Pol.* 1278a26–34), suggests the size of the citizen body as a cause; moderns speak of discouraging aristocratic alliances with citizens of other states (Humphreys 1974, 93), closing a loophole as the base of power broadened in the democracy (Davies 1978a, 117–18), a desire for racial purity (e.g., Hignett, *HAC* 346), a political threat to the party of Cimon, himself a μητρόξενος (Jacoby, *FGrHist* 3B suppl., 1:477–81), or unwillingness to share the privileges and monetary rewards of empire (E. M. Walker, *CAH* 5:102–3). Patterson's argument, 1981, 104–7, is persuasive: despite the serious casualties of the 450s, in Egypt and elsewhere, the citizen population of Athens had grown considerably since the Persian Wars, because of natural growth and because of the casual enrollment policies of some demes. The new law was an attempt by the demos to gain centralized control and set a standard qualification for citizenship. Differentiation from the permanent residents of Attica and an awareness of the newly won privileges and powers of the Athenian citizen would have played an important part. Though we hear most about marriages with non-Athenians in aristocratic circles, there would have been frequent temptation for marriage between Athenian citizens and well-established resident aliens; Pericles and the demos clearly felt that this needed to be stopped (cf. Rhodes, *CAAP* 334). Walters 1983, 331–36, also notes that the law would prevent fathers from enrolling their sons by slave concubines (naturally of foreign origin) as citizens.

The law denied citizenship to a large class previously admitted, children of legitimate couples of whom one (usually the wife) was foreign. Effectively it meant that marriages with non-Athenians were no longer recognized in Athenian law as a means of begetting citizen children or continuing the *oikos*. We are not told how it was put into operation, but as it did not affect men like Cimon or his son Lacedaemonius (also a μητρόξενος) it must not have been retroactive. Presumably the law affected children who after 451/50 were presented formally to their deme at age eighteen, not those who had already been accepted by the deme and therefore into the citizen rolls.

Interestingly enough, P. did not choose to report this in its chronological position: presumably he did not see how it related to the struggle for power with Cimon and Thucydides. Nor can we, for it is probable that Cimon would have shared in the desire to define the citizen body more precisely, even though his own children had a foreign mother. P.'s omission provides evidence for the selectivity of his account in chapters 9–14.

ἀκμάζων: not a date, simply a contrast to his difficult situation in 430 and 429.

πρὸ πάνυ πολλῶν χρόνων: "a long time before." Again, a flexible expression, which could refer to centuries or a few years. Cf. *Alex.* 48.4, the same phrase referring to the period of three years between the capture of Damascus and the death of Philotas. P. frequently uses the plural in such expressions, where English expects the singular.

37.4

τοῦ βασιλέως . . . πέμψαντος: This grain distribution apparently is that mentioned in a fragment of Philochorus, μήποτε δὲ περὶ τῆς ἐξ Αἰγύπτου δωρεᾶς λέγει, ἣν Φιλόχορός φησι Ψαμμήτιχον πέμψαι τῷ δήμῳ ἐπὶ Λυσιμαχίδου [445/44] μυριάδας τρεῖς—πλὴν τὰ τοῦ ἀριθμοῦ οὐδαμῶς συμφωνεῖ—πέντε ἑκάστῳ δὲ Ἀθηναίων μεδίμνους· τοὺς γὰρ λαβόντας γενέσθαι μυρίους τετρακισχιλίους διακοσίους μ' (*FGrHist* 328 F119 = schol. Ar. *Wasps* 718), and slightly differently in the second scholion to *Wasps* 718, σιτοδείας ποτὲ γενομένης ἐν τῇ Ἀττικῇ Ψαμμίτιχος, ὁ τῆς Λιβύης βασιλεύς, ἀπέστειλε σῖτον τοῖς Ἀθηναίοις αἰτήσασιν αὐτόν. τῆς δὲ διανομῆς γενομένης τοῦ σίτου ξενηλασίαν ἐποιήσαν Ἀθηναῖοι, καὶ ἐν τῷ διακρίνειν τοὺς αὐθιγενεῖς εὗρον καὶ ἑτέρους ͵δψξ' ξένους παρεγγεγραμμένους. This Psammetichus is not known: the instigator of the Egyptian revolt whom the Athenians aided in the 450s was Inarus, son of Psammetichus, "the king of Libya who managed everything concerning Egypt," and who was killed when the revolt failed (Thuc. 1.110.3; cf. 1.104.1; Hdt. 3.12.4, 3.15.3, 7.7). Another Egyptian, Amyrtaeus, received assistance from Athens at the time of Cimon's Cyprian expedition (Thuc. 1.112.3). By 445/44 Thannyras and Pausiris were ruling, the children of these two (Hdt. 3.15.3). Psammetichus might be another name for Thannyras, or his brother. Cf. Jacoby, commentary to 328 F119, n. 5.

The only other suggestion of a shortage of grain at this time is an undated and fragmentary inscription, *IG* I³ 30, which refers to σίτου ἐνδεί[α. The revolt of Euboea, a major source of grain to Athens, the year before (cf. 22.1, 23.3–4) would certainly have caused a temporary instability in the grain supply. We hear of donations of grain in the sixth century by Amasis of Egypt (schol. Ar. *Plut.* 178) and in 299/98 by Lysimachus (*IG* II² 657). Cf. Salmon 1965, 209–13, and, on the importance of grain imports for Athens, de Ste. Croix, *OPW* 46–49.

τετρακισμυρίους πυρῶν μεδίμνους: Philochorus F119 has 30,000. Neither figure is enormous; the total annual imports of grain a century later, in the 350s, are calculated at ca. 800,000. The Athenian medimnus was about 41.5 liters (*RE* s.v., XV [1931] 86–87), or approximately 1.2 bushels. Philochorus' figure would represent about 1,080 tons of wheat, P.'s about 1,440. We have no way to decide between them.

διανέμεσθαι τοὺς πολίτας: certainly all the citizens, not just the poorer class as suggested by, e.g., Beloch 1886, 76.

πολλαὶ . . . ἐξετάσθησαν: Though this has been interpreted as referring to a full διαψήφισις, or review by the demes of the entire citizen roll, such as occurred in 346/45, neither P. nor Philochorus speak in those terms, and it is more likely that there was a series of ad hoc accusations. See the discussion by Jacoby, commentary to Androtion, *FGrHist* 324 F52; Rhodes, *CAAP* 188, 332–33, 500–501. Ar. *Wasps* 715–18 refers to a narrow escape from a prosecution for being a noncitizen (γραφὴ ξενίας) in connection with a distribution of grain, which may be this one. It is difficult to imagine what actually happened in 445/44: one thinks of distribution at Piraeus with deme magistrates present, or in the demes. As men presented themselves, some were challenged, either by the magistrates or by onlookers, as not being citizens, for other reasons and because they did not meet the criterion of the Periclean law. (There is no evidence that there was any general review of the rolls when Pericles' law was passed, or that there was any direct connection between the law and the proceedings of 445/44.) Because the last known διαψήφισις had been after the expulsion of the tyrants (*Ath. pol.* 13.5), many ξένοι might since have become falsely accepted as citizens. The difficulty is presented by the large numbers of such παρέγγραφοι and the proportion they represented of the citizen body. Both Jacoby and Rhodes, e.g., find the figures incredible. Given our ignorance of internal Athenian affairs, we cannot be sure: How serious was the famine? How many strangers had been living in Attica as citizens for years? How many had married Athenians and now found their children excluded by Pericles' law? And how quick to prosecute and condemn were demesmen and jurors? The notice suggests the existence of a highly emotional issue that might have caused strong feeling and rash action: cf. the treatment of American citizens of Japanese descent during World War II. This event followed close on the revolts of Euboea and Megara and the Peloponnesian invasion of Attica (446). P., of course, includes the incident because he thinks it related to the feelings behind the citizenship law, but we cannot know the proportion of those who were denied citizen rights on that basis. It is possible also that the law was now applied retroactively, though before it had not been. Labarbe 1961, 191–207, rightly argues that because of the uncertainty of so many factors, it is impossible to draw any demographic conclusions from this notice.

ἀνεφύοντο: "sprang up like weeds"; cf. *Thes.* 17.1, *Arist.* 26.2.

γράμματος: "law," but emphasizing its written, and therefore man-made, rather than customary nature. The plural only is listed for this sense in LSJ s.v. III.4, but for the singular see *Sol.* 19.5, *Ti. Gracch.* 8.3.

συκοφαντήμασι: prosecutions by συκοφάντεις, vexatious informers, usually with no true basis. Cf. MacDowell, *Law*, 62–66. The abstract noun is found in P. only here, at *Pel.* 25.4, and at *Eum.* 16.4.

ἀπεκρίθησαν: "were rejected after examination." Cf. LSJ s.v. ἀποκρίνω III; Plut. *Symp.* 637A; Plato, *Leg.* 751D. This is Coraes's emendation, accepted by Ziegler, for the mss.' ἐπράθησαν, "were sold as slaves." The harshness of the penalty has encouraged many attempts at emendation, including Coraes's. However, the sale of those who were rejected by their demesmen, yet appealed to a court and lost, is well established: cf. *Ath. pol.* 41.2; Rhodes, *CAAP* 501–2; Peremans 1973. The vaguer statement of schol. Ar. *Wasps* 718, φησὶν οὖν ὁ Φιλόχορος αὖθις ποτὲ τετρακισχιλίους ἑπτακοσίους ξ' ὀφθῆναι παρεγγράφους (328 F119), cannot be used to reject P.'s report. To pretend falsely to be a citizen served to annul one's status as a free man.

The figures represent a rounding off from those of Philochorus—4,760 and 14,240 respectively—for a total of 19,000 (somewhere in the Plutarchean tradition διακόσιοι has dropped out). That Philochorus' figures total to a round number suggests that he originally had two numbers: the round number itself (the pre-445 total of citizens), and the total of those to whom grain was distributed. He then would have assumed that the difference equaled those excluded from citizenship, there being no record of the number of lawsuits (cf. Jacoby, commentary to 328 F119, pp. 464–65). The numbers have been very important for estimates of the citizen body and total population of Athens, but interpretations vary widely, depending on whether the 19,000 is thought to include all male citizens or only certain classes. Cf. Jacoby, 465–66 and notes; Beloch 1886, 75–81; Gomme 1933, 16–17; Ehrenberg 1969, 30–32; Hansen 1982. Standard ancient figures for the citizen body were 30,000 (Hdt. 5.97.2) or 20,000 (Ar. *Wasps* 709, a totally unreliable context, and [Dem.] 25.51). Modern estimates for free adult male citizens in mid-fifth century run between 20,000 and 43,000.

37.5

ὄντος . . . δεινοῦ: "although it was extraordinary"; cf. *Pel.* 21.2, δεινοῦ δὲ καὶ παρανόμου τοῦ προστάγματος αὐτῷ φανέντος; *Rom.* 23.2, *Publ.* 9.4.

δυστυχία . . . περὶ τὸν οἶκον: cf. Hdt. 8.102, οὐδεμία συμφορὴ μεγάλη ἔσται . . . περὶ οἶκον τὸν σόν; LSJ s.v. περὶ C.I.5.

ὑπεροψίας . . . μεγαλαυχίας: cf. 5.3.

ἐπέκλασε: "broke the hearts of, moved to pity," a frequent expression in P., though usually in the passive: cf. *Oth.* 15.3, *Cam.* 35.3, *Marc.* 20.11, etc. The expression appears already in Thucydides' Plataean debate: cf. 3.59.1, φείσασθαι δὲ καὶ ἐπικλασθῆναι τῇ γνώμῃ οἴκτῳ σώφρονι λαβόντας, and 3.67.2, μὴ . . . ἐπικλασθῆτε; cf. also 4.37.1.

νεμεσητά . . . παθεῖν: "to have suffered just retribution." Νεμεσητός in this sense is frequent in P.: cf. *Mar.* 26.5, πρᾶγμα νεμεσητὸν παθεῖν; *Aem.* 26.8, *Luc.* 36.1, *Ages.* 22.2, *Pomp.* 38.1, 42.3; and οὐ

. . . ἀνεμεσητός at *Aem.* 36.6 and *Cat. Mai.* 24.1, both of deaths in the family.

ἀνθρωπίνων: "proper and natural for a mortal man (to ask)"; a frequent word in P. both to contrast the divine and the human and to emphasize the weakness and uncertainty of human life, human nature, or human reason.

ἀπογράψασθαι . . . φράτορας: "to enroll his illegitimate son among the members of his phratry." The phratry was an association, between the level of deme and tribe, united by real or fictitious kinship, religious ties, and civil duties. Membership in a phratry usually preceded membership in a deme and was considered evidence for citizenship. Bastards could not belong. Awards of citizenship regularly granted permission to enroll in tribe, phratry, and deme. Cf. Hignett, *HAC* 55–56; Rhodes, *CAAP* 68–71, 496–501. In this case the demos did not repeal the law but granted Pericles an exception for his son.

The phrase could have been added by P. to give color to this anecdote, but there are only two other references to phratries in P. (at *Pel.* 18.3 and *Symp.* 618D; *Rom.* 14.7, 20.3, and *Publ.* 7.8 refer to Roman curiae), which suggests that this is probably taken over from his source. P. himself was δημοποίητος at Athens and had been enrolled in the tribe Leontis (*Symp.* 628A).

The younger Pericles belonged to the deme Cholargus like his father, was elected Hellenotamias in 410/9 (ML 84, l. 8, etc.) and general in 406/5 (Xen. *Hell.* 1.5.16; Diod. 13.74.1). He must have been born before 440: cf. Davies, *APF* 458. His immediate enrollment in a phratry suggests that he had already come of age (sixteen for entry into a phratry) and hence was born by 446. Cf. Carter 1967. The usual time for enrollment in a phratry apparently was the feast of the Apaturia, in the month Pyanopsion, October–November, but other occasions were possible (Harrison, *Law*, 1:89–90; Mikalson 1983, 85). Pericles probably died before the Apaturia of 429 (see note to 38.1), so unless he had been reelected almost at once, before October 429, he would have presented his son on a different occasion. P.'s silence on enrollment in a deme suggests that Pericles may have died before he could present his son to the deme (cf. the case of Boeotus, Dem. 39.5).

The offices that the younger Pericles held indicate that he inherited his father's property after his death.

ὄνομα θέμενον: the name given upon enrollment in the phratry, which need not have been his original name; cf. Dem. 39.5, 22. It is unusual but not unheard of for the son to be named after the father: Index I in Davies, *APF*, records sixteen instances, including Megacles the cousin of Pericles and the orator Demosthenes, among some four hundred with both names preserved.

37.6

ὕστερον . . . συστρατήγων: The generals commanding the fleet at the battle of Arginusae in 406, including Pericles, defeated the Lacedaemonian fleet but were prevented by a storm from collecting the survivors of the wrecked ships. An angry demos recalled them, tried together the six who returned, and condemned them to death (Xen. *Hell.* 1.6.28–7.35; Diod. 13.97.3–100.4, 101.1–103.2). Pericles' kinsman Euryptolemus—probably not the man mentioned at 7.5—tried to defend him (Xen. *Hell.* 1.7.16–33). Socrates as president of the boule tried to block the trial as illegal, as all were being tried as a body: Xen. *Hell* 1.7.15, *Mem.* 1.1.18, 4.4.2; Plat. *Apol.* 32B, [Plat.] *Axioch.* 368D.

38–39

Two non-Thucydidean anecdotes of Pericles' deathbed sayings flow smoothly into an evaluation of the man. The qualities of φρόνημα, ἀσφαλεία, and πρᾳότης recalled by the anecdotes are made explicit in 39.1, which is then followed by the rhetorical elaboration of 39.2, suitable for a peroration.

Theophrastus perhaps is the source for all of 38, although cited only for 38.2. Cf. Meinhardt, 65–66.

38.1

τότε: P. skips at once from Pericles' reelection to his last sickness, cutting out any reference to the Spartan and Athenian campaigns of 429 (cf. Thuc. 2.71–92). Thucydides too mentions Pericles' death immediately after his reelection and is silent on Pericles' participation in events between the two dates. Thucydides puts his death two years and six months after the outbreak of the war (2.65.6). That date is disputed: Rawlings 1981, 13–44, has made a strong case for Thucydides' believing that the war began toward the end of winter, 432/31, when the last Spartan embassy was rejected sometime before the attack on Plataea (cf. Thuc. 1.145). This would put Pericles' death in late August or early September 429; dating the war from the attack on Plataea (6 or 7 March 429) or the invasion of Attica (end of May) would move the death correspondingly, to early September or late November 429. Diod. 12.46.1 and Athen. 5.217E place it simply in the third year of the war, when Epaminon was archon (429/28).

τότε δὲ . . . τῆς ψυχῆς: "It was at this time, apparently, that the plague made an attack on Pericles, not an acute or intense one, as with others, but one that killed his body and undermined his spirit a little at a time by a feeble disease, prolonged by various ups and downs." The emphatic role in the sentence of λαβήν, "attack, on-set," makes it difficult to put the sentence into English. Most of the terms are frequent in medical writers. Λαμβάνω is used of the onset of disease or a fever: see Thuc. 2.49.2; LSJ s.v. I.2. Βληχρός, "feeble, slow," describes low-grade fevers: cf. Hippoc. Aph. 5.64, ἐν πυρετοῖσι μακροῖσι βληχροῖσι, etc. Note that Thucydides (2.49.2) says that the fever of the plague was ἰσχυρός. P. uses βληχρός at Sert. 8.4, De tu. san. 133E, De facie 933D, and in a quote from Pindar at De lat. viv. 1130D, not in medical contexts. Διαχρωμένην here takes the acc. σῶμα, with the sense "destroy, ruin." This is the only example among sixteen in P. where its object is not personal and the sense is not simply to kill oneself or another. The word clearly had strong emotional overtones, for it is used in such famous passages as Hdt. 1.24.3 (the Arion story) and Thuc. 3.36.3 (the decision to execute the Mytileneans). For ὑπερείπουσαν . . . ψυχῆς cf. Crass. 18.4, τὸ θράσος ὑπήρειπε; Brut. 7.7, τὸν θυμὸν ὑπερείποντα. The phrase φρόνημα ψυχῆς is frequent in P.: cf. Per. 36.8, Agis 4.1, 43.2, Praec. ger. rep. 824E, Adv. Colot. 1119C, and, contrasted with physical strength or beauty, Cam. 27.4, Cim. 1.2.

ὁ λοιμός: Our only statement on the cause of Pericles' death. How-ever, if P.'s description is accurate, he must have died of something else, as the symptoms of the plague (Thuc. 2.49) were quite different: cf. Busolt, *Gr. Gesch.* 3.2:984n. 2.

38.2

Theophrastus: F146 Wimmer, *Ethics* L21 Fortenbaugh; cf. the Introduction, 3.2.d. See also Gellius *NA* 1.3, which is based on Theophrastus' *On Friendship* and cites a deathbed saying of the sage Chilon and an apophthegm of Pericles (1.3.20, found in a different form in P., *Reg. et imp. apophtheg.* 186C, *De vit. pud.* 531C, and *Praec. ger. rep.* 808A, but not in *Pericles*). The question whether virtue could be affected by fortune, or character by external factors, was frequently debated; for a full discussion cf. Gill 1983. Several other lives consider apparent changes in character at the end: cf. *Fab.* 26.2, ταῦτα μὲν οὖν ἐδόκει πολιτεύεσθαι πρὸς τὴν ἑαυτοῦ φύσιν ὁ Φάβιος; *Sull.* 30.6, *Arat.* 51.4, *Comp. Cim.–Luc.* 1.3–4. Closest, perhaps, to this passage is *Sert.* 10.5–7, where after noting Sertorius' special virtues, Plutarch adds, καίτοι δοκεῖ περὶ τὸν ἔσχατον αὐτοῦ βίον ὠμότητος καὶ βαρυθυμίας τὸ περὶ τοὺς ὁμήρους πραχθὲν ἔργον ἐπιδεῖξαι τὴν φύσιν οὐκ οὖσαν ἥμερον, ἀλλ' ἐπαμπεχομένην λογισμῷ διὰ τὴν ἀνάγκην. ἐμοὶ δ' ἀρετὴν μὲν εἰλικρινῆ καὶ κατὰ λόγον συνεστῶσαν οὐκ ἄν ποτε δοκεῖ τύχη τις ἐκστῆσαι πρὸς τοὐναντίον· ἄλλως δὲ προαιρέσεις καὶ φύσεις χρηστὰς ὑπὸ συμφορῶν μεγάλων παρ' ἀξίαν κακωθείσας οὐκ ἀδύνατον τῷ δαίμονι συμμεταβαλεῖν τὸ ἦθος. ὃ καὶ Σερτώριον οἶμαι παθεῖν, ἤδη τῆς τύχης αὐτὸν ἐπιλειπούσης ἐκτραχυνόμενον ὑπὸ τῶν πραγμάτων γινομένων πονηρῶν πρὸς τοὺς ἀδικοῦντας. Note also Alexander (*Alex.* 75.1), who becomes superstitious and filled by those around him with ἀβελτερίας καὶ φόβου. For other uses of ἀβελτερία as foolish superstition cf. *De adul. et amic.* 66C, *Conj. praec.* 145C.

διαπορήσας: "after having raised the question"; cf. 24.2, 36.5.

ἐξίσταται: "degenerate from"; cf. LSJ s.v. B.II.4.

ἐπισκοπουμένῳ: "visiting"; cf. Matthew 25:36, ἠσθένησα καὶ ἐπεσκέψασθέ με.

περίαπτον: "an amulet." They were commonly used at times of sickness and fever: cf. Plato *Rep.* 426B; Plut. *De facie* 920B, ὡς γὰρ οἱ ἐν νοσήμασι χρονίοις πρὸς τὰ κοινὰ βοηθήματα καὶ τὰς συνήθεις διαίτας ἀπειπόντες ἐπὶ καθαρμοὺς καὶ περίαπτα καὶ ὀνείρους τρέπονται. The word appears only in these two passages in P.; more common is φυλακτήριον, a case containing a magical charm, such as the one said to have been used by Demosthenes to hold the poison that killed him (*Dem.* 30.2), or that worn by the goddess Isis when pregnant (*De Is.* 377B, 378B). However, the usage is more often figurative, as at *Caes.* 57.8: Caesar put on his neck goodwill as the finest and most secure φυλακτήριον (cf. *Arat.* 25.7, *Praec. ger. rep.* 820F, 821B). For an interesting example of a phylactery see Kotansky 1983. For a general account of ancient amulets see *Reallexikon für Antike und Christentum* (Stuttgart 1950) 1:397–411, s.v. Amulett. Various sorts of fever amulets have been discovered in Egypt: see C. Bonner 1950, 67–68, and esp. 5, with reference to *Per.* 38.2: "the amulet (περίαπτον) may have been a bronze plaque or a small bag containing some of the well-known 'similars' supposed to be suited to the sick man's case." For papyrus texts used as amulets see, e.g., P. Erlangen 15, reedited by Maltomini 1982. A similar story is told of Bion of Borysthenes: ἐμπεσὼν εἰς νόσον . . . περίαπτα λαβεῖν ἐπείσθη (Diog. Laer. 4.54). DeVries 1975 notes the irony in Pericles' comment, σφόδρα . . . ἀβελτερίαν, which he thinks might be authentic.

38.3

οἱ περιόντες: "the survivors"; cf. 36.7, on the death of his friends from the plague.

τῶν τροπαίων τὸ πλῆθος: P. has only mentioned one, at 19.2. Thucydides mentions none: where did the figure nine come from? It is used also at *Comp. Per.–Fab.* 2.1, Περικλῆς δ' ἐννέα τρόπαια κατὰ γῆν καὶ κατὰ θάλατταν ἔστησεν ἀπὸ τῶν πολεμίων. Trophies, composed of captured arms, were regularly erected after every battle, even minor skirmishes: cf. Pritchett 1974, 246–75, who notes, 270, that Thucydides records some fifty-eight trophies. There is nothing unreasonable about the number P. ascribes to Pericles.

38.4

καθῃρημένου τὴν αἴσθησιν: "having lost consciousness."

εἰς μέσον: "out loud."

πρὸς τύχης . . . κοινά: "gifts of fortune available to all." Cf. P.'s own opinion at 2.3.

οὐδεὶς . . . περιεβάλετο: "No citizen has put on mourning because of me." For the black himation as a sign of mourning cf. Eur. *Alc.* 215–17, 923; Xen. *Hell.* 1.7.8; Hippoc. *Morb. sacr.* 1.17 Grensemann. The same anecdote is given as an example of the correct perspective on accomplishments at *De laude ipsius* 543B–C (cf. *Reg. et imp. apophtheg.* 186D) and elaborated by Julian *Or.* 3.128C–D. As P. explains in 39.1, the point is that Pericles did not win power by violence or civil war. But in the context in which it appears, immediately after the reference to trophies, it recalls also Pericles' *ἀσφάλεια*: despite the many battles and the Peloponnesian War, no Athenian deaths could be attributed to Pericles' lack of care, self-control, or foresight (cf. 18.1–3). P. chooses to ignore the many deaths in military actions that might have been avoided by a different policy, most notably during the Peloponnesian War itself. For the high value placed on refusing to kill fellow citizens compare Epaminondas' refusal to participate in the freeing of Thebes because "he never would kill a citizen without trial, unless absolutely necessary" (*De gen. Socr.* 594B). This second anecdote provides a corrective to the first: Pericles still preserved his *φρόνημα ψυχῆς*, despite his illness.

Ziegler accepts Cobet's emendation, 1873b, 372, correcting *ὄντων* to *πολιτῶν* and rejecting *Ἀθηναίων* as a gloss. However, it may be that the simpler solution, suggested also by the parallels in *De laude ipsius* and *Reg. et imp. apophtheg.*, is simply to delete *ὄντων*: "no Athenian has put on mourning. . . ."

39.1

θαυμαστὸς οὖν: P. offers his interpretation of the preceding anecdote: it demonstrates Pericles' reasonableness and calm (cf., after the same anecdote at *De laude ipsius* 543C, the reference to πρᾳότης and δικαιοσύνη) and his high-mindedness (alluded to in 38.2). Ἐπιείκεια, although not mentioned before, is a natural complement to πρᾳότης: cf. *Sert.* 25.6, *Caes.* 15.4, *Comp. Per.–Fab.* 3.2. The word is used especially of avoidance of harshness toward fellow citizens. The construction with θαυμαστός is the genitive of cause after a verbal adjective implying emotion (Smyth 1405, 1435): cf. *Publ.* 14.8, θαυμαστὸς οὖν ὁ ἀνὴρ τῆς εὐσταθείας; *Cat. Mai.* 6.1, τῆς δ' ἄλλης ἐγκρατείας ὑπερφυῶς θαυμαστὸς ὁ ἀνὴρ; *Flam.* 13.3. P. also uses the adjective with the accusative (*Per.* 27.3, *Aem.* 12.5, etc.) and the dative (*Arist.* 14.5, *Cim.* 6.1, etc.).

εἰ . . . ἀνηκέστῳ: "in that he considered the finest of his works to be that he had never on the basis of his enormous power indulged either envy or passion, nor treated any enemy as irreconcilable." Εἰ here means "the fact that," as regularly in expressions with θαυμαστόν: cf. *Pomp.* 14.6, *Cat. Min.* 49.4, etc. Μήτε . . . θυμῷ: control of these passions was a product of philosophical training, as Dion explains, *Dion* 47.4.

ἀπὸ . . . δυνάμεως: cf. *Pyrrh.* 14.11, τῆς Ἑλλάδος ἄρχειν ὑπάρξει βεβαίως ἀπὸ τηλικαύτης δυνάμεως; *Lys.* 30.2, ἀπὸ χρημάτων πολλῶν καὶ δυνάμεως . . . μηδὲ μίκρον ἐπιλαμπρύναντος τὸν οἶκον; *Phil.* 10.1, *Nic.* 3.1.

ἀνηκέστῳ: For quite different reasons, Crassus never made an irreconcilable enemy; cf. *Crass.* 7.7. For the expression see *Flam.* 19.8, *Mar.* 29.6, *De coh. ira* 456E, *De frat. am.* 483D. The only example given by P., in fact, is his recall of Cimon (10.4) and leniency at his trial (10.6). P.'s rhetoric leads him to generalize.

39.2

A rich and complex sentence, comparing P. to the Olympians, almost an apotheosis. P. employs the *topos apo onomatos* (cf. Arist. *Rhet.* 1400b18–26; [Longinus] 4.3) to praise his subject, as in *Arist.* 6. Aelius Aristides develops the same topos on this epithet of Pericles in his *On the Four* (123–24 Lenz and Behr). The sentence is tripartite: καὶ . . . προσαγορεύεσθαι, stating the major point; καθάπερ . . . ὄντων, explaining the true character of the gods; and οὐχ ὥσπερ . . . προσηκόντων, combating the stories of the poets. The weight of the last third is borne by the two contrasting participial phrases, τὸν μὲν τόπον . . . καλοῦντες . . . περιλαμπόμενον (supplemented by the genitive absolute, ὡς . . . πρεπούσης) and αὐτοὺς δὲ τοὺς θεοὺς . . . ἀποφαίνοντες . . . προσηκόντων. His quarrel with the poets allows P. to expand upon the tranquility of Olympus, similar to that of Pericles, and upon the turmoil of the passions. Although he suggests that this subject is a digression, belonging in another work (39.3), it has a rhetorical purpose here. Note the very frequent doubling of adjectives and nouns, typical of P.'s high style.

προσωνυμίαν: i.e. "the Olympian." P. first introduced the epithet at 8.3 but has delayed connecting it with πρᾳότης until he is ready to deliver this encomium. Val. Max. 5.10.ext. 1 relates the epithet to Pericles' self-control when his sons died. In P.'s day the Athenians had awarded the title to a Phoenician benefactor, and Dio Chrysostom (Or. 31.116, 48.10) refers to awards of this title as a common practice. We know from inscriptions of other instances (cf. L. Robert 1949, 7:80–81; J. and L. Robert 1953, 193 no. 19). The title became the most common honorific of the emperor Hadrian in the Greek East, especially in connection with his dedication of the Olympeion and foundation of the Panhellenion at Athens in 131/32; see Benjamin 1963. Would this passage have influenced the emperor to employ this title?

οὕτως . . . προσαγορεύεσθαι: appositive to ἐν τοῦτο.

ἐν ἐξουσίᾳ: again stressing the temptation of power, as ἀπὸ τηλικαύτης δυνάμεως above. Cf. 15.3.

ἀμίαντον: "unsullied," a poetic word rare in the lives (Num. 9.10, 9.12, Nic. 9.7), but often used in the Moralia (Qu. Rom. 267C, 270F, De Is. 382E, 383B, De E 388F, De Pyth. or. 395E, De tranq. 477B, Cons. ad uxor. 612B).

καθάπερ: in opposition to οὐχ ὥσπερ below.

ἀξιοῦμεν: "consider it right that."

αἴτιον . . . πεφυκός: cf. Plat. *Rep.* 379B–C, of the Good, τῶν μὲν εὖ ἐχόντων αἴτιον, τῶν δὲ κακῶν ἀναίτιον, and of God, ὀλίγων μὲν [good things] τοῖς ἀνθρώποις αἴτιος, πολλῶν δὲ [bad things] ἀναίτιος.

ἁλίσκονται . . . μυθεύμασι: "condemned by (the inconsistency of) their own fictions." P. uses μύθευμα especially of poetic fabrications. Cf. *De Is.* 358E, again rejecting the false stories of the poets about the gods.

ἀσφαλὲς ἕδος: This is a paraphrase of Homer's description of Olympus, *Od.* 6.42–45:

> . . . ὅθι φασὶ θεῶν ἕδος ἀσφαλὲς αἰεὶ
> ἔμμεναι· οὔτ' ἀνέμοισι τινάσσεται οὔτε ποτ' ὄμβρῳ
> δεύεται οὔτε χιὼν ἐπιπίλναται, ἀλλὰ μάλ' αἴθρη
> πέπταται ἀνέφελος, λευκὴ δ' ἐπιδέδρομεν αἴγλη.

προσηκόντων: modifying παθῶν.

39.3

ἑτέρας . . . πραγματείας: cf. 6.5. This aside on the nature of the gods, like its companion in chapter 6, reminds us of the importance of the divine in P.'s moral philosophy. P. treated the nature of the gods in a variety of works, from several perspectives. Concerning their "Olympian" calmness cf. the words he ascribes to his teacher Ammonius, *De E* 393A: ἀλλ' ἔστιν ὁ θεός, εἰ χρὴ φάναι, καὶ ἔστι κατ' οὐδένα χρόνον ἀλλὰ κατὰ τὸν αἰῶνα τὸν ἀκίνητον καὶ ἄχρονον καὶ ἀνέγκλιτον καὶ οὐ πρότερον οὐδέν ἐστιν οὐδ' ὕστερον οὐδὲ μέλλον οὐδὲ παρῳχημένον οὐδὲ πρεσβύτερον οὐδὲ νεώτερον.

τοῦ δὲ . . . πράγματα: "Events produced in the Athenians a swift perception and manifest longing for Pericles." Their perception of the man changed when he was compared with those that followed (cf. 37.1; Thuc. 2.65.10–13).

ἀνωμολογοῦντο . . . τρόπον: "(They) were agreed that never had there been a character more moderate in (despite its) self-importance, or more awesome in (despite its) mildness." Ὄγκος and σεμνότης were potentially opprobrious (cf. 5.3, 7.6); P., by noting the balance of Pericles' character, shifts them to praise. Note the chiasmus of thought (μετριώτερον pairing with πρᾳότητι, and ὄγκῳ with σεμνότερον) countering the parallelism of syntax.

39.4

ἡ δ' ἐπίφθονος . . . γενομένη: a figure of redefinition, made famous by Thuc. 3.82.4–5. It is called παραδιαστολή or distinctio (Quint. 9.3.65; Rhet. ad Her. 3.3.6). Cf., e.g., Tac. Agr. 30.6, ubi solitudinem faciunt, pacem appellant; Cic. Phil. 12.14. In this case the redefinition praises Pericles.

μοναρχία καὶ τυραννίς: cf. 9.1, 11.1, 16.1–2. Now, however, in the grandness of the final sentences, monarchy is no longer a charge to be avoided, but a boast, and brings to mind not the humble work of the local magistrate in a provincial city but the burden of responsibility for the whole state borne by the emperor himself.

σωτήριον ἔρυμα: cf. Praec. ger. rep. 802C, [Pericles' eloquence] τῇ πόλει σωτηρίαν ἔφερε; Mar. 14.2, τὸ γὰρ ἐν ἀρχῇ σκυθρωπὸν αὐτοῦ καὶ περὶ τὰς τιμωρίας δυσμείλικτον ἐθισθεῖσι μηδὲν ἁμαρτάνειν μηδ' ἀπειθεῖν ἅμα τῷ δικαίῳ σωτήριον ἐφαίνετο; Xen. Anab. 2.6.11, καὶ γὰρ τὸ στυγνὸν τότε φαιδρὸν . . . ἔφασαν φαίνεσθαι καί τὸ χαλεπὸν ἐρρωμένον πρὸς τοὺς πολεμίους ἐδόκει εἶναι, ὥστε σωτήριον, οὐκέτι χαλεπὸν ἐφαίνετο. For this figurative use of ἔρυμα cf. Phoc. 21.5, ὡς ἔρυμα πανταχόθεν ἀνάλωτον ὑπὸ τοῦ χρυσίου; Cat. Min. 29.8, [Cato] ἔρυμα καὶ πρόβλημα μέγα πρὸς τὸν Πομπηΐου δύναμιν.

τοσαύτη . . . γενέσθαι: "So abundant a crop, so large a multitude of evils lay upon the state, which he had kept from sight, making them weak and unimposing, and had prevented from becoming incurable in their strength." Φορά, "crop, abundance," is much preferable to mss. φθορά. Cf. De cur. 519B, [as butchers pray for a φορὰ of fattened animals, and fishermen of fish,] οὕτως οἱ πολυπράγμονες εὔχονται φορὰν κακῶν καὶ πλῆθος πραγμάτων καὶ καινότητας καὶ μεταβολάς; and De comm. not. 1067D, κακίας μὲν φορὰν τοσαύτην τὸ πλῆθος; De fort. Rom. 321A, φλεγμαῖνον ὑπὸ πλήθους καὶ φορᾶς γάλακτος. Πράγμασιν, "affairs of state, the state"; cf. 33.7.

In the enthusiasm of this peroration P. neglects a feature common in the *Lives*: the place of burial. The tomb of Pericles was a tourist site, in the Keramaikos: cf. Cic. *De fin.* 5.5, *paulum ad dexteram a via declinavi, ut ad Pericli sepulcrum accederem*; Paus. 1.29.3; Stupperich 1977, 25. Although the general evaluation of a hero, such as P. here gives Pericles, is unusual in the *Lives*, the reference to events after the hero's death is not.

The *Fabius* begins immediately with τοιούτου δὲ τοῦ Περικλέους ἐν τοῖς ἀξίοις μνήμης γεγονότος, ὡς παρειλήφαμεν, ἐπὶ τὸν Φάβιον τὴν ἱστορίαν μετάγομεν.

Comparison

On the importance of the idea of comparison in the *Parallel Lives* see the Introduction, 1.3; on this pair, see the Introduction, 2.2, and Stadter 1975. Ziegler's edition continues the chapter numeration of the *Fabius* as well as separate numbers.

1 (28).1

πολιτικῆς καὶ πολεμικῆς ἀρετῆς: This phrase establishes the structure of the comparison of the two men. The different nature of their two accomplishments, with an emphasis on the military, is set out in chapter 1. Pericles kept the city safe, once its greatness had been established; Fabius rescued the city after disaster. But it was easier for Fabius to control a humbled city than for Pericles to rein in a successful one. Military excellence is treated in chapter 2, political in chapter 3.

1 (28).2

Cimon: cf. note to 7.3. The campaigns of Cimon are alluded to at 9.5 and described more fully at *Cim.* 7–8, 12–14.

Myronides: cf. note to 16.3.

Leocrates: cf. note to 16.3.

Tolmides: cf. note to 18.2.

1 (28).3

The sentence recalls in overtly rhetorical fashion the situation after the Roman defeats at the Trebia (218), and Lake Trasimene (217) (cf. *Fab.* 2–3), before Fabius became dictator.

1 (28).4

ταπεινὴν . . . γενομένην: an adjective and a participial phrase modifying πόλιν, in emphatic position. Τοῦ φρονοῦντος κατήκοον, "obedient to someone who thinks clearly."

σπαργῶντι: "swollen with passion"; used also by Plato of the wanton steed in his myth of the soul, *Phaedr.* 256A. For the demos as a horse needing a bridle, see *Per.* 7.8, 11.4, 15.1.

2 (29)

The chapter sets out in balanced form the military exploits of the two. The siege of Samos (*Per.* 25–28) is set against that of Tarentum (*Fab.* 22–23); the recapture of Euboea (*Per.* 22–23) against the winning of Campania, Pericles' nine trophies (*Per.* 38.3) against Fabius' single triumph (*Fab.* 2.1). Two acts of Fabius are made to balance each other out: his rescue of Minucius and the Roman army (*Fab.* 11–12), and his deception by Hannibal (*Fab.* 6–10). Pericles seems to have the better of it.

2 (29).1

τὰς περὶ Καμπανίαν πόλεις: The recapture of Capua or other Campanian cities is not described in the *Fabius*, but cf. *Marc.* 26.8. Appius Claudius Pulcher and Q. Fulvius Flaccus as consuls in 212 were active in Campania and invested Capua; it capitulated in 211 when they were proconsuls. The reference here is a salutary reminder to the modern reader that Plutarch does not include in his *Lives* all that he knows about a hero or the historical context.

2 (29).3

ὡς Περικλῆς προέγνω καὶ προεῖπεν: cf. Thuc. 2.65.13.

παρὰ τοὺς Φαβίου λογισμούς: cf. *Fab.* 25-27.

3 (30)

The chapter lists charges and counter-charges against the heroes' actions in politics. Pericles caused the Peloponnesian War, but Fabius would certainly not have yielded to the Carthaginians. Pericles fought against and finally ostracized Cimon and Thucydides, but Fabius was patient with Minucius. However, Pericles' acquisition of power allowed him to restrain other generals, as Fabius could not. Both were honest, but Pericles had more opportunity to profit from his position. Pericles' building program was unrivaled. Although P. does not say it in so many words, Pericles clearly emerges superior from the comparison.

3 (30).1

ἔγκλημα: cf. *Per.* 29.8, 31.1.

3 (30).2

ἡ μέντοι . . . πρᾳότης: cf. esp. *Fab.* 5.5–8, 10.2–7, 13.

τὸν . . . στασιασμόν: cf. *Per.* 9–14.

3 (30).3

προσέπταισε: cf. *Per.*18.3.

3 (30).5

λυσάμενος: cf. *Fab.* 7.5–8. However, P. errs in his calculations. According to *Fab.* 7.5–6 Fabius had to pay 250 drachmas each for 240 men, a total of 60,000 drachmas or 10 talents.

3 (30).6

ἀδωρότατον . . . ἐφύλαξεν: cf. *Per.* 15.3.

3 (30).7

ἔργων . . . οἰκοδομημάτων: cf. *Per.* 12–13. Jones, *Plutarch*, 109, notes P.'s partiality to Athens in preference to other Greek cities with splendid buildings.

APPENDIX 1

Differences from the Editions of Ziegler and Flacelière

The text I have reproduced is that of Ziegler's third edition. Differences from this text in the Budé edition of Flacelière and in my commentary (Stad.) are listed below.

1.2 τὴν πληγὴν Zieg. page 1, line 13; Stad.
τῆς πληγῆς Flac.

3.5 καραΐέ Zieg. 4,2; Stad.
καράνιε Flac.

3.6 "ποτὲ μὲν" . . . "καρηβαροῦντα, ποτὲ δὲ
μόνον, Zieg. 4,3–4; Flac.
ποτὲ μὲν . . . "καρηβαροῦντα," ποτὲ δὲ "μόνον, Stad.

4.6 ἄλλοις Zieg. 5,13; Stad.
ὅλοις Flac.

5.3 ⟨συμ⟩περιφοραῖς Zieg. 6,9; Stad.
περιφοραῖς Flac.

7.7 ῥήτορας ἑτέρους Zieg. 8,23; Stad.
ἑταίρους ῥήτορας Flac.

7.8 ἀλλ' ⟨ἐν⟩δάκνειν Zieg. 8,30
ἀλλὰ δάκνειν Flac., Stad.

8.6 [μηδὲ] Zieg. 10,1
μηδὲ Flac., Stad.

9.2 ⟨Δάμωνος τοῦ⟩ Zieg. 11,5
no addition Flac., Stad.

10.4 ἐπανελθὼν Zieg. 12,10
κατελθὼν Flac., Stad.

10.6 διαπράσσειν Zieg. 12,24; Stad.
πράσσειν Flac.

11.5 ⟨τοὺς⟩ Zieg. 14,10
no addition Flac., Stad.

12.6 λινουργοὶ Zieg. 15,32; Flac.
λιθουλκοὶ Stad.

13.10 ὅδε / προσέρχεται [Περικλέης] Zieg. 17,20–21
ὅδε / προσέρχεται Flac.
ὁδί προσέρχεται / Περικλέης Stad.

13.14 [εἶναι] Zieg. 18,12; Stad.
 εἶναι Flac.
13.15 εἰς ταὐτὸ Zieg. 18,16; Flac.
 εἰς τὰ ἔργα Stad.
15.3 διέθεντο ⟨τοῖς⟩ ἐκείνου Zieg. 20,20–21
 διέθεντο, ἐκεῖνος Flac.
 διέθεντο, [ἐκεῖνος] Stad.
17.1 [τῆς] Zieg. 22,22; Stad.
 τῆς Flac.
23.3 εὐθὺς Zieg. 27,7; Stad.
 αὖθις Flac.
24.10 Μυρωνίδην Zieg. 29,7; Flac.
 Πυρωνίδην Stad.
26.4 φορτοφορεῖν Zieg. 31,11, Flac.
 ποντοπορεῖν Stad.
27.2 ⟨εἰς⟩ Zieg. 31,24; Stad.
 no addition Flac.
27.3 παρ⟨ασχ⟩όντος Zieg. 32,3; Stad.
 παρόντος Flac.
28.6 ⟨σου⟩ Zieg. 33,11
 no addition Flac., Stad.
28.7 γραῦς, ἠλείφεο Zieg. 33,18; Stad.
 γρῆϋς, ἠλείφεν Flac.
31.3 πᾶν Zieg. 37,4; Stad.
 πάνυ Flac.
32.5 φοβηθεὶς ⟨τὸ δικαστήριον⟩ ἐξέκλεψε καὶ προύπεμψεν Zieg.
 38,9–10
 φοβηθεὶς ἐξέπεμψεν Flac., Stad.
32.6 [φοβηθεὶς τὸ δικαστήριον] Zieg. 38,11–12; Stad.
 φοβηθεὶς τὸ δικαστήριον Flac.
33.7 αὐτῷ Zieg. 39,26; Stad.
 αὐτοῦ Flac.
34.2 [ὅμως] Zieg. 40,18
 ὅμως Flac., Stad.
34.5 χωρικοῦ Zieg. 41,10
 χωριτικοῦ Flac., Stad.
36.1 ⟨τῇ⟩ Zieg. 42,24; Stad.
 no addition Flac.
37.4 δωρεὰν Zieg. 44,18; Stad.
 δωρεὰς Flac.
37.4 ἀπεκρίθησαν Zieg. 44,23
 ἐπράθησαν Flac., Stad.

39.4 φορὰ Zieg. 47,6; Stad.
      φθορὰ Flac.

Comparison

1.2 ⟨ἐν⟩εορτάσαι Zieg. 82,1; Stad.
      ἐνεορτάσαι Flac.
1.3 [ἐν] τῷ Zieg. 82,7; Stad.
      τῷ Flac.
1.4 [τῷ] δήμῳ Zieg. 82,13; Stad.
      δήμῳ Flac.

APPENDIX 2

A Chronology of Pericles' Life

References to the *Pericles* are in parentheses.

ca. 495	Pericles born (3.1)
490	Expedition of Darius against Athens, battle of Marathon
485/84	Xanthippus ostracized (*Ath. pol.* 22.6)
480	Xerxes' invasion of Greece, battles of Thermopylae, Artemisium, and Salamis
	Athens evacuated
479	Battles of Plataea and Mycale
	Xanthippus captures Sestus
478/77	Delian League established
ca. 472	Themistocles ostracized and flees to Persia
472	Pericles choregus for Aeschylus' *Persians* (Xanthippus presumably already dead)
ca. 470	Pericles becomes active in politics (7.3–4)
ca. 468	Cimon's victory at Eurymedon
463	Pericles a public prosecutor against Cimon (10.6)
462?	Cimon brings Athenian help to Spartans at Messene
462/61	Reform of the Areopagus, ostracism of Cimon (9.2–5)
458–453	Athenian expedition to Egypt
ca. 458	Pericles' son Xanthippus born
457?	Battle of Tanagra, recall of Cimon (?) (10.1–4)
454?	Pericles' expedition in the Corinthian Gulf (19.2)
454	League treasury moved to Athens
451	Pericles' citizenship law (37.3)
450?	Cimon dies (10.8)
	Athenian victory at Salamis on Cyprus
	Cleruchies to Naxos and Andros (11.5)
448	Spartan and Athenian campaigns to Delphi (21.1–2)
447	Beginning of construction of Parthenon
	Athenian defeat at Coronea (18.3)
	Pericles' campaign and cleruchy to the Chersonese (19.1, 11.5)

446	Revolts of Euboea and Megara, Peloponnesian invasion of Attica (22–23)
446/45	Thirty-year peace between Athens and Sparta (24.1)
ca. 445–443	Building of middle Long Wall (13.7)
445/44	Psammetichus of Egypt gives grain to Athens. Purging of citizen rolls (37.4)
444?	Foundation of Thurii (11.5)
443?	Ostracism of Thucydides son of Melesias (14.3)
440–439	Samian revolt (25–28)
438	Foundation of Amphipolis (11.5)
438/37	Dedication of Parthenos statue (13.14) Prosecution of Phidias? (31)
437–432	Construction of the Propylaea (13.12)
435?	Pericles' Pontic expedition (20.1–2)
433	Athenian aid to Corcyra, battle of Sybota (29.1–3) Congress of Peloponnesians at Sparta (29.4–6)
432/31	Winter: last embassies to Athens (29.7–30.1), Pericles opposes repeal of Megarian decree (30.2, 31.1, 32.6)
431	May: Peloponnesian invasion of Attica (33.4) Summer: Athenian expedition against Peloponnese (34.1–3) and removal of Aeginetans (34.2) 3 August: solar eclipse (35.2) Fall: Athenian invasion of Megara (34.4)
430	Spring: the plague strikes Athens (34.5), second Peloponnesian invasion Pericles' expedition against Epidaurus (35.1, 3), reinforcements to Potidaea (35.3) Summer: Pericles deposed from office (35.4) Deaths of Pericles' sons Xanthippus and Paralus, a sister, and other relatives (36.6–8)
429?	Pericles reelected as general (37.1–2) Pericles begs for citizenship for his bastard son (37.5)
429	Fall: Pericles' death (38)

BIBLIOGRAPHY

See also the List of Abbreviations.

Aalders, G. J. D. 1977. "Political Theory in Plutarch's *Convivium Septem Sapientium*." *Mnemosyne*, ser. 4, 30:28–39.

_____. 1982. *Plutarch's Political Thought*. Amsterdam.

Accame, S. 1982. "Stesimbroto di Taso e la pace di Callia." *Miscellanea greca e romana* 8:125–52.

Adcock, F., and D. J. Mosley. 1975. *Diplomacy in Ancient Greece*. London.

Alessandrì, S. 1985. "Le civette di Gilippo (Plut. *Lys.*, 16–17)." *ASNP*, ser. 3, 15:1081–93.

Alexiou, M. 1974. *The Ritual Lament in the Greek Tradition*. Cambridge.

Allen, W. S. 1974. *Vox Graeca*². Cambridge.

Altheim, F., and R. Stiehl. 1962. "Neue Fragmente Zenons von Kition aus dem Arabischen." *F & F* 36:12–14, 372–75.

Ambaglio, D. 1980. "Plutarco, Erodoto e la tradizione storica frammentaria." *Rend. Ist. Lomb.* 114:123–41.

Ameling, W. 1981. "Komödie und Politik zwischen Kratinos und Aristophanes: Das Beispiel Perikles." *Quaderni Catanesi di studi classici e medievali* 3:383–424.

_____. 1985. "Plutarch, Perikles 12–14." *Historia* 34:47–63.

_____. 1986. "Zu einem neuen Datum des Phidiasprozesses." *Klio* 68:63–66.

Amit, M. 1965. *Athens and the Sea*. Brussels.

_____. 1970. "Hostages in Ancient Greece." *RFIC* 98:129–47.

_____. 1971. "The Boeotian Confederation during the Pentekontaetia." *Rivista di Storia Antica* 1:49–64.

Anderson, J. K. 1954. "A Topographical and Historical Study of Achaea." *ABSA* 49:72–92.

Anderson, W. D. 1966. *Ethos and Education in Greek Music*. Cambridge, Mass.

Andrewes, A. 1959. "Thucydides on the Causes of War." *CQ*, n.s. 9:223–39.

_____. 1963. *The Greek Tyrants*. New York.

_____. 1966. "The Government of Classical Sparta." In *Ancient Society and*

Institutions: Studies . . . V. Ehrenberg, 1–20. Oxford.
――――. 1977. "Kleisthenes' Reform Bill." *CQ*, n.s. 27:241–48.
――――. 1978. "The Opposition to Perikles." *JHS* 98:1–8.
Arnim, H. von. 1903–24. *Stoicorum Veterum Fragmenta.* 4 vols. Leipzig.
――――. 1921. *Plutarch über Dämonen und Mantik.* Amsterdam.
Asheri, D. 1969. "The Site of Brea." *AJP* 90:337–40.
Austin, C. 1973. *Comicorum Graecorum Fragmenta in Papyris Reperta.* Berlin and New York.
Avery, H. 1973. "Sophokles' Political Career." *Historia* 22:509–14.
Avigad, N. 1986. *Hebrew Bullae from the Time of Jeremiah: Remnants of a Burnt Archive.* Jerusalem.
Babut, D. 1978. "Anaxagore jugé par Socrate et Platon." *REG* 91:44–76.
Badian, E. 1987. "The Peace of Callias." *JHS* 107:1–39.
Balcer, J. M. 1974. "Separatism and Anti-Separatism in the Athenian Empire (478–433 B.C.)." *Historia* 23:21–39.
――――. 1978. *The Athenian Regulations for Chalkis: Studies in Athenian Imperial Law.* Wiesbaden.
Barber, G. L. 1935. *The Historian Ephorus.* Cambridge.
Barns, J. W. B. 1950, 1951. "A New Gnomologium with Some Remarks on Gnomic Anthologies." *CQ* 44:126–37, 45 (n.s. 1):1–19.
――――, and H. Lloyd-Jones. 1963. "Un nuovo frammento papiraceo dell'elegia ellenistica." *SIFC* 35:221–22.
Barron, J. P. 1962. "Milesian Politics and Athenian Propaganda ca. 460–440 B.C." *JHS* 82:1–6.
――――. 1966. *The Silver Coins of Samos.* London.
Barrow, R. H. 1967. *Plutarch and His Times.* London.
Beare, J. I. 1906. *Greek Theories of Elementary Cognition.* Oxford.
Becatti, G. 1951. *Problemi Fidiaci.* Milan and Florence.
Behr, C. A. 1968. *Aelius Aristides and the Sacred Tales.* Amsterdam.
Bekker, I. 1814–21. *Anecdota Graeca.* 3 vols. Reprinted Graz 1965.
Beloch, [K.] J. 1886. *Die Bevölkerung der griechisch-römischen Welt.* Leipzig.
――――. 1912–27. *Griechische Geschichte*[2]. 4 vols. in 8. Strassburg (vols. 1–2); Berlin and Leipzig (vols. 3–4). Reprinted 1927.
Bengtson, H. 1962. *Die Staatsverträge des Altertums.* Vol. 2. Munich.
Benjamin, A. S. 1963. "The Altars of Hadrian in Athens and Hadrian's Panhellenic Program." *Hesperia* 32:57–86.
Benseler, G. E. 1841. *De Hiatu in Oratoribus Atticis et Historicis Graecis Libri Duo.* Freiburg.
Berger, E., ed. 1984. *Parthenon-Kongress: Basel, 4.–8. April 1982. Referate und Berichte.* Mainz.
Berthelot, M. 1888. *Collection des anciens alchemistes grecs.* Paris.

Bicknell, P. J. 1972. *Studies in Athenian Politics and Genealogy. Historia* Einzelschrift 19. Wiesbaden.

———. 1982. "Axiochus Alkibiadou, Aspasia, and Aspasios." *AC* 51:248–49.

Blackman, D. 1969. "The Athenian Navy and Allied Naval Contributions in the Pentecontaetia." *GRBS* 10:179–216.

Blass, F. 1874–93. *Die attische Beredsamkeit*. 3 vols. Leipzig.

———, and A. Debrunner. 1961. *A Greek Grammar of the New Testament.* Trans. by R. W. Funk. Chicago and London.

Bloch, H. 1959. Review of Jacoby, *FGrHist* vol. 3B suppl. *Gnomon* 31:487–99.

Bloedow, E. F. 1987. "Pericles' Powers in the Counter-Strategy of 431." *Historia* 36:9–27.

Blomqvist, J. 1969. *Greek Particles in Hellenistic Prose*. Lund.

Blümner, H. 1875–87. *Technologie und Terminologie der Gewerbe und Künste bei Griechen und Römern*. 4 vols. Leipzig.

Blumenthal, A. von. 1939. *Ion von Chios: Die Reste seine Werke*. Stuttgart.

Boardman, J. 1980. *The Greeks Overseas*. London.

———. 1982. "Heracles, Theseus, and the Amazons." In *The Eye of Greece: Studies in the Art of Athens*, edited by D. Kurtz and B. Sparkes, 18–20. Cambridge.

———. 1985. *Greek Sculpture: The Classical Period*. London.

Boegehold, A. L. 1972. "The Establishment of a Central Archive at Athens." *AJA* 76:23–30.

Boersma, J. S. 1970. *Athenian Building Policy from 561/0 to 405/4 B.C.* Groningen.

Bonner, C. 1950. *Studies in Magical Amulets, Chiefly Graeco-Egyptian*. Ann Arbor.

Bonner, R. J., and G. Smith. 1938. *The Administration of Justice from Homer to Aristotle*. Vol. 2. Chicago.

Bosworth, A. B. 1971. "The Congress Decree: Another Hypothesis." *Historia* 20:600–616.

Bothmar, D. von. 1957. *Amazons in Greek Art*. Oxford.

Boulanger, A. 1923. *Aelius Aristides et la sophistique dans la province d'Asie au IIe siècle de notre ère*. Paris. Reprinted 1968.

Boulter, C. 1953. "Pottery of the Mid-Fifth Century from a Well in the Athenian Agora." *Hesperia* 22:59–115.

Bowra, C. M. 1938. "The Epigram on the Fallen of Coronea." *CQ* 32:80–88.

Bradeen, D. W. 1974. *The Athenian Agora*. Vol. 17, *Inscriptions: The Funerary Monuments*. Princeton.

Brandhofer, F.-J. 1971. *Untersuchungen zur athenischen Westpolitik im Zeitalter des Perikles*. Munich.

Brasinskij, I. B. 1958. "L'expédition pontique de Périclès" (in Russian). *VDI* 65:110–21.

Breebaart, A. B. 1971. "Plutarch and the Political Development of Pericles." *Mnemosyne*, ser. 4, 24:260–72.

Bremmer, J. 1981. "Plutarch and the Naming of Greek Women." *AJP* 102:425–27.

Brenk, F. E. 1977. *In Mist Apparelled*. Leiden.

Breslin, J. 1980. "The Athenian Board of Generals in Samos 439/8 B.C. (*IG* I² 50 = ML 56)." *AncW* 3:104–6.

Bridges, A. P. 1980. "The Athenian Treaty with Samos, ML 56." *JHS* 100:185–88.

Brochard, V. 1923. *Les sceptiques grecs*². Paris. Reprinted 1959.

Brommer, F. 1967. *Die Metopes des Parthenon*. Mainz.

Brunt, P. A. 1951. "The Megarian Decree." *AJP* 72:269–82.

————. 1966. "Athenian Settlements Abroad in the Fifth Century B.C." In *Ancient Society and Institutions: Studies . . . V. Ehrenberg*, 71–92. Oxford.

————. 1973. "Aspects of the Social Thought of Dio Chrysostom and the Stoics." *Proc. Cambr. Philol. Soc.*, n.s. 19:9–34.

————. 1980. "Free Labor and Public Works at Rome." *JRS* 70:81–100.

Buchanan, J. J. 1962. *Theorika*. Locust Valley, N.Y.

Bucher-Isler, B. 1972. *Norm und Individualität in den Biographien Plutarchs*. Stuttgart.

Buck, R. J. 1970. "The Athenian Domination of Boeotia." *CP* 65:217–27.

Buckler, J. 1978. "Plutarch on the Trials of Pelopidas and Epaminondas." *CP* 73:36–42.

Bundgaard, J. A. 1957. *Mnesicles: A Greek Architect at Work*. Stockholm.

————. 1976. *Parthenon and the Mycenaean City on the Heights*. Copenhagen.

Bureth, P. 1964. *Les titulatures impériales dans les papyrus, les ostraca et les inscriptions d'Egypte (30 a.C.–284 p.C)*. Brussels.

Burford, A. 1963. "The Builders of the Parthenon." In *Parthenos and Parthenon*, 23–35. *Greece and Rome* suppl. 10. Oxford.

————. 1965. "The Economics of Greek Temple Building." *PCPhS* 191:21–32.

————. 1969. *The Greek Temple Builders at Epidauros*. Liverpool.

————. 1972. *Craftsmen in Greek and Roman Society*. London.

Burkert, W. 1986. "Der Autor von Derveni: Stesimbrotus *peri teleton*?" *ZPE* 62:1–5.

Busolt, G. 1893–1904. *Griechische Geschichte bis zur Schlacht bei Chaeronea*². 3 vols. in 4. Gotha.

_____, and H. Swoboda. 1920–26. *Griechische Staatskunde*³. 2 vols. Munich.

Buttrey, T. 1977. "Ὑπο in Aristophanes and ὑποκριτής." *GRBS* 18:5–23.

Cadell, H. 1965. Review of *Plutarque: Vies*, vol. 3, *Périclès–Fabius Maximus, Alcibiade–Coriolan*, edited by R. Flacelière and E. Chambry. *REA* 57:498–501.

Caizzi, F. 1966. *Antisthenis Fragmenta*. Milan.

Calder, W. M., III. 1971. "Sophoclean Apologia: *Philoctetes*." *GRBS* 12:153–74.

Camp, J. M. 1986. *The Athenian Agora*. London.

Carawan, E. 1987. "*Eisangelia* and *Euthyna*: The Trials of Miltiades, Themistocles, and Cimon." *GRBS* 28:167–208.

Carney, T. F. 1960. "Plutarch's Style in the Marius." *JHS* 80:24–31.

Carpenter, R. 1970. *The Architects of the Parthenon*. Harmondsworth.

Carrara, P. 1987. "On the Nature of P. Petrie I.iii.1: Gnomologium or Work about Plagiarism?" *ZPE* 68:14–18.

Carrière, J. C. 1977. "A propos de la *Politique* de Plutarque." In *Dialogues d'histoire ancienne*, 3:237–51. Annales littéraires de l'Université de Besançon 202. Paris.

Carter, J. M. 1967. "Eighteen Years Old?" *BICS* 14:51–57.

Cassio, A. C. 1982. "Arte compositiva e politica in Aristofane: il discorso di Ermete nella *Pace* (603–648)." *RFIC* 110:22–44.

Casson, L. 1958. "Hemiolia and Triemiolia." *JHS* 78:14–18.

Cawkwell, G. L. 1969. "Anthemocritus and the Megarians and the Decree of Charinus." *REG* 82:327–35.

_____. 1975. "Thucydides' Judgment of Periclean Strategy." *YClS* 24:53–70.

Chambers, M. 1957. Review of Jacoby, *FGrHist* vol. 3B. *CP* 52:130–32.

_____. 1967. "The Berlin Fragments of the *Ath. Pol.*" *TAPA* 98:49–66.

Cherniss, H., ed. 1957. *Plutarch's Moralia*. Vol. 12. Cambridge, Mass.

Clairmont, C. 1979. "New Light on Some Public Athenians of the 5th and 4th Century." *ZPE* 36:123–30.

Clay, D. 1982. "Epicurus in the Archives of Athens." In *Studies in Attic Epigraphy, History, and Topography Presented to Eugene Vanderpool*, 17–26. *Hesperia* suppl. 19. Princeton.

Clerc, M. 1893. *Les Métèques Athéniens*. Paris. Reprinted 1979.

Cobet, C. G. 1873a. "Miscellanea Philologica et Critica." *Mnemosyne*, n.s. 1:97–142.

_____. 1873b. *Variae Lectiones*². Leiden.

_____. 1878. "Ad Plutarchi Βίους Παραλλήλους." *Mnemosyne*, n.s. 6:113–73.

Cohen, B. 1985. "Kresilas' *Perikles* and the Riace Bronzes: New Evidence for Schinocephaly." *AIA Abstracts*, p. 30.

Cole, J. R. 1974. "Cimon's Dismissal, Ephialtes' Revolution and the Peloponnesian Wars." *GRBS* 15:369–85.

Connor, W. R. 1962a. "Charinus' Megarean Decree." *AJP* 83:225–46.

———. 1962b. "Vim Quamdam Incredibilem: A Tradition Concerning the Oratory of Pericles." *Classica et Mediaevalia* 23:23–33.

———. 1963. "Two Notes on Diopeithes the Seer." *CP* 58:115–18.

———. 1967. "Two Notes on Cimon." *TAPA* 98:67–75.

———. 1968. *Theopompus and Fifth-Century Athens*. Cambridge, Mass.

———. 1970. "Charinus' Megarean Decree Again." *REG* 83:305–8.

———. 1971. *The New Politicians of Fifth-Century Athens*. Princeton.

Conomis, C. N. 1975. In *Φίλτρα: Festschrift S. G. Kapsomenos* (*Τιμητικὸς τόμος Σ. Γ. Καψωμένου*). Thessalonike.

Coraes, A., ed. 1809–14. *Πλουτάρχου Βίοι Παράλληλοι*. Paris.

Corbetta, C. 1977. "La fallita spedizione di Pericle a Cipro." *Rendiconti Ist. Lombardo*, Cl. lett. e sc. mor. e stor., 111:155–66.

Corso, A. 1986. *Monumenti Periclei: Saggio critico sulla attivitá edilizia di Pericle*. Ist. Veneto di scienze, lettere ed arti, *Memorie*, classe di sc. mor., lett. ed arti, 40, fasc. 1. Venice.

Coulton, J. J. 1977. *Ancient Greek Architects at Work*. Ithaca, N.Y.

Cromey, R. D. 1982. "Pericles' Wife: Chronological Calculations." *GRBS* 23:203–12.

———. 1984. "On Deinomache." *Historia* 33:385–401.

Dale, A. M. 1968. *The Lyric Metres of Greek Drama*[2]. Cambridge.

Dareste, R. 1902. "Droit de représailles chez les Grecs." In *Nouvelles études d'histoire du droit*, pp. 305–21. Paris.

Daux, G. 1936. *Pausanias à Delphes*. Paris.

Davies, J. K. 1971. *Athenian Propertied Families, 600–300 B.C.* Oxford.

———. 1978a. "Athenian Citizenship: The Descent Group and the Alternatives." *CJ* 73:105–21.

———. 1978b. *Democracy and Classical Greece*. London.

Davison, J. A. 1953. "Protagoras, Democritus and Anaxagoras." *CQ* 47:33–45.

———. 1958. "Notes on the Panathenaea." *JHS* 78:23–42. Reprinted in *From Archilochus to Pindar*, pp. 28–69. London and New York 1968.

DeLacy, P. 1966. "Galen and the Greek Poets." *GRBS* 7:259–66.

Denniston, J. D. 1954. *The Greek Particles*[2]. Oxford.

Derenne, E. 1930. *Les procès d'impiété intentés aux philosophes à Athènes au Vme et au IVme siècles avant J.-C.* Liège. Reprinted New York 1976.

Deubner, L. 1956. *Attische Feste*. Berlin.

DeVries, G. J. 1975. "Theophrastus on Pericles' Last Illness." *Mnemosyne*, ser. 4, 28:193.

de Wet, B. X. 1981. "Aspects of Plutarch's Portrayal of Pompey." *Acta Classica* 24:119–32.

Diels, H. 1901. *Poetarum Philosophorum Fragmenta*. Berlin.

———, and W. Kranz. 1951–52. *Die Fragmente der Vorsokratiker*[6]. Zurich and Berlin.

DiGregorio, L. 1979, 1980. "Lettura diretta e utilizzazione di fonti nelle citazioni plutarchee dei tre grandi tragici." *Aevum* 53:11–50, 54:46–79.

Dinsmoor, W. B. 1950. *The Architecture of Ancient Greece*[3]. London.

Dinsmoor, W. B., Jr. 1980. *The Propylaia to the Athenian Acropolis*. Vol. 1, *The Predecessors*. Princeton.

Dittmar, H. 1912. *Aeschines von Sphettos*. Philologische Untersuchungen 12. Berlin. Reprinted New York 1976.

Dodds, E. R. 1959. *Plato: Gorgias*. Oxford.

Donnay, G. 1967. "Les comptes de l'Athéna chryséléphantine du Parthénon." *BCH* 91:50–86.

———. 1968. "La date du procès de Phidias." *AntCl* 37:19–36.

Douglas, A. E. 1966. *M. Tulli Ciceronis Brutus*. Oxford.

Dove, W. Franklin. 1936. "Artificial Production of the Fabulous Unicorn." *Scientific Monthly* 42:431–36.

Dover, K. J. 1960. "Δέκατος αὐτός." *JHS* 80:61–77.

———. 1966. "Anthemocritus and the Megarians." *AJP* 87:203–9.

———. 1967. "Portrait-Masks in Aristophanes." In *Κωμῳδοτραγήματα: Studia Aristophanea W. J. W. Koster in Honorem*, 16–28. Amsterdam.

———. 1968. *Aristophanes: Clouds*. Oxford.

———. 1972. *Aristophanic Comedy*. Berkeley and Los Angeles.

———. 1974. *Greek Popular Morality in the Time of Plato and Aristotle*. Berkeley and Los Angeles.

———. 1975. "The Freedom of the Intellectual in Greek Society." *Talanta* 7:24–54.

———. 1978. *Greek Homosexuality*. Cambridge, Mass.

Dow, S. 1961. "Thucydides and the Number of Acharnian *Hoplitai*." *TAPA* 92:66–80.

———. 1963. "The Attic Demes Oa and Oe." *AJP* 84:166–81.

Ducrey, P. 1968. *Le traitement des prisonniers de guerre dans la Gréce antique*. Paris.

Durić, M. 1953. "Ein plutarchisches Zeugnis über Protagoras" (in Serbian). *ZAnt* 3:65–73.

Eddy, S. K. 1968. "Athens' Peacetime Navy in the Age of Pericles." *GRBS* 9:141–56.

———. 1973. "The Cold War between Athens and Persia, ca. 448–442 B.C." *CP* 68:241–59.

———. 1977. "The Gold in the Athena Parthenos." *AJA* 81:107–11.

Edmonds, J. 1957–61. *Fragments of Attic Comedy.* 3 vols. Leiden.

Ehlers, B. 1966. *Eine vorplatonische Deutung des sokratischen Eros: Der Dialog Aspasia des Sokratikers Aischines.* Zetemata 41. Munich.

Ehrenberg, V. 1948. "The Foundation of Thurii." *AJP* 69:149–70.

———. 1951. *The People of Aristophanes.* London. Reprinted New York 1962.

———. 1952. "Thucydides on Athenian Colonization." *CP* 47:143–49.

———. 1954. *Sophocles and Pericles.* Oxford.

———. 1969. *The Greek State.* London.

Emperius, A. 1847. *Opuscula Philologica et Historica,* pp. 286–96. Göttingen.

Erbse, H. 1952. "Plutarchs Schrift περὶ δεισιδαιμονίας." *Hermes* 80:296–314.

———. 1956. "Die Bedeutung der Synkrisis in den Parallelbiographien Plutarchs." *Hermes* 84:398–424.

———. 1961. Review of *Plutarch: Vitae Parallelae,* edited by Cl. Lindskog and K. Ziegler. *Gnomon* 33:38–44.

Erdmann, Walter. 1934. *Die Ehe im alten Griechenland.* Munich.

Eriksson, K. 1943. *Das Praesens historicum in der nachklassischen griechischen Historiographie.* Diss. Lund.

Ewbank, L. C. 1982. *Plutarch's Use of Non-literary Sources in the Lives of Sixth- and Fifth-Century Greeks.* Diss. Chapel Hill.

Ferguson, W. S. 1904. "The Historical Value of the Twelfth Chapter of Plutarch's Life of Pericles." *TAPA* 35:5–20.

Ferrarese, P. 1974. "La spedizione di Pericle nel Ponto Eusino." In *Propaganda e persuasione occulta nell'antichità,* 7-19. Contributi dell'Istituto di storia antica, 2. Pubbl. dell'Università Cattolica del Sacro Cuore, Sc. stor. 8. Milano.

Ferrero, L. 1963. "Tra poetica e storia: Duride di Samo." In *Miscellanea di studi alessandrini . . . Rostagni,* 68–100. Turin.

Ferretto, C. 1984. *La città dissipatrice: studi sull'excursus del libro decimo dei Philippika di Teopompo.* Genoa.

Figueira, T. J. 1986. "Xanthippos, Father of Perikles, and the *Prutaneis* of the *Naukraroi.*" *Historia* 35:257–79.

Flacelière, R. 1937. *Sur les oracles de la Pythie.* Paris.

———. 1951. "Plutarque et les éclipses de lune." *REA* 53:203–21.

———. 1965. *Daily Life in Ancient Greece at the Time of Pericles.* New York.

———. 1969. "Etat présent des études sur Plutarque." In *Actes du VIIIe Congrès Guillaume Budé,* 483–506. Paris.

———, and E. Chambry. 1964. *Plutarque: Vies.* Vol. 3, *Périclès–Fabius Maximus, Alcibiade–Coriolan.* Paris. Reprinted 1969.

Fogazza, G. 1970. "Aspasia minore." *La Parola del Passato* 25:420–22.

Fornara, C. W. 1971a. *The Athenian Board of Generals from 501 to 404.* *Historia* Einzelschrift 16. Wiesbaden.

―――. 1971b. *Herodotus: An Interpretative Essay.* Oxford.

―――. 1975. "Plutarch and the Megarian Decree." *YCS* 24:213–28.

―――. 1979. "On the Chronology of the Samian War." With "Additional Note" by D. M. Lewis. *JHS* 99:7–19.

Forrest, W. G. 1966. *The Emergence of Greek Democracy.* London.

―――, and D. L. Stockton. 1987. "The Athenian Archons: A Note." *Historia* 36:235–40.

Fortenbaugh, W. W. 1984. *Quellen zur Ethik Theophrasts.* Amsterdam.

Foucart, P. 1889. "Décret athénien de l'année 352 trouvé à Eleusis." *BCH* 13:433–67.

Fraenkel, E. 1955. "Neues Griechisch in Graffiti." *Glotta* 34:42–47.

Frazier, F. 1987. "A propos de la composition des couples dans les 'Vies parallèles' de Plutarque." *RPh* 61:65–75.

Fritz, K. von. 1954. *The Theory of the Mixed Constitution in Antiquity.* New York.

Frost, F. 1961. "Some Documents in Plutarch's Lives." *Classica et Mediaevalia* 22:182–94.

―――. 1964a. "Pericles and Dracontides." *JHS* 84:69–72.

―――. 1964b. "Pericles, Thucydides Son of Melesias, and Athenian Politics before the War." *Historia* 13:385–99.

―――. 1980. *Plutarch's Themistocles.* Princeton.

―――. 1984. "Plutarch and Theseus." *CB* 60:65–71.

Fuhrmann, F. 1964. *Les images de Plutarque.* Paris.

Gall, H. von. 1979. "Das Zelt des Xerxes und seiner Rolle als persischer Raumtyp in Griechenland." *Gymnasium* 86:444–62.

Gardiner, E. N. 1910. *Greek Athletic Sports and Festivals.* London.

Gauthier, P. 1973. "A propos des clérouquies athéniennes du Ve siècle." In *Problèmes de la terre en Grèce ancienne*, edited by M. I. Finley, 163–78. Paris and The Hague.

Geiger, J. 1981. "Plutarch's Parallel Lives: The Choice of Heroes." *Hermes* 109:85–104.

―――. 1985. *Cornelius Nepos and Ancient Political Biography.* Stuttgart.

Gernet, L. 1924. "Sur l'exécution capitale." *REG* 37:291–93. Reprinted in English translation in Gernet 1981.

―――. 1981. *The Anthropology of Ancient Greece.* Baltimore and London.

Gershenson, D. E., and D. A. Greenberg. 1964. *Anaxagoras and the Birth of Physics.* New York.

Giannantoni, G. 1983. *Socraticorum Reliquiae.* Vol. 2. Rome and Florence.

Giglioni, G. Bodei. 1974. *Lavori pubblici e occupazione nell'antichità classica.* Bologna.

Gilbert, G. 1895. *The Constitutional Antiquities of Sparta and Athens.* London.

Gill, C. 1983. "The Question of Character-Development: Plutarch and Tacitus." *CQ,* n.s. 33:469–87.

Godolphin, F. R. B. 1931. "The Nemesis of Cratinus." *CP* 26:423–26.

Goergemanns, H. 1970. *Untersuchungen zu Plutarchs Dialog De facie in orbe lunae.* Heidelberg.

Gomme, A. W. 1933. *The Population of Athens in the Fifth and Fourth Centuries B.C.* Oxford.

———. 1945–56. *A Historical Commentary to Thucydides.* 3 vols. (to 5.24). Vols. 4 and 5 completed by K. J. Dover and A. Andrewes. Oxford.

Gossage, A. J. 1967. "Plutarch." In *Latin Biography,* edited by T. Dorey, 45–78. London.

Gottschalk, H. B. 1980. *Heraclides of Pontus.* Oxford.

Gould, J. 1980. "Law, Custom, and Myth: Aspects of the Social Position of Women in Classical Athens." *JHS* 100:38–59.

Graham, A. J. 1964. *Colony and Mother City in Ancient Greece.* New York.

Green, J. R., and R. K. Sinclair. 1970. "Athenians in Eretria." *Historia* 19:515–27.

Griffith, G. T. 1978. "A Note on Plutarch *Pericles* 17." *Historia* 27:218–19.

Griffiths, J. Gwyn. 1970. *Plutarch: De Iside et Osiride.* Cambridge.

Groot, A. W. de. 1915. "The Rhythm of Greek Prose." *CQ* 9:231–44.

———. 1918. *A Handbook of Antique Prose-Rhythm.* Groningen.

Guthrie, W. K. C. 1962–81. *A History of Greek Philosophy.* 6 vols. Cambridge.

Habicht, C. 1957. "Samische Volksbeschlüsse der hellenistischen Zeit." *MDAI(A)* 72:154–64.

———. 1961. "Falsche Urkunden zur Geschichte Athens im Zeitalter der Perserkriege." *Hermes* 89:1–35.

———. 1985. *Pausanias' Guide to Ancient Greece.* Berkeley and Los Angeles.

Hamilton, J. R. 1969. *Plutarch's Alexander.* Oxford.

Hammond, N. G. L., and G. T. Griffith. 1979. *A History of Macedonia.* Vol. 2. Oxford.

Hands, A. R. 1975. "In Favour of a Peace of Kallias." *Mnemosyne,* ser. 4, 28:193–95.

Hansen, M. H. 1975. *Eisangelia.* Oxford.

———. 1980. "Eisangelia in Athens: A Reply." *JHS* 100:89–95.

———. 1982. "Demographic Reflections on the Number of Athenian Citizens 451–309 B.C." *AJAH* 7:172–89.

Harris, B. F. 1970. "The Portrait of Autocratic Power in Plutarch's Lives." In *Auckland Classical Essays presented to E. M. Blaiklock,* 185–202. Auckland.

Harris, H. A. 1964. *Greek Athletes and Athletics.* London.

Harrison, A. R. W. 1968. *Law of Athens*. Vol. 1, *The Family and Property*. Oxford.

————. 1971. *Law of Athens*. Vol. 2, *Procedure*. Oxford.

Harrison, E. 1966. "The Composition of the Amazonomachy on the Shield of Athena Parthenos." *Hesperia* 35:107–33.

————. 1981. "Motifs of the City-siege on the Shield of the Athena Parthenos." *AJA* 85:281–317.

Headlam, W. 1966. *Herodas: The Mimes and Fragments*. Edited by A. D. Knox. Cambridge.

Heichelheim, F. M. 1964. *Ancient Economic History*. Vol. 2. Leiden.

Heilmeyer, W. D. 1981. "Antike Werkstättenfunde in Griechenland." *AA* 440–53.

Hein, A. 1914. *De Optativi apud Plutarchum Usu*. Diss. Breslau.

Helmbold, W. C., and E. N. O'Neill. 1959. *Plutarch's Quotations*. N.p.

Henderson, J. J., ed. 1987. *Aristophanes' Lysistrata*. Oxford.

Henry, A. S. 1983. *Honours and Privileges in Athenian Decrees*. Hildesheim, Zurich, and New York.

Herbert, K. B. J. 1954. *Ephorus in Plutarch's Lives: A Source Problem*. Diss. Harvard. Résumé in *HSCP* 63 (1958) 510–13.

————. 1957. "The Identity of Plutarch's Lost Scipio." *AJP* 78:83–88.

Herington, C. J. 1955. *Athena Parthenos and Athena Polias*. Manchester.

Herman, G. 1987. *Ritualised Friendship and the Greek City*. Cambridge.

Hershbell, J. 1982. "Plutarch and Anaxagoras." *ICS* 7:141–58.

Herwerden, H. van. 1880. "Ad Plutarchi Vitas." *RhM* 35:456–68, 529–42.

Hignett, C. 1951. *A History of the Athenian Constitution to the End of the Fifth Century*. Oxford.

Hill, G. F. 1951. *Sources for Greek History between the Persian and Peloponnesian Wars*. New ed. by R. Meiggs and A. Andrewes. Oxford.

Hiller von Gaertringen, F. 1919. "Voreuklidische Steine." *Sitzungsberichte der Preussischen Akademie der Wissenschaften*, 660–72.

Himmelmann, N. 1977. "Phidias und die Parthenon-Skulpturen." In *Bonner Festgabe Johannes Straub*, 67–90. Bonn.

Hind, J. G. F. 1983–84. "Greek and Barbarian Peoples on the Shores of the Black Sea." *AR* 30:71–97.

Hirzel, R. 1912. *Plutarch*. Leipzig.

Hock, R. F. 1976. "Simon the Shoemaker as an Ideal Cynic." *GRBS* 17:41–53.

Hoelscher, T. 1975. "Die Aufstellung des Perikles-Bildnisses und ihre Bedeutung." *WJA*, n.s. 1:187–99.

————, and E. Simon. 1976. "Die Amazonenschlacht auf dem Schild der Athena Parthenos." *MDAI(A)* 91:115–48.

Hoepfner, W. 1976. *Kerameikos.* Vol. 10, *Das Pompeion und seine Nachfolgerbauten.* Berlin.

Holden, H. A. 1894. *Plutarch's Life of Pericles.* London and New York. Reprinted Chicago, n.d.

Holladay, A. J. 1986. "The Detente of Kallias." *Historia* 35:503–7.

Homeyer, H. 1963. "Beobachtungen zu den hellenistischen Quellen des Plutarch-Viten." *Klio* 41:145–57.

Humphreys, S. C. 1974. "The Nothoi of Kynosarges." *JHS* 94:88–95.

———. 1978. *Anthropology and the Greeks.* London.

Huxley, G. 1965. "Ion of Chios." *GRBS* 6:29–46.

———. 1972. "On Aristotle's Historical Methods." *GRBS* 13:157–69.

Immerwahr, H. R. 1985. "The Date of the Construction of Solon's *Axones.*" *BAPS* 22:23–35.

Ingenkamp, H. G. 1971. *Plutarchs Schriften über die Heilung der Seele.* Hypomnemata 34. Göttingen.

Irigoin, J. 1976. "Les manuscrits de Plutarque à 32 lignes et à 22 lignes." In *Actes du XIVe Congrès international des études byzantins, Bucarest, 6–12 septembre 1971,* 3:83–87. Bucharest.

———. 1982–83. "La formation d'un corpus: un problème d'histoire des textes dans la tradition des *Vies parallèles* de Plutarque." *Rev.Hist.Textes* 12–13:1–12.

Jacoby, F. 1923–. *Die Fragmente der griechischen Historiker.* Berlin and Leiden.

———. 1944. "*Patrios Nomos.*" *JHS* 64:37–66. Reprinted in *Abhandlungen zur griechischen Geschichtsschreibung,* edited by H. Bloch, 260–315. Leiden 1956.

———. 1947. "Some Remarks on Ion of Chios." *CQ* 41:1–17. Reprinted in *Abhandlungen zur griechischen Geschichtsschreibung,* edited by H. Bloch, 144–68. Leiden 1956.

———. 1949. *Atthis.* Oxford.

———. 1956. *Griechische Historiker.* Stuttgart.

Jaeger, W. 1948. *Aristotle*[2]*.* Oxford.

Jahn, O., and A. Michaelis. 1901. *Arx Athenarum.* Bonn. Reprinted as *The Acropolis of Athens.* Chicago 1956.

Jameson, M. H. 1955. "Seniority in the Strategia." *TAPA* 86:63–87.

———. 1971. "Sophocles and the Four Hundred." *Historia* 20:541–68.

———. 1977–78. "Agriculture and Slavery in Classical Athens." *CJ* 73:122–45.

Jebb, R. C. 1900. *Sophocles.* Part 2, *The Oedipus Coloneus.* Cambridge.

Jeppesen, K. 1958. *Paradeigmata.* Aarhus.

Jones, C. P. 1966a. "The Teacher of Plutarch." *HSCP* 71:205–13.

_____. 1966b. "Towards a Chronology of Plutarch's Works." *JRS* 56:61–74.

_____. 1970. "Sura and Senecio." *JRS* 60:98–104.

_____. 1971. *Plutarch and Rome.* Oxford.

_____. 1978. *The Roman World of Dio Chrysostom.* Cambridge, Mass.

_____. 1987. "Stigma: Tattooing and Branding in Graeco-Roman Antiquity." *JRS* 77:139–55.

Jones, R. M. 1916. *The Platonism of Plutarch.* Diss. Chicago.

Jordan, B. 1975. *The Athenian Navy in the Classical Period.* Berkeley, Los Angeles, and London.

Judeich, W. 1925. "Zum 'Pheidias-Papyrus.' " *Hermes* 60:50–58.

_____. 1931. *Topographie von Athen²*. Munich.

Kagan, D. 1969. *The Outbreak of the Peloponnesian War.* Ithaca, N.Y.

_____. 1974. *The Archidamian War.* Ithaca, N.Y.

Kahrstedt, U. 1932. "Die Landgrenzen Athens." *MDAI(A)* 57:8–28.

Kalbfleisch, K. 1925. "Griechische Komödienbruchstücke aus einer Anthologie." In *Raccolta di scritti in onore di G. Lumbroso,* 29–35. Milan.

Karamoutsos, S. N. 1979. " Ἡ ἐκστρατεία τοῦ Περικλῆ στὸν Πόντο" (with English résumé). *Δωδώνη* 8:9–36.

Karavites, P. 1976. "Tradition, Scepticism, and Sophocles' Political Career." *Klio* 58:359–65.

_____. 1985. "Enduring Problems of the Samian Revolt." *RhM* 128:40–56.

Kassel, R., and C. Austin. 1983–. *Poetae Comici Graeci.* Vol. 3.2, *Aristophanes,* 1984. Vol. 4, *Aristophon–Crobylus,* 1983. Vol. 5, *Damoxenus–Magnes,* 1986. Berlin and New York.

Kebric, R. B. 1977. *In the Shadow of Macedon: Duris of Samos. Historia* Einzelschrift 29. Wiesbaden.

Kennedy, G. 1963. *The Art of Persuasion in Greece.* Princeton.

Keramopoullos, A. 1923. Ὁ ἀποτυμπανισμός. Athens.

Kerferd, G. B. 1981. *The Sophistic Movement.* Cambridge.

Kett, P. 1966. *Prosopographie der historischen griechischen Manteis.* Erlangen.

Keuls, E. 1985. *The Reign of the Phallus.* New York.

Kienast, D. 1953. "Der innenpolitische Kampf in Athen von der Rückkehr des Thukydides bis zu Perikles' Tod." *Gymnasium* 60:210–29.

Kinkel, G. 1877. *Epicorum Graecorum Fragmenta.* Vol. 1. Leipzig.

Kirchner, J. E. 1901–3. *Prosopographia Attica.* 2 vols. Reprinted Berlin 1966.

Kirk, G. S., J. E. Raven, and M. Schofield. 1983. *The Presocratic Philosophers²*. Cambridge.

Klein, R. 1979. "Die Innenpolitische Gegnerschaft gegen Perikles." In

BIBLIOGRAPHY

Perikles und seine Zeit, edited by G. Wirth, 494–533. Darmstadt.

Kleiner, D. 1983. *The Monument of Philopappus in Athens.* Rome.

Knell, H. 1968. "Iktinos, Baumeister der Parthenon und des Apollontempel von Phigalia-Bassae?" *JDAI* 83:110–17.

————. 1979. *Perikleische Baukunst.* Darmstadt.

Knigge, U. 1972. "Die Gesandtenstelen im Kerameikos." *Athens Annals of Archaeology* 5:258–65.

Kock, T. 1880–88. *Comicorum Atticorum Fragmenta.* 3 vols. Leipzig.

Korres, G. S. 1970. Τὰ μετὰ κεφαλῶν κριῶν κράνη: ἡ κεφαλὴ κριοῦ ὡς ἔμβλημα ἀρχῆς (with English résumé). Athens.

Kotansky, R. 1983. "A Silver Phylactery for Pain." *J. Paul Getty Museum Journal* 11:167–78.

Krauss, H. 1911. *Aeschinis Socratici Reliquiae.* Leipzig.

Krech, P. 1888. *De Crateri Psephismaton Synagoge.* Griefswald. Reprinted under the title *Craterus: The Fragments from His Collection of Attic Decrees.* Chicago 1970.

Krentz, P. 1984. "The Ostracism of Thoukydides, Son of Melesias." *Historia* 33:499–504.

Kunze, E. 1959. *Neue deutsche Ausgrabungen in Mittelmeergebiet und im vordern Orient.* Berlin.

Kurtz, D. C., and J. Boardman. 1971. *Greek Burial Customs.* Ithaca, N.Y.

Labarbe, J. 1961. "La distribution de blé de 445/4 à Athènes et ses incidences démographiques." In *Sozialökonomische Verhältnisse im alten Orient und im klassichen Altertum,* 191–207. Berlin.

Lacey, W. K. 1968. *The Family in Ancient Greece.* Ithaca, N.Y.

Lampe, G. W. H. 1961. *A Patristic Greek Lexicon.* Oxford.

Langmuir, A. D., T. D. Worthen, J. Solomon, C. G. Ray, and E. Petersen. 1985. "The Thucydides Syndrome: A New Hypothesis for the Plague at Athens." *New England Journal of Medicine* 313:1027–30.

Lanza, D. 1966. *Anassagora: testimonianze e frammenti.* Florence.

Lasserre, F. 1954. *Plutarque: De la musique.* Lausanne.

————. 1979. "Prose grecque classicisante." In *Le classicisme à Rome aux Iers siècles avant et après J.-C.,* edited by H. Flashar, 134–63. Entretiens Hardt 25. Vandoeuvres and Geneva.

Lawrence, A. W. 1957. *Greek Architecture.* London.

Leaf, W. 1916. "The Commerce of Sinope." *JHS* 36:1–15.

Lee, H. D. P. 1936. *Zeno of Elea.* Cambridge. Reprinted Amsterdam 1967.

Legon, R. P. 1972. "Samos in the Delian League." *Historia* 21:145–58.

————. 1981. *Megara.* Ithaca, N.Y.

Leipen, N. 1971. *Athena Parthenos: A Reconstruction.* Toronto.

Lenardon, R. 1959. "The Chronology of Themistokles' Ostracism and Exile." *Historia* 8:23–48.

Leo, F. 1901. *Die griechische-römische Biographie.* Leipzig.

Leutsch, E. L., and F. G. Schneidewin. 1839. *Corpus Paroemiographorum Graecorum.* Göttingen. Reprinted Hildesheim 1958.

Lewis, D. M. 1961. "Double Representation in the *Stragegia.*" *JHS* 81:118–23.

———. 1974. "Entrenchment Clauses in Attic Decrees." In Φόρος: *Tribute to Benjamin Dean Meritt,* 81–89. Locust Valley, N.Y.

———. 1977. *Sparta and Persia.* Leiden.

Linfert, A. 1982. "Athenen des Phidias." *MDAI(A)* 97:57–77.

Littman, R. J., and M. L. Littman. 1969. "The Athenian Plague: Smallpox." *TAPA* 100:261–75.

Livrea, E. 1985. "P. Harris 171: gnomologio con testi comici." *ZPE* 58:11–20.

Lloyd-Jones, H., and P. Parsons. 1983. *Supplementum Hellenisticum.* Berlin and New York.

Long, A. A. 1974. *Hellenistic Philosophy.* London.

———. 1978. "Timon of Phlius: Pyrrhonist and Satirist." *PCPS,* n.s. 24:68–91.

Loraux, N. 1986. *The Invention of Athens: The Funeral Oration in the Classical City.* Cambridge, Mass., and London.

Lotze, D. 1962. "Μόθακες." *Historia* 11:427–35.

Lozza, G. 1980. *Plutarco: De superstitione.* Milan.

Luppe, W. 1967. "Wie lange las man noch Kratinos-komödien." *WZHalle* 16:389–95.

———. 1974. "Die Nemesis des Kratinos: Mythos und politischer Hintergrund." *WZHalle* 23, no. 4:49–60.

McArthur, W. P. 1954. "The Athenian Plague: A Medical Note." *CQ,* n.s. 4:171–74.

MacDonald, B. R. 1982. "The Authenticity of the Congress Decree." *Historia* 31:120–23.

———. 1983. "The Megarian Decree." *Historia* 32:385–400.

MacDowell, D. M. 1963. *Athenian Homicide Law in the Age of the Orators.* Manchester.

———. 1976. "Bastards as Athenian Citizens." *CQ,* n.s. 26:88–91.

———. 1978. *The Law in Classical Athens.* Ithaca, N.Y.

———, ed. 1962. *Andokides: On the Mysteries.* Oxford.

———. 1971. *Aristophanes: Wasps.* Oxford.

McGregor, M. F. 1982. "Athens and Hestiaia." In *Studies in Attic Epigraphy, History and Topography Presented to Eugene Vanderpool,* 101–11. *Hesperia* suppl. 19. Princeton.

Madvig, J. N. 1871. *Adversaria Critica ad Scriptores Graecos et Latinos.* Vol. 1. Copenhagen.

Magnien, Victor. 1907. "Deux fragments comiques dans Plutarque (Vie de Périclès ch. III)." *RPh* 31:22–27.

Mallwitz, A. 1972a. *100 Jahre deutsche Ausgrabung in Olympia*. Munich.

_____. 1972b. *Olympia und seine Bauten*. Munich.

_____, and W. Schiering. 1964. *Die Werkstatt des Phidias*. Part 1, *Olympische Forschungen*, vol. 5. Berlin.

Malten, L. 1961. *Die Sprache des menschlichen Antlitzes im frühen Griechentum*. Berlin.

Maltomini, F. 1982. "Osservazioni al testo di alcuni papiri magici greci, III." *SCO* 32:235–40.

Manfredini, M. 1968. "La cleruchia ateniese in Calcide." *Studi classici e orientali* 17:199–212.

_____. 1977. "La tradizione manoscritta della *Vita Solonis* di Plutarco." *ASNP*, ser. 3, 7:945–98.

_____. 1979. "Gli scoli alle vite di Plutarco." *JOEByz* 28:83–119.

_____. 1981. "Nuovo contributo allo studio della tradizione manoscritta di Plutarco: le *Vitae Lycurgi et Numae*." *ASNP*, ser. 3, 7:33–68.

_____. 1983. "Note sulla tradizione manoscritta delle *Vitae Thesei–Romuli* e *Themistoclis–Camilli* di Plutarco." *CCC* 4:401–7.

_____. 1987. "La tradizione manoscritta delle Vite." In *Plutarco, Vite Parallele: Alessandro, Cesare*, x–xx. Milan.

Mansfeld, J. 1979. "The Chronology of Anaxagoras' Athenian Period and the Date of His Trial, I: The Length and Dating of the Athenian Period." *Mnemosyne*, ser. 4, 32:36–69.

_____. 1980. "The Chronology of Anaxagoras' Athenian Period and the Date of His Trial, II: The Plot against Pericles and His Associates." *Mnemosyne*, ser. 4, 33:17–95.

Marasco, G. 1976. "I processi d'empietà nella democrazia ateniese." *Atene e Roma* 21:113–31.

Marrou, H. I. 1964. *A History of Education in Antiquity*. New York.

Martin, H. 1960. "The Concept of *Praotes* in Plutarch's Lives." *GRBS* 3:65–73.

_____. 1961. "The Concept of *Philanthropia* in Plutarch's Lives." *AJP* 82:164–75.

_____. 1969. "Plutarch's Citation of Empedocles at *Amatorius* 756D." *GRBS* 10:57–70.

Martin, R. 1965. *Manuel d'architecture grecque*. Vol. 1, *Matériaux et techniques*. Paris.

Mastrocinque, A. 1979. "Demetrios tragodoumenos." *Athenaeum* 57:260–76.

Mattingly, H. B. 1961. "The Athenian Coinage Decree." *Historia* 10:148–88.

_____. 1971–72. "Facts and Artifacts: The Researcher and His Tools."

Univ. of Leeds Review 14:277–97.

_____. 1977. "Poets and Politicians in Fifth-Century Greece." In *Greece and the Mediterranean in Ancient History and Prehistory: Studies . . . F. Schachermeyr*, edited by K. H. Kinzl, 231–45. Berlin.

Meiggs, R. 1963. "The Political Implications of the Parthenon." *G&R* suppl. 10:36–45.

_____. 1972. *The Athenian Empire*. Oxford.

_____. 1982. *Trees and Timber in the Ancient World*. Oxford.

_____, and D. Lewis. 1969. *A Selection of Greek Historical Inscriptions to the End of the Fifth Century B.C.* Oxford.

Meineke, A. 1839–57. *Fragmenta Comicorum Graecorum*. 5 vols. Berlin. Reprinted 1970.

Meinel, R. 1980. *Das Odeion*. Frankfurt.

Meinhardt, E. 1957. *Perikles bei Plutarch*. Frankfurt.

Meister, K. 1973. "Damon, der politische Berater des Perikles." *Rivista storica dell'antichità* 3:29–45.

_____. 1978. "Stesimbrotos' Schrift über die athenischen Staatsmänner und ihre historische Bedeutung (*FGrHist* 107 F1–11)." *Historia* 27:274–94.

_____. 1982. *Die Ungeschichtlichkeit des Kalliasfriedens und deren historische Folgen*. Wiesbaden.

Meritt, B. D. 1937. *Documents on Athenian Tribute*. Cambridge.

_____. 1972. "The Tribute Quota List of 454–453 B.C." *Hesperia* 41:403–17.

_____. 1984. "The Samian Revolt from Athens in 440–439 B.C." *PAPhS* 128:123–33.

_____, and H. T. Wade-Gery. 1963. "The Dating of Documents to the Mid-Fifth Century." *JHS* 83:100–117.

_____, H. T. Wade-Gery, and M. F. McGregor. 1939–53. *The Athenian Tribute Lists*. 4 vols. Cambridge, Mass. (vol. 1); Princeton (vols. 2–4).

Merkelbach, R. 1986. "Nochmals das Xanthippos-Ostrakon." *ZPE* 62:57–62.

Mewaldt, J. 1907. "Selbstcitate in den Biographien Plutarchs." *Hermes* 42:564–78.

Meyer, E. 1899. "Die Biographie Kimons." In *Forschungen zur alten Geschichte*, 2:1–87. Halle.

Meyer, H. D. 1967. "Thukydides Melesiou und die oligarchische Opposition gegen Perikles." *Historia* 16:141–65.

Mickwitz, G. 1937. "Economic Rationalism in Greco-Roman Agriculture." *English Historical Review* 52:577–89.

Mikalson, J. D. 1975. *The Sacred and Civil Calendar of the Athenian Year*. Princeton.

_____. 1983. *Greek Popular Religion*. Chapel Hill.

Milne, M. J. 1941. "The Use of τορεύω and Related Words." *AJA* 45:390–98.

———, and D. von Bothmer. 1953. "Καταπύγων, καταπύγαινα." *Hesperia* 2:215–24.

Moellering, H. 1963. *Plutarch on Superstition.* Boston.

Molitor, M. V. 1986. "The Third Scholion on *Vespae* 947." *Hermes* 114:306–14.

Momigliano, A. 1971. *The Development of Greek Biography.* Cambridge, Mass.

Mommsen, A. 1898. *Feste der Stadt Athen.* Leipzig.

Montuori, M. 1977–78. "Di Aspasia Milesia." *AFLN* 20:63–85.

———. 1981. "De Aspasia Milesia." In *Corolla Londiniensis,* edited by G. Giangrande, 1:87–109. Amsterdam.

Mooren, G. E. J. 1948. *Plutarchus' Leven van Pericles.* Nijmegen.

Morrison, J. S., and R. T. Williams. 1968. *Greek Oared Ships 900–322 B.C.* Cambridge.

Mosley, D. J. 1971. "Cimon and the Spartan Proxeny." *Athenaeum* 49:131–32.

———. 1973. *Envoys and Diplomacy in Ancient Greece. Historia* Einzelschrift 22.

Muehll, P. von der. 1954. "Direkte Benützung des Ephoros und Theopomp bei Plutarch." *MH* 11:243–44.

Mylonas, G. E. 1961. *Eleusis and the Eleusinian Mysteries.* Princeton.

Nesselhauf, H. 1933. *Untersuchungen zur Geschichte der delisch-attischen Symmachie. Klio* Beiheft 30. Leipzig.

———. 1934. "Die diplomatischen Verhandlungen vor dem Peloponnesischen Kriege." *Hermes* 69:286–99.

Nisbet, R. G. M., and M. Hubbard. 1970. *A Commentary on Horace: Odes Book 1.* Oxford.

Noack, F. 1927. *Eleusis: Die baugeschichtliche Entwicklung des Heiligtums.* Berlin and Leipzig.

Nock, A. D. 1928. "Notes on Ruler-Cult." *JHS* 48:21–44.

North, H. 1966. *Sophrosyne.* Ithaca, N.Y.

Norwood, G. 1932. *Greek Comedy.* Boston.

Ober, J. 1984. *Fortress Attica. Mnemosyne* suppl. 84. Leiden.

Oliver, J. H. 1960. *Demokratia, the Gods, and the Free World.* Baltimore.

Orlandos, A. K. 1966. *Les matériaux de construction et la technique architecturale des anciens grecs.* Vol. 1. Paris.

———. 1977–78. Ἡ ἀρχιτεκτονικὴ τοῦ Παρθενῶνος. 2 vols. Athens.

Osborne, M. J. 1981. "Entertainment in the Prytaneion at Athens." *ZPE* 41:153–70.

Ostwald, M. 1969. *Nomos and the Beginnings of Athenian Democracy.* Oxford.

———. 1986. *From Popular Sovereignty to the Sovereignty of Law.* Berkeley and Los Angeles.

Overbeck, J. 1868. *Die antike Schriftquellen zur Geschichte der bildenden Künste bei den Griechen.* Leipzig. Reprinted Hildesheim 1959.

Pack, R. A. 1965. *The Greek and Latin Literary Texts from Greco-Roman Egypt²*. Revised. Ann Arbor.

Page, D. L. 1950. *Select Papyri.* Vol. 3. Cambridge, Mass. and London.

———. 1962. *Poetae Melici Graeci.* Oxford.

Pareti, L. 1909. "Il processo di Fidia ed un papiro di Ginevra." *MDAI(R)* 24:271–316.

Parke, H. W. 1977. *Festivals of the Athenians.* Ithaca, N.Y.

Parker, R. 1983. *Miasma: Pollution and Purification in Early Greek Religion.* Oxford.

Patrucco, R. 1972. *Lo Sport nella Grecia antica.* Florence.

Patterson, C. 1981. *Pericles' Citizenship Law of 451–50 B.C.* New York.

Pearson, A. C. 1917. *The Fragments of Sophocles.* Cambridge.

Pečírka, J. 1973. "Homestead Farms in Classical and Hellenistic Hellas." In *Problèmes de la terre en Grèce ancienne*, edited by M. I. Finley, 113–47. Paris and The Hague.

Pelling, C. B. 1979. "Plutarch's Method of Work in the Roman Lives." *JHS* 99:74–96.

———. 1980. "Plutarch's Adaptation of His Source Material." *JHS* 100:127–40.

———. 1985. "Plutarch and Catiline." *Hermes* 113:311–29.

———. 1986a. "Plutarch and Roman Politics." In *Past Perspectives: Studies in Greek and Roman Historical Writing*, edited by I. Moxon et al., 159–87. Cambridge.

———. 1986b. "Synkrisis in Plutarch's Lives." In *Miscellanea Plutarchea*, edited by F. Brenk and I. Gallo, 83–96. Quaderni del *Giornale filologico ferrarese* 8. Ferrara.

Peper, L. 1912. *De Plutarchi "Epaminonda."* Jena.

Peremans, W. 1973. "Sur le droit de cité à Athènes au Ve s. av. J.-C." In *Zetesis: Album Amicorum . . . E. de Strycker*, 531–40. Antwerp and Utrecht.

Perlman, S. 1958. "A Note on the Political Implications of Proxenia in the Fourth Century B.C." *CQ*, n.s. 8:185–91.

———. 1976. "Panhellenism, the Polis and Imperialism." *Historia* 25:1–30.

Perrin, B. 1910. *Plutarch's Cimon and Pericles.* New York.

Pfeiffer, R., ed. 1949. *Callimachus.* Vol. 1, *Fragmenta.* Oxford.

Philippides, M. 1985. "King Pleistonax and the Spartan Invasion of Attica in 446 B.C." *Ancient World* 11:33–41.

Phillips, D. J. 1982. "Athenian Ostracism." In *Hellenika*, edited by G. H. Horsley, 21–43. North Ryde, N.S.W.

Phillips, E. D. 1973. *Aspects of Greek Medicine.* New York.

Phillipson, C. 1911. *International Law and Custom of Ancient Greece and Rome.* London.

Piccirilli, L. 1975. *Μεγαρικά: Testimonianze e frammenti.* Pisa.

————. 1982. "*Γυνὴ κλειτορία, κλιτορία, ἀλιτηρία* moglie di Cimone?" *RFIC* 110:278–82.

————. 1987. "L'assassinio di Efialte." *ASNP* 17.1:9–17.

————. 1989. *Efialte.* Genoa.

Pickard-Cambridge, A. 1968. *The Dramatic Festivals of Athens*[2]. Rev. by D. Lewis and J. P. Gould. Oxford.

Piérart, M. 1974. "A propos de l'élection des stratèges athéniens." *BCH* 98:125–46.

Plepelits, K. 1970. *Die Fragmente der Demen des Eupolis.* Vienna.

Podlecki, A. J. 1971. "Cimon, Skyros, and Theseus' Bones." *JHS* 91:141–43.

————. 1985. "Theophrastus on History and Politics." In *Theophrastus of Eresus: On His Life and Work*, edited by W. W. Fortenbaugh, pp. 231–49. Rutgers University Studies in Classical Humanities. New Brunswick.

————. 1987. *Plutarch: Life of Pericles.* A companion to the Penguin translation by I. Scott-Kilvert. Bristol.

Pollitt, J. J. 1965. *The Art of Greece 1400–31 B.C.: Sources and Documents.* Englewood Cliffs, N.J.

Pomeroy, S. B. 1975. *Goddesses, Whores, Wives, and Slaves.* New York.

Poole, J. C. F., and A. J. Holladay. 1979. "Thucydides and the Plague of Athens." *CQ*, n.s. 29:282–300.

Prandi, L. 1977. "I processi contro Fidia, Aspasia, Anassagora e l'opposizione a Pericle." *Aevum* 51:10–26.

Prees, L. 1967. *Olympia.* Stuttgart.

Preisigke, F. 1931. *Wörterbuch der griechischen Papyrusurkunden.* Vol. 3. Berlin.

Preisshofen, F. 1974. "Phidias-Daedalus auf dem Schild der Athena Parthenos?" *JDAI* 89:50–69.

Pritchett, W. K. 1969. "The Transfer of the Delian Treasury." *Historia* 18:17–21.

————. 1974. *The Greek State at War.* Vols. 1–2. Berkeley and Los Angeles.

Quinn, T. J. 1981. *Athens and Samos, Lesbos and Chios.* Manchester.

Radt, S. L. 1977. *Tragicorum Graecorum Fragmenta.* Vol. 4, *Sophocles.* Göttingen.

————. 1980. "Noch einmal Aischylos, Niobe fr. 162 N.[2] (278 M.): pt. I,

BIBLIOGRAPHY

Die Bedeutung von οἱ περὶ Τάνταλον." *ZPE* 38:47–56.

Rankin, H. D. 1986. *Antisthenes Sokratikos*. Amsterdam.

Raubitschek, A. E. 1947. "The Ostracism of Xanthippos." *AJA* 51:257–62.

_____. 1949. (With the collaboration of L. H. Jeffery.) *Dedications from the Athenian Akropolis*. Cambridge, Mass.

_____. 1954. "The New Homer." *Hesperia* 23:317–19.

_____. 1954–55. "Kimons Zurückberufung." *Historia* 3:379–80.

_____. 1955a. "Damon." *C&M* 16:78–83.

_____. 1955b. "Menon, Son of Menekleides." *Hesperia* 24:286–89.

_____. 1958. "Theophrastus on Ostracism." *C&M* 19:78–109.

_____. 1960a. "The Covenant of Plataea." *TAPA* 91:178–83.

_____. 1960b. "Theopompus on Thucydides the Son of Melesias." *Phoenix* 14:81–95.

_____. 1966. "The Peace Policy of Pericles." *AJA* 70:37–41.

_____. 1973. "The Speech of the Athenians at Sparta." In *The Speeches in Thucydides*, edited by P. A. Stadter, 32–48. Chapel Hill.

_____. 1973–74. "Zur Periklesstatue des Kresilas." *Archeologia Classica* 25–26:620–21.

_____. 1976. "Epilogue." In *La paz de Calias*, edited by C. Schrader, 215–17. Barcelona.

_____. 1984. "Zur Überschrift von *IG* I³ 259." *AUS* 77:2.

Rawlings, H. R. 1981. *The Structure of Thucydides' History*. Princeton.

Reece, D. W. 1950. "The Battle of Tanagra." *JHS* 70:75–76.

Reinhold, M. 1976. "The Generation Gap in Antiquity." In *The Conflict of the Generations in Ancient Greece and Rome*, edited by S. Bertman, 15–54. Amsterdam.

Renoirte, T. 1951. *Les "Conseils politiques" de Plutarque*. Louvain.

Rhodes, P. J. 1970. "Thucydides on Pausanias and Themistocles." *Historia* 19:395–400.

_____. 1972. *The Athenian Boule*. Oxford.

_____. 1978. "Bastards as Athenian Citizens." *CQ*, n.s. 28:89–92.

_____. 1979. "Εἰσαγγελία in Athens." *JHS* 99:103–14.

_____. 1981. *A Commentary on the Aristotelian Athenaion Politeia*. Oxford.

_____. 1986. "Political Activity in Classical Athens." *JHS* 106:132–44.

Richardson, N. J. 1975. "Homeric Professors in the Age of the Sophists." *PCPhS* 201 (n.s. 21):65–81.

Richter, G. M. A. 1965. *The Portraits of the Greeks*. Vol. 1. London.

_____. 1970. *The Sculpture and Sculptors of the Greeks*⁴. New Haven.

Ridgeway, B. 1981. *Fifth Century Styles in Greek Sculpture*. Princeton.

Robert, J., and L. Robert. 1953. "Bulletin épigraphique." *REG* 66:113–212.

_____. 1961. "Bulletin épigraphique." *REG* 74:119–268.

————. 1982. "Bulletin épigraphique." *REG* 95:322–432.

Robert, L. 1940–65. *Hellenica*. 13 vols. Paris.

Roberts, C. H., and T. C. Skeat. 1983. *The Birth of the Codex*. London.

Roberts, J. T. 1982. *Accountability in Athenian Government*. Madison.

Robertson, M. 1975a. *A History of Greek Art*. Cambridge.

————. 1975b. *A History of Greek Sculpture*. 2 vols. Cambridge.

Robertson, N. 1982. "The Decree of Themistocles in Its Contemporary Setting." *Phoenix* 36:1–44.

————. 1985. "The Origin of the Panathenaea." *RhM* 128:231–95.

Robkin, A. L. H. 1979. "The Odeion of Perikles: The Date of Its Construction and the Periklean Building Program." *Ancient World* 2:3–12.

Roebuck, Carl. 1959. *Ionian Trade and Colonization*. New York.

Roesch, P. 1982. *Etudes béotiennes*. Paris.

Rohde, E. 1966. *Psyche*. New York.

Romilly, J. de. 1979. *La douceur dans la pensée grecque*. Paris.

————. 1988. "Plutarch and Thucydides or the Free Use of Quotations." *Phoenix* 42:22–34.

Rose, V. 1886. *Aristotelis Qui Ferebantur Librorum Fragmenta*. Leipzig.

Rostovtzeff, M. 1922. *Iranians and Greeks in South Russia*. New York.

Rowe, C. J. 1986. *Plato: Phaedrus*. Warminster.

Rudhardt, J. 1960. "La définition du délit d'impiété d'après la législation attique." *MH* 17:87–105.

Ruschenbusch, E. 1966. "Ephialtes." *Historia* 15:369–76.

————. 1975. "Die Wahl der Strategen im 5. und 4. JH. v. Chr. in Athen." *Historia* 24:112–14.

————. 1979. "Die Einfuhrung des Theorikon." *ZPE* 36:303–8.

————. 1980. "Theopompea: ἀντιπολιτεύεσθαι." *ZPE* 39:81–90.

Russell, D. A. 1963. "Plutarch's Life of Coriolanus." *JRS* 53:21–28.

————. 1966. "On Reading Plutarch's Lives." *G&R* 13:139–54.

————. 1972. *Plutarch*. London and New York.

————. 1982. "Plutarch and the Antique Hero." *Yearbook of English Studies* 12:24–34.

————. 1983. *Greek Declamation*. Cambridge.

Rutter, N. K. 1973. "Diodorus and the Foundation of Thurii." *Historia* 22:155–76.

Ste. Croix, G. E. M. de. 1954–55. "The Character of the Athenian Empire." *Historia* 3:1–41.

————. 1964. Review of *Theorika*, by J. J. Buchanan. *CR*, n.s. 78:190–92.

————. 1972. *The Origins of the Peloponnesian War*. Ithaca, N.Y.

————. 1981. *The Class Struggle in the Ancient Greek World*. London.

Salmon, P. 1965. *La politique égyptienne d'Athènes (VIe et Ve siècle avant J.-C.)*.

BIBLIOGRAPHY

Acad. Roy. de Belgique, Cl. des lettres, Mémoires 57, fasc. 6. Brussels.

Sandbach, F. H. 1939. "Rhythm and Authenticity in Plutarch's Moralia." *CQ* 33:194–203.

——. 1969. *Plutarch: Moralia.* Vol. 15, *Fragments.* London and Cambridge, Mass.

——. 1975. *The Stoics.* London.

——. 1982. "Plutarch and Aristotle." *ICS* 7:207–32.

Sansone, D. 1988. "Notes on Plutarch: *Pericles and Fabius.*" *ICS* 13:311–18.

Sartori, F. 1975. *Una pagina di storia ateniese in un frammento dei "Demi" Eupolidei.* Rome.

Sauppe, H. 1863. "Zum Komiker Telekleides." *Philologus* 20:174–76.

Scardigli, B. 1979. *Die Römerbiographien Plutarchs.* Munich.

Schachermeyr, F. 1965. "Stesimbrotos und seine Schrift über die Staatsmänner." *SAWW* 247, 5.

——. 1968. "Religionspolitik und Religiosität bei Perikles." *SAWW* 258, 3.

——. 1969. "Damon." In *Beiträge zur alten Geschichte und deren Nachleben: Festschrift für F. Altheim,* 1:192–204. Berlin.

Schaps, D. 1977. "The Woman Least Mentioned: Etiquette and Women's Names." *CQ,* n.s. 27:323–30.

Schellens, J. 1864. *De Hiatu in Plutarchi Moralibus.* Bonn.

Schläpfer, H. 1950. *Plutarch und die klassischen Dichter.* Zurich.

Schmid, W. 1887–97. 5 vols. *Der Atticismus.* Stuttgart.

Schofield, M. 1980. *An Essay on Anaxagoras.* Cambridge.

Schwartz, E. 1959. *Griechische Geschichtsschreiber.* Leipzig.

Schwarze, J. 1971. *Die Beurteilung des Perikles durch die attische Komödie und ihre historische und historiographische Bedeutung.* Zetemata 51. Munich.

Schweitzer, B. 1940. "Phidias und der Parthenonmeister." *JDAI* 55:170–241.

——. 1963. "Der bildende Künstler und der Begriff des Künstlerischen in der Antike." In *Zur Kunst der Antike,* 11–104. Tübingen.

Schwyzer, E., and A. Debrunner. 1959. *Griechische Grammatik.* Vol. 2. Munich.

Seager, R. 1967. "The Congress Decree: Some Doubts and a Hypothesis." *Historia* 18:129–41.

Sealey, R. 1956. "The Entry of Pericles into History." *Hermes* 84:234–47.

——. 1958. "P. Strassburg 84 verso." *Hermes* 86:440–46.

——. 1964. "Ephialtes." *CP* 59:11–22.

——. 1973. "The Origins of *demokratia.*" *CSCA* 6:253–95.

——. 1975. "The Causes of the Peloponnesian War." *CP* 70:89–109.

———. 1976. *A History of the Greek City-States 700–338 B.C.* Berkeley, Los Angeles, and London.

Shear, I. M. 1963. "Kallikrates." *Hesperia* 32:375–424.

Shear, T. L. 1941. "The Campaign of 1940." *Hesperia* 10:1–8.

Shear, T. L., Jr. 1966. *Studies in the Early Projects of the Periklean Building Program.* Diss. Princeton.

———. 1982. "The Demolished Temple at Eleusis." In *Studies in Athenian Architecture, Sculpture, and Topography Presented to Homer A. Thompson,* 128–40. *Hesperia* suppl. 20. Princeton.

Sherwin-White, S. M. 1985. "Ancient Archives: The Edict of Alexander to Priene, A Reappraisal." *JHS* 105:69–89.

Shipley, G. 1987. *A History of Samos, 800–180 B.C.* Oxford.

Sider, D. 1981. *The Fragments of Anaxagoras.* Meisenheim.

Siefert, O., and F. Blass. 1909. *Plutarchs ausgewählte Biographien für den Schulgebrauch erklärt.* Vol. 3, *Themistokles und Perikles.* Edited by B. Kaiser. Leipzig and Berlin.

Siegel, R. E. 1970. *Galen on Sense Perception.* Basel and New York.

Siewart, P. 1977. "The Ephebic Oath in Fifth-Century Athens." *JHS* 97:102–11.

Sintenis, C. 1856. *Ausgewählte Biographien des Plutarch.* Vol. 3, *Themistokles und Perikles*². Berlin.

Sisson, S., and J. D. Grossman. 1953. *The Anatomy of the Domestic Animals*⁴. Philadelphia and London.

Smith, M. 1975. "De Superstitione." In *Plutarch's Theological Writings and Early Christian Literature,* edited by H. D. Betz, 1–35. Leiden.

Smyth, H. W. 1956. *Greek Grammar.* Rev. by Gordon M. Messing. Cambridge, Mass.

Soffel, J. 1974. *Die Regeln Menanders für die Leichenrede.* Beiträge zur klassischen Philologie 57. Meisenheim am Glan.

Sokolowski, F. 1969. *Lois sacrées des cités grecques.* Paris.

Sommerstein, A. 1980. "The Naming of Women in Greek and Roman Comedy." *Quaderni di Storia* 11:393–409.

Sordi, M. 1973. Review of *The Athenian Empire,* by R. Meiggs. *Athenaeum* 51:416–19.

Sparkes, B. A. 1960. "Kottabos: An Athenian After-dinner Game." *Archaeology* 13:202–7.

Spuler, C. 1973. *Opaion und Laterne.* Hamburg.

Stadter, P. A. 1965. *Plutarch's Historical Methods.* Cambridge, Mass.

———. 1973b. "Thucydidean Orators in Plutarch." In *The Speeches in Thucydides,* edited by P. A. Stadter, 109–23. Chapel Hill.

———. 1975. "Plutarch's Comparison of Pericles and Fabius Maximus." *GRBS* 16:77–85.

———. 1983. "The Motives for Athens' Alliance with Corcyra (Thuc. 1.44)." *GRBS* 24:131–36.

———. 1983–84. "Searching for Themistocles." *CJ* 79:356–63.

———. 1984. "Plutarch, Charinus, and the Megarian Decree." *GRBS* 25:351–72.

———. 1987. "The Rhetoric of Plutarch's *Pericles*." *Ancient Society* 18:251–69.

———. 1988. "The Proems of Plutarch's *Lives*." *ICS* 13:275–95.

———, ed. 1973a. *The Speeches in Thucydides*. Chapel Hill.

Stanier, R. S. 1953. "The Cost of the Parthenon." *JHS* 73:68–76.

Stegmann, K. 1882. *Über den Gebrauch der Negationen bei Plutarch*. Progr. Geestemünde.

Steidle, W. 1951. *Sueton und die antike Biographie*. Zetemata 1. Munich.

Steinhausen, J. 1910. *Komodoumenoi*. Bonn.

Stevens, G. P. 1957. "How the Parthenos Was Made." *Hesperia* 26:350–61.

Stillwell, R., ed. 1976. *Princeton Encyclopedia of Classical Sites*. Princeton.

Stockton, D. 1959. "The Peace of Callias." *Historia* 8:61–79.

———. 1982. "The Death of Ephialtes." *CQ*, n.s. 32:227–28.

Stoltz, C. 1929. *Zur relativen Chronologie der Parallelbiographien Plutarchs*. Lund.

Strasburger, H. 1986. "Aus den Anfängen der griechischen Memoirenkunst." In *Forma et Subtilitas: Festschrift für Wolfgang Schöne zum 75. Geburtstag*, 1–11. Berlin.

Strocka, V. M. 1967. *Piraeusreliefs und Parthenosschild*. Bochum.

———. 1984. "Das Schildrelief: Zum Stand des Forschung." In *Parthenon-Kongress, Basel, 4.–8. April 1982: Referate und Berichte*, edited by E. Berger, 188–96, 409–10. Mainz.

Stroud, R. S. 1974. "An Athenian Law on Silver Coinage." *Hesperia* 43:157–88.

Stupperich, R. 1977. *Staatsbegräbnis und Privatgrabmal im klassischen Athen*. Diss. Münster.

Svoboda, K. 1934. "Les idées esthétiques de Plutarque." In *Mélanges Bidez*, 917–46. Brussels.

Szegedy-Maszak, A., ed. 1981. *The Nomoi of Theophrastus*. New York.

Taran, L. 1965. *Parmenides*. Princeton.

Taylor, A. E. 1917. "On the Date of the Trial of Anaxagoras." *CQ* 11:81–87.

Theander, C. 1950–51. *Plutarch und die Geschichte*. Lund.

———. 1959. "Plutarchs Forschungen im Rom: Zur mündlichen Überlieferung als Quelle der Biographien." *Eranos* 57:99–131.

Thompson, D. B. 1960. "The House of Simon the Shoemaker." *Archaeology* 13:235–40.

Thompson, H. A. 1952. "Excavations in the Athenian Agora." *Hesperia* 21:83–113.

———. 1961. "The Panathenaic Festival." *AA* 224–31.

Thompson, H. A., and R. E. Wycherley. 1972. *The Athenian Agora.* Vol. 14, *The Agora of Athens: The History, Shape, and Use of an Ancient City Center.* Princeton.

Thompson, H. A., et al. 1976. *The Athenian Agora: A Guide to the Excavation and Museum.* Athens.

Thompson, W. E. 1969. "Euryptolemus." *TAPA* 100:583–86.

———. 1970. "The Kinship of Perikles and Alkibiades." *GRBS* 11:27–33.

———. 1971. "Leagros." *Athenaeum*, n.s. 49:328–35.

———. 1972. "Athenian Marriage Patterns: Remarriage." *CSCA* 5:211–25.

Thomsen, R. 1972. *The Origin of Ostracism.* Copenhagen.

Tod, M. N. 1901–2. "Some Unpublished 'Catalogi paterarum argentearum.'" *ABSA* 8:197–230.

———. 1948. *A Selection of Greek Historical Inscriptions.* Vol. 2, *From 403 to 323 B.C.* Oxford.

Toynbee, A. 1969. *Some Problems in Greek History.* London.

Traill, J. S. 1975. *The Political Organization of Attica: Study of the Demes, Trittyes, and Phylai and Their Representation in the Athenian Council.* *Hesperia* suppl. 14. Princeton.

Travlos, J. 1950–51. "Τὸ ἀνάκτορον τῆς Ἐλευσῖνος." *Archaiologike Ephemeris* 89–90:1–16.

———. 1971. *A Pictorial Dictionary of Ancient Athens.* London.

Treves, P. 1941. "Herodotus, Gelon, and Pericles." *CP* 36:321–45.

Triantaphyllopoulos, J. 1985. *Das Rechtsdenken der Griechen.* Munich.

Triebel-Schubert, C. 1983. "Zur Datierung des Phidiasprozesses." *MDAI(A)* 98:101–12.

Tuplin, C. J. 1984. "Pausanias and Plutarch's Epaminondas." *CQ*, n.s. 34:346–58.

Turner, E. G. 1968. *Greek Papyri.* Oxford.

Ullman, B. L. 1942. "History and Tragedy." *TAPA* 73:25–53.

Untersteiner, M. 1954. *The Sophists.* Oxford.

Unz, R. K. 1986. "The Chronology of the Pentecontaetea." *CQ*, n.s. 36:68–85.

Valgiglio, E. 1976. *Plutarco: Praecepta gerendae reipublicae.* Milano.

Vanderpool, E. 1970. *Ostracism at Athens.* Cincinnati.

———. 1974. "Ostraka from the Athenian Agora, 1970–72." *Hesperia* 43:189–93.

Van der Valk, M. 1982. "Notes on the Composition and Argument of the

Biographies of Plutarch." In *Studi in onore di Aristide Colonna*, 301–37. Perugia.

Van Ooteghem, J. 1932. "Démosthène et le théoricon." *LEC* 1:388–407.

Verbeke, G. 1960. "Plutarch and the Development of Aristotle." In *Aristotle and Plato in the Mid-Fourth Century*, edited by I. Düring and G. L. Owen, 236–47. Göteborg.

Veyne, P. 1976. *Le pain et le cirque: sociologie historique d'un pluralisme politique*. Paris.

Vinogradov, J. G. 1981. "Sinope und Olbia im 5. JH v. u. Z: Das Problem der Staatsordnung" (in Russian). *VDI* 156:65–90, 157:49–75.

Wade-Gery, H. T. 1932. "Thucydides Son of Melesias." *JHS* 52:205–27. Reprinted in Wade-Gery 1958, 239–70.

———. 1938. "Two Notes on Theopompos, Philippika 10." *AJP* 59:129–34. Reprinted in Wade-Gery 1958, 233–38.

———. 1940. "The Peace of Kallias." *HSCP* suppl. 1:121–56. Reprinted in Wade-Gery 1958, 201–32.

———. 1945. "The Question of Tribute in 449–448 B.C." *Hesperia* 14:212–29.

———. 1958. *Essays in Greek History*. Oxford.

———, and B. D. Meritt. 1957. "Athenian Resources in 449 and 431 B.C." *Hesperia* 26:163–97.

Walbank, F. W. 1955. "Tragic History: A Reconsideration." *BICS* 2:4–14.

Walbank, M. B. 1978. *Athenian Proxenies of the Fifth Century B.C.* Toronto and Sarasota.

Wallace, M. B. 1970. "Early Greek Proxenoi." *Phoenix* 24:189–208.

Wallace, R. W. 1974. "Ephialtes and the Areopagos." *GRBS* 15:259–69.

Wallace-Hadrill, A. 1983. *Suetonius*. London and New Haven.

Walsh, J. 1981. "The Authenticity and the Dates of the Peace of Callias and the Congress Decree." *Chiron* 11:31–63.

Walters, K. R. 1983. "Perikles' Citizenship Law." *ClAnt* 2:314–36.

Wardman, A. 1974. *Plutarch's Lives*. London.

Weber, L. 1922. "Perikles Samische Leichenrede." *Hermes* 57:375–95.

Webster, T. B. L. 1949. "The Masks of Greek Comedy." *BRL* 32:97–133.

Wehrli, F. 1953. *Die Schule des Aristoteles*. Vol. 3, *Herakleides Pontikos*. Basel.

———. 1959. *Die Schule des Aristoteles*. Vol. 10, *Hieronymus von Rhodos, Kritolaos und seine Schüler. Rückblick: Der Peripatos in vorchristlicher Zeit. Register*. Basel.

———. 1973. "Gnome, Anekdote, und Biographie." *MH* 30:193–203.

Weil, R. 1960. *Aristote et l'histoire: essai sur la Politique*. Paris.

Weissenberger, B. 1895. *Die Sprache Plutarchs und die pseudoplutarchische Schriften*. Part 1. Straubing.

Weissert, D. 1975. "Plutarch, Perikles 15,3: Ein neuer Konjekturvorschlag, ἐπιτόκια." *SCI* 2:157–62.

Weizsäcker, A. 1931. *Untersuchungen zur Plutarchs biographische Technik.* Berlin.

Welsh, D. 1983. "The Chorus of Aristophanes' *Babylonians.*" *GRBS* 24:137–50.

Wéry, L. M. 1966. "Le meurtre des hérauts de Darius en 491 et l'inviolabilité du héraut." *AntClas* 35:468–86.

Wesenberg, B. 1982. "Wer erbauete den Parthenon?" *MDAI(A)* 97:99–125.

Westermann, A. 1839. Παραδοξογράφοι: *Scriptores Rerum Mirabilium Graeci.* Braunschweig and London. Reprinted Amsterdam 1963.

Westlake, H. D. 1948. "Athenian Food Supplies from Euboea." *CR* 62:2–5.

―――. 1968. *Individuals in Thucydides.* Cambridge.

White, M. E. 1964. "Some Agiad Dates: Pausanias and His Sons." *JHS* 84:140–52.

Whitehead, D. 1977. *The Ideology of the Athenian Metic.* Cambridge.

Whitman, C. 1965. *Homer and the Homeric Tradition.* New York.

Wilamowitz-Moellendorff, U. von. 1893. *Aristoteles und Athen.* 2 vols. Berlin.

―――. 1919. "Lesefrüchte." *Hermes* 54:46–74.

―――. 1967. *Reden und Vorträge.* Dublin and Zurich.

Wilcken, U. 1907. "Der Anonymus Argentinensis." *Hermes* 42:374–418.

Wilhelm, A. 1909. *Beiträge zur griechischen Inschriftenkunde.* Vienna.

―――. 1949. "Zum Ostrakismos des Xanthippos, des Vaters des Perikles." *AnzWien* 86:237–43.

Will, E. 1972. *Le monde grec et l'Orient.* Vol. 1. Paris.

Williams, D. 1983. "Women on Athenian Vases: Problems of Interpretation." In *Images of Women in Antiquity,* edited by A. Cameron and A. Kuhrt, 92–106. Detroit.

Willis, W. H. 1968. "A Census of the Literary Papyri from Egypt." *GRBS* 9:205–41.

Wimmer, F. 1862. *Theophrasti Eresii Opera.* Vol. 3, *Fragmenta.* Leipzig.

Woodbury, L. 1970. "Sophocles among the Generals." *Phoenix* 24:209–24.

―――. 1981. "Anaxagoras and Athens." *Phoenix* 35:295–315.

Woodhead, A. G. 1952. "The Site of Brea: Thucydides 1.61.4." *CQ,* n.s. 2:57–62.

―――. 1960. "Thucydides' Portrait of Cleon." *Mnemosyne,* ser. 4, 13:289–317.

―――. 1973–74. "The Date of the Springhouse Decree." *Archeologia Classica* 25–26:751–61.

Wycherley, R. E. 1957. *The Athenian Agora*. Vol. 3, *Literary and Epigraphical Testimonia*. Princeton.

———. 1968. "The Agora of Pericles." *Journal of Historical Studies* 1:246–56.

———. 1978. *The Stones of Athens*. Princeton.

Wylie, J. A. H., and H. W. Stubbs. 1983. "The Plague at Athens, 430–428 B.C.: Epidemic and Epizootic." *CQ*, n.s. 33:6–11.

Yalouris, N. 1976. *Athletics in Ancient Greece*. Athens.

Ziebarth, E. 1929. *Beiträge zur Geschichte des Seeraubs und Seehandels im alten Griechenland*. Hamburg.

Ziegler, K. 1907. *Die Überlieferungsgeschichte der vergleichende Lebensbeschreibungen Plutarchs*. Leipzig. Reprinted Aalen 1974.

———. 1949. *Plutarchos von Chaironeia*. Stuttgart. Reprinted in *RE* s.v. Plutarchos 2, XXI, 1 (1951) 636–962; and separately, Stuttgart 1964.

———. 1964. Lindskog, Cl., and K. Ziegler. *Plutarchi Vitae Parallelae*. Vol. 1.2. Tert. recensuit K. Ziegler. Leipzig.

Ziehen, L. 1906. I. de Prott and L. Ziehen, *Leges Graecorum Sacrae e Titulis Collectae*. Vol. 2.1, *Leges Graeciae et insularum*, edited by L. Ziehen. Leipzig.

Zimmermann, R. 1930. "Die Quellen Plutarchs in der Biographie des Marcellus." *RhMus* 79:55–64.

INDEX OF AUTHORS AND PASSAGES

INDEX OF GREEK WORDS

GENERAL INDEX